4th Edition

UNDERSTANDING COMPUTERS
IN A CHANGING SOCIETY

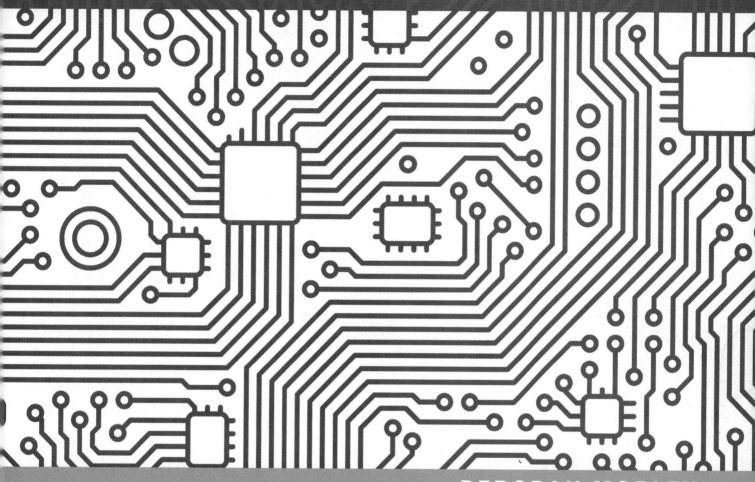

DEBORAH MORLEY

COURSE TECHNOLOGY
CENGAGE Learning™

Australia • Brazil • Japan • Korea • Mexico • Singapore • Spain • United Kingdom • United States

Kelly.Tamfe@students.msbcollege-.edu
pass - Kota-last 4 S.S.

COURSE TECHNOLOGY
CENGAGE Learning™

**Understanding Computers in a Changing Society,
4th Edition**
Deborah Morley

Vice President of Publishing: Nicole Jones Pinard

Executive Editor: Marie Lee

Associate Acquisitions Editor: Brandi Shailer

Senior Product Manager: Kathleen Finnegan

Product Manager: Leigh Hefferon

Associate Product Manager: Julia Leroux-Lindsey

Editorial Assistant: Zina Kresin

Senior Marketing Manager: Ryan DeGrote

Marketing Coordinator: Kristen Panciocco

Development Editor: Pam Conrad

Content Project Manager: Heather Hopkins

Print Buyer: Fola Orekoya

Proofreader: Brandy Lilly

Indexer: Elizabeth Cunningham

Composition: Integra Software Services

Text and Cover Designer: Marissa Falco

For product information and technology assistance, contact us at
Cengage Learning Customer & Sales Support, 1-800-354-9706

For permission to use material from this text or product, submit all requests online at **cengage.com/permissions**
Further permissions questions can be emailed to
permissionrequest@cengage.com

Library of Congress Control Number: 2010921533

Student Edition ISBN 13: 978-0-538-75448-4

Student Edition ISBN 10: 0-538-75448-6

Course Technology
20 Channel Center Street
Boston, MA 02210
USA

Cengage Learning is a leading provider of customized learning solutions with office locations around the globe, including Singapore, the United Kingdom, Australia, Mexico, Brazil, and Japan. Locate your local office at:
international.cengage.com/region

Cengage Learning products are represented in Canada by Nelson Education, Ltd.

For your course and learning solutions, visit **www.cengage.com**

Purchase any of our products at your local college store or at our preferred online store **www.CengageBrain.com**

Printed in the United States of America
1 2 3 4 5 6 7 16 15 14 13 12 11 10

PREFACE

In today's computer-oriented society, computers and technology impact virtually everyone's life. *Understanding Computers in a Changing Society, 4th Edition* (formerly *Computers and Technology in a Changing Society*) is designed to ensure that students are current and informed in order to thrive in our technologically oriented, global society. With this new edition, students not only learn about relevant cutting-edge technology trends, but they also gain a better understanding of technology in general and the important issues surrounding technology today. This information gives students the knowledge they need to succeed in today's world.

This nontechnical, introductory text explains in straightforward terms the importance of learning about computers, the various types of computer systems and their components, the principles by which computer systems work, the practical applications of computers and related technologies, the ways in which the world is being changed by these technologies, and the associated risks and other potential implications of computers and related technologies. The goal of this text is to provide readers with a solid knowledge of computer fundamentals, an understanding of the impact of our computer-oriented society, and a framework for using this knowledge effectively in their lives.

KEY FEATURES

Just like its previous editions, *Understanding Computers in a Changing Society, 4th Edition* provides current and comprehensive coverage of important topics. Flexible organization and an engaging presentation, combined with a variety of learning tools associated with each chapter, help students master important concepts. Numerous marginal notations direct students to the Understanding Computers in a Changing Society Web site where they can access **Online Videos**, **Podcasts**, **Video Podcasts**, and **Further Exploration** links, as well as other **Interactive Activities**, **Testing Activities**, **Study Tools**, and **Additional Resources**.

Currency and Accuracy

The state-of-the-art content of this book and its Web site reflect the latest technologies, trends, and classroom needs. To ensure the content is as accurate and up to date as possible, numerous **Industry Expert Reviewers** provided feedback and suggestions for improvements to the content in their areas of expertise. Throughout the writing and production stages, enhancements were continually made to ensure that the final product is as current and accurate as possible.

Comprehensiveness and Depth

Accommodating a wide range of teaching styles, *Understanding Computers in a Changing Society, 4th Edition* provides comprehensive coverage of traditional topics while also covering relevant, up-to-the-minute new technologies and important societal issues, such as netbooks, UMPCs, USB monitors, Wi-Fi SD cards, and other new and emerging types of hardware; wireless power, one-time password (OTP) cards, Digital Copy DVDs, thin-film solar panels, portable fuel cell chargers, gesture input, and other hardware technologies; cloud computing, thumb drive PCs, and other computing concepts; new software products and technologies, such as Google Chrome, cloudware, Microsoft Office 2010, and browser-based operating systems; new and growing Internet applications, such as mobile voice search, unified communications (UC), Twittering, social network management services, online financial alerts, business 3D worlds, private browsing, mobile phone check deposits, and geobrowsing; new security threats (such as real-time credit card data theft, rogue antivirus programs, and drive-by pharming) and new security trends (such as social engineering tests, people-driven security, and two-factor authentication); and important new societal issues, such as typosquatting, cyberbullying, and sexting.

Readability

We remember more about a subject if it is presented in a straightforward way and made interesting and exciting. This book is written in a conversational, down-to-earth style—one designed to be accurate without being intimidating. Concepts are explained clearly and simply, without the use of overly technical terminology. More complex concepts are explained in an understandable manner and with realistic examples from everyday life.

Chapter Learning Tools

1. **Outline**, **Learning Objectives**, **and Overview**: For each chapter, an **Outline** of the major topics covered, a list of student **Learning Objectives**, and a **Chapter Overview** help instructors put the subject matter of the chapter in perspective and let students know what they will be reading about.

2. **Boldfaced Key Terms and Running Glossary**: Important terms appear in boldface type as they are introduced in the chapter. These terms are defined at the bottom of the page on which they appear and in the end-of-text glossary.

3. **Chapter Boxes**: In each chapter, a **Trend** box provides students with a look at current and upcoming developments in the world of computers; an **Inside the Industry** box provides insight into some of the practices that have made the computer industry unique and fascinating; a **How It Works** box explains in detail how a technology or product works; and a **Technology and You** box takes a look at how computers and technology are used in everyday life.

4. **Ask the Expert Boxes**: In each chapter, three **Ask the Expert** boxes feature a question about a computing concept, a trend, or how computers are used on the job or otherwise in the real world along with the response from an expert. Experts for this edition include a guitarist from a rock band, a software engineer from Walt Disney Imagineering, and executives from notable companies like McDonald's, Jack in the Box, Google, Kingston, RealNetworks, The Computer Ethics Institute, EPIC, and Symantec.

NEW

5. **Marginal Tips and Caution Elements**: **Tip** marginal elements feature time-saving tips or ways to avoid a common problem or terminology mistake, or present students with interesting additional information related to the chapter content. New **Caution** elements warn of a possible problem students should avoid.

6. **Illustrations and Photographs**: Instructive, current, full-color illustrations and photographs are used to illustrate important concepts. Figures and screenshots show the latest hardware and software and are annotated to convey important information.

TIP

To help prevent identity theft, do not include your Social Security number on your résumé or any other document posted online.

CAUTION CAUTION CAUTIC

When upgrading your mobile phone, be c phone to others. Before disposing of or re settings to clear all personal data from the

7. **Online Video Marginal Element**: **Online Video** marginal elements direct students to the Understanding Computers in a Changing Society Web site to watch a short video (provided by Google, IBM, Symantec, and other companies) related to the topic in that section of the text.

 8. **Video Podcast Marginal Elements**: **Video Podcast** marginal elements direct students to the Understanding Computers in a Changing Society Web site to download and watch a practical "How To" video podcast related to the chapter content. Audio podcasts of the Expert Insight features are also available via this book's Web site.

9. **Summary and Key Terms**: The end-of-chapter material includes a concise, section-by-section **Summary** of the main points in the chapter. The chapter's Learning Objectives appear in the margin next to the relevant section of the summary so that students are better able to relate the Learning Objectives to the chapter material. Every boldfaced key term in the chapter also appears in boldface type in the summary.

10. **Review Activities**: End-of-chapter **Review Activities** allow students to test themselves on what they have just read. A matching exercise of selected **Key Terms** helps students test their retention of the chapter material. A **Self-Quiz** (with the answers listed at the end of the book) consists of ten true-false and completion questions. Five additional easily graded matching and short-answer **Exercises** are also included. Two short **Discussion Questions** for each chapter provide a springboard to jump-start classroom discussions.

 11. **Projects**: End-of-chapter **Projects** require students to extend their knowledge by doing research and activities beyond merely reading the book. Organized into six types of projects (**Hot Topics**, **Short Answer/Research**, **Hands On**, **Ethics in Action**, **Balancing Act**, and **Web Activities**, the projects feature explicit instructions so that students can work through them without additional directions from instructors. A special marginal icon denotes projects that require Internet access.

12. **Understanding Computers in a Changing Society Web Site**: Throughout each chapter, **Further Exploration** marginal elements direct students to the Understanding Computers in a Changing Society Web site where they can access collections of links to Web sites containing more in-depth information on a given topic from the text, as well as streaming videos and downloadable podcasts. At the end of every chapter, students are directed to the Understanding Computers in a Changing Society Web site to access a variety of other **Interactive Activities**, as well as **Testing Activities**, **Study Tools**, and **Additional Resources**.

References and Resources Guide
A **References and Resources Guide** at the end of the book brings together in one convenient location a collection of computer-related references and resources, including a **Computer History Timeline**, a **Guide to Buying a PC**, **A Closer Look at Numbering Systems** feature, and a **Coding Charts** feature.

NEW and Updated Expert Insight Features
In this exciting feature located at the end of each of the first seven chapters, industry experts provide students with personal insights on topics presented in the book, including their personal experiences with technology, key points to remember, and advice for the future. The experts, professionals from these major companies—**D-Link**, **Acer**, **Microsoft**, **Symantec**, **eBay**, **ACM/Google**, and **Dell**—provide a unique perspective on the book's content and how the topics discussed in the text impact their lives and their industry, what it means for the future, and more!

ONLINE VIDEO
Go to the Chapter 1 page at www.cengage.com/computerconcepts/np/uccs4 to watch the "Searching the Web on Your iPhone" video clip.

VIDEO PODCAST
Go to the Chapter 1 page at www.cengage.com/computerconcepts/np/uccs4 to download or listen to the "How To: Control Your Computer with Twitter" video podcast.

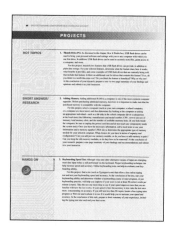

FURTHER EXPLORATION
Go to the Chapter 1 page at www.cengage.com/computerconcepts/np/uccs4 for links to information about computer certification programs.

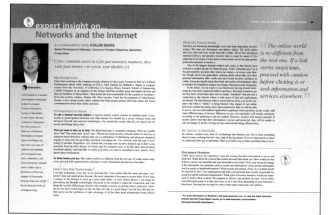

Expanded Web Site Content

The **Understanding Computers in a Changing Society Web site** includes a wealth of information at your fingertips to help enhance the classroom experience and to help students master the material covered in the book. Some of the content featured on the site includes new and updated **Key Term Matching**, **Self-Quizzes**, **Exercises**, and **Practice Tests**; interactive activities, such as **Student Edition Labs**, **Crossword Puzzles**, **Video Podcasts**, **Podcasts**, **Online Videos**, and **Further Exploration** links; and many other resources, including **Online Study Guides**, **Online Summaries**, **Online Glossaries**, **Expert Insights**, and **Online References and Resources Guide** content.

Student and Instructor Support Materials

Understanding Computers in a Changing Society, 4th Edition is available with a complete package of support materials for instructors and students. Included in the package are the Understanding Computers in a Changing Society Web site, Instructor Resources (available on CD and online), and SAM Computer Concepts.

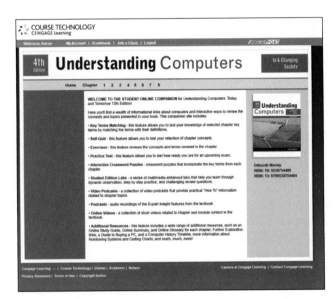

The Understanding Computers in a Changing Society Web Site

The Understanding Computers in a Changing Society Web site, which is located at **www.cengage.com/computerconcepts/np/uccs4**, provides media-rich support for each chapter of the book. The Web site includes the following:

> **Key Term Matching**—this feature allows students to test their knowledge of selected chapter key terms.

> **Self-Quiz**—this feature allows students to test their retention of chapter concepts.

> **Exercises**—this feature reviews the concepts and terms covered in the chapter.

> **Practice Test**—this feature allows students to test how ready they are for upcoming exams.

> **Crossword Puzzles**—this feature incorporates the key terms from each chapter into an online interactive crossword puzzle.

> **Student Edition Labs**—this interactive feature reinforces and expands the concepts covered in the chapters.

> **Video Podcasts**—this feature includes several downloadable video podcasts per chapter that provide practical "How To" information related to chapter topics.

> **Podcasts**—this feature includes downloadable audio podcasts of the Expert Insight features.

> **Online Videos**—this feature includes several streaming videos per chapter related to the topics in that chapter.

> **Further Exploration**—this feature includes links to additional information about content covered in each chapter.

> **Additional Resources**—this feature includes a wide range of additional resources, such as **Expert Insights**; an **Online Study Guide**, **Online Summary**, and **Online Glossary** for each chapter; a **Guide to Buying a PC** and a **Computer History Timeline**; and more information about **Numbering Systems** and **Coding Charts**.

Instructor Resources

Course Technology instructional resources and technology tools provide instructors with a wide range of tools that enhance teaching and learning. These tools can be accessed from the Instructor Resources CD or at **www.cengage.com/ coursetechnology**.

Electronic Instructor's Manual

The Instructor's Manual is written to provide instructors with practical suggestions for enhancing classroom presentations. For each chapter, the Instructor's Manual provides: **Lecture Notes, Teacher Tips, Quick Quizzes, Classroom Activities, Discussion Questions, Key Terms**, a **Chapter Quiz**, and more!

ExamView Test Bank

This textbook is accompanied by ExamView, a powerful testing software package that allows instructors to create and administer printed, computer (LAN-based), and Internet exams. ExamView includes 800 questions that correspond to the topics covered in this text, enabling instructors to create exams mapping exactly to the content they cover. The computer-based and Internet testing components allow instructors to administer exams over the computer and also save time by grading each exam automatically.

PowerPoint Presentations

This book comes with **Microsoft PowerPoint presentations** for each chapter. These are included as a teaching aid for classroom presentation, to make available to students on a network for chapter review, or to be printed for classroom distribution. Instructors can customize these presentations to cover any additional topics they introduce to the class. **Figure Files** for all figures in the textbook are also on the Instructor Resource CD.

Online Learning:

Course Technology has partnered with the leading distance learning solution providers and class-management platforms today. To access this material, Instructors can go to **www.cengage.com/coursetechnology** to visit our password-protected instructor resources. Instructor resources include the following: additional case projects, sample syllabi, PowerPoint presentations per chapter, and more. For additional information or for an instructor username and password, please contact your sales representative. For students to access this material, they must have purchased a WebTutor PIN-code specific to this title and your campus platform. The resources for students may include (based on instructor preferences) but are not limited to topic review, review questions, and practice tests.

SAM: Skills Assessment Manager

SAM 2007 is designed to help bring students from the classroom to the real world. It allows students to train and test on important computer skills in an active, hands-on environment. SAM's easy-to-use system includes powerful interactive exams, training and projects on the most commonly used Microsoft Office applications. SAM simulates the Office 2007 application environment, allowing students to demonstrate their knowledge and think through the skills by performing real-world tasks such as bolding text in Word or setting up slide transitions in PowerPoint. Add in live-in-the-application projects and students are on their way to truly learning and applying skills to business-centric documents.

Designed to be used with the New Perspectives Series, SAM includes handy page references, so students can print helpful study guides that match the New Perspectives Series textbooks used in class. For instructors, SAM also includes robust scheduling and reporting features.

ACKNOWLEDGEMENTS

We would like to extend a special thank you to all of the industry professionals who reviewed module content and provided their expertise for the **Expert Insight** features:

Joe Melfi, Associate Director of Business Solutions, D-Link Systems
Sumit Agnihotry, Vice President, Product Marketing, Acer Pan America
Graham Watson, Senior Community Lead, Technical Audience Global Marketing, Microsoft
Collin Davis, Senior Development Manager, Consumer Product Solutions, Symantec Corporation
Jim Griffith, Dean of eBay Education, eBay
Stuart Feldman, Past President of ACM and Vice President, Engineering, Google
Frank Molsberry, Technologist, Dell Inc.

In addition, we are very grateful to the numerous Industry Expert Reviewers that performed technical reviews and provided helpful suggestions to ensure this book is as accurate and current as possible. We would also like to thank the Educational Reviewers, who have helped to define and improve the quality of this text over the years. In particular, we would like to thank the following individuals:

Industry Expert Reviewers

Mike Hall, Corporate Communications, Seagate Technology
Kevin Curtis, CTO, InPhase Technologies
Sriram K. Peruvemba, Vice President, Marketing, E Ink Corporation
Jim Sherhart, Senior Director of Marketing, Data Robotics
Jack Dollard, Marketing, Mitek Systems
Joe Melfi, Associate Director of Business Solutions, D-Link Systems
Dave Gelvin, President, Tranzeo Wireless USA
Kevin Raineri, Director, Sales and Marketing, Innovative Card Technologies
Bill Shribman, Executive Producer, WGBH Interactive
Mike Markham, Vice President of Sales, Cadre Technologies
Renee Cassata, Marketing Manager, iDashboards
Russell T. Cross, Vice President of AAC Products, Prentke Romich Company
Dr. Kimberly Young, Director, The Center for Internet Addiction Recovery

Industry Expert Reviewers—Previous Editions

Jason Taylor, Worldwide Director of Corporate Communications, MobiTV; Nicole Rodrigues, Public Relations Manager, MobiTV; Stephen Yeo, Worldwide Strategic Marketing Director, IGEL Technology; Bob Hirschfeld, Public Information Officer, Lawrence Livermore National Lab; Bryan Crum, Vice President of Communication, Omnilert, LLC; David Bondurant, MRAM Product Manager, Freescale Semiconductor, Inc.; Rick McGowan, Vice President & Senior Software Engineer, Unicode, Inc.; Margaret Lewis, Director of Commercial Solutions, AMD; Mark Tekunoff, Senior Technology Manager, Kingston Technology; Billy Rudock, Customer Service Staff Engineer, Seagate Technology; James M. DePuydt, Ph.D., Technology Director, Imation Corporation; Dan Bloom, Sr. PR Manager, SanDisk; Kevin Curtis, CTO, InPhase Technologies; Gail Levy, Director of Marketing, TabletKiosk; Novell Marketing; John McCreesh, Marketing Project Lead, OpenOffice.org; Jackson Dunlap, ESP Systems; Laura Abram, Director of Corporate Marketing, Dust Networks; Kevin Schader, Communications Director, ZigBee Alliance; Mauro Dresti, Linksys Product Marketing Manager; Lianne Caetano, Executive Director, WirelessHD, LLC; Brad Booth; Howard Frazier; Bob Grow; Michael McCormack; George Cravens, Technical Marketing, D-Link; Christiaan Stoudt, Founder, HomeNetworkHelp.Info; Douglas M. Winneg, President, Software Secure, Inc.; Frank Archambeault, Director of Network Services, Dartmouth College; Adam Goldstein, IT Security Engineer, Dartmouth College; Ellen Young, Manager of Consulting Services, Dartmouth College; Becky Waring, Executive Editor, JiWire.com; Ellen Craw, General Manager, Ilium Software; Michael Behr, Senior Architect, TIBCO; Joe McGlynn, Director of Product Management, CodeGear; John Nash, Vice President of Marketing, Visible Systems; Josh Shaul, Director of Technology Strategy, Application Security, Inc.; Jodi Florence, Marketing Director, IDology, Inc.; Dr. Maressa Hecht Orzack, Director, Computer Addiction Services; Janice K. Mahon, Vice President of Technology Commercialization, Universal Display Corporation; Dr. Nhon Quach, Next Generation Processor Architect, AMD; Jos van Haaren, Department Head Storage Physics, Philips Research Laboratories; Terry O'Kelly, Technical Communications Manager, Memorex; Randy Culpepper, Texas Instruments RFID Systems; Aaron Newman, CTO and Co-Founder,

Application Security Inc.; Alan Charlesworth, Staff Engineer, Sun Microsystems; Khaled A. Elamrawi, Senior Marketing Engineer, Intel Corporation; Timothy D. O'Brien, Senior Systems Engineer, Fujitsu Software; John Paulson, Manager, Product Communications, Seagate Technology; Omid Rahmat, Editor in Chief, Tom's Hardware Guide; Jeremy Bates, Multimedia Developer, R & L Multimedia Developers; Charles Hayes, Product Marketing Manager, SimpleTech, Inc.; Rick McGowan, Vice President & Senior Software Engineer, Unicode, Inc.; Russell Reynolds, Chief Operating Officer & Web Designer, R & L Multimedia Developers; Rob Stephens, Director, Technology Strategies, SAS; Dave Stow, Database Specialist, OSE Systems, Inc.

Educational Reviewers

Marc Forestiere, Fresno City College; Beverly Amer, Northern Arizona University; James Ambroise Jr., Southern University, Louisiana; Virginia Anderson, University of North Dakota; Robert Andree, Indiana University Northwest; Linda Armbruster, Rancho Santiago College; Michael Atherton, Mankato State University; Gary E. Baker, Marshalltown Community College; Richard Batt, Saint Louis Community College at Meremec; Luverne Bierle, Iowa Central Community College; Fariba Bolandhemat, Santa Monica College; Jerry Booher, Scottsdale Community College; Frederick W. Bounds, Georgia Perimeter College; James Bradley, University of Calgary; Curtis Bring, Moorhead State University; Brenda K. Britt, Fayetteville Technical Community College; Cathy Brotherton, Riverside Community College; Chris Brown, Bemidji State University; Janice Burke, South Suburban College; James Buxton, Tidewater Community College, Virginia; Gena Casas, Florida Community College, Jacksonville; Thomas Case, Georgia Southern University; John E. Castek, University of Wisconsin-La Crosse; Mario E. Cecchetti, Westmoreland County Community College; Jack W. Chandler, San Joaquin Delta College; Alan Charlesworth, Staff Engineer, Sun Microsystems; Jerry M. Chin, Southwest Missouri State University; Edward W. Christensen, Monmouth University; Carl Clavadetscher, California State Polytechnic University; Vernon Clodfelter, Rowan Technical College, North Carolina; Joann C. Cook, College of DuPage; Laura Cooper, College of the Mainland, Texas; Cynthia Corritore, University of Nebraska at Omaha; Sandra Cunningham, Ranger College; Marvin Daugherty, Indiana Vocational Technical College; Donald L. Davis, University of Mississippi; Garrace De Groot, University of Wyoming; Jackie Dennis, Prairie State College; Donald Dershem, Mountain View College; John DiElsi, Marcy College, New York; Mark Dishaw, Boston University; Eugene T. Dolan, University of the District of Columbia; Bennie Allen Dooley, Pasadena City College; Robert H. Dependahl Jr., Santa Barbara City College; William Dorin, Indiana University Northwest; Mike Doroshow, Eastfield College; Jackie O. Duncan, Hopkinsville Community College; John Dunn, Palo Alto College; John W. Durham, Fort Hays State University; Hyun B. Eom, Middle Tennessee State University; Michael Feiler, Merritt College; Terry Felke, WR Harper College; J. Patrick Fenton, West Valley Community College; James H. Finger, University of South Carolina at Columbia; William C. Fink, Lewis and Clark Community College, Illinois; Ronald W. Fordonski, College of Du Page; Connie Morris Fox, West Virginia Institute of Technology; Paula S. Funkhouser, Truckee Meadows Community College; Janos T. Fustos, Metropolitan State; Gene Garza, University of Montevallo; Timothy Gottleber, North Lake College; Dwight Graham, Prairie State College; Wade Graves, Grayson County College; Kay H. Gray, Jacksonville State University; David W. Green, Nashville State Technical Institute, Tennessee; George P. Grill, University of North Carolina, Greensboro; John Groh, San Joaquin Delta College; Rosemary C. Gross, Creighton University; Dennis Guster, Saint Louis Community College at Meremec; Joe Hagarty, Raritan Valley Community College; Donald Hall, Manatee Community College; Jim Hanson, Austin Community College; Sallyann Z. Hanson, Mercer County Community College; L. D. Harber, Volunteer State Community College, Tennessee; Hank Hartman, Iowa State University; Richard Hatch, San Diego State University; Mary Lou Hawkins, Del Mar College; Ricci L. Heishman, Northern Virginia Community College; William Hightower, Elon College, North Carolina; Sharon A. Hill, Prince George's Community College, Maryland; Alyse Hollingsworth, Brevard College; Fred C. Homeyer, Angelo State University; Stanley P. Honacki, Moraine Valley Community College; L. Wayne Horn, Pensacola Junior College; J. William Howorth, Seneca College, Ontario, Canada; Mark W. Huber, East Carolina University; Peter L. Irwin, Richland College, Texas; John Jasma, Palo Alto College; Elizabeth Swoope Johnson, Louisiana State University; Jim Johnson, Valencia Community College; Mary T. Johnson, Mt. San Antonio College; Susan M. Jones, Southwest State University; Amardeep K. Kahlon, Austin Community College; Robert T. Keim, Arizona State University; Mary Louise Kelly, Palm Beach Community College; William R. Kenney, San Diego Mesa College; Richard Kerns, East Carolina University, North Carolina; Glenn Kersnick, Sinclair Community College, Ohio; Richard Kiger, Dallas Baptist University; Gordon C. Kimbell, Everett Community College, Washington; Robert Kirklin, Los Angeles Harbor Community College; Judith A. Knapp, Indiana University Northwest; Mary Veronica Kolesar, Utah State University; James G. Kriz, Cuyahoga Community College, Ohio; Joan Krone, Denison University; Fran Kubicek, Kalamazoo Valley Community College; Rose M. Laird, Northern Virginia Community College; Robert Landrum, Jones Junior College; Shelly Langman, Bellevue Community College; James F. LaSalle, The University of Arizona; Chang-Yang Lin, Eastern Kentucky University; Linda J. Lindaman, Black Hawk College; Alden Lorents,

Northern Arizona University; Paul M. Lou, Diablo Valley College; Deborah R. Ludford, Glendale Community College; Kent Lundin, Brigham Young University-Idaho; Barbara J. Maccarone, North Shore Community College; Wayne Madison, Clemson University, South Carolina; Donna L. Madsen, Kirkwood Community College; Randy Marak, Hill College; Gary Marks, Austin Community College, Texas; Kathryn A. Marold, Ph.D., Metropolitan State College of Denver; Cesar Marron, University of Wyoming; Ed Martin, Kingsborough Community College; Vickie McCullough, Palomar College; James W. McGuffee, Austin Community College; James McMahon, Community College of Rhode Island; William A. McMillan, Madonna University; Don B. Medley, California State Polytechnic University; John Melrose, University of Wisconsin—Eau Claire; Dixie Mercer, Kirkwood Community College; Mary Meredith, University of Southwestern Louisiana; Marilyn Meyer, Fresno City College; Carolyn H. Monroe, Baylor University; William J. Moon, Palm Beach Community College; Marilyn Moore, Purdue University; Marty Murray, Portland Community College; Don Nielsen, Golden West College; George Novotny, Ferris State University; Richard Okezie, Mesa Community College; Joseph D. Oldham, University of Kentucky; Dennis J. Olsen, Pikes Peak Community College; Bob Palank, Florissant Community College; James Payne, Kellogg Community College; Lisa B. Perez, San Joaquin Delta College; Savitha Pinnepalli, Louisiana State University; Delores Pusins, Hillsborough CC; Mike Rabaut, Hillsborough CC; Robert Ralph, Fayetteville Technical Institute, North Carolina; Herbert F. Rebhun, University of Houston-Downtown; Nicholas John Robak, Saint Joseph's University; Arthur E. Rowland, Shasta College; Kenneth R. Ruhrup, St. Petersburg Junior College; John F. Sanford, Philadelphia College of Textiles and Science; Kammy Sanghera, George Mason University; Carol A. Schwab, Webster University; Larry Schwartzman, Trident Technical College; Benito R. Serenil, South Seattle Community College; Allanagh Sewell, Southeastern Louisiana University; Tom Seymour, Minot State University; John J. Shuler, San Antonio College, Texas; Gayla Jo Slauson, Mesa State College; Harold Smith, Brigham Young University; Willard A. Smith, Tennessee State University; David Spaisman, Katherine Gibbs; Elizabeth Spooner, Holmes Community College; Timothy M. Stanford, City University; Alfred C. St. Onge, Springfield Technical Community College, Massachusetts; Michael L. Stratford, Charles County Community College, Maryland; Karen Studniarz, Kishwaukee College; Sandra Swanson, Lewis & Clark Community College; Tim Sylvester, Glendale Community College; Semih Tahaoglu, Southeastern Louisiana University; Jane J. Thompson, Solano Community College; Sue Traynor, Clarion University of Pennsylvania; William H. Trueheart, New Hampshire College; James D. Van Tassel, Mission College; James R. Walters, Pikes Peak Community College; Joyce V. Walton, Seneca College, Ontario, Canada; Diane B. Walz, University of Texas at San Antonio; Joseph Waters, Santa Rosa Junior College, California; Liang Chee Wee, University of Arizona; Merrill Wells, Red Rocks Community College; Fred J. Wilke, Saint Louis Community College; Charles M. Williams, Georgia State University; Roseanne Witkowski, Orange County Community College; David Womack, University of Texas, San Antonio; George Woodbury, College of the Sequoias; Nan Woodsome, Araphoe Community College; James D. Woolever, Cerritos College; Patricia Joann Wykoff, Western Michigan University; A. James Wynne, Virginia Commonwealth University; Robert D. Yearout, University of North Carolina at Asheville; Israel Yost, University of New Hampshire; and Vic Zamora, Mt. San Antonio College.

We would also like to thank the people on the Course team—their professionalism, attention to detail, and enormous enthusiasm make working with them a pleasure. In particular, we'd like to thank Marie Lee, Heather Hopkins, Brandi Shailer, Leigh Hefferon, and Pam Conrad for all their ideas, support, and tireless efforts during the design, writing, rewriting, and production of this book. Thanks to Julia Leroux-Lindsey for managing the instructor resources and Ryan DeGrote and Kristen Panciocco for their efforts on marketing this text. We would also like to thank Marissa Falco for the new interior and cover design, and Tintu Thomas for all her help managing the production of the book. Thanks also to Nicole Jones Pinard.

We are also very appreciative of the numerous individuals and organizations that were kind enough to supply information and photographs for this text, the many organizations that generously allowed us to use their videos in conjunction with this text to continue to include the Online Video feature, and Daniel Davis of Tinkernut.com who kindly permitted us to incorporate his video podcasts into this edition of the text to create the new Video Podcast feature.

We sincerely hope you find this book interesting, informative, and enjoyable to read. If you have any suggestions for improvement, or corrections that you'd like to be considered for future editions, please send them to deborah.morley@cengage.com.

Deborah Morley

BRIEF CONTENTS

Preface iii

Chapter 1
Introduction to the World of Computers 2
Expert Insight on Personal Computers 44

Chapter 2
A Closer Look at Hardware and Software 46
Expert Insight on Hardware 90

Chapter 3
The Internet and the World Wide Web 92
Expert Insight on Software 140

Chapter 4
Network and Internet Security 142
Expert Insight on Networks and the Internet 186

Chapter 5
Computer Security and Privacy 188
Expert Insight on Web-Based Multimedia
and E-Commerce 230

Chapter 6
Intellectual Property Rights and Ethics 232
Expert Insight on Systems 260

Chapter 7
Health, Access, and the Environment 262
Expert Insight on Computers and Society 292

Chapter 8
Emerging Technologies 294

References and Resources Guide R-1
Credits C-1
Glossary/Index I-1

CONTENTS

Preface iii

Chapter 1 Introduction to the World of Computers 2
Overview 3
Computers in Your Life 3
> Why Learn About Computers? 3
> Computers in the Home 5
> Computers in Education 5
> Computers on the Job 6
> Computers on the Go 7
What Is a Computer and What Does It Do? 8
> Data vs. Information 9
> Computers Then and Now 10
> Hardware 12
> Software 14
> Computer Users and Professionals 16
Computers to Fit Every Need 17
> Embedded Computers 18
> Mobile Devices 18
> Personal Computers (PCs) 19
> Midrange Servers 23
> Mainframe Computers 24
> Supercomputers 24
Computer Networks and the Internet 25
> What Are the Internet and the World Wide Web? 25
> Accessing a Network or the Internet 27
> Surfing the Web 31
> Searching the Web 32
> E-Mail 32
Computers and Society 34
> Benefits of a Computer-Oriented Society 34
> Risks of a Computer-Oriented Society 34
> Differences in Online Communications 36
> The Anonymity Factor 37
> Information Integrity 37
Summary 38
Review Activities 40
Projects 42

TECHNOLOGY AND YOU M-Learning on Campus 7
TREND Cloud Computing 17
INSIDE THE INDUSTRY Mobile Phone Use on the Job? 20
HOW IT WORKS Campus Emergency Notification Systems 30

 Expert Insight on Personal Computers 44

Chapter 2 A Closer Look at Hardware and Software 46
Overview 47
Digital Data Representation 47
> Bits and Bytes 47
> Numbering Systems and Coding Systems 48
Input Hardware 49
> Keyboards 49
> Pointing Devices 49
> Scanners, Readers, and Digital Cameras 53
> Other Input Devices 56
Processing Hardware and Other Hardware Inside the System Unit 57
> The Motherboard 57
> The Central Processing Unit (CPU) 58
> Memory 60

Output Hardware 62
> Display Devices 62
> Printers 63
> Other Output Devices 65
Storage Hardware 65
> Storage System Characteristics 65
> Hard Drives 66
> Optical Discs 69
> Flash Memory 72
> Other Types of Storage Systems 75
> Evaluating Your Storage Alternatives 76
Communications Hardware 77
> Network Adapters and Modems 78
> Other Networking Hardware 78
Software Basics 79
> Software Ownership Rights 79
> Installed vs. Web-Based Software 80
> Desktop vs. Mobile Software 80
> Common Software Commands 81
> Working with Files and Folders 83
Summary 84
Review Activities 86
Projects 88

TECHNOLOGY AND YOU Mobile Phone
Check Deposits 56
INSIDE THE INDUSTRY Watson, the
Ultimate Future *Jeopardy!* Contestant 59
HOW IT WORKS Thumb Drive PCs 74
TREND Microsoft Office 2010 81

**Expert Insight on
Hardware 90**

Chapter 3 The Internet and the World
Wide Web 92
Overview 93
Evolution of the Internet 93
> From ARPANET to Internet2 93
> The Internet Community Today 96
> Myths About the Internet 98

Getting Set Up to Use the Internet 99
> Type of Device 99
> Type of Connection and Internet
  Access 101
> Selecting an ISP and Setting Up Your
  Computer 105
Searching the Internet 106
> Search Sites 106
> Search Strategies 108
> Evaluating Search Results 110
> Citing Internet Resources 111
Beyond Browsing and E-Mail 111
> Other Types of Online
  Communications 111
> Social Networking 115
> Online Shopping and Investing 118
> Online Entertainment 119
> Online News, Reference, and
  Information 122
> Online Education and Writing 125
Censorship and Privacy Issues 128
> Censorship 129
> Web Browsing Privacy 130
> E-Mail Privacy 133
Summary 134
Review Activities 136
Projects 138

INSIDE THE INDUSTRY ISP Bandwidth
Limits 100
TREND Geobrowsing 113
TECHNOLOGY AND YOU Social
Networking Management Services 117
HOW IT WORKS Podcasting 124

**Expert Insight on
Software 140**

Chapter 4 Network and Internet
Security 142
Overview 143

Why Be Concerned About Network
And Internet Security? 143
Unauthorized Access and Unauthorized
Use 144
> Hacking 144
> War Driving and Wi-Fi Piggybacking 146
> Interception of Communications 147
Protecting Against Unauthorized Access
and Unauthorized Use 147
> Access Control Systems 147
> Firewalls, Encryption, and Virtual Private
Networks (VPNs) 152
> Additional Public Hotspot
Precautions 157
> Sensible Employee Precautions 157
Computer Sabotage 160
> Botnets 160
> Computer Viruses and Other Types
of Malware 160
> Denial of Service (DoS) Attacks 163
> Data, Program, or Web Site
Alteration 164
Protecting Against Computer
Sabotage 165
> Security Software 165
> Other Security Precautions 166
Online Theft, Online Fraud, and Other Dot
Cons 166
> Theft of Data, Information, and Other
Resources 167
> Identity Theft, Phishing, and
Pharming 168
> Online Auction Fraud 171
> Other Internet Scams 172
Protecting Against Online Theft, Online
Fraud, and Other Dot Cons 173
> Protecting Against Data and Information
Theft 173
> Protecting Against Identity Theft, Phishing,
and Pharming 173
> Protecting Against Online Auction Fraud
and Other Internet Scams 176
Personal Safety Issues 177
> Cyberbullying and Cyberstalking 177
> Online Pornography 178

Protecting Against Cyberbullying,
Cyberstalking, and Other Personal Safety
Concerns 178
> Safety Tips for Adults 178
> Safety Tips for Children and Teens 178
Network and Internet Security
Legislation 179
Summary 180
Review Activities 182
Projects 184

HOW IT WORKS Securing a Wireless
Home Router 153
TREND Evil Twins 158
INSIDE THE INDUSTRY New Tools to
Fight Malware 167
TECHNOLOGY AND YOU Online
Financial Alerts 175

 Expert Insight on Networks
and the Internet 186

Chapter 5 Computer Security
and Privacy 188
Overview 189
Why Be Concerned About Computer
Security? 189
Hardware Loss, Hardware Damage,
and System Failure 189
> Hardware Loss 190
> Hardware Damage 190
> System Failure and Other Disasters 190
> Protecting Against Hardware Loss,
Hardware Damage, and System
Failure 191
Software Piracy and Digital
Counterfeiting 200
> Software Piracy 200
> Digital Counterfeiting 201
> Protecting Against Software Piracy and
Digital Counterfeiting 202

Why Be Concerned about Information
Privacy? 204

Databases, Electronic Profiling, Spam,
and Other Marketing Activities 205
> Databases and Electronic Profiling 205
> Spam and Other Marketing
Activities 208
> Protecting the Privacy of Personal
Information 209

Electronic Surveillance and
Monitoring 214
> Computer Monitoring Software 215
> Video Surveillance 217
> Employee Monitoring 219
> Presence Technology 220
> Protecting Personal and Workplace
Privacy 221

Computer Security and Privacy
Legislation 222

Summary 224
Review Activities 226
Projects 228

TREND Social Engineering Tests 192
HOW IT WORKS Self-Destructing
Devices 194
TECHNOLOGY AND YOU Protecting
Your PC 198
INSIDE THE INDUSTRY Data
Killers 215

**Expert Insight on Web-Based
Multimedia and E-Commerce 230**

Chapter 6 Intellectual Property Rights
and Ethics 232

Overview 233

Intellectual Property Rights 233
> Copyrights 234
> Trademarks 235
> Patents 237

Ethics 238
> Ethical Use of Copyrighted Material 240
> Ethical Use of Resources and
Information 243
> Computer Hoaxes and Digital
Manipulation 247
> Ethical Business Practices and Decision
Making 249

Related Legislation 253
Summary 254
Review Activities 256
Projects 258

TREND High-Tech Anticounterfeiting
Systems 236
TECHNOLOGY AND YOU Virtual Gold
and Income Taxes 239
HOW IT WORKS Digital Copy
Movies 244
INSIDE THE INDUSTRY Click Fraud 249

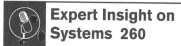

**Expert Insight on
Systems 260**

Chapter 7 Health, Access, and the
Environment 262

Overview 263

Computers and Health 263
> Physical Health 263
> Emotional Health 269

Access to Technology 274
> The Digital Divide 274
> Assistive Technology 277

Environmental Concerns 279
> Green Computing 279
> Recycling and Disposal of Computing
Equipment 281

Related Legislation 285
Summary 286
Review Activities 288
Projects 290

TECHNOLOGY AND YOU Mobile Coupons 272
HOW IT WORKS Mobile Voice Search 278
TREND Portable Fuel Cell Chargers 282
INSIDE THE INDUSTRY E-Paper 283

 Expert Insight on Computers and Society 292

Chapter 8 Emerging Technologies 294
Overview 295
The Computer of the Future 295
> Emerging Hardware 296
> The Impact of Nanotechnology 304
> Quantum and Optical Computers 306
Emerging Networking Technologies 307
> Wired Networking Improvements 308
> Wireless Networking Improvements 310
Artificial Intelligence (AI) 313
> What Is Artificial Intelligence (AI)? 313
> AI Applications 314
Technological Advances in Medicine 318
> Electronic Monitoring and Electronic Implants 318
> Telemedicine and Telesurgery 319
Technological Advances in the Military 320
> Battlefield Robots 320
> Exoskeleton Systems 321
Societal Implications of Emerging Technology 321

Summary 322
Review Activities 324
Projects 326

TREND Gesture Input 297
TECHNOLOGY AND YOU The "Morph" Concept 305
HOW IT WORKS The Browser OS 308
INSIDE THE INDUSTRY Wireless Power 311

References and Resources Guide R-1
Computer History Timeline R-2
Guide to Buying a PC R-8
> Analyzing Needs R-8
> Listing Alternatives R-9
A Look at Numbering Systems R-11
> The Decimal and Binary Numbering System R-11
> The Hexadecimal Numbering System R-11
> Converting Between Numbering Systems R-12
> Computer Arithmetic R-13
> Using a Scientific Calculator R-14
Coding Charts R-15
> ASCII and EBCDIC R-15
> Unicode R-16
Answers to Self-Quiz R-17

Credits C-1
Glossary/Index I-1

4th Edition

UNDERSTANDING COMPUTERS
IN A CHANGING SOCIETY

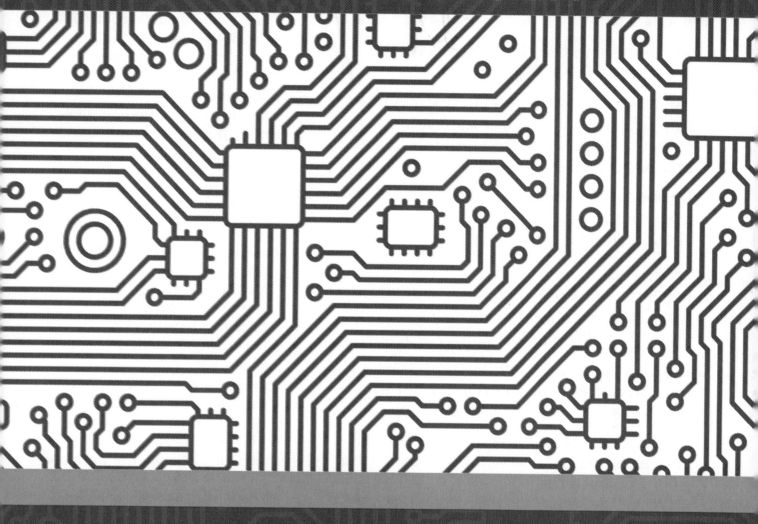

chapter 1

Introduction to the World of Computers

After completing this chapter, you will be able to do the following:

1. Explain why it is essential to learn about computers today and discuss several ways computers are integrated into our business and personal lives.

2. Define a computer and describe its primary operations.

3. List some important milestones in computer evolution.

4. Identify the major parts of a personal computer, including input, processing, output, storage, and communications hardware.

5. Define software and understand how it is used to instruct the computer what to do.

6. List the six basic types of computers, giving at least one example of each type of computer and stating what that computer might be used for.

7. Explain what a network, the Internet, and the World Wide Web are, as well as how computers, people, and Web pages are identified on the Internet.

8. Describe how to access a Web page and navigate through a Web site.

9. Discuss the societal impact of computers, including some benefits and risks related to their prominence in our society.

outline

Overview

Computers in Your Life
Why Learn About Computers?
Computers in the Home
Computers in Education
Computers on the Job
Computers on the Go

What Is a Computer and What Does It Do?
Data vs. Information
Computers Then and Now
Hardware
Software
Computer Users and Professionals

Computers to Fit Every Need
Embedded Computers
Mobile Devices
Personal Computers (PCs)
Midrange Servers
Mainframe Computers
Supercomputers

Computer Networks and the Internet
What Are the Internet and the World Wide Web?
Accessing a Network or the Internet
Surfing the Web
Searching the Web
E-Mail

Computers and Society
Benefits of a Computer-Oriented Society
Risks of a Computer-Oriented Society
Differences in Online Communications
The Anonymity Factor
Information Integrity

OVERVIEW

Computers and other forms of technology impact our daily lives in a multitude of ways. We encounter computers in stores, restaurants, and other retail establishments. We use computers and the Internet regularly to obtain information, experience online entertainment, buy products and services, and communicate with others. Many of us carry a mobile phone or other mobile device with us at all times so we can remain in touch with others on a continual basis and can access Internet information as we need it. It is even possible to use these portable devices to pay for purchases, play online games with others, watch TV and movies, and much, much more.

Businesses also use computers extensively, such as to maintain employee and customer records, manage inventories, maintain online stores and other Web sites, process sales, control robots and other machines in factories, and provide business executives with the up-to-date information they need to make decisions. The government uses computers to support our nation's defense systems, for space exploration, for storing and organizing vital information about citizens, for law enforcement and military purposes, and other important tasks. In short, computers and computing technology are used in an endless number of ways.

Understanding Computers in a Changing Society is a guide to computers and related technology, how they are being used in the world today, and their impact on our society. It will provide you with an introduction to computer concepts and terminology and give you a solid foundation for future computer-related courses. It will also provide you with the basic knowledge you need to understand and use computers in school, on the job, and in your personal life, as well as give you an understanding of the various societal issues related to technology, such as security and privacy issues, ethical considerations, and environmental concerns.

Chapter 1 is designed to help you understand what computers are, how they work, and how people use them. It introduces the important terms and concepts that you will encounter throughout this text and in discussions about computers with others, as well as includes an overview of the history of computers. It also takes a brief look at how to use a computer to perform basic tasks and to access resources on the Internet and the World Wide Web, in order to provide you with the knowledge, skills, and tools you need to complete the projects and online activities that accompany this textbook. The chapter closes with an overview of the societal impact of computers. ■

PODCAST

Go to **www.cengage.com/ computerconcepts/np/uccs4** to download or listen to the "Expert Insight on Personal Computers" podcast.

TIP

Most of the computer concepts and issues related to computers and society that are introduced in this chapter are discussed in more detail in subsequent chapters of this text.

COMPUTERS IN YOUR LIFE

Computers today are used in virtually every aspect of most individuals' lives—at home, at school, at work, and while on the go. The next few sections provide an overview of the importance of computers and some of the most common computer-related activities that individuals may encounter every day.

Why Learn About Computers?

Fifty years ago, computers were used primarily by researchers and scientists. Today, computers are an integral part of our lives. Experts call this trend *pervasive computing*, in which few aspects of daily life remain untouched by computers and computing technology. With pervasive computing—also referred to as *ubiquitous computing*—computers are found virtually everywhere and computing technology is integrated into an ever-increasing number of devices to give those devices additional functionality, such as enabling them to communicate with other devices on an on-going basis. Because of the prominence of computers in our society, it is important to understand what a computer is, a little about how a computer works, and the implications of living in a computer-oriented society.

Prior to about 1980, computers were large and expensive, and few people had access to them. Most computers used in organizations were equipped to do little more than carry out high-volume processing tasks, such as issuing bills and keeping track of product inventories. The average person did not need to know how to use a computer for his or her job, and it was uncommon to have a computer at home. Furthermore, the use of computers generally required a lot of technical knowledge and the use of the *Internet* was reserved primarily for researchers and educational institutions. Because there were few good reasons or opportunities for learning how to use computers, the average person was unfamiliar with them.

Beginning in the early 1980s, things began to change. *Microcomputers*—inexpensive *personal computers* that you will read about later in this chapter—were invented and computer use increased dramatically. The creation of the *World Wide Web* (*WWW*) in the late 1980s and the graphical *Web browser* in the 1990s brought personal computing to a whole new level and began the trend of individuals buying and using computers for personal use. Today, more than 80% of all U.S. households include a personal computer, and most individuals use some type of computer on the job. Whether you become a teacher, attorney, doctor, engineer, restaurant manager, salesperson, professional athlete, musician, executive, or skilled tradesperson, you will likely use a computer to obtain and evaluate information, to facilitate necessary on-the-job tasks, and to communicate with others. Today's computers are very useful tools for these purposes; they are also taking on new roles in our society, such as delivering entertainment on demand. In fact, computers and the traditional communication and entertainment devices that we use every day—such as telephones, televisions, and home entertainment systems—are *converging* into single units with multiple capabilities. For instance, you can check your *e-mail* (electronic messages), watch videos, and view other Internet content on your living room TV; you can make telephone calls via your personal computer; and you can view Internet content and watch TV on your *mobile phone*. As a result of this *convergence* trend (see Figure 1-1), the personal computer has moved beyond an isolated productivity tool to become an integral part of our daily lives.

Just as you can learn to drive a car without knowing much about car engines, you can learn to use a computer without understanding the technical details of how a computer works. However, a little knowledge gives you a big advantage. Knowing something about cars can help you make wise purchasing decisions and save money on repairs. Likewise, knowing something about computers can help you buy the right one for your needs, get the most efficient use out of it, be able to properly *upgrade* it as your needs change, and have a much higher level of comfort and confidence along the way. Therefore, basic **computer literacy**—knowing about and understanding computers and their uses—is an essential skill today for everyone.

Ⓥ FIGURE 1-1

Convergence.

Today's computers typically take on the role of multiple devices.

MOBILE DEVICES
Typically include the functions of a telephone, organizer, digital media player, gaming device, Web browser, and digital camera.

HOME COMPUTERS
Can often be used as a telephone, television, and stereo system, in addition to their regular computing functions.

> **Computer literacy.** The knowledge and understanding of basic computer fundamentals.

Computers in the Home

Home computing has increased dramatically over the last few years as computers and Internet access have become less expensive and as an increasing number of computer-related consumer activities have become available. Use of the Internet at home to look up information, exchange e-mail, shop, watch TV and videos, download music and movies, research products, pay bills and manage bank accounts, check news and weather, store and organize *digital photos*, play games, make vacation plans, and so forth is now the norm for many individuals (see Figure 1-2). Many individuals also use a computer at home for work-related tasks, such as to review work-related documents or check work e-mail from home.

As computers, the Internet, television, *digital video recorders* (*DVRs*), and *gaming consoles* continue to converge, the computer is also becoming a central part of home entertainment. *Wireless networking* has added to the convenience of home computing, allowing the use of computers in virtually any location and the ability to stream content wirelessly from one device to another. You can also use a computer to make telephone calls (referred to as *Voice over IP* or *VoIP*) via a personal computer, a special telephone adapter connected to your *landline phone*, or a *dual-mode mobile phone* (a mobile phone that can make phone calls over the Internet via a *Wi-Fi network*, in addition to making phone calls via a *cellular network*).

Computing technologies also make it possible to have *smart appliances*—traditional appliances (such as refrigerators or ovens) with some type of built-in computer or communications technology that allows them to be controlled by the user via a telephone or the Internet, to access and display Internet information, or to perform other computer-related functions. *Smart homes*—homes in which household tasks (such as watering the lawn, turning the air conditioning on or off, making coffee, monitoring the security of the home and grounds, and managing home entertainment content) are controlled by a main computer in the home or by the homeowner remotely via a mobile phone—have arrived, and they are expected to be the norm in less than a decade. Some believe that one primary focus of smart appliances and smart homes will be energy conservation—for instance, the ability to perform tasks (such as running the dishwasher and watering the lawn) during non-peak energy periods and to potentially transfer waste heat from one appliance (such as an oven) to another appliance (such as a dishwasher) as needed.

Computers in Education

Today's youth can definitely be called the *computing generation*. From *handheld gaming devices* to mobile phones to computers at school and home, most children and teens today have been exposed to computers and related technology all their lives. Although the amount of computer use varies from school to school and from grade level to grade level, most students today have access to computers either in a classroom or in a computer lab. Many schools (particularly college campuses) today also have *wireless hotspots* that allow students to use their personal computers to connect wirelessly to the college network and the Internet from anywhere on campus (see Figure 1-3). Today, students at all levels are typically required to use a computer to some extent as part of their normal coursework—such as for preparing papers, practicing skills, doing Internet research, accessing Internet content (for instance, class *Web pages* or their campus *YouTube* channel), or delivering presentations—and some colleges require a computer for enrollment. For a look at how mobile phones are beginning to be used as a teaching tool at some colleges, see the Technology and You box.

Computers are also used to facilitate *distance learning*—an alternative to traditional classroom learning in which students participate, typically at their own pace, from their

REFERENCE AND COMMUNICATIONS
Many individuals today have access to the Internet at home; retrieving information, obtaining news, viewing recipes, shopping online, and exchanging e-mail are popular home computer activities.

PRODUCTIVITY
Home computers are frequently used for editing and managing digital photos and home videos, creating and editing work-related documents, and other productivity tasks.

ENTERTAINMENT
Home computers and gaming consoles are becoming a central hub for entertainment, such as the delivery of photos, videos, music, games, and recorded TV.

 FIGURE 1-2
Computer use at home.

COMPUTER LABS AND CLASSROOMS
Many schools today have computers available in a lab or the library, as well as computers or Internet connections in classrooms, for student use.

CAMPUS WIRELESS HOTSPOTS
Many college students can access the Internet from anywhere on campus to do research, check e-mail, and more, via a campus hotspot.

DISTANCE LEARNING
With distance learning, students—such as these U.S. Army soldiers—can take classes from home or wherever they happen to be at the moment.

 FIGURE 1-3
Computer use in education.

 FIGURE 1-4
Computer use on the job.

current location (via their computers and Internet connections) instead of physically going to class. Consequently, distance learning gives students greater flexibility to schedule class time around their personal, family, and work commitments, as well as allows individuals located in very rural areas or stationed at military posts overseas to take courses when they are not able to attend classes physically.

Computers on the Job

Although computers have been used on the job for years, their role is continually evolving. Computers were originally used as research tools for computer experts and scientists and then as productivity tools for office workers. Today, computers are used by all types of employees in all types of businesses—including corporate executives, retail store clerks, traveling sales professionals, artists and musicians, engineers, police officers, insurance adjusters, delivery workers, doctors and nurses, auto mechanics and repair personnel, and professional athletes. In essence, the computer has become a universal tool for on-the-job decision making, productivity, and communications (see Figure 1-4). Computers are also used extensively for access control at many businesses and organizations, such as *authentication systems* that allow only authorized individuals to enter an office building, punch in or out of work, or access the company network via an access card or a fingerprint or hand scan, as shown in Figure 1-4 and discussed in detail in Chapter 4. In addition to jobs that require the use of computers by employees, many new jobs have been created simply because computers

DECISION MAKING
Many individuals today use a computer to help them make on-the-job decisions.

PRODUCTIVITY
Many individuals today use a computer to perform on-the-job tasks efficiently and accurately.

OFFSITE COMMUNICATIONS
Many individuals use portable computers or mobile devices to record data, access data, or communicate with others when they are out of the office.

AUTHENTICATION
Many individuals use authentication systems to punch in and out of work, access facilities, log on to company computers, or perform other security-related tasks.

TECHNOLOGY AND YOU

M-Learning on Campus

While mobile phones have been banned from many class-rooms in past years, the tide may be turning. Despite concerns about cheating and distractions, some educators are now viewing mobile phones as a tool to enhance learning. One such school is Abilene Christian University (ACU) in Texas where entering freshman receive either an *iPhone 3G* or an *iPod Touch.* The devices are being used to facilitate *m-learning* (*mobile learning*) by providing the means for students to access class schedules, podcasts, flashcards, Google Apps, campus directories, news, and other student tools, as well as to facilitate real-time class polls, live assessments, and other in-class activities. These in-class activities can provide both instructors and students with immediate feedback, as well as keep students engaged and interested in the content being presented and discussed in class. ACU has a special mobile learning Web site (see the accompanying figure) to help students access available resources, which are expected to grow as the program evolves.

While notebook and tablet computers are used more often than mobile phones for m-learning activities on college campuses today, the time for mobile phone-based learning may have arrived. ACU considered notebook computers as their m-learning platform, but determined that the screens created a barrier between the teacher and the students and so selected the mobile phone as their m-learning platform instead. With the vast majority of college students already owning a mobile phone, and with Web-enabled mobile phones becoming the norm, m-learning could be the next logical step for education.

exist, such as jobs in electronics manufacturing, online retailing, and technology-related computer support.

Computers are also used extensively by military personnel for communications and navigational purposes, as well as to control missiles and other weapons, identify terrorists and other potential enemies, and perform other necessary national security tasks. To update their computer skills, many employees in all lines of work periodically take computer training classes or enroll in computer certification programs.

FURTHER EXPLORATION Go

Go to the Chapter 1 page at **www.cengage.com/ computerconcepts/np/uccs4** for links to information about computer certification programs.

Computers on the Go

In addition to using computers in the home, at school, and on the job, most people encounter and use all types of computers in other aspects of day-to-day life. For example, it is common for consumers to use *consumer kiosks* (small self-service computer-based stations that provide information or other services to the public, including those used for ATM transactions, bridal registries, ticketing systems, and more), *point-of-sale (POS) systems* (such as

PORTABLE COMPUTERS
Many people today carry a portable computer or mobile device with them at all times or when they travel in order to remain in touch with others and Internet resources.

CONSUMER KIOSKS
Electronic kiosks are widely available to view conference or gift registry information, print photographs, order products or services, and more.

M-COMMERCE SYSTEMS
Allow individuals to pay for purchases using a mobile phone or other device.

CONSUMER AUTHENTICATION SYSTEMS
Allow access to facilities for authorized members only, such as for theme park annual pass holders, as shown here.

 FIGURE 1-5
Computer use while on the go.

TIP

To protect your notebook computer against falls or other damage while going through airport security scans, use a *checkpoint-friendly notebook bag* so your notebook can remain in its bag during X-ray screening.

those found at most retail stores to check customers out), and *self-checkout systems* (which allow retail store customers to scan their purchases and pay for them without a salesclerk) while in retail stores and other public locations. Individuals may also need to use a computer-based consumer authentication system to gain access to a local health club, theme park, or other membership-based facility (see Figure 1-5).

In addition, many individuals carry a *portable computer* or Web-enabled *mobile device* with them on a regular basis to remain electronically in touch with others and to access information (such as stock quotes, driving directions, airline flight updates, movie times, news headlines, and more) as needed while on the go. These portable devices are also increasingly being used to watch TV, download and listen to music, access *Facebook* and other *social networking sites*, and perform other mobile entertainment options, as well as to pay for products and services via *m-commerce systems* (refer again to Figure 1-5). GPS (*global positioning system*) capabilities are also frequently built into mobile phones, cars, and other devices to provide individuals with driving directions and other geographical or navigational information while traveling or hiking.

WHAT IS A COMPUTER AND WHAT DOES IT DO?

A **computer** can be defined as a programmable, electronic device that accepts data, performs operations on that data, presents the results, and stores the data or results as needed. The fact that a computer is *programmable* means that a computer will do whatever the instructions—called the *program*—tell it to do. The programs used with a computer determine the tasks the computer is able to perform.

The four operations described in this definition are more technically referred to as *input*, *processing*, *output*, and *storage*. These four primary operations of a computer can be defined as follows:

> **Input**—entering data into the computer.

> **Processing**—performing operations on the data.

> **Computer.** A programmable, electronic device that accepts data input, performs processing operations on that data, and outputs and stores the results. > **Input.** The process of entering data into a computer; can also refer to the data itself. > **Processing.** Performing operations on data that has been input into a computer to convert that input to output.

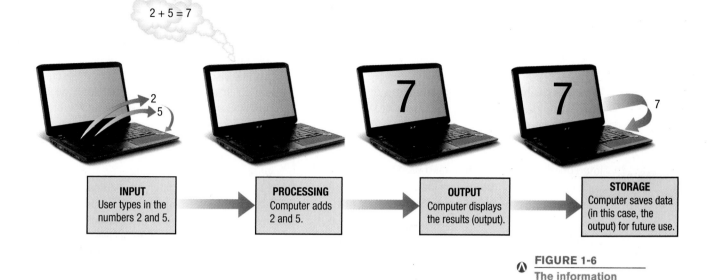

Ⓐ FIGURE 1-6
The information
processing cycle.

> **Output**—presenting the results.

> **Storage**—saving data, programs, or output for future use.

For example, assume that you have a computer that has been programmed to add two numbers. As shown in Figure 1-6, input occurs when data (in this example, the numbers 2 and 5) is entered into the computer, processing takes place when the computer program adds those two numbers, and output happens when the sum of 7 is displayed on the computer screen. The storage operation occurs any time the data, a change to a program, or some output is saved for future use.

For an additional example, look at a supermarket *barcode reader* to see how it fits this definition of a computer. First, the grocery item being purchased is passed over the barcode reader—input. Next, the description and price of the item are looked up—processing. Finally, the item description and price are displayed on the cash register and printed on the receipt—output—and the inventory, ordering, and sales records are updated—storage.

This progression of input, processing, output, and storage is sometimes referred to as the *IPOS cycle* or the *information processing cycle*. In addition to these four primary computer operations, today's computers also typically perform **communications** functions, such as sending or retrieving data via the Internet, accessing information located in a shared company database, or exchanging e-mail messages. Therefore, communications—technically an input or output operation, depending on which direction the information is going—is increasingly considered the fifth primary computer operation.

Data vs. Information

As just discussed, a user inputs **data** into a computer, and then the computer processes it. Almost any kind of fact or set of facts can become computer data, such as the words in a letter to a friend, the numbers in a monthly budget, the images in a photograph, the notes in a song, or the facts stored in an employee record. When data is processed into a meaningful form, it becomes **information**.

> **Output.** The process of presenting the results of processing; can also refer to the results themselves. > **Storage.** The operation of saving data, programs, or output for future use. > **Communications.** The transmission of data from one device to another. > **Data.** Raw, unorganized facts.
> **Information.** Data that has been processed into a meaningful form.

ASK THE EXPERT

Paul Baker, Senior Principal Software Engineer, Walt Disney Imagineering.

Would a college student graduating with a computer degree qualify for a job at Walt Disney Imagineering?

Computers play a large role at Walt Disney Imagineering, so a degree based on computers could be a great match if the course load includes science, math, and engineering courses. Every Disney ride is run by a computer and in many cases by several computers. In fact, some of the rides have computers on each and every vehicle. Unlike typical desktop computers, these "ride computers" are specialized for performing specific, distinct tasks and interfacing to the electronic devices that control and monitor mechanical equipment. Consequently, the algorithms used to run these rides—and ensure they operate in a dependable, predictable manner—are heavily based on engineering and physics. Two types of computer-related jobs that exist at Imagineering are Ride Engineering and Pre-Visualization—both require computer skills, as well as strong math, science, and engineering skills.

Information is frequently generated to answer some type of question, such as how many of a restaurant's employees work less than 20 hours per week, how many seats are available on a particular flight from Los Angeles to San Francisco, or what is Hank Aaron's lifetime home run total. Of course, you don't need a computer system to process data into information; for example, anyone can go through time cards or employee files and make a list of people who work a certain number of hours. If this work is done by hand, however, it could take a lot of time, especially for a company with a large number of employees. Computers, however, can perform such tasks almost instantly, with accurate results. *Information processing* (the conversion of data into information) is a vital activity today for all computer users, as well as for businesses and other organizations.

Computers Then and Now

The basic ideas of computing and calculating are very old, going back thousands of years. However, the computer in the form in which it is recognized today is a fairly recent invention. In fact, personal computers have only been around since the late 1970s. The history of computers is often referred to in terms of *generations*, with each new generation characterized by a major technological development. The next sections summarize some early calculating devices and the different computer generations.

Precomputers and Early Computers (before approximately 1946)

Based on archeological finds, such as notched bones, knotted twine, and hieroglyphics, experts have concluded that ancient civilizations had the ability to count and compute. The *abacus* is considered by many to be the earliest recorded calculating device; it was used primarily as an aid for basic arithmetic calculations. Other early computing devices include the *slide rule*, the *mechanical calculator*, and Dr. Herman Hollerith's *Punch Card Tabulating Machine and Sorter.* This latter device (see Figure 1-7) was the first electromechanical machine that could read *punch cards*—special cards with holes punched in them to represent data. Hollerith's machine was used to process the 1890 U.S. Census data and it was able to complete the task in two and one half years, instead of the decade it usually took to process the data manually. Consequently, this is considered to be the first successful case of an information processing system replacing a paper-and-pen-based system. Hollerith's company eventually became *International Business Machines* (*IBM*).

First-Generation Computers (approximately 1946—1957)

The first computers were enormous, often taking up entire rooms. They were powered by thousands of *vacuum tubes*—glass tubes that look similar to large, cylindrical light bulbs—which needed replacing constantly, required a great deal of electricity, and generated a lot of heat. *First-generation computers* could solve only one problem at a time since they needed to be physically rewired with cables to be reprogrammed (see Figure 1-7), which typically took several days (sometimes even weeks) to complete and several more days to check before the computer could be used. Usually paper punch cards and paper tape were used for input, and output was printed on paper.

Two of the most significant examples of first-generation computers were *ENIAC* and *UNIVAC*. ENIAC, shown in Figure 1-7, was the world's first large-scale, general-purpose computer. Although it was not completed until 1946, ENIAC was developed during World War II to compute artillery-firing tables for the U.S. Army. Instead of the 40 hours required for a person to compute the optimal settings for a single weapon under a single set of conditions using manual calculations, ENIAC could complete the same calculations in less than two minutes. UNIVAC, released in 1951, was initially built for the U.S. Census Bureau and was used to analyze votes in the 1952 U.S. presidential election. Interestingly, its correct prediction of an Eisenhower victory only 45 minutes after the polls closed was not publicly aired because the results were not trusted. Despite this initial mistrust of its capabilities, UNIVAC did go on to become the first computer to be mass produced for general commercial use.

PRECOMPUTERS AND EARLY COMPUTERS
Dr. Herman Hollerith's Punch Card Tabulating Machine and Sorter is an example of an early computing device. It was used to process the 1890 U.S. Census data.

FIRST-GENERATION COMPUTERS
First-generation computers, such as ENIAC shown here, were large and bulky, used vacuum tubes, and had to be physically wired and reset to run programs.

SECOND-GENERATION COMPUTERS
Second-generation computers, such as the IBM 1401 mainframe shown here, used transistors instead of vacuum tubes so they were smaller, faster, and more reliable than first-generation computers.

THIRD-GENERATION COMPUTERS
Third-generation computers used integrated circuits which allowed the introduction of smaller computers, such as the IBM System/360 mainframe shown here.

Second-Generation Computers (approximately 1958–1963)

The second generation of computers began when the *transistor*—a small device made of *semiconductor* material that acts like a switch to open or close *electronic circuits*—started to replace the vacuum tube. Transistors allowed *second-generation computers* to be physically smaller, less expensive, more powerful, more energy-efficient, and more reliable than first-generation computers. Typically, programs and data were input on punch cards and *magnetic tape*, output was on punch cards and paper printouts, and magnetic tape was used for storage (see Figure 1-7). *Magnetic hard drives* and *programming languages* (such as *FORTRAN* and *COBOL*) were developed and implemented during this generation.

FOURTH-GENERATION COMPUTERS
Fourth-generation computers, such as the original IBM PC shown here, are based on microprocessors. Most of today's computers fall into this category.

FIGURE 1-7
A brief look at computer generations.

Third-Generation Computers (approximately 1964–1970)

The replacement of the transistor with *integrated circuits* (*ICs*) marked the beginning of the third generation of computers. Integrated circuits incorporate many transistors and electronic circuits on a single tiny silicon *chip*, allowing *third-generation computers* to be even smaller and more reliable than computers in the earlier computer generations. Instead of punch cards and paper printouts, *keyboards* and *monitors* were introduced for input and output; magnetic hard drives were typically used for storage. An example of a widely used third-generation computer is shown in Figure 1-7.

✓ **TIP**

For a more detailed timeline regarding the development of computers, see the "Computer History Timeline" located in the References and Resources Guide at the end of this book.

Go **FURTHER EXPLORATION**

Go to the Chapter 1 page at **www.cengage.com/computerconcepts/np/uccs4** for links to information about the history of computers.

Fourth-Generation Computers (approximately 1971–present)

A technological breakthrough in the early 1970s made it possible to place an increasing number of transistors on a single chip. This led to the invention of the *microprocessor* in 1971, which ushered in the fourth generation of computers. In essence, a microprocessor contains the core processing capabilities of an entire computer on one single chip. The original *IBM PC* (see Figure 1-7) and *Apple Macintosh* computers, and most of today's modern computers, fall into this category. *Fourth-generation computers* typically use a keyboard and *mouse* for input, a monitor and *printer* for output, and magnetic *hard drives*, *flash memory media*, and *optical discs* for storage. This generation also witnessed the development of *computer networks*, *wireless technologies*, and the Internet.

Fifth-Generation Computers (now and the future)

Although some people believe that the fifth generation of computers has not yet begun, most think it is in its infancy stage. *Fifth-generation computers* have no precise classification, since experts tend to disagree about the definition for this generation of computers. However, one common opinion is that fifth-generation computers will be based on *artificial intelligence*, allowing them to think, reason, and learn. Voice and touch are expected to be a primary means of input, and computers may be constructed differently than they are today, such as in the form of *optical computers* that process data using light instead of electrons, tiny computers that utilize *nanotechnology*, or as entire general-purpose computers built into desks, home appliances, and other everyday devices.

FIGURE 1-8
Common hardware listed by operation.

Hardware

The physical parts of a computer (the parts you can touch and discussed next) are called **hardware**. The instructions or programs used with a computer—called *software*—are discussed shortly. Hardware components can be *internal* (located inside the main box or *system unit* of the computer) or *external* (located outside the system unit and connected to the system unit via a wired or wireless connection). There are hardware devices associated with each of the five computer operations previously discussed (input, processing, output, storage, and communications), as summarized in Figure 1-8 and illustrated in Figure 1-9. Both hardware and software are discussed in more detail in Chapter 2.

INPUT	PROCESSING
Keyboard	CPU
Mouse	**OUTPUT**
Microphone	Monitor
Scanner	Printer
Digital camera	Speakers
Digital pen/stylus	Headphones/headsets
Touch pad/touch screen	Data projector
Joystick	**STORAGE**
Fingerprint reader	Hard drive
COMMUNICATIONS	CD/DVD disc
Modem	CD/DVD drive
Network adapter	Flash memory card
	Flash memory card reader
	USB flash drive

Input Devices

An *input device* is any piece of equipment that is used to input data into the computer. The input devices shown in Figure 1-9 are the *keyboard*, *mouse*, and *microphone*. Other common input devices include *scanners*, *digital cameras*, *digital pens* and *styluses*, *touch pads* and *touch screens*, *fingerprint readers*, and *joysticks*.

Processing Devices

The main *processing device* for a computer is the *central processing unit* (*CPU*). The CPU is a *computer chip* located inside the system unit that performs the calculations and comparisons

>**Hardware.** The physical parts of a computer system, such as the keyboard, monitor, printer, and so forth.

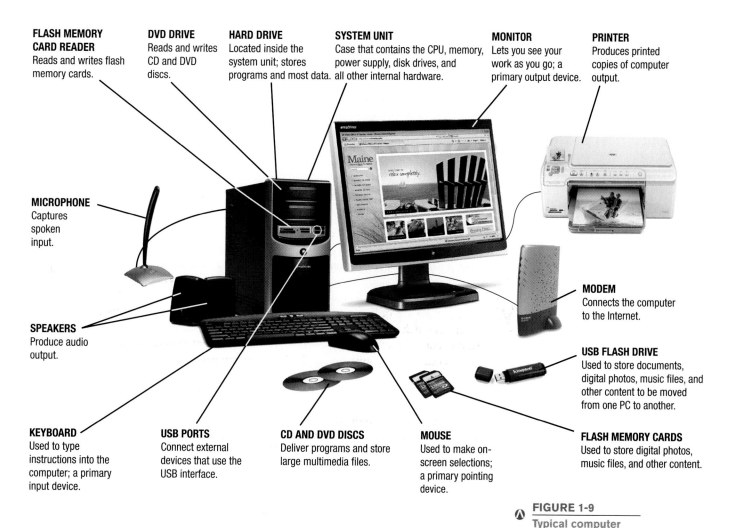

FLASH MEMORY CARD READER
Reads and writes flash memory cards.

DVD DRIVE
Reads and writes CD and DVD discs.

HARD DRIVE
Located inside the system unit; stores programs and most data.

SYSTEM UNIT
Case that contains the CPU, memory, power supply, disk drives, and all other internal hardware.

MONITOR
Lets you see your work as you go; a primary output device.

PRINTER
Produces printed copies of computer output.

MICROPHONE
Captures spoken input.

SPEAKERS
Produce audio output.

MODEM
Connects the computer to the Internet.

USB FLASH DRIVE
Used to store documents, digital photos, music files, and other content to be moved from one PC to another.

KEYBOARD
Used to type instructions into the computer; a primary input device.

USB PORTS
Connect external devices that use the USB interface.

CD AND DVD DISCS
Deliver programs and store large multimedia files.

MOUSE
Used to make on-screen selections; a primary pointing device.

FLASH MEMORY CARDS
Used to store digital photos, music files, and other content.

FIGURE 1-9
Typical computer hardware.

needed for processing; it also controls the computer's operations. For these reasons, the CPU is often considered the "brain" of the computer. Also involved in processing are various types of *memory*—additional chips located inside the system unit that the computer uses to store data and instructions while it is working with them.

Output Devices

An *output device* accepts processed data from the computer and presents the results to the user, most of the time on the computer screen (*monitor*), on paper (via a *printer*), or through a *speaker*. Other common output devices include *headphones* and *headsets* (used to deliver audio output to a single user) and *data projectors* (used to project computer images onto a projection screen).

Storage Devices

Storage devices (such as *CD/DVD drives* and *flash memory card readers*) are used to store data on or access data from *storage media* (such as *CD discs*, *DVD discs*, or *flash memory cards*). Some storage hardware (such as a *hard drive* or a *USB flash drive*) includes both a storage device and storage medium in a single piece of hardware. Storage devices are used to save data, program settings, or output for future use; they can be installed inside the computer, attached to the computer as an external device, or accessed remotely through a network or wireless connection.

Communications Devices

Communications devices allow users to communicate electronically with others and to access remote information via the Internet or a home, school, or company computer network. Communications hardware includes *modems* (used to connect a computer to the Internet) and *network adapters* (used to connect a computer to a computer network). A variety of modems and network adapters are available because there are different types of Internet and network connections—a modem used to connect to the Internet via a cable connection is shown in Figure 1-9. Communications hardware is discussed in more detail in Chapter 2; connecting to the Internet is covered in Chapter 3.

Software

The term **software** refers to the programs or instructions used to tell the computer hardware what to do. Software is traditionally purchased on a CD or DVD or is downloaded from the Internet; in either case, the software needs to be *installed* on a computer before it can be used. A rapidly growing alternative is running programs directly from the Internet (via Web pages) without installing them on your computer—referred to as *Web-based software*, *Software as a Service* (*SaaS*), and *cloud computing* (see the Trend box) and discussed in more detail in Chapter 2.

Computers use two basic types of software: *system software* and *application software*. The differences between these types of software are discussed next.

VIDEO PODCAST

Go to the Chapter 1 page at **www.cengage.com/ computerconcepts/np/uccs4** to download or listen to the "How To: Control Your Computer with Twitter" video podcast.

System Software

The programs that allow a computer to operate are collectively referred to as *system software*. The main system software is the **operating system**, which starts up the computer and controls its operation. Common operating system tasks include setting up new hardware, allowing users to run other software, and allowing users to manage the documents stored on their computers. Without an operating system, a computer cannot function. Common operating systems for personal computers are *Windows*, *Mac OS*, and *Linux*.

To use a computer, first turn on the power to the computer by pressing the power button, and then the computer begins to **boot**. During the *boot process*, part of the computer's operating system is loaded into memory, the computer does a quick diagnostic of itself, and then it launches any programs—such as an *antivirus* or *instant messaging* (*IM*) program—designated to run each time the computer starts up. You may need to *log on* to your computer or the appropriate computer network to finish the boot process.

Once a computer has booted, it is ready to be used and waits for input from the user. Most software today uses a variety of graphical objects (such as *icons* and *buttons*) that are selected with the mouse (or with a finger or stylus for a computer that supports touch or pen input) to tell the computer what to do. For instance, the **Windows desktop** (the basic workspace for computers running the Windows operating system; that is, the place where documents, folders, programs, and other objects are displayed when they are being used), along with some common graphical objects used in Windows and many other software programs, are shown in Figure 1-10.

>**Software.** The instructions, also called computer programs, that are used to tell a computer what it should do. >**Operating system.** A type of system software that enables a computer to operate and manage its resources and activities. >**Boot.** To start up a computer. >**Windows desktop.** The background work area displayed on the screen in Microsoft Windows.

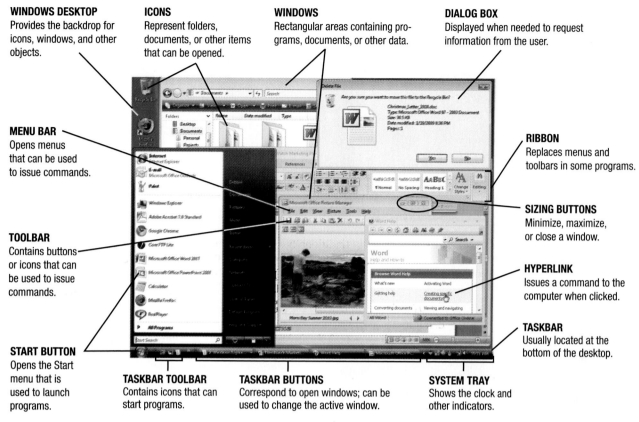

WINDOWS DESKTOP
Provides the backdrop for icons, windows, and other objects.

ICONS
Represent folders, documents, or other items that can be opened.

WINDOWS
Rectangular areas containing programs, documents, or other data.

DIALOG BOX
Displayed when needed to request information from the user.

MENU BAR
Opens menus that can be used to issue commands.

RIBBON
Replaces menus and toolbars in some programs.

SIZING BUTTONS
Minimize, maximize, or close a window.

TOOLBAR
Contains buttons or icons that can be used to issue commands.

HYPERLINK
Issues a command to the computer when clicked.

TASKBAR
Usually located at the bottom of the desktop.

START BUTTON
Opens the Start menu that is used to launch programs.

TASKBAR TOOLBAR
Contains icons that can start programs.

TASKBAR BUTTONS
Correspond to open windows; can be used to change the active window.

SYSTEM TRAY
Shows the clock and other indicators.

FIGURE 1-10
The Windows desktop.

Application Software

Application software (see Figure 1-11) consists of programs designed to allow people to perform specific tasks using a computer, such as creating letters (*word processing software*), preparing budgets (*spreadsheet software*), managing inventory and customer databases (*database software*), playing games (*gaming software*), watching videos or listening to music (*multimedia software*), editing digital photographs (*image editing software*), viewing Web pages (*Web browsers*), and exchanging e-mail (*e-mail programs*). Application software can be sold as individual stand-alone programs; related programs are sometimes bundled together into a *software suite*, such as the popular *Microsoft Office* software suite. Application software is launched via the operating system (such as by using the *Windows Start menu* shown in Figure 1-10 for Windows computers).

There are also application programs that help users write their own programs in a form the computer can understand using a *programming language* like *BASIC*, *Visual Basic*, *COBOL*, *C++*, *Java*, or *Python*. Some languages are traditional programming languages for developing applications; others are designed for use with Web pages or multimedia programming. For overall Web page development, *markup languages*—such as *Hypertext Markup Language (HTML)* and *Extensible Hypertext Markup Language (XHTML)*—can be used. Markup languages use text-based *tags* embedded into Web pages to indicate where and how the content of a Web page should be displayed. *Scripting languages* (such as *JavaScript* or *VBScript*) are often used to create interactive Web pages.

> **Application software.** Programs that enable users to perform specific tasks on a computer, such as writing letters or playing games.

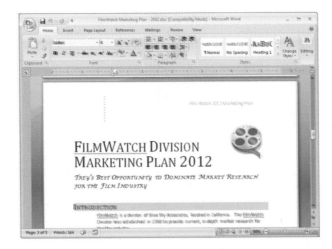

WORD PROCESSING PROGRAMS
Allow users to create written documents, such as reports, letters, and memos.

MULTIMEDIA PROGRAMS
Allow users to perform tasks, such as playing music or videos and transferring content to CDs and DVDs.

WEB BROWSERS
Allow users to view Web pages and other information located on the Internet.

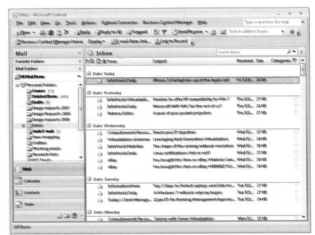

E-MAIL PROGRAMS
Allow users to compose, send, receive, and manage electronic messages sent over the Internet or a private network.

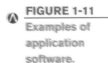
FIGURE 1-11
Examples of application software.

Computer Users and Professionals

In addition to hardware, software, data, and *procedures* (the predetermined steps to be carried out in particular situations), a computer system includes people. *Computer users*, or *end users*, are the people who use computers to perform tasks or obtain information. Anyone who uses a computer is a computer user, including an accountant electronically preparing a client's taxes, an office worker using a word processing program to create a letter, a supervisor using a computer to check and see whether or not manufacturing workers have met the day's quotas, a parent e-mailing his or her child's teacher, a college student analyzing science lab data, a child playing a computer game, and a person bidding at an *online auction* over the Internet.

Programmers, on the other hand, are computer professionals who write the programs that computers use. Other *computer professionals* include *systems analysts* (who design computer systems to be used within their companies), *computer operations personnel* (who are responsible for the day-to-day computer operations at a company, such as maintaining systems or troubleshooting user-related problems), and *security specialists* (who are responsible for securing the company computers and networks against *hackers* and other intruders who are discussed in more detail in Chapter 4).

TREND

Cloud Computing

In general, the term *cloud computing* refers to computing in which tasks are performed by a "cloud" of servers, typically via the Internet. This type of network has been used for several years to create the supercomputer-level power needed for research and other power-hungry applications, but it was more typically referred to as *grid computing* in this context. Today, *cloud computing* typically refers to accessing Web-based applications and data using a personal computer, mobile phone, or any other Internet-enabled device (see the accompanying illustration). While many of today's cloud applications (such as Google Apps, Windows Live, Facebook, and YouTube) are consumer-oriented, business applications are also available and are expected to grow in the near future. Consequently, the term is also used to refer to businesses purchasing computing capabilities as they need them, such as through the *Amazon Elastic Compute Cloud* (*Amazon EC2*) service or other *cloud providers* that provide Web-based applications, computing power, *cloud storage,* and other cloud services.

Advantages of cloud computing include easy scalability, lower capital expenditure, and access to data from anywhere. It is also beneficial to business travelers and other individuals whose computers, mobile phones, or other devices may be lost or otherwise compromised while the individual is on the go—if no personal or business data is stored on the device, none can be compromised. Disadvantages include a possible reduction in performance of applications if they run more slowly via the cloud than they would run if installed locally, and the potentially high expense related to data transfer for companies with high bandwidth applications. In addition, numerous security concerns exist, such as how the data is protected against unauthorized access and data loss.

Despite the potential risks, many believe that cloud computing is the wave of the future and will consist of millions of computers located in data centers around the world that are connected together via the Internet. They also view cloud computing as a way to enable all of an individual's devices to stay synchronized and, and as a result, allow an individual to work with his or her data and applications on a continual basis.

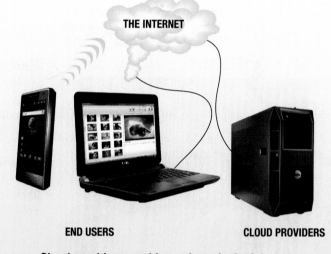

Cloud providers provide services via the Internet.

COMPUTERS TO FIT EVERY NEED

The types of computers available today vary widely—from the tiny computers embedded in consumer devices and appliances, to the pocket-sized computers and mobile phones that do a limited number of computing tasks, to the powerful and versatile *desktop computers* and *portable computers* found in homes and businesses, to the superpowerful computers used to control the country's defense systems. Computers are generally classified in one of six categories, based on size, capability, and price.

> - *Embedded computers*—tiny computers embedded into products to perform specific functions or tasks for that product.

> - *Mobile devices*—mobile phones and other small personal devices that contain built-in computing or Internet capabilities.

> - *Personal computers*—fully-functioning portable or desktop computers that are designed to be used by a single individual at a time.

> *Midrange servers*—computers that host data and programs available to a small group of users.

> *Mainframe computers*—powerful computers used to host a large amount of data and programs available to a wide group of users.

> *Supercomputers*—extremely powerful computers used for complex computations and processing.

In practice, classifying a computer into one of these six categories is not always easy or straightforward. For example, some high-end personal computers today are as powerful as midrange servers, and some personal computers today are nearly as small as a mobile phone. In addition, technology changes too fast to have precisely defined categories and the computer of the future may not look anything like today's computers. In fact, future predictions envision personal computers built into a variety of useful objects to best fit a person's lifestyle—such as a ring or watch for an older person, eyeglasses for a technical worker, and a flexible mobile device that can physically change its shape as needed (as discussed in the Chapter 8 Technology and You box) for general consumer use. Future devices are also expected to use voice, touch, or gesture input instead of a keyboard and mouse, and to project output on any appropriate surface instead of using a monitor. Nevertheless, these six categories are commonly used today to refer to groups of computers designed for similar purposes.

FIGURE 1-12

Embedded computers. This car's embedded computers control numerous features, such as notifying the driver when a car enters his or her blind spot.

A light indicates that a moving vehicle is in the driver's blind spot.

A camera located under the mirror detects moving vehicles in the driver's blind spot.

Embedded Computers

An **embedded computer** is a tiny computer embedded into a product designed to perform specific tasks or functions for that product. For example, computers are often embedded into household appliances (such as dishwashers, microwaves, ovens, coffee makers, and so forth), as well as into other everyday objects (such as thermostats, answering machines, treadmills, sewing machines, DVD players, and televisions), to help those appliances and objects perform their designated tasks. Typically, cars also use many embedded computers to assist with diagnostics, to notify the user of important conditions (such as an underinflated tire or an oil filter that needs changing), to control the use of the airbag and other safety devices (such as cameras that alert a driver that a vehicle is in his or her blind spot—see Figure 1-12—or auto braking systems that engage when a front collision is imminent), to facilitate the car's navigational or entertainment systems, and to help the driver perform tasks. Embedded computers are designed for specific tasks and specific products and so cannot be used as general-purpose computers.

ONLINE VIDEO

Go to the Chapter 1 page at **www.cengage.com/ computerconcepts/np/uccs4** to watch the "Wireless O ROKR Sunglasses" video clip.

Mobile Devices

A **mobile device** is loosely defined as a very small communications device (such as a mobile phone) that has built-in computing or Internet capability. Mobile devices can typically be used to make telephone calls, send *text messages* (short text-based messages), view Web pages, take digital photos, play games, download and play music, watch TV shows, and access calendars and other personal productivity features. Most (but not all) mobile phones today include computing and Internet capabilities; these phones (such as the one in Figure 1-13) are sometimes referred to as **smartphones**; an older term is *PDA*

>**Embedded computer.** A tiny computer embedded in a product and designed to perform specific tasks or functions for that product. >**Mobile device.** A very small communications device that has built-in computing or Internet capability. >**Smartphone.** A mobile device based on a mobile phone.

(*personal digital assistant*), though some devices referred to as PDAs do not include telephone capabilities. Handheld gaming devices (such as the *Sony PSP* and the *Nintendo DSi*) and *portable digital media players* (such as the *iPod Touch* and *Zune*) that include Internet capabilities can also be referred to as mobile devices, though they have less overall capabilities than conventional mobile devices.

Today's mobile devices typically have small screens and keyboards. Because of this, mobile devices are most appropriate for individuals wanting continual access to e-mail, timely Web content (such as breaking news, weather forecasts, driving directions, and updates from Web sites like Facebook), and music collections, rather than for those individuals wanting general Web browsing and computing capabilities. This is beginning to change, however, as mobile devices continue to grow in capabilities, as wireless communications continue to become faster, and as mobile input options (such as voice input) continue to improve. For instance, some mobile devices can perform Internet searches and other tasks via voice commands, some can be used to pay for purchases while you are on the go, and many can view and edit documents stored in a common format, such as *Microsoft Office* documents. For a look at some recent issues surrounding the use of mobile devices on the job, see the Inside the Industry box.

FIGURE 1-13
Smartphones. Most mobile devices today are based on the mobile phone.

Personal Computers (PCs)

A **personal computer** (**PC**) or **microcomputer** is a small computer designed to be used by one person at a time. Personal computers are widely used by individuals and businesses today and range in size from *desktop computers* to *ultra-mobile PCs* (*UMPCs*), as discussed next. Because many personal computers today are continually connected to the Internet, securing those computers—such as protecting them against *computer viruses* and *hackers* as discussed more later in this chapter and in Chapter 4—is an essential concern for both individuals and businesses.

Desktop Computers

Conventional personal computers that are designed to fit on or next to a desk (see Figure 1-14) are often referred to as **desktop computers**. The most common style of desktop computer today uses a *tower case*; that is, a system unit that is designed to sit vertically, typically on the floor. Desktop computers can also have a *desktop case* that is designed to be placed horizontally on a desk's surface, or an *all-in-one case* that incorporates the monitor and system unit into a single piece of hardware (a tower case and all-in-one case are shown in Figure 1-14).

FIGURE 1-14
Desktop computers.

Desktop computers typically cost between $350 and $1,000 and usually conform to one of two standards or *platforms*: *PC-compatible* or *Macintosh*. PC-compatible computers (sometimes referred to as *Windows PCs* or *IBM-compatible PCs*) evolved from the original IBM PC—the first personal computer widely accepted for business

TOWER CASES

ALL-IN-ONE CASES

INSIDE THE INDUSTRY

Mobile Phone Use on the Job?

While there are numerous jobs for which having access to a mobile phone and the Internet are needed and extremely useful, there are times when this isn't necessarily the case. One of the most well-known recent issues surrounding mobile phone use on the job was the decision involving President Obama's desire to continue to use his Blackberry after taking office. While the President was eventually allowed to keep his device to stay in touch with senior staff and a small group of personal friends—a first for any U.S. president—the decision brought the issue of mobile phone use on the job to the forefront, especially as it relates to security issues. Security experts stress the importance of protecting the content on mobile phones by using tools such as logon passwords, encryption, remote wiping features, and other security tools discussed in detail in Chapter 4.

In addition to security concerns, the issue of the appropriateness of mobile phone use on the job is also under scrutiny. While the ability to stay in touch with others and post information on a regular basis is often a useful business and personal tool, it can also violate company policy, laws, and even social norms. For instance, one professional basketball player was recently reprimanded for posting a Twitter update during halftime from the locker room and judges across the country are having to deal with the issue of mobile phone use by jurors to obtain and disseminate information about cases during trials.

From researching defendants online, to using Google Maps to determine walking or driving time between locations discussed in the trial, to Twittering about upcoming verdicts, juror mobile phone use is resulting in numerous mistrials and is raising many questions about jury instructions and juror access to technology during trials. Another issue is discretion and taste, as in the case of a newspaper reporter who recently posted Twitter updates during the funeral of a three-year-old boy. Mobile phone use is already prohibited in some public locations (see the accompanying illustration), such as theaters (for courtesy reasons) and airplanes and hospitals (for safety reasons). With mobile phones becoming ubiquitous, it is increasingly important for individuals to ensure that they use their mobile phones only in an appropriate and secure manner, both on the job and off.

ASK THE EXPERT

Debra Jensen, Vice President and Chief Information Officer, Jack in the Box Inc.

How long will it be until paying for fast-food purchases by mobile phone is the norm?

The technology exists today to allow for the payment of fast-food purchases by mobile phone and it's being used in Europe and Japan. Though it's also being tested in the United States, there are still some hurdles, primarily the adoption of the technology by cell phone providers and retailers, and consumers' willingness to use it. Another hurdle is consumer concerns about the technology being secure. It will likely be 2011 before there is widespread use.

use—and are the most common type of personal computer used today. In general, PC-compatible hardware and software are compatible with all brands of PC-compatible computers—such as those made by Dell, Hewlett-Packard, NEC, Acer, Lenovo, Fujitsu, and Gateway—and these computers typically run the Microsoft Windows operating system. Macintosh (*Mac*) computers are made by Apple, use the Mac OS operating system, and often use different hardware and software than PC-compatible computers. Although PC-compatible computers are by far the most widely used in the United States, the Mac is traditionally the computer of choice for artists, designers, and others who require advanced graphics capabilities. Extra powerful desktop computers designed for computer users running graphics, music, film, architecture, science, and other powerful applications are sometimes referred to as *workstations*.

Portable Computers

Portable computers are computers that are designed to be carried around easily, such as in a briefcase or pocket, depending on their size. Like mobile devices, portable computers are designed to be powered by rechargeable batteries so they can be used while on the go, though many can also be powered by electricity. Portable computers now outsell desktop computers and are often the computer of choice for students and for individuals buying a new home computer, as well as for many businesses. In fact, portable computers are essential for many workers, such as salespeople who need to make presentations or take orders from clients off-site, agents who need to collect data at remote locations, and managers who need computing and communications resources as they travel. Portable computers are available in a variety of configurations, as discussed next and shown in Figure 1-15.

NOTEBOOKS

SLATE TABLETS

NETBOOKS

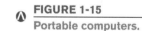

ULTRA-MOBILE PCS (UMPCs)

FIGURE 1-15
Portable computers.

> ➤ **Notebook computers** (also called **laptop computers**)—computers that are about the size of a paper notebook and open to reveal a screen on the top half of the computer and a keyboard on the bottom. They are typically comparable to desktop computers in features and capabilities.

> ➤ **Tablet computers**—notebook-sized computers that are designed to be used with a digital pen or stylus. They can be either *slate tablets* (which are one-piece computers with just a screen on top and no keyboard, such as the one shown in Figure 1-15) or *convertible tablets* (which use the same *clamshell* design as notebook computers but the top half of the computer can be rotated and folded shut so it can also be used as a slate tablet.

> ➤ **Netbooks** (also called *mini-notebooks*, *mini-laptops*, and *ultraportable computers*)—notebook computers that are smaller (a 10-inch-wide screen is common), lighter (typically less than three pounds), and less expensive than conventional notebooks, so they are especially appropriate for students and business travelers. They typically don't include a CD or DVD drive and they have a smaller keyboard than a notebook computer. The market for this new category of portable computer is growing rapidly and it is expected to reach 50 million by 2012, according to the research firm Gartner.

> ➤ **Ultra-mobile PCs** (UMPCs) (also sometimes called **handheld computers**)—computers that are small enough to fit in one hand. UMPCs are smaller (with a typical screen size of seven inches or smaller) and lighter (usually less than two pounds) than netbooks. They can support keyboard, touch, and/or pen input, depending on the particular design being used.

It is important to realize that while a portable computer offers the convenience of mobility, it typically isn't as comfortable to use for a primary home or work computer as a desktop computer is, without additional hardware. For instance, many individuals find it more convenient to connect and use a conventional monitor, keyboard, and mouse when using a notebook

>**Portable computer.** A small personal computer, such as a notebook, tablet, netbook, or ultra-mobile PC (UMPC), designed to be carried around easily. >**Notebook computer.** A fully functioning portable computer that opens to reveal a screen and keyboard; also called a **laptop computer**. >**Tablet computer.** A portable computer about the size of a notebook that is designed to be used with an electronic pen. >**Netbook.** A very small notebook computer. >**Ultra-mobile PC (UMPC).** A portable personal computer that is small enough to fit in one hand; also called a **handheld computer.**

ASK THE EXPERT

Martin Smekal, President and Founder, TabletKiosk

How will personal computers five years from now be different than today?

I believe that five years from now people will rely even more on their computers than they do today. They will likely create a personal computing ecosystem that combines the stability of a desktop system with the portability of a mobile computer and that has full wireless access to key files and applications. Hopefully, this will evolve to one single adaptable computing device that is capable of meeting all of these needs by incorporating "always-on" wireless connectivity and a touch screen interface.

In general, the computers of the future will be smaller, lighter, and have a much longer battery life than today's models. Traditional modes of input like the keyboard and mouse could become obsolete as we begin to rely more on touch input, speech recognition, and improved handwriting recognition.

computer at a desk for a long computer session. This hardware can be connected individually to many portable computers via a wired or wireless connection; there are also special *docking stations* that can be used to connect a portable computer easily to the hardware devices that are attached to the docking station. Docking stations and other *ergonomic*-related topics are discussed in more detail in Chapter 7.

Thin Clients and Internet Appliances

Most personal computers today are sold as stand-alone, self-sufficient units that are equipped with all the necessary hardware and software needed to operate independently. In other words, they can perform input, processing, output, and storage without being connected to a network, although they can be networked if desired. In contrast, a device that must be connected to a network to perform processing or storage tasks is referred to as a *dumb terminal*. Two types of personal computers that may be able to perform a limited amount of independent processing (like a desktop or notebook computer) but are designed to be used with a network (like a dumb terminal) are *thin clients* and *Internet appliances*.

A **thin client**—also called a *network computer* (*NC*)—is a device that is designed to be used in conjunction with a company network. Instead of using local hard drives for storage, programs are typically accessed from and data is stored on a *network server*. The main advantage of thin clients over desktop computers is lower cost (such as for overall hardware and software, computer maintenance, and power and cooling costs), increased security (since data is not stored locally), and easier maintenance (since all software is located on a central server). Disadvantages include having limited or no local storage (although this is an advantage for companies with highly secure data that need to prevent data from leaving the facility) and not being able to function as a stand-alone computer when the network is not working. Thin clients are used by businesses to provide employees with access to network applications; they are also sometimes used to provide Internet access to the public. For instance, the thin client shown in Figure 1-16 is installed in a hotel in Boston, Massachusetts, and is used to provide guests with Internet access, hotel and conference information, room-to-room calling, and free phone calls via the Internet.

Network computers or other devices designed primarily for accessing Web pages and/or exchanging e-mail are called **Internet appliances** (sometimes referred to as *Internet devices*). Typically, Internet appliances are designed to be located in the home and can be built into another product (such as a refrigerator or telephone console) or can be stand-alone Internet devices (such as the *Chumby* device shown in Figure 1-16 that is designed to deliver news, sports scores, weather, and other personalized Web-based information). Gaming consoles (such as the *Nintendo Wii* shown in Figure 1-16 and the *Sony*

>**Thin client.** A personal computer designed to access a network for processing and data storage, instead of performing those tasks locally; also called a network computer (NC). >**Internet appliance.** A specialized network computer designed primarily for Internet access and/or e-mail exchange.

THIN CLIENTS   **STAND-ALONE INTERNET DEVICES**   **INTERNET-ENABLED GAMING CONSOLES**

PlayStation 3) that can be used to view Internet content, in addition to their gaming abili-ties, can also be classified as Internet appliances when they are used to access the Internet. There are also Internet capabilities beginning to be built into television sets, which make these TVs Internet appliances, as well.

FIGURE 1-16
Ⓐ Thin clients and Internet appliances.

Midrange Servers

A **midrange server**—also sometimes called a *minicomputer* or *midrange computer*—is a medium-sized computer used to host programs and data for a small network. Typically larger, more powerful, and more expensive than a desktop computer, a midrange server is usually located in a closet or other out-of-the-way place and can serve many users at one time. Users connect to the server through a network, using their desktop computer, por-table computer, thin client, or a dumb terminal consisting of just a monitor and keyboard (see Figure 1-17). Midrange servers are often used in small- to medium-sized businesses (such as medical or dental offices), as well as in school computer labs. There are also spe-cial *home servers* designed for home use, which are often used to *back up* (make duplicate copies of) the content located on all the computers in the home automatically and to host music, photos, movies, and other media to be shared via a *home network*.

FIGURE 1-17
Ⓥ **Midrange servers.**
Midrange servers are used to host data and programs on a small network, such as a school computer lab or medical office network.

Some midrange servers consist of a collection of individ-ual *circuit boards* called *blades*; each blade contains the hard-ware necessary to provide the complete processing power of one personal computer. These servers—called *blade servers*—are much easier to expand and upgrade than traditional serv-ers, have lower overall power and cooling costs, and are more secure. With some blade servers, the processing power of the blades is shared among users. With others, each user has an individual blade, which functions as that individual's personal computer, but the blades are locked in a secure location instead of having that hardware located on each employee's desk. In either case, the thin client designed specifically to access a blade server is sometimes called a *blade workstation*.

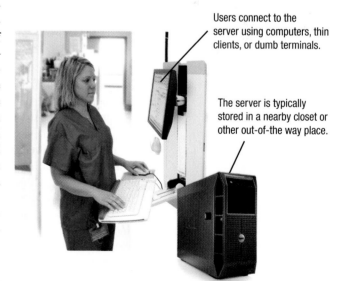

Users connect to the server using computers, thin clients, or dumb terminals.

The server is typically stored in a nearby closet or other out-of-the way place.

One trend involving midrange servers (as well as the *main-frame computers* discussed next) today is **virtualization**—creating *virtual* (rather than actual) versions of a comput-ing resource; in this case, separate server environments that, although physically located on the same computer, function

---

> **Midrange server.** A medium-sized computer used to host programs and data for a small network. > **Virtualization.** Creating virtual (rather than actual) versions of a computing resource, such as several separate environments that are located on a single server but act like different servers.

as separate servers and do not interact with each other. For instance, all applications for an organization can be installed in virtual environments on one or more physical servers instead of using a separate server for each application. Using a separate server for each application often wastes resources since the servers are typically not used to full capacity—one estimate is that about only 10% of server capability is frequently utilized. With virtualization, companies can fulfill their computing needs with fewer servers, which translates into reduced costs for hardware and server management, as well as lower power and cooling costs. Consequently, one of the most significant appeals of *server virtualization* today is increased efficiency. The concepts of virtualization are also beginning to be applied to other computing areas, such as networking and storage.

Mainframe Computers

Ⓥ **FIGURE 1-18**
Mainframe
computers.

A **mainframe computer** is a powerful computer used by many large organizations—such as hospitals, universities, large businesses, banks, and government offices—that need to manage large amounts of centralized data. Larger, more expensive, and more powerful than midrange servers, mainframes can serve thousands of users connected to the mainframe via personal computers, thin clients, or dumb terminals, in a manner similar to the way users connect to midrange servers. Mainframe computers are typically located in climate-controlled *data centers* and connect to the rest of the company computers via a computer network. During regular business hours, a mainframe typically runs the programs needed to meet the different needs of its wide variety of users. At night, it commonly performs large processing tasks, such as payroll and billing. Today's mainframes are sometimes referred to as *high-end servers* or *enterprise-class servers* and they usually cost at least several hundred thousand dollars each.

One issue facing businesses today is the high cost of electricity to power and cool the mainframes, servers, and personal computers used in an organization. Consequently, making the computers located in a business—particularly mainframes and servers—more energy efficient is a high priority today. For example, IBM recently consolidated approximately 4,000 servers located in its data centers into just 30 mainframes (one of the new mainframes is shown in Figure 1-18). This new environment is expected to consume approximately 80 percent less energy and result in significant savings in energy, software, and system support costs. Energy efficiency and other *green computing* topics are discussed in more detail in Chapter 7.

Supercomputers

Some applications require extraordinary speed, accuracy, and processing capabilities—for example, sending astronauts into space, controlling missile guidance systems and satellites, forecasting the weather, exploring for oil, and assisting with some kinds of scientific research. **Supercomputers**—the most powerful and most expensive type of computer available—were developed to fill this need. Some relatively new supercomputing applications include hosting extremely complex Web sites and *decision support systems* for corporate executives, as well as *three-dimensional applications* (such as 3D medical imaging, 3D image projections, and 3D architectural modeling). Unlike mainframe computers, which typically run multiple applications simultaneously to serve a wide variety of users, supercomputers generally run one program at a time, as fast as possible.

Conventional supercomputers can cost several million dollars each. To reduce the cost, supercomputers today are often built by connecting hundreds of smaller and less

>**Mainframe computer.** A computer used in large organizations (such as hospitals, large businesses, and colleges) that need to manage large amounts of centralized data and run multiple programs simultaneously. >**Supercomputer.** The fastest, most expensive, and most powerful type of computer.

expensive computers (increasingly midrange servers) into a **supercomputing cluster** that acts as a single supercomputer. The computers in the cluster usually contain multiple CPUs each and are dedicated to processing cluster applications. For example, IBM's *Roadrunner* supercomputer (shown in Figure 1-19)—currently the fastest computer in the world—contains approximately 19,000 CPUs. This supercomputing cluster, built for the U.S. Department of Energy, is installed at Los Alamos National Lab in California and is used primarily to ensure the safety and reliability of the nation's nuclear weapons stockpile. Roadrunner, which cost about $100 million and occupies about 5,200 square feet, is the first supercomputer to reach *petaflop* (quadrillions of *floating point operations per second*) speeds. This supercomputer is also one of the most energy efficient computers in the *TOP500* list of the 500 fastest computers in the world. A new IBM supercomputer named *Sequoia* that is currently under development for the Lawrence Livermore National Laboratory is expected to use approximately 1.6 million CPUs and perform at 20 petaflops.

FIGURE 1-19
The Roadrunner supercomputer. Supercomputers are used for specialized situations in which immense processing speed is required.

COMPUTER NETWORKS AND THE INTERNET

A **computer network** is a collection of computers and other devices that are connected together to enable users to share hardware, software, and data, as well as to communicate electronically with each other. Computer networks exist in many sizes and types. For instance, home networks are commonly used to allow home computers to share a single printer and Internet connection, as well as to exchange files. Small office networks enable workers to access company records stored on a *network server*, communicate with other employees, share a high-speed printer, and access the Internet (see Figure 1-20). School networks allow students and teachers to access the Internet and school resources, and large corporate networks often connect all of the offices or retail stores in the corporation, creating a network that spans several cities or states. Public wireless networks—such as those available at some coffeehouses, restaurants, public libraries, and parks—provide Internet access to individuals via their portable computers and mobile devices. Most computers today connect to a computer network.

What Are the Internet and the World Wide Web?

The **Internet** is the largest and most well-known computer network in the world. It is technically a network of networks, since it consists of thousands of networks that can all access each other via the main *backbone* infrastructure of the Internet. Individual users connect to the Internet by connecting their computers to servers belonging to an **Internet service provider (ISP)**—a company that provides Internet access, usually for a fee. ISPs (which include conventional and mobile telephone companies like AT&T, Verizon, and Sprint; cable providers like Comcast and Time Warner; and stand-alone ISPs like NetZero and EarthLink) function as gateways or onramps to the Internet, providing Internet access to their subscribers. ISP servers are continually connected to a larger network, called a *regional network*, which, in turn, is connected to one of the major high-speed networks within a country, called a *backbone network*. Backbone networks within a country are connected to each other and to backbone networks in other countries. Together they form one enormous network of networks—the Internet. Tips for selecting an ISP are included in Chapter 3.

VIDEO PODCAST

Go to the Chapter 1 page at **www.cengage.com/computerconcepts/np/uccs4** to download or listen to the "How To: Share a Printer over a Network" video podcast.

TIP

Although some people use the terms *Internet* and *Web* interchangeably, technically the Web—the collection of Web pages available over the Internet—is only one resource available via the Internet.

> **Supercomputing cluster.** A supercomputer comprised of numerous smaller computers connected together to act as a single computer.
> **Computer network.** A collection of computers and other hardware devices that are connected together to share hardware, software, and data, as well as to communicate electronically with one another. > **Internet.** The largest and most well-known computer network, linking millions of computers all over the world. > **Internet service provider (ISP).** A business or other organization that provides Internet access to others, typically for a fee.

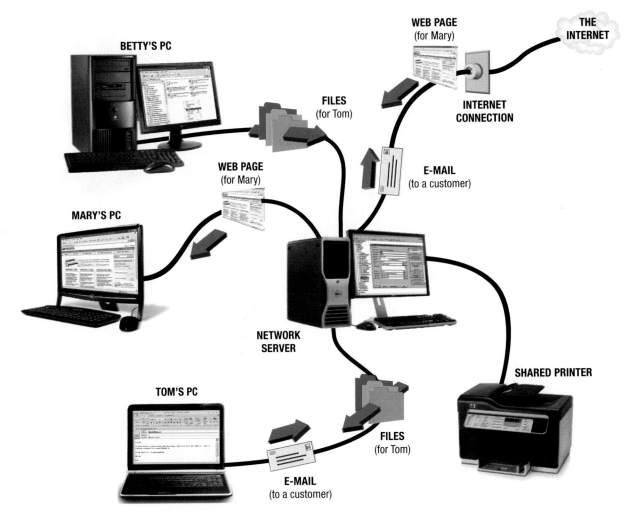

WEB PAGE
(for Mary)

THE INTERNET

BETTY'S PC

FILES
(for Tom)

INTERNET
CONNECTION

WEB PAGE
(for Mary)

E-MAIL
(to a customer)

MARY'S PC

NETWORK
SERVER

SHARED PRINTER

TOM'S PC

FILES
(for Tom)

E-MAIL
(to a customer)

FIGURE 1-20
Example of a
computer network.

Millions of people and organizations all over the world are connected to the Internet. Some of the most common Internet activities today are exchanging e-mail and instant messages (IMs), and accessing content located on *Web pages*. While the term *Internet* refers to the physical structure of that network, the **World Wide Web** (**WWW**) refers to one resource—a collection of documents called **Web pages**—available through the Internet. A group of Web pages belonging to one individual or company is called a **Web site**. Web pages are stored on computers (called **Web servers**) that are continually connected to the Internet; they can be accessed at any time by anyone with a computer (or other Web-enabled device) and an Internet connection. A wide variety of information is available via Web pages, such as company and product information, government forms and publications, maps, telephone directories, news, weather, sports results, airline schedules, and much, much more. You can also use Web pages to shop, bank, trade stock, and perform other types of online financial transactions; access *social networks* like *Facebook* and *MySpace*; and listen to music, play games, watch television shows, and perform other entertainment-oriented activities (see Figure 1-21). Web pages are viewed using a **Web browser**, such as *Internet Explorer (IE)*, *Chrome*, *Safari*, *Opera*, or *Firefox*.

>**World Wide Web (WWW).** The collection of Web pages available through the Internet. >**Web page.** A document, typically containing hyperlinks to other documents, located on a Web server and available through the World Wide Web. >**Web site.** A collection of related Web pages usually belonging to an organization or individual. >**Web server.** A computer that is continually connected to the Internet and hosts Web pages that are accessible through the Internet. >**Web browser.** A program used to view Web pages.

ACCESSING PRODUCT INFORMATION

LOOKING UP REFERENCE INFORMATION

READING NEWS

SHOPPING

ACCESSING SOCIAL NETWORKS

WATCHING TV SHOWS AND MOVIES

Accessing a Network or the Internet

To access a local computer network (such as a home network, a school or company network, or a public wireless hotspot), you need to use a network adapter (either built into your computer or attached to it) to connect your computer to the network. With some computer networks you need to supply logon information (such as a *username* and a password) to *log on* to a network. Once you are connected to the network, you can access network resources, including the network's Internet connection. If you are connecting to the Internet without going through a computer network, your computer needs to use a modem to connect to the communications media (such as a telephone line or cable connection) used by your ISP. Network adapters and modems are discussed in more detail in Chapter 2.

Most Internet connections today are *direct* (or *always-on*) *connections*, which means the computer or other device being used to access the Internet is continually connected to the ISP's computer. With a direct connection, you only need to open your Web browser to begin using the Internet. With a dial-up connection, you must start the program that instructs your computer to dial and connect to the ISP's server via a telephone line, and then open a Web browser, each time you want to access the Internet.

To request a Web page or other resource located on the Internet, its **Internet address**—a unique numeric or text-based address—is used. The most common types of Internet addresses are *IP addresses* and *domain names* (to identify computers), *URLs* (to identify Web pages), and *e-mail addresses* (to identify people).

FIGURE 1-21
Some common Web activities.

>**Internet address.** An address that identifies a computer, person, or Web page on the Internet, such as an IP address, domain name, or e-mail address.

HOW IT WORKS

Campus Emergency Notification Systems

Recent on-campus tragedies, such as the Virginia Tech shootings in 2007, have increased attention on ways organizations can quickly and effectively notify a large number of individuals. Following the Virginia Tech tragedy, which involved a shooting rampage lasting about two hours and killing more than 30 individuals, the *Higher Education Opportunity Act* was signed into law. The law provides grants and other assistance to colleges and universities to create an emergency communications system that can be used to contact students when a significant emergency or dangerous situation emerges. In response, colleges across the U.S. are implementing emergency notification systems to notify students, faculty, staff, and campus visitors of an emergency, severe weather condition, campus closure, or other critical event.

Since nearly all college students in the U.S. today have mobile phones, sending emergency alerts via text message is a natural option for many colleges. To be able to send a text message to an entire campus typically requires the use of a company that specializes in this type of mass communications. One such company is *Omnilert*, which has systems installed in more than 600 colleges and universities around the country. With the Omnilert campus notification system—called *e2Campus*—the contact information of the students, faculty, and staff to be notified is entered into the system and then the individuals can be divided into groups, depending on the types of messages each individual should receive. When an alert needs to be sent, an administrator sends the message (via a mobile phone or computer) and it is distributed to the appropriate individuals (see the accompanying illustration). In addition to text messages, alerts can also be sent simultaneously and automatically via virtually any voice or text communications medium, such as voice messages, e-mail messages, RSS feeds, instant messages, Twitter feeds, Facebook pages, school Web pages, personal portal pages, desktop pop-up alerts, digital signage systems (such as signs located inside dorms and the student union), indoor and outdoor campus public address (PA) systems, and more.

To facilitate campus emergency notification systems, some colleges now require all undergraduate students to have a mobile phone. Some campuses also implement other useful mobile services, such as tracking campus shuttle buses, participating in class polls, and accessing class assignments and grades. An additional safety feature available at some schools is the ability to use the phones to activate an alert whenever a student feels unsafe on campus; these alerts automatically send the student's physical location (determined via the phone's GPS coordinates) to the campus police so the student can be quickly located.

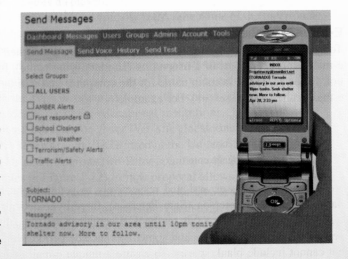

TIP

The *home page* for a Web site is the starting page of that particular site; the *home page* for your browser is the Web page designated as the first page you see each time the browser is opened.

Pronouncing Internet Addresses

Because Internet addresses are frequently given verbally, it is important to know how to pronounce them. A few guidelines are listed next, and Figure 1-24 shows some examples of Internet addresses and their proper pronunciations.

> ▸ If a portion of the address forms a recognizable word or name, it is spoken; otherwise, it is spelled out.

> ▸ The @ sign is pronounced *at.*

> ▸ The period (.) is pronounced *dot.*

> ▸ The forward slash (/) is pronounced *slash.*

TYPE OF ADDRESS	SAMPLE ADDRESS	PRONUNCIATION
Domain name	berkeley.edu	berkeley dot e d u
URL	microsoft.com/windows/ie/default.asp	microsoft dot com slash windows slash i e slash default dot a s p
E-mail address	president@whitehouse.gov	president at whitehouse dot gov

Surfing the Web

Once you have an Internet connection, you are ready to begin *surfing the Web*—that is, using a Web browser to view Web pages. The first page that your Web browser displays when it is opened is your browser's starting page or *home page.* Often this is the home page for the Web site belonging to your browser, school, or ISP. However, you can use your browser's customization options to change the current home page to any page that you plan to visit regularly. From your browser's home page, you can move to any Web page you desire, as discussed next.

Using URLs and Hyperlinks

To navigate to a new Web page for which you know the URL, type that URL in the appropriate location for your Web browser (such as Internet Explorer's *Address bar*, as shown in Figure 1-25) and press Enter. Once that page is displayed, you can use the *hyperlinks*—graphics or text linked to other Web pages—located on that page to display other Web pages. In addition to Web pages, hyperlinks can also be linked to other types of files, such as to enable Web visitors to view or download images, listen to or download music files, view video clips, or download software programs.

The most commonly used Web browsers include Internet Explorer (shown in Figure 1-25), Chrome (shown in Figure 1-26), and Firefox. The newest versions of these browsers include *tabbed browsing* (which allows you to have multiple Web pages open at the same time), improved *crash recovery* and security, and improved ability to search for and *bookmark* Web pages, as discussed shortly. *Internet Explorer 8 (IE 8)* also includes the ability to subscribe to *Web Slices*—small pieces of a Web site, such as a particular online

FIGURE 1-24
Pronouncing Internet addresses.

TIP

If you get an error message when typing a URL, first check to make sure you typed it correctly. If it is correct, edit the URL to remove any folder or filenames and press Enter to try to load the home page of that site.

FIGURE 1-25
Surfing the Web with IE 8. URLs, hyperlinks, and favorites can be used to display Web pages.

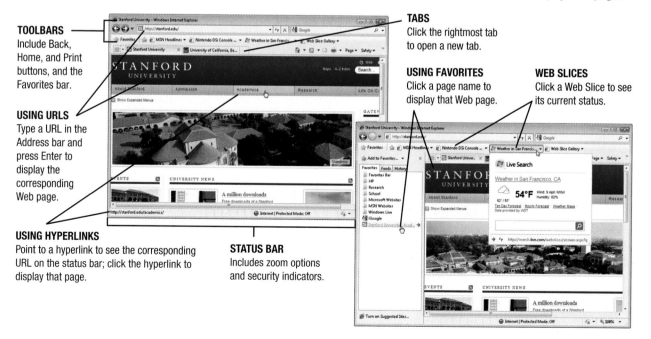

TOOLBARS
Include Back, Home, and Print buttons, and the Favorites bar.

USING URLS
Type a URL in the Address bar and press Enter to display the corresponding Web page.

USING HYPERLINKS
Point to a hyperlink to see the corresponding URL on the status bar; click the hyperlink to display that page.

STATUS BAR
Includes zoom options and security indicators.

TABS
Click the rightmost tab to open a new tab.

USING FAVORITES
Click a page name to display that Web page.

WEB SLICES
Click a Web Slice to see its current status.

auction or a particular Facebook page—and see the current status of that Web Slice without leaving your current page (refer again to Figure 1-25). In any browser, you can use the Back button on the browser's toolbar to return to a previous page. To print the current Web page, click the browser's Print button or select *Print* from the browser's menu or toolbar.

Using Favorites and the History List

All Web browsers have a feature (usually called *Favorites* or *Bookmarks* and accessed via a Favorites or Bookmarks menu or button) that you can use to save Web page URLs. Once a Web page is saved as a favorite or a bookmark, you can redisplay that page without typing its URL—you simply select its link from the Favorites or Bookmarks list. You can also use this feature to save a group of tabbed Web pages to open the entire group again at a later time. Web browsers also maintain a *History list*, which is a record of all Web pages visited during a period of time specified in the browser settings; you can revisit a Web page located on the History list by displaying the History list and selecting that page.

Most Web browsers today allow you to delete, move into folders, and otherwise organize your favorites/bookmarks, as well as to search your favorites/bookmarks or History list to help you find pages more easily. Chrome goes one step further by displaying thumbnails of your most visited sites, a list of your most recent bookmarks, and a history search box each time you open a new browser tab.

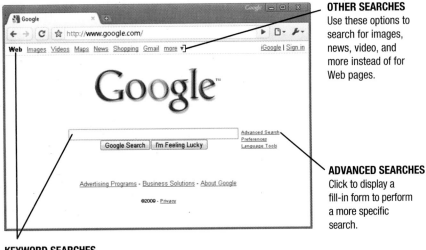

OTHER SEARCHES
Use these options to search for images, news, video, and more instead of for Web pages.

ADVANCED SEARCHES
Click to display a fill-in form to perform a more specific search.

KEYWORD SEARCHES
Since the Web option is selected, type keywords here and press Enter to see a list of Web pages matching your search criteria.

FIGURE 1-26
The Google search site displayed in the Chrome browser.

Searching the Web

People typically turn to the Web to find specific types of information. There are a number of special Web pages, called *search sites*, available to help you locate what you are looking for on the Internet. One of the most popular search sites—*Google*—is shown in Figure 1-26. To conduct a search, you typically type one or more *keywords* into the search box on a search site, and a list of links to Web pages matching your search criteria is displayed (many browsers also allow you to type search terms in the Address bar instead of a URL and an Internet search will be performed). There are also numerous *reference sites* available on the Web to look up addresses, phone numbers, ZIP codes, maps, and other information. To find a reference site, type the information you are looking for (such as "ZIP code lookup" or "topographical maps") in a search site's search box to see links to sites with that information. Searching the Web is discussed in more detail in Chapter 3.

E-Mail

Electronic mail (more commonly called **e-mail**) is the process of exchanging electronic messages between computers over a network—usually the Internet. E-mail is one of the

>**Electronic mail (e-mail).** Electronic messages sent from one user to another over the Internet or other network.

most widely used Internet applications—Americans alone send billions of e-mail messages daily and worldwide e-mail traffic is expected to exceed one-half trillion messages per day by 2013, according to the Radicati Group. You can send an e-mail message from any Internet-enabled device (such as a desktop computer, portable computer, or mobile device) to anyone who has an Internet e-mail address. As illustrated in Figure 1-27, e-mail messages travel from the sender's computer to his or her ISP's *mail server*, and then through the Internet to the mail server being used by the recipient's ISP. When the recipient logs on to the Internet and requests his or her e-mail, it is displayed on the computer he or she is using. In addition to text, e-mail messages can include attached files, such as photos and other documents.

E-mail can be sent and received via an *e-mail program*, such as *Microsoft Outlook*, installed on the computer being used (sometimes referred to as *conventional e-mail*) or via a Web page belonging to a Web mail provider such as *Gmail* or *Windows Live Mail* (referred to as *Web-based e-mail* or just *Web mail*). Using an installed e-mail program is convenient for individuals who use e-mail often and want to have copies of sent and received e-mail messages stored on their computer. To use an installed e-mail program, however, it must first be set up with the user's name, e-mail address, incoming mail server, and outgoing mail server information. Web-based e-mail does not require this set up and a user's e-mail can be accessed from any computer with an Internet connection by just displaying the appropriate Web mail page and logging on. Consequently, Web-based e-mail is more flexible than conventional e-mail since it can be accessed easily from any computer with an Internet connection. However, Web-based e-mail is typically slower than conventional e-mail and messages can only be viewed when the user is online and logged on to his or her Web mail account, unless the Web-based e-mail provider offers *offline e-mail* service. Despite these limitations, use of Web-based e-mail for both personal and business use is growing and, according to a Gartner estimate, as much as 20% of business e-mail accounts are expected to be Web-based by 2012—up from only 2% in 2007.

Web-based e-mail is typically free and virtually all ISPs used with personal computers include e-mail service in their monthly fee. Some plans from mobile phone providers that provide Internet service for mobile phones include a limit on the number and/or size of e-mail messages that can be sent or received during a billing period; messages after that point result in additional fees. Other types of mobile communications, such as text messages that typically use the *Short Message Service* (*SMS*) protocol when sent between mobile phones, may also incur a fee. Messaging and other types of online communications that can be used in addition to e-mail are discussed in Chapter 3.

FIGURE 1-27
How e-mail works.

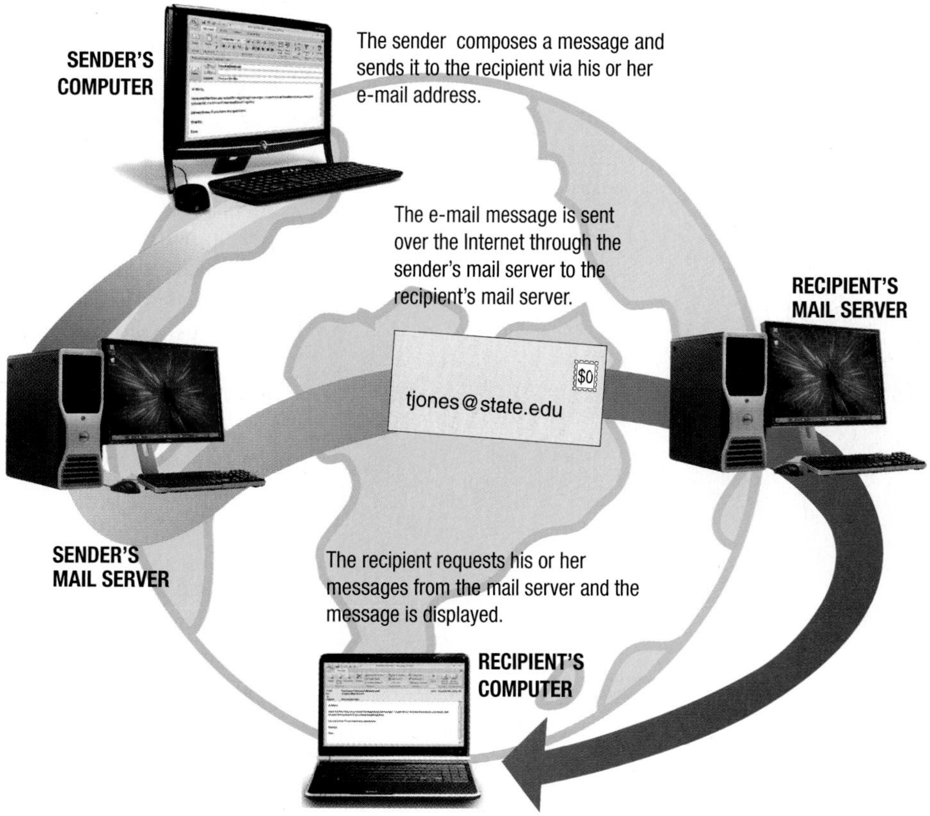

SENDER'S COMPUTER

The sender composes a message and sends it to the recipient via his or her e-mail address.

The e-mail message is sent over the Internet through the sender's mail server to the recipient's mail server.

RECIPIENT'S MAIL SERVER

tjones@state.edu

$0

SENDER'S MAIL SERVER

The recipient requests his or her messages from the mail server and the message is displayed.

RECIPIENT'S COMPUTER

COMPUTERS AND SOCIETY

The vast improvements in technology over the past decade have had a distinct impact on daily life, both at home and at work. Computers have become indispensable tools in our personal and professional lives, and related technological advancements have changed the way our everyday items—cars, microwaves, coffee pots, toys, exercise bikes, telephones, televisions, and more—look and function. As computers and everyday devices become smarter, they tend to do their intended jobs faster, better, and more reliably than before, as well as take on additional capabilities. In addition to affecting individuals, computerization and technological advances have changed society as a whole. Without computers, banks would be overwhelmed by the job of tracking all the transactions they process, moon exploration and the space shuttle would still belong to science fiction, and some scientific advances—such as DNA analysis and gene mapping—would be nonexistent. In addition, we as individuals are getting accustomed to the increased automation of everyday activities, such as shopping and banking, and we depend on having fast and easy access to information via the Internet and rapid communications via e-mail and instant messaging. In addition, many of us would not think about making a major purchase without first researching it online. In fact, it is surprising how fast the Internet and its resources have become an integral part of our society. But despite all its benefits, *cyberspace* has some risks. Some of the most important societal implications related to computers and the Internet are introduced next; many of these issues are covered in more detail in later chapters of this text.

Benefits of a Computer-Oriented Society

The benefits of having such a computer-oriented society are numerous, as touched on throughout this chapter. The capability to virtually design, build, and test new buildings, cars, and airplanes before the actual construction begins helps professionals create safer end products. Technological advances in medicine allow for earlier diagnosis and more effective treatment of diseases than ever before. The benefit of beginning medical students performing virtual surgery using a computer instead of performing actual surgery on a patient is obvious. The ability to shop, pay bills, research products, participate in online courses, and look up vast amounts of information 24 hours a day, 7 days a week, 365 days a year via the Internet is a huge convenience. In addition, a computer-oriented society generates new opportunities. For example, technologies—such as *speech recognition software* and Braille input and output devices—enable physically- or visually-challenged individuals to perform necessary job tasks and to communicate with others more easily.

In general, technology has also made a huge number of tasks in our lives go much faster. Instead of experiencing a long delay for a credit check, an applicant can get approved for a purchase, loan, or credit card almost immediately. Documents and photographs can be e-mailed or faxed in mere moments, instead of taking at least a day to be mailed physically. We can watch many of our favorite TVs shows online (see Figure 1-28) and access up-to-minute news at our convenience. And we can download information, programs, music files, movies, and more on demand when we want or need them, instead of having to order them and then wait for delivery or physically go to a store to purchase the desired items.

▼ FIGURE 1-28
Episodes of many televisions shows are available online to be viewed at the user's convenience.

Risks of a Computer-Oriented Society

Although there are a great number of benefits from having a computer-oriented society and a *networked economy*, there are risks as well. A variety of problems have emerged from our extensive computer use, ranging from stress and health concerns, to the proliferation of *spam* (unsolicited e-mails) and *malware* (harmful programs that can be installed on our computers without our knowledge), to security and privacy issues, to legal and ethical dilemmas. Many of the security and privacy concerns stem from the fact that so much of our personal business takes place online—or at least ends up as data in a computer database somewhere—and the potential for misuse of this data is enormous. Another concern is the repercussions of collecting such vast amounts of information electronically. Some people worry about creating a "Big Brother" situation, in which the government or another organization is watching everything that we do. Although the accumulation and distribution of information is a necessary factor of our networked economy, it is one area of great concern to many individuals. And some Internet behavior, such as downloading music or movies from an unauthorized source or viewing pornography on an office computer, can get you arrested or fired.

Security Issues

One of the most common online security risks today is your computer becoming infected with a malware program, such as a *computer virus*—a malicious software program designed to change the way a computer operates. Malware often causes damage to the infected computer, such as erasing data or bogging down the computer so it does not function well; it can also be used to try to locate sensitive data on your computer (such as Web site passwords or credit card numbers) and send that data to the malware creator. Malware can be attached to a program (such as one downloaded from a Web page), as well as attached to, or contained within, an e-mail message. To help protect your computer, never open an e-mail attachment from someone you do not know or that has an executable *file extension* (the last three letters in the filename preceded by a period), such as *.exe*, *.com*, or *.vbs*, without checking with the sender first to make sure the attachment is legitimate. You should also be careful about what files you download from the Internet. In addition, it is crucial to install *security software* on your computer and to set up the program to monitor your computer on a continual basis (see Figure 1-29). If a virus or other type of malware attempts to install itself on your computer (such as through an e-mail message attachment or a downloaded file), the antivirus program will block it. If malware does find its way onto your computer, the antivirus program will detect it during a regular scan, notify you, and attempt to remove it.

Another ongoing security problem is *identity theft*—in which someone else uses your identity, typically to purchase goods or services. Identity theft can stem from personal information discovered from offline means—like discarded papers or stolen mail—or from information found online, stolen from an online database, or obtained via a malware program. *Phishing*—in which identity thieves send fraudulent e-mails to people masquerading as legitimate businesses to obtain Social Security numbers or other information needed for identity theft—is also a major security issue today. Common security concerns and precautions, such as protecting your computer from malware and protecting yourself against identity theft and phishing schemes, are discussed in detail in Chapter 4.

FIGURE 1-29
Antivirus software.
Antivirus software is crucial for protecting your computer from viruses and other types of malware.

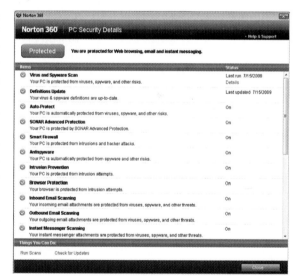

Privacy Issues

Some individuals view the potential risk to personal privacy as one of the most important issues regarding our networked society. As more and more data about our everyday activities is collected and stored on computers accessible via the Internet, our privacy is at risk because the potential for privacy violations increases. Today, data is collected about practically anything we buy online or offline, although offline purchases may not be associated with our identity unless we use a credit card or a membership or loyalty card. At issue is not that data is collected—with virtually all organizations using computers for recordkeeping, that is unavoidable—but rather how the collected data is used and how secure it is. Data collected by businesses may be used only by that company or, depending on the businesses' *privacy policy*, may be shared with others. Data shared with others often results in *spam*—unsolicited e-mails. Spam is an enormous problem for individuals and businesses today, and it is considered by many to be a violation of personal privacy. Privacy concerns and precautions are discussed in detail in Chapter 5.

CAUTION CAUTION CAUTION CAUTION CAUTION CAUTION CAUT

Using your primary e-mail address when shopping online or signing up for a sweepstake or other online activity will undoubtedly result in spam being sent to that e-mail address. Use a *throw-away e-mail address* (a free e-mail address from Gmail or another free e-mail provider that you can change easily) for these activities instead to help protect your privacy and cut back on the amount of spam delivered to your regular e-mail account.

Differences in Online Communications

There is no doubt that e-mail, instant messaging, and other online communications methods have helped speed up both personal and business communications and have made them more efficient (such as avoiding the telephone tag problem). As you spend more and more time communicating online, you will probably notice some differences between online communications methods (such as e-mail and instant messaging) and traditional communications methods (such as telephone calls and written letters). In general, online communications tend to be much less formal. This may be because people usually compose e-mail messages quickly and just send them off, without taking the time to reread the message content or check the spelling or grammar. However, you need to be careful not to be so casual—particularly in business—that your communications appear unprofessional or become too personal with people you do not know.

To help in that regard, a special etiquette—referred to as *netiquette*—has evolved to guide online behavior. A good rule of thumb is always to be polite and considerate of others and to refrain from offensive remarks. This holds true whether you are asking a question via a company's e-mail address, posting a message on someone's *Facebook Wall*, or IMing a friend. When the communication involves business, you should also be very careful with your grammar and spelling, to avoid embarrassing yourself. Some specific guidelines for what is considered to be proper online behavior are listed in Figure 1-30.

Another trend in online communications is the use of abbreviations and *emoticons*. Abbreviations or *acronyms*, such as BTW for "by the way," are commonly used to save time in all types of communications today. They are being used with increased frequency in text messaging and e-mail exchanged via mobile phones to speed up the text entry process. Emoticons are illustrations of faces showing smiles, frowns, and other expressions that are created with keyboard symbols—such as the popular :-) smile emoticon—and allow people to add an emotional tone to written online communications. Without these symbols, it is sometimes difficult to tell if the person who sent the online communication is serious or joking, since you

FIGURE 1-30

Netiquette. Use these netiquette guidelines and common sense when communicating online.

RULE	EXPLANATION
Use descriptive subject lines	Use short, descriptive subject lines for e-mail messages and discussion group posts. For example, "Question regarding MP3 downloads" is much better than a vague title, such as "Question".
Don't shout	SHOUTING REFERS TO TYPING YOUR ENTIRE E-MAIL MESSAGE OR DISCUSSION GROUP POST USING CAPITAL LETTERS. Use capital letters only when it is grammatically correct to do so or for emphasizing a few words.
Watch what you say	Things that you say or write online can be interpreted as being sexist, racist, ethnocentric, xenophobic, or in just general bad taste. Also check spelling and grammar—typos look unprofessional and nobody likes wading through poorly written materials.
Avoid e-mail overload	Don't send spam mail, which is unsolicated bulk e-mail and the Internet equivalent of junk mail. The same goes for forwarding e-mail chain letters or every joke you run across to everyone in your address book.
Be cautious	Don't give out personal information—such as your real name, telephone number, or credit card information—to people you meet in a chat room or other online meeting place.
Think before you send	Once you send an e-mail or text message or post something online, you lose control of it. Don't send messages that include content (such as compromising photos) that you would not want shared with others.

cannot see the individual's face or hear his or her tone of voice. While most people would agree that using abbreviations and emoticons with personal communications is fine, they are not usually viewed as appropriate for formal business communications.

The Anonymity Factor

By their very nature, online communications lend themselves to *anonymity*. Since recipients usually do not hear senders' voices or see their handwriting, it is difficult to know for sure who the sender is. Particularly on *message boards* (online discussions in which users post messages and respond to other posts), in *virtual worlds* (online worlds that users can explore), and other online activities where individuals use made-up names instead of real names, there is an anonymous feel to being online.

Being anonymous gives many individuals a sense of freedom, which makes them feel able to say or do anything online. This sense of true freedom of speech can be beneficial. For example, a reserved individual who might never complain about a poor product or service in person may feel comfortable lodging a complaint by e-mail. In political discussion groups, many people feel they can be completely honest about what they think and can introduce new ideas and points of view without inhibition. Anonymous e-mail is also a safe way for an employee to blow the whistle on a questionable business practice, or for an individual to tip off police to a crime or potential terrorist attack.

But, like all good things, online anonymity can be abused. Using the Internet as their shield, some people use rude comments, ridicule, profanity, and even slander to attack people, places, and things they do not like or agree with. Others may use multiple online identities (such as multiple usernames on a message board) to give the appearance of increased support for their points of view. Still others may use multiple identities to try to manipulate stock prices (by posting false information about a company to drive the price down, for instance), to get buyers to trust an online auction seller (by posting fictitious positive feedback about themselves), or to commit other illegal or unethical acts.

It is possible to hide your true identity while browsing or sending e-mail by removing personal information from your browser and e-mail program or by using privacy software that acts as a middleman between you and Web sites and hides your identity, as discussed in more detail in Chapter 5. But, in fact, even when personal information is removed, ISPs and the government may still be able to trace communications back to a particular computer when a crime has occurred, so it is difficult—perhaps impossible—to be completely anonymous online.

Information Integrity

The Web contains a vast amount of information on a wide variety of topics. While much of the information is factual, other information may be misleading, biased, or just plain wrong. As more and more people turn to the Web for information, it is crucial that they take the time to determine if the information they obtain and pass on to others is accurate. There have been numerous cases of information intended as a joke being restated on a Web site as fact, statements being quoted out of context (which changed the meaning from the original intent), and hoaxes circulated via e-mail. Consequently, use common sense when evaluating what you read online, and double-check information before passing it on to others.

One way to evaluate online content is by its source. If you obtain information from a news source that you trust, you should feel confident that the accuracy of its online information is close to that of its offline counterpart. For information about a particular product, go to the originating company. For government information, government Web sites are your best source for fact checking. There are also independent Web sites (such as the *Snopes* Web site shown in Figure 1-31) that report on the validity of current online rumors and stories.

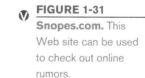

FIGURE 1-31

Snopes.com. This Web site can be used to check out online rumors.

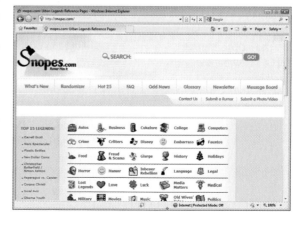

SUMMARY

COMPUTERS IN YOUR LIFE

Chapter Objective 1:
Explain why it is essential to learn about computers today and discuss several ways computers are integrated into our business and personal lives.

Computers appear almost everywhere in today's world, and most people need to use a computer or a computerized device frequently on the job, at home, at school, or while on the go. **Computer literacy**, which is being familiar with basic computer concepts, helps individuals feel comfortable using computers and is a necessary skill for everyone today.

Computers abound in today's homes, schools, workplaces, and other locations. Most students and employees need to use a computer for productivity, research, or other important tasks. Individuals often use computers at home and/or carry portable computers or devices with them to remain in touch with others or to use Internet resources on a continual basis. Individuals also frequently encounter computers while on the go, such as *consumer kiosks* and *point-of-sale (POS) systems*.

WHAT IS A COMPUTER AND WHAT DOES IT DO?

Chapter Objective 2:
Define a computer and describe its primary operations.

A **computer** is a *programmable* electronic device that accepts **input**; performs **processing** operations; **outputs** the results; and provides **storage** for data, programs, or output when needed. Most computers today also have **communications** capabilities. This progression of input, processing, output, and storage is sometimes called the *information processing cycle*.

Data is the raw, unorganized facts that are input into the computer to be processed. Data that the computer has processed into a useful form is called **information**. Data can exist in many forms, representing text, graphics, audio, and video.

Chapter Objective 3:
List some important milestones in computer evolution.

One of the first calculating devices was the *abacus*. Early computing devices that predate today's computers include the *slide rule*, the *mechanical calculator*, and Dr. Herman Hollerith's *Punch Card Tabulating Machine and Sorter*. *First-generation computers*, such as *ENIAC* and *UNIVAC*, were powered by *vacuum tubes*; *second-generation computers* used *transistors*; and *third-generation computers* were possible because of the invention of the *integrated circuit (IC)*. Today's *fourth-generation computers* use *microprocessors* and are frequently connected to the *Internet* and other *networks*. Some people believe that *fifth-generation computers* will likely be based on *artificial intelligence*.

Chapter Objective 4:
Identify the major parts of a personal computer, including input, processing, output, storage, and communications hardware.

A computer is made up of **hardware** (the actual physical equipment that makes up the computer system) and **software** (the computer's programs). Common hardware components include the *keyboard* and *mouse (input devices)*, the *CPU (a processing device)*, *monitors* and *printers (output devices)*, and *storage devices* and *storage media* (such as *CDs, DVD drives, hard drives, USB flash drives*, and *flash memory cards*). Most computers today also include a *modem, network adapter*, or other type of *communications device* to allow users to connect to the Internet or other network.

Chapter Objective 5:
Define software and understand how it is used to instruct the computer what to do.

All computers need *system software*, namely an **operating system** (usually *Windows, Mac OS*, or *Linux*), to function. The operating system assists with the **boot** process, and then controls the operation of the computer, such as to allow users to run other types of software and to manage their files. Most software programs today use a variety of graphical objects that are selected to tell the computer what to do. The basic workspace for a Windows' users is the **Windows desktop**.

Application software consists of programs designed to allow people to perform specific tasks or applications, such as word processing, Web browsing, photo touch-up, and so on. Software programs are written using a *programming language*. Programs are written by *programmers*; *computer users* are the people who use computers to perform tasks or obtain information.

COMPUTERS TO FIT EVERY NEED

Embedded computers are built into products (such as cars and household appliances) to give them added functionality. **Mobile devices** are small devices with computing or Internet capabilities; a mobile device based on a mobile phone is called a **smartphone**.

Small computers used by individuals at home or work are called **personal computers** (**PCs**) or **microcomputers**. Most personal computers today are either **desktop computers** or **portable computers** (**notebook computers**, **laptop computers**, **tablet computers**, **netbooks**, or **ultra-mobile PCs** (**UMPC**)—also called **handheld computers**) and typically conform to either the *PC-compatible* or *Macintosh* standard. Tablet computers come in both *slate tablet* and *convertible tablet* formats. **Thin clients** are designed solely to access a network; **Internet appliances** are designed specifically for accessing the Internet and e-mail.

Medium-sized computers, or **midrange servers**, are used in many businesses to host data and programs to be accessed via the company network. A growing trend is **virtualization**—creating separate virtual environments on a single server that act as separate servers. The powerful computers used by most large businesses and organizations to perform the information processing necessary for day-to-day operations are called **mainframe computers**. The very largest, most powerful computers, which typically run one application at a time, are **supercomputers**. A supercomputer comprised of numerous smaller computers connected together to act as a single computer is a **supercomputing cluster**.

COMPUTER NETWORKS AND THE INTERNET

Computer networks are used to connect individual computers and related devices so that users can share hardware, software, and data as well as communicate with one another. The **Internet** is a worldwide collection of networks. Typically, individual users connect to the Internet by connecting to computers belonging to an **Internet service provider** (**ISP**)—a company that provides Internet access, usually for a fee. One resource available through the Internet is the **World Wide Web** (**WWW**)—an enormous collection of **Web pages** located on **Web servers**. The starting page for a **Web site** (a related group of Web pages) is called the *home page* for that site. Web pages are viewed with a **Web browser**, are connected with *hyperlinks*, and can be used for many helpful activities.

To access a computer network, you need some type of *modem* or *network adapter*. To access the Internet, an Internet service provider (ISP) is also used. **Internet addresses** are used to identify resources on the Internet and include numerical **IP addresses** and text-based **domain names** (used to identify computers), **uniform resource locators** or **URLs** (used to identify Web pages), and **e-mail addresses** (a combination of a **username** and domain name that is used to send an individual e-mail messages).

Web pages are displayed by clicking hyperlinks or by typing appropriate URLs in the browser's *Address bar. Favorites/Bookmarks* and the *History list* can be used to redisplay a previously-visited Web page and *search sites* can be used to locate Web pages matching specified criteria. **Electronic mail** (**e-mail**) is used to send electronic messages over the Internet.

COMPUTERS AND SOCIETY

Computers and devices based on related technology have become indispensable tools for modern life, making ordinary tasks easier and quicker than ever before and helping make today's worker more productive than ever before. In addition to the benefits, however, there are many risks and societal implications related to our heavy use of the Internet and the vast amount of information available through the Internet. Issues include privacy and security risks and concerns (such as *malware*, *identity theft*, *phishing*, and *spam*), the differences in online and offline communications, the anonymity factor, and the amount of unreliable information that can be found on the Internet.

Chapter Objective 6:
List the six basic types of computers, giving at least one example of each type of computer and stating what that computer might be used for.

Chapter Objective 7:
Explain what a network, the Internet, and the World Wide Web are, as well as how computers, people, and Web pages are identified on the Internet.

Chapter Objective 8:
Describe how to access a Web page and navigate through a Web site.

Chapter Objective 9:
Discuss the societal impact of computers, including some benefits and risks related to their prominence in our society.

REVIEW ACTIVITIES

KEY TERM MATCHING

a. computer

b. hardware

c. Internet

d. netbook

e. processing

f. software

g. storage

h. supercomputer

i. uniform resource locator (URL)

j. Web site

Instructions: Match each key term on the left with the definition on the right that best describes it.

1. _____ A collection of related Web pages usually belonging to an organization or individual.

2. _____ An Internet address, usually beginning with http://, that uniquely identifies a Web page.

3. _____ A programmable, electronic device that accepts data input, performs processing operations on that data, and outputs and stores the results.

4. _____ A very small notebook computer.

5. _____ Performing operations on data that have been input into a computer to convert that input to output.

6. _____ The operation of saving data, programs, or output for future use.

7. _____ The fastest, most expensive, and most powerful type of computer.

8. _____ The instructions, also called computer programs, that are used to tell a computer what it should do.

9. _____ The largest and most well-known computer network, linking millions of computers all over the world.

10. _____ The physical parts of a computer system, such as the keyboard, monitor, printer, and so forth.

SELF-QUIZ

Instructions: Circle **T** if the statement is true, **F** if the statement is false, or write the best answer in the space provided. **Answers for the self-quiz are located in the References and Resources Guide at the end of the book.**

1. **T** **F** A mouse is one common input device.

2. **T** **F** Software includes all the physical equipment in a computer system.

3. **T** **F** A computer can run without an operating system if it has good application software.

4. **T** **F** One of the most common types of home computers is the midrange server.

5. **T** **F** An example of a domain name is *microsoft.com.*

6. _____ is the operation in which data is entered into the computer.

7. A(n) _____ computer can come in convertible or slate form.

8. _____ is frequently used with servers today to create several separate environments on a single server that act as separate servers.

9. Electronic messages sent over the Internet that can be retrieved by the recipient at his or her convenience are called _____.

10. Write the number of the term that best matches each of the following descriptions in the blank to the left of its description.

a. _____ Allows access to resources located on the Internet.

b. _____ Supervises the running of all other programs on the computer.

c. _____ Enables users to perform specific tasks on a computer.

d. _____ Allows the creation of application programs.

1. Application software
2. Operating system
3. Programming language
4. Web browser

---

1. For the following list of computer hardware devices, indicate the principal function of each device by writing the appropriate letter—I (input device), O (output device), S (storage device), P (processing device), or C (communications device)—in the space provided.

a. CPU _____   d. Keyboard _____   g. Speakers _____

b. Monitor _____   e. Hard drive _____   h. DVD drive _____

c. Mouse _____   f. Modem _____   i. Microphone _____

2. Supply the missing words to complete the following statements.

a. The Internet is an example of a(n) _____, a collection of computers and other devices connected together to share resources and communicate with each other.

b. The starting page for a Web site is called the site's _____.

c. For the e-mail address *jsmith@cengage.com*, *jsmith* is the _____ and *cengage.com* is the _____ name.

d. The e-mail address pronounced *bill gee at microsoft dot com* is written _____.

3. What are three differences between a desktop computer and an ultra-mobile PC (UMPC)?

4. List two reasons why a business may choose to network its employees' computers.

5. If a computer manufacturer called Apex created a home page for the Web, what would its URL likely be? Also, supply an appropriate e-mail address for yourself, assuming that you are employed by that company.

---

1. There is usually a positive side and a negative side to each new technological improvement. Select a technology you use every day and consider its benefits and risks. What benefits does the technology provide? Are there any risks involved and, if so, how can they be minimized? If you chose not to use this technology because of the possible risks associated with it, how would your life be affected? Who should determine if the benefits of a new technology outweigh the potential risks? Consumers? The government?

2. The ubiquitous nature of mobile phones today brings tremendous convenience to our lives, but will misuse of new improvements to this technology result in the loss of that convenience? For instance, camera phones are now banned in many fitness centers, park restrooms, and other similar facilities because some people have used them inappropriately to take compromising photos, and mobile phones are banned in many classrooms because of the disruption of constant text messaging and the use of the phone by dishonest students to cheat on exams. Do you think these reactions to mobile phone misuse are justified? Is there another way to ensure the appropriate use of mobile phones without banning their use for all individuals? Should there be more stringent consequences for those who use technology for illegal or unethical purposes?

PROJECTS

1. **Mobile TV** As discussed in this chapter, TV is one of the newest entertainment options available for mobile phones. From live TV to video clips and movies, mobile TV is taking off.

   For this project, investigate the mobile TV options available today. Find at least two services and compare features, such as cost, compatibility, channels, and programming. Do your selected services offer live TV, video-on-demand, or both? If you have a mobile phone, are any of the services available through your mobile provider? Are there currently Web sites where mobile users can view episodes of TV shows for free, like personal computer users can? What is the current status of the push by the *Open Mobile Video Coalition* to have a free mobile TV standard across the United States? Have you ever watched TV on a mobile phone? If so, how do you rate your experience and would you do it again? If not, would you want to watch TV on a mobile phone? Do you think mobile TV is the wave of the future? Why or why not? At the conclusion of your research, prepare a one-page summary of your findings and opinions and submit it to your instructor.

2. **Buying a New PC** New personal computers are widely available directly from manufacturers, as well as in retail, computer, electronic, and warehouse stores. Some stores carry only standard configurations as set up by the manufacturers; others allow you to customize a system.

   For this project, assume that you are in the market for a new personal computer. Give some thought to the type of computer (such as desktop, notebook, or netbook computer) that best fits your lifestyle and the tasks you wish to perform (such as the application programs you wish to use, how many programs you wish to use at one time, and how fast you desire the response time to be). Make a list of your hardware and software requirements (refer to the "Guide for Buying a PC" in the References and Resources Guide at the end of this book, if needed), being as specific as possible. By researching newspaper ads, manufacturer Web sites, and/or systems for sale at local stores, find three systems that meet your minimum requirements. Prepare a one-page comparison chart, listing each requirement and how each system meets or exceeds it. Also include any additional features each system has, and information regarding the brand, price, delivery time, shipping, sales tax, and warranty for each system. On your comparison sheet, mark the system that you would prefer to buy and write one paragraph explaining why. Turn in your comparison sheet and summary to your instructor, stapled to copies of the printed ads, specifications printed from Web sites, or other written documentation that you collected during this project.

3. **The Internet** The Internet and World Wide Web are handy tools that can help you research topics covered in this textbook, complete many of the projects, and perform the online activities available via the textbook's Web site that are designed to enhance your learning and help you prepare for exams on the content covered in this textbook.

   For this project, find an Internet-enabled computer on your campus, at home, or at your public library and access the Understanding Computers Web site located at **www.cengage.com/ computerconcepts/np/uccs4**. Once you are at the site, note the types of information and activities that are available to you as a student and select a few of them by using your mouse to click the hyperlinks corresponding to the options you want to explore. At the conclusion of this task, prepare a one-page summary describing the resources available through this textbook's Web site, and your opinion about their usefulness in enhancing your learning experience and/or preparing for exams related to this text, and submit it to your instructor.

4. **Gossip Sites** A recent trend on college campuses today is the use of campus gossip sites, where students can post campus related news, rumors, and basic gossip. These sites were originally set up to promote free speech and to allow participants to publish comments anonymously without repercussions from school administrators, professors, and other officials. However, they are now being used to post vicious comments about others. What do you think of campus gossip sites? Is it ethical to post a rumor about another individual on these sites? How would you feel if you read a posting about yourself on a gossip site? School administrators cannot regulate the content since the sites are not sponsored or run by the college, and federal law prohibits Web hosts from being liable for the content posted by its users. Is this ethical? What if a posting leads to a criminal act, such as a rape, murder, or suicide? Who, if anyone, should be held responsible?

For this project, form an opinion about the ethical ramifications of gossip Web sites and be prepared to discuss your position (in class, via an online class discussion group, in a class chat room, or via a class blog, depending on your instructor's directions). You may also be asked to write a short paper expressing your opinion.

5. **Traditional vs. Online Education** The amount of distance learning available through the Internet and World Wide Web has exploded recently. A few years ago, it was possible to take an occasional course online—now, an entire college degree can be earned online. But are traditional and online educations equal? Do the potential advantages of online education (such as convenience, flexibility, and the ability to take classes when you are not physically located near a university) outweigh the potential disadvantages (such as technological dependency and lack of face-to-face interactions with other students and with instructors)? Will potential employers question the integrity of a degree earned online (where there is more potential for cheating if online exams are used) more than one earned in person? Or does the ability to take a wider range of classes online versus in person put the online student at an advantage?

For this project, consider the pros and cons of online learning versus traditional learning and form an opinion about online education. Be prepared to discuss both sides of this issue and your opinion (in class, via an online class discussion group, in a class chat room, or via a class blog). You may also be asked to write a short paper or prepare a short presentation expressing your opinion, depending on your instructor's directions.

Instructions: Go to the Chapter 1 page at **www.cengage.com/computerconcepts/np/uccs4** to work the following Web Activities.

6. **Interactive Activities** Work the interactive **Crossword Puzzle**, watch the **Video Podcasts** and **Online Videos**, and explore the **Further Exploration** links associated with this chapter.

If you have a SAM user profile, you may have access to hands-on instruction, practice, and assessment of the skills covered in this chapter. Check with your instructor for instructions and the correct URL/Web site to access those assignments.

7. **Student Edition Labs** Work the following interactive **Student Edition Labs.**
    - ➤ **Using Windows**
    - ➤ **E-Mail**
    - ➤ **Word Processing**
    - ➤ **Spreadsheets**
    - ➤ **Databases**
    - ➤ **Presentation Software**

8. **Test Yourself** Review the **Online Study Guide** for this chapter, then test your knowledge of the terms and concepts covered in this chapter by completing the **Key Term Matching** exercise, the **Self-Quiz**, the **Exercises**, and the **Practice Test**.

SAM

Student Edition Labs

Personal Computers

D-Link®
Building Networks for People

Joe Melfi is the
Associate Director of
Business Solutions for
D-Link Systems. He has
worked in the area of
communications and
electronics technologies
for more than 25 years,
including as a Systems
Engineer, Software
Engineer, Application
Engineer, and Technical
Marketing Engineer,
before accepting his cur-
rent position at D-Link.
Joe holds a Bachelor
of Science degree in
Electrical Engineering,
as well as several tech-
nical certificates. He
has also been a college
instructor, teaching
courses in microproces-
sor systems, data com-
munications, and digital
electronics.

A conversation with JOE MELFI
Associate Director of Business Solutions, D-Link Systems

"*. . . it is important to be cautious about what information is shared online because, once it is out there, it can't be taken back.*"

My Background . . .

In my youth, I had an endless curiosity about how things worked. I took everything apart to see what was inside, which led me down the path to become an electrical engineer. Eventually, I found my calling in computer communications. All in all, I have more than 25 years of applied experience in a wide range of communications and electronics technologies. Currently, I serve as Associate Director of Business Solutions for D-Link, a leading company in the area of business and consumer networking hardware. My primary responsibilities include driving marketing programs, creating sales materials, and overseeing technical aspects of the marketing department.

Throughout my career, I've found I favor roles that merge technology with marketing. I credit my engineering education and experience; my hands-on experience as a technician and hobbyist; my teaching experience; and my experience as a techie working with sales teams and making presentations with giving me the experience and skills needed to succeed in my chosen career.

It's Important to Know . . .

Computers are everywhere, and take many forms. Computers are more than the PC on your desk. They are in your cars, your televisions, your phones, and so many other places. The smartphone is one current technology that may end up having the biggest impact on our lives. Today's mobile phones typically can be used for much more than placing phone calls. They often include a camera, GPS capabilities, a voice recorder, Internet connectivity, multimedia functions, and access to e-mail, calendars, contact information, and more. It will be interesting to see how far this technology goes.

Computers are ubiquitous on the job. They are an integral part of almost any job today. Therefore, you can never know enough about computers and how to utilize them effectively.

Computers have also affected social behavior. While computers increase productivity and enhance functionality, we should not forget that sometimes human interaction is needed. And, when dealing with people, we should remember that people are not computers and shouldn't be treated as such—they require patience and emotional consideration.

How I Use this Technology . . .

I use computers in almost every aspect of my life, both professional and personal. My home is completely networked with computers on every floor, cameras for surveillance, servers and storage devices for managing all my data, and centralized printers and scanners accessible throughout the network. I also have networked media players that deliver video and audio from my home computers, storage devices, or the Internet to my big screen TV and entertainment systems. In addition, I have wireless home control, which is something that I expect to become more popular in the near future. My mobile phone also syncs data from my network so I can take essential information with me wherever I go.

What the Future Holds . . .

There was a time when individuals and businesses hesitated to embrace the Internet, but that has clearly changed in recent years. We are surely becoming a connected society and computers, computer communications, and the Internet have changed the way businesses operate in so many ways. Mobile phones are quickly replacing landline phones, and they are becoming handheld computers that bring us amazing capabilities, including allowing us to be more mobile than ever before. And, with Internet usage becoming such an integral part of our business and personal lives, high-speed networking is changing from optional to commonplace.

But there is more change to come. The new wireless standards that are on the horizon will continue to improve communication performance and functionality in the near future. We will have Internet access everywhere, anytime, via handheld devices, and entertainment will use the Internet as a significant method of delivery. This continued evolution of computers and communications will provide us with easier access to goods and services, instant accomplishment of tasks, and an endless assortment of entertainment and productivity options at our disposal.

It is important to remember, however, that while our increasingly connected society has many benefits, it also brings additional security and privacy risks. Computers and the Internet allow more ways for the curious and the deviant to peek into our lives and access data that has traditionally been private. In addition, many individuals today voluntarily provide personal data without hesitation, and social networking has made it so easy for a person's voice to be heard that many people spend a great deal of time posting their opinions online. But it is important to be cautious about what information is shared online because, once it is out there, it can't be taken back.

"Computers are an integral part of almost any job today. Therefore, you can never know enough about computers and how to utilize them effectively."

My Advice to Students . . .

Embrace computers as productivity tools and entertainment appliances, in whatever form they take. Overcome the fear that keeps many people from taking full advantage of computers. I highly recommend learning how computers function by learning what hardware is located inside. In fact, I build computers for fun and learning; there is no better way to learn than with a hands-on experience.

Discussion Question

Joe Melfi views the mobile phone as one current technology that may end up having the biggest impact on our lives in the future. Think about which tasks you use your mobile phone for and which ones you cannot. What changes need to be made in the future in order to perform all of these tasks on a mobile phone? Will they be primarily hardware or software changes? Is the mobile phone the computer of the future? Be prepared to discuss your position (in class, via an online class discussion group, in a class chat room, or via a class blog, depending on your instructor's directions). You may also be asked to write a short paper expressing your opinion.

> **For more information on D-Link Systems, visit www.dlink.com.**

chapter 2

A Closer Look at Hardware and Software

After completing this chapter, you will be able to do the following:

1. Understand how data is represented to a computer.

2. Identify several types of input devices and explain their functions.

3. Explain the functions of the primary hardware components found inside the system unit, namely the motherboard, the CPU, and memory.

4. List several output devices and explain their functions.

5. Understand the difference between storage and memory, as well as between a storage device and a storage medium.

6. Name several types of storage systems and explain the circumstances under which they are typically used.

7. Describe the purpose of communications hardware.

8. Understand basic software concepts and commands.

outline

Overview

Digital Data Representation
Bits and Bytes
Numbering Systems and Coding Systems

Input Hardware
Keyboards
Pointing Devices
Scanners, Readers, and Digital Cameras
Other Input Devices

Processing Hardware and Other Hardware Inside the System Unit
The Motherboard
The Central Processing Unit (CPU)
Memory

Output Hardware
Display Devices
Printers
Other Output Devices

Storage Hardware
Storage System Characteristics
Hard Drives
Optical Discs
Flash Memory
Other Types of Storage Systems
Evaluating Your Storage Alternatives

Communications Hardware
Network Adapters and Modems
Other Networking Hardware

Software Basics
Software Ownership Rights
Installed vs. Web-Based Software
Desktop vs. Mobile Software
Common Software Commands
Working with Files and Folders

OVERVIEW

When you hear the phrase "computer system," you probably picture hardware—a desktop or notebook computer, a printer, or maybe a mobile phone. But a computer system involves more than just hardware. As you already know from Chapter 1, computers need software in order to function. It is the software that tells the hardware what to do and when to do it. Computers also need data input, which is used to begin the information processing cycle.

This chapter opens with a discussion of data and how it is represented to a computer. Next, we take a closer look at the hardware that makes up a computer system. Since it is not possible to mention all of the hardware products available today, a sampling of the most common hardware products used for input, processing, output, storage, and communications is covered in this chapter. Although a complete discussion of software is also beyond the scope of this book, the chapter concludes with a brief look at some basic software concepts and operations.

The basic hardware and software concepts and terminology covered in this chapter are important for all computer users to understand. In addition, these concepts will provide you with a solid foundation for discussing the important societal issues featured throughout this text. Many of you will apply this chapter's content to conventional personal computers—such as desktop and notebook computers. However, it is important to realize that the principles and procedures discussed in this chapter apply to other types of computers as well, such as those embedded in toys, consumer devices, household appliances, cars, and other devices, and those used with mobile devices, powerful servers, mainframes, and supercomputers. ■

PODCAST

Go to **www.cengage.com/ computerconcepts/np/uccs4** to download or listen to the "Expert Insight on Hardware" podcast.

DIGITAL DATA REPRESENTATION

Virtually all computers today—such as the embedded computers, mobile devices, personal computers, midrange servers, mainframes, and supercomputers discussed in Chapter 1—are *digital computers*. Most digital computers are *binary computers*, which can understand only two states, usually thought of as *off* and *on* and represented by the digits 0 and 1. Consequently, all data processed by a binary computer must be in binary form (0s and 1s). Fortunately, the computer takes care of translating input into the form needed by the computer being used and then, after processing, translates and outputs the resulting information into a form that can be understood by the user.

Bits and Bytes

The 0s and 1s used to represent data can be represented in a variety of ways, such as with an open or closed circuit, the absence or presence of an electronic charge, the absence or presence of a magnetic spot or depression on a storage medium, and so on.

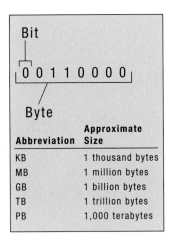

Abbreviation	Approximate Size
KB	1 thousand bytes
MB	1 million bytes
GB	1 billion bytes
TB	1 trillion bytes
PB	1,000 terabytes

 FIGURE 2-1

Bits and bytes. Document size, storage capacity, and memory capacity are all measured in bytes.

FIGURE 2-2

Some extended ASCII code examples.

CHARACTER	ACSII
0	00110000
1	00110001
2	00110010
3	00110011
4	00110100
5	00110101
A	01000001
B	01000010
C	01000011
D	01000100
E	01000101
F	01000110
+	00101011
!	00100001
#	00100011

Regardless of their physical representations, these 0s and 1s are commonly referred to as *bits*, a computing term derived from the phrase *binary digits*. A **bit** is the smallest unit of data that a binary computer can recognize. Therefore, the input you enter via a keyboard, the software program you use to play your music collection, the term paper stored on your computer, and the digital photos located on your mobile phone are all just groups of bits. Consequently, binary can be thought of as the computer's "native language."

A bit by itself typically represents only a fraction of a piece of data. Consequently, large numbers of bits are needed to represent a written document, computer program, digital photo, music file, or virtually any other type of data. Eight bits grouped together are collectively referred to as a **byte**. It is important to be familiar with this concept because *byte* terminology is frequently used in a variety of computer contexts, such as to indicate the size of a document or digital photo, the amount of memory a computer has, or the amount of room left on a storage medium. Since these quantities often involve thousands or millions of bytes, prefixes are commonly used in conjunction with the term *byte* to represent larger amounts of data (see Figure 2-1). For instance, a **kilobyte (KB)** is equal to 1,024 bytes, but is usually thought of as approximately 1,000 bytes; a **megabyte (MB)** is about 1 million bytes; a **gigabyte (GB)** is about 1 billion bytes; a **terabyte (TB)** is about 1 trillion bytes; and a **petabyte (PB)** is about 1,000 terabytes (2^{50} bytes). Therefore, 5 KB is about 5,000 bytes, 10 MB is about 10 million bytes, and 2 TB is about 2 trillion bytes.

Numbering Systems and Coding Systems

A *numbering system* is a way of representing numbers. The numbering system we commonly use is called the **decimal numbering system** because it uses 10 symbols—the digits 0, 1, 2, 3, 4, 5, 6, 7, 8, and 9—to represent all possible numbers. Numbers greater than nine, such as 21 and 683, are represented using combinations of these 10 symbols. The **binary numbering system** uses only two symbols—the digits 0 and 1—to represent all possible numbers. Consequently, binary computers use the binary numbering system to represent numbers and perform math computations.

In both numbering systems, the position of each digit determines the power, or exponent, to which the *base number* (10 for decimal or 2 for binary) is raised. In the decimal numbering system, going from right to left, the first position or column (the ones column) represents 10^0 or 1; the second column (the tens column) represents 10^1 or 10; the third column (the hundreds column) represents 10^2 or 100; and so forth. Therefore, although 101 represents "one hundred one" in the decimal number system, it equals "five" ($1 \times 2^2 + 0 \times 2^1 + 1 \times 2^0$ or $4 + 0 + 1$ or 5) using the binary number system. For more information about numbering systems and some examples of converting between numbering systems, see the "A Look at Numbering Systems" section in the References and Resources Guide at the end of this book.

To represent text-based data, special fixed-length binary *coding systems*—namely, *ASCII* and *Unicode*—were developed. These codes represent all characters that can appear in text data, including numeric characters, alphabetic characters, and special characters such as the dollar sign ($) and period (.). **ASCII (American Standard Code for Information Interchange)** is the coding system traditionally used with personal computers. ASCII is a 7-digit (7-bit) code, although there are several different 8-bit *extended* versions of ASCII that contain additional symbols not included in the 7-bit ASCII code, such as to represent non-English characters, graphics symbols, and mathematical symbols. The extended ASCII character sets represent each character as a unique combination of 8 bits (see Figure 2-2). One group of 8 bits (one byte) allows 256 (2^8) unique combinations. Therefore, an 8-bit code (like extended ASCII) can represent 256 characters.

Unlike ASCII, which is limited to only the Latin alphabet used with the English language, **Unicode** is a universal international coding standard designed to represent text-based data written in any ancient or modern language, including those with different alphabets, such as Chinese, Greek, Hebrew, Amharic, Tibetan, and Russian (see Figure 2-3). Unicode uniquely identifies each character using 0s and 1s, no matter which language, program, or computer platform is being used. It is a longer code, consisting of 1 to 4 bytes (8 to 32 bits) per character, and can represent over one million characters, which is more than enough unique combinations to represent the standard characters in all the world's written languages, as well as thousands of mathematical and technical symbols, punctuation marks, and other symbols and signs. The biggest advantage of Unicode is that it can be used worldwide with consistent and unambiguous results.

CHINESE   GREEK   HEBREW

AMHARIC   TIBETAN   RUSSIAN

FIGURE 2-3
Unicode. Many characters, such as these, can be represented by Unicode but not by ASCII.

INPUT HARDWARE

As discussed in Chapter 1, *input* is the process of entering data into a computer. An **input device** is any piece of hardware that is used to perform data input. Traditional input devices include the *keyboard* and *mouse*, but there are also many other types of input devices in use today.

Keyboards

Most computers today are designed to be used with a **keyboard**—a device used to enter characters at the location on the screen marked by the *insertion point* or *cursor* (typically a blinking vertical line). An *integrated keyboard* is built into a device, a *wired keyboard* is connected via a cable to the computer's *system unit* (typically via a *USB port* or *keyboard port*), and a *wireless keyboard* is powered by batteries and connected via a wireless connection (such as *Bluetooth*). Most keyboards today contain standard alphanumeric keys along with a variety of special keys for specific purposes. However, the order and layout of the keys on a mobile device may be different from the order and layout on a conventional keyboard, and the keyboard layout may vary from device to device.

Virtually all desktop computers include a keyboard. Notebook and netbook computers usually have a keyboard that is similar to a desktop keyboard, but it is typically smaller, contains fewer keys (it often has no numeric keypad, for instance), and the keys are typically placed somewhat closer together. Increasingly, ultra-mobile PCs (UMPCs) and mobile devices today have an integrated keyboard; often these are *slide-out keyboards* that can be revealed when needed and hidden when not in use. Mobile devices that do not include a physical keyboard may support an *on-screen keyboard* or rely on other means of input (such as *pen input* or *touch input*, discussed shortly) instead. A mobile device with a slide-out keyboard is shown in Figure 2-4; a typical desktop keyboard is shown in Figure 2-5.

Pointing Devices

In addition to a keyboard, most computers today are used in conjunction with some type of **pointing device**. Pointing devices are used to select and manipulate objects, to input certain types of data (such as handwritten

FIGURE 2-4
Slide-out keyboards.

>**Unicode.** An international coding system that can be used to represent text-based data in any written language. >**Input device.** A piece of hardware that supplies input to a computer. >**Keyboard.** An input device containing numerous keys that can be used to input letters, numbers, and other symbols. >**Pointing device.** An input device that moves an on-screen pointer, such as an arrow, to allow the user to select objects on the screen.

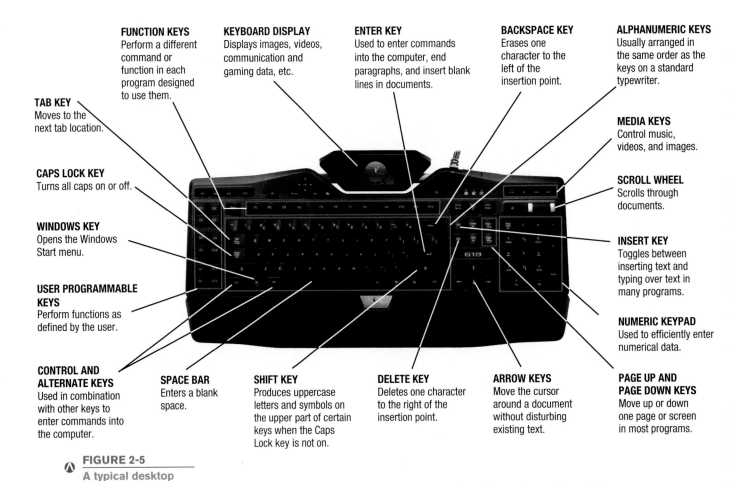

FUNCTION KEYS
Perform a different command or function in each program designed to use them.

KEYBOARD DISPLAY
Displays images, videos, communication and gaming data, etc.

ENTER KEY
Used to enter commands into the computer, end paragraphs, and insert blank lines in documents.

BACKSPACE KEY
Erases one character to the left of the insertion point.

ALPHANUMERIC KEYS
Usually arranged in the same order as the keys on a standard typewriter.

TAB KEY
Moves to the next tab location.

MEDIA KEYS
Control music, videos, and images.

CAPS LOCK KEY
Turns all caps on or off.

SCROLL WHEEL
Scrolls through documents.

WINDOWS KEY
Opens the Windows Start menu.

INSERT KEY
Toggles between inserting text and typing over text in many programs.

USER PROGRAMMABLE KEYS
Perform functions as defined by the user.

NUMERIC KEYPAD
Used to efficiently enter numerical data.

CONTROL AND ALTERNATE KEYS
Used in combination with other keys to enter commands into the computer.

SPACE BAR
Enters a blank space.

SHIFT KEY
Produces uppercase letters and symbols on the upper part of certain keys when the Caps Lock key is not on.

DELETE KEY
Deletes one character to the right of the insertion point.

ARROW KEYS
Move the cursor around a document without disturbing existing text.

PAGE UP AND PAGE DOWN KEYS
Move up or down one page or screen in most programs.

FIGURE 2-5
A typical desktop keyboard.

data or edits to images), and to issue commands to the computer. Two of the most common pointing devices are the *mouse* and the *pen/stylus*, which are used to *click* screen objects and perform *pen input*, respectively; a common pointing device that uses *touch input* is the *touch screen*.

Mice

The **mouse** is the most common pointing device for a desktop computer. It typically rests on the desk or other flat surface close to the user's computer, and it is moved across the surface with the user's hand in the appropriate direction to point to and select objects on the screen. As it moves, an on-screen *mouse pointer*—usually an arrow—moves accordingly. Once the mouse pointer is pointing to the desired object on the screen, the buttons on the mouse are used to perform actions on that object (such as to open a hyperlink or to resize an image). Older *mechanical mice* have a ball exposed on the bottom surface of the mouse to control the pointer movement. Most mice today are *optical mice* or *laser mice* that track movements with light. Mice are used to start programs; open, move around, and edit documents; draw or edit images; and more. Some of the most common mouse commands are described in Figure 2-6. Similar to keyboards, mice today typically connect via a USB or mouse port, or via a wireless connection. In addition to being used with desktop computers, mice can also be used with portable computers (such as notebook and netbook computers), as long as an appropriate port (such as a USB port) is available.

> **Mouse.** A common pointing device that the user slides along a flat surface to move a pointer around the screen and clicks its buttons to make selections.

Pens/Styluses

Many devices today, including some desktop computers and many tablet computers and mobile devices, can accept *pen input*; that is, input by writing, drawing, or tapping on the screen with a pen-like device called a **stylus**. Sometimes, the stylus (also called a *digital pen*, *electronic pen*, or *tablet pen*) is simply a plastic device with no additional functionality; more commonly, it is a pressure-sensitive device that transmits the pressure applied by the user to the device that the stylus is being used with in order to allow more precise input. These more sophisticated styluses also are

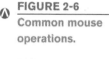

POINT
Move the mouse until the mouse pointer is at the desired location on the screen.

CLICK
Press and release the left mouse button.

RIGHT-CLICK
Press and release the right mouse button.

DOUBLE-CLICK
Press and release the left mouse button twice, in rapid succession.

DRAG-AND-DROP
When the mouse pointer is over the appropriate object, press and hold down the left mouse button, drag the object to the proper location on the screen by moving the mouse, and then drop the object by releasing the mouse button.

SCROLL WHEEL/BUTTON
If your mouse has a wheel or button on top, use it to scroll through the displayed document.

typically powered by the device that they are being used with, have a smooth rounded tip so they don't scratch the screen, and contain buttons or switches to perform actions such as erasing content or right-clicking.

The idea behind pen-based input and *digital writing* in general is to make using a computer or other device as convenient as writing with a pen, while adding the functionality that pen input can provide (such as converting pen-based input to editable typed text or retrieving and editing stored digitally-written documents). Pen input is also a useful alternative to touch input for mobile device users who have long fingernails, who wear gloves in the winter, or who have a device with a screen that is too small to have accurate touch input via a finger.

Although their capabilities depend on the type of computer and software being used, pen input can be used with a variety of computer types (see Figure 2-7). Most often, pens are used with mobile devices, UMPCs, and tablet computers to both input handwritten text and sketches, and to manipulate objects (such as to select an option from a menu, select text, or resize an image). They can also be used with desktop computers if the monitor supports pen input and they are used increasingly for photography, graphic design, animation, industrial design, document processing, and healthcare applications. Depending on the software being used, handwritten input can be stored as an image, stored as handwritten characters that can be recognized by the

FIGURE 2-6
Common mouse operations.

FIGURE 2-7
Examples of digital pen use.

Stylus
MOBILE DEVICES

TABLET COMPUTERS

GRAPHICS TABLETS

SIGNATURE CAPTURE DEVICES

> **Stylus.** An input device that is used to write electronically on the display screen.

computer, or converted to editable, typed text. For the latter two options, software with *handwriting recognition* capabilities must be used. The use of handwriting recognition technology in conjunction with *digital forms* (forms that are filled out using a computer and digital pen instead of on paper) is growing rapidly and is expected to continue to grow as companies increasingly move toward digital records and digital documents, such as *electronic health records*. Other devices that use digital pens are *graphics tablets* (flat, touch-sensitive tablets used in conjunction with a digital pen to transfer input drawn or written on the graphics tablet to the connected computer) and *signature capture devices* (devices used to electronically record signatures for deliveries and to authorize credit card purchases).

Touch Screens

Touch screens allow the user to touch the screen with his or her finger to select commands or otherwise provide input to the computer associated with the touch screen (see Figure 2-8). Their use is becoming common with personal computers, mobile phones, and mobile devices to provide easy input. Some touch screens (such as the one used on the iPhone 3G) are *multi-touch*; that is, they can recognize input from more than one finger at a time. Touch screens are also used in consumer kiosk and other point-of-sale (POS) systems, and they are useful for on-the-job applications (such as factory work) where it might be impractical to use a keyboard or mouse. While touch screens make many devices today (computers, mobile phones, televisions, and many other consumer electronics) more convenient for the majority of individuals to use, there is also concern that these devices and their applications are not accessible to blind individuals, users with limited mobility, and other individuals with a disability; accessibility and pointing devices designed for users with limited mobility are discussed in detail in Chapter 7.

Other common pointing devices include the following (refer again to Figure 2-8):

TOUCH SCREENS
Commonly found on mobile devices and are increasingly being used with many types of computers today.

BUTTONS AND WHEELS
Commonly found on portable digital media players and other consumer devices.

Thumb wheel

Select button

TOUCH PADS
Commonly found on notebook and netbook computers.

 FIGURE 2-8
Examples of other common pointing devices.

> *Buttons* and *wheels*—used to select items and issue commands on many consumer devices today, such as portable digital media players, GPS devices, and handheld gaming devices.

> *Touch pads*—rectangular pad across which a fingertip or thumb slides to move the on-screen pointer; most often found on notebook and netbook computers.

> *Gaming devices*—joysticks, gamepads, steering wheels, guitars, dance pads, and other devices commonly used with computer games and gaming consoles like the Wii, Xbox 360, and Playstation 3.

>**Touch screen.** A display device that is touched with the finger to issue commands or otherwise provide input to the connected device.

Scanners, Readers, and Digital Cameras

Some input devices are designed either to convert data that already exists in physical form to digital form or to capture data initially in digital form. Three of the most common types of these input devices—*scanners*, *readers*, and *digital cameras*—are discussed next.

Scanners and Readers

There are various types of scanners and readers that can be used to capture data from a *source document* (a document containing data that already exists in physical form, such as an order form, photograph, invoice, check, price label, or shipping label) and convert it into input that the computer can understand. Capturing data electronically from a source document can save a great deal of time and is much more accurate than inputting that data manually.

FIGURE 2-9
Scanners and readers transform data from physical form into digital form.

A **scanner**, more officially called an *optical scanner*, captures the image of a usually flat object (such as a printed document, photograph, or drawing) in digital form and then transfers that data to a computer. Typically, the entire document (including both text and images) is input as a single graphical image that can be resized, inserted into other documents, posted on a Web page, e-mailed to someone, printed, or otherwise treated like any other graphical image. The text in the image, however, cannot be edited unless *optical character recognition* (*OCR*) software is used in conjunction with the scanner to input the scanned text as individual text characters.

Scanners are frequently used by individuals to input photographs and other personal documents into a computer. Businesses are increasingly using scanners to convert paper documents into electronic format for archival or document processing purposes. The most common type of scanner is the *flatbed scanner* (see Figure 2-9), which is designed to scan flat objects one page at a time. *Portable scanners* are designed to capture text and other data while on the go. They are typically powered by batteries, the scanned content is stored in the scanner, and the content is transferred to a computer (via a cable or a wireless connection) when needed. The quality of scanned images

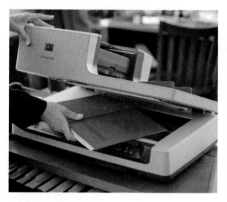

FLATBED SCANNERS
Used to input photos, sketches, slides, bound books, and other relatively flat documents into the computer.

PORTABLE BARCODE READERS
Used to read barcodes when portability is needed.

RFID READERS
Used to read RFID tags, such as the portal RFID reader shown here that reads all of the RFID tags on a palette at one time, as it passes between the readers.

BIOMETRIC READERS
Used to control access to facilities or computer systems, such as to the notebook computer shown here.

> **Scanner.** An input device that reads printed text and graphics and transfers them to a computer in digital form.

is indicated by *resolution*, which is usually measured in the number of *dots per inch* (*dpi*) and can be specified when an item is scanned or when it is later modified using an *image editing program*. A higher resolution results in a better image but also results in a larger file size. A higher resolution is needed, however, if the image is to be enlarged significantly or if only one part of the image is to be extracted and enlarged.

A **barcode** is an *optical code* that represents data with bars of varying widths or heights. Barcodes are read with **barcode readers**, which use either light reflected from the barcode or imaging technology to interpret the bars contained in the barcode as the numbers or letters they represent. Two of the most familiar barcodes are *UPC* (*Universal Product Code*)—the barcode found on packaged goods in supermarkets and other retail stores—and *ISBN* (*International Standard Book Number*)—the type of barcode used with printed books. Businesses and organizations can also create and use custom barcodes to fulfill their unique needs. For instance, shipping organizations (such as FedEx, UPS, and the U.S. Postal Service) use custom barcodes to mark and track packages; hospitals use custom barcodes to match patients with their charts and medicines; libraries and video stores use custom barcodes for checking out and checking in materials, such as books and movies; researchers use custom barcodes to tag and track the migration habits of animals; and law enforcement agencies use custom barcodes to mark evidence. *Fixed barcode readers* are frequently used in point-of-sale (POS) systems; *portable barcode readers* (see Figure 2-9) are also available.

Radio frequency identification (*RFID*) is a technology that can store, read, and transmit data located in *RFID tags*. **RFID tags** contain tiny chips and radio antennas and can be attached to objects, such as products, ID cards, assets, shipping containers, and more. The data in RFID tags is read by **RFID readers** and can be unique so that each item containing an RFID tag can be individually identified. Whenever an RFID-tagged item is within range of an RFID reader (from two inches to up to 300 feet or more, depending on the type of tag and the radio frequency being used), the tag's built-in antenna allows the information located within the RFID tag to be sent to the reader. Because RFID tags are read by radio waves (not by light like barcodes), the tags only need to be within range (not within line of sight) of a reader. This enables RFID readers to read the data stored in many RFID tags at the same time and read them through cardboard and other materials. In addition, RFID chips can be updated during the life of a product (such as to record information about a product's origin, shipping history, and the temperature range the item has been exposed to) and that information can be read when needed (such as at a product's final destination), and RFID can be used in conjunction with GPS to include location information. Consequently, RFID can be used for many different purposes, including for tracking the movement of the items the tags are attached to, for tracking the movement of inventory pallets and shipping containers during transit, as a replacement for barcodes on tickets and other consumer products, and as part of an electronic payment system. *Handheld RFID readers* look similar to handheld barcode readers; *portal RFID readers* (such as the one shown in Figure 2-9) can be used to read all the RFID tags inside a shipping box or palette when it passes through the portal.

Despite all its advantages, a number of privacy and security issues need to be resolved before RFID gains widespread use at the consumer level. Privacy advocates are concerned about linking RFID tag data with personally-identifiable data contained in corporate databases, such as to track consumer movements or shopping habits. As of now, no long-term solution to this issue has been reached. However, precautions against fraudulent use—such as using high-frequency tags that need to be within a few inches of the reader and requiring a PIN code, signature, or other type of authorization when an RFID payment

---

>**Barcode.** A machine-readable code that represents data as a set of bars. >**Barcode reader.** An input device that reads barcodes. >**RFID tag.** A device containing a tiny chip and a radio antenna that is attached to an object so it can be identified using RFID technology. >**RFID reader.** A device used to read RFID tags.

system is used—are being developed. Currently, a price limit (such as $25) for completely automated purchases (without a signature or other authorization) is being debated as a compromise between convenience and security.

Biometric readers (refer again to Figure 2-9) read *biometric data* (measurable biological characteristics, such as an individual's fingerprint, hand geometry, face, iris, or voice) in order to identify or authenticate individuals, as discussed in more detail in Chapter 4. Biometric readers can be stand-alone or built into another piece of hardware, such as a keyboard, a portable computer, an external hard drive, or a USB flash drive. Other types of readers include *optical mark readers* (*OMRs*), which input data from special forms to score or tally exams, questionnaires, ballots, and so forth; *optical character recognition* (*OCR*) *readers*, which are used to read *optical characters* printed on documents, such as invoices and utility bills; and *magnetic ink character recognition* (*MICR*) *readers*, which are used to read the MICR-encoded bank and account information on checks, in order to sort and process the checks.

Digital Cameras

Digital cameras work much like conventional film cameras, but instead of recording images on film they record them on a digital storage medium, such as a *flash memory card*, *digital tape cartridge*, built-in *hard drive*, or *DVD disc* (see Figure 2-10). Digital cameras are usually designated either as *still* cameras (which take individual still photos) or *video* cameras (which capture moving video images), although many cameras today take both still images and video. In addition to stand-alone still and video cameras, digital camera capabilities are integrated into many portable computers and mobile phones today. For a look at how the digital camera in your phone can be used to remotely deposit checks into your bank account, see the Technology and You box.

Digital still cameras are available in a wide variety of sizes and capabilities, such as inexpensive point-and-shoot digital cameras designed for consumers, professional digital cameras with removable lenses, and digital cameras integrated into mobile phones and other mobile devices. The primary appeal of digital still cameras is that the images are immediately available for viewing or printing, instead of having to have the film developed first. Digital still cameras most often use flash memory cards for storage; the number of digital photos that can be stored at one time depends on the capacity of the card being used, as well as the photo resolution being used. Photos taken with a digital camera are typically transferred to a computer or printer via the flash memory card containing the images or by connecting the camera to the computer or printer using a wired or wireless connection. Once the photos have been transferred to a computer, they can be retouched with image editing software; saved, printed, posted to a Web page; or burned onto a CD or DVD disc, just like any other digital image. The images on the storage medium can be deleted at any time to make room for more photos.

Digital video cameras include *digital camcorders* (such as the one shown in Figure 2-10) and small digital video cameras used in conjunction with computers and other devices. Both types of digital video cameras are commonly used by individuals and businesses today to capture or

FIGURE 2-10
Digital cameras.

Virtually all digital cameras let you display and erase images.

Most cameras use removable storage media in addition to, or instead of, built-in storage.

DIGITAL STILL CAMERAS
Typically store photos on flash memory media.

DIGITAL CAMCORDERS
Typically store video on a built-in hard drive (as in this camera) or on DVD discs.

TECHNOLOGY AND YOU

Mobile Phone Check Deposits

You use your mobile phone today for a wide number of functions—such as phone calls, texting, accessing Web information, and storing music and photos—but depositing your paychecks? Yes, now you can, thanks to a new technology developed by Mitek Systems.

While the use of remote deposit by businesses is growing, this new technology opens the door to remote deposit by individuals. In order to make a remote deposit via your mobile phone, you need to have the mobile deposit application on your mobile phone (if it is not included in your mobile banking software, you can typically download it). To make a remote deposit, you simply need to log on to your mobile banking service, and then you can enter the amount of the check and use your phone's built-in camera to take a photo of the front and back of the check (see the accompanying photo) in order to deposit that check into your bank account. After the software optimizes the image and verifies it meets the *Check 21 Law* image standards, the check images and deposit data are transmitted to your bank and you receive a confirmation text message. The software can be used with virtually any mobile banking system and a secure connection is used to protect the data as it is being transmitted.

Mobile phone cameras can be used to submit check images for remote deposit.

ONLINE VIDEO

Go to the Chapter 2 page at **www.cengage.com/ computerconcepts/np/uccs4** to watch the "How Mobile Deposit Works" video clip.

FURTHER EXPLORATION

Go to the Chapter 2 page at **www.cengage.com/ computerconcepts/np/uccs4** for links to information about digital cameras and digital photography.

transmit video images. Digital video cameras can also be used for identification purposes, such as in conjunction with face recognition technology to authorize access to a secure facility or computer resource, as discussed in more detail in Chapter 4. Digital camcorders are similar to conventional *analog* camcorders, but they store images on digital media—typically on built-in hard drives or rewritable DVDs for conventional-sized camcorders or flash memory for pocket-sized camcorders. Once a video is recorded, it can be transferred to a computer, edited with software as needed, and saved to a DVD or other type of storage medium. It can also be *compressed* (made smaller), if needed, and then uploaded to video-sharing sites, such as YouTube. Some digital video cameras today can take high-definition (HD) video. Video cameras used with personal computers—commonly called *PC cams* or *Web cams*—are typically used to transmit still or video images over the Internet (such as during a *videoconference* or *video phone call*) or to broadcast images continually to a Web page.

Other Input Devices

Other input devices include *microphones* or *headsets* (used for voice input, such as issuing commands or dictating documents to a computer (via *speech recognition software*), placing telephone calls via a computer (referred to as *Voice over IP* or *VoIP*), or recording spoken voice for a *podcast* (a recorded audio file that is distributed via the Internet). Music can be input into a computer via a CD, a DVD, or a Web download. For original compositions, conventional computer keyboards, special keyboards that contain piano keys, and microphones can be used. Once the music is input into the computer, it can be saved, modified, played, inserted into other programs, or burned to a CD or DVD. *Adaptive input devices* (designed for users with a physical disability) and *ergonomic input devices* (designed to lessen the physical impact of computer use) are discussed in detail in Chapter 7; types of emerging input devices are covered in Chapter 8.

PROCESSING HARDWARE AND OTHER HARDWARE INSIDE THE SYSTEM UNIT

The **system unit** is the main case of a computer. It houses the *processing hardware* for that computer (namely, a *motherboard*, one or more *CPUs*, and several types of *memory*), as well as a few other devices, such as storage devices, the power supply, and cooling fans. In addition, the system unit contains interfaces used to connect external *peripheral devices* (such as printers) to the computer, storage devices to be used with that computer, the power supply, and cooling fans. The system unit for a desktop computer often looks like a rectangular box, although other shapes and sizes are available, such as the all-in-one computer illustrated in Figure 1-14; the inside of a system unit for a typical desktop computer system is shown in Figure 2-11. Portable computers (like notebook computers and ultra-mobile PCs (UMPCs)) and mobile devices have similar components, but the system unit and components are usually smaller and the system unit is usually combined with the computer screen to form a single piece of hardware.

The Motherboard

A *circuit board* is a thin board containing *computer chips*—very small pieces of silicon or other semiconducting material—and other electronic components. The main circuit board inside the system unit is called the **motherboard**. As shown in Figure 2-11, the

FIGURE 2-11

Inside a typical system unit. The system unit houses the CPU, memory, and other important pieces of hardware.

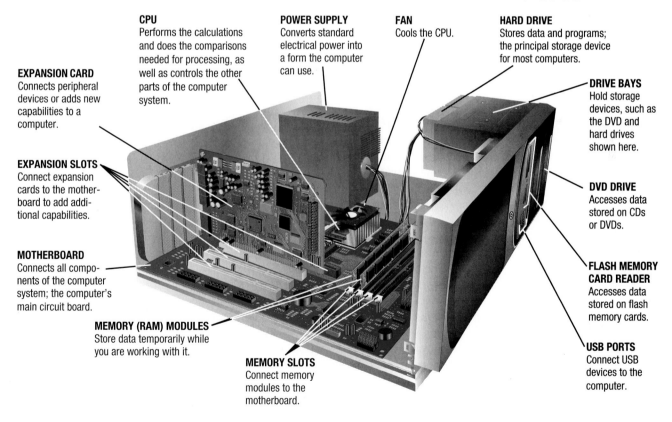

CPU
Performs the calculations and does the comparisons needed for processing, as well as controls the other parts of the computer system.

POWER SUPPLY
Converts standard electrical power into a form the computer can use.

FAN
Cools the CPU.

HARD DRIVE
Stores data and programs; the principal storage device for most computers.

EXPANSION CARD
Connects peripheral devices or adds new capabilities to a computer.

DRIVE BAYS
Hold storage devices, such as the DVD and hard drives shown here.

EXPANSION SLOTS
Connect expansion cards to the motherboard to add additional capabilities.

DVD DRIVE
Accesses data stored on CDs or DVDs.

MOTHERBOARD
Connects all components of the computer system; the computer's main circuit board.

FLASH MEMORY CARD READER
Accesses data stored on flash memory cards.

MEMORY (RAM) MODULES
Store data temporarily while you are working with it.

USB PORTS
Connect USB devices to the computer.

MEMORY SLOTS
Connect memory modules to the motherboard.

> **System unit.** The main box of a computer that houses the CPU, motherboard, memory, and other devices. > **Motherboard.** The main circuit board of a computer, located inside the system unit, to which all computer system components connect.

POWER CONNECTOR
Connects the computer to a power outlet.

VGA MONITOR PORT
Connects a VGA monitor.

USB PORTS
Connect a keyboard, mouse, scanner, flash memory drive, printer, digital camera, or other USB devices.

HDMI PORT
Connects a high-definition monitor.

FIREWIRE PORT
Connects FireWire devices.

NETWORK PORT
Connects the computer to a network.

AUDIO PORTS
Connect speakers, headphones, and a microphone.

EMPTY SLOTS
Ports located on new expansion cards added to the computer will be accessible here.

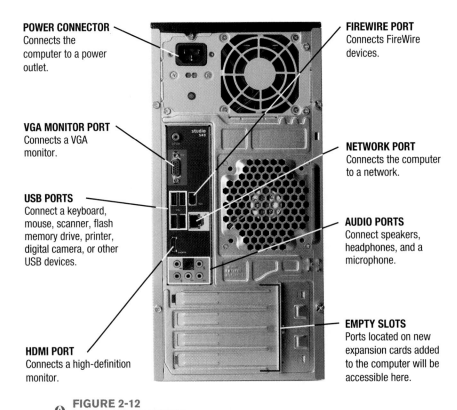

FIGURE 2-12
Ports are used to connect external devices to the motherboard.

motherboard has a variety of chips and boards attached to it; in fact, all devices used with a computer need to be connected in one way or another to the motherboard. To accomplish this, a variety of *ports*—special connectors exposed through the exterior of the system unit case—are either built into the motherboard or are created via an *expansion card* inserted into an *expansion slot* on the motherboard. These ports are used to connect *external* devices (such as monitors, keyboards, mice, and printers) to the computer.

The most common ports for a desktop computer are shown in Figure 2-12. Notebook, netbook, and other portable computers often have some of these ports (such as USB ports, *FireWire* ports, and network ports). In addition, notebook and netbook computers typically contain an *ExpressCard slot* designed for *ExpressCard modules*; mobile devices often have an *SD slot* that can be used with the *Secure Digital (SD)* type of flash memory media discussed later in this chapter, as well as with peripheral devices (such as barcode readers and GPS receivers) adhering to the *Secure Digital Input/ Output (SDIO)* standard.

The Central Processing Unit (CPU)

The **central processing unit (CPU)** consists of a variety of circuitry and components that are packaged together and connected directly to the motherboard. The CPU—also called the **microprocessor** (when talking about personal computers) or just the **processor** (when speaking in general terms for any computer)—does the vast majority of the processing for a computer. The CPU has two principal parts. The *arithmetic/logic unit (ALU)* is the section of the CPU that performs arithmetic (addition, subtraction, multiplication, and division) involving integers and logical operations (such as comparing two pieces of data to see if they are equal or determining if a specific condition is true or false). In other words, it is the part of the CPU that computes. The *control unit* coordinates and controls the operations and activities taking place within the CPU, such as retrieving data and instructions and passing them on to the ALU for execution. For a look inside a computer that may one day be able to compete with human contestants on the *Jeopardy!* TV show, see the Inside the Industry box.

There are CPUs designed for desktop computers, servers and workstations, conventional portable computers (like notebook and tablet computers), and very small portable computers (like netbooks and UMPCs). In addition, there are also processors designed for mobile phones and embedded computers, such as the CPUs incorporated into digital media players, gaming consoles, cars, and other devices. Most personal

INSIDE THE INDUSTRY

Watson, the Ultimate Future *Jeopardy!* Contestant

While game shows traditionally have human contestants, IBM is working on an advanced computing system that will be capable of competing with humans on the popular quiz show, *Jeopardy!* (see the accompanying illustration). This system, codenamed *Watson*, uses software called *Question Answering* (QA) and is designed to understand complex questions and answer them with enough precision and speed to make it a viable *Jeopardy!* contestant. Like human contestants, Watson will not have access to the Internet or any other outside assistance. However, it will have access to its self-contained data, and researchers are teaching it how to go beyond basic data retrieval and analyze its data deeply. For example, they are teaching Watson to use context to "understand" how words relate to each other, to consider factors such as keywords and statistical paraphrasing, and to deal with puns and wordplay in order to come up with a proper response to a question (or to come up with a question to match an answer, as is the case with *Jeopardy!*). To achieve this with the speed and accuracy required for *Jeopardy!*, Watson will need to be based on a supercomputer platform, such as the IBM Blue Gene/P platform, which can contain over one million CPU cores to obtain close to petaflop performance.

While creating a computer that can play *Jeopardy!* is entertaining and newsworthy, IBM plans to make the same technology available for other, perhaps more practical, applications, such as in medical systems used to diagnose patients and in business intelligence systems used for making business decisions. IBM also envisions the technology being used with consumer applications—most likely via cloud computing on a fee per question or fee per minute basis. But, before that happens, we can enjoy Watson's *Jeopardy!* debut—currently targeted for late 2010.

computers today use CPUs manufactured by *Intel* or *Advanced Micro Devices* (*AMD*). Many CPUs today are **multi-core CPUs**; that is, CPUs that contain the processing components or *cores* of multiple independent processors on a single CPU. For example, **dual-core CPUs** contain two cores and **quad-core CPUs** contain four cores. Up until just a few years ago, most CPUs designed for desktop computers had only a single core and a common way to increase the amount of processing performed by the CPU was to increase the speed of the CPU. However, heat constraints are making it progressively more difficult to continue to increase CPU speed, so CPU manufacturers today are focusing on multi-core CPUs to increase the amount of processing that a CPU can do in a given time period. One measurement of the *processing speed* for a CPU is *CPU clock speed*, which is rated in *megahertz (MHz)* or *gigahertz (GHz)*. A higher CPU clock speed means that more instructions can be processed per second than the same CPU with a lower CPU clock speed. For instance, a Core 2 Duo processor running at 3.0 GHz would be faster than a Core 2 Duo running at 2.4 GHz, if all other components remain the same. Although CPU clock speed is an important factor in computer performance, other factors (such as the number of cores, the amount of memory, and

ONLINE VIDEO ▷

Go to the Chapter 2 page at **www.cengage.com/ computerconcepts/np/uccs4** to watch the "A Look at Watson, the Ultimate Future *Jeopardy!* Contestant" video clip.

> **Multi-core CPU.** A CPU that contains the processing components or core of more than one processor in a single CPU. > **Dual-core CPU.** A CPU that contains two separate processing cores. > **Quad-core CPU.** A CPU that contains four separate processing cores.

Four cores

Shared Level 3 cache memory

FIGURE 2-13
CPUs. CPUs today typically have multiple cores.

FURTHER EXPLORATION

Go

Go to the Chapter 2 page at **www.cengage.com/ computerconcepts/np/uccs4** for links to information about CPUs.

FIGURE 2-14
RAM memory modules.

the speed of external storage devices) greatly affect the overall processing speed of the computer. As a result, computers today are beginning to be classified less by CPU clock speed and more by the computer's overall processing speed or performance.

Multi-core CPUs (such as the Intel quad-core CPU designed for desktop computers that is shown in Figure 2-13) allow computers to work simultaneously on more than one task at a time, such as burning a DVD while surfing the Web, as well as to work faster within a single application if the software is designed to take advantage of multiple cores. Another benefit of multi-core CPUs is that they typically experience fewer heat problems than *single-core CPUs* because each core typically runs slower than a single-core CPU, although the total processing power of the multi-core CPU is greater. In addition to heat reduction, goals of CPU manufacturers today include creating CPUs that are as energy-efficient as possible (in order to reduce power consumption and increase battery life) and that use materials that are not toxic when disposed of (in order to lessen the e-trash impact of computers, as discussed in detail in Chapter 7).

Memory

Memory refers to chip-based storage. When the term *memory* is used alone, it refers to chip-based storage used by the computer—usually the amount of the computer's main memory (called **random access memory** or **RAM**), which is located inside the system unit. In contrast, the term *storage* refers to the amount of long-term storage available to a computer—usually in the form of the computer's hard drive or removable storage media, such as CDs, DVDs, flash memory cards, and USB flash drives, all discussed later in this chapter. RAM is used to store the essential parts of the operating system while the computer is running, as well as the programs and data that the computer is currently using. RAM is **volatile**, which means its content is lost when the computer is shut off. Data in RAM is also deleted when it is no longer needed, such as when the program using that data is closed. If you want to retrieve a document at a later time, you need to save the document on a storage medium before closing it. There are several forms of *nonvolatile RAM* (*NVRAM*) under development that may be a possibility for the future; this and other types of emerging processing hardware are discussed in more detail in Chapter 8.

Like the CPU, RAM consists of circuits etched onto chips. These chips are arranged onto circuit boards called *memory modules* (see Figure 2-14) which, in turn, are plugged into the motherboard. RAM capacity is measured in bytes and most notebook and desktop computers sold today have at least 1 GB of RAM. It is important for a computer to have sufficient RAM since more RAM allows more applications to run at one time and the computer to respond more quickly when a user switches from task to task.

In addition to RAM, computer users should be aware of four other types of computer memory. Two of these—*cache memory* and *registers*—are volatile like RAM; the other two—*read-only memory* (*ROM*) and *flash memory*—are *nonvolatile*.

The memory module contains memory chips.

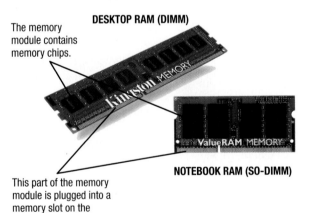

DESKTOP RAM (DIMM)

NOTEBOOK RAM (SO-DIMM)

This part of the memory module is plugged into a memory slot on the motherboard.

Cache memory is a special group of very fast memory chips located on or close to the CPU. Cache memory is used to speed up processing by storing the data and instructions that may be needed next by the CPU in handy locations. Cache memory level numbers indicate the order in which the various caches are accessed by the CPU when it requires new data or instructions. *Level 1 (L1) cache* (which is the fastest type of cache but typically holds less data than other levels of cache) is checked first, followed by *Level 2 (L2) cache*, followed by *Level 3 (L3) cache* if it exists. If the data or instructions are not found in cache memory, the computer looks for them in RAM, which is slower than cache memory. If the data or instructions cannot be found in RAM, then they are retrieved from the hard drive—an even slower operation. Typically, more cache memory results in faster processing. Most multi-core CPUs today have some cache memory (such as a L1 and L2 cache) dedicated to each core; they may also use a larger shared cache memory (such as L3 cache, as shown back in Figure 2-13) that can be accessed by any core as needed.

Registers are another type of high-speed memory built into the CPU. Registers are used by the CPU to temporarily store data and intermediary results during processing. Registers are the fastest type of memory used by the CPU, even faster than Level 1 cache. Generally, the more data a register can contain at one time, the faster the CPU performs.

ROM (*read-only memory*) consists of nonvolatile chips that permanently store data or programs. Like RAM, these chips are attached to the motherboard inside the system unit, and the data or programs are retrieved by the computer when they are needed. An important difference, however, is that you can neither write over the data or programs in ROM chips (which is the reason ROM chips are called *read-only*), nor destroy their contents when you shut off the computer's power. ROM is used for storing permanent instructions used by a computer (referred to as *firmware*); ROM is increasingly being replaced with *flash memory*, as discussed next, for any data that may need to be updated during the life of the computer.

Flash memory is a type of nonvolatile memory into which data can be stored and retrieved. Flash memory chips have begun to replace ROM for storing system information, such as a computer's *BIOS* or *basic input/output system*—the sequence of instructions the computer follows during the boot process. By storing this information in flash memory instead of in ROM, the BIOS information can be updated as needed. Similarly, firmware for personal computers and other devices (such as mobile phones and networking hardware) are now typically stored in flash memory that is embedded in the device so the firmware can be updated over the life of the product. In addition to built-in flash memory chips that are used only by the computer, computers and storage devices can include built-in flash memory chips designed to be used by the user for storage purposes, as discussed shortly.

ASK THE EXPERT

Kingston TECHNOLOGY **Mark Tekunoff,** Senior Technology Manager, Kingston Technology

What's the best way to find out if more memory can be added to a particular computer and the type of memory that is needed?

The best way to upgrade is to go to a Web site that has a list of PCs and other products along with a list of the memory options available to support those PCs and products. A good example is Kingston's Web site at www.kingston.com, where Kingston supports over 20,000 products with a variety of memory solutions.

In general, Windows Vista and basic Windows 7 users typically will want at least 2 GB of memory for good functionality. For advanced 32-bit Windows 7 users, we recommend 3 to 4 GB of RAM; power users with 64-bit Windows 7 are better off with 4 to 8 GB of RAM.

VIDEO PODCAST

Go to the Chapter 2 page at **www.cengage.com/ computerconcepts/np/uccs4** to download or listen to the "How To: Deal with a Blue Screen of Death" video podcast.

TIP

To avoid confusion, when you are referring to the amount of room on your hard drive, use the proper term—*storage* space, not *memory*.

FURTHER EXPLORATION

Go to the Chapter 2 page at **www.cengage.com/ computerconcepts/np/uccs4** for links to information about memory.

OUTPUT HARDWARE

Output hardware consists of all the devices that are used to produce the results of processing—usually, output is displayed on a computer screen, printed on paper, or presented as audio output. Hardware devices that produce output are called **output devices**. The most common output devices are discussed next; types of emerging output devices are discussed in Chapter 8.

Display Devices

A **display device**—the most common form of output device—presents output visually on some type of screen. The display device for a desktop computer is more formally called a **monitor**; the display device for a notebook computer, netbook computer, UMPC, mobile phone, or other device for which the screen is built into the device is typically called a **display screen**. In addition to being used with computers and mobile devices (see Figure 2-15), display screens are also built into handheld gaming devices, home entertainment devices (like remote controls, televisions, and portable DVD players), and kitchen appliances. They are also an important component in *digital photo frames* (stand-alone or wall mounted photo frames, which display digital photos that are typically transferred to the frame via a flash memory card or a wireless networking connection), *e-book readers* (which display electronic versions of books), portable digital media players, and other consumer products. A *data projector* is a display device that projects computer output onto a wall or projection screen for a large group presentation; *digital signage systems* display digital signs (such as for billboards, restaurant menus, and advertising signs in retail stores) whose content can be changed throughout the day as needed.

The *CRT monitor* used to be the norm for desktop computers. CRTs use *cathode-ray tube* technology to display images; as a result they are large, bulky, and heavy like conventional televisions. While CRT monitors are still in use, most computers today (as well as most television sets) use the thinner and lighter *flat-panel display*. Flat-panel display technology is also used in the display screens integrated into mobile phones and consumer electronics. Flat-panel displays form images by manipulating electronically charged chemicals or gases sandwiched between thin panes of glass or other transparent material. Flat-panel displays consume less power than CRTs. They also take up less desk space, which makes it possible to use multiple monitors working together to increase the amount of data the user can view at one time.

Regardless of the technology used, the screen of a display device is divided into a fine grid of small areas or dots called **pixels** (from the phrase *picture element*). A pixel is the smallest colorable area in an electronic image. The number of pixels used on a display screen determines the *screen resolution*, which affects the amount of information that can be displayed on the screen at one time. When a higher resolution is selected, such as 1,280 pixels horizontally by 1,024 pixels vertically for a standard computer monitor (written as 1,280 × 1,024 and read as *1280 by 1024*), more information can fit on the screen, but everything will be displayed smaller than with a lower resolution, such as 1,024 × 768 (see Figure 2-16). The screen resolution on many computers today can be changed by users to match their preferences and the software being used. On Windows computers, display options are changed using the Control Panel. When multiple monitors are used, typically the screen resolution of each display can be set independently of the others. Very high-resolution monitors are available for special applications, such as viewing digital X-rays.

FIGURE 2-15

Many consumer products today, such as the mobile phone shown here, have a display screen.

> **Output device.** A piece of hardware that presents the results of processing in a form the user can understand. > **Display device.** An output device that contains a viewing screen. > **Monitor.** A display device for a desktop computer. > **Display screen.** A display device built into a notebook computer, netbook, UMPC, or other device. > **Pixel.** The smallest colorable area in an electronic image, such as a scanned image, a digital photograph, or an image displayed on a display screen.

Display devices today are typically *color displays*, which form colors by mixing combinations of three colors—red, green, and blue. Screen size is usually measured diagonally from corner to corner, in a manner similar to the way TV screens are measured; some monitors today support pen and touch input.

1,024 × 768

1,280 × 1,024

Printers

Instead of the temporary, ever-changing soft copy output that a monitor produces, **printers** produce *hard copy*; that is, a permanent copy of the output on paper. Most desktop computers are connected to a printer; portable computers can use printers as well. Printers designed to be connected to a single computer are referred to as *personal printers*; *network printers* are designed to be shared by multiple users via a network.

Printers produce images through either impact or nonimpact technologies. *Impact printers*, like old ribbon typewriters, have a print mechanism that actually strikes the paper to transfer ink to the paper. Most printers today are *nonimpact printers*, meaning they form images without the print mechanism actually touching the paper. Impact printers, such as the older *dot-matrix printers*, are primarily used today for producing multipart forms, such as invoices, packing slips, and credit card receipts. Nonimpact printers usually produce higher-quality images and are much quieter than impact printers. Both impact and nonimpact printers form images with dots, similar to the way monitors display images using pixels. Because of this, printers are very versatile and can print text in virtually any size, as well as print photos and other graphical images. Printers can be *color printers* or *black-and-white printers*, printer quality is measured in dots per inch (dpi), and printer speed is measured in *pages per minute* (*ppm*). Most personal printers today connect to a computer via a USB connection; some have the option of connecting via a *Wi-Fi* wireless connection (a widely used standard for connecting devices wirelessly to a network or the Internet, as discussed more in Chapter 8), as well. In addition, many personal printers can receive data to be printed via a flash memory card. The two most common types of printers today are *laser printers* and *ink-jet printers*, both of which are nonimpact printers.

Laser Printers

Laser printers are the standard for business documents and come in both personal and network versions; they are also available as both color and black-and-white printers. To print a document, the laser printer first uses a laser beam to charge the appropriate locations on a drum to form the page's image, and then *toner powder* (powdered ink) is released from a *toner cartridge* and sticks to the drum. The toner is then transferred to a piece of paper when the paper is rolled over the drum, and a heating unit fuses the toner powder to the paper to permanently form the image (see Figure 2-17). Laser printers print one entire page at a time and are typically faster and have better quality output than *ink-jet printers*, discussed next. Common print resolutions for laser printers are between 600 and 2,400 dpi; speeds for personal laser printers range from about 15 to 30 ppm.

FIGURE 2-16
Screen resolution.
A higher screen resolution (measured in pixels) displays more content than a lower screen resolution, but everything is displayed smaller.

> **TIP**

Printers that offer more than just printing capabilities (such as printing, copying, scanning, and faxing) are referred to as *multifunction devices* (*MFD*) or *all-in-ones*.

> **TIP**

To save money, consider buying *recharged* (refilled) toner cartridges when your laser printer cartridge runs out of toner powder. Recharged cartridges typically cost about one-third less than new cartridges and last at least as long.

> **Printer.** An output device that produces output on paper. > **Laser printer.** An output device that uses toner powder and technology similar to that of a photocopier to produce images on paper.

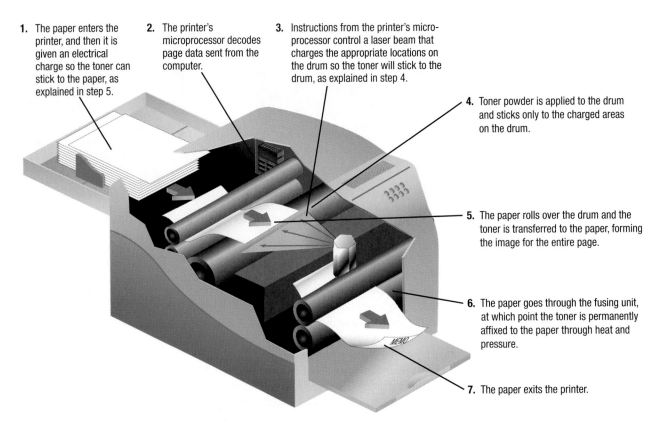

1. The paper enters the printer, and then it is given an electrical charge so the toner can stick to the paper, as explained in step 5.

2. The printer's microprocessor decodes page data sent from the computer.

3. Instructions from the printer's microprocessor control a laser beam that charges the appropriate locations on the drum so the toner will stick to the drum, as explained in step 4.

4. Toner powder is applied to the drum and sticks only to the charged areas on the drum.

5. The paper rolls over the drum and the toner is transferred to the paper, forming the image for the entire page.

6. The paper goes through the fusing unit, at which point the toner is permanently affixed to the paper through heat and pressure.

7. The paper exits the printer.

FIGURE 2-17

How black-and-white laser printers work.

Ink-Jet Printers

Ink-jet printers form images by spraying tiny drops of liquid ink from one or more *ink cartridges* onto the page, one printed line at a time (see Figure 2-18). Some printers print with one single-sized ink droplet; others print using different-sized ink droplets and using multiple nozzles or varying electrical charges for more precise printing. The print head for ink-jet printers typically travels back and forth across the page, which is one reason why ink-jet printers are slower than laser printers. Because they are relatively inexpensive, have good-quality output, and can print in color, ink-jet printers are usually the printer of choice for home use. With the use of special photo paper, most ink jet printers can also print photograph quality digital photos. Ink-jet printers are typically less expensive than laser printers, although the cost of the replaceable ink cartridges can add up, especially if you do a lot of color printing.

Special-Purpose Printers

Although both laser and ink-jet printers can typically print on a variety of media—including sheets of labels, envelopes, transparencies, photo paper, and even fabric—in addition to various sizes of paper, some printers are designed for a particular purpose. For instance, *photo printers* are color printers designed to print photographs; *barcode printers* enable businesses and other organizations to print custom barcodes on price tags, shipping labels, and other documents for identification or pricing purposes; *portable printers* are small, lightweight printers that can be used on the go, such as with a notebook computer

>**Ink-jet printer.** An output device that sprays droplets of ink to produce images on paper.

or mobile device; *wide-format ink-jet printers* are designed to produce charts, drawings, maps, blueprints, advertising banners, and other large documents; and *3D printers* form output in layers using molten plastic during a series of passes to build a 3D version of the desired output.

Other Output Devices

Other types of output devices include **speakers**, such as those that connect to a computer and provide audio output for computer games, music, video clips and TV shows, videoconferencing, and other applications. *Headphones* can be used instead of speakers so the audio output does not disturb others (such as in a school computer lab or public library). *Headsets* are headphones with a built-in microphone and are often used for dictating to a computer and when making telephone calls or participating in videoconferences using a computer; wireless headsets are commonly used in conjunction with mobile phones. Even smaller than headphones are the *earphones* and *earbuds* often used with portable digital media players, handheld gaming devices, and other mobile devices.

Each ink cartridge is made up of multiple tiny ink-filled firing chambers; to print images, the appropriate color ink is ejected through the appropriate firing chamber.

Ink-jet printer

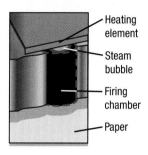
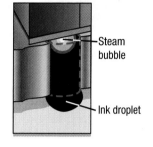
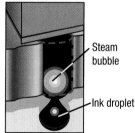

Heating element
Steam bubble
Firing chamber
Paper

Steam bubble
Ink droplet

Steam bubble
Ink droplet

1. A heating element makes the ink boil, which causes a steam bubble to form.

2. As the steam bubble expands, it pushes ink through the firing chamber.

3. The ink droplet is ejected onto the paper and the steam bubble collapses, pulling more ink into the firing chamber.

FIGURE 2-18
How ink-jet printers work.

STORAGE HARDWARE

Unlike RAM, which is volatile and holds data only temporarily, *storage systems* are nonvolatile and are used anytime you want to save a document for future use. The basic characteristics of storage systems are discussed first, followed by a look at the most common types of storage systems.

Storage System Characteristics

All storage systems have specific characteristics, such as consisting of a *storage device* and a *storage medium*, the amount of *portability* they have, and the type of storage technology used.

Storage Media and Storage Devices

There are two parts to any storage system: the **storage medium** and the **storage device**. A storage medium is the hardware where data is actually stored (for example, a *CD* or a *flash memory card*); a storage medium is inserted into its corresponding storage device

---

>**Speakers.** Output devices that provide audio output. >**Storage medium.** The part of a storage system where data is stored, such as a DVD disc. >**Storage device.** A piece of hardware, such as a DVD drive, into which a storage medium is inserted to be read from or written to.

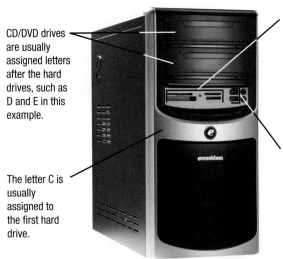

CD/DVD drives are usually assigned letters after the hard drives, such as D and E in this example.

The letter C is usually assigned to the first hard drive.

The various slots in a built-in flash memory card reader are typically assigned next, such as the letters F, G, H and I, in this example.

Other letters, beginning with J in this example, are used for any other storage devices attached to the computer, such as via these USB ports.

FIGURE 2-19

Storage device identifiers. To keep track of storage devices in an unambiguous way, the computer system assigns letter of the alphabet or names to each of them.

(such as a *CD drive* or a *flash memory card reader*) in order to be read from or written to. Often the storage device and storage medium are two separate pieces of hardware (that is, the storage medium is *removable*), although with some systems—such as a *hard drive* or most *USB flash drives*—the two parts are permanently sealed together to form one piece of hardware.

Storage devices can be *internal* (located inside the system unit), *external* (plugged into an external port on the system unit), or *remote* (located on another computer, such as a network server). Internal devices have the advantage of requiring no additional desk space and are usually faster than their external counterparts. External devices, however, can be easily transported from one location to another (such as to share data with others, to transfer data between a work computer and a home computer, or to take digital photos to a photo store). They can also be removed from the computer and stored in a secure area, when needed (such as for backup purposes or to protect sensitive data). Remote devices are accessed over a network. Some remote storage devices, such as those accessed via the Internet, have the additional advantage of being accessible from any computer with an Internet connection. Regardless of how storage devices are connected to a computer, letters of the alphabet and/or names are typically assigned to each storage device so that the user can identify each device easily when it needs to be used (see Figure 2-19).

Type of Storage Technology Used

Data is stored *magnetically* or *optically* on many types of storage media. With magnetic storage systems, such as conventional hard drives, data is stored magnetically on the storage medium, which means the data (0s and 1s) is represented using different magnetic alignments. The storage device can change the magnetic alignment when needed, so data can be written to the medium, deleted from the medium, or rewritten to the medium. Optical storage media (such as CDs and DVDs) store data optically using laser beams. On some optical media, the laser burns permanent marks to represent 0s and 1s into the surface of the medium so the data cannot be erased or rewritten. With *rewritable* optical media, the laser changes the reflectivity of the medium to represent 0s and 1s but it does not permanently alter the disc surface so the reflectivity of the medium can be changed back again as needed. Consequently, the data stored on a rewritable optical disc can be changed.

Some storage systems use a combination of magnetic and optical technology. Others use a different technology altogether, such as *flash memory storage systems* that represent data using *electrons*. Some of the most widely used storage systems are discussed in the next few sections.

Hard Drives

With the exception of computers designed to use only network storage devices (such as network computers and some Internet appliances), virtually all personal computers come with a **hard drive** that is used to store most programs and data. *Internal hard drives* (those

>**Hard drive.** The primary storage system for most computers; used to store most programs and data used with a computer.

located inside the system unit) are not designed to be removed, unless they need to be repaired or replaced. *External hard drives* typically connect to a computer via a USB or FireWire port and are frequently used for additional storage (such as for digital photos, videos, and other large multimedia files), to move files between computers, and for backup purposes. In addition to being used with computers, hard drives are also increasingly being incorporated into other consumer products, such as mobile phones, portable digital media players, digital video recorders (DVRs), gaming consoles, digital camcorders, and more.

For security purposes, both internal and external hard drives today are increasingly coming with built-in *encryption* that automatically encrypts all data stored on the hard drive and protects access to the hard drive with a *secure password*; external hard drives may use a built-in *fingerprint reader* to grant only authorized users access to the hard drive. Encryption, secure passwords, and fingerprint readers are discussed in detail in Chapter 4.

Magnetic Hard Drives

A **magnetic hard drive** (usually what individuals are referring to when they use the term *hard drive*) contains one or more round pieces of metal (called *hard disks* or *platters*) that are coated with a magnetizable substance. These hard disks are permanently sealed inside the hard drive case, along with the *read/write heads* used to store (*write*) and retrieve (*read*) data and an *access mechanism* used to move the read/write heads in and out over the surface of the hard disks (see Figure 2-20). The surface of a hard disk is organized into *tracks* (concentric rings) and pie-shaped groups of *sectors* (small pieces of tracks). The read/write heads magnetize particles a certain way on the disk surface to represent

FIGURE 2-20
Magnetic hard drives.

MOUNTING SHAFT
The mounting shaft spins the hard disks at a speed of several thousand revolutions per minute while the computer is turned on.

SEALED DRIVE
The hard disks and the drive mechanism are hermetically sealed inside a case to keep them free from contamination.

READ/WRITE HEADS
There is a read/write head for each hard disk surface, and they move in and out over the disks together.

HARD DISKS
There are usually several hard disk surfaces on which to store data. Most hard drives store data on both sides of each disk.

ACCESS MECHANISM
The access mechanism moves the read/write heads in and out together between the hard disk surfaces to access required data.

INSIDE A 3.5-INCH HARD DRIVE

2.5-INCH HARD DRIVE LOCATED INSIDE A NOTEBOOK COMPUTER

>**Magnetic hard drive.** A hard drive consisting of one or more metal magnetic disks permanently sealed, with an access mechanism and read/write heads, inside its drive.

the data's 0s and 1s. The particles retain their magnetic orientation until the orientation is changed again, so data can be stored, rewritten to the disk, and deleted as needed. The computer uses a *file system* to record where each document (called a *file*) is physically stored on the hard drive and what *filename* the user has assigned to it. When the user requests a document (always by filename), the computer uses its file system to retrieve it.

Hard drives designed for desktop computers (sometimes referred to as *desktop hard drives*) typically use 2.5-inch or 3.5-inch hard disks and notebook hard drives typically use 2.5-inch hard disks. Portable digital media players, mobile phones, and other mobile devices that include a magnetic hard drive typically use tiny 1.5-inch or smaller hard drives instead. Regardless of the size, one hard drive usually contains a stack of several hard disks; if so, there is a read/write head for each hard disk surface (top and bottom), and these heads move in and out over the disk surfaces simultaneously.

> ### CAUTION CAUTION CAUTION CAUTION CAUTION CAUTION CAUT
>
> Because you never know when a head crash or other hard drive failure will occur—there may be no warning whatsoever—be sure to *back up* the data on your hard drive on a regular basis. Backing up data—that is, creating a second copy of important files—is critical not only for businesses but also for individuals and is discussed in more detail in Chapter 5.

Data is stored in flash memory chips located inside the drive; there are no moving parts like in magnetic hard drives.

FIGURE 2-21
Solid-state drives (SSDs).

Solid State Drives (SSDs) and Hybrid Hard Drives

Solid-state drives (SSDs) are hard drives that use flash memory technology instead of spinning hard disk platters and magnetic technology; consequently, data is stored as electrical charges on *flash memory media* (see Figure 2-21) and SSDs have no moving parts. These characteristics mean that SSDs (along with the other types of flash memory storage systems discussed later in this chapter) are not subject to mechanical failures like magnetic hard drives, and are, therefore, more resistant to shock and vibration. They also consume less power, make no noise, and boot faster. Consequently, SSDs are an especially attractive option for portable computers and mobile devices. Although previously too expensive for all but specialty applications, prices of SSDs (also sometimes called *flash memory hard drives*) have fallen significantly over the past few years and they are becoming the norm for netbooks and other very portable computers.

SSDs are available in the same dimensions as conventional magnetic 2.5-inch hard drives so they can easily be used instead of conventional magnetic hard drives in notebooks, netbooks, and other personal computers. There are also smaller 1.8-inch SSDs available that can be used when a smaller physical size is needed, such as for a portable digital media player or mobile phone. SSDs are currently available in capacities up to 512 GB. **Hybrid hard drives** include both flash memory and a magnetic hard drive—this combination is less expensive than an SSD, can extend the battery life of portable computers and mobile devices, and can allow encryption or other security measures to be built into the drive (encryption is discussed in Chapter 4).

> **Solid-state drive (SSD).** A hard drive that uses flash memory media instead of metal magnetic hard disks. > **Hybrid hard drive.** A hard drive that contains both a large amount of flash memory and magnetic hard disks.

Internal and External Hard Drives

Internal hard drives are permanently located inside a computer's system unit and typically are not removed unless there is a problem with them. Virtually all computers have at least one internal hard drive (either a magnetic hard drive or an SSD) that is used to store programs and data. *External hard drives* are commonly used to transport a large amount of data from one computer to another (by moving the entire hard drive to another computer), for backup purposes, and for additional storage. Today, because of their large capacity, full-sized external hard drives (which typically are magnetic hard drives and hold between 500 GB and 4 TB) are often used by individuals to store their digital photos, digital music, home movies, recorded TV shows, and other multimedia content to be distributed to the computers and entertainment devices located in the home. While full-sized external hard drives can be moved from computer to computer when needed, *portable hard drives* are smaller external hard drives specifically designed for that purpose (see Figure 2-22). Unlike full-sized hard drives (which typically need to be plugged into a power outlet to be used), portable hard drives are often powered via the computer they are being used with instead. Portable magnetic hard drives typically hold up to 500 GB; the capacity of portable SSD hard drives at the present time is smaller—up to 128 GB. Most external desktop and portable hard drives connect to the computer via a USB connection. However, some can connect via a wired or wireless networking connection instead, and *ExpressCard hard drives* connect via an ExpressCard slot.

FIGURE 2-22
Portable hard drives.

PORTABLE HARD DRIVES (MAGNETIC)
Are about the size of a 3 by 5-inch index card, but thicker; this drive holds 500 GB.

EXPRESSCARD HARD DRIVES (SSD)
Fit into an ExpressCard slot; this drive holds 32 GB.

Optical Discs

Data stored on **optical discs** (such as *CDs*, *DVDs*, and *Blu-ray Discs* (*BDs*)) is stored and read *optically*; that is, using laser beams. Optical discs are thin circular discs made out of molded *polycarbonate substrates*—essentially a type of very strong plastic—that are topped with layers of other materials and coatings used to store data and protect the disc. Data can be stored on one or both sides of an optical disc, depending on the disc design, and some types of discs use multiple recording layers on each side of the disc to increase capacity. To keep data organized, optical discs are divided into tracks and sectors like magnetic disks but use a single grooved spiral track beginning at the center of the disc (see Figure 2-23), instead of a series of concentric tracks. Data is written to an optical disc in one of two ways. With *read-only optical discs* like movie, music, and software CDs and DVDs, the surface of the disc is molded or stamped appropriately to represent the data. With *recordable* or *rewritable optical discs* that can be written to using an *optical drive* such as a *CD drive* or *DVD drive*, the reflectivity of the disc is changed using a laser to represent the data. In either case, the disc is read with a laser and the computer interprets the reflection of the laser off the disc surface as 1s and 0s.

To accomplish this with molded or stamped optical discs, tiny depressions (when viewed from the top side of the disc) or bumps (when viewed from the bottom) are created on the disc's surface. These bumps are called *pits*; the areas on the disc that are not changed are called

>**Optical disc.** A type of storage medium read from and written to using a laser beam.

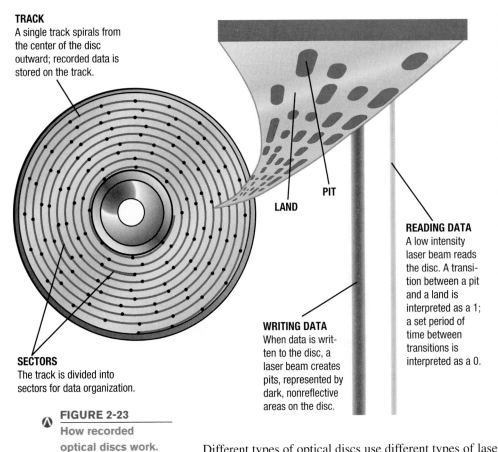

TRACK
A single track spirals from the center of the disc outward; recorded data is stored on the track.

SECTORS
The track is divided into sectors for data organization.

LAND

PIT

READING DATA
A low intensity laser beam reads the disc. A transition between a pit and a land is interpreted as a 1; a set period of time between transitions is interpreted as a 0.

WRITING DATA
When data is written to the disc, a laser beam creates pits, represented by dark, nonreflective areas on the disc.

FIGURE 2-23
How recorded optical discs work.

lands. Although many people think that each individual pit and land represents a 1 or 0, that is not completely accurate—it is the transition between a pit and land that represents a 1. When the disc is read, the amount of laser light reflected back from the disc changes when the laser reaches a transition between a pit and a land. When the optical drive detects a transition, it is interpreted as a 1; no transition for a specific period of time indicates a 0.

With a CD or DVD that is recorded using a CD or DVD drive, the recording laser beam changes the reflectivity of the appropriate areas on the disc to represent the data stored there— dark, nonreflective areas are pits; reflective areas are lands, as illustrated in Figure 2-23. The transition between a pit and a land still represents a 1 and no transition for a specific distance along the track represents a 0.

Different types of optical discs use different types of laser beams. Conventional **CD discs** use *infrared* lasers; conventional **DVD discs** use *red* lasers, which allow data to be stored more compactly on the same size disc; and high-definition **Blu-ray Discs (BD)** use *blue-violet lasers*, which can store data even more compactly on a disc.

Standard-sized optical discs are 120-mm (approximately 4½-inch) discs (see Figure 2-24). There are also smaller 80-mm (approximately 3-inch) *mini discs*, most often used in conjunction with digital video cameras. In addition, optical discs can be made into a variety of sizes and shapes—such as a heart, triangle, irregular shape, or the hockey-rink shape commonly used with *business card CDs*—because the track starts at the center of the disc and the track just stops when it reaches an outer edge of the disc. One of the biggest advantages of optical discs is their large capacity. Standard-sized *single-layer* CD discs normally hold either 650 MB or 700 MB, standard-sized single-layer DVD discs hold 4.7 GB, and standard-sized single-layer BD discs hold 25 GB. To further increase capacity, many discs are available as *dual-layer discs* (also called *double-layer discs*) that store data in two layers on a single side of the disc, so the capacity is approximately doubled. Discs can also be *double sided*, which doubles the capacity; however, the disc must be turned over to access the second side. Double-sided discs are most often used with movies and other prerecorded content, such as to store a *widescreen version* of a movie on one side of a DVD disc and a *standard version* on the other side. Small optical discs have a smaller storage capacity than their larger counterparts: typically, single-layer, single-sided 3-inch mini CD, DVD, and BD discs hold about 200 MB, 1.4 GB, and 7.5 GB, respectively, and business-card-sized CD and DVD discs hold about 50 MB and 325 MB, respectively.

STANDARD 120 MM (4.7 INCH) SIZED DISC

MINI 80 MM (3.1 INCH) SIZED DISC

CUSTOM-SHAPED BUSINESS CARD DISC

FIGURE 2-24
Optical discs are available in a variety of sizes, appearances, and capacities.

Read-Only Discs: CD-ROM, DVD-ROM, and BD-ROM Discs

CD-ROM (*compact disc read-only memory*) *discs* and *DVD-ROM* (*digital versatile disc read-only memory*) *discs* are *read-only optical discs* that come prerecorded with commercial products, such as software programs, clip art and other types of graphics collections, music, and movies. For high-definition content (such as feature films), *BD-ROM* (*Blu-ray Disc read-only memory*) *discs* are available. There are also additional read-only disc formats for specific gaming devices, such as the *UMD* (*Universal Media Disc*) format used with the Sony PSP handheld gaming device and the proprietary discs used with the Wii, Xbox, and Playstation gaming consoles. The data on a read-only disc cannot be erased, changed, or added to because the pits that are molded into the surface of the disc when the disc is produced are permanent.

Recordable Discs: CD-R, DVD-R, DVD+R, and BD-R Discs

Recordable optical discs (also sometimes called *write-once discs*) can be written to, but the discs cannot be erased and reused. Recordable CDs are referred to as *CD-R discs*. Single-layer recordable DVDs are called either *DVD-R discs* or *DVD+R discs*, depending on the standard being used, and dual-layer recordable DVDs are called *DVD+R DL* and *DVD-R DL discs*. Recordable BD discs are also available in both single-layer and dual-layer (*BD-R discs* and *BD-R DL discs*, respectively). The capacities of recordable optical discs are the same as the read-only formats. Recordable optical discs are written to using an appropriate optical drive, such as a *CD-R drive* for CD-R discs or a *DVD-R drive* for DVD-R discs, although optical drives are usually *downward-compatible*, meaning that they can be used with lower formats, such as using a DVD-R drive to burn a CD-R disc.

Recordable CDs are commonly used for backing up files, sending large files to others, and creating custom music CDs (for example, from MP3 files legally downloaded from the Internet or from songs located on a music album purchased on CD). DVD-Rs can be used for similar purposes when more storage space is needed, such as for backing up large files and for storing home movies, digital photos, and other multimedia files. BD-R discs can be used when an even greater amount of storage is needed, such as very large backups or high-definition multimedia files. Because of their widespread use of CDs and DVDs, most personal computers today come with an internal optical drive; one exception is netbooks, which typically do not include an optical drive. An *external optical drive* that connects via a USB port (see Figure 2-25) can be used with these computers whenever an optical drive is temporarily needed.

FIGURE 2-25
External optical drives. Can be connected as needed, typically via a USB port, such as to the netbook shown here.

Rewritable Discs: CD-RW, DVD-RW, DVD+RW, and BD-RE Discs

Rewritable optical discs can be written to, erased, and overwritten just like magnetic hard disks. The most common types of rewritable optical media are *CD-RW*, *DVD-RW*, *DVD+RW*, and *BD-RE discs*; BD-RE discs are also available as dual-layer discs (*BD-RE DL discs*). The capacities of rewritable discs are the same as their read-only and recordable counterparts.

CD-RW discs can be written to using a *CD-RW drive* and can be read by most CD and DVD drives. DVD-RW and DVD+RW discs are recorded using a *DVD-RW* or *DVD+RW drive*, respectively, and can be read by most DVD drives. BD-RE discs are recorded and read by *rewritable Blu-ray Disc drives*. Instead of permanently altering the surface of the disc, rewritable optical discs use *phase change* technology and a heating and cooling process to make the appropriate areas of the disc nonreflective to function as pits (the reflective areas function as lands). To erase the disc, the heating and cooling process is used to change the areas to be erased back to their original reflective state. The capacities of rewritable discs are the same as their read-only and recordable counterparts.

Rewritable optical discs are used for many of the same purposes as recordable optical discs. However, they are particularly appropriate for situations in which data written to the optical disc can be erased at a later time so the disc can be reused (such as transferring large files from one computer to another or temporarily storing TV shows recorded on your computer that you will later watch using your living room TV and DVD player).

Flash Memory

Flash memory is a chip-based storage medium that represents data using electrons. Because they have no moving parts, flash memory storage systems are not subject to mechanical failures like hard drive and optical disc systems, and, therefore, are more resistant to shock and vibration. They also consume less power and make no noise. Flash memory media is rewritable and has a longer expected life than magnetic media, though it is typically more expensive per MB. In addition to the SSDs and hybrid hard drives already discussed, flash memory media is increasingly being embedded directly into a variety of consumer products—such as portable digital media players, digital cameras, handheld gaming devices, GPS devices, mobile phones, and even sunglasses and wristwatches—to provide built-in data storage. There are also a variety of types of *flash memory cards* and *USB flash drives* available to use with computers and other devices for data storage and data transfer, as discussed next.

Flash Memory Cards

One of the most common types of flash memory media is the **flash memory card**—a small card containing one or more flash memory chips, a controller chip, other electrical components, and metal contacts to connect the card to the device or reader with which it is being used. Flash memory cards are available in a variety of formats, such as *CompactFlash (CF)*, *Secure Digital (SD)*, *Secure Digital High Capacity (SDHC)*, *xD Picture Card (xD)*, and *Memory Stick (MS)* (see Figure 2-26). Flash memory cards come in a variety of capacities; one of the most widely used types of flash memory media—Secure Digital (SD)—is also available in different physical sizes. For instance, standard-sized SD cards are often used in digital cameras and computers; the smaller *miniSD* and *microSD* (about one-half and one-quarter the size of a standard SD card, respectively) are designed to be used with mobile phones and other mobile devices.

FURTHER EXPLORATION

Go to the Chapter 2 page at **www.cengage.com/ computerconcepts/np/uccs4** for links to information about DVD technology.

> **Flash memory.** Nonvolatile memory chips that can be used for storage by the computer or user; can be built into a computer or a storage medium. > **Flash memory card.** A small, rectangular flash memory medium, such as a CompactFlash (CF) or Secure Digital (SD) card; often used with digital cameras and other portable devices.

COMPACTFLASH (CF) CARDS

MEMORY STICKS

SECURE DIGITAL (SD) CARDS

XD PICTURE CARDS

FLASH MEMORY CARD READERS
Can be built-in or external and usually support several different types of flash memory media; external readers, such as this one, typically connect to a computer via a USB port.

Flash memory cards are the most common type of storage media for digital cameras, portable digital media players, mobile phones, and other portable devices. They can also be used to store data for a personal computer, as needed, as well as to transfer data from a portable device to a computer. Consequently, most desktop and notebook computers today come with a *flash memory card reader* capable of reading flash memory cards; an external flash memory card reader (that typically connects via a USB port and is shown in Figure 2-26) can be used if a built-in reader is not available. The capacity of flash memory cards is continually growing and is up to about 4 GB for standard cards and 32 GB for *high-capacity cards*; the even higher capacity *extended capacity cards* are just beginning to become available and are expected to reach capacities of 2 TB by 2014.

USB Flash Drives

USB flash drives (sometimes called *USB flash memory drives*, *thumb drives*, or *jump drives*) consist of flash memory media integrated into a self-contained unit that connects to a computer or other device via a standard USB port and is powered via the USB port. USB flash drives are designed to be very small and very portable (see Figure 2-27). In order to appeal to a wide variety of users, USB flash drives are available in a range of sizes, colors, and appearances—including those designed to be attached to backpacks or worn on a lanyard around the neck; those built into necklaces, wristbands, or wristwatches; those thin enough to fit easily into a wallet; and those made into custom shapes for promotional or novelty purposes. For a device to read from or write to a USB flash drive, you just plug it into a USB port. If the USB flash drive is being used with a computer, it is assigned a drive letter by the computer, just like any other type of attached drive, and files can be read from or written to the USB flash

FIGURE 2-26
Flash memory cards. Shown here are some of the most widely used types of flash memory cards and a multicard reader.

FIGURE 2-27
USB flash drives are often used to store data and transfer files from one computer to another.

> **USB flash drive.** A small storage device that plugs into a USB port and contains flash memory media.

HOW IT WORKS

Thumb Drive PCs

We all know that USB flash drives are a great way to transport documents from one location to another, but what about using one to take a personalized computer with you wherever you go? It's possible and easy to do with the use of *portable applications* (also called *portable apps*)—computer programs that are designed to be used with portable devices like USB flash drives. When the device is plugged into the USB port of any computer, you have access to the software and personal data (including your browser bookmarks, calendar, e-mail and instant messaging contacts, and more) stored on that device, just as you would on your own computer. And when you unplug the device, none of your personal data is left behind because all programs are run directly from the USB flash drive. Many portable applications (such as the PortableApps suite shown in the accompanying illustration) are free and include all the basics you might want in a single package. For instance, PortableApps includes a menu structure, antivirus program, Web browser, e-mail program, calendar program, the OpenOffice.org office suite, and more. To set up a USB flash drive as a portable computer, you need to perform the following steps:

1. Download your desired portable applications (such as the PortableApps suite) to your desktop or notebook computer.

2. Plug in your USB flash drive and run the portable apps installation program, using your USB flash drive as the destination folder.

3. Open a file management program such as Windows Explorer, double-click your USB flash drive, and then launch your portable apps software to test it.

4. Download and install any additional portable apps you would like to use (it is a good idea to include an antivirus program to try to prevent the USB flash drive from becoming infected with a computer virus).

To use your thumb drive computer, plug it into the USB port of any computer—many portable apps will launch automatically and display a main menu, such as the one shown in the accompanying illustration. Portable apps can also be installed on an iPod or other portable digital media player (instead of a USB flash drive) if you prefer to use that device as your portable computer.

1. USB flash drive is plugged into a computer.

2. This menu is displayed; all programs run off the USB flash drive.

VIDEO PODCAST

Go to the Chapter 2 page at **www.cengage.com/ computerconcepts/np/uccs4** to download or listen to the "How To: Use Portable Applications with a USB Flash Drive" video podcast.

drive until it is unplugged from the USB port. The capacity of most USB flash drives today ranges from 1 GB to 64 GB. USB flash drive use has become commonplace for individuals, students, and employees to transport files from one computer to another, as well as to quickly back up important files.

In addition to providing basic data storage and data portability, USB flash drives can provide additional capabilities. For instance, they can be used to lock a computer and to issue Web site passwords; they can also include *biometric features*—such as a built-in fingerprint reader—to allow only authorized individuals access to the data stored on the USB flash drive or to the computer with which the USB flash drive is being used. For a look at how you can carry your personal computer with you on a USB flash drive, see the How It Works box.

Other Types of Storage Systems

Two additional types of storage systems that are frequently used are *remote storage systems* and *smart cards*. Types of emerging storage systems are discussed in Chapter 8.

Remote Storage Systems

Remote storage refers to using a storage device that is not connected directly to the user's computer; instead, the device is accessed through a local network or through the Internet. Using a remote storage device via a local network (referred to as *network storage*) works in much the same way as using *local storage* (the storage devices and media that are directly attached to the user's computer). To read data from or write data to a remote storage device (such as a hard drive in another computer being accessed via a network), the user just selects it (see Figure 2-28) and then performs the necessary tasks in the normal fashion. Network storage is common in businesses; it is also used by individuals with home networks for backup purposes or to share files with another computer in the home.

Remote storage devices accessed via the Internet are often referred to as **online storage** or **cloud storage**. While these terms are often used interchangeably, some view cloud storage as a specific type of online storage that can be accessed on demand by various Web applications. Most online applications (such as *Google Docs*, the *Flickr* photo sharing service, and social networking sites like *Facebook*, for instance) provide online storage for these services. There are also sites whose primary objective is to allow users to store documents online, such as Microsoft *SkyDrive* (see Figure 2-28). The ability to store documents online (or "in the cloud") is growing in importance as more and more applications are becoming Web based and as individuals increasingly want access to their files from anywhere with any Internet-enabled device, such as a portable computer or mobile phone.

FIGURE 2-28
Remote storage.

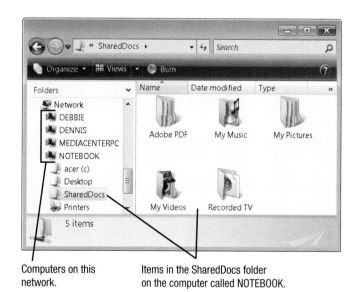

Computers on this network.

Items in the SharedDocs folder on the computer called NOTEBOOK.

NETWORK STORAGE
Shared folders on network computers appear and are accessed in a manner similar to local folders.

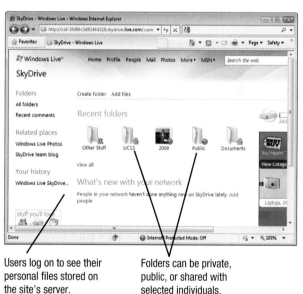

Users log on to see their personal files stored on the site's server.

Folders can be private, public, or shared with selected individuals.

CLOUD STORAGE
Files and folders are stored and accessed online; this site provides 25 GB of free storage.

>**Remote storage.** A storage device that is not directly connected to the computer being used, such as one accessed through a local network or the Internet. >**Online storage.** Remote storage devices accessed via the Internet; also called **cloud storage**.

Online storage is also increasingly being used for backup purposes. In fact, some online storage sites have an automatic backup option that uploads the files in designated folders on your computer to your online account at regular specified intervals, as long as your computer is connected to the Internet. Many Web sites providing online storage to individuals offer the service for free (for instance, SkyDrive gives each individual 25 GB of free storage space); others charge a small fee, such as $10 per month for 50 GB of storage space. Typically, online/cloud storage sites are password-protected and allow users to specify uploaded files as private files or as shared files that designated individuals can access.

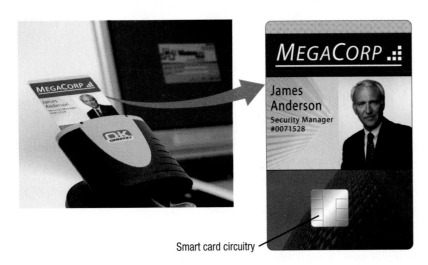

Smart card circuitry

FIGURE 2-29
Smart cards.

Smart Cards

A **smart card** is a credit card-sized piece of plastic that contains computer circuitry and components—typically a processor, memory, and storage (see Figure 2-29). Smart cards today store a relatively small amount of data (typically 64 KB or less) that can be used for payment or identification purposes. For example, a smart card can store a prepaid amount of *digital cash*, which can be used for purchases at a smart card-enabled vending machine or computer—the amount of cash available on the card is reduced each time the card is used. Smart cards are also commonly used worldwide for national and student ID cards, credit and debit cards, and cards that store identification data for accessing facilities or computer networks. Although these applications have used conventional *magnetic stripe* technology in the past, the processor integrated into a smart card can perform computations—such as to authenticate the card and encrypt the data on the card to protect its integrity and secure it against unauthorized access—and data can be added to the card or modified on the card as needed. The increased capabilities of smart cards has also allowed for new applications, such as storing biometric data (the characteristics of a fingerprint or hand, for instance) and other identifying data needed to accelerate airport security and to link patients to the electronic health records increasingly being used by hospitals.

To use a smart card, it must either be inserted into a *smart card reader* (if it is the type of card that requires contact, as in Figure 2-29) or placed close to a smart card reader (if it is a *contactless* card) built into or attached to a computer, keyboard, vending machine, or other device. Once a smart card has been verified by the card reader, the transaction—such as making a purchase or unlocking a door—can be completed. For an even higher level of security, some smart cards today store biometric data in the card and use that data to ensure the authenticity of the card's user before authorizing the smart card transaction (biometrics, encryption, and other security procedures are discussed in more detail in Chapter 4).

Evaluating Your Storage Alternatives

Storage alternatives are often compared by weighing a number of product characteristics and cost factors. Some of these product characteristics include speed, compatibility, storage capacity, convenience, and the portability of the media. Keep in mind that each storage alternative normally involves trade-offs. For instance, most systems with removable media are slower than those with fixed media, and external drives are typically slower than internal ones. Although cost is a factor when comparing similar devices, it is often not the most compelling reason to choose a particular technology. For instance, although USB flash drives are relatively expensive per GB compared to optical discs and external hard drives, many users find them essential for transferring files between work and home or for taking presentations or other files with them as they travel. For drives that use a USB interface, the type of USB port is also significant. For example, storage devices that connect via a USB port adhering to the original *USB 1.0* standard transfer data at up to 12 *Mbps* (millions of bits per second)—*USB 2.0* devices are about 40 times faster and the emerging *USB 3.0* devices will be about 10 times as fast as USB 2.0 devices.

With so many different storage alternatives available, it is a good idea to research which devices and media are most appropriate for your personal situation. In general, most users today need a hard drive (for storing programs and data), some type of recordable or rewritable optical drive (for installing programs, backing up files, and sharing files with others), and a flash memory card reader (for transferring photos, music, and other content between portable devices and the computer). Users who plan to transfer music, digital photos, and other multimedia data on a regular basis between devices—such as a computer, digital camera, mobile phone, and printer—will want to select and use the flash memory media that are compatible with the devices they are using. They will also need to obtain the necessary adapter for their computer if it does not include a compatible built-in flash memory reader. Virtually all computer users today will also need at least one convenient free USB port to be used to connect external hard drives, USB flash drives, and other USB-based storage hardware, as well as USB devices that contain storage media, such as digital cameras and portable digital media players.

ONLINE VIDEO

Go to the Chapter 2 page at **www.cengage.com/ computerconcepts/np/uccs4** to watch the "What Is Bluetooth?" video clip.

FURTHER EXPLORATION

Go to the Chapter 2 page at **www.cengage.com/ computerconcepts/np/uccs4** for links to information about wired and wireless communications media.

COMMUNICATIONS HARDWARE

Most computers today include *communications hardware* to enable the user to communicate with others over a network or the Internet. The type of **communications device** used depends on the device being used (desktop computer, notebook computer, or mobile phone, for instance), as well as the *communication standard* (such as *Ethernet* for wired networks, *Wi-Fi* or *WiMAX* for wireless networks, *Bluetooth* for short-range wireless connections, or a *cellular standard* for a mobile phone) being used. Common communications devices include *network adapters*, *modems*, *cabling*, and other networking hardware as discussed next; emerging communications standards and devices are discussed in more detail in Chapter 8.

ASK THE EXPERT

Dave Weick, Senior Vice President, Chief Information Officer, McDonald's Corporation

How has the emergence of Wi-Fi affected companies such as McDonalds?

The emergence of Wi-Fi has fueled our customers' expectations of having immediate access to information. Our customers and employees love the convenience and relevance of McDonald's "hotspots." Through wireless connectivity, Wi-Fi is creating a more modern and relevant experience for our customers. The ability to conveniently check e-mail or download music or games can be a deciding factor in choosing a place to eat—a trend we don't see ending anytime soon.

> **Communications device.** A piece of hardware that allows one device to communicate with other devices via a network or the Internet.

Network Adapters and Modems

A **network adapter**, also called a *network interface card* (*NIC*) when it is in the form of an expansion card, is used to connect a computer to a network. A **modem** (derived from the terms *modulate* and *demodulate*) is used to connect a computer to a network over telephone lines. However, in everyday use, the term *modem* is also used to refer to any device that connects a computer to a *broadband Internet connection*, such as a *cable modem* used for cable Internet service. As a result, there are a number of different types of modems in use today, each matching a particular type of Internet connection, such as *conventional dial-up*, *cable*, *fixed wireless*, and *DSL* (the types of Internet services that utilize these modems are discussed in detail in Chapter 3).

Most computers and mobile devices today come with a network adapter and/or modem built in; the type of network adapter and modem used depends on the type of network (such as Ethernet, Wi-Fi, or cellular) and Internet access being used. For instance, to connect a computer to an Ethernet network, an Ethernet network adapter is used. To connect a computer to a cable Internet connection, typically both a cable modem and an Ethernet network adapter are used. To connect a computer to a Wi-Fi or WiMAX network or public hotspot, a Wi-Fi or WiMAX network adapter, respectively, is used. Network adapters and modems can be internal devices that connect directly to the motherboard, USB devices that connect to the computer via a USB port, or ExpressCard devices that connect via an ExpressCard slot (see Figure 2-30 for some examples of network adapters and modems).

Other Networking Hardware

To connect the devices on a network together, typically a central device is needed. This device can be a *hub*, *switch*, or *router* for wired networks; networks designed for wireless users typically use a *wireless access point* or *wireless router* instead (a Wi-Fi wireless router is shown in Figure 2-30). To increase the range of a network, *repeaters*, *range extenders*, and *antennas* can be used. To connect the wired devices to the network, *cabling* (typically *twisted-pair*, *coaxial cable*, or *fiber-optic cable*) is used.

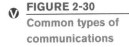

FIGURE 2-30
Common types of communications hardware.

Port for twisted-pair Ethernet cable

PCI EXPRESS GIGABIT ETHERNET ADAPTERS FOR DESKTOP COMPUTERS

Connects to USB port

USB WI-FI ADAPTERS FOR DESKTOP OR NOTEBOOK COMPUTERS

Slides into ExpressCard slot

EXPRESSCARD WI-FI ADAPTERS FOR NOTEBOOK COMPUTERS

Connects to USB port

USB 3G CELLULAR MODEMS FOR DESKTOP OR NOTEBOOK COMPUTERS

Incoming coaxial cable from cable provider and either a USB or Ethernet cable coming from the computer or router connect to the back of the modem.

USB/ETHERNET CABLE MODEMS

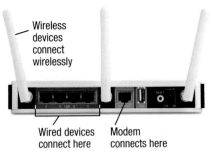
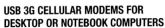

Wireless devices connect wirelessly

Wired devices connect here

Modem connects here

WI-FI WIRELESS ROUTERS

>**Network adapter.** A network interface, such as an expansion card or external network adapter. >**Modem.** A device that enables a computer to communicate over telephone lines.

SOFTWARE BASICS

As discussed in Chapter 1, all computers need an operating system (such as Windows, Linux, or Mac OS) in order to function. The operating system is used to boot the computer, control its operation, and allow users to run application software—the programs used to perform specific tasks on the computer. Although features and capabilities vary from program to program, most software programs today use similar basic features and operations. While covering how to use specific software programs is beyond the scope of this book, an understanding of basic software concepts and operations is an important part of becoming familiar with computers. An overview of booting a computer, using the Windows user interface, and some common types of application software was included in Chapter 1. Other important software basics—including software ownership rights, installation options, common software commands, and the concept of *file management*— are discussed in the remainder of this chapter.

Software Ownership Rights

The *ownership rights* of a software program specify the allowable use of that program. After a software program is developed, the developer (typically an individual or an organization) holds the ownership rights for that program and decides whether or not the program can be sold, shared with others, or otherwise distributed. When a software program is purchased, the buyer is not actually buying the software. Instead, the buyer is acquiring a **software license** that permits him or her to use the software. This license specifies the conditions under which a buyer can use the software, such as the number of computers on which it may be installed (many software licenses permit the software to be installed on just one computer). In addition to being included in printed form inside the packaging of most software programs, the licensing agreement is usually displayed and must be agreed to by the end user at the beginning of the software installation process

There are four basic categories of software: *commercial software* (software that is developed and sold for a profit), *shareware* (software that is distributed on the honor system), *freeware* (software that is given away free of charge), and *public domain software* (software that is not copyrighted). In addition, software that falls into any of these four categories can also be *open source software*—programs whose source code is available to the general public. An open source program can be copyrighted, but individuals and businesses are allowed to modify the program and redistribute it—the only restrictions are that changes must be shared with the open source community and the original copyright notice must remain intact.

ASK THE EXPERT

Greg Weir, Webmaster, Tucows

Why should an individual or business pay for shareware?

In short, because it's the right thing to do. You are obligated to pay for shareware if you continue to use it past the end of the trial period. The fact that shareware publishers allow you to try their software on your computer at your leisure so you can be certain the software meets your needs before you pay for it is testament to their belief in the quality of their product.

There are a number of good reasons for paying for shareware beyond personal or business ethics. In some cases, the title will cease to function after its trial period or will display an annoying "nag" screen every time you start the program to remind you to pay. In addition, payment allows the publisher to enhance the product, fix bugs, and provide support. Continued use of a shareware product past its trial period without paying for it should rightly be considered theft.

> **Software license.** An agreement, either included in a software package or displayed on the screen during installation, that specifies the conditions under which a buyer of the program can use it.

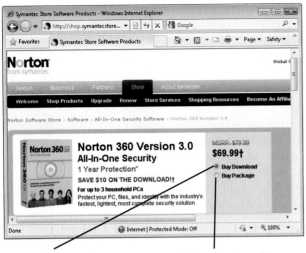

Downloaded version will be downloaded to the buyer's computer.

Packaged version will be shipped to the buyer.

FIGURE 2-31

Installed software. Installed software can be purchased in a physical package or downloaded via the Internet.

ONLINE VIDEO

Go to the Chapter 2 page at **www.cengage.com/ computerconcepts/np/uccs4** to watch the "Using Google Docs Offline" video clip.

ONLINE VIDEO

Go to the Chapter 2 page at **www.cengage.com/ computerconcepts/np/uccs4** to watch the "Using Google Mobile App Voice Search" video clip.

Installed vs. Web-Based Software

Software also differs in how it is accessed by the end user. It can be **installed software** that is installed on and run from the end user's computer, or it can be **Web-based software** that is accessed by the end user over the Internet. Installed software is the most common type of software at the present time and is either purchased in physical form (such as on a CD or DVD) or downloaded from the Internet (see Figure 2-31). Web-based software (also referred to as *Software as a Service (SaaS)* and *cloudware*) is delivered on demand via the Web to wherever the user is at the moment, provided he or she has an Internet connection (and has paid to use the software, if a payment is required). The use of Web-based software is growing rapidly. In fact, research firm Gartner predicts that 25% of new business software will be delivered via the Web by 2011, up from 5% of new software purchases in 2006, and *Microsoft Office 2010* (which is scheduled to be released in 2010) will include a Web-based version of the program. For a look at this new version of Office, see the Trend box.

One advantage of Web-based software over installed software is that the programs and your documents can be accessed from any computer with an Internet connection regardless of the type of computer or operating system used; some can also be accessed via a mobile phone, portable digital media player, or other type of mobile devices. Some potential disadvantages of Web-based software are that online applications tend to run more slowly than applications stored on a local hard drive, that many online applications have a limit regarding the file size of the documents you create, and that the cost may eventually exceed the cost of buying a similar installed software program. In addition, you cannot access the Web-based program and your data if the server on which they reside goes down or if you are in a location with no Internet access, such as while traveling or in a rural area. To eliminate this last concern, a growing trend is for Web-based software to also function, at least in part, offline. For instance, Google Docs added offline capabilities so that users can access the Google Docs applications and their documents locally on their computers, when needed. Edits are stored locally on the computer when a user is offline and, when the user reconnects to the Internet, the changes are synchronized with the documents stored on the Google Docs servers.

Desktop vs. Mobile Software

Notebook computers, tablet computers, UMPCs, and other portable computers typically run the same application software as desktop computers. However, mobile phones and other mobile devices typically require *mobile software*; that is, software specifically designed for a specific type of mobile phone or other mobile device. Mobile software is typically downloaded and a wide range of mobile software is available today. For instance, there are mobile versions of popular programs like Word or PowerPoint, games and media players, business tools that record inventory data or keep track of your business expenses, calendars and programs that allow you to organize notes and voice recordings, applications that allow you to broadcast your current location to friends, and Web browsers for accessing Web sites. Mobile software tends to have a more compact,

---

TREND

Microsoft Office 2010

The upcoming version of Microsoft Office—*Office 2010*—takes advantage of the trends of cloud computing and mobile computing and has specific versions of Office available for those users, in addition to the traditional installed version. The *Web version* of Office enables users to store, access, and collaborate on documents online, such as from the Windows Live *SkyDrive* online storage service. The *Mobile version* is designed for mobile phones and other mobile devices; desktop users can also create a portable version of Office to carry with them on a USB flash drive, when needed.

The overall appearance of Office 2010 is similar to Office 2007 (see the accompanying illustration). The Ribbon is still used for most commands, though the Office button is now the *File tab*, which opens the *Backstage view* containing tasks that allow you to open, share, save, print, and publish your documents. New features include improved image editing tools, improved document protection features to better manage permissions and metadata associated with documents, extended printing capabilities from within Office applications, and the *jump lists* introduced in Microsoft Windows 7 to provide quick access to commonly used tasks.

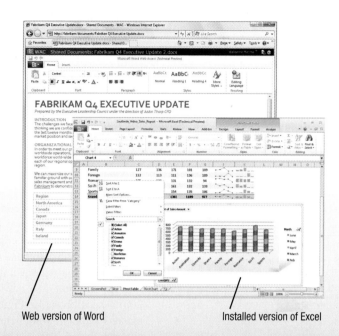

Web version of Word   Installed version of Excel

Office 2010 comes in both installed and Web versions.

efficient appearance than *desktop software*, and many mobile applications include features for easier data input, such as an on-screen keyboard, a phrase list, or handwriting recognition capabilities.

Common Software Commands

Application programs today have a number of concepts and commands in common. For example, many programs allow you to create a new document (such as a letter, drawing, house plan, or greeting card) and then *save* it. To reopen the document at a later time, you use the *open* command; to print the document, you use the *print* command. One of the greatest advantages of using software instead of paper and pencil to create documents is that you can make changes without erasing or recreating the entire document because the document is created in RAM and then saved on a storage medium, instead of it being created directly on paper. Consequently, the document can be retrieved, modified, saved, and printed as many times as needed. Many programs also include tools to help you as you create documents, such as a *spelling and grammar check* feature to locate and help you correct possible spelling and grammar errors in your documents, and a *styles* feature that allows you to apply a common format to a series of documents or a group of similar headings within a single document.

Toolbars, Menus, Keyboard Shortcuts, and the Ribbon

Most commands in an application program are issued through *menus*, *keyboard shortcuts*, or *command buttons* located on a *toolbar* or *Ribbon*. As shown in Figure 1-10 in Chapter 1, the *menu bar* appears at the top of many windows and contains text-based lists (menus),

VIDEO PODCAST

Go to the Chapter 2 page at **www.cengage.com/ computerconcepts/np/uccs4** to download or listen to the "How To: Use Free Web App Alternatives to Expensive Software" video podcast.

FURTHER EXPLORATION Go

Go to the Chapter 2 page at **www.cengage.com/ computerconcepts/np/uccs4** for links to information about application software resources.

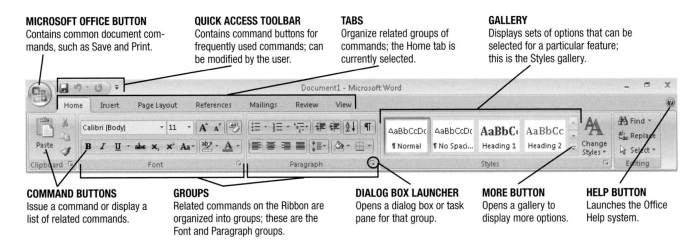

MICROSOFT OFFICE BUTTON
Contains common document commands, such as Save and Print.

QUICK ACCESS TOOLBAR
Contains command buttons for frequently used commands; can be modified by the user.

TABS
Organize related groups of commands; the Home tab is currently selected.

GALLERY
Displays sets of options that can be selected for a particular feature; this is the Styles gallery.

COMMAND BUTTONS
Issue a command or display a list of related commands.

GROUPS
Related commands on the Ribbon are organized into groups; these are the Font and Paragraph groups.

DIALOG BOX LAUNCHER
Opens a dialog box or task pane for that group.

MORE BUTTON
Opens a gallery to display more options.

HELP BUTTON
Launches the Office Help system.

FIGURE 2-32
The Microsoft Office 2007 Ribbon.

which provide access to commands that can be selected to perform actions in that program. Many programs also have toolbars—sets of *icons* or command buttons that are clicked with the mouse to issue commands. *Keyboard shortcuts* are key combinations that correspond to specific commands, such as Ctrl+S for the Save command (this keyboard shortcut is issued by holding down the Ctrl key and pressing the S key).

The **Ribbon** is a new feature in versions of Microsoft Office starting with Office 2007. The Ribbon (see Figure 2-32) consists of *tabs*, which contain *groups* of related commands for the program being used. For convenience, most programs have a *Home tab* that contains the most frequently used commands in that program. In addition to the standard Ribbon tabs that are available whenever the program is open, additional *contextual tabs* are displayed as needed, depending on the action being taken. For instance, selecting a picture or other graphic in Word displays the *Picture Tools tab* that contains commands related to a picture, such as to crop, resize, rotate, or recolor the picture. Clicking a command button on the Ribbon either carries out that command or displays a *gallery* of choices from which the user can select the desired action. The *Microsoft Office Button* (in Microsoft Office 2007) and the *File tab* (in Microsoft Office 2010) replace the File menu used in older versions of Office and contain commands commonly used with documents, such as to open, save, print, send, and publish them.

Editing a Document

Editing a document refers to changing the content of the document, such as adding or deleting text. Most application programs that allow text editing have an insertion point that looks like a blinking vertical line on the screen and shows where the next change will be made to the document currently displayed on the screen. To insert text, just start typing and the text will appear at the insertion point location. To delete text, press the Delete key to delete one character to the right of the insertion point or press the Backspace key to delete one character to the left of the insertion point. If the insertion point is not in the proper location for the edit, it must be moved to the appropriate location in the document by using the arrow keys on the keyboard or by pointing and clicking with the mouse. To select an object or block of text, click the object or drag the mouse over the text. Usually, once an object or some text is selected, it can be manipulated, such as to be moved, deleted, copied, or *formatted*.

Formatting a Document

While editing changes the actual content of a document, **formatting** changes the appearance of the document. One common type of formatting is changing the appearance of selected text in a document. You can change the *font face* or *typeface* (a named collection of text characters that share a common design, such as Calibri or Times New Roman), *font size* (which is measured in *points*), *font style* (such as bold, italic, or underline), and *font color*. Other common types of formatting include changing the *line spacing* or *margins* of a document; adding *page numbers*; and adding *shading* or *borders* to a paragraph, image, or other item.

Working with Files and Folders

It is important for software users to understand the concepts of *files* and *folders* and be able to work with them quickly and efficiently. Anything (such as a program, letter, digital photograph, or song) stored on a storage medium is referred to as a **file**. Data files are also often called *documents*. When a document that was just created (such as a memo or letter in a word processing program) is saved, it is stored as a new file on the storage medium that the user designates. During the storage process, the user is required to give the file a name, called a **filename**; that filename is used to retrieve the file later. To keep files organized, related documents are often stored in **folders** located on the storage medium. For example, one folder might contain memos to business associates while another might hold a set of budgets (see Figure 2-33). To organize files further, you can create *subfolders* (*subdirectories*) within a folder. For instance, you might create a subfolder within the *Budgets* subfolder for each fiscal year. In Figure 2-33, both *Budgets* and *Memos* are subfolders inside the *Documents* folder; the *Budgets* subfolder contains two additional subfolders (*2010* and *2011*).

File management programs (such as *Windows Explorer*) allow you to perform file management tasks, such as looking to see which files are stored on a storage medium, and copying, moving, deleting, and renaming folders and files. For instance, you can see the folders and files stored on your hard drive, USB flash drive, or any other storage medium by clicking the appropriate letter or name for that medium in the Windows Explorer window, and you can copy a file or folder by selecting the desired item, issuing the *Copy* command (such as by using the Organize button in Window Explorer or pressing Ctrl+C), displaying the location where you want the copy to go, and then issuing the *Paste* command (such as by pressing Ctrl+V). You can delete an item by selecting it and pressing the Delete key on the keyboard.

FIGURE 2-33
Windows Explorer.

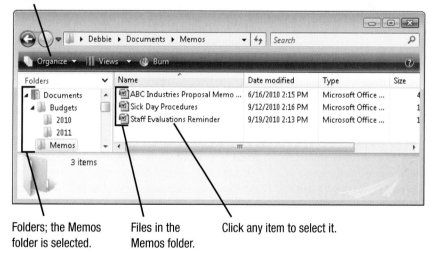

Use the Organize button to copy or move the selected file or folder.

Folders; the Memos folder is selected.

Files in the Memos folder.

Click any item to select it.

SUMMARY

DIGITAL DATA REPRESENTATION

Chapter Objective 1:
Understand how data is
represented to a computer.

Data must be represented appropriately (using 0s and 1s) in order to be used by a computer. A single 0 or 1 is called a **bit**; 8 bits together is referred to as a **byte.** A **kilobyte (KB)** equals 1,024 bytes, a **megabyte (MB)** is about 1 million bytes, a **gigabyte (GB)** is about 1 billion bytes, a **terabyte (TB)** is about 1 trillion bytes, and a **petabyte (PB)** is about 1,000 terabytes. To represent numbers and do mathematical operations, computers use the **binary numbering system** instead of the **decimal numbering system** that people are accustom to using; for representing characters, coding systems, such as **ASCII (American Standard Code for Information Interchange)** and **Unicode**, are used.

INPUT HARDWARE

Chapter Objective 2:
Identify several types of input
devices and explain their
functions.

An **input device** is any piece of hardware that is used to input data into a computer. Two of the most common input devices are the **keyboard** and **mouse**. While a keyboard is designed to enter input by pressing keys, a mouse is a **pointing device** that is used to select objects and commands on the screen. Another common pointing device is the **stylus** (also called an *electronic pen* or *digital pen*), which is used with computers and other devices to input handwritten data and select options. **Touch screens** are touched with the finger to select commands or provide input. Other pointing devices include *graphics tablets*, *gaming devices*, *buttons* and *wheels*, and *touch pads*.

To input data that already exists, a **scanner** (either *flatbed* or *handheld*) can be used. When used with *optical character recognition* (*OCR*) software, the computer system recognizes scanned text characters and stores them digitally so they can be manipulated by the computer. If not, the scanned data is input as an image. Other types of scanners or readers include **barcode readers** (used to read **barcodes** on consumer products and other objects), **RFID readers** (used to read **RFID tags**), and **biometric readers** (used to read *biometric data* belonging to an individual). **Digital cameras** (both *still* and *video cameras*) are used to capture images in digital form and record images on some type of digital storage medium. *Microphones*, *headsets*, and *MIDI* devices can be used for input, as well.

PROCESSING HARDWARE AND OTHER HARDWARE INSIDE THE SYSTEM UNIT

Chapter Objective 3:
Explain the functions of the
primary hardware components
found inside the system unit,
namely the motherboard, the
CPU, and memory.

Processing hardware is located inside the **system unit**, along with other important components. The **motherboard** or *system board* is the main *circuit board* for a personal computer. All hardware used with a computer must be connected to the motherboard, either directly or via a *port*. Every computer has at least one **central processing unit (CPU)**—also called a **processor**, or a **microprocessor** when referring to personal computers—attached to its motherboard that performs the processing for the computer. CPUs today are often **multi-core CPUs**, such as **dual-core** (two cores) and **quad-core** (four cores) **CPUs.** The term *memory* is usually used to refer to **random access memory (RAM)**—groups of chips that are also attached to the motherboard and provide temporary storage for the computer to use. RAM is **volatile**, so all data in RAM is erased when the power to the computer goes off. Other types of memory used by the computer include *cache memory*, *registers*, *read-only memory* (*ROM*), and *flash memory*.

OUTPUT HARDWARE

Output devices present the result of processing to the user, usually in the form of a **display device**—also called a **monitor** or a **display screen**—or a **printer**. The common types of monitors are *CRTs* and *flat-panel displays*. Monitors form images using **pixels**, and the number of pixels used to display an image determines the *screen resolution*.

The most widely-used printers today are **laser printers** (the standard for business documents) and **ink-jet printers** (used in homes and for inexpensive color printouts). Specialty printers, such as *photo printers*, *barcode printers*, and *portable printers* are also available. Other output devices include **speakers**, *headphones*, and *headsets*.

Chapter Objective 4:
List several output devices and explain their functions.

STORAGE HARDWARE

Storage systems make it possible to save programs, data, and processing results for later use. All storage systems have a **storage medium** (which holds the data) and a **storage device** (which reads from and writes to the medium). Data is stored either *magnetically* or *optically* on most storage media. Storage devices can be *internal*, *external*, or *remote*. They are typically assigned letters by the computer, which are used to identify the drive.

Hard drives are used in most computers to store programs and data. Conventional hard drives are **magnetic hard drives**; a newer type of hard drive that uses flash memory instead of magnetic disks is the **solid-state drive** (**SSD**). Hard drives can be *internal* or *external*; external hard drives can be full-sized or portable. **Hybrid hard drives** are a combination of a magnetic hard drive and an SSD, designed to provide increased performance while reducing power consumption.

Optical discs (such as **CD discs**, **DVD discs**, and **Blu-ray Discs** (**BDs**)) store data *optically* using laser beams, and they can store data much more densely than magnetic disk technology. Optical discs can be *read-only*, *recordable*, or *rewritable*.

Flash memory storage systems use nonvolatile memory chips and so have no moving parts. **Flash memory cards** are commonly used with a variety of devices, and come in many formats. **USB flash drives** connect to a computer via a USB port and are a convenient method of transferring files between computers. Other possibilities for storage include **remote storage**—storage accessed through the Internet (**online storage** or **cloud storage**) or another network—and **smart cards** (that contain small amounts of data, such as digital cash or personal data, for a variety of purposes).

Chapter Objective 5:
Understand the difference between storage and memory, as well as between a storage device and a storage medium.

Chapter Objective 6:
Name several types of storage systems and explain the circumstances under which they are typically used.

COMMUNICATIONS HARDWARE

Communications devices, such as **network adapters** and **modems**, enable users to communicate with others over a network. Other networking hardware (such as *hubs*, *routers*, *wireless access points*, and *cabling*) is used to connect the devices on a network; *repeaters*, *range extenders*, and *antennas* can be used to extend the range of a network.

Chapter Objective 7:
Describe the purpose of communications hardware.

SOFTWARE BASICS

A program's **software license** explains the allowable use of the program. Most software today is *commercial*, *shareware*, *freeware*, or *public domain* and can be either **installed software** or **Web-based software**. **Editing** refers to making changes to the content of a document; **formatting** refers to changing its appearance. To issue commands to a software program, user interface tools such as *menus*, *keyboard shortcuts*, *toolbar buttons*, and the **Ribbon** are used. Anything stored on a storage medium (such as a document, a program, or an image) is called a **file** and is given an identifying **filename** by the user. To keep files organized, related documents can be stored inside **folders**. Users can open, copy, move, and delete files and folders, using a *file management program*, such as *Windows Explorer*.

Chapter Objective 8:
Understand basic software concepts and commands.

REVIEW ACTIVITIES

KEY TERM MATCHING

a. byte

b. central processing unit (CPU)

c. file

d. keyboard

e. laser printer

f. modem

g. motherboard

h. optical disc

i. software license

j. USB flash drive

Instructions: Match each key term on the left with the definition on the right that best describes it.

1. _____ A device that enables a computer to communicate over telephone lines.

2. _____ A group of 8 bits.

3. _____ An agreement, either included in a software package or displayed on the screen during installation, that specifies the conditions under which a buyer of the program can use it.

4. _____ An input device containing numerous keys that can be used to input letters, numbers, and other symbols.

5. _____ An output device that uses toner powder and technology similar to that of a photocopier to produce images on paper.

6. _____ A small storage device that plugs into a USB port and contains flash memory media.

7. _____ A type of storage medium read from and written to using a laser beam.

8. _____ Something stored on a storage medium, such as a program, a document, or an image.

9. _____ The chip located on the motherboard of a computer that performs the processing for a computer. Also called the processor.

10. _____ The main circuit board of a computer, located inside the system unit, to which all computer system components connect.

SELF-QUIZ

Instructions: Circle **T** if the statement is true, **F** if the statement is false, or write the best answer in the space provided. **Answers for the self-quiz are located in the References and Resources Guide at the end of the book.**

1. **T** **F** A storage medium that can hold 256 GB can hold about 256 billion characters.

2. **T** **F** A mouse is an example of a pointing device.

3. **T** **F** An ink-jet printer normally produces a better image than a laser printer.

4. **T** **F** A hybrid hard drive contains both magnetic hard disks and optical discs.

5. **T** **F** Changing the font size in a document is an example of a formatting operation.

6. A(n) _____ can be used to convert flat printed documents, such as a drawing or photograph, into digital form.

7. A CPU with four separate processing cores is referred to as a(n) _____ CPU.

8. Secure Digital (SD) cards are one type of _____ medium.

9. Files can be stored inside _____ to keep them organized.

10. Match each input device to its input application, and write the corresponding number in the blank to the left of the input application.

a. _____ Pen-based computing	**1.**	Keyboard
b. _____ Consumer kiosk	**2.**	Stylus
c. _____ Text-based data entry	**3.**	RFID tag
d. _____ Secure facility access	**4.**	Biometric reader
e. _____ Tracking goods	**5.**	Touch screen

1. Number the following terms from 1 to 6 to indicate their size from smallest to largest.

   a. _____ Petabyte   b. _____ Kilobyte   c. _____ Byte

   d. _____ Terabyte   e. _____ Gigabyte   f. _____ Megabyte

2. For the following list of hardware devices, write the appropriate abbreviation (I, P, O, S, or C) in the space provided to indicate whether each device is used for input (I), processing (P), output (O), storage (S), or communications (C).

   a. _____ Biometric reader   f. _____ Display device

   b. _____ Modem   g. _____ USB flash drive

   c. _____ Speaker   h. _____ Microphone

   d. _____ Photo printer   i. _____ Hard drive

   e. _____ CPU   j. _____ Network adapter

3. Supply the missing words to complete the following statements.

   a. The smallest piece of data that can be represented by a computer (0 or 1) is called a(n) _____.

   b. _____ is an international coding system that can be used to represent text-based data in any written language.

   c. A(n) _____ optical disc can hold either 25 GB or 50 GB and is designed for high-definition content, such as movies.

4. List one personal or business application that you believe is more appropriate for a dot-matrix printer, instead of another type of printer, and explain why.

5. Which types of storage media would be appropriate for someone who needed to exchange large (5 MB to 75 MB) files with another person? List at least three different types, stating under what specific conditions each might be the most appropriate type of storage medium to use.

1. People send their digital photos over the Internet in different ways. For instance, digital photos are often e-mailed to others, posted on Facebook pages and other social networking sites, and uploaded to a server (such as one belonging to Snapfish, Wal-Mart, or Costco) in order to order prints, enlargements, or other photo-based items. If you have ever sent photos over the Internet, were you concerned about someone other than the intended recipient intercepting or viewing your photo files? If you have ever uploaded files to a processing service for printing, did you check to see if the Web server being used was secure? Should individuals be concerned about sending their personal photos over the Internet? There are a number of advantages, but are there privacy risks, as well?

2. The choice of an appropriate input device for a product is often based on both the type of device being used and the target market for that device. For instance, a device targeted to college students and one targeted to older individuals may use different input methods. Suppose that you are developing a device to be used primarily for Internet access that will be marketed to senior citizens. What type of hardware would you select as the primary input device? Why? What are the advantages and disadvantages of your selected input device? How could the disadvantages be minimized?

PROJECTS

1. **Thumb Drive PCs** As discussed in the chapter How It Works box, USB flash drives can be used to bring your personal software and settings with you to any computer with which you use that drive. In addition, USB flash drives can be used to securely store files, grant access to a computer, and more.

    For this project, research two features that USB flash drives can provide, in addition to plain data storage. For your selected features, determine what the feature does, how it works, what benefits it provides, and some examples of USB flash drives that are currently being sold that include that feature. Is there an additional cost for drives that contain this feature? If so, do you think it is worth the extra cost? Do you think the feature is beneficial? Why or why not? At the conclusion of your research, prepare a one- to two-page summary of your findings and opinions and submit it to your instructor.

2. **Adding Memory** Adding additional RAM to a computer is one of the most common computer upgrades. Before purchasing additional memory, however, it is important to make sure that the purchased memory is compatible with the computer.

    For this project, select a computer (such as your own computer, a school computer, or a computer at a local store) and then determine (by looking at the computer or asking an appropriate individual—such as a lab aide in the school computer lab or a salesperson at the local store) the following: manufacturer and model number, CPU, current amount of memory, total memory slots, and the number of available memory slots. (If you look inside the computer, be sure to unplug the power cord first and do not touch any components inside the system unit.) Once you have the necessary information, call a local store or use your information and a memory supplier's Web site to determine the appropriate type of memory needed for your selected computer. What choices do you have in terms of capacity and configuration? Can you add just one memory module, or do you have to add memory in pairs? Can you keep the old memory modules, or do they have to be removed? At the conclusion of your research, prepare a one-page summary of your findings and recommendations and submit it to your instructor.

3. **Keyboarding Speed Test** Although voice and other alternative means of input are emerging, most data input today is still performed via the keyboard. Proper keyboarding technique can help increase speed and accuracy. Online keyboarding tests can help to evaluate your key-boarding ability.

    For this project, find a site (such as Typingtest.com) that offers a free online typing test and test your keyboarding speed and accuracy. At the conclusion of the test, rate your keyboarding ability and determine whether a keyboarding course or tutor program, or just keyboarding practice, will help you improve if your score is not at least 20 correct words per minute (cwpm). Take the test one more time to see if your speed improves now that you are familiar with how the test works. If your speed is fast, but accuracy is low, take the test once more, concentrating on accuracy. If you still test less than 20 cwpm, locate a free typing tutor program or Web site and evaluate it to see if it would help you to increase your speed and accuracy. At the conclusion of this task, prepare a short summary of your experience, including the typing test site used and your best score.

4. **Lost and Found** Portable computers, mobile phones, USB flash drives, and other portable devices are lost all the time today. They can be dropped out of a pocket or bag, inadvertently left on a table, and so forth. If the owner has identifying information (name, phone number, or e-mail address, for instance) printed on the device, the individual who finds the device can attempt to return it to the owner. But what if there is no identifying information clearly visible on the device? Should the finder look at the contents of the device to try to determine the owner? If the device is lost in a location where there is a responsible party (such as an airplane or a restaurant), the finder can turn over the device to that authority (such as a flight attendant or a manager). But, is it ethical for the responsible party to look at the contents in order to identify the owner? If you lost a device, would you want someone to look at the contents to try to determine your identity? Why or why not? Is looking at the contents on a found device ever ethical? Should it be illegal?

   For this project, form an opinion about the ethical ramifications of lost devices and be prepared to discuss your position (in class, via an online class discussion group, in a class chat room, or via a class blog, depending on your instructor's directions). You may also be asked to write a short paper expressing your opinion.

5. **Open Source Software: Software Development Benefit or Hindrance?** A number of open source software products (such as the Linux operating system) are available today. One reason individuals and organizations are switching to Linux and other open source software is cost. Proponents of open source software also believe that if programmers who are not concerned with financial gain work on an open source program, they will produce a more useful and error-free product much faster than the traditional commercial software development process. However, what is the impact of open source software on software development in general? Will it force existing commercial software companies to streamline their development process in order to cut costs to better compete with open source products? Or will commercial software companies simply go out of business? Would commercial software manufacturers be justified in raising their prices to make up for revenue lost to open source competitors? Would you prefer to use open source software or commercial software? Why?

   For this project, consider the pros and cons of open source software and form an opinion about its impact on the software industry and software in general. Be prepared to discuss both sides of this issue and your opinion (in class, via an online class discussion group, in a class chat room, or via a class blog). You may also be asked to write a short paper or prepare a short presentation expressing your opinion, depending on your instructor's directions.

Instructions: Go to the Chapter 2 page at **www.cengage.com/computerconcepts/np/uccs4** to work the following Web Activities.

6. **Interactive Activities** Work the interactive **Crossword Puzzle**, watch the **Video Podcasts** and **Online Videos**, and explore the **Further Exploration** links associated with this chapter.

   If you have a SAM user profile, you may have access to hands-on instruction, practice, and assessment of the skills covered in this chapter. Check with your instructor for instructions and the correct URL/Web site to access those assignments.

SAM

Student Edition
Labs

7. **Student Edition Labs** Work the following interactive **Student Edition Labs**.
   - ➤ **Binary Numbers**   ➤ **Understanding the Motherboard**   ➤ **Using Input Devices**
   - ➤ **Peripheral Devices**   ➤ **Managing Files and Folders**

8. **Test Yourself** Review the **Online Study Guide** for this chapter, then test your knowledge of the terms and concepts covered in this chapter by completing the **Key Term Matching** exercise, the **Self-Quiz**, the **Exercises**, and the **Practice Test**.

expert insight on...

Hardware

ACER

Sumit Agnihotry is the Vice President of Product Marketing for Acer Pan America. In his 15+ years in the computer field, he has held various positions in computer product marketing. He started at the Acer Group in 1998 as a product manager, and he has successfully helped launch numerous Acer products through U.S. consumer channels. Sumit holds a Bachelor of Science Degree in Marketing and has attended Executive Education programs in Leadership Development and Cross-Cultural Negotiation at the Johns Hopkins University.

A conversation with SUMIT AGNIHOTRY
Vice President, Product Marketing, Acer Pan America

" . . . storage technology will need to continue to evolve to improve accessibility, performance, and capacity, and to support new high-definition and content-on-the-go applications. "

My Background . . .

I started in the computer industry when I got my first job as a manufacturer's representative while still in school, marketing computer peripherals and accessories to retailers. I began my career at the Acer Group in 1998 as a product manager for mobile products. I'm now the Vice President of product marketing for the Americas region and my responsibilities include working with engineers to develop the latest cutting-edge products, and then launching those products through various channels in North, Central, and South America. I also oversee the marketing of Acer notebooks, netbooks, desktop computers, and monitors. I believe that my ability to understand consumer needs and pain points, coupled with my knowledge of this industry and technology, has helped me succeed in this field and in my current position.

It's Important to Know . . .

Moore's Law is still valid. The trend of improvements in the area of computing hardware is well described by Moore's Law, which basically says that the number of transistors that can be placed inexpensively on an integrated circuit has increased exponentially since the invention of the integrated circuit in 1958 and will continue to do so. But, in addition to the density of components and transistors, many other measures of digital technology are improving at exponential rates as well, including computing performance, power consumption, battery life, and network capacity. This growth trend is expected to continue for at least another decade.

The world is becoming wireless. Consumers today want access to information anytime and anywhere. The desire of consumers to access digital and voice information on the go dictates that emerging devices will need to have wireless connectivity and high performance, as well as be able to support popular applications such as social networking. In addition, devices will need to be ultra thin and light, and have an all-day battery life. They must also be designed to appeal to the mass market, but still be affordable.

Storage technology will continue to evolve. Optical storage media (such as DVDs and CDs) and flash storage media (such as flash memory cards and USB flash drives) are widely used today. However, storage technology will need to continue to evolve to improve accessibility, performance, and capacity, and to support new high-definition and content-on-the-go applications. The potential impact of current and future technologies on the environment will need to be taken into consideration as well.

How I Use this Technology . . .

I spend a lot of time on the road visiting suppliers and customers so I use my BlackBerry and laptop throughout the day—basically anytime I am not sleeping or flying. When I don't have access to my laptop or it's not convenient to use it, I am still able to respond to e-mail messages and perform other mission-critical tasks in a timely manner using my BlackBerry. These devices also allow me to connect with my family easily when I am away from home. Of course, another personal favorite use of technology is entertainment and I frequently download movies and TV shows to watch while I'm on the go; for instance, I watched an episode of "The Office" that I downloaded from iTunes on a recent flight from San Francisco to Taipei.

What the Future Holds . . .

Over the past few decades, computing has evolved from mainframes, to desktop computers, to luggable so-called "portable" computers, to today's laptops and mobile devices. I believe that as consumers continue to embrace digital information consumption on the go, the vision of a "laptop for every lap" will come true. However, the device may not look like today's laptop. As the cost of creating wireless and mobile devices continue to drop, we will see huge improvements in portable computing products in the near future that will enable us to provide consumers with portable, yet affordable, devices that can be used to access the types of information that are important to them, whenever they want to do so.

My Advice to Students . . .

Technology has to adapt to market needs, not the other way around. So when you think about innovative technology, it has to be centered on improving consumer experience and pain points.

> *"The desire of consumers to access digital and voice information on the go dictates that emerging devices will need to have wireless connectivity and high performance . . ."*

Discussion Question

Sumit Agnihotry believes the vision of a "laptop for every lap" will become a reality in the near future. Think about the computing and communications tasks you wish to do on a daily basis, which tasks you prefer to do on the go, and the size and connectivity requirements for the optimal device to accomplish these tasks. What capabilities would the device need to have? Would your optimal device be based on today's mobile phone, notebook computer, netbook computer, or something entirely different? What other hardware characteristics would your optimal device need? Is the future of personal computing a mobile device? Be prepared to discuss your position (in class, via an online class discussion group, in a class chat room, or via a class blog, depending on your instructor's directions). You may also be asked to write a short paper expressing your opinion.

>For more information on Acer and Acer products, visit us.acer.com. For news about hot technology products, trends, and ideas, visit www.engadet.com and www.ted.com.

chapter 3

The Internet and the World Wide Web

After completing this chapter, you will be able to do the following:

1. Discuss how the Internet evolved and what it is like today.

2. Identify the various types of individuals, companies, and organizations involved in the Internet community and explain their purposes.

3. Describe device and connection options for connecting to the Internet, as well as some considerations to keep in mind when selecting an ISP.

4. Understand how to search effectively for information on the Internet and how to cite Internet resources properly.

5. List several ways to communicate over the Internet, in addition to e-mail.

6. List several useful activities that can be performed via the Web.

7. Discuss censorship and privacy, and how they are related to Internet use.

outline

Overview

Evolution of the Internet
From ARPANET to Internet2
The Internet Community Today
Myths About the Internet

Getting Set Up to Use the Internet
Type of Device
Type of Connection and Internet Access
Selecting an ISP and Setting Up Your Computer

Searching the Internet
Search Sites
Search Strategies
Evaluating Search Results
Citing Internet Resources

Beyond Browsing and E-Mail
Other Types of Online Communications
Social Networking
Online Shopping and Investing
Online Entertainment
Online News, Reference, and Information
Online Education and Writing

Censorship and Privacy Issues
Censorship
Web Browsing Privacy
E-Mail Privacy

OVERVIEW

With the prominence of the Internet in our personal and professional lives today, it is hard to believe that there was a time not too long ago that few people had even heard of the Internet, let alone used it. But technology is continually evolving and, in fact, it is only relatively recently that it has evolved enough to allow the use of multimedia applications—such as downloading music and movies, watching TV and videos, and playing multimedia interactive games—over the Internet to become everyday activities. Today, the Internet and the World Wide Web are household words, and, in many ways, they have redefined how people think about computers, communications, and the availability of news and information.

Despite the popularity of the Internet, however, many users cannot answer some important basic questions about it. What makes up the Internet? Is it the same thing as the World Wide Web? How did the Internet begin, and where is it heading? How can the Internet be used to find specific information? This chapter addresses these types of questions and more.

Chapter 3 begins with a discussion of the evolution of the Internet, followed by a look at the many individuals, companies, and organizations that make up the Internet community. Next, the chapter covers different options for connecting to the Internet, including the types of devices, Internet connections, and ISPs that are available today. Then, one of the most important Internet skills you should acquire— efficient Internet searching—is discussed. To help you appreciate the wide spectrum of resources and activities available over the Internet, we also take a brief look at some of the most common applications available via the Internet. The chapter closes with a discussion of a few of the important societal issues that apply to Internet use. ■

EVOLUTION OF THE INTERNET

The **Internet** is a worldwide collection of separate, but interconnected, networks accessed daily by millions of people using a variety of devices to obtain information, disseminate information, access entertainment, or communicate with others. While *Internet* has become a household word only during the past two decades or so, it has actually operated in one form or another for much longer than that.

From ARPANET to Internet2

The roots of the Internet began with an experimental project called *ARPANET*. The Internet we know today is the result of the evolution of ARPANET and the creation of the *World Wide Web* (WWW).

> **Internet.** The largest and most well-known computer network, linking millions of computers all over the world.

ARPANET

The U.S. Department of Defense *Advanced Research Projects Agency* (*ARPA*) created **ARPANET** in 1969. One objective of the ARPANET project was to create a computer network that would allow researchers located in different places to communicate with each other. Another objective was to build a computer network capable of sending or receiving data over a variety of paths to ensure that network communications could continue even if part of the network was destroyed, such as in a nuclear attack or by a natural disaster.

Initially, ARPANET connected four supercomputers and enabled researchers at a few dozen academic institutions to communicate with each other and with government agencies. As the project grew during the next decade, students were granted access to ARPANET as hundreds of college and university networks were connected to it. These networks consisted of a mixture of different computers so, over the years, protocols were developed for tying this mix of computers and networks together, for transferring data over the network, and for ensuring that data was transferred intact. Additional networks soon connected to ARPANET, and this *internet*—or network of networks—eventually evolved into the present day Internet.

The Internet infrastructure today can be used for a variety of purposes, such as researching topics of interest; exchanging e-mail and instant messages; participating in videoconferences and making telephone calls; downloading software, music, and movies; purchasing goods and services; watching TV and video online; accessing computers remotely; and sharing files with others. Most of these activities are available through the primary Internet resource—the *World Wide Web* (*WWW*).

The World Wide Web

In its early years, the Internet was used primarily by the government, scientists, and educational institutions. Despite its popularity in academia and with government researchers, the Internet went virtually unnoticed by the public and the business community for over two decades because 1) it required a computer and 2) it was hard to use (see the left image in Figure 3-1). As always, however, computer and networking technology improved and new applications quickly followed. Then, in 1989, a researcher named *Tim Berners-Lee* proposed the idea of the **World Wide Web** (**WWW**). He envisioned the World Wide Web as a way to organize information in the form of pages linked together through selectable text or images (today's hyperlinks) on the screen. Although the introduction of Web pages did not replace all other Internet resources (such as e-mail and collections of downloadable files), it became a popular way for researchers to provide written information to others.

In 1993, a group of professors and students at the University of Illinois *National Center for Supercomputing Applications* (*NCSA*) released the *Mosaic* Web browser. Soon after, use

FIGURE 3-1

Using the Internet: Back in the "old days" versus now.

EARLY 1990s
Even at the beginning of the 1990s, using the Internet for most people meant learning how to work with a cryptic sequence of commands. Virtually all information was text-based.

TODAY
Today's Web organizes much of the Internet's content into easy-to-read pages that can contain text, graphics, animation, video, and interactive content that users access via hyperlinks.

> **ARPANET.** The predecessor of the Internet, named after the Advanced Research Projects Agency (ARPA), which sponsored its development.
> **World Wide Web (WWW).** The collection of Web pages available through the Internet.

of the World Wide Web began to increase dramatically because Mosaic's *graphical user interface (GUI)* and its ability to display images on Web pages made using the World Wide Web both easier and more fun than in the past. Today's Web pages are a true multimedia, interactive, experience (see the right image in Figure 3-1). They can contain text, graphics, animation, sound, video, and three-dimensional virtual reality objects.

A growing number of today's Web-based applications and services are referred to as *Web 2.0* applications. Although there is no precise definition, Web 2.0 generally refers to applications and services that use the Web as a platform to deliver rich applications that enable people to collaborate, socialize, and share information online. Some Web 2.0 applications (such as cloud computing) have been discussed in previous chapters; others (such as *social networking sites, RSS feeds, podcasts, blogs*, and *wikis*) are covered later in this chapter.

Although the Web is only part of the Internet, it is by far the most widely used part. Today, most companies regard their use of the Internet and their World Wide Web presence as indispensable competitive business tools, and many individuals view the Internet—and especially the Web—as a vital research, communications, and entertainment medium.

One remarkable characteristic of both the Internet and World Wide Web is that they are not owned by any person or business, and no single person, business, or organization is in charge. Web pages are developed by

ASK THE EXPERT

Dave Weick, Senior Vice President, Chief Information Officer, McDonald's Corporation

i'm lovin' it

How important is it for a business to have a Web site today if it doesn't sell products and services online?

For McDonald's, our online presence is about extending the McDonald's experience to our customers. Mcdonalds.com allows our customers another channel to engage with our brand without ever entering a restaurant. Through our Web site, customers can find promotions and nutritional information on all of our products. On the Open for Discussion blog, customers are talking about McDonald's corporate sustainability efforts. Happymeal.com is connecting kids across the globe in fun, interactive, and uniquely McDonald's ways. Finally, customers can download podcasts about food safety.

For McDonald's, our Web site allows us the opportunity to connect with our customers on topics that are important to them and in the way that they want to connect. In addition, in some parts of the world you can order off the menu located on our Web site and have it delivered to your door. As our customers demand even more convenience and control over the "ordering process," this may become even more prevalent in the future.

individuals and organizations, and are hosted on Web servers owned by individuals, schools, businesses, or other entities. Each network connected to the Internet is privately owned and managed individually by that network's administrator, and the primary infrastructure that makes up the *Internet backbone* is typically owned by communications companies, such as telephone and cable companies. In addition, the computers and other devices used to access the Internet belong to individuals or organizations. So, while individual components of the Internet are owned by individuals and organizations, the Internet as a whole has no owner or network administrator. The closest the Internet comes to having a governing body is a group of organizations that are involved with issues such as establishing the protocols used on the Internet, making recommendations for changes, and encouraging cooperation between and coordinating communications among the networks connected to the Internet.

Internet2

Internet2 is a consortium of researchers, educators, and technology leaders from industry, government, and the international community that is dedicated to the development of revolutionary Internet technologies. Internet2 uses high-performance networks linking over 200 member institutions to deploy and test new network applications and capabilities. It is important to realize, however, that the Internet2 network is not a new network designed to eventually replace the Internet—it is simply a research and development tool to help develop technologies that ensure the Internet in the future can handle tomorrow's applications. Much of Internet2 research is focused on speed. For instance, the *Internet2 Land Speed Record* is an ongoing contest for the highest-bandwidth end-to-end network. The current record is an average speed of 9.08 Gbps while transferring 20.42 TB of data across about 30,000 miles of network.

The Internet Community Today

The Internet community today consists of individuals, businesses, and a variety of organizations located throughout the world. Virtually anyone with a computer or other Web-enabled device can be part of the Internet, either as a user or as a supplier of information or services. Most members of the Internet community fall into one or more of the following groups.

Users

Users are people who use the Internet to retrieve content or perform online activities, such as to look up a telephone number, read the day's news headlines or top stories, browse through an online catalog, make an online purchase, download a music file, watch an online video, make a phone call, or send an e-mail message. According to the Pew Internet & American Life Project, approximately 75% of the United States population are Internet users, using the Internet at work, home, school, or another location. The availability of low-cost computers, low-cost or free Internet access (such as at libraries, school, and other public locations), and bundled pricing for obtaining Internet service in conjunction with telephone and/or television service has helped Internet use begin to approach the popularity and widespread use of telephones and TVs.

Internet Service Providers (ISPs)

Internet service providers (**ISPs**) are businesses or other organizations (see some examples in Figure 3-2) that provide Internet access to others, typically for a fee. ISPs (sometimes called *wireless ISPs* or *WISPs* when referring to ISPs that offer service via a wireless network) include most communications and media companies, such as conventional and mobile phone companies, cable providers, and satellite providers. Some ISPs (such as cable and cellular phone companies) offer Internet service over their private networks; other ISPs provide Internet service over the regular telephone lines or the airwaves. While many ISPs (such as Road Runner and EarthLink) provide service nationwide, others provide service to a more limited geographical area. Regardless of their delivery method and geographical coverage, ISPs are the onramp to the Internet, providing their subscribers with access to the World Wide Web, e-mail, and other Internet resources. In addition to Internet access, some ISPs provide proprietary online services available only to their subscribers. A later section of this chapter covers ISPs in more detail, including factors to consider when selecting an ISP.

V FIGURE 3-2
Companies that provide Internet access today include telephone, cable, and satellite companies.

Internet Content Providers

Internet content providers supply the information that is available through the Internet. Internet content providers can be commercial businesses, nonprofit organizations, educational institutions, individuals, and more. Some examples of Internet content providers are listed next.

> A photographer who posts samples of her best work on a Web page.

> An individual who publishes his opinion on various subjects to an online journal or *blog*.

> A software company that creates a Web site to provide product information and soft-ware downloads.

> A national news organization that maintains an online site to provide up-to-the-minute news, feature stories, and video clips.

> A television network that develops a site for its TV shows, including episode summaries, cast information, and links to watch past episodes online.

Application Service Providers (ASPs) and Web Services

Application service providers (**ASPs**) are companies that manage and distribute Web-based software services to customers over the Internet. Instead of providing access to the Internet like ISPs do, ASPs provide access to software applications via the Internet. In essence, ASPs rent access to software programs to companies or individuals—typically, customers pay a monthly or yearly fee to use each application. As discussed in Chapter 2, this software can be called *Web-based software, Software as a Service (SaaS),* and *cloud-ware.* Common ASP applications for businesses include office suites, collaboration and communications software, accounting programs, and e-commerce software.

One type of self-contained business application designed to work over the Internet or a company network is a **Web service**. A Web service can be added to Web pages to provide a service that would otherwise not be feasible (such as the inclusion of mapping information on a Web site or in a Web application using Microsoft's *MapPoint .NET Web service*). A Web service can also be used to provide a service via a user's computer and the Internet. For instance, the *FedEx QuickShip Web service* allows users to create a shipment to any Microsoft Outlook contact from within Microsoft Outlook (by right-clicking the contact's name, as shown in Figure 3-3, or using the FedEx QuickShip toolbar displayed in Microsoft Outlook); the toolbar can also be used to track packages, order pickups, check rates, and more. It is impor-tant to realize that Web services are not stand-alone applications and, therefore, do not have a user interface—they are simply a standardized way of allowing different applications and comput-ers to share data and processes via a network so they can work together with other Web services and be used with many differ-ent computer systems. A company that provides Web services is sometimes referred to as a *Web services provider.*

FIGURE 3-3

Web services. Once downloaded and installed, this Web service allows users to create and manage FedEx shipments from within Microsoft Outlook.

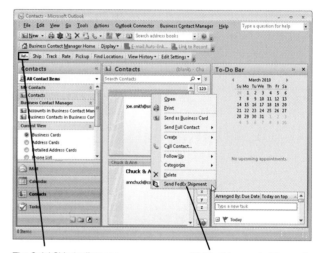

The QuickShip toolbar can be used for a variety of shipping tasks.

Right-click a contact to create a shipment to that individual.

Infrastructure Companies

Infrastructure companies are the enterprises that own or operate the paths or "roadways" along which Internet data travels, such as the Internet backbone and the communications networks connected to it. Examples of infrastructure companies include conventional and mobile phone companies, cable companies, and satellite Internet providers.

Hardware and Software Companies

A wide variety of hardware and software companies make and distribute the products used with the Internet and Internet activities. For example, companies that create or sell the software used in conjunction with the Internet (such as Web browsers, e-mail programs, e-commerce

---

>**Application service provider (ASP).** A company that manages and distributes software-based services over the Internet. >**Web service.** A self-contained business application that operates over the Internet.

and multimedia software, and Web development tools) fall into this category. So, too, do the companies that make the hardware (network adapters, modems, cables, routers, servers, computers, and mobile phones, for instance) that is used with the Internet.

The Government and Other Organizations

Many organizations influence the Internet and its uses. Governments have the most visible impact; their laws can limit both the information made available via Web servers located in a particular country and the access individuals residing in that country have to the Internet. For example, in France, it is illegal to sell items or post online content related to racist groups or activities; in China, there are tight controls imposed on what information is published on Web servers located in China, as well as on the information available to its citizens. And in the United States, anything illegal offline (illegal drugs, child pornography, and so forth) is illegal online.

Legal rulings also can have a large impact on the communications industry in general. For example, the 1968 *Carterfone Decision* allowed companies other than AT&T to utilize the AT&T infrastructure and the 1996 *Telecommunications Act* deregulated the entire communications industry so that telephone companies, cable TV and satellite operators, and firms in other segments of the industry were free to enter each other's markets. A petition to apply the Carterfone Decision to wireless networks in order to allow open access to wireless networks so that any phone can be used with any network is under consideration now by the Federal Communications Commission (FCC). In addition to making these types of decisions, the FCC also greatly influences the communications industry through its ability to allocate radio frequencies (which are used with most types of wireless communications) and to implement policies and regulations related to interstate and international communications via radio, television, wire, satellite, and cable. The ability of the government to approve or block potential mergers between communications companies and to break apart companies based on antitrust law to prevent new monopolies also impacts the Internet and communications industry.

Key Internet organizations are responsible for many aspects of the Internet. For example, the *Internet Society* (*ISOC*) provides leadership in addressing issues that may impact the future of the Internet. It also oversees the groups responsible for Internet infrastructure standards, such as determining the protocols that can be used and how Internet addresses are constructed. *ICANN* (*Internet Corporation for Assigned Names and Numbers*) coordinates activities related to the Internet's naming system, such as IP address allocation and domain name management. The *World Wide Web Consortium* (*W3C*) is a group of over 450 organizations dedicated to developing new protocols and specifications to promote the evolution of the Web and to ensure its interoperability. In addition, many colleges and universities support Internet research and manage blocks of the Internet's resources.

Myths About the Internet

Because the Internet is so unique in the history of the world—and its content and applications keep evolving—several widespread myths about it have surfaced.

Myth 1: The Internet Is Free

This myth stems from the fact that there has traditionally been no cost associated with accessing online content—such as news and product information—or with e-mail exchange, other than what the Internet users pay their ISPs for Internet access. And many people—such as students, employees, and consumers who opt for free Internet service or use free access available at public libraries or other public locations—pay nothing for Internet access. Yet it should also be obvious that someone, somewhere, has to pay to keep the Internet up and running.

Businesses, schools, public libraries, and most home users pay Internet service providers flat monthly fees to connect to the Internet. In addition, businesses, schools, libraries, and other large organizations might have to lease high-capacity communications lines (such as from a telephone company) to support their high level of Internet traffic.

Mobile users that want Internet access while on the go typically pay hotspot providers or mobile phone providers for this access. ISPs, phone companies, cable companies, and other organizations that own part of the Internet infrastructure pay to keep their parts of the Internet running smoothly. ISPs also pay software and hardware companies for the resources they need to support their subscribers. Eventually, most of these costs are passed along to end users through ISP fees. ISPs that offer free Internet access typically obtain revenue by selling on-screen ads that display on the screen when the service is being used.

Another reason that the idea the Internet is free is a myth is the growing trend of subscription or per-use fees to access Web-based resources. For instance, downloadable music and movies are very common today (see Figure 3-4) and some journal or newspaper articles require a fee to view them online. In fact, some newspapers and magazines have moved entirely online and most charge a subscription fee to view the level of content that was previously published in a print version. In lieu of a mandatory fee, some Web sites request a donation for use of the site. Many experts expect the use of fee-based Internet content to continue to grow at a rapid pace.

FIGURE 3-4
Fee-based Web content. The use of fee-based Web content, such as downloadable movies and music, is growing.

Myth 2: Someone Controls the Internet

As already discussed, no single group or organization controls the Internet. Governments in each country have the power to regulate the content and use of the Internet within their borders, as allowed by their laws. However, legislators often face serious obstacles getting legislation passed into law—let alone getting it enforced. Making governmental control even harder is the "bombproof" design of the Internet itself. If a government tries to block access to or from a specific country or Web site, for example, users can use a third party (such as an individual located in another country or a different Web site) to circumvent the block. This occurred recently in Iran when the Iranian government blocked access to social networking sites after the 2009 elections—some Iranian citizens were able to send and read Twitter updates via third-party sites.

Myth 3: The Internet and the World Wide Web Are Identical

Since you can now use a Web browser to access most of the Internet's resources, many people think the Internet and the Web are the same thing. Even though in everyday use many people use the terms *Internet* and *Web* interchangeably, they are not the same thing. Technically, the Internet is the physical network, and the Web is the collection of Web pages accessible over the Internet. A majority of Internet activities today take place via Web pages, but there are Internet resources other than the Web that are not accessed via a Web browser. For instance, files can be uploaded and downloaded using an *FTP (File Transfer Protocol) program* and conventional e-mail can be accessed using an e-mail program.

GETTING SET UP TO USE THE INTERNET

Getting set up to use the Internet typically involves three decisions—determining the type of device you will use to access the Internet, deciding which type of connection is desired, and selecting the Internet service provider to be used. Once these determinations have been made, your computer can be set up to access the Internet.

Type of Device

The Internet today can be accessed using a variety of devices. The type of device used depends on a combination of factors, such as the devices available to you, if you need

INSIDE THE INDUSTRY

ISP Bandwidth Limits

Internet traffic has increased tremendously recently as individuals are watching TV and videos online, downloading music and movies, playing online multiplayer gaming, using online backup services, and otherwise performing high-bandwidth activities (see the accompanying illustration). This has created the issue of ISPs potentially running out of bandwidth available for customers, resulting in outages or delays. In response, some ISPs have, at times, blocked selected traffic to and from their customers, such as cable giant Comcast blocking the use of P2P sites like BitTorrent that is often used to download movies, music, and other large files. Other ISPs are slowing down traffic to and from heavy users during peak Internet usage periods or experimenting with *bandwidth caps* as Internet usage management tools. For instance, Comcast is currently testing slowing down traffic to and from heavy users during peak periods, Time Warner Cable is testing tiered pricing based on usage in certain areas, and AT&T is testing bandwidth caps for new customers in certain areas. With a bandwidth cap, customers either temporarily lose Internet access or are charged an additional fee if they exceed their download limit (often 5 GB to 150 GB per month).

Comcast, like most ISPs, includes a statement in its terms of service agreement that allows it to use tools to "efficiently manage its networks" in order to prevent customers from using a higher than normal level of bandwidth. However, many considered Comcast's blocking of P2P content to be a blatant *net neutrality* issue since Comcast was blocking access to multimedia from a source other than its own cable source and the Internet is designed for all content to be treated equally. There are also concerns about bandwidth caps and that overcharges will grow to an unreasonable level—particularly by cable companies and other providers who may want to stifle Internet multimedia to protect their TV advertising revenues. To protect against this, the *Broadband Internet Fairness Act* has been introduced in the U.S. to require broadband providers to submit tiered pricing plans to the FTC to ensure they are not unreasonable or discriminatory. While it is unclear at this time as to the outcome of this bill, as well as whether or not bandwidth caps will be part of the future of home Internet service, it is clear that, as Internet usage by the average consumer continues to grow, the issue of a finite amount of Internet bandwidth versus an increasing demand for online multimedia content will remain.

Online TV, videos, and other multimedia content require a great deal of bandwidth.

access just at home or while on the go, and what types of Internet content you want to access. Some possible devices are shown in Figure 3-5 and discussed next.

Personal Computers

Most users who have access to a personal computer (such as a desktop or notebook computer) at home, work, or school will use it to access the Internet. One advantage of using personal computers for Internet access is that they have relatively large screens for viewing Internet content, and they typically have a full keyboard for easier data entry. They can also be used to view or otherwise access virtually any Web page content, such as graphics, animation, music files, games, and video clips. In addition, they typically have a large hard drive and are connected to a printer so Web pages, e-mail messages, and downloaded files can be saved and/or printed easily.

Mobile Phones

Mobile phones are increasingly being used to view Web page content, exchange e-mail and instant messages, and download music and other online content. In fact, mobile Web

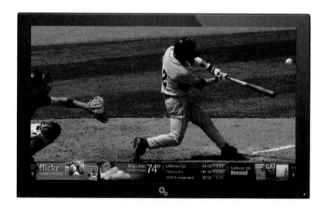

PERSONAL COMPUTERS   **MOBILE PHONES**   **TELEVISIONS**

use—or *wireless Web*, as it is sometimes called—is one of the fastest growing uses of the Internet today. While mobile phones are convenient to use on the go, they typically have a relatively small display screen. As discussed in Chapter 1, some devices include a built-in or sliding keyboard for easier data entry; others utilize pen or touch input instead.

FIGURE 3-5

A variety of devices can be used to access the Internet.

Gaming Devices and Televisions

Another option is using a gaming device (such as a gaming console or handheld gaming device) to access Web content, in addition to using that device to play games. For instance, the Sony PlayStation 3, Sony PSP, Nintendo Wii, and Nintendo DSi all have Web browsers that can be used to access Web content. In addition to gaming consoles that can connect to television sets to display Internet content, an emerging option is *broadband-enabled TVs* that have Internet capabilities built-in in order to display Web pages and other Web content (such as the weather, stock quote, and other information displayed at the bottom of the TV screen shown in Figure 3-5) without any additional hardware.

Type of Connection and Internet Access

In order to use the Internet, your computer needs to be connected to it. Typically, this occurs by connecting the computer or other device you are using to a computer or a network (usually belonging to your ISP, school, or employer) that is connected continually to the Internet.

As discussed in Chapter 2, communications hardware is used to connect a computer to another device or to the Internet. Most types of Internet connections today are *broadband* or high-speed connections. In fact, more than 60% of all home Internet connections in the U.S. are broadband connections, and that percentage is expected to climb to 77% by 2012, according to a recent Gartner study. As applications requiring high-speed connections continue to grow in popularity, access to broadband Internet speeds are needed in order to take full advantage of these applications. For instance, high-definition television, video-on-demand (VOD), and other multimedia applications all benefit from fast broadband connections (see Figure 3-6). For a look at a topic related to the increased use of multimedia Internet content—*ISP bandwidth limits*—see the Inside the Industry box.

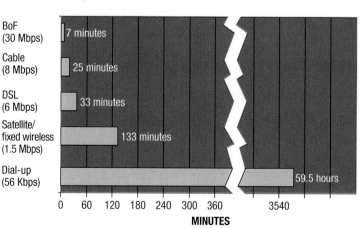

BoF
(30 Mbps)   7 minutes

Cable
(8 Mbps)   25 minutes

DSL
(6 Mbps)   33 minutes

Satellite/
fixed wireless 133 minutes
(1.5 Mbps)

Dial-up
(56 Kbps)   59.5 hours

0   60 120 180 240 300 360   3540
MINUTES

FIGURE 3-6

Length of time to download a 1.5 GB movie using different home Internet options.

The difference between *dial-up* and *direct* Internet connections are discussed next, followed by an overview of the most common types of Internet connections used for personal use today; these types of Internet connections are also summarized in Figure 3-7. Many providers today offer bundles (such as cable TV, telephone, and Internet service) to lower an individual's overall total cost for the services. Additional home Internet alternatives—such

TYPE OF INTERNET CONNECTION	AVAILABILITY	APPROXIMATE MAXIMUM SPEED*	APPROXIMATE MONTHLY PRICE
Conventional dial-up	Anywhere there is telephone service	56 Kbps	Free–$20
Cable	Virtually anywhere cable TV service is available	5–20 Mbps	$40–60
DSL	Within 3 miles of a switching station that supports DSL	1–7 Mbps	$20–40
Satellite	Anywhere there is a clear view to the southern sky and where a satellite dish can be mounted and receive a signal	1–1.5 Mbps	$60–80
Fixed wireless	Selected areas where service is available	1–2 Mbps	$40–60
Broadband over fiber (BoF)	Anywhere fiber has been installed to the building	10–50 Mbps	$50–145
Mobile wireless (3G)	Virtually anywhere cellular phone service is available	700 Kbps–1.7 Mbps	Varies greatly; often bundled with mobile phone service

* Download speed; most connections have slower upload speeds.

FIGURE 3-7
Typical home Internet connection options.

as the emerging *broadband over power lines* (*BPL*) standard discussed in Chapter 8, which allows people to connect to the Internet through their power outlets—will likely be available in the future.

Dial-Up vs. Direct Connections

While some Internet connections are *dial-up connections* (in which your computer dials up and connects to your ISP's computer only when needed), most are *direct* (or *always-on*) *connections* (in which you have a continuous connection to your ISP).

Dial-up connections usually work over standard telephone lines. To connect to the Internet, your computer dials its modem and then connects to a modem attached to a computer belonging to your ISP via the telephone lines. While you are connected to your ISP, your computer can access Internet resources. To end your Internet session, you disconnect from your ISP. One advantage of a dial-up connection is security. Since you are not continually connected to the Internet, it is much less likely that anyone (such as a *hacker*, as discussed in Chapter 4) will gain access to your computer via the Internet, either to access the data located on your computer or, more commonly, to use your computer in some type of illegal or unethical manner. However, dial-up connections are much slower than other types of connections; they are also inconvenient, since you have to instruct your computer to dial up your ISP every time you want to connect to the Internet. Also, your telephone line will be tied up while you are accessing the Internet, unless you have a second phone line. The most common type of dial-up Internet service is *conventional dial-up*.

Direct connections keep you continually connected to your provider and, therefore, continually connected to the Internet. With a direct connection (such as *cable*, *DSL*, *satellite*, or *fixed wireless*), you access the Internet simply by opening a Web browser, such as Internet Explorer, Chrome, or Firefox. Direct Internet connections are typically broadband connections, are commonly used in homes and businesses, and are often connected to a LAN to share the Internet connection with multiple devices within the home or business. Because direct connections keep your computer connected to the Internet at all times (as long as your computer is powered up), it is important to protect your computer from unauthorized access or hackers. Consequently, all computers with a direct Internet connection should use a *firewall* program. Firewall programs block access to a computer from outside computers and enable each user to specify which programs on his or her computer are allowed to have access to the Internet. Firewalls, as well as other network and Internet security precautions, are discussed in more detail in Chapter 4.

> **Dial-up connection.** A type of Internet connection in which the computer or other device must dial up and connect to a service provider's computer via telephone lines before being connected to the Internet. > **Direct connection.** A type of Internet connection in which the computer or other device is connected to the Internet continually.

Conventional Dial-Up

Conventional dial-up Internet access uses a *conventional dial-up modem* connected to a standard telephone jack with regular twisted-pair telephone cabling. Conventional dial-up Internet service is most often used with home computers for users who don't need, or do not want to pay for, broadband Internet service. Advantages include inexpensive hardware, ease of setup and use, and widespread availability. The primary disadvantage is slow connection speed, since conventional dial-up modems connect to the Internet at a maximum of 56 *Kbps* (thousands of bits per second).

Cable

Cable Internet access uses a direct connection and is the most widely used type of home broadband connection, with over half of the home broadband market. Cable connections are very fast (typically between 5 and 20 Mbps, though some faster services are available for a premium fee) and are available wherever cable TV access is available, provided the local cable provider supports Internet access. Consequently, cable Internet is not widely available in rural areas. Cable Internet service requires a *cable modem*.

DSL

DSL (Digital Subscriber Line) Internet access is a type of direct connection that transmits via standard telephone lines, but it does not tie up your telephone line. DSL requires a *DSL modem* and is available only to users who are relatively close (within three miles) to a telephone switching station and who have telephone lines capable of handling DSL. DSL speeds are about one-half of cable speeds and the speed of the connection degrades as the distance between the modem and the switching station gets closer and closer to the three-mile limit. Consequently, DSL is usually only available in urban areas. Download speeds are typically between 1 and 7 Mbps.

Satellite

Satellite Internet access uses a direct connection, but is slower and more expensive than cable or DSL access (typically up to around 1.5 Mbps). However, it is often the only broadband option for rural areas. In addition to a *satellite modem*, it requires a *transceiver* satellite dish mounted outside the home or building to receive and transmit data to and from the satellites being used. Installation requires an unobstructed view of the southern sky (to have a clear line of sight between the transceiver and appropriate satellite), and performance might degrade or stop altogether during very heavy rain or snowstorms.

Fixed Wireless

Fixed wireless Internet access uses a direct connection and is similar to satellite Internet in that it uses wireless signals, but it uses radio transmission towers (either stand-alone towers like the one shown in Figure 3-8 or transmitters placed on existing cell phone towers) instead of satellites. Fixed wireless Internet access requires a modem and, sometimes, an outside-mounted transceiver. Fixed wireless companies typically use Wi-Fi and/or *WiMAX* technology to broadcast the wireless signals to customers. Speeds are typically up to about 2 Mbps, though the speed depends somewhat on the distance between

FIGURE 3-8
WiMAX towers. This tower is installed at the peak of Whistler Mountain in British Columbia.

>**Conventional dial-up Internet access.** Dial-up Internet access via standard telephone lines. >**Cable Internet access.** Fast, direct Internet access via cable TV lines. >**DSL (Digital Subscriber Line) Internet access.** Fast, direct Internet access via standard telephone lines. >**Satellite Internet access.** Fast, direct Internet access via the airwaves and a satellite dish. >**Fixed wireless Internet access.** Fast, direct Internet access available in some areas via the airwaves.

the tower and the customer, the types and number of obstacles in the path, and the type and speed of the connection between the wireless transmitter and the Internet.

Broadband over Fiber (BoF)

A new type of direct connection available to homes and businesses in areas where there is fiber-optic cabling available all the way to the building is generically called **broadband over fiber (BoF)** or **fiber-to-the-premises (FTTP) Internet access**, with other names being used by individual providers, such as Verizon's *fiber-optic service* (*FiOS*). These fiber-optic networks are most often installed by telephone companies in order to upgrade their overall infrastructures and, where installed, are used to deliver telephone and TV service, in addition to Internet service. However, some cities are creating fiber-optic networks that include connections to businesses and homes to provide very fast broadband Internet services. Where available, download speeds for BoF service typically range between 10 Mbps and 50 Mbps and the cost varies accordingly. BoF requires a special networking terminal installed at the building to convert the optical signals into electrical signals that can be sent to a computer or over a LAN.

Mobile Wireless

Mobile wireless Internet access is the type of direct connection most commonly used with mobile phones and other mobile devices to keep them connected to the Internet via a mobile phone network, even as they are carried from place to place. Some mobile wireless services can be used with notebook computers and other computers as well. For instance, AT&T's DataConnect service allows you to access the Internet on your notebook or netbook computer via the AT&T wireless network, and some mobile phones can be connected to a notebook computer to act as a modem to connect that computer to the mobile phone's wireless network. The speed of mobile wireless depends on the cellular standard being used—*3G networks* (the current cellular standard) typically have speeds between 1 and 1.7 Mbps. Costs for mobile wireless Internet access vary widely, with some packages including unlimited Internet, some charging by the number of minutes of Internet use, and some charging by the amount of data transferred.

Wi-Fi Hotspots

While not typically used for primary Internet access, another option for Internet access is a **Wi-Fi hotspot**—a location with a direct Internet connection and a wireless access point that allows users to connect wirelessly (via Wi-Fi) to the hotspot to use its Internet connection (see Figure 3-9). Public Wi-Fi hotpots are widely available

FIGURE 3-9

Wi-Fi hotspots. Hotspots are used to wirelessly connect to the Internet via the Internet connection belonging to a business, city, school, or other organization.

COFFEEHOUSES AND OTHER PUBLIC LOCATIONS
Often fee-based, though some are available for free.

HOSPITALS, BUSINESSES, AND OTHER ORGANIZATIONS
Usually designed for employees but are sometimes also available free to visitors.

COLLEGE CAMPUSES
Usually designed for students and faculty; sometimes used directly in class for student assignments, as shown here.

today, such as at many coffeehouses and restaurants; at hotels, airports, and other locations frequented by business travelers; and in or nearby public areas such as libraries, subway stations, and parks. Some public Wi-Fi hotspots are free; others charge per hour, per day, or on a subscription basis. College campuses also typically have Wi-Fi hotspots to provide Internet access to students; many businesses and other organizations have Wi-Fi hotspots for use by employees in their offices, as well as by employees and guests in conference rooms, waiting rooms, lunchrooms, and other onsite locations.

Selecting an ISP and Setting Up Your Computer

Once the type of Internet access to be used is determined, the final steps to getting connected to the Internet are selecting an ISP and setting up your system. While this discussion is geared primarily toward a home Internet connection used with a personal computer, some of the concepts apply to business or mobile users as well.

Selecting an ISP

The type of device used (such as a personal computer or mobile phone), the type of Internet connection and service desired (such as cable Internet or mobile wireless), and your geographical location (such as metropolitan or rural) will likely determine your ISP options. The pricing and services available through any two ISPs will probably differ somewhat, based on the speed of the service, as well as other services available. The questions listed in Figure 3-10 can help you narrow your ISP choices and determine the questions you want answered before you decide on an ISP. A growing trend is for ISPs to offer a number of *tiers*; that is, different levels (speeds) of service for different prices so users requiring faster service can get it, but at a higher price.

Setting Up Your Computer

The specific steps for setting up your computer to use your selected type of Internet connection depend on the type of device, the type of connection, and the ISP you have chosen to use. Some types of Internet connections, such as satellite and broadband over fiber, require professional installation, after which you will be online; with other types, you can install the necessary hardware (typically a modem that connects to your computer or wireless router via an *Ethernet cable*) yourself. You will usually need to select a username and your desired payment method at some point during the ordering or setup process. This username is needed to log on to some types of Internet connections; it is also used in your e-mail address that will be associated with that Internet service.

After one computer is successfully connected to the Internet, you may need to add additional hardware to connect other computers and devices that you want to be able to access the Internet. For instance, to

FURTHER EXPLORATION (Go)

Go to the Chapter 3 page at **www.cengage.com/ computerconcepts/np/uccs4** for links to information about types of Internet access and ISPs.

FIGURE 3-10

Choosing an ISP. Some questions to ask before making your final selection.

AREA	QUESTIONS TO ASK
Services	Is the service compatible with my device?
	Is there a monthly bandwidth limit?
	How many e-mail addresses can I have?
	What is the size limit on incoming and outgoing e-mail messages and attachments?
	Do I have a choice between conventional and Web-based e-mail?
	Is there dial-up service that I can use when I'm away from home?
	Are there any special member features or benefits?
	Does the service include Web site hosting?
Speed	How fast are the maximum and usual downstream (ISP to my PC) speeds?
	How fast are the maximum and usual upstream (my PC to ISP) speeds?
	How much does the service slow down under adverse conditions, such as high traffic or poor weather?
Support	Is 24/7 telephone technical support available?
	Is Web-based technical support (such as via e-mail) available?
	Is there ever a charge for technical support?
Cost	What is the monthly cost for the service? Is it lower if I prepay a few months in advance? Are different tiers available?
	Is there a set-up fee? If so, can it be waived with a 6-month or 12-month agreement?
	What is the cost of any additional hardware needed, such as modem or transceiver? Can the fee be waived with a long-term service agreement?
	Are there any other services (telephone service, or cable or satellite TV, for instance) available from this provider that I have or want and that can be combined with Internet access for a lower total cost?

share a broadband connection, you can connect other computers directly to the modem (via an Ethernet cable or Wi-Fi connection) if the modem contains a built-in switch or wireless router. If the modem does not include switching or wireless routing capabilities, you will need to connect a switch or wireless router to the modem (typically via an Ethernet cable), and then connect your devices to the switch or router, in order to share the Internet connection with those devices.

SEARCHING THE INTERNET

Most people who use the Internet turn to it to find specific information. For instance, you might want to find out the lowest price of the latest *Pirates of the Caribbean* DVD, the flights available from Los Angeles to New York on a particular day, a recipe for clam chowder, the weather forecast for the upcoming weekend, a video of President Obama's inaugural address, or a map of hiking trails in the Grand Tetons. The Internet provides access to a vast array of interesting and useful information, but that information is useless if you cannot find it when you need it. Consequently, one of the most important skills an Internet user can acquire today is how to search for and locate information on the Internet successfully. Basic Internet searching was introduced in Chapter 1, but understanding the various types of search sites available and how they work, as well as some key searching strategies, can help you perform more successful and efficient Internet searches. These topics are discussed next.

Search Sites

Search sites (such as *Google, Bing, Yahoo! Search, Microsoft Live Search, Ask.com, Cuil,* and so forth) are Web sites designed specifically to help you find information on the Web. Most search sites use a **search engine**—a software program—in conjunction with a huge database of information about Web pages to help visitors find Web pages that contain the information they are seeking. Search site databases are updated on a regular basis; for example, Google estimates that its entire index is updated about once per month. Typically, this occurs using small, automated programs (often called *spiders* or *webcrawlers*) that use the hyperlinks located on Web pages to jump continually from page to page. At each Web page, the spider program records important data about the page into the search site's database, such as the page's URL, its title, the keywords that appear frequently on the page, and the keywords and descriptive information added to the page's code by the Web page author when the page was created. Spider programs can be tremendously fast, visiting millions of pages per day. In addition to spider programs, search site databases also obtain information from Web page authors who submit Web page URLs and keywords associated with their Web sites to the search site. The size of the database used varies with each particular search site, but typically includes information collected from several billion Web pages; at the time of this writing, for instance, the spider used with the Cuil search site had crawled a total of 186 billion Web pages. Designing a Web site so it is classified properly by search sites and is listed in the search results when appropriate keywords are typed is referred to as *search site optimization (SSO)*.

To begin a search using a search site, type the URL for the desired search site in the Address bar of your browser. Most search sites today are designed for *keyword searches*; some sites allow *directory searches* as well. These two types of searches are discussed next. In addition, as the ability to search becomes more and more important, new types of searching are being developed. One emerging possibility is *real-time search engines* that search the Web

> **Search site.** A Web site designed to help users search for Web pages that match specified keywords or selected categories. > **Search engine.** A software program used by a search site to retrieve matching Web pages from a search database.

live, instead of relying on a search site database (one such service—called *MyLiveSearch*—was in development at the time of this writing). Another emerging search site—*ChaCha Search*—uses human guides that you can chat with via the ChaCha Search page if you can't find the information you are looking for. Searching by mobile phone is another growing area, including *mobile voice search*, which is discussed in the Chapter 7 How It Works box.

Keyword Search

The most common type of Internet search is the **keyword search**—that is, when you type appropriate **keywords** (one or more key terms) describing what you are looking for into a search box. The site's search engine then uses those keywords to return a list of Web pages (called *hits*) that match your search criteria; you can view any one of these Web pages by clicking its corresponding hyperlink (see Figure 3-11). Search sites differ in determining how close a match must be between the specified search criteria and a Web page before a link to that page is displayed, so the number of hits from one search site to another may vary. To reduce the number of hits displayed, good search strategies (discussed shortly) can be used. Search sites also differ with respect to the order in which the hits are displayed. Some sites list the most popular sites (usually judged by the number of Web pages that link to it) first; others list Web pages belonging to organizations that pay a fee to receive a higher rank (typically called *sponsored links*) first.

The keyword search is the most commonly used search type. It is used not only on conventional search sites like the Google search site shown in Figure 3-11, but also on many other Web sites. For instance, Web pages like the one shown in Figure 3-12 often include a keyword search box so visitors can search that Web site to find information (such as items for sale via the site or specific documents or Web pages located on that site). Many of these Web site searches are powered by search engine technology, such as by *Google Site Search*.

Directory Search

An alternate type of Internet search available on some search sites is the **directory search**, which uses lists of categories instead of a search box. To perform a directory search, click the category that best matches what you are looking for in order to display a list of more specific subcategories within the main category. You can then click specific subcategories to drill down to more specific topics until you see hyperlinks to Web pages matching the information you are looking for.

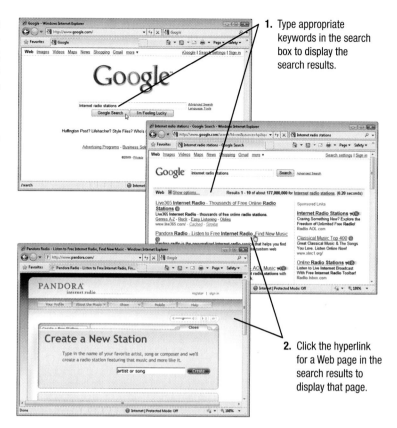

1. Type appropriate keywords in the search box to display the search results.

2. Click the hyperlink for a Web page in the search results to display that page.

FIGURE 3-11
Using a search site.

FIGURE 3-12
Web page keyword searches. Allow users to search the Web site for the desired content.

Search box

FUNCTION	EXPLANATION
Calculator	Enter a mathematical expression or a conversion to see the result.
Currency converter	Enter an amount and currency type to see the corresponding value.
Dictionary	Enter the term *define* followed by a term to view definitions for that term from online sources.
Flight information	Enter an airline and a flight number to see status information.
Movie showtimes	Enter the term *movie* followed by a ZIP code to view movies showing in that area.
Number search	Enter a UPS, FedEx, or USPS tracking number; an area code; or a UPC code to view the associated information.
Phonebook	Enter a name followed by a city and a state, a ZIP code, or an area code to look up that person's address and phone number.
Reverse phonebook	Enter a telephone number to look up the person or business associated with that number.
Stock quotes	Enter one or more stock ticker symbols to retrieve stock quotes.
Street maps	Enter an address to find a map to that location.
Time	Enter the term *time* followed by a city name to see the current time in that city.
Travel conditions	Enter an airport code followed by the term *airport* to view current conditions at that airport.
Weather	Enter the term *weather* followed by a city name or ZIP code to view the weather for that location.
Yellow pages	Enter a type of business and city name or ZIP code to view businesses in that local area.

EXAMPLES:

10 miles in feet — Search
10 miles = 52 800 feet

weather san francisco — Search
Weather for San Francisco, CA
68°F Mostly Cloudy
Wind: NW at 1 mph
Humidity: 76%
Wed 65°F | 50°F Thu 68°F | 52°F Fri 70°F | 52°F

time paris — Search
10:10pm Wednesday (CEST)
Time in Paris, France

FIGURE 3-13
Google search tools.

ONLINE VIDEO
Go to the Chapter 3 page at www.cengage.com/computerconcepts/np/uccs4 to watch the "Google 15 Second Search Tips" video clip.

Search Site Tools

Many search sites contain a variety of tools that can be used to find specific types of information. For instance, many search sites include links next to the search box that allow you to search for items other than Web pages, such as music files, videos, images, maps, news articles, products for sale—even files on your computer. Google is one of the most versatile search sites at the present time and is continually adding new search options. In addition to the options just listed, Google allows a variety of special searches to be conducted by typing specific search criteria in its search box to find other useful information, such as to quickly track a shipped package, look up a telephone number, check on the status of an airline flight, or make a calculation or conversion. Some examples of search tools that can be performed using the Google search box are listed in Figure 3-13.

Search Strategies

There are a variety of strategies that can be used to help whittle down a list of hits to a more manageable number (some searches can return billions of Web pages). Some search strategies can be employed regardless of the search site being used; others are available only on certain sites. Some of the most useful search strategies are discussed next.

Using Phrases

One of the most straightforward ways to improve the quality of the hits returned is to use *phrase searching*—essentially typing more than one keyword in a keyword search. Most search engines automatically list the hits that include all the keywords first, followed by hits matching most of the keywords, continuing down to hits that fit only one of the keywords. To force this type of sorting, virtually all search engines allow you to use some type of character—often quotation marks—to indicate that you want to search for the entire phrase together. Because search options vary from site to site, it is best to look for a search tips link on the search site you are using; the search tips should explain all of the search options available for that site. Examples of the results based on different search phrases to find Web pages about hand signals used with dogs and conducted at two search sites are listed in Figure 3-14. Notice that while the last two search phrases shown in Figure 3-14

SEARCH PHRASE USED	SEARCH SITE	NUMBER OF PAGES FOUND	TITLE OF FIRST TWO NONSPONSORED PAGES FOUND*
dogs	Google	48,600,000	Dogs & Puppies – Next Day Pets Dogs – Dog Information, Pictures and Reviews for over 350 Dogs
	Yahoo!	633,000,000	American Kennel Club (AKC) Animal Planet's Dog Guide
hand signals	Google	58,600,000	Hand Signals Bicycle Safety – Hand Signals
	Yahoo!	45,100,000	Hand Signals – Wikipedia, the free encyclopedia Bicycle Safety – Hand Signals
dog hand signals	Google	1,010,000	DDEAF Training Hand Signals How to Teach a Dog Hand Signals | eHow.com
	Yahoo!	7,660,000	How to Train a Dog Using Hand Signals | eHow.com Dog Training – Hand Signals – Amazingdogtrainingman.com
"dog hand signals"	Google	713	How to Teach a Dog Hand Signals | eHow.com D for Dog – Deaf dog hand signals sign language
	Yahoo!	213	How to Train a Dog Using Hand Signals | eHow.com Dog Training – Hand Signals – Amazingdogtrainingman.com

* Highlighted entries indicate Web pages about dog hand signals.

FIGURE 3-14

Examples of phrase searching. Using different search phrases and different search sites can dramatically change the search results.

both returned relevant (and similar) Web pages, the number of Web pages found varied dramatically (hundreds of pages versus millions).

Using Boolean Operators

To further specify exactly what you want a search engine to find, *Boolean operators*—most commonly AND, OR, and NOT—can often be used in keyword searches. For example, if you want a search engine to find all documents that cover *both* the Intel and AMD microprocessor manufacturers, you can use the search phrase *Intel AND AMD* if the search engine supports Boolean operators. If, instead, you want documents that discuss *either* of these companies, the search phrase *Intel OR AMD* can be used. On the other hand, if you want documents about microprocessors that are cataloged with no mention of Intel, *microprocessors NOT Intel* can be used. Just as with other operators, the rules for using Boolean operators might vary from search site to search site (for instance, Google automatically assumes the AND operator as the default operator any time more than one search term is listed and uses a minus sign (–) instead of the word *NOT*). Be sure to check the search tips for the search site that you are using to see what operators can be used on that site. Some search sites also include an *Advanced Search* option that helps you specify Boolean conditions and other advanced search techniques using a fill-in-the-blank form.

Using Multiple Search Sites

Most users have a favorite search site that they are most comfortable using. However, as illustrated in Figure 3-14, different search sites can return different results. It is important to realize that sometimes a different search site might perform better than the one you use regularly. If you are searching for something and are not making any progress with one search site, then try another search site.

Using Appropriate Keywords, Synonyms, Variant Word Forms, and Wildcards

When choosing the keywords to be used with a search site, it is important to select words that represent the key concept you are searching for. For example, if you want to find out about bed and breakfasts located in the town of Leavenworth, Washington, a keyword

FIELD TYPE	EXAMPLE	EXPLANATION
Title	title:"tax tips"	Searches for Web pages containing the words "tax tips" in the page title.
URL	url:taxtips	Searches for Web pages containing "taxtips" in the page URL.
Text	text:"tax tips"	Searches for Web pages containing "tax tips" in the text of the page.
Site	forms site:irs.gov	Searches for Web pages associated with the keyword "forms" that are located only on the irs.gov Web site.
Domain	tax tips site:*.gov	Searches for Web pages associated with the keywords "tax tips" that are located on government Web sites (they can have anything for the first part of the domain name, but must have a .gov TLD).

FIGURE 3-15

Field searching.

Field searches limit search results to just those pages that match specific field criteria, in addition to any specified search criteria.

phrase (such as *Leavenworth Washington bed and breakfast*) should return appropriate results. If your initial search does not produce the results you are hoping for, you can try *synonyms*—words that have meanings similar to other words. For example, you could replace *bed and breakfast* with *hotel* or *lodging*. To use synonyms in addition to the original keywords, Boolean operators can be used, such as the search phrase *"bed and breakfast" OR hotel OR lodging AND Leavenworth AND Washington.*

Variant—or alternate—word forms are another possibility. Try to think of a different spelling or form of your keywords, if your search still does not work as desired. For example, *bed and breakfast* could be replaced or supplemented with the variants *bed & breakfast* and *B&B*, and the *hand signals* keywords used in Figure 3-14 could be replaced with the variants *hand signal* and *hand signaling*. Using alternative spellings is a form of this strategy, as well. Another strategy that is sometimes used with keywords is the *wildcard* approach. A wildcard is a special symbol that is used in conjunction with a part of a word to specify the pattern of the terms you want to search for. For instance, the asterisk wildcard (*) is used to represent one or more letters at the asterisk location, so on many sites searching for *hand sign** would search for *hand sign, hand signal, hand signals, hand signaling*, and any other keywords that fit this specific pattern.

Using Field Searches

Another strategy that can be used when basic searching is not producing the desired results is *field searching*. A field search limits the search to a particular search characteristic (or *field*), such as the page title, URL, page text, top-level domain, or Web site (see Figure 3-15). When a field search is performed, only the hits associated with the Web pages that match the specified criteria in the specified field are displayed. You can also use field searching in conjunction with regular search terms, such as to search for a particular keyword on just Web sites that use a specific domain. Many, but not all, search engines support some type of field searching. Check the search tips for the particular search site you are using to see if it has that option.

Evaluating Search Results

Once a list of Web sites is returned as the result of a search, it is time to evaluate the sites to determine their quality and potential for meeting your needs. Two questions to ask yourself before clicking a link in the search results are as follows:

> Does the title and listed description sound appropriate for the information you are seeking?

> Is the URL from an appropriate company or organization? For example, if you want technical specifications about a particular product, you might want to start with information on the manufacturer's Web site. If you are looking for government publications, stick with government Web sites.

After an appropriate Web page is found, the evaluation process is still not complete. To determine if the information can be trusted, you should evaluate both the author and the

FURTHER EXPLORATION

Go to the Chapter 3 page at **www.cengage.com/ computerconcepts/np/uccs4** for links to information about citing online references.

TYPE OF RESOURCE	CITATION EXAMPLE
Web page article (magazine)	Dvorak, John (2009, May 5). Data Mining and the Death of Privacy. *PC Magazine.* Retrieved February 14, 2010, from http://www.pcmag.com/article2/0,1895,2346287,00.asp
Web page article (journal)	Sensmeier, Joyce (2009, March). Advancing the EHR (Electronic Health Record): Are We There Yet? *Nursing Management,* 40 no. 3. Retrieved June 21, 2010, from http://www.nursingcenter.com/library/JournalArticle.asp?Article_ID=850211
Web page article (not appearing in a periodical)	Baldor, Lolita (2009, May 6). Air Traffic Systems Vulnerable to Cyber Attack. MSNBC. Retrieved March15, 2010, from http://www.msnbc.msn.com/id/30602242
Web page content (not an article)	*Browse the Web Safely.* (n.d.) Retrieved April 11, 2010 from http://www.symantec.com/norton/security_response/browsewebsafely.jsp
E-mail (cited in text, not reference list)	Maria Rodriquez (personal communication, March 28, 2010).

source to decide if the information can be considered reliable and whether or not it is biased. Be sure to also check for a date to see how up-to-date the information is—many online articles are years old. If you will be using the information in a report, paper, or other document in which accuracy is important, try to verify the information with a second source.

Citing Internet Resources

According to the online version of the Merriam-Webster Dictionary, the term *plagiarize* means "to steal and pass off the ideas or words of another as one's own" or to "use another's production without crediting the source." To avoid plagiarizing Web page content, you need to credit Web page sources—as well as any other Internet resources—when you use them in papers, on Web pages, or in other documents.

The guidelines for citing Web page content are similar to those for written sources. In general, the author, date of publication, and article or Web page title are listed along with a "Retrieved" statement listing the date the article was retrieved from the Internet and the URL of the Web page used to retrieve the article. Some citation examples based on the guidelines obtained from the *American Psychological Association (APA)* Web site are shown in Figure 3-16. If in doubt when preparing a research paper, check with your instructor as to the style manual (such as APA, *Modern Language Association (MLA)*, or *Chicago Manual of Style*) he or she prefers you to follow and refer to that guide for direction.

BEYOND BROWSING AND E-MAIL

In addition to basic browsing and e-mail (discussed in Chapter 1), there are a host of other activities that can take place via the Internet. Some of the most common of these Web-based applications are discussed next.

Other Types of Online Communications

Many types of online communications methods exist. E-mail, discussed in Chapter 1, is one of the most common; other types of online communications are discussed in the next few sections. While originally the programs that supported the various types of online communications discussed next were dedicated to a single task, today's programs often can be used for a variety of types of online communications. For instance, many *instant messaging (IM) programs* today (such as the one shown in Figure 3-17) can also be used to exchange *text messages,*

FIGURE 3-16

Citing Web sources. It is important to properly credit your Web sources. These examples follow the American Psychological Association (APA) citation guidelines.

FIGURE 3-17

Online messaging programs can often be used to perform a variety of communications tasks.

1. After signing in to your messaging program, select a contact in order to start an IM or initiate a voice call, video call, game, or other activity with that individual.

2. IMs show up on both the sender's and the recipient's computers.

Message Boards

For asking questions of, making comments to, or initiating discussions with a large group of individuals, **message boards** (also called *discussion groups, newsgroups,* and *online forums*) can be used. Message boards are Web pages designed to facilitate written discussions between people on specific subjects, such as TV shows, computers, movies, investing, gardening, music, photography, or politics. When a participant posts a message, it is displayed for anyone accessing the message board to read and respond to. Messages are usually organized by topics (called *threads*); participants can post new messages in response to an existing message and stay within that thread, or they can post discussion group messages that start new threads. Participants in discussion groups do not have to be online at the same time because participants can post and respond to messages at their convenience.

Voice over Internet Protocol (VoIP)

Internet telephony is the original industry term for the process of placing telephone calls over the Internet. Today, the standard term for placing telephone calls over the Internet or any other type of data network is **Voice over Internet Protocol** (**VoIP**) and it can take many forms. At its simplest level, VoIP calls can take place from computer to computer, such as by starting a voice conversation with an online buddy using an IM program and a headset or microphone connected to the computer. Computer to computer calls (such as via the popular *Skype* service, as well as via messaging programs that support voice calls) are generally free. Often calls can be received from or made to conventional or mobile phones for a small fee, such as two cents per minute for domestic calls.

More permanent VoIP setups (sometimes referred to as *digital voice, broadband phone,* or *Internet phone service*) are designed to replace conventional landline phones in homes and businesses. VoIP is offered through some ISPs, such as cable, telephone, and mobile phone companies; it is also offered through dedicated VoIP providers, such as *Vonage.* Permanent VoIP setups require a broadband Internet connection and a *VoIP phone adapter* (also called an *Internet phone adapter*) that goes between a conventional phone and a broadband router, as shown in Figure 3-19. Once your phone calls are routed through your phone adapter and router to the Internet, they travel to the recipient's phone, which can be another VoIP phone, a mobile phone, or a landline phone. VoIP phone adapters are typically designed for a specific VoIP provider. With these more permanent VoIP setups, most users switching from landline phone service can keep their existing telephone number.

The biggest advantage of VoIP is cost savings, such as unlimited local and long-distance calls for as little as $25 per month, or cable and VoIP services bundled together for about $50 per month. One of the biggest disadvantages of VoIP at the present time is that it does not function during a power outage or if your Internet connection (such as your cable connection for cable Internet users) goes down.

ⓥ **FIGURE 3-19**

Voice over IP (VoIP).
Permanent VoIP setups allow telephone calls to be placed via a broadband Internet connection using a conventional telephone.

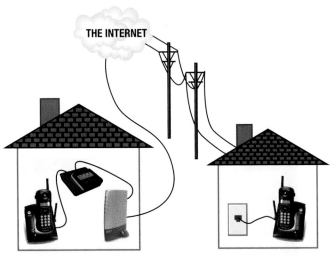

THE INTERNET

1. A conventional phone is plugged into a VoIP adapter, which is connected to a broadband modem.

2. Calls coming from the VoIP phone travel over the Internet to the recipient's phone.

Web Conferences and Webinars

The term *videoconferencing* refers to the use of computers, video cameras, microphones, and other communications technologies to conduct face-to-face interactive meetings

---

between people in different locations. Videoconferencing that takes place via the Internet is often called *Web conferencing* or *online conferencing*. **Web conferences** typically take place via a personal computer or mobile phone and are used by businesses and individuals. Basic Web conferences (such as a video call between individuals as in Figure 3-20) can be performed via any online communications program (such as an instant messaging program) that supports video phone calls. Business Web conferences that require multiple participants or other communication tools (such as a shared whiteboard or the ability for attendees to share the content on their computer screens) may need to use *Web conferencing software* or services instead. Business Web conferencing is often used for meetings between individuals located in different geographical locations, as well as for employee training, sales presentations, customer support, and other business applications.

FIGURE 3-20
Web conferencing.
Allows individuals to talk with and see each other in real time, such as this student talking to her family from her dorm room.

Webinars (Web seminars) are similar to Web conferences, but typically have a designated presenter and an audience. Although interaction with the audience is usually included (such as question and answer sessions), a Webinar is typically more one-way communication than a Web conference.

Social Networking

A **social networking site** can be loosely defined as any site that creates a community of individuals who can communicate with and/or share information with one another. Some examples are *MySpace* and *Facebook* that allow users to post information about themselves for others to read, *Meetup.com* that connects people with common hobbies and interests, video sharing sites like *YouTube*, and photo sharing sites like *Flickr* and *Fotki*. Social networking can be performed via personal computers, though the use of *mobile social networking*—social networks accessed with a mobile phone or other mobile device—is growing rapidly. In fact, Jupiter Research predicts the number of active mobile social networking users will rise from 54 million today to 730 million in five years, and MySpace expects half of its traffic to come from mobile devices within a few years. Some reasons for this include that most individuals carry a mobile phone with them all the time, many individuals like to communicate with others via the Web while they are on the go, and the use of a mobile phones enables location applications to be integrated into the social networking experience.

Social networking sites are used most often to communicate with existing friends.

ASK THE EXPERT

THROW THE FIGHT

Ryan Baustert, Guitarist, Throw the Fight

What impact has the Internet and social networking sites had on your band's success?

The Internet has had a major impact on us. The best marketing is when the distance between artist and audience is short and direct. Due to sites like MySpace, Purevolume, and Facebook, we are able to stay better connected and interact with our fans on a more personal level. We can also gauge how our music is received by peoples' reactions and comments online.

It's much easier to promote shows, tours, and album releases, as well. More recently, with the explosion of Twitter, we can go one step further and give fans more insight into what is going on in our lives behind the scenes. This, in turn, helps us build brand loyalty.

>**Web conference.** A face-to-face meeting taking place via the Web; typically uses video cameras and microphones to enable participants to see and hear each other. >**Webinar.** A seminar presented via the Web. >**Social networking site.** A site that enables a community of individuals to communicate and share information.

FIGURE 3-21

Social networking sites. A variety of social networking sites are available to meet different needs.

Facebook, for instance (shown in Figure 3-21), allows you to post photos, videos, music, and other content for your *Facebook friends* (individuals you have chosen to communicate with via Facebook) to view. You can also chat with your Facebook friends who are currently online, and publish notes and status updates (similar to Twitter tweets) on your *Facebook wall*, as well as the walls of your friends' Facebook pages. For privacy purposes, you can limit access to your Facebook page to the individuals you identify (such as just to your Facebook friends). To help keep track of all your friends' social networking activities, *social networking management services* can help, as discussed in the Technology and You box.

In addition to being used to communicate with existing friends, social networking sites are also used to learn about individuals you currently don't know. For instance, one new application for social networks like Facebook is their use by college-bound students to meet other incoming freshmen before the school year starts. Class pages for many colleges in the United States emerge prior to the fall semester so that incoming freshmen can "facestalk" (view the profiles of) other students in their graduating class, look up the profiles of their dorm roommates, find fellow students with common interests, and more—all before actually setting foot on campus.

In addition to being used for personal use, social networking sites today are also viewed as a business marketing tool. For instance, MySpace, Facebook, and YouTube are often used by businesses, political candidates, emerging musicians, and other professionals or professional organizations to increase their online presence. There are also business social networking sites designed for business networking. These sites (such as LinkedIn shown in Figure 3-21) are used for recruiting new employees, finding new jobs, building professional contacts, and other business activities. Other specialized social networking sites include sites designed for children (these usually work in a manner similar to

TECHNOLOGY AND YOU

Social Networking Management Services

With the popularity of social networking sites comes the problem of trying to keep up with the seemingly endless stream of input (such as Flickr photos, Twitter tweets, MySpace messages, Facebook posts, and so forth) generated by friends and contacts. There are a number of different *social networking management tools* available now that can help. These tools typically display new content from your friends and contacts (such as from your Facebook friends and/or people in your IM or e-mail contact list) in a central location to make it easier to follow all of your friends' activities at one time.

Some social networking management capabilities are built into portal pages and IM programs. For instance, the *What's New* area at the bottom of the *Windows Live Messenger* screens displays updates about activities the people you have specified as being in your Live network have performed recently, such as new blog posts or new uploaded photos. Other services are more universal, such as the *Yoono* browser plug-in that contains various widgets located on the left side of your browser to conveniently display different types of information aggregated from the Web. The *Friends Widget* (shown in the accompanying illustration) displays your friend's social networking activities continuously, and the updates can be displayed in chronological order, by social network, or by friend. The Friends Widget also provides one-click access to e-mail and IM, and allows you to upload media to your favorite social networks.

With the popularity and use of social networks still growing at an astounding rate, expect to see many more types of social management services in the future.

Most recent activity (Facebook posts and Twitter tweets in this example) by friends.

MySpace, but they have safeguards in place to prevent personal information from being posted, to monitor language, and so forth) and families (such as to exchange messages, view online tasks lists, and access a shared family calendar).

When using a social networking site, adults and children should be cautious about revealing too much personal information via these sites, both for personal safety reasons and to prevent the information from being used in personalized, targeted *spear phishing* attacks, discussed in Chapter 4. In addition, social networking content is increasingly being monitored by colleges (to find inappropriate behavior by students and to research college applicants) and employers (to find unprofessional behavior by current employees and to research potential job candidates). Because of this, all individuals should be careful about the types of photos and other content they post online. There have been numerous cases over the past few years of students being disciplined or not admitted to a college, and individuals being fired or not hired, due to content posted to a social networking site. Consequently, it is a good idea for individuals to take a close look at their online posts and photos and remove anything that might be potentially embarrassing if viewed by current or future employers, a future partner, or other people important to them now or in the future.

Another emerging issue is what happens to social networking content when someone dies unexpectedly, since family members and heirs cannot access the sites without logon information or access to the deceased's e-mail for password recovery purposes. In response, some special services have emerged to help individuals store information about their online assets and to designate a beneficiary—the person designated to receive that information upon the individual's death. These services can be used to store logon information for Web sites and e-mail accounts and to leave e-mail messages to be distributed to designated individuals when the individual dies, such as to loved ones, online and offline friends, online gaming companions, and other individuals. An alternative is for individuals to leave the necessary online contact and access information, as well as instructions regarding how to notify online friends and sites, with a trusted friend or relative who is instructed to use the information only in the event of the individual's death.

Online Shopping and Investing

Online shopping and *online investing* are examples of *e-commerce*—online financial transactions. It is very common today to order products, buy and sell stock, pay bills, and manage financial accounts online. However, since *online fraud, credit card fraud*, and *identity theft* (a situation in which someone gains enough personal information to pose as another person) are continuing to grow at a rapid pace, it is important to be cautious when participating in online financial activities. To protect yourself, use a credit card or *online payment service* (such as *PayPal*) whenever possible when purchasing goods or services online so that any fraudulent activities can be disputed. Also, be sure to enter your payment information only on a *secure Web page* (look for a URL that begins with *https* instead of *http*). Online financial accounts should also be protected with *strong user passwords* that are changed frequently. Internet security and strong passwords are discussed in detail in Chapter 4.

Online Shopping and Online Auctions

Online shopping is commonly used to purchase both physical products (such as clothing, books, DVDs, shoes, furniture, and more) and downloadable products (such as software, movies, music, and e-books) via Web pages. Typically, shoppers locate the items they would like to purchase using an online shopping site (one example is shown in Figure 3-22), and then they add those items to their online *shopping carts* or *shopping bags*. The site's *checkout* process—including supplying the necessary billing and shipping information—is then used to complete the sale. After the payment is processed, the item is either shipped to the customer (if it is a physical product), or the customer is given instructions on how to download it (if it is a downloadable product). Forrester Research predicts that U.S. online sales will reach approximately $335 billion by 2012.

Online auctions are the most common way to purchase items online from other individuals. Sellers list items for sale on an auction site (such as *eBay* or *Yahoo! Auctions*) and pay a small listing fee (and a commission to the auction site if the item is sold). Individuals can visit the auction site and enter bids on auction items until the end of the auction. At that time, the person with the highest bid is declared the successful bidder (provided the minimum selling price, if one was established, was met) and arranges payment for and delivery of the item directly with

FIGURE 3-22

Online shopping.

Allows you to purchase goods and services online.

>**Online shopping.** Buying products or services over the Internet. >**Online auction.** An online activity for which bids are placed for items, and the highest bidder purchases the item.

the seller. Another common way to purchase items from other individuals is via online classified ads, such as those posted on the popular *Craigslist* site.

Online Banking and Online Investing

Many banks today offer **online banking** as a free service to their customers to enable customers to check balances on all their accounts (such as checking, credit cards, mortgage, and investment accounts), view cashed checks and other transactions, transfer funds between accounts, pay bills electronically, and perform other activities related to their bank accounts. Online banking is continually growing—according to the Pew Internet & American Life Project, close to one-half of all U.S. adults now bank online.

Buying and selling of stocks, bonds, mutual funds, and other types of securities is referred to as **online investing**. Although it is common to see stock quote capabilities on many search and news sites, trading stocks and other securities requires an *online broker*. The biggest advantages of online investing include lower transaction fees and the ability to quickly buy or sell stock when desired—a convenience for those investors who do a lot of trading. Common online investing services include the ability to order sales and purchases; access performance histories, corporate news, and other useful investment information; and set up an *online portfolio* that displays the status of the stocks you specify. On some Web sites, stock price data is delayed 20 minutes; on other sites, real-time quotes are available. Like other Web page data, most stock price data is current at the time it is retrieved via a Web page, but it will not be updated (and you will not see current quotes, for instance) until you reload the Web page using your browser's Refresh or Reload toolbar button. An exception to this rule is if the Web page is designed to refresh the content automatically on a regular basis. For example, the portfolio shown in Figure 3-23 uses a *Java applet*—a small program built into a Web page—to redisplay updated data continuously.

FIGURE 3-23

Online investing.

Allows you to buy and sell stock, view your portfolio, get real-time quotes, and more.

Online Entertainment

There are an ever-growing number of ways to use the Web for entertainment purposes, such as listening to music, watching TV and videos, and playing online games. Some applications can be accessed with virtually any type of Internet connection; others are only practical with a broadband connection. Many online entertainment applications require the use of a *media player program* or *plug-in* (such as *QuickTime Player* or *Silverlight*) to deliver multimedia content.

Online Music

There are a number of options available today for **online music**, such as listening to live radio broadcasts via an *online radio station*, watching music videos on *MTV.com* or *Yahoo! Music*, or downloading music from *online music stores*, such as the *iTunes Music Store, Rhapsody MP3 Store*, or *Wal-Mart MP3 Music Downloads*. Online radio

>**Online banking.** Performing banking activities via the Web. >**Online investing.** Buying and selling stocks or other types of investments via the Web. >**Online music.** Music played or obtained via the Web.

Online News, Reference, and Information

There is an abundance of news and other important information available through the Internet. The following sections discuss some of the most widely used news, reference, and information resources.

News and Reference Sites

News organizations, such as television networks, newspapers, and magazines, nearly always have Web sites that are updated on a continual basis to provide access to current local and world news, as well as sports, entertainment, health, travel, politics, weather, and other news topics (see Figure 3-25). Many news sites also have searchable archives to look for past articles, although some require a fee to view back articles. Once articles are displayed, they can typically be saved, printed, or sent to other individuals via e-mail. A growing trend is for newspapers and magazines to abandon print subscriptions and to provide Web-only service—primarily for cost reasons. Although some subscribers miss the print versions, there are some advantages to digital versions, such as the ability to easily search through content in some digital publications. Other online news resources include news radio programs that are broadcast over the Internet, as well as the wide variety of news video clips available through many Web sites.

News can also be delivered via gadgets displayed on computer desktops, TVs, dashboards, and other objects. News gadgets typically display headlines, and clicking a headline displays that news story. Recent versions of Windows include a number of gadgets that can be added to the Windows desktop.

Reference sites are designed to provide users access to specific types of useful information. For example, reference sites can be used to generate maps (see Figure 3-25), check the weather forecast, look up the value of a home, or provide access to encyclopedias, dictionaries, ZIP code directories, and telephone directories. One potential downside to the increased availability of online reference sites is use by criminals. For instance, one California lawmaker has introduced a bill requiring mapping sites to blur out details of schools, churches, and government buildings after being informed that some terrorists have used these maps to plan bombings and other attacks.

FIGURE 3-25
Online news and reference.

NEWS SITES
News organizations typically update their sites several times per day to provide access to the most current news and information.

REFERENCE SITES
Reference Web sites provide access to specific types of useful information, such as the maps and driving directions available via this Web site.

Portal Pages, RSS Feeds, and Podcasts

Portal Web pages are Web pages designed to be selected as a browser's home page and visited on a regular basis. Portal pages typically include search capabilities, news headlines, weather, and other useful content, and can usually be customized by users to display their requested content (see Figure 3-26). Once the portal page is customized, each time the user visits the portal page, the specified information is displayed. Popular portals include *My Yahoo!*, *iGoogle*, *My MSN*, and *AOL.com*.

RSS (Really Simple Syndication) is an online news tool designed for facilitating the delivery of news articles and other content regularly published to a Web site. Provided the content has an associated *RSS feed*, individuals can *subscribe* (usually for free) to that feed. You typically subscribe to an RSS feed by clicking a *subscribe* link on the associated Web page to add the feed content to your browser feed list or by copying the URL for the RSS feed to your portal page. To view the feed content, you can select that feed from your browser's feed list (such as the *Favorites Feeds* list in Internet Explorer) or you can click the appropriate link on your portal page, such as the links shown on the portal page in Figure 3-26. In either case, as new content for the subscribed feed becomes available, it will be accessible via the feed links. In addition to computers, RSS feeds today can also be delivered to mobile phones and other mobile devices. In the future, we will likely see RSS feeds delivered directly to televisions—and perhaps even to watches, refrigerators, and other consumer devices that have a display screen.

Another Web resource that can provide you with useful information is a **podcast**—a recorded audio or video file that can be downloaded via the Internet, such as the audio and video podcasts available for download via the Web site that accompanies this text. The term *podcast* is derived from the iPod portable digital media player (the first widely used device for playing digital audio files), although podcasts today can also be listened to using a computer or mobile phone.

Podcasting (creating a podcast) enables individuals to create self-published, inexpensive Internet radio broadcasts, such as to share their knowledge, express their opinions on particular subjects, or share original poems, songs, or short stories with interested individuals. Originally created and distributed by individuals, podcasts are now also being created and distributed by businesses. Some commercial radio stations are making portions of their broadcasts available via podcasts, and a growing number of news sites and corporate sites now have regular podcasts available. In fact, some view podcasts as the new and improved radio since it is an easy way to listen to your favorite radio broadcasts on your own schedule. Podcasts are typically uploaded to the Web on a regular basis, and RSS feeds can be used to notify subscribers when a new podcast is available. For a look at how to create an audio podcast, see the How It Works box.

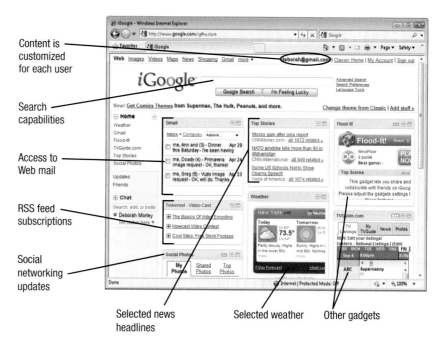

Content is customized for each user
Search capabilities
Access to Web mail
RSS feed subscriptions
Social networking updates
Selected news headlines
Selected weather
Other gadgets

FIGURE 3-26
Portal pages. Portal pages can contain a wide variety of customized news and information.

VIDEO PODCAST

Go to the Chapter 3 page at **www.cengage.com/ computerconcepts/np/uccs4** to download or listen to the "How To: Create an RSS Feed" video podcast.

VIDEO PODCAST

Go to the Chapter 3 page at **www.cengage.com/ computerconcepts/np/uccs4** to download or listen to the "How To: Create a Podcast" video podcast.

> **Portal Web page.** A Web page designed to be designated as a browser home page; typically can be customized to display personalized content.
> **RSS (Really Simple Syndication).** A tool used to deliver selected Web content to subscribers as the content is published to a Web site.
> **Podcast.** A recorded audio or video file that can be played or downloaded via the Web.

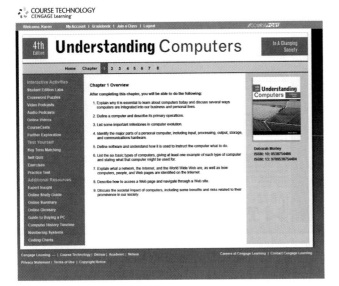

FIGURE 3-28

Web-based learning.
The Understanding
Computers Web site
provides a variety of
Web-based learning
opportunities for
readers of this textbook.

Web links, downloadable audio and video podcasts, streaming videos, and other online resources for students taking a course that uses this textbook (see Figure 3-28). There are also Web-based *learning management systems* (such as *Blackboard*) that can be used to deliver course content, manage assignments and grades, and more; and the use of *student response systems*—where students use a special device or their mobile phone to respond to surveys or review questions during in-class lectures is growing. The next few sections take a look at some of the most widely used online education applications.

Web-Based Training and Distance Learning

The term **Web-based training** (**WBT**) refers to any instruction delivered via the Web. It is commonly used for employee training, as well as for delivering instruction in an educational setting. **Distance learning** occurs whenever students take classes from a location—often home or work—which is different from the one where the delivery of instruction takes place. Distance learning today typically includes Web-based training or other online learning tools (and so is also called *online learning* and *e-learning*) and is available through many high schools, colleges, and universities, as well as organizations that provide professional certifications. Distance learning can be used to learn just one task or new skill; it can also be used to complete a college course or an entire degree program. Typically the majority of distance learning coursework is completed over the Internet via class Web pages, YouTube videos, Webinars, podcasts, discussion groups, and e-mail, although schools might require some in-person contact, such as sessions for orientation and testing.

The biggest advantage of Web-based training and distance learning is that they are typically experienced individually and at the user's own pace. Online content for Web-based training components is frequently customized to match the pace of each individual user and can be completed at the user's convenience. Web-based content can be updated as needed and online content and activities (such as exercises, exams, and animations) typically provide immediate feedback to the student. One disadvantage is the possibility of technological problems—since students need a working computer and Internet connection to access the material, they cannot participate if they have no access to a computer or if their computer, their Internet connection, or the Web server hosting the material goes down. Another concern among educators is the lack of face-to-face contact, and security issues—such as the difficulty in ensuring that the appropriate student is completing assignments or taking exams. Some possible solutions for this later concern are discussed in the next section.

Online Testing

In both distance learning and traditional classes, *online testing*—which allows students to take tests via the Internet—is a growing trend. Both objective tests (such as those containing multiple choice or true/false questions) and performance-based exams (such as those given in computer classes to test student mastery of software applications) can be administered and taken online. For instance, there are *SAM (Skills Assessment Manager)*

>**Web-based training (WBT).** Instruction delivered on an individual basis via the Web. >**Distance learning.** A learning environment in which the student is physically located away from the instructor and other students; commonly, instruction and communications take place via the Web.

tests available for use in conjunction with this textbook to test both Microsoft Office software skills and computer concepts. Typically online tests are graded automatically, freeing up the instructor's time for other activities, as well as providing fast feedback to the students.

One challenge for online testing is ensuring that an online test is taken by the appropriate individual and in an authorized manner, in order to avoid cheating. Some distance learning programs require students to go physically to a testing center to take the test or to find an acceptable test proctor (such as an educator at a nearby school or a commanding officer for military personnel). Other options are using smart cards, fingerprint scans, and other means to authenticate students taking an online exam from a remote location. For instance, one secure testing solution being used at a number of schools nationwide to enable students to take online tests from their remote locations while still ensuring the integrity of the exams is the *Securexam Remote Proctor* system shown in Figure 3-29. This system uses a device that first authenticates the individual taking the test via a fingerprint scan, and then captures real-time audio and video during the exam. The device's camera points to a reflective ball, which allows it to capture a full 360-degree image of the room, and the recording is uploaded to a server so it can be viewed by the instructor from his or her location. The Securexam software locks down the computer so that it cannot be used for any purpose not allowed during the test (such as performing an Internet search). It also flags suspicious behavior (such as significant noises or movements) in the recording so that the instructor can review those portions of the recording to see if any unauthorized behavior (such as leaving the room or making a telephone call) occurred during the testing period.

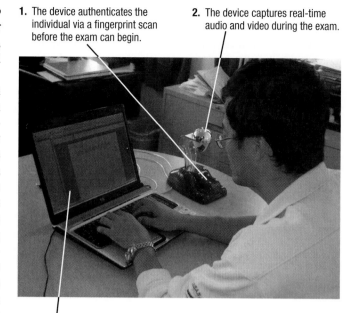

1. The device authenticates the individual via a fingerprint scan before the exam can begin.

2. The device captures real-time audio and video during the exam.

3. The computer is locked down during the exam so it can only be used for authorized activities.

FIGURE 3-29
Secure online testing.

FIGURE 3-30
Blogs. Allow individuals to post entries to an online personal journal.

Blogs, Wikis, and Other Types of Online Writing

A **blog**—also called a *Web log*—is a Web page that contains short, frequently updated entries in chronological order, typically as a means of expression or communication (see Figure 3-30). In essence, a blog is an online personal journal accessible to the public that is usually created and updated by one individual. Blogs are written by a wide variety of individuals—including ordinary people, as well as celebrities, writers, students, and experts on particular subjects—and can be used to post personal commentary, research updates, comments on current events, political opinions, celebrity gossip, travel diaries, television show recaps, and more.

Blogging software, which is available via blogging sites such as Blogger.com, is usually used to easily create and publish blogs and blog updates to the Web. Blogs are also frequently published on school, business, and personal Web sites. Blogs

> **Blog.** A Web page that contains short, frequently updated entries in chronological order, typically by just one individual.

✓ TIP

There are numerous online blog search engines and directories—such as Technorati.com—to help you find blogs that meet your interests.

are usually updated frequently, and entries can be posted via computers, e-mail, and mobile phones. Blogs often contain text, photos, and video clips. With their increased use and audiences, bloggers and the *blogosphere* (the complete collection of blogs on the Internet) are beginning to have increasing influence on businesses, politicians, and individuals today. One new ethical issue surrounding blogging relates to bloggers who are paid to blog about certain products. Although some Web sites that match up bloggers with advertisers require that the blogger reveal that he or she receives payment for "sponsored" posts, some believe that commercializing blogging will corrupt the blogosphere. Others, however, view it as a natural evolution of word-of-mouth advertising.

Another form of online writing sometimes used for educational purposes is the **wiki**. Wikis, named for the Hawaiian phrase *wiki wiki* meaning *quick*, are a way of creating and editing collaborative Web pages quickly and easily. Similar to a blog, the content on a wiki page can be edited and republished to the Web just by pressing a Save or Submit button. However, wikis are intended to be modified by others and so are especially appropriate for collaboration, such as for class Web pages or group projects. To protect the content of a wiki from sabotage, the entire wiki or editing privileges for a wiki can be password protected.

One of the largest wikis is *Wikipedia* (shown in Figure 3-31), a free online encyclopedia that contains over eight million articles written in 250 languages, is updated by more than 75,000 active contributors, and is visited by hundreds of thousands of individuals each day. While most Wikipedia contributors edit articles in a responsible manner, there are instances of erroneous information being added to Wikipedia pages intentionally. As with any resource, visitors should carefully evaluate the content of a Wikipedia article before referencing it in a report, Web page, or other document, as discussed earlier in this chapter.

Ⓐ FIGURE 3-31

Wikis. Wikis, such as the Wikipedia collaborative online encyclopedia shown here, can be edited by any authorized individual.

An **e-portfolio**, also called an *electronic portfolio* or *digital portfolio*, is a collection of an individual's work accessible through a Web site. Today's e-portfolios are typically linked to a collection of student-related information, such as résumés, papers, projects, and other original works. Some e-portfolios are used for a single course; others are designed to be used and updated throughout a student's educational career, culminating in a comprehensive collection of information that can be used as a job-hunting tool.

CENSORSHIP AND PRIVACY ISSUES

There are many important societal issues related to the Internet. One important issue—network and Internet security—is covered in Chapter 4. Two other important issues—*censorship* and *privacy*—are discussed next, in the context of Internet use. Other societal issues—including computer security, ethics, health, and the environment—related to computer use are discussed in further detail in Chapters 5, 6, and 7.

>**Wiki.** A collaborative Web page that is designed to be edited and republished by a variety of individuals. >**E-portfolio.** A collection of an individual's work accessible via the Web.

Censorship

The issue of Internet censorship affects all countries that have Internet access. In some countries, Internet content is filtered by the government, typically to hinder the spread of information from political opposition groups, to filter out subjects deemed offensive, or to block information from sites that could endanger national security. Increasingly, some countries are also blocking information (such as blogs and personal Web pages) from leaving the country, and have occasionally completely shut down Internet access to and from the country during political protests to stop the flow of information in and out of that country.

In the United States, the First Amendment to the U.S. Constitution guarantees a citizen's right to free speech. This protection allows people to say things to others without fear of arrest. But how does the right to free speech relate to potentially offensive or indecent materials available over the Internet where they might be observed by children or by people who do not wish to see them? There have been some attempts in the United States and other countries to regulate Internet content—what some would view as *censorship*—in recent years, but the courts have had difficulty defining what is "patently offensive" and "indecent" as well as finding a fair balance between protection and censorship. For example, the *Communications Decency Act* was signed into law in 1996 and made it a criminal offense to distribute patently indecent or offensive material online in order to protect children from being exposed to inappropriate Web content. In 1997, however, the Supreme Court overturned the portion of this law pertaining to indecent material on the basis of free speech, making this content legal to distribute via the Internet and protecting Web sites that host third-party content from being liable for that content.

Another example of legislation designed to protect children from inappropriate Web content is the *Children's Internet Protection Act (CIPA)*. CIPA requires public libraries and schools to implement Internet safety policies and technologies to block children's access to inappropriate Web content in order to receive certain public funds. While this law was intended to protect children, it was fought strenuously by free speech advocacy groups and some library associations on the basis that limiting access to some Internet content violates an individual's First Amendment rights to free speech. While CIPA was ruled unconstitutional by a federal court in 2002, the Supreme Court reversed the lower court decision in 2003 and ruled that the law is constitutional because the need for libraries to prevent minors from accessing obscene materials outweighs the free speech rights of library patrons and Web site publishers. However, the Court also modified the law to require the library to remove the technologies for an adult library patron at the patron's request.

One technology commonly used to conform to CIPA regulations, as well as by parents and employees, is **Internet filtering**—the act of blocking access to particular Web pages or types of Web pages. It can be used on home computers (for instance, by individuals to protect themselves from material they would view as offensive or by parents to protect their children from material they feel is inappropriate). It is also commonly used by employers to keep employees from accessing non-work-related sites, by some ISPs and search sites to block access to potentially objectionable materials, and by many schools and libraries to control the Web content that children are able to view. Internet filtering typically restricts access to Web pages that contain offensive language, sex/pornography, racism, drugs, or violence (based on either the keywords contained

---

>**Internet filtering.** Using a software program or browser option to block access to particular Web pages or types of Web pages.

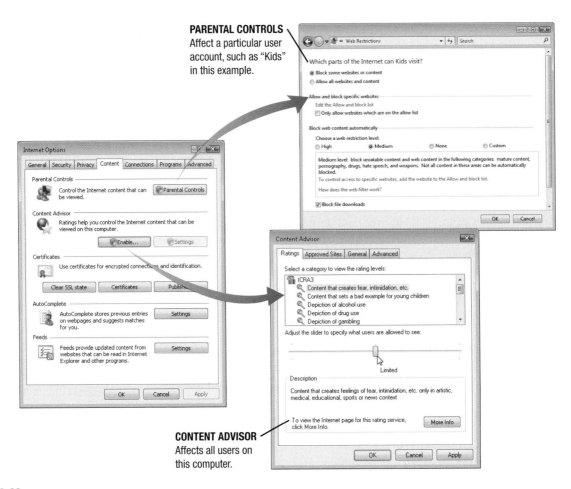

PARENTAL CONTROLS
Affect a particular user account, such as "Kids" in this example.

CONTENT ADVISOR
Affects all users on this computer.

FIGURE 3-32

Internet filtering.
Browser settings can be changed to deny access to Web pages with objectionable content.

on each site or a database of URLs containing restricted content). It can also be used to block access to specific sites (such as social networking sites, YouTube, or eBay), as well as to restrict the total number of hours or the time of day that the Internet can be used.

Most browsers include some Internet filtering options. For instance, Internet Explorer's *Content Advisor* (see Figure 3-32) can be used to filter the Web sites displayed for all users of a particular computer (although blocked Web sites can be viewed if the user knows the appropriate password); and *Parental Controls* can be used to set restrictions for individual users, such as the Web sites that can be viewed, whether or not the user can download files, and so forth. More comprehensive Internet filtering can be obtained with stand-alone filtering programs, such as *NetNanny* or *Safe Eyes*.

Web Browsing Privacy

Privacy, as it relates to the Internet, encompasses what information about individuals is available, how it is used, and by whom. As more and more transactions and daily activities are being performed online, there is the potential for vast amounts of private information to be collected and distributed without the individual's knowledge or permission. Therefore, it is understandable that public concern regarding privacy and the Internet is on the rise. Although personal privacy will be discussed in more detail in Chapter 5, a few issues that are of special concern to Internet users regarding Web browsing privacy and e-mail privacy are discussed in the next few sections.

Cookies

Many Web pages today use **cookies**—small text files that are stored on your hard drive by a Web server—to identify return visitors and their preferences. While some individuals view all cookies as a potential invasion of privacy, Web sites can read only their own cookie files and the use of cookies can provide some benefits to consumers. For example, cookies can enable a Web site to remember preferences for customized Web site content (for instance, displaying customized content on a portal page, such as the one shown in Figure 3-26), as well as to retrieve a shopping cart containing items selected during a previous session. Some Web sites also use cookies to keep track of which pages on their Web sites each person has visited, in order to recommend products on return visits that match that person's interests. A use of cookies that is more objectionable to some is the use of *third-party cookies* (cookies placed on your hard drive by a company other than the one associated with the Web page that you are viewing—typically a Web advertising company). Third-party cookies target advertisements to Web site visitors based on their activities on the site (such as products viewed or advertisements clicked).

The information stored in a cookie file typically includes the name of the cookie, its expiration date, and the domain that the cookie belongs to. In addition, a cookie contains either personal information that you have entered while visiting the Web site or an ID number assigned by the Web site that allows the Web site's server to retrieve your personal information from its database. Such a database can contain two types of information: *personally identifiable information (PII)* and *non-personally identifiable information (Non-PII)*. Personally identifiable information is connected with a specific user's identity—such as his or her name and address—and is typically given during the process of ordering goods or services. Non-personally identifiable information is anonymous data—such as which product pages were viewed or which advertisements located on the site were clicked—that is not directly associated with the visitor's name or another personally identifiable characteristic.

Cookies stored on your computer's hard drive can be looked at, if desired, although sometimes deciphering the information contained in a cookie file is difficult. Internet Explorer users can view and/or delete cookies and other temporary files by using Internet Explorer's Tools menu to open the Internet Options dialog box and selecting the appropriate options in the *Browsing history* section on the General tab. The Privacy tab in this dialog box (shown in Figure 3-33) can be

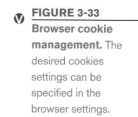

FIGURE 3-33
Browser cookie management. The desired cookies settings can be specified in the browser settings.

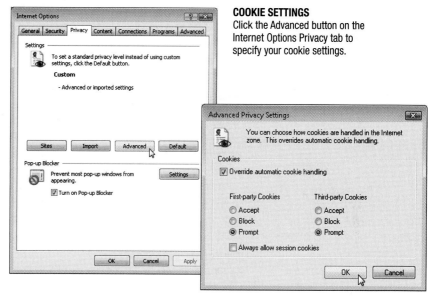

COOKIE SETTINGS
Click the Advanced button on the Internet Options Privacy tab to specify your cookie settings.

COOKIE PROMPTS
After selecting the "Prompt" option, you will be prompted to accept or reject cookies as they are encountered.

Web sites requesting cookie use

> **Cookie.** A small file stored on a user's hard drive by a Web server; commonly used to identify personal preferences and settings for that user.

ONLINE VIDEO

Go to the Chapter 3 page at **www.cengage.com/ computerconcepts/np/uccs4** to watch the "Google Search Privacy: Plain and Simple" video clip.

used to specify which type of cookies (if any) are allowed to be used, such as permitting the use of regular cookies, but not third-party cookies or cookies using personally identifiable information.

Turning off cookies entirely might make some features—such as a shopping cart—on some Web sites inoperable. The *Medium High* privacy option in Internet Explorer is a widely used setting since it allows the use of regular cookies but blocks third-party cookies that use personally identifiable information without explicit permission. Users who want more control over their cookies can choose to accept or decline cookies as they are encountered in most browsers. Although this option interrupts your Web surfing frequently, it is interesting to see the cookies generated from each individual Web site. For example, the two cookie prompts shown in the bottom of Figure 3-33 were generated while visiting the BestBuy.com Web site. Although one cookie request is from the BestBuy.com Web site directly, the other is a third-party cookie from an online marketing company.

Another alternative is the *private browsing* option available with many Web browsers, including Internet Explorer, Chrome, and Safari. As discussed more in Chapter 5, this option allows you to browse the Web without leaving any history (including browsing history, form data, cookies, usernames, and passwords) on the computer you are using. Private browsing is useful for individuals using school, library, or other public computers to visit password-protected sites, research medical information, or perform other tasks that the user may prefer to keep private. Individuals using a computer to shop for presents or other surprises for family members who share the same computer may find the feature useful, as well.

CAUTION CAUTION CAUTION CAUTION CAUTION CAUTION CAU

Cookies (typically placed by advertising companies) that attempt to track your activities across a Web site or the Web sites belonging to an advertising network are referred to as *tracking cookies*. If your security software includes tracking cookie protection, be sure it is enabled to avoid these cookies from being stored on your computer. Setting your browser's privacy settings to block third-party cookies can offer you some additional protection against tracking cookies.

Spyware and Adware

Spyware is the term used for any software program that is installed without the user's knowledge and that secretly gathers information about the user and transmits it through his or her Internet connection. Spyware is sometimes used to provide advertisers with information used for marketing purposes, such as to help select advertisements to display on each person's computer. The information gathered by the spyware software is usually not associated with a person's identity. But spyware is a concern for privacy advocates because it is typically installed without a user's direct knowledge (such as at the same time another program is installed, often when a program is downloaded from a Web site or a P2P service) and conveys information about a user's Internet activities. Spyware can also be used by criminals to retrieve personal data stored on your computer for use in criminal activities, as discussed in more detail in Chapter 4.

>**Spyware.** A software program that is installed without the user's permission and that secretly gathers information to be sent to others.

Unfortunately, spyware use is on the rise and can affect the performance of a computer (such as slowing it down or causing it to work improperly), in addition to its potential security risks. And the problem will likely become worse before it gets any better. Some spyware programs—sometimes referred to as *stealthware*—are getting more aggressive, such as delivering ads regardless of the activity you are doing on your computer, changing your browser home page or otherwise altering your browser settings (referred to as *browser hijacking*), and performing other annoying actions. The worst spyware programs rewrite your computer's main instructions—such as the Windows registry—to change your browser settings back to the hijacked settings each time you reboot your computer, undoing any changes you may have made to your browser settings.

A related type of software is *adware*, which is free or low-cost software that is supported by on-screen advertising. Many free programs that can be downloaded from the Internet, such as the free version of the *NetZero* e-mail program, include some type of adware, which results in on-screen advertising. The difference between spyware and adware is that adware typically does not gather information and relay it to others via the Internet (although it can), and it is not installed without the user's consent. Adware might, however, be installed without the user's direct knowledge, since many users do not read licensing agreements before clicking OK to install a new program. When this occurs with a program that contains adware, the adware components are installed without the user's direct knowledge.

Both spyware and adware can be annoying and use up valuable system resources, in addition to revealing data about individuals. As discussed in detail in Chapter 4, *firewalls* and *antispyware programs* can be used to protect against spyware.

E-Mail Privacy

Many people mistakenly believe that the e-mail they send and receive is private and will never be read by anyone other than the intended recipient. Since it is transmitted over public media, however, only *encrypted* (electronically scrambled) e-mail can be transmitted safely, as discussed in Chapter 4. Although unlikely to happen to your personal e-mail, *nonencrypted* e-mail can be intercepted and read by someone else. Consequently, from a privacy standpoint, a nonencrypted e-mail message should be viewed more like a postcard than a letter (see Figure 3-34).

It is also important to realize that your employer and your ISP have access to the e-mail you send through those organizations. Businesses and ISPs typically archive (keep copies of) e-mail messages that travel through their servers and are required to comply with subpoenas from law enforcement agencies for archived e-mail messages.

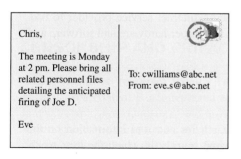

REGULAR (NONENCRYPTED E-MAIL) = POSTCARD

ENCRYPTED E-MAIL = SEALED LETTER

FIGURE 3-34
You cannot assume e-mail messages are private, unless they are encrypted.

Microsoft®

Graham Watson is a Senior Community Lead in the Technical Audience Group Marketing Team at Microsoft. He has worked for Microsoft for 16 years, initially as an enterprise infrastructure consultant. In all, he has over 30 years of experience working in the computer industry, beginning as a computer operator and then as a support engineer. Graham has a Bachelor of Arts degree in Computer Studies and runs a blog at blogs.technet.com/grahamtwatson.

A conversation with GRAHAM WATSON

Senior Community Lead, Technical Audience Global Marketing, Microsoft

" . . . as computers become smaller, more powerful, and more connected, additional opportunities open up."

My Background . . .

I actually got started with computers at school when I discovered I could either take a lesson where I played with a computer terminal or one involving cross-country running in winter! I quickly worked out that the computer was more fun! I'm now part of the Technical Audience Global Marketing Group at Microsoft. My specific responsibilities include making sure that the IT Professional and Developer User Groups around the world—representing over four million people—have the connection they need with Microsoft.

It's Important to Know . . .

About computer systems. No matter how directly you will be involved with computer systems in your career, everyone will need to know enough about systems to be able to make appropriate decisions as to how to use technology to help them in their work and daily lives in general. For example, everyone needs to know how to at least send an e-mail and create, edit, and print a document. Think about the business tasks you need to complete each day, and make sure you can efficiently use the right tools on your computer to help you work more effectively.

The impact of Windows 7. One of the biggest impacts on society that Windows 7 will have is enhanced security for users. One problem with the connectivity that computers provide is that it can also provide thieves and other miscreants with access to you. Each version of Windows improves on previous versions and, although Windows Vista was the most secure mass-marketed operating system when it was launched, Windows 7 continues this evolution and its use will further improve resilience against most forms of attack.

How IT affects your chosen career. It is important to understand the business impact and future trends within the IT space and how it can affect your chosen career. For example, think about the way the retail sales industry has changed over the past ten years. Depending on your chosen career, computer power, graphics, communications capabilities, or mobility may be particularly important to you. You will also need to keep abreast of the latest trends and understand the benefits, costs, risks, and details of how to implement solutions to business problems successfully, taking into account the needs of the customer and the user.

How I Use this Technology . . .

There are two main areas where computers affect me personally. The first one is the most obvious—it provides me with highly enjoyable employment! It's interesting, though, how my current role is more related to computers as a social tool, given my responsibilities toward technical communities. The second one is the same as for many people—my family and friends are all connected, and I often communicate with my wife and children via e-mail or IM. I also do most of my shopping via the Internet—I think I got most of my Christmas shopping done last year without leaving my desk. It's hard to imagine how I would live my life without Windows!

What the Future Holds . . .

Connectivity is probably the biggest thing—not just between people, but also between parts of computer applications. Web services will continue to grow in importance, and Windows 7, together with .NET 3.0 and Microsoft "Azure," will further enable the ability to develop applications quickly by "stitching together" services obtained from a variety of companies and building on them to fulfill specific needs. Mobility is another interesting area—as computers become smaller, more powerful, and more connected, additional opportunities open up. On one hand, we are finding some devices becoming more general purpose (for example, your cell phone may also take pictures and play music), but at the same time there is an opposite movement toward more dedicated devices which work better. Some people just want a simple-to-use cell phone.

I expect that the software we know today will continue to evolve and get more sophisticated but be simpler to use—for example, Microsoft Office continues to improve on its ability to create professional documents very easily. There will probably be at least one "left field" innovation—something that will be obvious once it's taken off, but almost unnoticed until that time. Examples of this from the last few years include digital video recorders (such as TiVo or Windows Media Center Edition), Voice over IP, and social media tools (such as Twitter). One possibility for the future is intelligent search–something that Microsoft is making significant progress on with *Bing* (imagine being able to ask your computer almost any question in the same way you would ask a friend, and get a single, correct answer). Another possibility we'll likely see in the near future is improved connectivity between computers and devices (imagine phoning friends and arranging to meet them, and then automatically getting directions given to you by your car, meetings set up and moved, flights booked, etc.).

> *"Use technology to become a better informed and connected person and use the information and connections gained to move forward in your chosen career."*

My Advice to Students . . .

Use technology to become a better informed and connected person and use the information and connections gained to move forward in your chosen career. Technology should be used as an enabler to achieve your goals, improve your life, and improve the lives of others.

Discussion Question

Graham Watson believes that every employee needs to know at least how to send an e-mail and how to create, edit, and print a document. Think about the jobs available today. Are there any that may not require computer skills? If so, would computer skills give that employee an advantage, even if it's not required? Should companies be required to teach any necessary computer skills or is it reasonable to require basic computer skills for any job today? Be prepared to discuss your position (in class, via an online class discussion group, in a class chat room, or via a class blog, depending on your instructor's directions). You may also be asked to write a short paper expressing your opinion.

> For more information on Microsoft, visit www.microsoft.com. For interesting IT-related information, visit technet.microsoft.com and msdn.microsoft.com. To check if your PC is Windows 7 ready, go to www.microsoft.com/windows/windows-7/get/upgrade-advisor.aspx

chapter 4

Network and Internet Security

After completing this chapter, you will be able to do the following:

1. Explain why computer users should be concerned about network and Internet security.

2. List several examples of unauthorized access and unauthorized use.

3. Explain several ways to protect against unauthorized access and unauthorized use, including access control systems, firewalls, and encryption.

4. Provide several examples of computer sabotage.

5. List how individuals and businesses can protect against computer sabotage.

6. Discuss online theft, identity theft, spoofing, phishing, and other types of dot cons.

7. Detail steps an individual can take to protect against online theft, identity theft, spoofing, phishing, and other types of dot cons.

8. Identify personal safety risks associated with Internet use.

9. List steps individuals can take to safeguard their personal safety when using the Internet.

10. Discuss the current state of network and Internet security legislation.

outline

Overview

Why Be Concerned about Network and Internet Security?

Unauthorized Access and Unauthorized Use
Hacking
War Driving and Wi-Fi Piggybacking
Interception of Communications

Protecting Against Unauthorized Access and Unauthorized Use
Access Control Systems
Firewalls, Encryption, and Virtual Private Networks (VPNs)
Additional Public Hotspot Precautions
Sensible Employee Precautions

Computer Sabotage
Botnets
Computer Viruses and Other Types of Malware
Denial of Service (DoS) Attacks
Data, Program, or Web Site Alteration

Protecting Against Computer Sabotage
Security Software
Other Security Precautions

Online Theft, Online Fraud, and Other Dot Cons
Theft of Data, Information, and Other Resources
Identity Theft, Phishing, and Pharming
Online Auction Fraud
Other Internet Scams

Protecting Against Online Theft, Online Fraud, and Other Dot Cons
Protecting Against Data and Information Theft
Protecting Against Identity Theft, Phishing, and Pharming
Protecting Against Online Auction Fraud and Other Internet Scams

Personal Safety Issues
Cyberbullying and Cyberstalking
Online Pornography

Protecting Against Cyberbullying, Cyberstalking, and Other Personal Safety Concerns
Safety Tips for Adults
Safety Tips for Children and Teens

Network and Internet Security Legislation

OVERVIEW

As discussed in the last few chapters, networks and the Internet help many of us be more efficient and effective workers, as well as add convenience and enjoyment to our personal lives. However, there is a downside, as well. The widespread use of home and business networks and the Internet increases the risk of unauthorized computer access, theft, fraud, and other types of computer crime. In addition, the vast amount of business and personal data stored on computers accessible via company networks and the Internet increases the chances of data loss due to crime or employee errors. Some online activities can even put your personal safety at risk, if you are not careful.

This chapter looks at a variety of security concerns stemming from the use of computer networks and the Internet in our society, including unauthorized access and use, computer viruses and other types of sabotage, and online theft and fraud. Safeguards for each of these concerns are also covered, with an explanation of precautions that can be taken to reduce the chance that these security problems will happen to you. Personal safety issues related to the Internet are also discussed, and the chapter closes with a look at legislation related to network and Internet security. ∎

PODCAST

Go to **www.cengage.com/computerconcepts/np/uccs4** to download or listen to the "Expert Insight on Networks and the Internet" podcast.

WHY BE CONCERNED ABOUT NETWORK AND INTERNET SECURITY?

From a *computer virus* making your computer function abnormally, to a *hacker* using your personal information to make fraudulent purchases, to someone harassing you online in a discussion group, a variety of security concerns related to computer networks and the Internet exist. Many Internet security concerns today can be categorized as **computer crimes**. Computer crime—sometimes referred to as *cybercrime*—includes any illegal act involving a computer. Many computer crimes today are committed using the Internet or another computer network and include theft of financial assets or information, manipulating data (such as grades or account information), and acts of sabotage (such as releasing a computer virus or shutting down a Web server). Cybercrime is an important security concern today. It is a multibillion-dollar business that is often performed by seasoned criminals. In fact, according to the FBI, organized crime organizations in many countries are increasingly turning to computer crime to target millions of potential victims easily, and *phishing attacks* and other *Internet scams* (discussed shortly) are expected to increase in reaction to the recent troubled economy. These and other computer crimes that are carried out via the Internet or another computer network are discussed in this chapter. Other types of computer crime (such as using a computer to create counterfeit currency or make illegal copies of a DVD) are covered in Chapter 5.

>**Computer crime.** Any illegal act involving a computer.

SMART CARDS
Are read by a smart card reader to provide access to a facility or computer system.

USB SECURITY TOKENS
Are inserted into one of the computer's USB ports to provide access to that computer system.

 FIGURE 4-6
Possessed objects.
Help protect against unauthorized access; some can also store additional security credentials.

 TIP

Cuts or other changes to a finger may prevent access via a fingerprint reader. To avoid this problem, be sure to enroll more than one finger, if possible, whenever you are being set up in a system that uses a fingerprint reader. Many systems allow the user to enter images for more than one finger and any of the registered fingers may be used for access.

 ONLINE VIDEO

Go to the Chapter 4 page at **www.cengage.com/ computerconcepts/np/uccs4** to watch the "How the Eikon Personal Biometric Reader Works" video clip.

to provide other security features—are also being used. Access cards (like the one shown in Figure 4-5) and other devices used to supply the OTPs used to log on to Web sites and other resources are another type of *security token* possessed object.

One disadvantage of using possessed objects is that the object can be lost or, like passwords, can be used by an unauthorized individual if that individual has possession of the object. This latter disadvantage can be overcome by using a second factor, such as requiring the user to supply a username/password combination or be authenticated by a fingerprint or other type of *biometric* data in order to use the possessed object.

Biometric Access Systems

Biometrics is the study of identifying individuals using measurable, unique physiological or behavioral characteristics. **Biometric access systems** typically identify users by a particular unique biological characteristic (such as a fingerprint, a hand, a face, or an iris), although personal traits are used in some systems. For instance, some systems today use *keystroke dynamics* to recognize an individual's unique typing pattern to authenticate the user as he or she types in his or her username and password; other systems identify an individual via his or her voice, signature, or gait. Because the means of access (usually a part of the body) cannot typically be used by anyone other than the authorized individual, biometric access systems can perform both identification and authentication.

To identify and authenticate an individual, biometric access systems typically use a biometric reader (such as a *fingerprint reader* or *hand geometry reader* to identify an individual based on his or her fingerprint or hand image) or a digital camera (to identify an individual based on his or her face or iris), in conjunction with software and a database. The system matches the supplied biometric data with the biometric data that was stored in the database when the individual was enrolled in the system and authenticates the individual if the data matches. To speed up the process, many biometric access systems require users to identify themselves first (such as by entering a username or swiping a smart card), and then the system uses that identifying information to verify that the supplied biometric data matches the identified person.

Biometric access systems are used to control access to secure facilities (such as corporate headquarters and prisons); to log users on to computers, networks, and secure Web sites (by using an external reader or one built into the computer); to punch employees in and out of work; and to confirm consumers' identities at ATM machines and check-cashing services. Biometric readers are also increasingly being built into notebook computers, external hard drives, USB flash drives, and other hardware to prevent unauthorized use of those devices.

>**Biometric access system.** An access control system that uses one unique physical characteristic of an individual (such as a fingerprint, face, or voice) to authenticate that individual.

In addition to being used to control access to computers, networks, and other resources, biometrics are an important part of the systems used by law enforcement agencies and the military to identify individuals. For instance, the border control systems in many countries use biometrics to identify citizens, travelers, criminal suspects, and potential terrorists, and biometric identification systems are used extensively by law enforcement agencies and the military in areas of conflict. For example, biometric identification systems are being used in Iraq to identify members of the Iraqi police and military, prisoners, prison guards, authorized gun owners, citizens, contract employees, known criminals, and criminal suspects. In addition, *face recognition systems* (biometric systems that use cameras and a database of photos to attempt to identify individuals as they walk by the cameras) are used in many airports and other public locations to help identify known terrorists and criminal suspects.

Biometric access systems are very accurate. In fact, the odds of two different individuals having identical irises is 1 in 10^{78} and the statistical probability of two different irises being declared a match are 1 in 1.2 million—even identical twins (who have the same DNA structure) have different fingerprints and irises. Systems based on biological characteristics (such as a person's iris, hand geometry, face, or

FINGERPRINT RECOGNITION SYSTEMS
Typically used to protect access to office computers, to automatically supply Web site passwords on home computers, and to pay for products or services.

HAND GEOMETRY SYSTEMS
Typically used to control access to facilities (such as government offices, prisons, and military facilities) and to punch in and out of work.

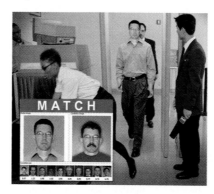

FACE RECOGNITION SYSTEMS
Typically used to control access to highly secure areas, as well as to identify individuals for law enforcement purposes.

IRIS RECOGNITION SYSTEMS
Typically used to control access to highly secure areas and by the military; also beginning to be used to authenticate ATM users and other consumers.

fingerprint) tend to be more accurate than those based on a personal trait (such as a person's voice or written signature) because biological traits do not change, but physical traits might change (such as an individual's voice, which might be affected by a cold, or a written signature, which might be affected by a broken wrist). In addition, biometric characteristics cannot be lost (like an access card), cannot be forgotten (like a password), and do not have to be pulled out of a briefcase or pocket (like an access card or other type of possessed object).

The primary disadvantages of biometric access systems are that much of the necessary hardware and software is expensive, and the data used for authentication (such as a fingerprint or an iris image) cannot be reset if it is compromised. In addition, fingerprint and hand geometry systems typically require contact with the reader device, though some systems under development (such as one that identifies individuals based on the veins in their hands) are contactless systems.

Some examples of the most commonly used types of biometric access and identification systems are shown in Figure 4-7.

FIGURE 4-7
Types of biometric access and identification systems.

VIDEO PODCAST

Go to the Chapter 4 page at **www.cengage.com/ computerconcepts/np/uccs4** to download or listen to the "How To: Use Face Recognition with Your Computer" video podcast.

Controlling Access to Wireless Networks

As already discussed, wireless networks—such as Wi-Fi networks—are less secure, in general, than wired networks. There are Wi-Fi security procedures, however, that can be used to protect against unauthorized use of a wireless network and to *encrypt* data sent over the network so that it is unreadable if it is intercepted. The original Wi-Fi security standard was

Because the SSID is being broadcast, the user can select the network from the list.

The user must supply the appropriate network key or passphrase in order to connect to the network.

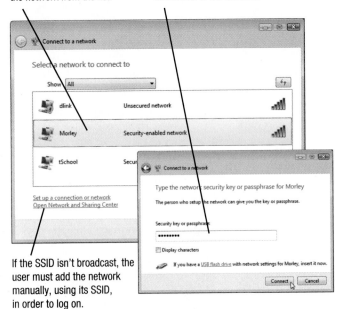

If the SSID isn't broadcast, the user must add the network manually, using its SSID, in order to log on.

Ⓐ **FIGURE 4-8**

Accessing a Wi-Fi network. To access a secure network, the appropriate passphrase must be supplied.

WEP (*Wired Equivalent Privacy*). WEP is now considered insecure and has been replaced with the more secure *WPA* (*Wi-Fi Protected Access*) and the even more secure *WPA2* standards. However, Wi-Fi security features only work if they are enabled. Most Wi-Fi hardware today is shipped with the security features switched off, and many network owners never enable them, leaving those networks unsecured.

To protect against unauthorized access, Wi-Fi network owners should secure their networks by changing the router or access point settings to enable one of the encryption standards and to assign a *network key* or *passphrase* (essentially a password) that must be supplied in order to access the secured network. In addition, the name of the network (called the *SSID*) can be hidden from view by switching off the SSID broadcast feature. While hiding the network name will not deter serious hackers, it may reduce the number of casual war drivers or neighbors accessing the network. Once a network is secured, users who want to connect to that network need to either select or supply the network SSID name (depending on whether or not the SSID is being broadcast) and then enter the network key assigned to that network (see Figure 4-8). For an overview of how you can secure your wireless home router, see the How It Works box.

Firewalls, Encryption, and Virtual Private Networks (VPNs)

In addition to the access control systems just discussed, there are a number of other tools that can be used to prevent access to an individual computer or to prevent data from being intercepted in an understandable form during transit. These tools are discussed next.

Firewalls

A **firewall** is a security system that essentially creates a barrier between a computer or network and the Internet in order to protect against unauthorized access. Firewalls are typically two-way, so they check all incoming (from the Internet to the computer or the network) and outgoing (from the computer or the network to the Internet) traffic and allow only authorized traffic to pass through the firewall. *Personal firewalls* are typically software-based systems that are geared toward protecting home computers from hackers attempting to access those computers through their Internet connections. All computers with direct Internet connections (such as DSL, cable, satellite, or fixed wireless Internet access) should use a firewall (computers using dial-up Internet access only are relatively safe from hackers). Personal firewalls can be stand-alone programs (such as the free *ZoneAlarm* program); they are also built into many operating systems (such as the *Windows Firewall* program shown in Figure 4-9). Many routers, modems, and other pieces of networking hardware also include built-in firewall capabilities to help secure the networks these devices are used with. Firewalls designed to protect business networks may be software-based, hardware-based, or a combination of the two. They can typically be used both to prevent network access by hackers and other outsiders, as well as to control employee Internet access.

> **Firewall.** A collection of hardware and/or software intended to protect a computer or computer network from unauthorized access.

HOW IT WORKS

Securing a Wireless Home Router

If you have a home wireless network, it is important to secure it properly so it cannot be used by unauthorized individuals. Security settings are specified in the router's configuration screen, such as the one shown in the accompanying illustration. To open your router's configuration screen to check or modify the settings, type the IP address assigned to that device (such as 192.168.0.1—check for a sticker on the bottom of your router or your router's documentation for its default IP address and username) in your browser's Address bar. Use the default password listed in your router documentation to log on the first time, and then change the password using the configuration screen to prevent unauthorized individuals from changing your router settings. To secure the router, enter the network name (SSID) you want to have associated with the router, select the appropriate security mode (such as WEP, WPA, or WPA2) to be used, and then type a secure passphrase to be used in order to log on to the network.

For additional security, *MAC (Media Access Control) address filtering* can be used to allow only the devices whose network adapter MAC addresses you enter into your router's settings access to the network. Because hackers can "spoof" MAC addresses by changing the MAC addresses of their devices to match an authorized MAC address (once the hacker determines those addresses), MAC address filtering should not be considered an alternative to using WPA or WPA2 encryption. However, it does add another layer of protection. Other precautions include designating specific times (such as when you are away from home) that the router will deny access to any device, and reducing the strength of the wireless signal if its current strength reaches farther than you need.

Use the router's IP address to display the router's configuration screen.

Use this tab to enable MAC address filtering.

Use this tab to change the administrator password used to access this configuration screen.

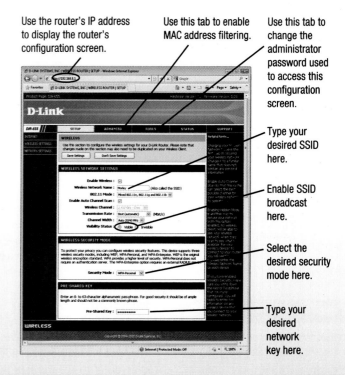

Type your desired SSID here.

Enable SSID broadcast here.

Select the desired security mode here.

Type your desired network key here.

Firewalls work by closing down all external *communications port addresses* (the electronic connections that allow a computer to communicate with other computers) to unauthorized computers and programs. While business firewalls are set up by the network administrator and those settings typically cannot be changed by end users, individuals may choose to change the settings for their personal firewall. For example, the user can choose to be notified when any application program on the computer is trying to access the Internet, to specify the programs that are allowed to access the Internet, or to block all incoming connections temporarily. In addition to protecting your computer from outside access, firewall programs also protect against

ONLINE VIDEO

Go to the Chapter 4 page at **www.cengage.com/computerconcepts/np/uccs4** to watch the "Securing Your Wireless Router" video clip.

FIGURE 4-9
A personal firewall program. The firewall is on, so only authorized traffic can access the computer.

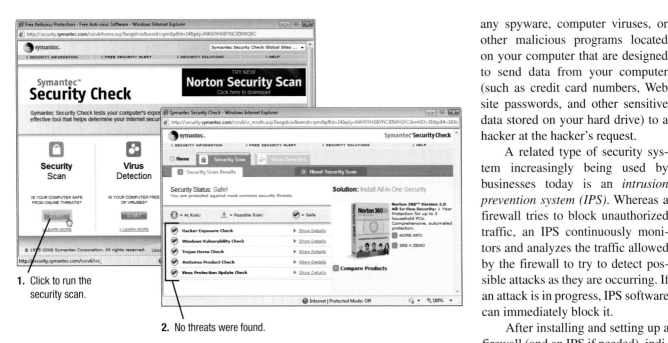

1. Click to run the security scan.

2. No threats were found.

⊘ **FIGURE 4-10**
Online security scans can check your system for vulnerabilities.

any spyware, computer viruses, or other malicious programs located on your computer that are designed to send data from your computer (such as credit card numbers, Web site passwords, and other sensitive data stored on your hard drive) to a hacker at the hacker's request.

A related type of security system increasingly being used by businesses today is an *intrusion prevention system (IPS)*. Whereas a firewall tries to block unauthorized traffic, an IPS continuously monitors and analyzes the traffic allowed by the firewall to try to detect possible attacks as they are occurring. If an attack is in progress, IPS software can immediately block it.

After installing and setting up a firewall (and an IPS if needed), individuals and businesses should test their systems to determine if vulnerabilities still exist. Individuals can use online security tests—such as the *Symantec Security Check* shown in Figure 4-10 or the tests at Gibson Research's *Shields Up* site—to check their computers; businesses may wish to hire an outside consultant to perform a comprehensive security assessment.

Encryption

Encryption is a way of temporarily converting data into a form, known as a *cipher*, which is unreadable until it is *decrypted* (unscrambled) in order to protect that data from being viewed by unauthorized individuals. As previously discussed, secure Wi-Fi networks use encryption to secure data that is transferred over the network. **Secure Web pages** use encryption so that sensitive data (such as credit card numbers) sent via the Web page is protected as it travels over the Internet. The most common security protocols used with secure Web pages are *Secure Sockets Layer (SSL)* and *Extended Validation Secure Sockets Layer (EV SSL)*. The URL for Web pages using either form of SSL begins with *https:* instead of *http:*.

Some Internet services (such as *Skype VoIP* calls and *HushMail* Web-based e-mails) use built-in encryption. Encryption can also be added manually to a file or an e-mail message before it is sent over the Internet to ensure that the content is unreadable if the file or message is intercepted during transit. In addition to securing files during transit, encryption can be used to protect the files stored on a hard drive so they will be unreadable if opened by an unauthorized person (such as if a hacker accesses a file containing sensitive data or if a computer containing sensitive files is lost or stolen). Increasingly, computers and hard drives (particularly those used with portable computers) are *self-encrypting*; that is, encrypting all data automatically and invisibly to the user, as discussed in Chapter 5. Windows, Mac OS, and other current operating systems support encryption and businesses are increasingly turning to encryption to prevent data loss, if a data breach should occur.

> **Encryption.** A method of scrambling the contents of an e-mail message or a file to make it unreadable if an unauthorized user intercepts it.
> **Secure Web page.** A Web page that uses encryption to protect information transmitted via that Web page.

The two most common types of encryption in use today are *public key encryption* (often used with content being transmitted over the Internet, such as secure Web pages and encrypted e-mail) and *private key encryption* (most often used to encrypt files or the content of a hard drive or other device). **Private key encryption**, also called *symmetric key encryption*, uses a single secret *private key* (essentially a password) to both encrypt and decrypt the file or message. It is often used to encrypt files stored on an individual's computer, since the individual who selects the private key is likely the only one who will need to access those files. Private key encryption can also be used to send files securely to others, provided both the sender and recipient agree on the private key that will be used to access the file. Private key encryption capabilities are incorporated into a variety of programs today, including Microsoft Office, the WinZip file compression program, and Adobe Acrobat (the program used to create PDF files). To encrypt a document in Microsoft Word, for instance, you use the *Prepare* option on the Office menu, choose *Encrypt Document*, type the desired password (private key), and then save the file. To open that document again (or any copies of the file, such as those sent via e-mail), the password assigned to that file must be entered correctly.

Public key encryption**, also called *asymmetric key encryption*, utilizes two encryption keys to encrypt and decrypt documents. Specifically, public key encryption uses a pair of keys (a private key and a *public key*) that are related mathematically to each other and have been assigned to a particular individual. An individual's public key is not secret and is available for anyone to use, but the corresponding private key is used only by the individual to whom it was assigned. Documents or messages encrypted with a public key can only be decrypted with the matching private key.

Public/private key pairs are generated by the program being used to perform the encryption or they are obtained via the Internet through a *Certificate Authority*, such as VeriSign or Thawte. Once obtained, encryption keys are stored in your browser, e-mail program, and any other program with which they will be used—this is typically done automatically for you when you obtain your key pairs. Obtaining a business public/private key pair usually requires a fee, but free key pairs for personal use are available through some Certificate Authorities. If a third-party encryption program is used (such as *Pretty Good Privacy* or *PGP*), the program typically takes care of obtaining and managing your keys for you.

To send someone an encrypted e-mail message or file using public key encryption, you need his or her public key. If that person has previously sent you his or her public key (such as via an e-mail message), it was likely stored by your e-mail program in your address book or contacts list, or by your encryption program in a central key directory used by that program. In either case, that public key is available whenever you want to send that person an encrypted document. If you do not already have the public key belonging to the individual to whom you wish to send an encrypted e-mail or file, you will need to request it from that individual. Once the recipient's public key has been used to encrypt the file or e-mail message and that document is received, the recipient uses his or her private key to decrypt the encrypted contents (see Figure 4-11).

To avoid the need to obtain the recipient's public key before sending that person an encrypted e-mail, *Web-based encrypted e-mail* can be used. Web-based encrypted e-mail works similarly to regular Web-based e-mail (in which e-mail is composed and viewed on a Web page belonging to a Web-based e-mail provider), but Web-based encrypted e-mail systems use secure Web servers to host the Web pages that are used to compose and read e-mail messages. Some Web-based encrypted e-mail systems—such as the popular free *HushMail* service that automatically encrypts all e-mail sent through the

VIDEO PODCAST

Go to the Chapter 4 page at **www.cengage.com/ computerconcepts/np/uccs4** to download or listen to the "How To: Create an Encrypted Partition On Your Hard Drive" video podcast.

FURTHER EXPLORATION

Go to the Chapter 4 page at **www.cengage.com/ computerconcepts/np/uccs4** for links to information about encryption.

> **Private key encryption.** A type of encryption that uses a single key to encrypt and decrypt the file or message. > **Public key encryption.** A type of encryption that uses key pairs to encrypt and decrypt the file or message.

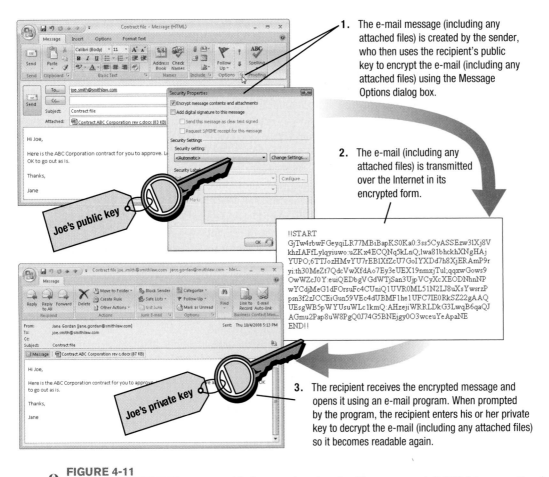

1. The e-mail message (including any attached files) is created by the sender, who then uses the recipient's public key to encrypt the e-mail (including any attached files) using the Message Options dialog box.

2. The e-mail (including any attached files) is transmitted over the Internet in its encrypted form.

3. The recipient receives the encrypted message and opens it using an e-mail program. When prompted by the program, the recipient enters his or her private key to decrypt the e-mail (including any attached files) so it becomes readable again.

FIGURE 4-11

Using public key encryption to secure an e-mail message.

service—require both the sender and recipient to have accounts. Others require only the sender to have an account and the recipient is sent an e-mail containing instructions regarding how to view the message on a secure Web page.

There are various strengths of encryption available; the stronger the encryption, the more difficult it is to crack. Older 40-bit encryption (which can only use keys that are 40 bits or 5 characters long) is considered *weak encryption*. Stronger encryption is available today, such as *strong 128-bit encryption* (which uses 16-character keys) and *military-strength 2,048-bit encryption* (which uses 256-character keys), although not without some objections from law enforcement agencies and the government because they state that terrorists routinely use encryption methods to communicate.

Virtual Private Networks (VPNs)

While e-mail and file encryption can be used to transfer individual messages and files securely over the Internet, a **virtual private network (VPN)** is designed to be used when a continuous secure channel over the Internet is needed. A VPN provides a secure private tunnel from the user's computer through the Internet to another destination and is most often used to provide remote employees with secure access to a company network. VPNs use encryption and other security mechanisms to ensure that only authorized users can access the remote network and that the data cannot be intercepted during transit. Since it uses the Internet instead of an expensive private physical network, a VPN can provide a secure environment over a large geographical area at a manageable cost. Once a VPN is set up, the user just needs to log on (such as with a username/password combination or a security token) in order to use the VPN.

VPNs are often used by both businesses and individuals at public Wi-Fi hotspots to prevent data interception when connecting to the Internet via the hotspot. While businesspeople will typically use a VPN set up by their companies, individuals can create *personal VPNs* using software designed for that purpose. This software automatically encrypts all inbound and outbound Internet traffic, including Web pages, e-mail messages, IMs, VoIP calls, and

>**Virtual private network (VPN).** A private, secure path over the Internet that provides authorized users a secure means of accessing a private network via the Internet.

so forth, and also acts as a personal firewall. Using a personal VPN at a public hotspot can help individuals from becoming the victim of a growing trend—*evil twin* Wi-Fi access points, discussed in the Trend box.

Additional Public Hotspot Precautions

The precautions already discussed (such as using firewall software, secure Web pages, VPNs, and encryption) are a good start for protecting against unauthorized access and unauthorized use at a public Wi-Fi hotspot. However, there are additional precautions individuals can use to avoid data (both that which is on their computers and that which is being sent over the Internet) from being compromised. These precautions are listed in Figure 4-12.

Sensible Employee Precautions

A significant number of business security breaches—over 60%, according to a recent University of Washington study—are the responsibility of insiders. Sometimes the employee deliberately performs the act; other times the employee makes a mistake, such as losing a portable computer or removable storage medium, or inadvertently providing access to sensitive data. Consequently, it pays for employers to be cautious with their employees. Some suggestions to avoid security breaches by employees are listed next.

PUBLIC HOTSPOT PRECAUTIONS
Turn off automatic connections and pay attention to the list of available hotspots to try to make sure you connect to a legitimate access point (not an evil twin).
Use a personal firewall to control the traffic going to and from your computer and temporarily use it to block all incoming connections.
Use a virtual private network (VPN) to secure all activity between your computer and the Internet.
Only enter passwords, credit card numbers, and other data on secure Web pages using a VPN.
If you're not using a VPN, encrypt all sensitive files before transferring or e-mailing them.
If you're not using a VPN, avoid online shopping, banking, and other sensitive transactions.
Turn off file sharing so others can't access the files on your hard drive.
Turn off Bluetooth and Wi-Fi when you are not using them.
Disable *ad hoc* capabilities to prevent another computer from connecting to your computer directly without using an access point.
Use antivirus software and make sure your operating system is up to date.

FIGURE 4-12
Sensible precautions for public Wi-Fi hotspot users.

Screen Potential New Hires Carefully

Employers should carefully investigate the background of all potential employees. Some people falsify résumés to get jobs. Others may have criminal records or currently be charged with a crime. One embarrassing mistake made by Rutgers University was to hire David Smith, the author of the *Melissa* computer virus, as a computer technician when he was out on bail following the arrest for that crime.

Watch for Disgruntled Employees and Ex-Employees

The type of employee who is most likely to commit a computer crime is one who has recently been terminated or passed over for a promotion, or one who has some reason to want to "get even" with the organization. Limiting access for each employee to only the resources needed for his or her job (referred to as the *Principle of Least Privilege*) and monitoring any attempts to access off-limit resources can help prevent some types of problems, such as unauthorized access of sensitive files, unintentional damage like deleting or changing files inadvertently, or sabotage like deleting or changing company files intentionally. In addition, it is vital that whenever an employee leaves the company for any reason, all access to the system for that individual (username, password, e-mail address, and so forth) should be removed immediately. For employees with high levels of system access, simultaneously removing access while the termination is taking place is even better. Waiting even a few minutes can be too late, since just-fired employees have been known to barricade themselves in their office immediately after being terminated in order to change passwords, sabotage records, and perform other malicious acts. Some wait slightly longer, such as one computer administrator at a Houston organ and tissue donation center who recently pled guilty to accessing the company computer system the evening of and day after being fired and intentionally deleting numerous software applications and important files, such as organ donation records, accounting files, and backup files. She was charged with one

TREND

Evil Twins

An *evil twin* is a fake Wi-Fi hotspot set up by a thief to masquerade as a legitimate Wi-Fi hotspot in order to gather personal or corporate information from individuals who connect to that hotspot thinking it is the legitimate one. Typically, the thief selects a legitimate hotspot and moves within range of that hotspot, uses software to discover the network name (SSID) and radio frequency being used by the legitimate hotspot, and then broadcasts his or her hotspot using the same SSID as the legitimate one. To the end user, the evil twin looks like the legitimate hotspot because it uses the same SSID and settings as the "good twin" it is impersonating. If an end user connects to the evil twin to access the Internet, the thief can intercept sensitive data sent to the Internet, such as passwords or credit card information. That information can then be used for *identity theft* and other fraudulent activities.

Because of the increased use of Wi-Fi hotspots and the availability of software enabling a would-be thief to set up an evil twin hotspot, evil twins are an increasing threat. To make matters worse, some evil twins are able to disconnect users from the legitimate hotspot in hopes the users will be reconnected automatically to the evil twin instead of the legitimate hotspot. To protect yourself, set up your portable computer to only connect manually to hotspots so you cannot be connected to an evil twin hotspot inadvertently. In addition, refrain from performing sensitive transactions (such as shopping and banking) at public hotspots. Businesspeople should use a VPN when connecting to the company server via a Wi-Fi hotspot; individuals needing to perform sensitive transactions should use a personal VPN, such as the one shown in the accompanying figure.

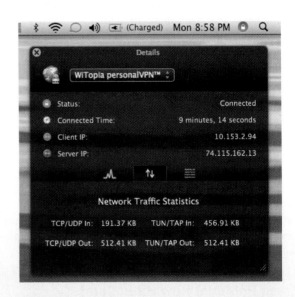

count of unauthorized computer access, sentenced to two years in prison, and ordered to pay more than $94,000 in restitution.

Develop Policies and Controls

All companies should develop policies and controls regarding security matters. As already mentioned, employees should be granted the least amount of access to the company network that they need to perform their job. Employees should be educated about the seriousness and consequences of hacking, data theft, and other computer crimes, and they should be taught what to do when they suspect a computer crime has been committed. Employees should also be instructed about proper computer and e-mail usage policies—such as whether or not downloading and installing software on company computers is allowed, whether or not employees are responsible for updating their computers, and the types of removable storage mediums (such as USB flash drives or portable digital media players) that may be used with company computers—in order to avoid inadvertently creating a security problem. Policies for removing computers and storage media containing sensitive data from the premises should also be implemented and enforced, and sensitive documents should be shredded when they are no longer needed. In addition, policies should be updated as needed to respond to new types of threats. For instance, the Pentagon banned USB flash drives in late 2008 due to a computer virus threat; it is unknown at this time when or if their use will be allowed again.

Employees who work from home or otherwise access the company network via the Internet also need to be educated about security policies for remote access and the proper precautions that need to be taken. These precautions include keeping their operating system and security software up to date, and using only encrypted storage devices (such as self-encrypting USB flash drives) when transporting documents between work and home. In addition, telecommuting workers and outside contractors should not be allowed to have peer-to-peer (P2P) software on computers containing company documents, since data is increasingly being exposed through the use of P2P networks. For instance, classified data about the U.S. presidential helicopter was discovered recently on a computer in Iran and traced back to a P2P network and the computer of a military contractor in Maryland, and the Social Security numbers and other personal data belonging to about 17,000 current and former Pfizer workers were leaked onto a P2P network in 2007 after an employee installed unauthorized P2P software on a company notebook computer provided for use at her home.

Use Data-Leakage Prevention and Enterprise Rights-Management Software

As employees are increasingly bringing portable devices (such as mobile phones, portable digital media players, and USB flash drives) that can interact with business networks to the office, the challenge of securing these devices (and the company network against these devices) has grown. Some companies now prohibit all portable devices; others allow only company-issued devices so they can ensure appropriate security measures, such as encryption, password protection, and the ability to wipe the device clean remotely if it is lost or stolen, are implemented.

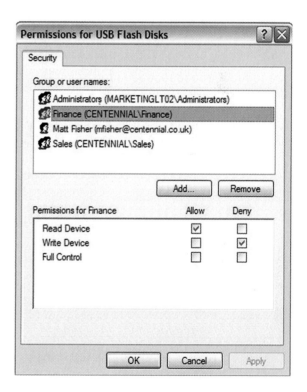

To protect against employees copying or sending confidential data to others either intentionally or accidentally, *data-leakage prevention systems* can be used. Data-leakage prevention systems are available as software and/or hardware systems, and have a range of capabilities, but the overall goal is to prevent sensitive data from exposure. For instance, some systems control which devices (such as USB flash drives and portable digital media players) can be connected to an employee's computer (see Figure 4-13) in order to prevent sensitive data from being taken home inadvertently or intentionally. Other data-leakage prevention systems—sometimes also called *outbound-content monitoring systems*—scan all outgoing communications (e-mail, transferred files, instant messages, and so forth) for documents containing Social Security numbers, intellectual property, and other confidential information. Some can also continually scan network devices to locate sensitive data in documents stored on computers to ensure that sensitive files are not on the computer of an employee who should not have access to them. For even stronger protection of confidential company documents, *enterprise rights-management software*, which encrypts confidential documents and limits functions such as printing, editing, and copying the data to only authorized users with the appropriate password, can be used.

FIGURE 4-13
Data-leakage prevention software can control which devices can be connected to an employee's computer.

Ask Business Partners to Review their Security

In this networked economy, many organizations provide some access to internal resources for business partners. If those external companies are lax with their security measures, however, attacks through the business partners' computers (such as via an employee or hacker) are possible. Consequently, businesses should make sure that their business partners maintain adequate security policies and controls. Regulations—such as the *Sarbanes-Oxley Act of 2002*—increasingly require businesses to ensure that adequate controls are in place to preserve the integrity of financial reports. This includes outside companies—such as business partners and *outsourcing companies* (outside vendors for specific business tasks)—if they have access to sensitive corporate data. Companies that utilize cloud computing also need to ensure that the cloud vendor's policies (such as for protecting access to stored data, using adequate encryption techniques and backup procedures, submitting to necessary audits, and storing data in locations with the desired security and privacy laws) match the company's requirements.

COMPUTER SABOTAGE

Computer sabotage—acts of malicious destruction to a computer or computer resource—is another common type of computer crime today. Computer sabotage can take several forms, including launching a *computer virus* or a *denial of service (DoS) attack*, altering the content of a Web site, or changing data or programs located on a computer. A common tool used to perform computer sabotage is a *botnet*, discussed next. Computer sabotage is illegal in the United States, and acts of sabotage are estimated to cost individuals and organizations billions of dollars per year, primarily for labor costs related to correcting the problems caused by the sabotage, lost productivity, and lost sales.

Botnets

A computer that is controlled by a hacker or other computer criminal is referred to as a **bot** or *zombie computer*; a group of bots that are controlled by one individual and can work together in a coordinated fashion is called a **botnet**. According to the FBI, an estimated one million U.S. computers are currently part of a botnet; consequently, botnets are a major security threat. Criminals (called *botherders*) are increasingly creating botnets to use for computer sabotage, such as to spread *malware* and to launch *denial of service (DoS) attacks*, discussed shortly. Botherders also often sell their botnet services to send spam and launch Internet attacks on their clients' behalf, as well as use them to steal identity information, credit card numbers, passwords, corporate secrets, and other sensitive data, which are then sold to other criminals or otherwise used in an illegal manner.

Computer Viruses and Other Types of Malware

Malware is a generic term that refers to any type of malicious software. Malware programs are intentionally written to perform destructive acts, such as damaging programs, deleting files, erasing an entire hard drive, or slowing down the performance of a computer. This damage can take place immediately after a computer is *infected* (that is, the malware software is installed) or it can begin when a particular condition is met. A malware program that activates when it detects a certain condition, such as when a particular keystroke is pressed or an employee's name is deleted from an employee file, is called a *logic bomb*. A logic bomb that is triggered by a particular date or time is called a *time bomb*.

Writing a computer virus or other type of malware or even posting the malware code on the Internet is not illegal, but it is considered highly unethical and irresponsible behavior. Distributing malware, on the other hand, is illegal, and virus writers who release their malware are being vigorously prosecuted. Malware can be very costly in terms of the labor costs associated with removing the viruses and correcting any resulting damage, as well as the cost of lost productivity of employees. One type of malware often used by computer criminals to send sensitive data secretly from

---

>**Computer sabotage.** An act of malicious destruction to a computer or computer resource. >**Bot.** A computer that is controlled by a hacker or other computer criminal. >**Botnet.** A group of bots that are controlled by one individual. >**Malware.** Any type of malicious software.

infected computers to the criminal—spyware—was discussed in Chapter 3. The most common other types of malware are discussed next.

Computer Viruses

One type of malware is the **computer virus**—a software program that is installed without the permission or knowledge of the computer user, that is designed to alter the way a computer operates, and that can replicate itself to infect any new media it has access to. Computer viruses are often embedded into program or data files (often games, videos, and music files downloaded from Web pages or shared via a P2P service). They are spread whenever the infected file is downloaded, is transferred to a new computer via an infected removable storage medium, or is e-mailed to another computer (see Figure 4-14). Viruses can also be installed when a recipient clicks a link in an e-mail message (often in an unsolicited e-mail message that resembles a legitimate e-mail message that normally contains a link, such as an electronic greeting card e-mail that contains a link to view the card), as well as through links in instant messages. Regardless of how it is obtained, once a copy of the infected file reaches a new computer it typically embeds itself into program, data, or system files on the new computer and remains there, affecting that computer according to its programmed instructions, until it is discovered and removed.

FIGURE 4-14
How a computer virus or other type of malicious software might spread.

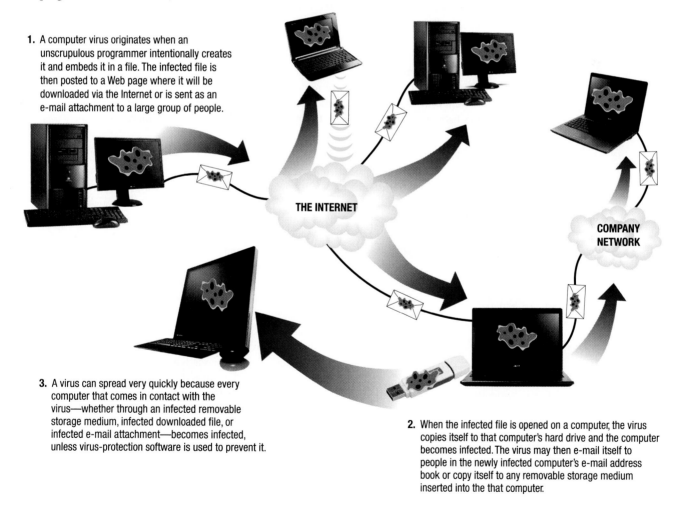

1. A computer virus originates when an unscrupulous programmer intentionally creates it and embeds it in a file. The infected file is then posted to a Web page where it will be downloaded via the Internet or is sent as an e-mail attachment to a large group of people.

THE INTERNET

COMPANY NETWORK

3. A virus can spread very quickly because every computer that comes in contact with the virus—whether through an infected removable storage medium, infected downloaded file, or infected e-mail attachment—becomes infected, unless virus-protection software is used to prevent it.

2. When the infected file is opened on a computer, the virus copies itself to that computer's hard drive and the computer becomes infected. The virus may then e-mail itself to people in the newly infected computer's e-mail address book or copy itself to any removable storage medium inserted into the that computer.

>**Computer virus.** A software program installed without the user's knowledge and designed to alter the way a computer operates or to cause harm to the computer system.

ONLINE VIDEO

Go to the Chapter 4 page at **www.cengage.com/ computerconcepts/np/uccs4** to watch the "How Worms Spread Using AutoPlay" video clip.

Computer Worms

Another common form of malware is the **computer worm**. Like a computer virus, a computer worm is a malicious program that is typically designed to cause damage. Unlike a computer virus, however, a computer worm does not infect other computer files on the infected computer in order to replicate itself; instead, it spreads by creating copies of its code and sending those copies to other computers via a network. Often, the worm is sent to other computers as an e-mail attachment. Usually after the infected e-mail attachment is opened by an individual, the worm inflicts its damage and then automatically sends copies of itself to other computers via the Internet or a private network, typically using addresses in the e-mail address book located on the newly infected computer. When those e-mail messages and their attachments are opened, the new computers become infected and the cycle continues. Because of its distribution method, a worm can spread very rapidly. For instance, the *Mydoom* worm (which was released in 2004 and is considered one of the fastest spreading worms ever) spread so rapidly that, at one point, one out of every 10 e-mails contained the worm.

Some newer worms do not require any action by the users (such as opening an e-mail attachment) to infect their computers. Instead, the worm scans the Internet looking for computers that are vulnerable to that particular worm and sends a copy of itself to those computers to infect them. Other worms just require the user to view an infected e-mail message or insert an infected removable storage medium (such as a USB flash drive) into the computer, in order to infect the computer. Still other worms are specifically written to take advantage of newly discovered *security holes* (vulnerabilities) in operating systems and e-mail programs. Worms and other types of malware that are designed to take advantage of a security hole and are released at a time when no security patch to correct the problem is available are referred to as *zero-day attacks*. Unfortunately, as malware writing tools become more sophisticated, zero-day attacks are becoming more common.

Trojan Horses

A **Trojan horse** is a type of malware that masquerades as something else—usually an application program (such as what appears to be a game or utility program). When the seemingly legitimate program is downloaded or installed, the malware part of the Trojan horse infects the computer. Many recent Trojan horses masquerade as normal ongoing activities (such as the Windows Update service or an *antivirus* or *antispyware program* telling you to download a file containing program updates) when they are installed to try to trick unsuspecting users into downloading another malware program or buying a useless program. For instance, after a *rogue antivirus program* like the one shown in Figure 4-15 is installed (usually without the user's direct knowledge or permission), the malware takes over the computer displaying warning messages or scan results (see Figure 4-15) indicating the computer is infected with malware. In addition, the rogue antivirus program typically prevents access to any Web sites other than its own and prompts the user to buy a fake antimalware program to get rid of the "malware." Usually the only malware on the computer is the rogue program,

FIGURE 4-15
Rogue antivirus programs. These programs try to trick victims into purchasing subscriptions to remove nonexistent malware supposedly installed on their computers.

> **Computer worm.** A malicious program designed to spread rapidly to a large number of computers by sending copies of itself to other computers.
> **Trojan horse.** A malicious program that masquerades as something else.

but it is often very intrusive (such as displaying constant messages on the desktop and in pop-up windows and hiding the options needed to change the hijacked settings back to normal), and it is extremely hard to remove.

Unlike viruses and worms, Trojan horses cannot replicate themselves. Trojan horses are usually spread by being downloaded from the Internet, though they may also be sent as an e-mail attachment, either from the Trojan horse author or from individuals who forward it, not realizing the program is a Trojan horse. Some Trojan horses today act as spyware and are designed to find sensitive information about an individual (such as a Social Security number or a bank account number) or about a company (such as corporate intellectual property like mechanical designs, electronic schematics, and other valuable proprietary information) located on infected computers and then send that information to the malware creator to be used in illegal activities. One emerging type of Trojan horse is called a *RAT* (*Remote-Access Trojan*). RATs are typically installed via small files obtained from an Internet download, such as free software, games, or electronic greeting cards. Once installed, RATs are designed to record every keystroke made on the infected computer and then send the sensitive information they recorded (such as account numbers and passwords) to criminals.

Mobile Malware

In addition to computers, malware also can infect mobile phones, portable digital media players, printers, and other devices that contain computing hardware and software. In fact, some GPS devices and portable digital media players (including some video iPods) shipped recently had malware already installed on them. Mobile phones with Bluetooth capabilities in particular are vulnerable since they can be infected via a Bluetooth connection just by being within range (about 30 feet) of a carrier. Some *mobile malware* is designed to crash the phone's operating system; others are designed to be a nuisance by changing icons or otherwise making the device more difficult to use. Still others are money-oriented, such as malware designed to steal credit card data located on the mobile phone. According to IBM, more malware directed to mobile phones and other devices—such as cars—that contain embedded computers is expected in the near future as those devices continue to incorporate more software components and, consequently, become more vulnerable to malware. However, the lack of a universal operating system for mobile devices (compared with the relatively few operating systems used with personal computers) at the present time limits the amount of mobile malware currently in circulation.

Denial of Service (DoS) Attacks

A **denial of service (DoS) attack** is an act of sabotage that attempts to flood a network server or Web server with so many requests for action that it shuts down or simply cannot handle legitimate requests any longer, causing legitimate users to be denied service. For example, a hacker might set up one or more computers to *ping* (contact) a server continually with a request to send a responding ping back to a false return address, or to request nonexistent information continually. If enough useless traffic is generated, the server has no resources left to deal with legitimate requests (see Figure 4-16). An emerging trend is DoS attacks aimed at mobile wireless networks. These attacks typically involve repeatedly establishing and releasing connections with the goal of overloading the network to disrupt service.

ONLINE VIDEO

Go to the Chapter 4 page at **www.cengage.com/ computerconcepts/np/uccs4** to watch the "Demonstration of a Rogue Antivirus Program Spread via Skype" video clip.

FURTHER EXPLORATION

Go to the Chapter 4 page at **www.cengage.com/ computerconcepts/np/uccs4** for links to information about malware and malware detection.

1. Hacker's computer sends several simultaneous requests; each request asks to establish a connection to the server but supplies false return information. In a distributed DoS attack, multiple computers send multiple requests at one time.

Hello? I'd like some info...

Hello? I'd like some info...

I'm busy, I can't help you right now.

LEGITIMATE COMPUTER

2. The server tries to respond to each request but can't locate the computer because false return information was provided. The server waits for a short period of time before closing the connection, which ties up the server and keeps others from connecting.

I can't find you, I'll wait and try again...

HACKER'S COMPUTER

3. The hacker's computer continues to send new requests, so as a connection is closed by the server, a new request is waiting. This cycle continues, which ties up the server indefinitely.

Hello? I'd like some info...

4. The server becomes so overwhelmed that legitimate requests cannot get through and, eventually, the server usually crashes.

WEB SERVER

FIGURE 4-16
How a denial of service (DoS) attack might work.

DoS attacks today are often directed toward popular sites (for example, Twitter was recently shut down for two hours due to a DoS attack) and typically are carried out via multiple computers (referred to as a *distributed denial of service attack* or *DDoS attack*). DDoS attacks are typically performed by botnets created by hackers; the computers in the botnet participate in the attacks without the owners' knowledge. Because home computers are increasingly using direct Internet connections but tend to be less protected than school and business computers, hackers are increasingly targeting home computers for botnets used in DDoS attacks and other forms of computer sabotage.

Denial of service attacks can be very costly in terms of business lost (such as when an e-commerce site is shut down), as well as the time and expense required to bring the site back online. Networks that use VoIP are particularly vulnerable to DoS attacks since the real-time nature of VoIP calls means their quality is immediately affected when a DoS attack slows down the network.

Data, Program, or Web Site Alteration

Another type of computer sabotage occurs when a hacker breaches a computer system in order to delete data, change data, modify programs, or otherwise alter the data and programs located there. For example, a student might try to hack into the school database to change his or her grade; a hacker might change a program located on a company server in order to steal money or information; or a disgruntled or former employee might perform a vengeful act, such as altering programs so they work incorrectly, deleting customer records or other critical data, or randomly changing data in a company's database. Like other forms of computer sabotage, data and program alteration is illegal.

Data on Web sites can also be altered by hackers. For instance, individuals sometimes hack into and alter other people's social networking accounts. In early 2009, for instance, the Twitter accounts of over 30 high-profile individuals (including then President-elect Obama) were accessed by an unauthorized individual who sent out fake (and sometimes embarrassing) tweets posing as those individuals. It is also becoming more common for hackers to compromise legitimate Web sites and then use those sites to perform malware attacks. Typically, a hacker alters a legitimate site to display an official-looking message that informs the user that a particular software program must be downloaded, or the hacker posts a rogue banner ad on a legitimate site that redirects the user to a malware site instead of the site for the product featured in the banner ad. According to a report released this year by security company Websense, more than half of the Web sites classified as malicious are actually legitimate Web sites that have been compromised.

PROTECTING AGAINST COMPUTER SABOTAGE

One of the most important protections against computer sabotage is using *security software*, and ensuring that it is kept current.

Security Software

To protect against becoming infected with a computer virus or other type of malware, all computers and other devices used to access the Internet or a company network in both homes and offices should have **security software** installed. Security software typically includes a variety of security features, including a firewall, protection against spyware and bots, and protection against some types of *online fraud*, discussed shortly. One of the most important components is **antivirus software**, which protects against computer viruses and other types of malware.

Antivirus software typically runs continuously whenever the computer is on to perform real-time monitoring of the computer and incoming e-mail messages, instant messages, Web page content, and downloaded files, in order to prevent malicious software from executing. Many antivirus programs also automatically scan any devices as soon as they are connected to a USB port in order to guard against infections from a USB flash drive, a portable digital media player, or other USB device. Antivirus software helps prevent malware from being installed on your computer since it deletes or *quarantines* (safely isolates) any suspicious content (such as e-mail attachments or downloaded files) as they arrive; regular full system scans can detect and remove any viruses or worms that find their way onto your computer (see Figure 4-17).

According to McAfee Security, a manufacturer of antivirus and security software, there are millions of threats in existence today, and research firm IDC estimates that 450 new viruses and other types of malware are released each day. Consequently, it is vital to keep your antivirus program up to date. Antivirus software is usually set up to download new *virus definitions* automatically from its associated Web site on a regular basis, as often as several times per day—a very important precaution. Most fee-based antivirus programs come with a year of access to free updates; users should purchase additional years after that to continue to be protected or they should switch to a free antivirus program, such as *AVG Free*, that can be updated regularly at no cost. Schools and businesses should also ensure

FIGURE 4-17
Security software. Most security software is set up to monitor your system on a continual basis, removing threats as they are discovered.

ANTIVIRUS SOFTWARE

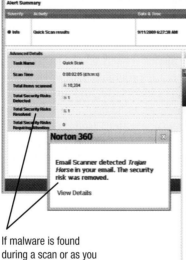

Both programs typically monitor your system on a continual basis, as well as periodically scanning your entire computer.

If malware is found during a scan or as you use your computer, the software removes it.

If spyware is found, the software recommends quarantining or removing it.

ANTISPYWARE SOFTWARE

>**Security software.** Software, typically a suite of programs, used to protect your computer against a variety of threats. >**Antivirus software.** Software used to detect and eliminate computer viruses and other types of malware.

VIRUS PREVENTION STRATEGIES

Use antivirus software to check incoming e-mail messages and files, and download updated virus definitions on a regular basis.

Limit the sharing of flash memory cards, USB flash drives, and other removable storage media with others.

Only download files from reputable sites.

Only open e-mail attachments that come from people you know and that do not have an executable file extension (such as .exe, .com, .bat, or .vbs); double-check with the sender before opening an unexpected, but seemingly legitimate, attachment.

For any downloaded file you are unsure of, upload it to a Web site (such as VirusTotal.com) that tests files for viruses before you open them.

Keep the preview window of your e-mail program closed so you will not view messages until you determine that they are safe to view.

Regularly download and install the latest security patches available for your operating system, browser, and e-mail programs.

Avoid downloading files from P2P sites.

FIGURE 4-18

Sensible precautions can help protect against computer virus infections.

TIP

If you suspect you are infected with a malware program that your antivirus software cannot detect or remove, try a software program that specializes in removing hard-to-remove malware, such as the free *MalwareBytes Anti-Malware* program.

that students and employees connecting to the campus or company network with personal computers are using up-to-date antivirus software so they will not infect the network with malware inadvertently. Some colleges now require new students to go through a *quarantine process*, in which students are not granted access to the college network until they complete a security process that checks their computers for security threats, updates their operating systems, and installs antivirus software. Some additional virus-prevention strategies are listed in Figure 4-18.

Many ISPs today also offer some malware protection to their subscribers. Typically, ISP antivirus software scans all incoming e-mail messages at the mail server level to filter out messages containing a virus. If a message containing a virus is detected, it is usually deleted and the recipient is notified that the message contained a virus and was deleted. Another type of program, which is currently in development and which is designed to protect against viruses sent via e-mail, is an *e-mail authentication system*. E-mail authentication systems are designed to tell recipients exactly where e-mail messages come from to help them determine which messages are safe to open and which might contain malware. For a look at an emerging tool in the fight against malware—*people-driven security* and *whitelisting*—see the Inside the Industry box.

Other Security Precautions

Individuals and businesses can protect against some types of computer sabotage (such as program, data, or Web site alteration) by controlling access to their computers and networks, as discussed earlier in this chapter. Intrusion protection systems can help businesses detect and protect against denial of service (DoS) attacks. For extra protection against spyware, rogue antivirus programs, and other specialized malware, specialized security programs (such as the antispyware program shown in Figure 4-17 for detecting and removing spyware) can be used. In addition, most Web browsers have security settings that can be used to help prevent programs from being installed on a computer without the user's permission, such as prompting the user for permission whenever a download is initiated. Enabling these security settings is a wise additional precaution.

ONLINE THEFT, ONLINE FRAUD, AND OTHER DOT CONS

A booming area of computer crime involves online fraud, theft, scams, and related activities designed to steal money or other resources from individuals or businesses—these are collectively referred to as **dot cons**. According to a report by the *Internet Crime Complaint Center (IC3)*, a joint venture of the FBI and the National White Collar Crime Center that receives cybercrime complaints from consumers and reports them to the appropriate law enforcement agency, online crime hit a record high in 2008. In all, more than

> **Dot con.** A fraud or scam carried out through the Internet.

INSIDE THE INDUSTRY

New Tools to Fight Malware

People-driven security refers to using the judgments of individuals to identify new threats. For instance, Google has a page where users can submit URLs of Web sites they believe are malicious (see the accompanying illustration), and antivirus companies like Symantec and McAfee rely on malware samples that they receive from users to help keep their virus lists and programs current. Many security experts believe that user involvement is crucial today in the fight against malware and phishing. People-driven security is also being used today to identify spammers.

The idea behind *whitelisting* is the opposite of blocking potentially dangerous applications from running on your computer; with whitelisting, only known good programs are allowed to run. While some users believe that whitelisting is annoying (because trying to run a program not on the whitelist requires responding to a pop-up alert message), many security companies believe that keeping track of known good software might be easier than trying to keep track of all the malware in existence today. Both Symantec and Kaspersky Lab are advocates of whitelisting and Kaspersky recently integrated the database

of Bit9, a company that maintains a list of over six billion known good applications, into its antivirus programs. While antivirus companies are currently working on maintaining their own whitelists to use in conjunction with their products, some view a central whitelist maintained by a neutral group and available to everyone as the most efficient solution for consumers.

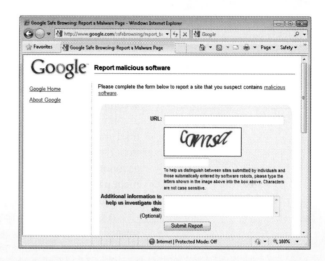

275,000 reports were received with an average individual loss of $931. Some of the most common types of dot cons are discussed next.

Theft of Data, Information, and Other Resources

Data theft or *information theft* is the theft of data or information located on or being sent from a computer. It can be committed by stealing an actual computer (as discussed in more detail in Chapter 5); it can also take place over the Internet or a network by an individual gaining unauthorized access to that data by hacking into the computer or by intercepting the data in transit. Common types of data and information stolen via the Internet or another network include customer data (such as Web site passwords or credit card information) and proprietary corporate information. Over the past years, there have been numerous examples of hackers stealing information from company databases. For instance, one hacker obtained the contact information of more than 1.6 million users of the Monster.com online job search service; another breached the systems of the Heartland credit and debit card processor and several retail stores, stealing more than 130 million credit and debit card numbers, according to the charges filed against the hacker. Stolen consumer data is often used in fraudulent activities, such as *identity theft*, as discussed shortly.

Money is another resource that can be stolen via a computer. Company insiders sometimes steal money by altering company programs to transfer small amounts of money—for example, a few cents' worth of bank account interest—from a very large number of transactions to an account controlled by the thieves. This type of crime is sometimes called *salami shaving*. Victims of salami-shaving schemes generally are unaware that their funds have been accessed because the amount taken from each individual is very small. However, added together, the amounts can be substantial. Another example of monetary theft performed via computers involves hackers electronically transferring money illegally from online bank accounts, traditional bank accounts, credit card accounts, or accounts at online payment services (such as PayPal).

Identity Theft, Phishing, and Pharming

A growing dot con trend is obtaining enough information about an individual to perform fraudulent financial transactions. Often, this is carried out in conjunction with *identity theft*; techniques frequently used to obtain the necessary personal information to commit identity theft are *phishing*, *spear phishing*, and *pharming*. These topics are discussed next.

Identity Theft

Identity theft occurs when someone obtains enough information about a person to be able to masquerade as that person—usually to buy products or services in that person's name (see Figure 4-19). Typically, identity theft begins with obtaining a person's name, address, and Social Security number, often from a discarded or stolen document (such as a preapproved credit card application that was sent in the mail), from information obtained via the Internet (such as from a résumé posted online), or from information located on a computer (such as on a stolen computer or hacked server, or information sent from a computer via a computer virus or spyware program installed on that computer). The thief may then order a copy of the individual's birth certificate, obtain a "replacement" driver's license, make purchases and charge them to the victim, and/or open credit or bank accounts in the victim's name. Identity theft is illegal and, in 1998, the federal government passed the *Identity Theft and Assumption Deterrence Act*, which made identity theft a federal crime.

Assuming the thief requests a change of address for these new accounts after they are opened, it may take quite some time—often until a company or collections agency contacts the victim about overdue bills—for the victim to become aware that his or her identity has been stolen. Although identity theft often takes place via a computer today, information used in identity theft can also be gathered from trash dumpsters, mailboxes, and other locations. Other commonly used techniques are *skimming* and *social engineering*. Skimming involves stealing credit card or debit card numbers by using an illegal device attached to an ATM machine or credit card reader that reads and stores the card numbers to be retrieved by the thief

FIGURE 4-19
How identity theft works.

1. The thief obtains information about an individual from discarded mail, employee records, credit card transactions, Web server files, or some other method.

2. The thief uses the information to make purchases, open new credit card accounts, and more in the victim's name. Often, the thief changes the address on the account to delay the victim's discovery of the theft.

3. The victim usually finds out by being denied credit or by being contacted about overdue bills generated by the thief. Clearing one's name after identity theft is time-consuming and can be very difficult and frustrating for the victim.

> **Identity theft.** Using someone else's identity to purchase goods or services, obtain new credit cards or bank loans, or otherwise illegally masquerade as that individual.

at a later time. Social engineering involves pretending—typically via phone or e-mail—to be a bank officer, potential employer, or other trusted individual in order to get the potential victim to supply personal information. One recent social engineering scheme placed phony parking tickets on cars instructing the owners to go to a particular Web site; going to that site installed software on the users' computers to capture their keystrokes.

Unfortunately, identity theft is a very real danger to individuals today. According to the Federal Trade Commission (FTC), millions of Americans have their identity stolen each year. Identity theft can be extremely distressing for victims, can take years to straighten out, and can be very expensive. Some identity theft victims, such as Michelle Brown, believe that they will always be dealing with their "alter reality" to some extent. For a year and a half, an identity thief used Brown's identity to obtain over $50,000 in goods and services, to rent properties—even to engage in drug trafficking. Although the culprit was eventually arrested and convicted for other criminal acts, she continued to use Brown's identity and was even booked into jail using Brown's stolen identity. As a final insult after the culprit was in prison, U.S. customs agents detained the real Michelle Brown when she was returning from a trip to Mexico because of the criminal record of the identity thief. Brown states that she has not traveled out of the country since, fearing an

ASK THE EXPERT

 Marian Merritt, Internet Safety Advocate, Symantec Corporation

What is the single most important thing computer users should do to protect themselves from online threats?

The single most important step to protect computer users from online threats is to make sure their Internet security solution is current and up to date. There are several all-in-one security solutions available, such as Symantec's Norton 360, which combine PC security, antiphishing capabilities, backup, and tuneup technologies.

It's also pivotal to maintain a healthy wariness when receiving online communications. Do not click on links in suspicious e-mails or instant messages (IMs). These links will often direct you to sites that will ask you to reveal passwords, PINs, or other confidential data. Genuine organizations or institutions do not send such e-mails, nor do they ask for confidential data (like your Social Security number) for ordinary business transactions. If you're unsure whether or not an e-mail is legitimate, type the URL directly in your browser or call the institution to confirm they sent you that e-mail. Finally, do not open attachments in e-mails of questionable origin, since they may contain viruses.

arrest or some other serious problem resulting from the theft of her identity, and estimates she has spent over 500 hours trying to correct all the problems related to the identity theft.

Phishing and Spear Phishing

Phishing (pronounced "fishing") is the use of a *spoofed* e-mail message (an e-mail appearing to come from eBay, PayPal, Bank of America, or another well-known legitimate organization, but is actually sent from a phisher) to trick the recipient into revealing sensitive personal information (such as Web site logon information or credit card numbers). Once obtained, this information is used in identity theft and other fraudulent activities. A phishing e-mail typically looks legitimate and it contains links in the e-mail that appear to go to the Web site of the legitimate business, but these links go to the phisher's Web site that is set up to look like the legitimate site instead—an act called *Web site spoofing*. Phishing e-mails are typically sent to a wide group of individuals and usually include an urgent message stating that the individual's credit card or account information needs to be updated and instructing the recipient of the e-mail to click the link provided in the e-mail in order

>**Phishing.** The use of spoofed e-mail messages to gain credit card numbers and other personal data to be used for fraudulent purposes.

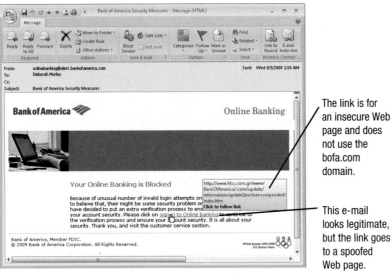

The link is for an insecure Web page and does not use the bofa.com domain.

This e-mail looks legitimate, but the link goes to a spoofed Web page.

FIGURE 4-20

Phishing. Phishing schemes use legitimate-looking e-mails to trick users into providing private information.

to keep the account active (see Figure 4-20). If the victim clicks the link and supplies the requested information via the spoofed site, the criminal gains access to all information provided by the victim, such as account numbers, credit card numbers, and Web site passwords. Phishing attempts can occur today via IM, text messages (called *smishing*), fake messages sent via eBay or MySpace, Twitter tweets, and pop-up security alert windows, in addition to via e-mail. Phishers also frequently utilize spyware; typically, clicking the link in the phishing e-mail installs the spyware on the victim's computer, and it will remain there (transmitting passwords and other sensitive data to a phisher) until it is detected and removed.

To fool victims into using the spoofed Web site, phishing e-mails and the spoofed Web sites often look legitimate. To accomplish this, phishers typically use copies of the spoofed organization's logo and other Web site content from the legitimate Web site. For spoofed banking Web pages and other pages where the victim would expect to see a secure Web page, some criminals use a secure connection between the victim and the criminal's server so the Web page looks secure with an *https:* in the Address bar. The domain name of the legitimate company (such as *ebay* for an eBay phishing page) is also often used as part of the URL of the phishing link (such as a URL starting with the text *ebay* even though the URL's domain is not ebay.com) to make it appear more legitimate. Other phishing schemes use a technique called *typosquatting*, which is setting up spoofed Web sites with addresses slightly different from legitimate sites. For example, a spoofed Web site using the URL www.amazom.com might be used to catch shoppers intending to reach the Amazon.com Web site located at www.amazon.com in hopes that customers making this error when typing the URL will not notice it and will supply logon information via the spoofed site when they arrive at it.

Another recent trend is the use of more targeted, personalized phishing schemes, known as **spear phishing**. Spear phishing e-mails are directly targeted to a specific individual and typically appear to come from an organization or person that the targeted individual has an association with. They also often include personalized information (such as the potential victim's name) to make the spear phishing e-mails seem even more legitimate. Several recent spear phishing attacks were targeted at users of social networking sites like MySpace since the personal information (name, age, hobbies, friends list, favorite music, and so forth) typically included on these sites makes them a good resource for spear phishers. Some of these attacks used spoofed logon pages for the social networking sites to obtain an individual's logon information and password. Since many individuals use the same logon information for a variety of sites, once a scammer has a valid username/password combination, he or she can try it on a variety of common e-commerce sites, such as shopping sites, online banking sites, and online payment services like PayPal. If the scammer is able to log on successfully to one of these sites, he or she can buy products, transfer money, and perform other types of financial transactions posing as the victim. Another recent tactic is to use the victim's social networking site logon information to log on to the victim's account and then post comments or send messages containing phishing links (posing as the victim) to the victim's friends, who are much more likely to click on the links because they appear to come from a friend.

> **Spear phishing.** A personalized phishing scheme targeted at an individual.

Spear phishers also target employees of selected organizations by posing as someone within the company, such as a human resources or technical support employee. These spear phishing e-mails often request confidential information (such as logon IDs and passwords) or direct the employee to click a link to supposedly reset his or her password. The goal for corporate spear phishing attacks is usually to steal intellectual property, such as software source code, design documents, or schematics. It can also be used to steal money. For instance, in one recent case, a grocery store received fraudulent e-mails that appeared to come from two approved suppliers. The e-mails instructed the grocery store chain to send future payments to new bank accounts listed in the e-mail—the grocery store chain deposited more than $10 million into two fraudulent bank accounts before the scam was discovered.

Pharming and Drive-By Pharming

Pharming is another type of scam that uses spoofing—specifically spoofed domain names used to obtain personal information for use in fraudulent activities. With pharming, the criminal reroutes traffic intended for a commonly used Web site to a spoofed Web site set up by the pharmer. Sometimes pharming takes place via malicious code sent to a computer via an e-mail message or other distribution method. More often, however, it takes place via changes made to a *DNS server*—a computer that translates URLs into the appropriate IP addresses needed to display the Web page corresponding to a URL. This type of pharming can take place at one of the 13 *root DNS servers* (the DNS servers used in conjunction with the Internet), but it more often takes place at a *company DNS server* (the DNS server for that company used to route Web page requests received via company Web site URLs to the appropriate company server). After hacking into a company DNS server (typically for a company with a commonly used Web site), the pharmer changes the IP addresses used in conjunction with a particular company URL (called *DNS poisoning*) so any Web page requests made via the legitimate company URL is routed (via the company's poisoned DNS server) to a phony spoofed Web page located on the pharmer's Web server. So, even though a user types the proper URL to display the legitimate company Web page in his or her browser, the spoofed page is displayed instead.

Since spoofed sites are set up to look like the legitimate sites, the user typically does not notice any difference, and any information sent via that site is captured by the pharmer. To avoid suspicion, some pharming schemes capture the user's account name and password as it is entered the first time on the spoofed site, and then display a password error message. The spoofed site then redirects the user back to the legitimate site where he or she is able to log on to the legitimate site, leaving the user to think that he or she must have just mistyped the password the first time. But, by then, the pharmer has already captured the victim's username and password and can use that information to gain access to the victim's account.

A recent variation of pharming is *drive-by pharming*. The goal is still to redirect victims to spoofed sites; however, the pharmer accomplishes this by changing the victim's designated DNS server (which is specified in the victim's router settings) to the pharmer's DNS server in order to direct the victim to spoofed versions of legitimate Web sites when the victim enters the URLs for those sites. Typically, the pharmer uses malicious JavaScript code placed on a Web page to changes the victim's DNS settings to use the pharmer's DNS server; this change can only occur on a router in which the default administrator password was not changed.

Online Auction Fraud

Online auction fraud (sometimes called *Internet auction fraud*) occurs when an online auction buyer pays for merchandise that is never delivered, or that is delivered but it is

---

>**Pharming.** The use of spoofed domain names to obtain personal information to be used in fraudulent activities. >**Online auction fraud.** When an item purchased through an online auction is never delivered after payment, or the item is not as specified by the seller.

not as represented. Online auction fraud is an increasing risk for online auction bidders. According to the Internet Crime Complaint Center (IC3), online auction fraud accounted for about 25% of all reported online fraud cases in 2008 for an average loss of around $600. Like other types of fraud, online auction fraud is illegal, but similar to many types of Internet cons, prosecution is difficult for online auction fraud because multiple jurisdictions are usually involved. Although most online auction sites have policies that suspend sellers with a certain number of complaints lodged against them, it is very easy for those sellers to come back using a new e-mail address and identity.

Other Internet Scams

There is a wide range of other scams that can occur via Web sites or unsolicited e-mails. The anonymity of the Internet makes it very easy for con artists to appear to be almost anyone they want to be, including a charitable organization or a reputable-looking business. Common types of scams include loan scams, work-at-home cons, pyramid schemes, bogus credit card offers and prize promotions, and fraudulent business opportunities and franchises. These offers typically try to sell potential victims nonexistent services or worthless information, or they try to convince potential victims to voluntarily supply their credit card details and other personal information, which are then used for fraudulent purposes. Some scammers use hacking as a means of obtaining a list of e-mail addresses for potential targets for a scam (such as stealing contact information from sites related to investing for a stock market scam) to increase the odds of a potential victim falling for the scam. A recent trend involves scammers who hack into Web mail and social networking accounts and send messages (posing as the victim) to the victim's entire contact list requesting money or urging recipients to buy specific products.

One ongoing Internet scam is the *Nigerian letter fraud* scheme. This scheme involves an e-mail message that appears to come from the Nigerian government and that promises the potential victim a share of a substantial amount of money in exchange for the use of the victim's bank account. Supposedly the victim's bank account information is needed to facilitate a wire transfer (but the victim's account is emptied instead) and/or up-front cash is needed to pay for nonexistent fees (that is kept by the con artist with nothing given in return). The theme of these scams often changes to fit current events, such as the war in Iraq or the Katrina hurricane. However, the scams always involve a so-called fortune that is inaccessible to the con artist without the potential victims' help (see Figure 4-21) and the victims always lose money when they pay fees or provide bank account information in the hope of sharing in the wealth. Despite the fact that this con is well known, people are still falling for it and with heavy losses—at $1,650, the Nigerian letter fraud scam had the third highest average dollar loss per individual for 2008 complaints, according to a report issued by the Internet Crime Complaint Center (IC3).

FIGURE 4-21
A Nigerian letter fraud e-mail.

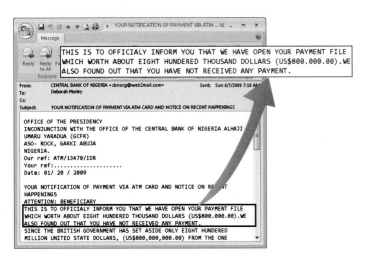

Other schemes involve con artists who solicit donations after disasters and other tragic events, but who keep the donations instead of giving them to any charitable organization. Another common scam involves setting up a pornographic site that requires a valid credit card, supposedly to prove that the visitor is of the required age (such as over 18), but which is then used for credit card fraud. A relatively new type of scam involves posting fake job listings on job search sites to elicit personal information (such as Social Security numbers) from job seekers. An even more recent twist is to hire individuals through online job sites for seemingly legitimate positions involving money handling (such as bookkeeping or accounting positions), but then use those individuals—often without their knowledge—as illegitimate go-betweens to facilitate Internet auction scams and other monetary scams.

PROTECTING AGAINST ONLINE THEFT, ONLINE FRAUD, AND OTHER DOT CONS

In a nutshell, the best protection against many dot cons is protecting your identity; that is, protecting any identifying information about you that could be used in fraudulent activities. There are also specific precautions that can help protect against online theft, identity theft, online auction fraud, and other types of dot cons, as discussed next. With any dot con, it is important to act quickly if you think you have been a victim. For instance, you should work with your local law enforcement agency, credit card companies, and the three major consumer credit bureaus (*Equifax*, *Experian*, and *TransUnion*) to close any accessed or fraudulent accounts, place fraud alerts on your credit report, and take other actions to prevent additional fraudulent activity while the fraud is being investigated.

Arrests and prosecutions by law enforcement agencies may also help cut down on cybercrimes. Prosecution of online scammers has been increasing and sentences are not light. For instance, one man—the first person convicted by a jury under the *CAN-SPAM Act of 2003* for operating a phishing scheme—was sentenced in mid-2007 to 70 months in federal prison and ordered to pay over one million dollars to his victims.

Protecting Against Data and Information Theft

Businesses and individuals can both help to prevent some types of data and information theft. For instance, businesses should use good security measures to protect the data stored on their computers. Individuals should be vigilant about protecting their private information by sending sensitive information via secure Web servers only and not disclosing personal information—especially a Social Security number or a mother's maiden name—unless it is absolutely necessary and they know how the information will be used and that it will not be shared with others. In addition, individuals should never give out sensitive personal information to anyone who requests it over the phone or by e-mail—businesses that legitimately need bank account information, passwords, or credit card numbers will not request that information via phone or e-mail. Encrypting computers and other hardware containing sensitive information, so it will not be readable if the hardware is lost or stolen, is another important precaution.

Protecting Against Identity Theft, Phishing, and Pharming

Some of the precautions used for other types of online theft (such as being careful to disclose your personal information only when it is necessary and only via secure Web pages) can help reduce the chance that identity theft will happen to you. So can using security software (and keeping it up to date) to guard against computer viruses, spyware, and other malware that can be used to send information from your computer or about your activities (the Web site passwords that you type, for example) to a criminal. In addition, to prevent someone from using the preapproved credit card offers and other documents containing personal information that frequently arrive in the mail, shred them before throwing them in the trash. To prevent the theft of outgoing mail containing sensitive information, don't place it in your mailbox—mail it at the post office or in a USPS drop box.

To avoid phishing schemes, never click a link in an e-mail message to go to a secure Web site—always type the URL for that site in your browser (not necessarily the URL shown in the e-mail message) instead. Phishing e-mails typically sound urgent and often contain spelling and grammatical errors—see Figure 4-22 for some tips to help you recognize phishing e-mails. Remember that

 FIGURE 4-22
Tips for identifying phishing e-mail messages.

A PHISHING E-MAIL OFTEN . . .

Tries to scare you into responding by sounding urgent, including a warning that your account will be cancelled if you do not respond, or telling you that you have been a victim of fraud.

Asks you to provide personal information, such as your bank account number, an account password, credit card number, PIN number, mother's maiden name, or Social Security number.

Contains links that do not go where the link text says it will go (point to a hyperlink in the e-mail message to view the URL for that link).

Uses legitimate logos from the company the phisher is posing as.

Appears to come from a known organization, but one you may not have an association with.

Appears to be text or text and images but is actually a single image; it has been created that way to avoid being caught in a spam filter (a program that sorts e-mail based on legitimate e-mail and suspected spam) since spam filters cannot read text that is part of an image in an e-mail message.

Contains spelling or grammatical errors.

TIPS FOR AVOIDING IDENTITY THEFT

Protect your Social Security number—give it out only when necessary.

Be careful with your physical mail and trash—shred all documents containing sensitive data.

Secure your computer—update your operating system and use up-to-date security (antivirus, antispyware, firewall, etc.) software.

Be cautious—never click on a link in an e-mail message or respond to a too-good-to-be-true offer.

Use strong passwords for your computer and online accounts.

Verify sources before sharing sensitive information—never respond to e-mail or phone requests for sensitive information.

Be vigilant while on the go—safeguard your wallet, mobile phone, and portable computer.

Watch your bills and monitor your credit reports—react immediately if you suspect fraudulent activity.

Use security software or browser features that warn you if you try to view a known phishing site.

FIGURE 4-23
Tips to reduce your risk of identity theft.

TIP

You can order your free credit reports online quickly and easily via Web sites like *AnnualCreditReport.com*.

FIGURE 4-24
Unsafe Web site alerts.

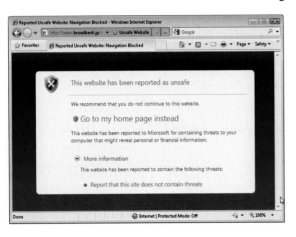

spear phishing schemes may include personalized information (such as your name)—do not let that fool you into thinking the phishing e-mail is legitimate. If you think an unsolicited e-mail message requesting information from you may be legitimate (for instance, if the credit card you use to make an automatic payment for an ongoing service is about to expire and you receive an e-mail message asking you to update your credit card information), type the URL for that site in your browser to load the legitimate site and then update your account information. To prevent a drive-by pharming attack, all businesses and individuals should change the administrator password for routers, access points, and other networking hardware from the default password to a strong password.

Keeping a close eye on your credit card bills and credit history is also important to make sure you catch any fraudulent charges or accounts opened by an identity thief as soon as possible. Make sure your bills come in every month (some thieves will change your mailing address to delay detection), and read credit card statements carefully to look for unauthorized charges. Be sure to follow up on any calls you get from creditors, instead of assuming it is just a mistake. Most security experts also recommend ordering a full credit history on yourself a few times a year to check for accounts listed in your name that you did not open and any other problems. The *Fair and Accurate Credit Transactions Act (FACTA)* enables all Americans to get a free copy of their credit report, upon request, each year from the three major consumer credit bureaus. Ideally, you should request a report from one of these bureaus every four months to monitor your credit on a regular basis. These reports contain information about inquiries related to new accounts requested in your name, as well as any delinquent balances or other negative reports. For another tool that you can use to help detect identity theft—*online financial alerts*—see the Technology and You box. You can also use browser-based *antiphishing* tools and *digital certificates* to help guard against identity theft and the phishing and pharming schemes used in conjunction with identity theft, as discussed next. Some additional tips for minimizing your risk of identity theft are listed in Figure 4-23.

Antiphishing Tools

Antiphishing tools are built into many e-mail programs and Web browsers to help notify users of possible phishing Web sites. For instance, some e-mail programs will disable links in e-mail messages identified as questionable, unless the user overrides it; many recent browsers warn users when a Web page associated with a possible phishing URL is requested (see Figure 4-24); and antiphishing capabilities are included in many recent security suites.

In addition, some secure Web sites are adding additional layers in security to protect against identity thieves. For example, some online banking sites analyze users' habits to look for patterns that vary from the norm, such as accessing accounts online at an hour unusual for that individual or a higher than normal level of online purchases. If a bank suspects the account may be compromised, it contacts the owner for verification. Bank of America and some other financial institutions have also added an additional step in their logon process—displaying an image or word preselected by the user and stored on the bank's server—to prove to the user that the site being viewed is the legitimate (not a phishing) site. In addition, if the system does not recognize the

TECHNOLOGY AND YOU

Online Financial Alerts

Want to know as soon as possible when a transaction that might be fraudulent is charged to your credit card? Well, *online financial alerts* might be the answer.

Many online banking services today allow users to set up e-mail alerts for credit card activity over a certain amount, low balances, and so forth. For individuals wishing to monitor multiple accounts, however, online money management aggregator services (such as *Mint.com*) make it easier. Once you have set up a free Mint.com account with your financial accounts (including credit cards and checking, savings, and PayPal accounts) and their respective passwords, you can see the status of all your accounts through the Mint.com interface. You can also set up alerts for any of the accounts based on your desired criteria, such as any transaction over a specified amount (see the accompanying illustration). The alerts are sent to you via e-mail or text message, depending on your preference, to help notify you as soon as possible if a suspicious activity occurs. And timeliness is of the essence, because the sooner identity theft is discovered, the less time the thief has to make additional fraudulent transactions. For security purposes, Mint.com doesn't store online banking usernames and passwords;

instead, a secure online financial services provider is used to connect Mint.com to the appropriate financial institutions as needed to update your activity. In addition, the Mint.com Web site cannot be used to move money out of or between financial accounts—it can be used only to view information.

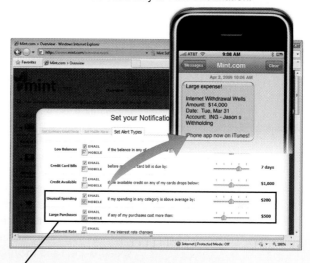

Unusual Spending and Large Purchases alerts can help you detect fraudulent charges to your financial accounts.

computer that the user is using to log on to the system, the user is required to go through an authentication process (typically by correctly answering cognitive authentication questions) before being allowed to access the system via that computer. The questions used are specifically designed to be "out of wallet" questions—easy for the individual to answer but difficult for hackers to guess the correct answer or find in a stolen wallet. Bank of America is also one bank offering customers the option of adding the use of one-time passwords (autogenerated by a security token like the one shown in Figure 4-5 or sent via text message to the individual's mobile phone) to their online banking logon procedure.

Digital Certificates and Digital Signatures

The purpose of a **digital certificate** is to authenticate the identity of an individual or organization. Digital certificates are granted by Certificate Authorities and typically contain the name of the person, organization, or Web site being certified along with a certificate serial number and an expiration date. Digital certificates also include a public/private key pair. In addition to being used by the certificate holder to encrypt files and e-mail messages (as discussed earlier in this chapter), these keys and the digital certificate are used with secure Web pages to guarantee the Web pages are secure and actually belong to the stated organization (so users can know for sure who their credit card number or other sensitive data is really being sent to, in order to protect against some online scams).

> **Digital certificate.** A group of electronic data that can be used to verify the identity of a person or organization; includes a key pair that can be used for encryption and digital signatures.

Red indicates a problem with the site's digital certificate.

Green indicates a valid EV SSL digital certificate.

Click to view certificate information.

⚓ **FIGURE 4-25**

EV SSL certificates.
The browser's Address bar reflects information about the digital certificate being used.

✓ **TIP**

According to the Electronic Signatures in Global and National Commerce Act, any form of electronic signature is as legally binding as a handwritten signature.

Secure Web sites can obtain either a normal *SSL digital certificate* or a newer *Extended Validation (EV) SSL digital certificate* that was developed to provide consumers with a higher level of trust while online. While both digital certificates require an application process, the verification process to obtain an EV SSL digital certificate is more thorough, requiring the use of reputable third-party sources to verify that the company has the right to use the Web site domain name in question and that the business requesting the certificate is authorized to do so. With both types of certificates, individuals can click the secure Web page icon in their browser window to view that site's digital certificate in order to ensure that the certificate is valid and issued to the company associated with the Web site being viewed. If an EV SSL certificate is used, however, additional information is displayed when the Web site is viewed in an EV-compliant browser, such as recoloring the Address bar green to indicate a site using a valid EV SSL certificate and displaying certificate information in the *Security Status bar* to the right of the Address bar, as shown in Figure 4-25.

The keys included in a digital certificate can also be used to authenticate the identity of a person sending an e-mail message or other document via a **digital signature**. To digitally sign an e-mail message or other document, the sender's private key is used and that key, along with the contents of the document, generates a unique digital signature; consequently, a digital signature is different with each signed document. When a digitally signed document is received, the recipient's computer uses the sender's public key to verify the digital signature. Since the document is signed with the sender's private key (that only the sender should know) and the digital signature will be deemed invalid if even one character of the document is changed after it is signed, digital signatures guarantee that the document was sent by a specific individual and that it was not tampered with after it was signed.

Digital signatures are an important component of the emerging *e-mail authentication systems* (such as the *DomainKeys* system used by Yahoo!, eBay, Google, PayPal, and other companies) that may help prevent some types of online fraud in the future as these systems become more widely used. These systems are designed to authenticate e-mail messages via digital signatures and so can help ISPs block phishing e-mails because messages coming from a participating company must be digitally signed by that company in order to be deemed authentic.

Protecting Against Online Auction Fraud and Other Internet Scams

The best protection against many dot cons is common sense. Be extremely cautious of any unsolicited e-mail messages you receive and realize that if an offer sounds too good to be true, it probably is. You should also be cautious when dealing with individuals online through auctions and other person-to-person activities. Before bidding on an auction item, check out the feedback rating of the seller to see comments written by other auction sellers and buyers. Always pay for auctions and other online purchases using a credit card or an online payment service (such as PayPal) that accepts credit card payments so you can dispute the transaction through your credit card company, if needed. Using an online payment service that bills the charge to your credit card, instead of allowing the seller to charge your credit card, has the extra advantage of keeping your credit card information private.

> **Digital signature.** A unique digital code that can be attached to a file or an e-mail message to verify the identity of the sender and guarantee the file or message has not been changed since it was signed.

In addition, some auction sites and online payment services offer free buyer protection against undelivered items or auction items that are significantly different from the description provided in the auction information. For instance, most eBay purchases paid for via PayPal have at least $200 of buyer protection coverage at no additional cost. For expensive items, consider using an *escrow service*, which allows you to ensure that the merchandise is as specified before your payment is released to the seller.

PERSONAL SAFETY ISSUES

In addition to being expensive and inconvenient, cybercrime can also be physically dangerous. Although most of us may not ordinarily view using the Internet as a potentially dangerous activity, cases of physical harm due to Internet activity do happen. For example, children and teenagers have become the victims of pedophiles who arranged face-to-face meetings by using information gathered via e-mail, message boards, social networking sites, or other online sources. There are also a growing number of incidents in which children are threatened by classmates via e-mail, Web site posts, or text messages. Adults may fall victim to unscrupulous or dangerous individuals who misrepresent themselves online, and the availability of personal information online has made it more difficult for individuals to hide from people who may want to do them harm, such as abused women trying to hide from their abusive husbands. Two of the most common ways individuals are harassed online—*cyberbullying* and *cyberstalking*—are discussed next.

Cyberbullying and Cyberstalking

Children and teenagers bullying other children or teenagers via the Internet—such as through e-mail, a text message, a social networking site, a blog, or other online communications method—is referred to as **cyberbullying**. Unfortunately, cyberbullying is common today—by some estimates, it affects as many as one-half of all U.S. teenagers. Cyberbullying can take place via direct online communication (such as with an e-mail or instant message), as well as via more subtle means. For instance, there have been cases of students posting videos on YouTube of other students being bullied and cases of individuals hacking into a student's MySpace or Facebook account and changing the content on the student's pages to harass that student. In one tragic instance, a 13-year-old girl hanged herself after the mother of one of the girl's classmates arranged to have a MySpace profile created for a nonexistent teenage boy in order to determine what the victim was saying about her daughter, and then cruelly ended the friendship. While the mother was convicted of three misdemeanor charges of unauthorized access to computers in conjunction with the case, her conviction was dismissed in 2009. However, the case prompted many states and schools to look at harassment statutes and bullying policies and resulted in several states implementing new laws or amending existing harassment laws to address cyberbullying.

Repeated threats or other harassment carried out online between adults is referred to as **cyberstalking**. Cyberstalkers sometimes find their victims online; for instance, someone in a discussion group who makes a comment or has a screen name that the cyberstalker does not like, or bloggers who are harassed and threatened with violence or murder because of their blogging activities. Other times, the attack is more personal, such as employers who are stalked online by ex-employees who were fired or otherwise left their position under adverse conditions, and celebrities who are stalked online by fans.

Cyberstalking typically begins with online harassment—such as sending harassing or threatening e-mail messages or unwanted files to the victim, posing as the victim in order to

FURTHER EXPLORATION (Go)

Go to the Chapter 4 page at **www.cengage.com/ computerconcepts/np/uccs4** for links to information about how to prevent and deal with identity theft and online auction fraud.

> **Cyberbullying.** Children or teenagers bullying other children or teenagers via the Internet. > **Cyberstalking.** Repeated threats or harassing behavior between adults carried out via e-mail or another Internet communications method.

sign the victim up for pornographic or otherwise offensive e-mail newsletters, publicizing the victim's home address and telephone number, or hacking into the victim's social networking pages to alter the content. Cyberstalking can also lead to offline stalking and possibly physical harm—in at least one case, it led to the death of the victim. While there are as yet no specific federal laws against cyberstalking, all states have made it illegal (and it is being increasingly prosecuted), and some federal laws do apply if the online actions include computer fraud or another type of computer crime, suggest a threat of personal injury, or involve sending obscene e-mail messages. Many cyberstalkers are not caught, however, due in part to the anonymity of the Internet, which assists cyberstalkers in concealing their true identities.

Online Pornography

A variety of controversial and potentially objectionable material is available on the Internet. Although there have been attempts to ban this type of material from the Internet, they have not been successful. For example, the *Communications Decency Act*, signed into law in 1996—which made it a criminal offense to distribute patently indecent or offensive material online—was ruled unconstitutional in 1997 by the U.S. Supreme Court. However, like its printed counterpart, online pornography involving minors is illegal. Because of the strong link they believe exists between child pornography and child molestation, many experts are very concerned about the amount of child pornography that can be found and distributed via the Internet. They also believe that the Internet makes it easier for sexual predators to act out, such as by striking up "friendships" with children online and convincing these children to meet them in real life. And this can have devastating consequences, as it did for a 13-year-old girl from Connecticut who was strangled to death in 2002 by a 25-year-old man she met originally online and eventually in person. Although the man confessed, he maintains that the strangling was accidental. The man was sentenced in late 2003 to a total of 40 years in prison for state and federal charges relating to the crime.

PROTECTING AGAINST CYBERBULLYING, CYBERSTALKING, AND OTHER PERSONAL SAFETY CONCERNS

The growing increase in attention to cyberbullying and cyberstalking is leading to more efforts to improve safeguards for children. For instance, social networking sites have privacy features that can be used to protect the private information of their members. In addition, numerous states in the U.S. have implemented cyberbullying and cyberstalking laws. While there is no surefire way to protect against cyberbullying, cyberstalking, and other online dangers completely, some common-sense precautions can reduce the chance of a serious personal safety problem occurring due to online activities.

Safety Tips for Adults

It is wise to be cautious and discreet online—especially in online profiles, message boards, and other online locations where individuals communicate with strangers. To protect yourself against cyberstalking and other types of online harassment, use gender-neutral, nonprovocative identifying names, such as *jsmith*, instead of *janesmith* or *iamcute*. Be careful about the types of photos you post of yourself online and do not reveal personal information—such as your real name, address, or telephone number—to people you meet online. In addition, do not respond to any insults or other harassing comments you may receive online. You may also wish to request that your personal information be removed from online directories—especially those associated with your e-mail address or other online identifiers.

Safety Tips for Children and Teens

Most experts agree that the best way to protect children from online dangers is to stay in close touch with them as they explore the Internet. In order for parents to be able to monitor

TIP

Search for yourself using search sites and online telephone books to see what personal information is available about you on the Internet.

TIP

Both adults and children should avoid including personal information on social networking sites that could be used by an online stalker.

their children's online activities, children and teenagers should use a computer in a family room or other public location, instead of their bedroom, and they should be told which activities are allowed, which types of Web sites are off-limits, and why. In addition, it should be made clear that they are never to reveal personal information about themselves online without a parent's permission. They should also be instructed to tell a parent (or teacher if at school) if an individual ever requests personal information or a personal meeting, or threatens or otherwise harasses the child, via any type of online communications medium. Older children should also be cautioned about sending compromising photos of themselves to others. This practice—referred to as *sexting*—is a growing problem. In one recent study, for instance, more than 20% of teens reported sending nude or seminude photos of them-

selves to others. Part of the problem is that many young people don't realize they lose control of photos and other compromising content once that information has been sent to others and, in one case, a teenage girl committed suicide after the nude photos she had sent her boyfriend were sent to other students once the couple broke up. Sexting has also resulted in child pornography charges being filed against teens for sending their own photos to others or having compromising photos of other children on their mobile phones.

NETWORK AND INTERNET SECURITY LEGISLATION

Although new legislation is passed periodically to address new types of computer crimes, it is difficult for the legal system to keep pace with the rate at which technology changes. In addition, there are both domestic and international jurisdictional issues because many computer crimes affect businesses and individuals located in geographic areas other than the one in which the computer criminal is located, and hackers can make it appear that activity is coming from a different location than it really is. Nevertheless, computer crime legislation continues to be proposed and computer crimes are being prosecuted. A list of selected federal laws concerning network and Internet security is shown in Figure 4-26.

FIGURE 4-26
Computer network and Internet security legislation.

DATE	LAW AND DESCRIPTION
2004	**Identity Theft Penalty Enhancement Act** Adds extra years to prison sentences for criminals who use identity theft (including the use of stolen credit card numbers) to commit other crimes, including credit card fraud and terrorism.
2003	**CAN-SPAM Act** Implements regulations for unsolicited e-mail messages.
2003	**Fair and Accurate Credit Transactions Act (FACTA)** Amends the Fair Credit Reporting Act (FCRA) to require, among other things, that the three nationwide consumer reporting agencies (Equifax, Experian, and TransUnion) provide to consumers, upon request, a free copy of their credit report once every 12 months.
2003	**PROTECT Act** Includes provisions to prohibit virtual child pornography.
2003	**Health Insurance Portability and Accountability Act (HIPAA)** Includes a Security Rule that sets minimum security standards to protect health information stored electronically.
2002	**Homeland Security Act** Includes provisions to combat cyberterrorism, including protecting ISPs against lawsuits from customers for revealing private information to law enforcement agencies.
2002	**Sarbanes-Oxley Act** Requires archiving a variety of electronic records and protecting the integrity of corporate financial data.
2001	**USA PATRIOT Act** Grants federal authorities expanded surveillance and intelligence-gathering powers, such as broadening the ability of federal agents to obtain the real identity of Internet users, intercept e-mail and other types of Internet communications, follow online activity of suspects, expand their wiretapping authority, and more.
1998	**Identity Theft and Assumption Deterrence Act of 1998** Makes it a federal crime to knowingly use someone else's means of identification, such as name, Social Security number, or credit card, to commit any unlawful activity.
1997	**No Electronic Theft (NET) Act** Expands computer piracy laws to include distribution of copyrighted materials over the Internet.
1996	**National Information Infrastructure Protection Act** Amends the Computer Fraud and Abuse Act of 1984 to punish information theft crossing state lines and to crack down on network trespassing.
1994	**Computer Abuse Amendments Act** Amends the Computer Fraud and Abuse Act of 1984 to include computer viruses and other harmful code.
1986	**Computer Fraud and Abuse Act of 1986** Amends the 1984 law to include federally regulated financial institutions.
1984	**Computer Fraud and Abuse Act of 1984** Makes it a crime to break into computers owned by the federal government. This act has been regularly amended over the years as technology has changed.

SUMMARY

WHY BE CONCERNED ABOUT NETWORK AND INTERNET SECURITY?

There are a number of important security concerns related to computers and the Internet. Many of these are **computer crimes**. Because computers and networks are so widespread and many opportunities for criminals exist, all computer users should be aware of the risks of using networks and the Internet so they can take appropriate precautions.

UNAUTHORIZED ACCESS AND UNAUTHORIZED USE

Two risks related to networks and the Internet are **unauthorized access** and **unauthorized use**. **Hacking** is using a computer to break into a computer. **War driving** and **Wi-Fi piggybacking** refer to the unauthorized use of unsecured Wi-Fi network. Data can be intercepted as it is transmitted over the Internet or a wireless network.

PROTECTING AGAINST UNAUTHORIZED ACCESS AND UNAUTHORIZED USE

Access control systems are used to control access to a computer, network, or other resource. These include **possessed knowledge access systems** that use **passwords** or other types of possessed knowledge; **possessed object access systems** that use physical objects; and **biometric access systems** that identify users by a particular unique biological characteristic, such as a fingerprint. Passwords should be *strong passwords*; **two-factor authentication systems** that use multiple factors are more effective than single-factor systems.

To protect wireless networks, they should be secured; **firewalls** protect against unauthorized access. Sensitive transactions should be performed only on **secure Web pages**; sensitive files and e-mails should be secured with **encryption**. **Public key encryption** uses a private key and matching public key; **private key encryption** uses only a private key. A **virtual private network (VPN)** can be used to provide a secure remote connection to a company network, as well as to protect individuals at public Wi-Fi hotspots. Employers should take appropriate precautions with current and former employees to limit the risk of unauthorized access and use, as well as accidental exposure of sensitive information.

COMPUTER SABOTAGE

Computer sabotage includes **malware** (**computer viruses**, **computer worms**, and **Trojan horses** designed to cause harm to computer systems), **denial of service (DoS) attacks** (designed to shut down a Web server), and data and program alteration. Computer sabotage is often performed via the Internet, increasingly by the **bots** in a **botnet**.

PROTECTING AGAINST COMPUTER SABOTAGE

Protection against computer sabotage includes using appropriate access control systems to keep unauthorized individuals from accessing computers and networks, as well as using **security software**. In particular, **antivirus software** protects against computer viruses and other types of malware. It is important to keep your security software up to date.

ONLINE THEFT, ONLINE FRAUD, AND OTHER DOT CONS

There are a variety of types of theft, fraud, and scams related to the Internet—collectively referred to as **dot cons**—that all Internet users should be aware of. Data, information, or money can be stolen from individuals and businesses. A common crime today is **identity theft**, in which an individual poses as another individual—typically to steal money or make purchases posing as the victim. The information used in identity theft is often gathered via **phishing**, **spear phishing**, and **pharming**. **Online auction fraud** is another common dot con.

Chapter Objective 6:
Discuss online theft, identity theft, spoofing, phishing, and other types of dot cons.

PROTECTING AGAINST ONLINE THEFT, ONLINE FRAUD, AND OTHER DOT CONS

To protect against identity theft, individuals should guard their personal information carefully. To check for identity theft, watch your bills and credit history. When interacting with other individuals online or buying from an online auction, it is wise to be conservative and use a credit card whenever possible. To avoid other types of dot cons, be very wary of responding to unsolicited offers and e-mails, and steer clear of offers that seem too good to be true. Never click a link in an e-mail message to update your personal information. To verify a Web site, a **digital certificate** can be used. To verity the sender of a document, a **digital signature** can be used. Digital certificates include key pairs that can be used to both digitally sign documents and to encrypt files.

Chapter Objective 7:
Detail steps an individual can take to protect against online theft, identity theft, spoofing, phishing, and other types of dot cons.

PERSONAL SAFETY ISSUES

There are also personal safety risks for both adults and children stemming from Internet use. **Cyberbullying** and **cyberstalking**—online harassment that frightens or threatens the victim—is more common in recent years, even though most states have passed laws against it. Cyberbully is a growing risk for children, as is the potential exposure to online pornography and other materials inappropriate for children, and the growing *sexting* trend.

Chapter Objective 8:
Identify personal safety risks associated with Internet use.

PROTECTING AGAINST CYBERBULLING, CYBERSTALKING, AND OTHER PERSONAL SAFETY CONCERNS

To protect their personal safety, adults and children should be cautious in online communications. They should be wary of revealing any personal information or meeting online acquaintances in person. To protect children, parents should keep a close watch on their children's online activities, and children should be taught never to reveal personal information to others online without a parent's consent.

Chapter Objective 9:
List steps individuals can take to safeguard their personal safety when using the Internet.

NETWORK AND INTERNET SECURITY LEGISLATION

The rapid growth of the Internet and jurisdictional issues have contributed to the lack of network and Internet security legislation. However, computer crime legislation continues to be proposed and computer crimes are actively prosecuted.

Chapter Objective 10:
Discuss the current state of network and Internet security legislation.

REVIEW ACTIVITIES

KEY TERM MATCHING

a. computer virus

b. denial of service (DoS) attack

c. dot con

d. encryption

e. firewall

f. hacking

g. identity theft

h. password

i. phishing

j. Trojan horse

Instructions: Match each key term on the left with the definition on the right that best describes it.

1. _____ A collection of hardware and/or software intended to protect a computer or computer network from unauthorized access.

2. _____ A fraud or scam carried out through the Internet.

3. _____ A malicious program that masquerades as something else.

4. _____ A method of scrambling the contents of an e-mail message or a file to make it unreadable if it is intercepted by an unauthorized user.

5. _____ A secret combination of characters used to gain access to a computer, computer network, or other resource.

6. _____ A software program installed without the user's knowledge and designed to alter the way a computer operates or to cause harm to the computer system.

7. _____ An act of sabotage that attempts to flood a network server or a Web server with so much activity that it is unable to function.

8. _____ The use of spoofed e-mail messages to gain credit card numbers and other personal data to be used for fraudulent purposes.

9. _____ Using a computer to break into another computer system.

10. _____ Using someone else's identity to purchase goods or services, obtain new credit cards or bank loans, or otherwise illegally masquerade as that individual.

SELF-QUIZ

Instructions: Circle **T** if the statement is true, **F** if the statement is false, or write the best answer in the space provided. **Answers for the self-quiz are located in the References and Resources Guide at the end of the book.**

1. **T F** A computer virus can only be transferred to another computer via a storage medium.

2. **T F** An access control system that uses passwords is a possessed knowledge access system.

3. **T F** Using a password that is two characters long is an example of two-factor authentication.

4. **T F** Secure Web pages use encryption to securely transfer data sent via those pages.

5. **T F** Cyberstalking is the use of spoofed e-mail messages to gain credit card numbers and other personal data to be used for fraudulent purposes.

6. Driving around looking for a Wi-Fi network to access is referred to as _____.

7. _____ access control systems use some type of unique physical characteristic of a person to authenticate that individual.

8. A(n) _____ can be used at a Wi-Fi hotspot to create a secure path over the Internet.

9. A(n) _____ can be added to a file or an e-mail message to verify the identity of the sender and guarantee the file or message has not been changed.

10. Match each computer crime to its description, and write the corresponding number in the blank to the left of the description.

    a. _____ A person working for the Motor Vehicle Division deletes a friend's speeding ticket from a database.

    b. _____ An individual does not like someone's comment on a message board and begins to send that individual harassing e-mail messages.

    c. _____ An individual sells the same item to 10 individuals via an online auction site.

    d. _____ A person accesses a computer belonging to the IRS without authorization.

1. Online auction fraud

2. Hacking

3. Data or program alteration

4. Cyberstalking

---

1. Write the appropriate letter in the blank to the left of each term to indicate whether it is related to unauthorized access (U) or computer sabotage (C).

    a. _____ Time bomb   c. _____ Malware   e. _____ War driving

    b. _____ DoS attack   d. _____ Wi-Fi piggybacking

2. Is the password *john1* a good password? Why or why not? If not, suggest a better password.

3. Supply the missing words to complete the following statements regarding public/private key pairs.

    a. With an encrypted e-mail message, the recipient's _____ key is used to encrypt the message, and the recipient's _____ key is used to decrypt the message.

    b. With a digital signature, the sender's _____ key is used to sign the document, and the sender's _____ key is used to validate the signature.

4. To secure files on your computer so they are unreadable to a hacker who might gain access to your computer, what type of encryption (public key or private key) would be the most appropriate? Explain.

5. List two precautions that individuals can take to secure a wireless router against unauthorized access.

---

1. The term *hacktivism* is sometimes used to refer to the act of hacking into a computer system for a politically or socially motivated purpose. While some view hacktivists no differently than they view other hackers, hacktivists contend that they break into systems in order to bring attention to political or social causes. Is hacktivism a valid method of bringing attention to specific causes? Why or why not? Should hacktivists be treated differently than other types of hackers when caught?

2. According to security experts, several worms released in past years contain more than just the virus code—they contain code to remove competing malware from the computers they infect and messages taunting other virus writers. The goal seems to be not only to gain control of an increasing number of infected machines—a type of "bot war" to build the biggest botnet—but also to one-up rivals. If this trend continues, do you think it will affect how hackers and other computer criminals will be viewed? Will they become cult heroes or be viewed as dangerous criminals? Will continuing to increase prosecution of these individuals help or hurt the situation?

PROJECTS

HOT TOPICS

1. **Wi-Fi Hotspot Safety** As discussed in the chapter, it is possible to inadvertently connect to an evil twin instead of the legitimate Wi-Fi hotspot you intended to connect to and, even if you are connected to a legitimate hotspot, any data you send unsecured via the hotspot can be intercepted by a criminal. In either case, if the thief intercepts your credit card number, Web site passwords, or other sensitive data, it can be used for identity theft and other criminal activities.

   For this project, research these and any other possible risks you can think of related to using a Wi-Fi hotspot. For each risk, identify a possible precaution that can be taken to guard against that risk. If you have ever used a Wi-Fi hotspot, were you at risk? Knowing what you do now, would you take any new precautions the next time you use one? Is it possible to surf safely using a Wi-Fi hotspot? At the conclusion of your research, prepare a one-page summary of your findings and opinions and submit it to your instructor.

SHORT ANSWER/ RESEARCH

2. **New Viruses** Unfortunately, new computer viruses and other types of malware are released all the time.

   For this project, identify a current virus or worm (most security companies, such as Symantec and McAfee, list the most recent security threats on their Web sites) and answer the following questions: When was it introduced? What does it do? How is it spread? How many computers have been affected so far? Is there an estimated cost associated with it? Is it still in existence? At the conclusion of your research, prepare a one-page summary of your findings and submit it to your instructor.

HANDS ON

3. **Virus Check** There are several Web sites that include a free virus check, as well as other types of diagnostic software.

   For this project, find a free virus check available on the Web site of a company that makes antivirus software (such as the Symantec Security Scan at **security.symantec.com**) and run the free virus check. NOTE: The programs may require temporarily downloading a small program or an ActiveX component. If you are unable to perform this task on a school computer, ask your instructor for alternate instructions. If the check takes more than 10 minutes and there is an option to limit the check to a particular drive and folder, redo the check but scan only part of the hard drive (such as the Documents folder) to save time. After the virus scan is completed, print the page displaying the result. Did the program find any viruses or other security threats? At the conclusion of this task, submit your printout with any additional comments about your experience to your instructor.

4. **Teaching Computer Viruses** Some college computer classes include instruction on writing computer viruses. At one university, precautions for containing code created during this course include only allowing fourth year students to take the course, not having a network connection in the classroom, and prohibiting the removal of storage media from the classroom. Do you think these precautions are sufficient? Should writing virus code be allowed as part of a computer degree curriculum? Some believe that students need to know how viruses work in order to be able to develop antivirus software; however, the antivirus industry disagrees, and most antivirus professionals were never virus writers. Is it ethical for colleges to teach computer virus writing? Is it ethical for students to take such a course? Will teaching illegal and unethical acts (such as writing virus code) in college classes help to legitimize the behavior in society? Would you feel comfortable taking such a course? Why or why not?

    For this project, form an opinion about the ethical implications of including the instruction of writing virus code in college classes and be prepared to discuss your position (in class, via an online class discussion group, in a class chat room, or via a class blog, depending on your instructor's directions). You may also be asked to write a short paper expressing your opinion.

5. **Security vs. Personal Freedom** We all depend on some types of security, such as depending on the military and police to keep us safe from terrorists and other criminals and expecting our employers to provide a safe workplace. What we view as potential danger tends to limit our personal freedom. For example, many citizens of large cities avoid walking the streets alone at night, even though they have the right to do so, and many Americans avoid traveling to the Middle East, South America, and other locations thought to be dangerous for Americans at the present time. Security measures established to protect us sometimes also limit our personal freedom—for example, having to submit to personal and baggage searches before boarding an airplane or having to show identification to gain admittance to your workplace. Most citizens are willing to give up some level of personal freedom in order to protect their personal safety, but the difficulty is determining the balance—how much loss of freedom is worth a certain level of additional security? Do you think it is necessary to sacrifice some degree of personal freedom in order to obtain the necessary level of national security? Why or why not? Do you think public support for a national ID card containing biometric data, public video surveillance systems, and other security measures will decrease or increase in the future? Why? Are you willing to give up some freedom for increased personal safety? For convenience?

    For this project, consider the issue of security versus personal freedom, and form an opinion regarding the optimal balance. Be prepared to discuss both sides of this issue and your opinion (in class, via an online class discussion group, in a class chat room, or via a class blog). You may also be asked to write a short paper or prepare a short presentation expressing your opinion, depending on your instructor's directions.

Instructions: Go to the Chapter 4 page at **www.cengage.com/computerconcepts/np/uccs4** to work the following Web Activities.

6. **Interactive Activities** Work the interactive **Crossword Puzzle**, watch the **Video Podcasts** and **Online Videos**, and explore the **Further Exploration** links associated with this chapter.

    If you have a SAM user profile, you may have access to hands-on instruction, practice, and assessment of the skills covered in this chapter. Check with your instructor for instructions and the correct URL/Web site to access those assignments.

7. **Student Edition Labs** Work the following interactive **Student Edition Lab**.

    ➤ **Wireless Networking**   ➤ **Keeping Your Computer Virus Free**
    ➤ **Advanced Databases**   ➤ **Careers and Technology**

8. **Test Yourself** Review the **Online Study Guide** for this chapter, then test your knowledge of the terms and concepts covered in this chapter by completing the **Key Term Matching** exercise, the **Self-Quiz**, the **Exercises**, and the **Practice Test**.

expert insight on...
Networks and the Internet

Collin Davis is a Senior Development Manager in the Consumer Product Solutions Group at Symantec Corporation. He has worked for Symantec for nine years, initially as a Software Development Intern while in college. He has over 12 years of experience working with computer systems, networks, and other computer-related areas. Collin has a Bachelor of Science degree in Computer Science from the UCLA Henry Samueli School of Engineering.

A conversation with COLLIN DAVIS

Senior Development Manager, Consumer Product Solutions, Symantec Corporation

"*Cyber criminals aren't in it for just notoriety anymore; they want your money—or worse, your identity.*"

My Background ...

I have been working in the computer security industry for nine years. I started in 2001 as a Software Development Intern while studying at UCLA. After earning my Bachelor's degree in computer science from the University of California, Los Angeles, Henry Samueli School of Engineering, I joined Symantec as an engineer on the Norton AntiVirus product team and helped develop and ship six iterations of that product. I then joined the team responsible for the creation of Symantec's all-in-one security solution, Norton 360. Most recently, I lead the development of OnlineFamily. Norton, a new, unique family safety solution that helps parents protect their kids online and fosters communication about their online activities.

It's Important to Know ...

To use a layered security system. A layered security system consists of multiple layers of protection to guard against intrusions and other threats. You should use a secure wireless router and advanced firewall and antivirus technologies. You should also ensure that all your passwords are secure and change them often.

That you need to stay up to date. The threat landscape is constantly changing. There are actually more "bad" files today than "good" ones. This has led some security software makers to rely less on signature-based detection. Instead, they use a combination of whitelisting and advanced reputation engines to trust only the good files and block everything else. Use software with this type of technology if possible. Regardless, it is critical that you keep your security products up to date to stay protected from the latest threats. It's fairly easy for computer users to do this since most products download updates automatically or notify you when you need to download a new version. Don't ignore these notifications.

To think before you act. The online world is no different from the real one. If a link seems suspicious, proceed with caution before clicking it or seek information and services elsewhere.

How I Use this Technology ...

I use this technology every day in my personal life. I also realize that the more and more "connected" data and applications become, the more important it becomes to secure them. Every time I connect to the Internet to send an e-mail, bank online, or view family photos, I am using the networking and Internet technologies discussed in this module to make the connection, and I am using the security technologies listed in this module to ensure my private data is protected. I don't always see these technologies as they do their job (this is a good thing!), but the fact that they are there gives me the confidence to take advantage of all the other great technologies being offered today.

What the Future Holds . . .

Our lives are becoming increasingly more and more dependent on technology. We store our documents and photos online. We work online and even date and form social networks online. All of this introduces increased privacy and security concerns that we must be aware of. It's important to be aware of what data is stored online and to use appropriate protection measures to secure it.

One of the biggest Internet-related risks today is that threats have evolved to exploit people for financial gain. Cyber criminals aren't in it for just notoriety anymore; they want your money—or worse, your identity. People need to be particularly cautious about whom they give their personal information (like credit card and Social Security numbers) to online. Everyone should check their bank and credit card statements often to monitor for fraudulent charges and change their passwords frequently.

In the future, we can expect to see businesses moving toward delivering an even more connected online experience. Personal computers are moving back toward their past role as simple "terminals" that provide a connection to the Internet where a wide array of data and applications are hosted. The line between what is stored and run from your local computer and what is "online" is being blurred. One impact of our online and local content becoming more interconnected is that we will be able to access our own personalized application experience from anywhere in the world, with many different types of devices. Wherever we are, our experience will remain consistent, according to our preferences and our content. However, security will remain essential. If people cannot trust that their information is secure and protected, they will be unable to take advantage of all the exciting services and benefits being offered today.

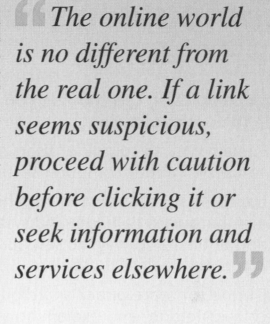

"The online world is no different from the real one. If a link seems suspicious, proceed with caution before clicking it or seek information and services elsewhere."

My Advice to Students . . .

Be curious—explore every facet of a technology that interests you. Try to learn everything about its inner workings but don't lose sight of the big picture. If you're interested in a career in a particular field, get an internship. There is no better way to learn something than to do it.

Discussion Question

Collin Davis stresses the importance of people trusting that their information is secure and protected. Think about the systems that contain personal data about you. How would you feel if those systems were breached and your information was stolen? Does your viewpoint change if the information was monetary (such as credit card information) versus private information (such as grades or health information)? What security precautions, if any, do you think should be imposed by laws? Are organizations that hold your personal data morally responsible for going beyond the minimum requirements? What types of security measures would you implement to protect these systems? Be prepared to discuss your position (in class, via an online class discussion group, in a class chat room, or via a class blog, depending on your instructor's directions). You may also be asked to write a short paper expressing your opinion.

> **For more information on Symantec, visit www.symantec.com. To view the latest Symantec Internet Security Threat Report results, go to www.symantec.com/business/ theme.jsp?themeid=threatreport.**

chapter 5

Computer Security and Privacy

After completing this chapter, you will be able to do the following:

1. Explain why all computer users should be concerned about computer security.

2. List some risks associated with hardware loss, hardware damage, and system failure, and understand ways to safeguard a computer against these risks.

3. Define software piracy and digital counterfeiting, and explain how they may be prevented.

4. Explain what information privacy is and why computer users should be concerned about it.

5. Describe some privacy concerns regarding databases, electronic profiling, spam, and telemarketing, and identify ways individuals can protect their privacy.

6. Discuss several types of electronic surveillance and monitoring, and list ways individuals can protect their privacy.

7. Discuss the status of computer security and privacy legislation.

outline

Overview

Why Be Concerned About Computer Security?

Hardware Loss, Hardware Damage, and System Failure
Hardware Loss
Hardware Damage
System Failure and Other Disasters
Protecting Against Hardware Loss, Hardware Damage, and System Failure

Software Piracy and Digital Counterfeiting
Software Piracy
Digital Counterfeiting
Protecting Against Software Piracy and Digital Counterfeiting

Why Be Concerned About Information Privacy?

Databases, Electronic Profiling, Spam, and Other Marketing Activities
Databases and Electronic Profiling
Spam and Other Marketing Activities
Protecting the Privacy of Personal Information

Electronic Surveillance and Monitoring
Computer Monitoring Software
Video Surveillance
Employee Monitoring
Presence Technology
Protecting Personal and Workplace Privacy

Computer Security and Privacy Legislation

OVERVIEW

The increasing use of computers in our society today has many advantages. It also, however, opens up new possibilities for problems (such as data loss due to a system malfunction or a disaster), as well as new opportunities for computer crime (such as hardware theft, software piracy, and digital counterfeiting). In addition, our networked society has raised a number of privacy concerns. Although we can appreciate that sometimes selected people or organizations have a legitimate need for some types of personal information, whenever information is provided to others there is always the danger that the information will be misused. For instance, facts may be taken out of context and used to draw distorted conclusions, or private information may end up being distributed to others without one's consent or knowledge. And, with the vast amount of information that is contained in databases accessible via the Internet today, privacy is an enormous concern for both individuals and businesses.

Chapter 4 discussed security risks related to network and Internet use. This chapter looks at other types of computer-related security concerns, as well as the computer-related privacy concerns facing us today. First, we explore hardware loss, hardware damage, and system failure, and the safeguards that can help reduce the risk of a problem occurring due to these security concerns. Next, software piracy and digital counterfeiting are discussed, along with the steps that are being taken to prevent these computer crimes. We then turn to privacy topics, including possible risks to personal privacy and precautions that can be taken to safeguard one's privacy. The chapter closes with a summary of legislation related to computer security and privacy. ■

PODCAST

Go to **www.cengage.com/ computerconcepts/np/uccs4** to download or listen to the "Expert Insight on Web-Based Multimedia and E-Commerce" podcast.

WHY BE CONCERNED ABOUT COMPUTER SECURITY?

Today, there are a number of security concerns surrounding computers and related technology that all individuals should be concerned about, including having your computer stolen, losing a term paper because the storage medium your paper was stored on becomes unreadable, losing your mobile phone containing your entire contact list and calendar, or running the risk of buying pirated or digitally counterfeited products. The most common security risks and computer crimes (including hacking, computer viruses, identity theft, and cyberbullying) that take place via networks and the Internet were discussed in Chapter 4, along with their respective precautions. While these concerns are extremely important today, there are additional computer security issues that are not related specifically to networks and the Internet. These computer security concerns, along with some precautions that users can take to reduce the risks of problems occurring due to these security concerns, are discussed in the next few sections.

HARDWARE LOSS, HARDWARE DAMAGE, AND SYSTEM FAILURE

Hardware loss can occur when a personal computer, USB flash drive, mobile device, or other piece of hardware is stolen or is lost by the owner. Hardware loss, as well as other security issues, can also result from *hardware damage* (both intentional and accidental) and *system failure*.

Hardware Loss

One of the most obvious types of hardware loss is **hardware theft**, which occurs when hardware is stolen from an individual or from a business, school, or other organization. Computers, printers, mobile phones, and other hardware can be stolen during a break-in; portable computers and mobile devices are also frequently stolen from cars, as well as from restaurants, airports, hotels, and other public locations. Although security experts stress that the vast majority of hardware theft is done for the value of the hardware itself, corporate executives and government employees may be targeted for computer theft for the information contained on their computers. In fact, *C-level attacks* (attacks aimed at C-level executives, such as CEOs and CIOs) are rapidly growing as executives are increasingly using e-mail and storing documents on their computers, as well as traveling more with portable computers, mobile phones, and other devices. And even if the data on a device is not the primary reason for a theft, any unencrypted sensitive data stored on the stolen device is at risk of being exposed or used for fraudulent purposes, and this is happening at unprecedented levels today.

Hardware loss also occurs when hardware is being transported in luggage or in a package that is lost by an airline or shipping company, or when an individual misplaces or otherwise loses a piece of hardware. With the vast number of portable devices that individuals carry with them today (such as portable computers, mobile phones, and USB flash drives), this latter type of hardware loss is a growing concern—by one estimate, more than 20 million people per year lose a mobile phone. While lost hardware may be covered by insurance and the data stored on a lost or stolen device may not be used in a fraudulent manner, having to replace the hardware and restore the data—or, worse yet, losing the data entirely if it was not backed up—is still a huge inconvenience. If any sensitive data (such as Social Security numbers, Web site passwords, or credit card data) was contained on the lost hardware, individuals risk identity theft (one study revealed that 80% of users store information that could be used for identity theft on their mobile phones). Businesses hosting sensitive data that is breached have to deal with the numerous issues and potential consequences of that loss, such as notifying customers that their personal information was exposed (as required by more than half of the states in the U.S.), responding to potential lawsuits, and trying to repair damage to the company's reputation.

Hardware Damage

Computer hardware often consists of relatively delicate components that can be damaged easily by power fluctuations, heat, dust, static electricity, water, and abuse. For instance, fans clogged by dust can cause a computer to overheat; dropping a computer will often break it; and spilling a drink on a keyboard or leaving a mobile phone in the pocket of your jeans while they go through the wash will likely cause some damage. In addition to accidental damage, burglars, vandals, disgruntled employees, and other individuals sometimes intentionally damage the computers and other hardware they have access to.

System Failure and Other Disasters

Although many of us may prefer not to think about it, **system failure**—the complete malfunction of a computer system—and other types of computer-related disasters do happen. From accidentally deleting a file to having your computer just stop working, computer problems can be a huge inconvenience, as well as cost you a great deal of time and money. When the system contains your personal documents and data, it is a problem; when it contains the only copy of your company records or controls a vital system—such as a nuclear power plant—it can be a disaster.

>**Hardware theft.** The theft of computer hardware. >**System failure.** The complete malfunction of a computer system.

System failure can occur because of a hardware problem, software problem, or computer virus. It can also occur because of a natural disaster (such as a tornado, fire, flood, or hurricane), sabotage, or a terrorist attack. The terrorist attack on the New York City World Trade Center Twin Towers on September 11, 2001, illustrated this all too clearly. When the Twin Towers collapsed, nearly 3,000 people were killed and hundreds of offices—over 13 million square feet of office space—were completely destroyed; another 7 million square feet of office space was damaged (see Figure 5-1). In addition to the devastating human loss, the offices located in the WTC lost their computer systems—including all the equipment, records, and data stored at that location. The ramifications of these system failures and the corresponding data loss were felt around the world by all the businesses and people connected directly or indirectly to these organizations.

FIGURE 5-1
System destruction.
The 9/11 attacks killed nearly 3,000 people and destroyed hundreds of business offices, including critical cables located in this Verizon office adjacent to Ground Zero.

Protecting Against Hardware Loss, Hardware Damage, and System Failure

To protect against hardware loss, hardware damage, and system failure, a number of precautions can be taken, as discussed next.

Door and Computer Equipment Locks

Locked doors and equipment can be simple deterrents to computer theft. For instance, doors to facilities should be secured with door locks, alarm systems, and whatever other access control methods (such as the possessed object and biometric access systems discussed in Chapter 4) are needed to make it difficult to gain access to hardware that might be stolen. In addition, employees should be trained regarding the proper procedures for ensuring visitors only have access to the parts of the facility that they are authorized to access. For a look at a new trend in evaluating security procedures—*social engineering tests* for employees—see the Trend box.

To secure computers and other hardware to a table or other object that is difficult to move, *cable locks* (see Figure 5-2) can be used. Cable locks are frequently used to secure desktop computers in schools and businesses. They can also be used to secure portable computers, external hard drives, and other portable pieces of hardware, and they are increasingly being used by college students and business travelers to secure their portable computers when they are not being used. To facilitate using a computer lock, nearly all computers today come with a *security slot*—a small opening built into the system unit case designed for computer locks. If a security slot is not available, *cable anchors* (which attach to a piece of hardware using industrial strength adhesive and which contain a connector through which the cable lock can be passed—refer again to Figure 5-2) can be used. Computer locks are available in both key and combination versions.

FIGURE 5-2
Cable locks can be used to secure computers and other hardware.

As an additional precaution with portable computers, *laptop alarm software* that emits a very loud alarm noise if the computer is unplugged, if USB devices are removed, or if the computer is shut down

NOTEBOOK COMPUTERS
This combination cable lock connects via a security slot built into the notebook computer.

DESKTOP COMPUTERS AND MONITORS
This keyed cable lock connects via a cable anchor attached to the back of the monitor.

TREND

Social Engineering Tests

With security and privacy breaches occurring on a regular basis today, a growing trend is for businesses to use security firms to perform security audits, also known as *vulnerability assessments*, on themselves. While some of these assessments focus on trying to breach security remotely, *social engineering tests* are designed to test a business's security policies and employees, such as whether or not employees will click a phishing e-mail message or give out sensitive information in response to a phishing telephone call, grant a potential thief physical access to the facility, or plug a USB flash drive found in the office (and potentially containing malware planted by a hacker) into their computers. And the use of these tests is growing. For instance, one security firm that performs social engineering tests—*TraceSecurity Inc.*—estimates that about 70% of its new customers are asking for social engineering tests, up from about 5% three years ago.

To perform a social engineering test, TraceSecurity engineers typically impersonate pest-control workers or fire inspectors in order to gain entry to server rooms and other locations where they can then access sensitive data. They sometimes precede their visit with a spoofed e-mail to office employees, such as announcing an upcoming pest inspection and requesting employees grant the pest control workers full access to check for infestation. Once at the office, TraceSecurity personnel attempt to talk their way into the building and into a room that allows access to the company network. As proof of access, they tag equipment with TraceSecurity stickers (see the accompanying photo), take photographs of the documents and data they were able to access, and sometimes even remove hardware from the building (assuming the business requests this and has granted the appropriate permission). The business receives a report detailing which tests employees passed and failed and, in a follow-up visit, the TraceSecurity employees explain how they were able to infiltrate the business and what

precautions should be taken to prevent this from happening again. Typical recommendations include not using e-mail alone to authorize company visitors; training employees to question any strangers they see in the office and to escort visitors that need access to sensitive areas of the business; and utilizing conventional precautions such as using access devices to secure facilities, using screen savers with passwords to lock computers when employees are away from their desks, not using any unauthorized portable storage devices, and encrypting all sensitive data.

While this type of vulnerability assessment may annoy or embarrass some employees, it tends to have a much greater impact on employees than receiving a memo or listening to a lecture on security policies. According to TraceSecurity's chief technology officer, "Sometimes you have to get burned to make you really understand."

The red and white sticker shown here marks equipment accessed during a TraceSecurity social engineering test.

without the owner's permission can be used. In addition to physically securing computers, it is also extremely important for businesses to ensure that employees follow security protocols related to portable storage media, such as signing in and out portable hard drives, USB flash drives, and other storage media, if required, and keeping those devices locked up when they are not in use.

Encryption and Self-Encrypting Hard Drives

As discussed in Chapter 4, encryption can be used to prevent a file from being readable if it is intercepted or viewed by an unauthorized individual. To protect the data on an entire computer in case it is lost or stolen, **full disk encryption (FDE)** can be used. FDE systems encrypt everything stored on the drive (the operating system, application programs, data, temporary files, and so forth) automatically without any user interaction, so users don't have to remember to encrypt sensitive documents and the encryption is always enabled. To access a hard drive that uses FDE (often referred to as a **self-encrypting hard drive**), a username and password or biometric characteristic is needed, typically before the computer containing the drive will boot.

While self-encrypting hard drives are used most often with portable computers (in fact, the U.S. federal government is in the process of implementing FDE on all government-owned portable computers and mobile devices), their use is also being expanded to desktop computers and servers. Because FDE requires no user input to enable it and the user has no say in which files are encrypted (since all files are encrypted automatically), these systems provide an easy way to ensure all data is protected, provided strong passwords are used in conjunction with the encryption system so the system cannot be easily hacked. As FDE technology continues to improve to reduce the additional disk access time required by the encryption system, use of self-encrypting hard drives is expected to grow past corporate and government use to individuals' personal computers.

Encryption can also be used to protect the data stored on removable media, such as flash memory cards and USB flash drives; either a strong password or a biometric feature (such as a built-in fingerprint reader, as shown in Figure 5-3) is used to provide access to the data on the drive. Many encrypted devices allow multiple users to be registered as authorized users (by assigning each individual a password or registering his or her fingerprint image, for instance), as well as allow a portion of the device to be designated as unencrypted for nonsensitive documents, if desired. Many businesses today are requiring that all desktop computers, portable computers, portable storage devices, and mobile phones issued to employees be encrypted, in order to protect against a data breach.

Computer Tracking Software and Antitheft Tools

Some software tools are not designed to prevent hardware from being stolen; instead, they are designed to aid in its recovery. This can be beneficial since, according to FBI statistics, the recovery rate of a stolen or lost computer is normally about 2% or 3%. One software tool that can be used to help increase the chances of a stolen or lost computer being recovered is *computer tracking software*. Computer tracking software sends identifying information (such as ownership information and location information determined from nearby Wi-Fi networks) to the computer tracking company on a regular basis, such as once per day if the computer is not reported stolen. When the computer is reported lost

FIGURE 5-3

Encrypted media.
The data on this encrypted USB flash drive cannot be accessed until the user is authenticated via a fingerprint scan.

> **Full disk encryption (FDE).** A technology that encrypts everything stored on a storage medium automatically, without any user interaction.
> **Self-encrypting hard drive.** A hard drive that uses full disk encryption (FDE).

HOW IT WORKS

Self-Destructing Devices

When a business or an individual is less concerned about recovering a stolen device than about ensuring the data located on the computer is not compromised, devices that self-destruct upon command are a viable option. Available as part of some computer tracking software programs (such as the one shown in the accompanying illustration), as well as stand-alone utilities, *kill switch* capabilities destroy the data on a device (typically by overwriting preselected files multiple times, rendering them unreadable) when instructed. Kill switches built into computer tracking systems are typically activated upon customer request when the device is determined to be lost or stolen. Once the kill switch is activated, all data on the computer is erased whenever it next connects to the Internet or when another predesignated remote trigger is activated (such as a certain number of unsuccessful logon attempts). Kill switch capabilities are also built into some mobile phone applications (such as the *MobileMe* iPhone app) and are typically activated by the owner logging onto an online account or sending the phone a text message containing the proper kill switch password—when the device receives the message, all data stored on the device is erased.

Kill switch technology is also beginning to be built into some USB flash drives and hard drives. For instance, hard drives with EDT's *Dead on Demand* technology contain a small canister filled with a corrosive chemical that completely destroys the drive when the drive is tampered with or when one of up to 17 remote triggers specified by the owner is activated. The self-destruction process does not damage the computer—only the hard drive—and the command to self-destruct can be activated even if the drive is not powered up or if it is removed from the computer. Not quite *Mission Impossible*, but when hardware containing sensitive data is stolen (which could impact an individual's personal privacy or a business's legal liability, reputation, and bottom line), kill switch technology could save the day.

VIDEO PODCAST

Go to the Chapter 5 page at **www.cengage.com/ computerconcepts/np/uccs4** to download or listen to the "How To: Track a Stolen Laptop" video podcast.

or stolen, however, the computer tracking software typically increases its contact with the computer tracking software company (such as sending new information every 15 minutes) so current location information can be provided to law enforcement agencies to help them recover the computer. Some software can even take video or photos of the person using the stolen computer (if the computer has a built-in video camera like many portable computers have today) to help identify and prosecute the thief.

Often any sign that computer tracking software is running on the computer or is sending information via the Internet is hidden from the user (this type of tracking software is sometimes called *stealth tracking software*), so the thief is usually not aware that a computer tracking system is installed on the computer. An alternative is tracking software that displays a message on the screen when the computer is lost or stolen. This message might be a plea to return the device for a reward or simply a message like "THIS COMPUTER IS STOLEN" in a big bright banner on the desktop to call attention to the fact that the computer is stolen (the owner can usually specify the message and messages typically reappear every 30 seconds, no matter how many times they are closed by the thief).

Computer tracking systems (the software and the support from the computer tracking company) usually cost between $30 and $50 per year. An alternative for protecting the data on a portable computer if it is stolen is to use a *kill switch*—technology that causes the device to self-destruct, as discussed in the How It Works box.

Another antitheft tool is the use of *asset tags* on hardware and other expensive assets. These labels usually identify the owner of the asset and are designed to be permanently attached to the asset. Some tags are designed to be indestructible; others are *tamper evident labels* that change their appearance if someone (such as a thief) tries to remove them. For instance, some labels have a printed message hidden underneath the label that is etched into the surface of the computer and is exposed when the label is removed. Both of these features alert a potential buyer to the fact that the item is likely stolen.

Additional Precautions for Mobile Users

With an increasing amount of personal data being stored on mobile phones and other mobile devices today, as well as the ability of some mobile phones to be used to make purchases and unlock doors, security features that guard against the unauthorized use of mobile devices are becoming increasingly more important. There is tracking software (similar to the computer tracking systems just discussed) available for mobile phones and other types of devices that are frequently lost or stolen (such as portable digital media players and USB flash drives) to help aid in the recovery of those devices. For instance, *mobile tracking software* can remotely lock down a lost or stolen phone, display a message on the phone containing instructions for returning the device, and/or play a sound to help the owner locate the phone if it is nearby. However, to avoid losing the device in the first place or to prevent someone from accessing the data stored on the device, other precautions should be used.

While on the go, the best antitheft measure is common sense. For example, you should never leave a portable computer or mobile device unattended in a public location (always keep a hand, finger, or other body part in contact with the device so, if you are distracted for a moment and glance away, it cannot be stolen without you noticing). When staying in a hotel, take your computer with you, use a cable lock to secure it to a piece of furniture, or lock it in a hotel safe (many hotel rooms today have room safes large enough to hold a portable computer) when you leave your hotel room for the day. Other sensible precautions include using a plain carrying case to make a portable computer less conspicuous and labeling your portable computer (and other portable hardware that you take with you on the go) with your contact information so a lost or stolen device can be returned to you when it is recovered. One additional possibility for protecting data while on the road is storing all data online or on the company server instead of on the computer you are using while traveling. Businesses can ensure no data is stored on the device by using a thin client portable computer that has no hard drive, such as the *SafeBook* computer. These computers look like ordinary notebook computers, but since all programs and data are stored on the company server and accessed via the Internet through a Wi-Fi, Ethernet, or 3G wireless connection, there is no data stored on the computer. As a result, no data can be compromised if the computer is lost or stolen. In addition, mobile users should disable wireless connections when they are not needed and enable password protection for accessing the device. These precautions are summarized in Figure 5-4.

MOBILE COMPUTING PRECAUTIONS

Install and use encryption, antivirus, antispyware, and firewall software.

Secure computers with boot passwords; set your mobile phone to autolock after a short period of time and require a passcode to unlock it.

Use only secure Wi-Fi connections and disable Wi-Fi and Bluetooth when they are not needed.

Never leave usernames, passwords, or other data attached to your computer or inside its carrying case.

Use a plain carrying case to make a portable computer less conspicuous.

Keep an eye on your devices at all times, especially when going through airport security.

Avoid setting your devices on the floor or leaving them in your hotel room; use a cable lock to secure the device to a desk or other object whenever this is unavoidable.

Back up the data stored on the device regularly.

Consider installing tracking or kill switch software.

FIGURE 5-4
Common sense precautions for portable computer and mobile device users.

FIGURE 5-5
Protective cases.

Proper Hardware Care

Proper care of hardware can help to prevent serious damage to a computer system. The most obvious precaution is to not harm your hardware physically, such as by dropping a portable computer, knocking a piece of hardware off a desk, or jostling a desktop computer's system unit. To help protect portable devices against minor abuse, *protective cases* (see Figure 5-5) can be used. These cases are typically padded or made from protective material to prevent

MOBILE PHONE CASES

NOTEBOOK CASES

RUGGED PORTABLE COMPUTERS

RUGGED MOBILE DEVICES

RUGGED MOBILE PHONES

> **FIGURE 5-6**
> Ruggedized devices.

> **FIGURE 5-7**
> Surge suppressors and uninterruptible power supplies (UPSs).

SURGE SUPPRESSOR FOR DESKTOP COMPUTERS

SURGE SUPPRESSOR FOR NOTEBOOK COMPUTERS

UPS FOR HOME COMPUTERS

UPS FOR SERVERS

damage due to occasional bumps and bangs; they also often have a thin protective layer over the device's display to protect against scratches. Some protective cases are water resistant to protect the device from rain or dust damage. There are also neoprene *laptop sleeves* available to protect portable computers from scratches and other damage when they are carried in a conventional briefcase or bag.

For users who need more protection than a protective case can provide, **ruggedized devices** (such as portable computers and mobile phones) are available (see Figure 5-6). These devices are designed to withstand much more physical abuse than conventional devices and range from *semirugged* to *ultrarugged*. For instance, semirugged devices typically have a more durable case and are spill-resistant. Rugged and ultrarugged devices go a few steps further—they are designed to withstand falls from three feet or more onto concrete, extreme temperature ranges, wet conditions, and use while being bounced around over rough terrain in a vehicle. Ruggedized devices are used most often by individuals who work out of the office, such as field workers, construction workers, outdoor technicians, military personnel, police officers, and firefighters.

To protect hardware from damage due to power fluctuations, it is important for all users to use a **surge suppressor** with a computer whenever it is plugged into a power outlet. When electrical power spikes occur, the surge suppressor prevents them from harming your system. For desktop computers, surge suppressors should be used with all of the powered components in the computer system (such as the system unit, monitor, printer, and scanner). Surge suppressors designed for portable computers are typically smaller and designed to connect only one device (see Figure 5-7). There are surge suppressors designed for business and industrial use, as well.

Users who want their desktop computers to remain powered up when the electricity goes off should use an

> **Ruggedized device.** A device (such as a portable computer or mobile phone) that is designed to withstand much more physical abuse than a conventional device. > **Surge suppressor.** A device that protects a computer system from damage due to electrical fluctuations.

uninterruptible power supply (UPS), which contains a built-in battery (see Figure 5-7). The length of time that a UPS can power a system depends on the type and number of devices connected to the UPS, the power capacity of the UPS device (typically measured in watts), and the age of the battery (most UPS batteries last only 3 to 5 years before they need to be replaced). Most UPS devices also protect against power fluctuations. UPSs designed for use by individuals usually provide power for a few minutes to keep the system powered up during short power blips, as well as to allow the user to save open documents and shut down the computer properly in case the electricity remains off. Industrial-level UPSs typically run for a significantly longer amount of time (such as a few hours), but not long enough to power a facility during an extended power outage such as those that happen periodically in some parts of the U.S. due to winter storms, summer rotating blackouts, and other factors. To provide longer-term power during extended power outages, as well as to provide continuous power to facilities (such as hospitals, nuclear power plants, and business data centers) that cannot afford to be without power for any period of time, *generators* can be used.

Dust, heat, static electricity, and moisture can also be dangerous to a computer, so be sure not to place your computer equipment in direct sunlight or in a dusty area. Small handheld vacuums made for electrical equipment can be used periodically to remove the dust from the keyboard and from inside the system unit, but be very careful when vacuuming inside the system unit. Also, be sure the system unit has plenty of ventilation, especially around the fan vents. To help reduce the amount of dust that is drawn into the fan vents, raise your desktop computer several inches off the floor. You should also avoid placing a portable computer on a soft surface, such as a couch or blanket, to help prevent overheating (*notebook cooling stands* can help provide air circulation). To prevent static electricity from damaging the inside of your computer when installing a new expansion card or other internal device, turn off the power to the computer and unplug the power cord from the computer before removing the cover from the system unit. Wearing an antistatic wristband is an additional good precaution. Unless your computer is ruggedized (like the one shown in Figure 5-8), do not get it wet or otherwise expose it to adverse conditions. Be especially careful with mobile phones and other mobile devices when you are near water (such as a swimming pool, lake, or large puddle) so you do not drop them into the water (more than 50% of the phones received by one data recovery firm are water damaged).

Both internal and external magnetic hard drives also need to be protected against jostling or other excess motion that can result in a *head crash*, which occurs when a hard drive's read/write heads actually touch the surface of a hard disk. Unless your portable computer contains a solid-state drive instead of a conventional magnetic hard drive, it is a good idea to turn off the computer, hibernate it, or put it into standby mode before moving it since magnetic hard drives are more vulnerable to damage while they are spinning. In addition, storage media—such as flash memory cards, hard drives, CDs, and DVDs—are all sensitive storage media that work well over time, as long as appropriate care is used. Don't remove a USB storage device (such as a USB flash drive or USB hard drive) when it is being accessed—use the *Safely Remove Hardware* icon in the system tray on a Windows computer to stop the device before unplugging it to avoid data loss and damage to the device. Keep CDs and DVDs in their protective *jewel cases* and handle them carefully to prevent fingerprints and scratches on the data sides of the discs (usually the bottom, unprinted side on a single-sided disc). *Screen protectors* (thin plastic film that covers the display screen of a mobile phone or mobile device) can be used to prevent scratches on the displays of pen-based devices. For more tips on how to protect your computer, see the Technology and You box.

FIGURE 5-8

Proper hardware care. Unless your computer is ruggedized (such as the one shown here), keep it out of the heat, cold, rain, water, and other adverse conditions.

FURTHER EXPLORATION   Go

Go to the Chapter 5 page at **www.cengage.com/computerconcepts/np/uccs4** for links to information about protecting your computer from theft or damage.

> **Uninterruptible power supply (UPS).** A device containing a built-in battery that provides continuous power to a computer and other connected components when the electricity goes out.

TECHNOLOGY AND YOU

Protecting Your PC

All computer users should take specific actions to protect their computers. In this world of viruses, worms, hackers, spyware, and "buggy" (error-prone) software, it pays to be cautious. Although safeguards have been covered in detail throughout this book, some specific precautionary steps all computer users should follow are summarized in this box.

Step 1: Protect your hardware.

Be sure to plug all components of your computer system (such as the system unit, monitor, printer, and scanner) into a surge suppressor. Be careful not to bump or move the computer when it is on. Don't spill food or drink onto the keyboard or any other piece of hardware. Store your flash memory cards and CDs properly. If you ever need to work inside the system unit, turn off the computer and unplug it before touching any component inside the system unit. When taking a portable computer on the road, don't ever leave it unattended, and be careful not to drop or lose it.

Step 2: Install and use security software.

Install a good antivirus program and set it up to scan your system on a continual basis, including checking all files and e-mail messages before they are downloaded to your computer. To detect the newest viruses and types of malware, keep your antivirus program up to date (have it automatically check for and install updates) and use a personal two-way firewall program to protect your computer from unauthorized access via the Internet, as well as to detect any attempts by spyware to send data from your computer to another party. For additional protection if you have a home network, enable file sharing only for files and folders that really need to be accessed by other users. Run an antispyware program—such as Ad-Aware or Spybot Search & Destroy—on a regular basis to detect and remove spyware.

Step 3: Back up regularly.

Once you have a new computer set up with all programs installed and the menus and other settings the way you like them, create a full backup so the computer can be restored to that configuration in case of a major problem with your computer or hard drive. Be sure also to back up your data files on a regular basis. Depending on how important your documents are, you may want to back up all of your data every night, or copy each document to a removable storage medium after each major revision. If you use local (instead of Web-based) e-mail, periodically back up the folder containing your e-mail, such as the *Outlook.pst* file used to store Microsoft Outlook mail. To facilitate data backup, keep your data organized using folders (such as storing all data files in a main folder called "Data"). For an even higher level of security, install (and regularly back up) a second hard drive just for data—if your main

hard drive ever becomes unstable and needs to be reformatted or replaced, your data drive will remain untouched. Backups should be stored in a different location than your computer, such as in a different building or in a fire-resistant safe. An easy way to accomplish this is to use an online backup service or upload your backup files to an online storage service.

Step 4: Update your operating system, browser, and e-mail program regularly.

Most companies that produce operating systems, Web browsers, or e-mail programs regularly post updates and patches—small programs that take care of software-specific problems, or bugs, such as security holes—on their Web sites on a regular basis. Some programs include an option within the program to check online for updates; for other programs, you will need to go to each manufacturer's Web site directly to check for any critical or recommended updates. For any programs—such as Windows and most antivirus and firewall programs—that have the option to check for updates automatically, enable that option. Windows users can check their current security settings using the *Windows Security Center* (called the *Action Center* in Windows 7), available through the Control Panel and shown in the accompanying illustration.

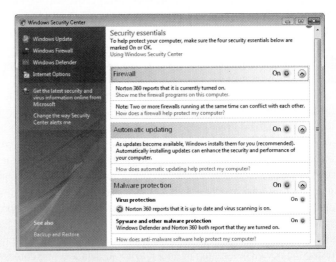

For optimal protection, all security essentials should be enabled.

Step 5: Test your system for vulnerabilities.

There are several free tests available through Web sites to see if your computer's ports are accessible to hackers or if your computer is infected with a virus or spyware. These tests, such as the one on the Symantec Web site shown in Figure 4-10 in Chapter 4 or the ShieldsUP test available on the Gibson Research Web site, should be run to check for any remaining vulnerabilities once you believe your antivirus software, firewall, and any other protective components you are using are set up correctly.

Backups and Disaster Recovery Plans

As mentioned in Chapter 1, creating a *backup* means making a duplicate copy of important files so that when a problem occurs (such as a hard drive failure or a stolen computer), you can restore those files using the backup copy. Data to be backed up includes company files, personal documents, photos, e-mail messages, and any other files that are important and the owner of the files would miss if they were lost. Backups can be performed for personal computers, servers, mobile phones, and other devices, depending on where the important data is located.

Businesses should make backups of at least all new data on a regular basis (such as once per day); individuals should make backups of important documents as they are created and back up the rest of their data periodically. Businesses and individuals that utilize cloud computing should also back up important data stored online.

After a backup is performed, the backup media used needs to be secured so that it will be intact when it is needed. If stored in-house, backup media should be placed in a fire-resistant safe; however, it is even better to store backup media in a different physical location. For instance, many businesses today use third-party *data storage companies* that store their backup media at a secure remote location; businesses can request their backups be returned whenever they are needed. To secure the data on the backup media while it is in transit and being stored, the data should be encrypted. *Online backup services* perform backups via the Internet so physically transporting backup media to the storage company location is not an issue.

For an even higher level of security than a scheduled backup, *continuous data protection* (*CDP*) can be used. A CDP backup system (most often used with company servers) records data changes on a continual basis so that data can be recovered from any point in time (even just a few minutes ago) with no data loss, and recovery can be as fast as five minutes after a failure. Although expensive, it is one of the best ways to ensure that company data is protected. In addition to business data, CDP is beginning to be used to adhere to the growing requirements for *e-discovery* of electronic business documents. In fact, the size of the e-mail archiving market alone in 2011 is expected to be $1.4 billion, according to research firm IDC.

To supplement backup procedures, businesses and other organizations should have a **disaster recovery plan** (also called a *business continuity* plan)—a plan that spells out what the organization will do to prepare for and recover from a disruptive event, such as a fire,

ONLINE VIDEO

Go to the Chapter 5 page at **www.cengage.com/ computerconcepts/np/uccs4** to watch the "The DriveSavers Data Recovery Service" video clip.

> **Disaster recovery plan.** A written plan that describes the steps a company will take following the occurrence of a disaster.

natural disaster, terrorist attack, power outage, or computer failure. Disaster recovery plans should include information about who will be in charge immediately after the disaster has occurred, what alternate facilities and equipment can be used, where backup media is located, the priority of getting each operation back online, disaster insurance coverage information, emergency communications methods, and so forth. If a *hot site*—an alternate location equipped with the computers, cabling, desks, and other equipment necessary to keep a business's operations going—is to be used following a major disaster, it should be set up ahead of time, and information about the hot site should be included in the disaster recovery plan. Businesses that cannot afford to be without e-mail service should also consider making arrangements with an *emergency mail system provider* to act as a temporary mail server if the company mail server is not functioning. Copies of the disaster recovery plan should be located off-site, such as at an appropriate employee's house or at the office of an associated organization located in a different city.

It is important to realize that disaster recovery planning isn't just for large businesses. In fact, disasters such as a fire or computer malfunction can cause a small company to go out of business if its data is not backed up. Measures as straightforward as backing up data daily and storing the backups in a fire-resistant safe at the owner's house with a plan regarding how that data can be quickly reinstated on a new system or otherwise used for business continuity can go a long way in protecting a small business. Companies that are considering using cloud computing services should find out what type of outages are to be expected (such as for regular maintenance) and what type of advance notice will be sent regarding these outages, as well as what type of disaster recovery services (such as switching to alternate servers if the main servers go down) are available.

The importance of a good disaster recovery plan was made obvious following the collapse of the World Trade Center Twin Towers in 2001. Minutes after the first airplane hit the towers, corporate executives, disaster recovery firms, and backup storage companies began arranging for employees and backup data to be moved to alternate sites. Employees at the data storage company Recall Corporation spent the day of the attack gathering backup tapes belonging to clients located in and near the attacks, using barcode scanners to locate the needed 30,000 tapes out of the 2 million in their secure storage facility. Bond trader Cantor Fitzgerald, which lost 700 employees and all the equipment and data located in its WTC offices, relocated to a prearranged hot site where employees received backup tapes the day after the attack, and it was able to begin trading the next morning. Although Cantor Fitzgerald—like the other organizations and businesses located in the WTC—suffered enormous human loss, good disaster recovery planning enabled Cantor Fitzgerald to restore the records containing client accounts and portfolios completely, avoiding an additional economic disaster related to this tragedy.

SOFTWARE PIRACY AND DIGITAL COUNTERFEITING

Instead of stealing an existing computer program, object, or other valuable that belongs to someone else, *software piracy* and *digital counterfeiting* involve creating duplicates of these items, and then selling them or using them as authentic items.

Software Piracy

Software piracy, the unauthorized copying of a computer program, is illegal in the United States and many other—but not all—countries. Because of the ease with which computers can create exact copies of a software program, software piracy is a widespread problem.

> **Software piracy.** The unauthorized copying of a computer program.

According to a 2009 report from the *Business Software Alliance* (*BSA*)—an organization that was formed by a number of the world's leading software developers and that has antipiracy programs in 65 countries worldwide—approximately 41% of all software installed on personal computers globally (and about 20% of all software in the United States) is installed illegally. The report estimates that the annual monetary loss to software vendors as the result of software piracy is more than $50 billion worldwide.

Software piracy can take many forms, including individuals making illegal copies of programs to give to friends, businesses installing software on more computers than permitted in the program's *end-user license agreement* or *EULA* (see Figure 5-9), computer retailers installing unlicensed copies of software on computers sold to consumers, and large-scale operations in which the software and its packaging are illegally duplicated and then sold as supposedly legitimate products. Pirated software—as well as pirated music CDs and movie DVDs—are commonly offered for sale at online auctions; they can also be downloaded from some Web sites and peer-to-peer file sharing services. Creating and distributing pirated copies of any type of *intellectual property* (such as software, music, and movies) is illegal. Intellectual property is discussed in more detail in Chapter 6.

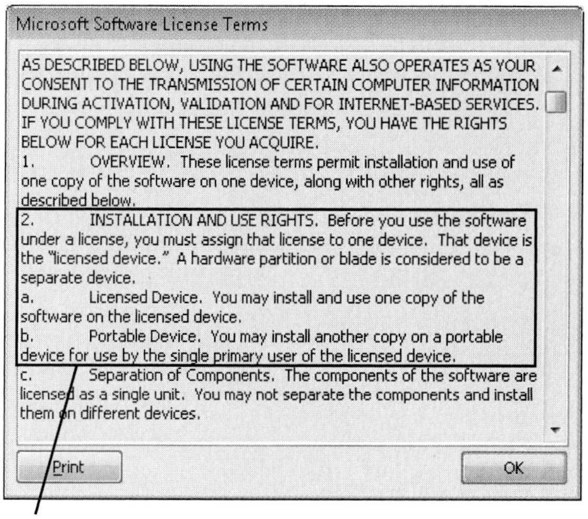

This software can be installed on one primary device and one portable device to be used by a single user.

FIGURE 5-9
An end-user license agreement (EULA). An EULA specifies the number of computers on which the software can be installed and other restrictions for use.

Digital Counterfeiting

The availability of high-quality, full-color imaging products (such as scanners, color printers, and color copiers) has made **digital counterfeiting**—creating counterfeit copies of items (such as currency and other printed resources) using computers and other types of digital equipment—easier and less costly than in the recent past. The U.S. Secret Service estimates that more than 60% of all counterfeit money today is produced digitally—up from 1% in 1996.

With digital counterfeiting, the bill (or other item to be counterfeited) is either color-copied or it is scanned into a computer and then printed. In addition to counterfeiting currency, other items that are digitally counterfeited include fake business checks, credit cards, printed collectibles (such as baseball cards or celebrity autographs), and fake identification papers (such as corporate IDs, driver's licenses, passports, and visas)—see Figure 5-10.

Counterfeiting is illegal in the United States and is taken very seriously. For creating or knowingly circulating counterfeit currency, for instance, offenders can face up to 15 years in prison for each offense. In spite of the risk of prosecution, counterfeiting of U.S. currency and other documents is a growing problem both in the United States and in other countries. Although the majority of counterfeit currency is produced by serious criminals (such as organized crime, gangs, and terrorist organizations), the Secret Service has seen an increase in counterfeiting among high school and college students. This is attributed primarily to the ease of creating counterfeit bills—although not necessarily high-quality counterfeit bills—using digital technology. Because the paper used with real U.S. bills is very expensive and cannot legally be made by paper

FIGURE 5-10
Digital counterfeiting. Documents commonly counterfeited include currency, credit cards, driver's licenses, passports, and checks.

>**Digital counterfeiting.** The use of computers or other types of digital equipment to make illegal copies of currency, checks, collectibles, and other items.

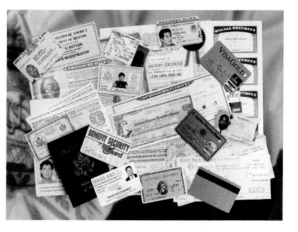

mills for any other purpose and because U.S. bills contain a number of other characteristics that are difficult to reproduce accurately, as discussed in more detail shortly, the majority of the counterfeit money made by amateurs is easily detectable.

Protecting Against Software Piracy and Digital Counterfeiting

Software piracy and digital counterfeiting affect individuals, as well as businesses and the government. For instance, some software companies charge higher prices and have less money available for research and development because of the losses from software pirates, which ultimately hurts law-abiding consumers. In addition, individuals and businesses that unknowingly accept counterfeit currency lose the face value of that currency if it is identified as counterfeit while it is in their possession, and they risk legal issues if they knowingly pass the counterfeit bills on to others. Some tools currently being used to curb software piracy and digital counterfeiting are discussed next.

Software Antipiracy Tools

One tool the software industry is using in an attempt to prevent software piracy is education. By educating businesses and consumers about the legal use of software and the possible negative consequences associated with breaking antipiracy laws, the industry hopes to reduce the use of illegal software significantly. To counteract piracy performed because of time or convenience issues, many software companies offer consumers the option of downloading software via the Internet—giving them a legal option for obtaining software that is as fast and convenient as downloading a pirated version. Some software manufacturers have launched extensive public relations campaigns—such as including information on their Web sites, in product information, and in advertisements—to inform consumers what software piracy is, and why they should not commit it or buy pirated software.

Another antipiracy tool is requiring a unique activation code (often called a *registration code* or *product key*) before the software can be installed (for commercial software) or before certain key features of a program are unlocked (for shareware or demo software). Typically the activation code is included in the product packaging (for software purchased on CD or DVD) or is displayed on the screen or sent to the user via e-mail once payment is made (for downloaded software). A related tool is checking the validity of a software installation before upgrades or other resources related to the program can be accessed. For instance, Microsoft checks a user's Windows installation before the user is allowed to download software from Microsoft's Web site (such as templates for Microsoft Office or gadgets for the Windows Vista Sidebar)—if their operating system is identified as invalid, users cannot download the resources. The goal of these techniques is to make pirated software unusable enough so that individuals will buy the licensed software.

Other antipiracy techniques used by software companies include watching online auction sites and requesting the removal of suspicious items, as well as buying pirated copies of software via Web sites and then filing lawsuits against the sellers. The increase in prosecution of consumers for illegally selling or sharing software (and other types of digital content, such as music and movies) may also help reduce some types of piracy and encourage individuals to obtain legal copies of these products. In 2009, for instance, *Operation Fastlink* (a Department of Justice initiative designed to combat online piracy worldwide that is credited with removing more than $50 million worth of illegally copied software, games, movies, and music from illicit distribution channels) resulted in its 60th felony conviction. In another recent instance, a Virginia man pleaded guilty to selling more than $1 million worth of counterfeit software on eBay and he is facing up to 25 years in prison.

One new option for software vendors is incorporating code into their programs that is designed to inform the vendor when pirated copies of its software is being used or when its software is being used in another manner that violates the terms of the software license. For instance, commercial software that contains the newest version of V.i Labs *CodeArmor Intelligence* software is designed to detect and report products in use that

ONLINE VIDEO

Go to the Chapter 5 page at **www.cengage.com/ computerconcepts/np/uccs4** to watch the "New Currency Design and Counterfeiting" video clip.

have been tampered with (such as products whose licensing features have been disabled and then resold as legitimate products), as well as products that are being used with more computers than allowed by the software license. Once piracy is detected, information about the infringement is sent to the software vendor's Web-based piracy dashboard. This information includes identifying data about the user of the pirated software (such as the user's domain name or IP address and a link to its location on Google Maps—see Figure 5-11) that can be used to help the vendor identify the user of the pirated software in order to pursue legal actions. It also provides the vendor with useful data about the overall state of piracy of their products, in order to help the company make appropriate business decisions regarding the distribution channels and the safeguards used with its products.

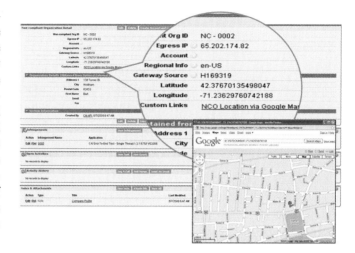

FIGURE 5-11
Antipiracy software.
This software identifies businesses (including their physical locations) using a pirated version of the vendor's software.

Digital Counterfeiting Prevention

To prevent the counterfeiting of U.S. currency, the Treasury Department releases new currency designs every 7 to 10 years. These new designs (such as the new $5 bill released in 2008 and shown in Figure 5-12) contain features (such as *microprinting, watermarks,* and a *security thread*) that make the new currency much more difficult to duplicate than older currency. Because the watermarks and security thread are embedded in the paper, counterfeiters are unable to duplicate those features when creating counterfeit bills either from scratch or by bleaching the ink out of existing lower-denomination bills and reprinting them with higher denominations. Consequently, counterfeit copies of bills using the new designs are easy to detect just by holding them up to the light and looking for the proper watermark or security thread. In addition, digital imaging equipment (such as color copiers and scanners) is equipped with technologies that can be used to track currency and other counterfeit items created with those devices. For example, many color copiers print invisible codes on copied documents, making counterfeit money copied on those machines traceable. This type of technology is also thought to be incorporated into many scanners. In fact, printer and scanner manufacturer Canon has revealed that it has been incorporating anticounterfeiting technologies into its products since 1992, but the company is prohibited by the government from disclosing any information about those technologies.

FIGURE 5-12
Anticounterfeiting measures used with U.S. currency.

Prevention measures for the counterfeiting of other types of documents—such as checks and identification cards—include using RFID tags, *digital watermarks,* and other difficult-to-reproduce content. As discussed in more detail in Chapter 6, a digital watermark is a subtle alteration that is not noticeable when the work is viewed or played but that can be read using special software to authenticate or identify the owner of the item. Finally, educating consumers about how the appearance of fake products differs from that of authentic products is a vital step in the ongoing battle against counterfeiting.

MICROPRINTING
Extremely small print that is very difficult to reproduce appears in three different locations on the front of the bill (in the left and right borders, at the top of the shield on the Great Seal, and in between the columns of the shield), though it is hard to see without a magnifying glass.

SECURITY THREAD
A plastic security thread embedded in the paper contains the letters "USA" followed by the number "5"; it can be seen when the bill is held up to the light and glows blue when placed in front of an ultraviolet light.

COLORS
Harder to match colors, such as shades of yellow and purple, have been added to some details.

WATERMARKS
Watermark images containing the number "5" located to the right and left of the portrait are incorporated into the paper itself and are visible when the bill is held up to the light (not visible in this photograph).

WHY BE CONCERNED ABOUT INFORMATION PRIVACY?

Privacy is usually defined as the state of being concealed or free from unauthorized intrusion. The term **information privacy** refers to the rights of individuals and companies to control how information about them is collected and used. The problem of how to protect personal privacy—that is, how to keep personal information private—existed long before computers entered the picture. For example, sealing wax and unique signet rings were used centuries ago to seal letters, wills, and other personal documents to guard against their content being revealed to unauthorized individuals, as well as to alert the recipient if such an intrusion occurred while the document was in transit. But today's computers, with their ability to store, duplicate, and manipulate large quantities of data—combined with the fact that databases containing our personal information can be accessed and shared via the Internet—have added a new twist to the issue of personal privacy.

As discussed in Chapters 3 and 4, one concern of many individuals is the privacy of their Web site activities and e-mail messages. Cookies and spyware are possible privacy risks, and e-mail and other documents can be read if intercepted by another individual during transit unless they are encrypted. For businesses and employees, there is the additional issue of whether or not Web activities, e-mail, and instant messages sent through a company network are private. In addition, businesses need to make sure they comply with privacy laws regarding the protection and the security of the private information they store on their servers. Recently, there has been an unprecedented number of high-profile data breaches—some via hacking and other network intrusions discussed in Chapter 4, and others due to lost or stolen hardware, or carelessness with papers or storage media containing Social Security numbers or other sensitive data. Since every data breach occurring today is a risk to information privacy, protecting the data stored in databases today is an important concern for everyone. Other privacy concerns are *spam* and other marketing activities, *electronic surveillance*, and *electronic monitoring*. These concerns, along with precautions that can be taken to safeguard information privacy, are discussed throughout the remainder of this chapter.

ASK THE EXPERT

epic.org   **Lillie Coney,** Associate Director, Electronic Privacy Information Center

What is the biggest Internet-related privacy risk for individuals today?

The biggest Internet-related privacy risk for individuals is the rapid consolidation of personal information based on online activity. Today, Web sites often include privacy statements or policies. However, the online experience allows the collection of unlimited amounts of personal information, such as search engine requests and Web sites visited, and the information you choose to share online may be sold to strangers or otherwise shared with others. For instance, in 2007, Facebook introduced the "Beacon" application, which monitored Facebook users who shopped at third-party Web sites and shared users' purchases with their friends via Facebook. The "Beacon" application resulted in a number of lawsuits and Facebook has suspended its use.

The race to monetize Internet activities also leaves the privacy of users in a vulnerable position because of the lack of regulation and government oversight. Furthermore, Internet privacy protection is undermined when online service providers promote anti-privacy proposals as privacy protection.

>**Privacy.** The state of being concealed or free from unauthorized intrusion. >**Information privacy.** The rights of individuals and companies to control how information about them is collected and used.

DATABASES, ELECTRONIC PROFILING, SPAM, AND OTHER MARKETING ACTIVITIES

There are marketing activities that can be considered privacy risks or, at least, a potential invasion of privacy. These include *databases, electronic profiling*, and *spam*.

Databases and Electronic Profiling

Information about individuals can be located in many different databases. For example, most educational institutions have databases containing student information, most organizations use an employee database to hold employee information, and most physicians and health insurance providers maintain databases containing individuals' medical information. If these databases are adequately protected from hackers and other unauthorized individuals and if the data is not transported on a portable computer or other device that may be vulnerable to loss or theft, these databases do not pose a significant privacy concern to consumers because the information can rarely be shared without the individuals' permission. However, the data stored in these types of databases is not always sufficiently protected and has been breached quite often in the past. Consequently, these databases, along with two other types of databases—*marketing databases* and *government databases*—that are typically associated with a higher risk of personal privacy violations and are discussed next, are of growing concern to privacy advocates.

Marketing databases contain marketing and demographic data about people, such as where they live and what products they buy. This information is used for marketing purposes, such as sending advertisements that fit each individual's interests (via regular mail or e-mail) or trying to sign people up over the phone for some type of service. Virtually anytime you provide information about yourself online or offline—for example, when you subscribe to a magazine, fill out a sweepstakes entry or product registration card, or buy a product or service using a credit card—there is a good chance that the information will find its way into a marketing database.

Marketing databases are also used in conjunction with Web activities, such as social network activity and searches performed via some personalized search services. For instance, the data stored on Facebook, MySpace, and other social networking sites can be gathered and used for advertising purposes by marketing companies, and the activities of users of personalized search services (where users log in to use the service) can be tracked and that data can be used for marketing purposes. There has been some objection to several of these possible privacy risks. For instance, Facebook met with significant objection to its *Beacon* advertising service. Beacon, introduced in late 2007, was designed to track members' Web purchases, movie rentals, and other Web activities on more than 40 partner sites and share those purchases and activities with the users' Facebook friends (one user discovered that his Facebook friends had been notified that he had bought an engagement ring before he had even proposed). In response to user complaints, Facebook changed the service to work only on an *opt-in* basis, where it would only be enabled at a member's request. However, it was still ordered to pay $9.5 million in late 2009 to fund a nonprofit privacy organization in response to one class action lawsuit related to the Beacon service. And Google, with its vast array of services that collect enormous amounts of data about individuals, worries many privacy advocates. For instance, Google may have data stored about your search history (Google search site), browsing history (Google Chrome), e-mail (Gmail), appointments (Google Calendar), telephone messages (Google Voice), photos (Picasa Web Albums), reading history (Google Books), and

ONLINE VIDEO

Go to the Chapter 5 page at **www.cengage.com/ computerconcepts/np/uccs4** to watch the "Google Search Privacy: Personalized Search" video clip.

>**Marketing database.** A collection of data about people that is stored in a large database and used for marketing purposes.

medical history (Google Health). While Google allows users to *opt out* of collecting some data (such as by not signing into a service) and states that the data stored on separate servers is not combined, the vast amount of collected data is a concern to some.

Information about individuals is also available in **government databases**. Some information, such as Social Security earnings and income tax returns, is confidential and can legally be seen only by authorized individuals. Other information—such as birth records, marriage certificates, and divorce information, as well as property purchases, assessments, liens, and tax values—is available to the public, including to the marketing companies that specialize in creating marketing databases. One emerging government database application is the creation of a *national ID system* that links driver's license databases across the country. Although controversial, this system is mandated by the *Real ID Act* that was passed in 2005, which also requires states to meet new federal standards for driver's licenses and other identification cards (such as the inclusion of a barcode or other machine-readable technology that can be used in conjunction with the ID database). If the proposed *Pass ID Act* that was introduced in 2009 passes, however, the requirement that all state databases be linked will be removed.

FIGURE 5-13

A variety of searchable databases are available via the Internet.

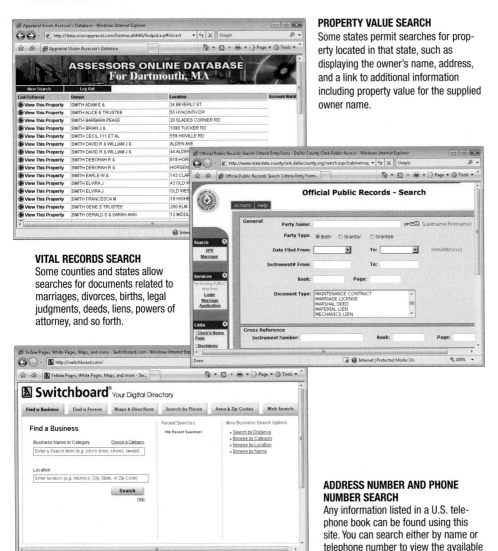

PROPERTY VALUE SEARCH
Some states permit searches for property located in that state, such as displaying the owner's name, address, and a link to additional information including property value for the supplied owner name.

VITAL RECORDS SEARCH
Some counties and states allow searches for documents related to marriages, divorces, births, legal judgments, deeds, liens, powers of attorney, and so forth.

ADDRESS NUMBER AND PHONE NUMBER SEARCH
Any information listed in a U.S. telephone book can be found using this site. You can search either by name or telephone number to view the available information.

In the past, the data about any one individual was stored in a variety of separate locations, such as at different government agencies, individual retail stores, the person's bank and credit card companies, and so forth. Because it would be extremely time consuming to locate all the information about one person from all these different places, there was a fairly high level of information privacy. Today, however, most of an individual's data is stored on computers that can communicate with each other via the Internet, which means accessing personal information about someone is much easier than it used to be. For example, a variety of public information about individuals is available free through the Internet (see Figure 5-13); there are also paid services that can perform online database searches for you. Although often this ability to search online databases

> **Government database.** A collection of data about people that is collected and maintained by the government.

When you make an electronic transaction, information about who you are and what you buy is recorded, usually in a database.

Databases containing the identities of people and what they buy are sold to marketing companies.

The marketing companies add the new data to their marketing databases; they can then reorganize the data in ways that might be valuable to other companies.

The marketing companies create lists of individuals matching the specific needs of companies; the companies buy the lists for their own marketing purposes.

FIGURE 5-14
How electronic profiling might work.

is an advantage—such as checking the background of a potential employee or looking up a misplaced phone number—it does raise privacy concerns. In response to the increased occurrence of identity theft (discussed in detail in Chapter 4), some local governments have removed birth and death information from their available online database records.

Collecting in-depth information about an individual is known as **electronic profiling**. Marketing companies often use data acquired from a variety of sources—such as from product and service purchases that are tied to personally identifiable information, as well as from public information like property values, vehicle registrations, births, marriages, and deaths—to create electronic profiles of individuals for marketing purposes. Electronic profiles are generally designed to provide specific information and can include an individual's name, current and previous addresses, telephone number, marital status, number and age of children, spending habits, and product preferences. The information retrieved from electronic profiles is then sold to companies upon request to be used for marketing purposes (see Figure 5-14). For example, one company might request a list of all individuals in a particular state whose street addresses are considered to be in an affluent area and who buy baby products. Another company might request a list of all SUV owners in a particular city who have not purchased a car in five years. Still another company may want a list of business travelers who fly to the East Coast frequently.

Most businesses and Web sites that collect personal information have a **privacy policy** (see Figure 5-15) that discloses how the personal information you provide will be used. As long as their actions do not violate their privacy policy, it is legal for businesses to sell the personal data that they collect. There are some problems with privacy policies, however, such as the fact that they are sometimes difficult to decipher and the reality that most people

FIGURE 5-15
Privacy policies. Web site privacy policies explain how your personal information might be used.

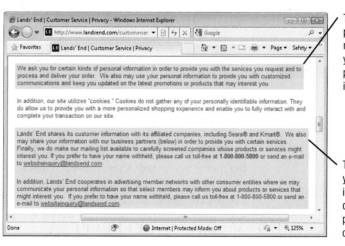

This indicates that your personal information may be used to keep you updated on products that might interest you.

This indicates that your personal information may be disclosed to third parties, unless you opt out.

>**Electronic profiling.** Using electronic means to collect a variety of in-depth information about an individual, such as name, address, income, and buying habits. >**Privacy policy.** A policy, commonly posted on a company's Web site, that explains how personal information provided to that company will be used.

do not take the time to read them before using a site. In addition, many businesses periodically change their privacy policies without warning, requiring consumers to reread privacy policies frequently or risk their personal information being used in a manner that they did not agree to when the information was initially provided. Some companies notify customers by e-mail when their privacy policies change but, more commonly, they expect customers to check the current policy periodically and notify the business if any new actions are objectionable.

Spam and Other Marketing Activities

Spam refers to unsolicited e-mail sent to a large group of individuals at one time. The electronic equivalent of junk mail (see Figure 5-16), spam is most often used to sell products or services to individuals. Spam is also used in phishing schemes and other dot cons and is sent frequently via botnets, as discussed in Chapter 4 (the text message spam shown in Figure 5-16 is an example of a phishing spam message). A great deal of spam involves health-related products (such as medicine or weight loss systems), counterfeit products (such as watches and medicine), pornography, and new—and often fraudulent—business opportunities and stock deals. Spam can also be generated by individuals forwarding e-mail messages they receive (such as jokes, recipes, or notices of possible new privacy or health concerns) to everyone in their address books. In addition to spam, most individuals receive marketing e-mails either from companies they directly provided with their e-mail addresses or from other companies that acquired their e-mail addresses from a third party to whom that information was provided (such as from a partner site or via a purchased mailing list). While these latter types of marketing e-mail messages do not technically fit the definition of spam since they were permission-based, many individuals consider them to be spam. Spam can also be sent via IM (called *spim*); to mobile phones (called *mobile phone spam* or *SMS spam*); to Facebook, MySpace, and Twitter pages and via other social networking communications methods; and to fax machines.

The sheer volume of spam is staggering today. For instance, Symantec's MessageLabs recently estimated that more than 90% of all e-mail messages are now spam. At best, large volumes of spam are an annoyance to recipients and can slow down a mail server's delivery of important messages. At worst, spam can disable a mail network completely, or it can cause recipients to miss or lose important e-mail messages because those messages have been caught in a *spam filter* (discussed shortly) or were accidentally deleted by the recipient while he or she was deleting a large number of spam e-mail messages. Most Internet users spend several minutes each day dealing with spam, making spam very expensive for businesses in terms of lost productivity, consumption of communications bandwidth, and drain of technical support. Spam sent to a mobile phone (either via text message or e-mail) is also expensive for end users that have a limited data or text message allowance.

FIGURE 5-16

Examples of spam.

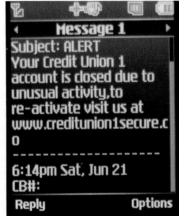

E-MAIL SPAM   TEXT MESSAGE SPAM

>**Spam.** Unsolicited, bulk e-mail sent over the Internet.

One of the most common ways of getting on a spam mailing list is by having your e-mail address entered into a marketing database, which can happen when you sign up for a free online service or use your e-mail address to register a product or make an online purchase. Spammers also use software to gather e-mail addresses from Web pages, message board posts, and social networking sites. Many individuals view spam as an invasion of privacy because it arrives on computers without permission and costs them time and other resources (bandwidth, mailbox space, and hard drive space, for instance).

Most spam is legal, but there are requirements that must be adhered to in order for it to be legal. For instance, the *CAN-SPAM Act of 2003* established requirements (such as using truthful subject lines and honoring remove requests) for commercial e-mailers, as well as specified penalties for companies and individuals that break the law. While the CAN-SPAM Act has not reduced the amount of spam circulated today, it has increased the number of spammers prosecuted for sending spam. In fact, several spammers have been convicted in recent years. They have either been fined or sent to prison, and more are awaiting trial. For instance, one spammer was recently ordered to pay $230 million to MySpace for spamming MySpace users and another was ordered to pay Facebook a record $873 million for spamming its members.

Protecting the Privacy of Personal Information

There are a number of precautions that can be taken to protect the privacy of personal information. Safeguarding your e-mail address and other personal information is a good start. You can also surf anonymously, *opt out* of some marketing activities, and use filters and other tools to limit your exposure to spam. Businesses also need to take adequate measures to protect the privacy of information stored on their servers and storage media. These precautions are discussed next.

Safeguard Your E-Mail Address

Protecting your e-mail address is one of the best ways to avoid spam. One way to accomplish this is to use one private e-mail address for family, friends, colleagues, and other trusted sources. For online shopping, signing up for free offers, message boards, product registration, and other activities that typically lead to junk e-mail, use a *disposable* or **throw-away e-mail address**— such as a second address obtained from your ISP or a free e-mail address from Yahoo! Mail, AOL Mail, Windows Live Hotmail, or Google's Gmail (see Figure 5-17). Although you will want to check your alternate e-mail address periodically (to check for online shopping receipts or shipping notifications, for instance), this precaution can prevent a great deal of spam from getting to your regular e-mail account.

Another advantage of using a throw-away e-mail address for only noncritical applications is that you can quit using it and obtain a new one if spam begins to get overwhelming or too annoying. To help with this, some ISPs (such as EarthLink) provide disposable anonymous e-mail addresses to their subscribers—e-mail messages sent to a subscriber's anonymous address are forwarded to the subscriber's account until the disposable address is deleted by the subscriber. Consequently, individuals can easily change disposable

FIGURE 5-17

Gmail. Free Web mail services like Gmail can be used for throw-away e-mail addresses, in addition to regular e-mail addresses.

>**Throw-away e-mail address.** An e-mail address used only for nonessential purposes and activities that may result in spam; the address can be disposed of and replaced if spam becomes a problem.

FIGURE 5-18
Anonymous surfing software can be used to protect your privacy online.

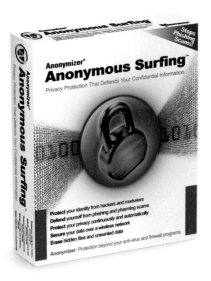

addresses when they begin to receive too much spam or when the disposable address is not needed any longer. There are also *anonymous e-mail services* (such as the one provided by Anonymizer *Nyms*) that allow users to create and delete anonymous e-mail addresses; messages sent to the anonymous e-mail addresses are forwarded to the user's specified e-mail account. These services typically cost about $20 per year.

To comply with truth-in-advertising laws, an *unsubscribe e-mail address* included in an unsolicited e-mail must be a working address. If you receive a marketing e-mail from a reputable source, you may be able to unsubscribe by clicking the supplied link or otherwise following the unsubscribe instructions. Since spam from less-legitimate sources often has unsubscribe links that do not work or that are present only to verify that your e-mail address is genuine—a very valuable piece of information for future use—many privacy experts recommend never replying to or trying to unsubscribe from any spam.

Be Cautious of Revealing Personal Information

In addition to protecting your real e-mail address, protecting your personal information is a critical step toward safeguarding your privacy. Consequently, it makes sense to be cautious about revealing your private information to anyone. Privacy tips for safeguarding personal information include the following:

> Read a Web site's privacy policy (if one exists) before providing any personal information. Look for a phrase saying that the company will not share your information with other companies under any circumstances. If the Web site reserves the right to share your information if the company is sold or unless you specifically notify them otherwise, it is best to assume that any information you provide will eventually be shared with others—do not use the site if that is unacceptable to you.

> Avoid putting too many personal details about yourself on your Web site or on a social networking site. If you would like to post photographs or other personal documents on a Web site for faraway friends and family members to see, consider using a photo sharing site that allows you to restrict access to your photos (such as *Flickr*, *Snapfish*, or *Fotki*).

> Beware of Web sites offering prizes or the chance to earn free merchandise in exchange for your personal information. Chances are good that the information will be sold to direct marketers, which will likely result in additional spam. If you choose to sign up for services from these Web sites, use your throw-away e-mail address.

> Consider using privacy software, such as *Anonymous Surfing* (see Figure 5-18) or *Privacy Guardian* to hide your personal information as you browse the Web so it is not revealed and your activities cannot be tracked by marketers.

> Just because a Web site or registration form asks for personal information, that does not mean you have to give it. Supply only the required information (these fields are often marked with an asterisk or are colored differently than nonrequired fields—if not, you can try leaving fields blank and see if the form will still be accepted). If you are asked for more personal information than you are comfortable providing, look for an alternate Web site for the product or information you are seeking. As a rule of thumb, do not provide an e-mail address (or else use a throw-away address) if you do not want to receive offers or other e-mail from that company.

> If you are using a public computer (such as at a school, a library, or an Internet café), be sure to remove any personal information and settings stored on the computer during your session. You can use browser options to delete this data manually from the computer before you leave (use the *Browsing history* option on the General tab of the Internet Options dialog box in Internet Explorer to delete this data). To prevent the deleted data from being recovered, run the Windows Disk Cleanup program on the hard drive, making sure that the options for Temporary

Internet Files and the Recycle Bin are selected during the Disk Cleanup process. An easier option is using the *private browsing* mode offered by some browsers (such as Internet Explorer's *InPrivate* or Chrome's *Incognito* modes (see Figure 5-19) that allow you to browse the Web without leaving any history (such as browsing history, temporary Internet files, form data, cookies, usernames, and passwords) on the computer you are using. In either case, be sure to log out of any Web sites you were using before leaving the computer.

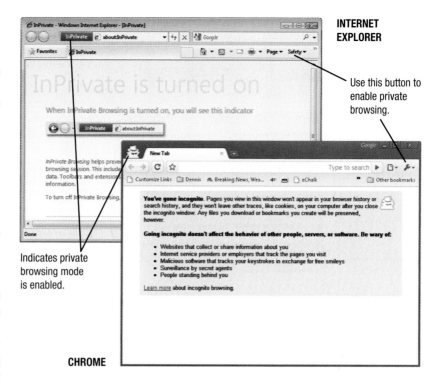

INTERNET EXPLORER

Use this button to enable private browsing.

Indicates private browsing mode is enabled.

CHROME

Use Filters and Opt Out

While keeping your personal information as private as possible can help to reduce spam and other direct marketing activities, *filtering* can also be helpful. Some ISPs automatically block all e-mail messages originating from known or suspected spammers so those e-mail messages never reach the individuals'

🅐 **FIGURE 5-19**
Private browsing
can protect your
Web surfing privacy
at public computers.

mailboxes; other ISPs flag suspicious e-mail messages as possible spam, based on their content or subject lines, to warn individuals that those messages may contain spam. To deal with spam that makes it to your computer, you can use an **e-mail filter**—a tool for automatically sorting your incoming e-mail messages. E-mail filters used to capture spam are called **spam filters**. Many e-mail programs have built-in spam filters that identify possible spam and either flag it or move it to a Spam or Junk E-mail folder. Individuals can typically change the spam settings used in their e-mail program to indicate the actions that should be taken with suspected spam. In addition, they can create e-mail filters in their e-mail program, or they can use third-party filtering software to customize their spam filtering further. Many spam filters can also "learn" what each user views as spam based on the user identifying e-mail messages that were classified incorrectly (either spam messages placed in the Inbox or legitimate messages placed in the Spam folder) by the spam filter. The user typically provides this information by clicking a button such as *Report Spam* or *Not Spam* when the message is selected; the spam filter uses this input to classify messages from that sender correctly in the future. Businesses can set up spam filters in-house, but they are increasingly turning to dedicated *antispam appliances* to filter out spam without increasing the load on the company e-mail server.

Custom e-mail filters are used to route messages automatically to particular folders based on stated criteria. For example, you can specify that e-mail messages with keywords frequently used in spam subject lines (such as *free, porn, opportunity, last chance, weight, pharmacy*, and similar terms) be routed into a folder named *Possible Spam*, and you can specify that all e-mail messages from your boss's e-mail address be routed into an *Urgent* folder. Filtering can help you find important messages in your Inbox by preventing it from becoming cluttered with spam. However, you need to be sure to check your Possible Spam or Junk E-mail folder periodically to locate any e-mail messages mistakenly filed

>**E-mail filter.** A tool that automatically sorts your incoming e-mail messages based on specific criteria. >**Spam filter.** An e-mail filter used to redirect spam from a user's Inbox.

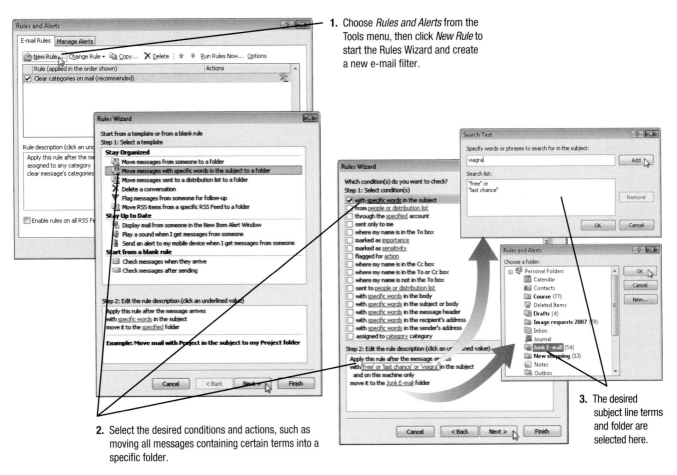

1. Choose *Rules and Alerts* from the Tools menu, then click *New Rule* to start the Rules Wizard and create a new e-mail filter.

2. Select the desired conditions and actions, such as moving all messages containing certain terms into a specific folder.

3. The desired subject line terms and folder are selected here.

FIGURE 5-20
E-mail filtering with Microsoft Outlook.

there—especially before you permanently delete those messages. Creating a new e-mail filter in Microsoft Outlook is shown in Figure 5-20.

Mobile users who receive Web-based e-mail via mobile phones can use the filters available via their Web mail provider to filter out spam. There are also some mobile spam filter applications available for some mobile phones. To block spam sent via text message, most carriers allow you to create an alias for your phone's e-mail address (which typically begins with your mobile phone number) and then block messages sent to that address, in order to prevent receiving text message spam sent by spammers simply guessing your mobile number.

Another alternative for reducing the amount of spam you receive is to **opt out**. *Opting out* refers to following a predesignated procedure to remove yourself from marketing lists, or otherwise preventing your personal information from being obtained by or shared with others. By opting out, you instruct companies you do business with (such as your bank, insurance company, investment company, or an online store) not to share your personal information with third parties. You can also opt out of being contacted by direct and online marketing companies.

To opt out from a particular company or direct marketing association, you can contact them directly—many organizations include opt-out instructions in the privacy policies posted on their Web sites. For Web sites that use registered accounts for repeat visitors,

> **Opt out.** To request that you be removed from marketing activities or that your information not be shared with other companies.

opt-out options are sometimes included in your personal settings and can be activated by modifying your personal settings for that site. Opt-out instructions for financial institutions and credit card companies are often included in the disclosure statements that are periodically mailed to customers; they can also often be found on the company's Web site.

To assist consumers with the opt-out process, there are a number of Web sites, such as the *Center for Democracy and Technology* and the *PrivacyRightsNow!* Web sites, which provide opt-out tools for consumers. For example, some sites help visitors create opt-out letters that can be sent to the companies in order to opt out. For online marketing activities, organizations—such as the *Network Advertising Initiative (NAI)*—have tools on their Web sites to help consumers opt out of online targeted ads. Typically, this process replaces an advertiser's marketing cookie with an *opt-out cookie*. The opt-out cookie prevents any more marketing cookies belonging to that particular advertiser from being placed on the user's hard drive as long as the opt-out cookie is present (usually until the user deletes the opt-out cookie file, either intentionally or unintentionally).

At the present time, opting-out procedures are confusing and time-consuming, and they do not always work well. Consequently, some privacy groups are pushing to change to an *opt-in* process, in which individuals would need to **opt in** (request participation in) to a particular marketing activity before companies can collect or share any personal data (as is the case in the European Union). In fact, Wal-Mart recently changed its privacy policy to share information with third parties only if customers opt in. However, the general practice in the U.S. business community today is to use your information as allowed for by each privacy policy unless you specifically opt out.

FURTHER EXPLORATION Go

Go to the Chapter 5 page at **www.cengage.com/ computerconcepts/np/uccs4** for links to information about protecting your privacy online.

Secure Servers and Otherwise Protect Personal Information

Any business that stores personal information about employees, customers, or other individuals must take adequate security measures to protect the privacy of that information. As discussed in Chapter 4, secure servers and encryption can protect the data stored on a server; firewalls and access systems can protect against unauthorized access. To prevent personal information from being sent intentionally or inadvertently via e-mail, organizations can use e-mail encryption systems that automatically encrypt e-mail messages containing certain keywords. For instance, some hospitals use encryption systems that scan all outgoing e-mail messages and attachments and then automatically encrypt all messages that appear to contain patient-identifiable information, such as a Social Security number, medical record number, patient name, or medical term like "cancer." The recipient of an encrypted e-mail message typically receives a link to a secure Web site to log in and view the encrypted e-mail message. Similar systems are used by banks and other businesses. Businesses also need to be very careful with papers, portable hard drives, and other media that contain personal data. For instance, many recent data breaches have occurred because of carelessness, such as papers containing personal information being found in dumpsters, lost in transit, or faxed to the wrong individual.

Ensuring that the private data stored by a business is adequately protected is increasingly the responsibility of a *chief privacy officer* (*CPO*)—a rapidly growing new position in business today. Typically, CPOs are responsible for ensuring privacy laws are complied with, identifying the data in a company that needs to be protected, developing policies to protect that data, and responding to any incidents that occur. Another issue that must

>**Opt in.** To request that you be included in marketing activities or that your information be shared with other companies.

be dealt with by CPOs is the changing definition of what information is regarded as personal and, therefore, needs to be safeguarded. For instance, the head of the European Union's group of data privacy regulators announced in early 2008 that IP addresses should be regarded as personal information. If that view becomes widespread or integrated into privacy laws, it will have major implications on search sites and other businesses that store the IP address of individuals using online services.

Properly Dispose of Hardware Containing Data

A final consideration for protecting the privacy of personal information for both individuals and businesses is protecting the information located on paper documents and hardware (such as old backup media, used CDs, obsolete computers, and old mobile phones) that are to be disposed of. Papers, CDs, DVDs, and other media containing sensitive data should be shredded (see Figure 5-21), and the hard drives of computers to be disposed of should be *wiped*— overwritten several times using special *disk-wiping* or *disk-erasing* software—before they are sold or recycled. Unlike the data on a drive that has merely been erased or even reformatted (which can still be recovered), data on a properly wiped drive is very difficult or impossible to recover.

FIGURE 5-21
Media disposal.
When disposing of CDs, DVDs, and other storage media, the media should be shredded to ensure the information on the media is destroyed.

Wiping is typically viewed as an acceptable precaution for deleting sensitive data (such as Web site passwords and tax returns) from hard drives and other storage media belonging to individuals, as well as for storage media to be reused within an organization. However, before disposing of storage media containing sensitive data, businesses should consider physically destroying the media, such as by shredding or melting the hardware. To help with this process, *data destruction services* can be used, as discussed in the Inside the Industry box. To ensure that all hardware containing business data is properly disposed of, it is important for all businesses today to develop and implement a policy (often called a *media sanitization* or *data destruction policy*) for destroying data that is no longer needed.

CAUTION **CAUTION** **CAUTION** **CAUTION** **CAUTION** **CAUTION** **CAUT**

When upgrading your mobile phone, be careful not to expose the personal data stored on your old phone to others. Before disposing of or recycling it, be sure to reset your mobile phone to its factory settings to clear all personal data from the phone.

ELECTRONIC SURVEILLANCE AND MONITORING

There are many ways electronic tools can be used to watch individuals, listen in on their conversations, or monitor their activities. Some of these tools—such as devices used by individuals to eavesdrop on wireless telephone conversations—are not legal. Other products and technologies, such as the GPS devices that are built into some cars so they can be located if they are stolen or the monitoring ankle bracelets used for offenders sentenced to house arrest, are used solely for law enforcement purposes. Still other electronic tools, such as *computer monitoring software, video surveillance* equipment, and *presence technology*, discussed next, can often be used legally by individuals, by businesses in conjunction with *employee monitoring*, and by law enforcement agencies.

INSIDE THE INDUSTRY

Data Killers

With the vast amount of sensitive and classified data stored on business computers today, disposing of those devices or removing the data from those devices so they can be reused is an important issue. Business computers typically contain a wide variety of sensitive data that needs to be protected if the hard drive containing that data needs to be disposed of or will be reused by another employee. *Data destruction services* are designed for this purpose.

Data destruction ranges from purging the data (such as wiping the drive clean or degaussing (demagnetizing) the drive so the data cannot be restored) to destroying the drive physically. The level of destruction needed depends on the type of data being deleted and where the hardware will go next. For instance, purging might be appropriate for personal hard drives being sold and for business hard drives that will be reused within the company, but all business hard drives that will no longer be used within the company and that contain sensitive data should be physically destroyed.

While data destruction can be performed in-house, there are data destruction services designed for this purpose. Such services typically can purge, degauss, or shred hard drives and other media, depending on the customer's preference. Once a hard drive has been shredded (see the accompanying photo), it is virtually impossible for any data to be recovered

from the pieces. However, for extra security, drives containing extremely sensitive data can be degaussed and then shredded. To ensure drives are not lost or compromised in transit, most data destruction companies offer secure transportation to the destruction facility using tamper proof locked cases, and will provide signed and dated Certificates of Purging or Certificates of Destruction, when requested. Some even offer destruction on site, if the customer desires. Purged hard drives are returned to the customer; shredded hard drives are typically recycled.

Computer Monitoring Software

Computer monitoring software is used specifically for the purpose of recording keystrokes, logging the programs or Web sites accessed, or otherwise monitoring someone's computer activity. These programs are typically marketed toward parents (to check on their children's online activities), spouses (to determine if a spouse is having an affair, viewing pornography, or participating in other activities that are unacceptable to the other spouse), law enforcement agencies (to collect evidence against suspected criminals), or employers (to ensure employees are using company computers and time only for work-related or otherwise approved activities). Computer monitoring programs can keep a log of all computer keystrokes performed on a computer, record the activities taking place (such as the amount of time spent on and tasks performed via the Web or installed software), take screen shots of the screen at specified intervals, and more (see Figure 5-22). Computer monitoring software designed for businesses also typically provides a summary of the activities (such as the programs used or the Web sites visited) performed by all company computers. In addition, some

> **Computer monitoring software.** Software that can be used to record an individual's computer usage, such as capturing images of the screen, recording the actual keystrokes used, or creating a summary of Web sites and programs accessed.

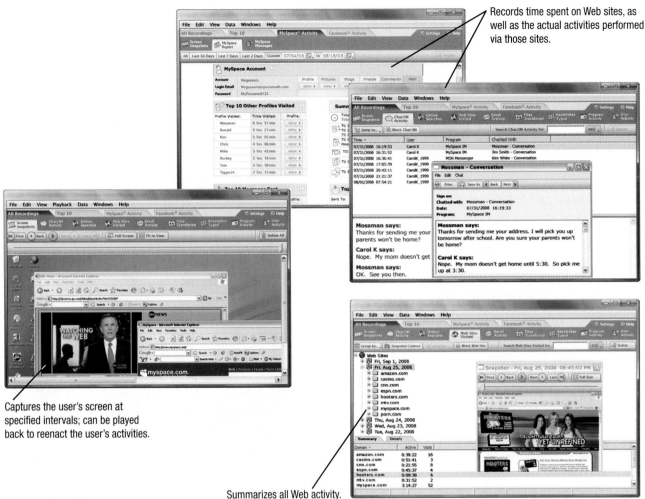

Records time spent on Web sites, as well as the actual activities performed via those sites.

Captures the user's screen at specified intervals; can be played back to reenact the user's activities.

Summarizes all Web activity.

FIGURE 5-22
Computer monitoring software.

computer monitoring software can block specific Web sites, as well as notify a designated party (such as the parent or computer administrator) if the individual using the computer being monitored uses specified keywords (such as inappropriate language for children or terms referring to company secrets for employees, for instance) or visits a Web site deemed inappropriate.

Although it is legal to use computer monitoring software on your own computer or on the computers of your employees, installing it on other computers without the owners' knowledge to monitor their computer activity is usually illegal. A growing illegal use of computer monitoring software is the use of a *keystroke logging system* by hackers. A keystroke logging system is typically software-based, but it can also be implemented via a small piece of hardware that is installed between the system unit and the keyboard of a computer. In either case, it is used to record all keystrokes performed on the computer in order to capture usernames, passwords, and other sensitive data entered into the computer via the keyboard. Keystroke logging software can be installed on an individual's computer via malware, or it can be installed on public computers in person if the proper precautions are not taken. For instance, in 2008, a Colombian man pled guilty to installing keystroke logging software on computers located in hotel business centers and Internet cafés around the world; the software collected the personal information he needed to access the bank, payroll, brokerage, and other financial accounts of over 600 individuals. He was sentenced in mid-2009 to nine years in prison and ordered to pay $347,000 in restitution.

In addition to computer monitoring products designed for individuals and businesses, there are also computer monitoring programs available for use only by law enforcement and other government agencies. Like wiretapping, electronic monitoring of computer activity requires a court order or similar authorization to be legal (although the *USA PATRIOT Act* does allow the FBI to conduct a limited form of Internet surveillance first, such as to capture e-mail addresses or IP addresses used with traffic going into or coming from a suspect's computer). With proper authorization and cooperation from a suspect's ISP, law enforcement agencies can use computer monitoring software to intercept files and e-mail messages sent to or from a suspect's computer. If the documents are encrypted, keystroke logging software can be used to record e-mail messages and documents before they are encrypted, as well as to record the private keys to encrypt messages and files.

Video Surveillance

The idea of **video surveillance** is nothing new. Many retail stores, banks, office buildings, and other privately owned facilities that are open to the public routinely use closed circuit security cameras to monitor activities taking place at those facilities for security purposes. In recent years, however, video surveillance has been expanded to a number of additional public locations (such as streets, parks, airports, sporting arenas, subway systems, and so forth) in many cities in the United States and

other countries for law enforcement purposes (worldwide, two of the most monitored cities are London and New York City). These cameras are typically located outside and attached to or built into fixtures, such as lamp posts (see Figure 5-23), or attached to buildings. Video surveillance cameras are also commonly installed in schools in the United States and other countries to enable administrators to monitor both teacher and student activities and to have a record of incidents as they occur. A snapshot of a live video feed from a camera installed inside a computer lab at a university in New York is shown in Figure 5-23.

Public video surveillance systems are often used in conjunction with face recognition technology to try to identify known terrorists and other criminals, to identify criminals when their crimes are caught on tape, and to prevent crimes from occurring. Video surveillance data is proving to be valuable to police for catching terrorists and other types of criminals, and it is routinely used to

FIGURE 5-23

Examples of public video surveillance.

OUTDOOR SURVEILLANCE
Many cameras placed in public locations are designed to blend into their surroundings to be less intrusive, such as the camera inside this light fixture on a Washington, D.C., street.

INDOOR SURVEILLANCE
Many cameras are placed inside businesses, schools, and other locations, such as the ones that broadcast live video from several locations at a university in New York; a snapshot from one of the video cameras is shown here.

> **Video surveillance.** The use of video cameras to monitor activities of individuals, such as employees or individuals in public locations, for work-related or crime-prevention purposes.

identify the individuals and cars used in attacks; this benefit is expected to increase as video surveillance moves to high definition. Some public video surveillance systems are also beginning to be used in conjunction with software to try to identify suspicious behavior (such as an unattended bag or a truck circling a skyscraper) and alert authorities to these possible threats.

Many privacy advocates object to the use of video surveillance and face recognition technology in public locations; their concerns are primarily based on how the video captured by these systems will be used. Privacy advocates also have doubts about the usefulness of these systems in protecting citizens against terrorism. They also object to the fact that, unlike private security video that is typically viewed only after a crime has occurred, the images from many public video cameras are watched all the time. In addition, networks of police video cameras that feed into a central operations center allow the observation of innocent people and activities on a massive scale. However, law enforcement agencies contend that face recognition systems and public video surveillance are no different than the many private video surveillance systems in place today in a wide variety of public locations, such as in retail stores and banks. They view this technology as just one more tool to be used to protect the public, similar to scanning luggage at the airport. Some privacy advocates also fear being under perpetual police surveillance and the eventual expansion of these security surveillance systems, such as using them to look for "deadbeat dads" or for other applications not vital for national security.

An emerging privacy issue related to public video cameras is their use with the display screens used to project advertisements in public places, such as a mall, health club, or retail store. This marketing technique uses tiny video cameras embedded in or on the edge of the screen, in conjunction with software, to identify characteristics of the individual looking at the screen (such as gender and approximate age) in order to display advertising content targeted to each viewer. The video cameras can also be used to determine if the displayed ads are reaching the intended demographic. While still in the infancy stage, this advertising tool is expected to be more prominent in the near future. To alleviate privacy concerns, developers state that no images are ever stored and individuals are not personally identified—only their characteristics. However, the idea of targeted advertisements based on physical appearance is a concern for some privacy advocates.

A related privacy concern is the inclusion of digital camera capabilities in most mobile phones today (see Figure 5-24). Although mobile phone digital cameras are increasingly being used to help law enforcement (such as being used by citizens to take photos of crimes as they are being committed) and camera functions are included for personal enjoyment and convenience, some fear that the ubiquitous nature of mobile phones will lead to increased privacy violations. In fact, some athletic clubs have banned mobile phones entirely to protect the privacy of their members while working out and in the dressing rooms. Many YMCAs, city parks and recreation departments, and other recreational facilities have banned camera phone use in locker rooms and restrooms to protect the privacy of both children and adults. Camera phones are also being banned by some schools to prevent cheating, by many courthouses to prevent witness or jury intimidation, and by many research and production facilities to prevent corporate espionage. Legally speaking, people typically have few rights to privacy in public places, but many believe that new technology—such as camera phones—will require the law to reconsider and redefine

FIGURE 5-24

Camera phones are ubiquitous today.

what is considered to be a public place and where citizens can expect to retain particular aspects of personal privacy.

Employee Monitoring

Employee monitoring refers to companies recording or observing the actions of employees while on the job. With today's technology, employee monitoring is very easy to perform, and much of it can be done through the use of computers. Common employee monitoring activities include screening telephone calls, reviewing e-mail, and tracking computer and Internet usage; with the growing inclusion of video cameras in computers and monitors today, employee monitoring via PC cams may become more prominent in the near future. Although many employees feel that being watched at work is an invasion of their personal privacy, it is legal and very common in the United States. According to the American Management Association (AMA), the vast majority of all U.S. companies use some type of electronic surveillance with their employees, and it is common for employers to discipline employees for misuse of e-mail or the Internet at work. Typically, the primary reason is to monitor Internet usage for legal liability, but monitoring employee productivity is another motivating factor. Many employers are finding that some employees waste large amounts of time on social networking sites and other Web activities. While access to these sites is frequently blocked by employers, many believe a better alternative is identifying employees who abuse their Internet access and then dealing with those employees directly. This can be accomplished using the computer monitoring software discussed in a previous section.

For monitoring the physical locations of employees, video cameras (such as video surveillance cameras or PC video cameras) can be used, but another possibility is the use of smart or RFID-enabled ID cards (sometimes called *proximity cards*). While these cards (such as the one shown in Figure 5-25) are most often used for access control—such as to facilitate access to a building or computer network, to automatically lock an employee's computer when he or she gets a certain distance away from it (to eliminate the problem of nosy coworkers), and to automatically unlock the computer when the employee returns (to eliminate the need for passwords)—they can also be used to track the physical location of employees. Other types of employee monitoring systems designed for tracking an employee's location are GPS-based systems, such as those systems that track an employee via his or her mobile phone or those that notify the employer if the employee's company vehicle exits a prescribed work area. Vehicle monitoring systems are discussed in more detail in Chapter 8.

Although some employees may view workplace monitoring as an invasion of their personal privacy, employers have several valid reasons for monitoring employee activities, such as security concerns, productivity measurement, legal compliance, and legal liability. For example, management has a responsibility to the company (and to its stockholders, for publicly held corporations) to make sure employees do the jobs that they are being paid to do. If any employees are spending too much time away from their desks chatting with other employees, answering their personal e-mail, or placing bids at online auctions, the company has the right to know and the responsibility to stop that misuse of company time and resources. For example, there have been many instances of employees viewing pornography, downloading pirated movies

The card is worn by an employee for continuous access and monitoring purposes.

Smart card circuitry

⚠ **FIGURE 5-25**

Smart ID cards. ID cards with smart card or RFID capabilities can be used for facility access, computer access, and employee monitoring.

> **Employee monitoring.** Observing or reviewing employees' actions while they are on the job.

or music, watching live sports video feeds—even running their own businesses—on company time and computers. In addition, the company needs to protect itself against lost business (due to employee incompetence or poor client skills, for example) and lawsuits (such as from employees when offensive e-mail messages are circulated within the office or when an employee includes statements that defame another business or reveal private information in a company blog). In addition, government regulations—such as the *Sarbanes-Oxley Act*, which requires publicly traded companies to keep track of which employees look at sensitive documents—may require it. However, some employees object to being monitored and some privacy advocates feel that some types of employee monitoring cross the line between valid employee monitoring and an invasion of privacy.

Comprehensive employee monitoring systems can be expensive; however, many companies view the cost as insignificant compared to the risk of a potential multimillion-dollar lawsuit. It is becoming increasingly common for U.S. firms to face sexual harassment and/or racial discrimination claims stemming from employee e-mail and Internet use and lawsuits can be costly—Chevron was once ordered to pay female employees $2.2 million to settle a sexual harassment lawsuit stemming from inappropriate e-mails sent by male employees.

To reduce cost and objections from employees, some businesses have found employee training and education to be an effective and cost-efficient alternative to continuous monitoring. Others use statistical-analysis software to detect unusual patterns in data collected about employee computer usage, and then use the reports to investigate only the employees and situations indicated as possible problems. Regardless of the techniques used, it is wise for businesses to inform employees about their monitoring practices (including what activities may be monitored and how long records of that monitoring will be archived), although they are not required by law in the U.S. at the current time to do so. However, bills have been introduced in several states in the United States that would prohibit employee monitoring without employee notification and some countries—such as in the European Union—are much more limiting with respect to the types of employee monitoring that can be performed without active notification. And legislation has been implemented or is being considered in several states to prevent employers from implanting employees with RFID chips without the employee's consent, in order to prevent employers from requiring that chips be implanted into employees for monitoring purposes, security access, or other work-related functions.

Presence Technology

Presence technology refers to the ability of one computing device (a desktop computer, portable computer, or mobile phone, for example) on a network (such as the Internet or a mobile phone network) to identify another device on the same network and determine its status. It can be used to tell when someone on the network is using his or her computer or mobile phone, as well as the individual's availability for communications; that is, whether or not the individual is able and willing to take a call or respond to an IM at the present time. For example, when an employee at a company utilizing presence technology (sometimes called *presence management* in a business context) has a question that needs answering, he or she can check the directory displayed on his or her computer or mobile phone to see which team members are available, regardless of where those team members are physically located. The employee can then call an available team member or send an instant message. Presence technology is expected to be used eventually on company Web

> **Presence technology.** Technology that enables one computing device (such as a computer or mobile phone) to locate and identify the current status of another device on the same network.

pages so that visitors—usually potential or current customers—can see which salespeople, service representatives, or other contacts are currently available. Another possible application is including dynamic presence buttons in e-mail messages—the presence button would display one message (such as "I'm online") if the sender is online at the time the e-mail message is read, and a different message (such as "I'm offline") if the sender is not online at that time.

Presence technology today can be implemented via software, as well as by GPS, RFID, or other technology. For instance, IM software indicates the current status of each buddy on an individual's contact list (based on each buddy's signed-in status). In addition, the presence technology built into many mobile phones today enables individuals to see when a contact is available (see Figure 5-26). The GPS capabilities integrated in many mobile phones today also allow you to keep track of your friends' physical locations, such as by using the Buddy Beacon, GyPSii, or Google Latitude application to view their current locations on a map. The GPS capabilities built into mobile phones can also be used by law enforcement to determine the location of a phone (such as one belonging to a missing individual or a criminal) when needed.

While some aspects of presence technology are useful and intriguing, such as being able to tell that a loved one's flight arrived safely when you notice that his or her mobile phone is on again, knowing if a friend or colleague is available for a telephone call before dialing the number, or identifying the location of your children at any point in time, privacy advocates are concerned about the use of this technology. They are concerned about presence technology being used to target ads and information to individuals based on their current physical location (such as close to a particular restaurant at lunchtime) and other activities that they view as potential privacy violations.

FIGURE 5-26
Presence technology. Presence icons indicate the status of individual contacts.

Protecting Personal and Workplace Privacy

There are not many options for protecting yourself against computer monitoring by your employer or the government, or against video surveillance systems. However, businesses should take the necessary security measures (such as protecting the company network from hackers, monitoring for intrusions, and using security software) to ensure that employee activities are not being monitored by a hacker or other unauthorized individual. Individuals should also secure their home computers to protect against keystroke logging or other computer monitoring software that may be inadvertently installed via an electronic greeting card, game, or other downloaded file, and that is designed to provide a hacker with account numbers, passwords, and other sensitive data that could be used in identity theft or other fraudulent activities. *Antispyware software*, such as the programs discussed in Chapter 4 and the example shown in Figure 5-27, can be used to detect and remove some types of illegal computer monitoring and spyware software.

FIGURE 5-27
Antispyware software. Antispyware software can detect and remove spyware used for computer monitoring purposes.

The Employer's Responsibilities

To protect the personal privacy of their employees and customers, businesses and organizations have a responsibility to keep private information about their employees, the company, and their customers safe. Strong security measures, such as firewalls and access-prevention methods for both computer data and facilities, can help to protect against unauthorized access by hackers. Businesses and organizations should take precautions against both intentional and accidental breaches of privacy by employees. Finally, businesses and organizations have the responsibility to monitor their employees' activities to ensure workers are productive. In general, businesses must maintain a safe and productive workplace environment and protect the privacy of their customers and employees, while at the same time ensure the company is not vulnerable to lawsuits.

All businesses should have an *employee policy* that informs employees about what personal activities (if any) are allowed during company time or on company equipment, as well as about what company communications (such as e-mail messages and blog postings) and what employee activities (such as Web surfing, e-mail, telephone calls, and downloading files to an office computer) may be monitored. Employee policies are usually included in an employee handbook or posted on the company intranet.

The Employees' Responsibilities

Employees have the responsibility to read a company's employee policy when initially hired and to review it periodically to ensure that they understand the policy and do not violate any company rules while working for that organization. In addition, since at-work activities may legally be monitored by an employer, it is wise—from a privacy standpoint—to avoid personal activities at work. From reading the organization's employee policy, an employee can determine if any personal activities are allowed at all (such as checking personal e-mail during the lunch hour), but it is safer to perform personal activities at home, regardless. Be especially careful with any activity, such as sending a joke via e-mail to a coworker, that might be interpreted as harassment. For personal phone calls, employees should use their mobile phones during their lunch hour or a rest break.

COMPUTER SECURITY AND PRIVACY LEGISLATION

The high level of concern regarding computer security and personal privacy has led state and federal legislators to pass a variety of laws since the 1970s. Internet privacy is viewed as one of the top policy issues facing Congress today, and numerous bills have been proposed in the last several years regarding spam, telemarketing, spyware, online profiling, and other very important privacy issues. However, Congress has had difficulty passing new legislation. There are several reasons for this, including that it is difficult for the legal system to keep pace with the rate at which technology changes, and there are jurisdictional issues domestically and internationally, since many computer crimes affect businesses and individuals located in geographic areas other than the one in which the computer criminal is located. In addition, privacy is difficult to define and there is a struggle to balance freedom of speech with the right to privacy.

Another issue is weighing the need to implement legislation versus the use of voluntary methods to protect computer security and personal privacy. For instance, the *Child Online Protection Act (COPA)* has been highly controversial since it was passed in 1998, and, in fact, it has never been implemented. This legislation prohibited making pornography or any other content deemed harmful to minors available to minors via the Internet and carried a $50,000 fine. This law was blocked by the U.S. Supreme Court several times, based on the likelihood that it violates the First Amendment and the possibility that less restrictive alternatives (such as Internet filtering) can be used instead to prevent the access of inappropriate materials by minors. A list of selected federal laws related to computer security and privacy are shown in Figure 5-28.

DATE	LAW AND DESCRIPTION
2006	**U.S. SAFE WEB Act of 2006** Grants additional authority to the FTC to help protect consumers from spam, spyware, and Internet fraud and deception.
2005	**Real ID Act** Establishes national standards for state-issued driver's licenses and identification cards; will be modified if the proposed Pass ID Act of 2009 is passed.
2005	**Junk Fax Prevention Act** Requires unsolicited faxes to have a highly-visible opt-out notice.
2003	**CAN-SPAM Act** Implements regulations for unsolicited e-mail messages and lays the groundwork for a federal Do Not E-Mail Registry.
2003	**Do Not Call Implementation Act** Amends the Telephone Consumer Protection Act to implement the National Do Not Call Registry.
2003	**Health Insurance Portability and Accountability Act (HIPAA)** Includes a Security Rule that sets minimum security standards to protect health information stored electronically.
2002	**Sarbanes-Oxley Act** Requires archiving a variety of electronic records and protecting the integrity of corporate financial data.
2001	**USA PATRIOT Act** Grants federal authorities expanded surveillance and intelligence-gathering powers, such as broadening the ability of federal agents to obtain the real identity of Internet users and intercept e-mail and other types of Internet communications.
1999	**Financial Modernization (Gramm-Leach-Bliley) Act** Extends the ability of banks, securities firms, and insurance companies to share consumers' non-public personal information, but requires them to notify consumers and give them the opportunity to opt out before disclosing any information.
1998	**Child Online Protection Act (COPA)** Prohibits online pornography and other content deemed harmful to minors; has been blocked by the Supreme Court.
1998	**Children's Online Privacy Protection Act (COPPA)** Regulates how Web sites can collect information from minors and communicate with them.
1998	**Telephone Anti-Spamming Amendments Act** Applies restrictions to unsolicited, bulk commercial e-mail.
1992	**Cable Act** Extends the Cable Communications Policy Act to include companies that sell wireless services.
1991	**Telephone Consumer Protection Act** Requires telemarketing companies to respect the rights of people who do not want to be called.
1988	**Computer Matching and Privacy Protection Act** Limits the use of government data in determining federal-benefit recipients.
1988	**Video Privacy Protection Act** Limits disclosure of customer information by video-rental companies.
1986	**Electronic Communications Privacy Act** Extends traditional privacy protections governing postal delivery and telephone services to include e-mail, cellular phones, and voice mail.
1984	**Cable Communications Policy Act** Limits disclosure of customer records by cable TV companies.
1974	**Education Privacy Act** Stipulates that, in both public and private schools that receive any federal funding, individuals have the right to keep the schools from releasing information such as grades and evaluations of behavior.
1974	**Privacy Act** Stipulates that the collection of data by federal agencies must have a legitimate purpose.
1970	**Fair Credit Reporting Act** Prevents private organizations from unfairly denying credit and provides individuals the right to inspect their credit records.
1970	**Freedom of Information Act** Gives individuals the right to inspect data concerning them that is stored by the federal government.

 FIGURE 5-28

Federal legislation
related to computer
security and privacy.

SUMMARY

WHY BE CONCERNED ABOUT COMPUTER SECURITY?

There are a number of important security concerns related to computers, such as having your computer stolen, losing data, and running the risk of buying pirated or digitally counterfeited products online. All computer users should be aware of possible security risks and the safeguards they can implement to prevent security problems since these problems can cost them time and money, as well as be an inconvenience.

HARDWARE LOSS, HARDWARE DAMAGE, AND SYSTEM FAILURE

Hardware loss (perhaps as a result of **hardware theft** or lost hardware), hardware damage (both intentional and unintentional), and **system failure** are important concerns. System failure can occur because of a hardware problem, or it can be the result of a natural or man-made disaster. To protect against hardware theft, door and equipment locks can be used. To protect against accidental hardware damage, **surge suppressors, uninterruptible power supplies** (UPSs), proper storage media care, and precautions against excess dust, heat, and static electricity are important. **Ruggedized devices** can be used when necessary. To protect against data loss, backups are essential for both individuals and businesses—most businesses should also develop a **disaster recovery plan** for natural and man-made disasters. Encryption can be used to protect individual files and the content of data stored on a storage medium. **Full disk encryption** (FDE) and **self-encrypting hard drives** can be used to encrypt all the content located on a hard drive automatically.

SOFTWARE PIRACY AND DIGITAL COUNTERFEITING

Software piracy (the unauthorized copying of a computer program) and **digital counterfeiting** (creating fake copies of currency and other resources) are illegal in the United States. They cost manufacturers billions of dollars each year, and some of these costs are passed on to law-abiding consumers. Various tools, such as consumer education, holograms, and software activation procedures, can be used to prevent software piracy. Many businesses are also aggressively pursuing software pirates in court in an attempt to reduce piracy. The government has various methods in place to prevent digital counterfeiting of currency, such as using difficult-to-reproduce materials and features like *security threads* and *watermarks*.

WHY BE CONCERNED ABOUT INFORMATION PRIVACY?

Privacy issues affect the lives of everyone. A number of important **privacy** concerns are related to computers and the Internet. For instance, **information privacy** refers to the rights of individuals and companies to control how information about them is collected and used. Other common concerns include the privacy of Web site activities and e-mail messages, as well as the high number of security breaches on systems that contain personal information. Businesses need to be concerned with protecting the privacy of the personal information they store because data breaches violate the privacy of their customers. In addition, data breaches are costly, and they can result in lawsuits and damaged reputations.

DATABASES, ELECTRONIC PROFILING, SPAM, AND OTHER MARKETING ACTIVITIES

The extensive use of **marketing databases** and **government databases** is of concern to many privacy organizations and individuals. Information in marketing databases is frequently sold to companies and other organizations; information in some government databases is available to the public. Some public information can be retrieved from databases via the Web. **Electronic profiling** is the collection of diverse information about an individual. An organization's **privacy policy** addresses how any personal information submitted to that company will be used. Another privacy issue that individuals need to be concerned about centers on the vast amount of **spam** (unsolicited bulk e-mail) that occurs today.

Protecting your e-mail address is one of the best ways to avoid spam. A **throw-away e-mail address** can be used for any activities that may result in spam; your permanent personal e-mail address can then be reserved for communications that should not result in spam. Before providing any personal information via a Web page, it is a good idea to review the Web site's privacy policy to see if the information will be shared with other organizations. Consider whether or not the Web site is requesting too much personal information, and only provide the required data. Do not provide personal details in chat rooms and personal Web sites. Unless you do not mind spam or are using a throw-away e-mail address, avoid completing online forms, such as to enter sweepstakes.

E-mail filters can be used to manage an individual's e-mail; **spam filters** are used to identify possible spam. To reduce the amount of spam, junk mail, online ads, and telemarketing calls received, an individual can **opt out** of marketing activities. It's possible that more marketing activities in the future will require individuals to **opt in** in order to participate. Individuals and businesses should be cautious when disposing of old hardware, such as hard drives and CDs, that contain sensitive data. Minimally, hard drives to be reused should be *wiped* clean; CDs, DVDs, and other media to be disposed of should be shredded.

Chapter Objective 5:
Describe some privacy concerns regarding databases, electronic profiling, spam, and telemarketing, and identify ways individuals can protect their privacy.

ELECTRONIC SURVEILLANCE AND MONITORING

Computer monitoring software that can record an individual's computer use is viewed as a privacy violation by some, as is the increased use of **video surveillance** in public locations. Although it is allowed by law, some employees view **employee monitoring** (such as monitoring computer use, telephone calls, and an individual's location using a smart ID card or video surveillance) as an invasion of their privacy. **Presence technology**—the ability of one computer on a network to know the status of another computer on that network—allows users of computers, mobile phones, and other communications devices to determine the availability of other individuals before contacting them.

To protect the privacy of employees and customers, businesses have a responsibility to keep private information about their employees, the company, and their customers safe. Firewalls, password-protected files, and encryption can help secure this information. Businesses have the responsibility to monitor employee activities in order to ensure that employees are performing the jobs they are being paid to do, are not causing lost business, and are not leaving the company open to lawsuits. To inform employees of allowable activities, an *employee policy* or code of conduct should be developed and distributed to employees. For the highest level of privacy while at the workplace, employees should perform only work-related activities on the job.

Chapter Objective 6:
Discuss several types of electronic surveillance and monitoring, and list ways individuals can protect their privacy.

COMPUTER SECURITY AND PRIVACY LEGISLATION

Although computer security and privacy are viewed as extremely important issues, legislating these issues is difficult due to ongoing changes in technology, jurisdictional issues, and varying opinions. Some legislation related to computer security has been enacted; new legislation is being considered on a regular basis.

Chapter Objective 7:
Discuss the status of computer security and privacy legislation.

Web-Based Multimedia and E-Commerce

eBay

Jim Griffith, aka "Griff," is the Dean of eBay Education, a roving eBay ambassador, an eBay spokesperson, the host of eBay Radio, and the author of *The Official eBay Bible*. An enthusiastic eBay buyer and seller since 1996, Griff spends nearly all his waking hours teaching others how to use eBay effectively, safely, and profitably, and spreading the word about eBay across print, radio, and TV. Griff has worked for eBay for 13 years.

A Conversation with JIM GRIFFITH

Dean of eBay Education, eBay

> *"In the future, more brick-and-mortar business owners will adopt the Internet as a primary or secondary channel for their businesses."*

My Background . . .

Although I have many roles at eBay, my most public role—Dean of eBay Education—is unique, slightly unorthodox, and best understood in the context of my history with the company. I was originally a user on eBay in the very early days (1996) and spent a lot of time assisting other buyers and sellers on eBay's one chat board. My posts came to the attention of eBay founder Pierre Omidyar who offered me a job as eBay's first customer support rep. I continued to be an active member of the eBay community along with my new duties at the time, which included assisting and teaching buyers, sellers, and eBay employees how to use eBay. Over time, I also became an eBay spokesperson, lead instructor of our eBay University program, author of *The Official eBay Bible* (now in its third edition), and host of eBay Radio.

In addition to the obvious knowledge of the eBay Web site, our policies, and the basics of business, the skills that proved to be most critical during my thirteen-year tenure at eBay (and I should say I am still refining them) would be diplomacy, empathy, civility, and a strong sense of self-deprecating humor.

It's Important to Know . . .

The basic principles behind successful e-commerce are no different than those behind traditional offline commerce. For example, the most valuable asset for any business, online or offline, is the customer. This is especially true for e-commerce where the competition for customers is fierce. Although the technologies and transaction experience for the Web and for traditional retail are markedly different, the standard, tried-and-true business basics (such as business planning, inventory procurement and management, and marketing) are as crucial to e-commerce as they are to traditional business.

The importance of an easy-to-use, well-designed, and appealing Web site. All of the inventory in the world is for naught if the buyer cannot search through it and purchase it with ease.

Online commerce technologies are constantly changing. What is cutting edge today will soon be passé. Anyone who makes his or her living online absolutely must stay on top of all online marketplace technology advances and adopt and implement them as necessary. Consumers in general—and online consumers in particular—are much more business and technology savvy than they were a mere 5 years ago. Demanding consumers will have little or no patience for online businesses that do not provide the best possible shopping experience.

How I Use this Technology . . .

Besides working for eBay, I am an avid consumer and seller online. I make at least one online purchase a day and I always have a selection of items up for sale (on eBay). My online e-commerce activity along with my job of instructing and assisting buyers and sellers to navigate and utilize eBay and PayPal requires an extensive working knowledge of and familiarity with our own Web sites (eBay and PayPal).

What the Future Holds . . .

The Internet revolution has in many ways changed the nature of human commerce forever. The most important impact of the Internet revolution has been the empowerment of the consumer. Never before has the buyer had so much control over the direction of the marketplace. This will only increase as time goes on, and the businesses that acknowledge this new reality and plan accordingly are the ones that will survive and thrive.

In the future, more brick-and-mortar business owners will adopt the Internet as a primary or secondary channel for their businesses. In addition, more small businesses will start up solely on the Internet as the cost of entry into the online marketplace continues to drop and the gap in the costs of starting an online and offline business continues to grow. This will lead to even more choices for the online consumer, who will continue to exert increasing service demands and pricing pressure on online sellers.

However, as the Internet becomes more a part of our day to day lives, the idea of the Internet as a unique environment will start to disappear, especially as access to the Internet becomes cheaper and more widespread (for example, embedded in appliances, cell phones, media devices, and even the walls of our homes!). Just like technologies before it (such as telegraph, telephone, radio, and television), we will soon take the Internet for granted as it matures and eventually becomes completely entwined within the matrix of our daily lives.

My Advice to Students . . .

Unless you're interested in pursuing a career in computer science, engineering, or programming, an academic study of the inner workings of the Internet or computers will not be a requirement for a career in an Internet-based industry. However, Internet companies will have an ever-increasing demand for inventive product marketing personnel, product designers, and intellectual property attorneys.

That said, whatever career you pursue, never forget that the direction of online commerce (and the world in general) is toward more control in the hands of the individual. Adjust your career path accordingly!

> *"Anyone who makes his or her living online absolutely must stay on top of all online marketplace technology advances and adopt and implement them as necessary."*

Discussion Question

Jim Griffith views the online buyer as an extremely influential part of the e-commerce marketplace. Think of online purchases you have made. How did your buying decision differ from shopping locally? What factors influenced your final decision? How does the increased number of online sources for products impact the online marketplace? Do consumers have more influence over online stores than over brick-and-mortar stores? Why or why not? If you were starting a business, would you have an e-commerce presence? A brick-and-mortar presence? Both? Be prepared to discuss your position (in class, via an online class discussion group, in a class chat room, or via a class blog, depending on your instructor's directions). You may also be asked to write a short paper expressing your opinion.

> For more information on eBay, visit www.ebay.com. For more information about e-commerce, read *FutureShop* by Daniel Nissanoff, and for more information about effective, safe, and successful buying or selling on eBay, refer to *The Official eBay Bible* by Jim "Griff" Griffith.

chapter 6

Intellectual Property Rights and Ethics

After completing this chapter, you will be able to do the following:

1. Understand the different types of intellectual property rights and how they relate to computer use.

2. Explain what is meant by the term "ethics."

3. Provide several examples of unethical behavior in the use of intellectual property and in computer-related matters.

4. Explain what computer hoaxes and digital manipulation are and how they relate to computer ethics.

5. Understand how ethics can impact business practices and decision making.

6. Discuss the current status of legislation related to intellectual property rights and ethics.

outline

Overview

Intellectual Property Rights
Copyrights
Trademarks
Patents

Ethics
Ethical Use of Copyrighted Material
Ethical Use of Resources and Information
Computer Hoaxes and Digital Manipulation
Ethical Business Practices and Decision Making

Related Legislation

OVERVIEW

While computers and related technology add convenience and enjoyment to our daily lives, they also can make it easier to perform some types of illegal or unethical acts. For example, computers can be used to launch computer viruses, create high-quality illegal copies of software programs and music CDs, and copy information from a Web page and present it as original work. However, just because technology enables us to do something, does that make it right? Is legality the only measuring stick, or are there some acts that are legal but still morally or ethically wrong? Is there only one set of ethics, or can ethics vary from person to person? This chapter continues where Chapter 5 left off by exploring computer-related societal issues. Two important issues—intellectual property rights and ethics—are discussed in this chapter; other societal issues are included in Chapter 7.

The chapter begins with a look at a legal issue that all computer users should be aware of—intellectual property rights. The specific types of intellectual property rights are discussed, along with examples of the types of property that each right protects. Next is a discussion of ethics, including what they are and a variety of ethical issues surrounding computer use by individuals and businesses. Topics include the ethical use of copyrighted material, ethical uses of resources and information, unethical use of digital manipulation, ethical business practices and decision making, and the impact of cultural differences with respect to ethics and business decisions. The chapter closes with a look at legislation related to the issues discussed in this chapter. ■

INTELLECTUAL PROPERTY RIGHTS

Intellectual property rights are the legal rights to which the creators of *intellectual property*—original creative works—are entitled. Intellectual property rights indicate who has the right to use, perform, or display a creative work and what can legally be done with that work. In addition, intellectual property rights determine how long the creator retains rights to the property, if the rights can be renewed, if the property ever reverts to the public domain, and other related restrictions. Examples of intellectual property include music and movies; paintings, computer graphics, and other works of art; poetry, books, and other types of written works; symbols, names, and designs used in conjunction with a business; architectural drawings; and inventions. Intellectual property rights can be claimed by individuals or by companies or other organizations. The three main types of intellectual property rights are *copyrights, trademarks*, and *patents*. Copyrights, trademarks, and patents are issued by individual countries; U.S. intellectual property rights are discussed in more detail next.

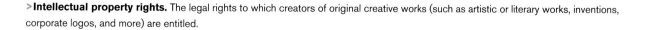

> **Intellectual property rights.** The legal rights to which creators of original creative works (such as artistic or literary works, inventions, corporate logos, and more) are entitled.

BOOK COPYRIGHT NOTICES

© Red Lobster. All rights reserved.

WEB SITE COPYRIGHT NOTICES

FIGURE 6-1

Copyright statements. Statements such as these are often included on books, Web sites, and other copyrighted works.

FURTHER EXPLORATION

Go

Go to the Chapter 6 page at **www.cengage.com/ computerconcepts/np/uccs4** for links to information about intellectual property rights.

Copyrights

A **copyright** is a form of protection available to the creator of an original artistic, musical, or literary work, such as a book, movie, software program, musical composition, or painting. It gives the copyright holder the exclusive right to publish, reproduce, distribute, perform, or display the work. A major revision to U.S. copyright legislation was the *1976 Copyright Act*. This act extended copyright protection to nonpublished works, so, immediately after creating a work in some type of material form (such as on paper, film, videotape, or a digital storage medium), the creator automatically owns the copyright of that work. Consequently, the creator is entitled to copyright protection of that work and has the right to make a statement, such as "Copyright © 2010 John Smith. All rights reserved." Although works created in the United States after March 1, 1989 are not required to display a copyright notice in order to retain their copyright protection, displaying a copyright statement on a published work (see Figure 6-1) reminds others that the work is protected by copyright law and that any use must comply with copyright law. Only the creator of a work (or his or her employer if the work is created as a *work for hire*; that is, within the scope of employment) can rightfully claim copyright. Copyrights can be registered with the *U. S. Copyright Office*. Although registration is not required for copyright protection, it does offer an advantage if the need to prove ownership of a copyright ever arises, such as during a copyright-infringement lawsuit. Most countries offer some copyright protection to works registered in other countries.

Anyone wishing to use copyrighted materials must first obtain permission from the copyright holder and pay any required fee. One exception is the legal concept of *fair use*, which permits limited duplication and use of a portion of copyrighted material for specific purposes, such as criticism, commentary, news reporting, teaching, and research. For example, a teacher may legally read a copyrighted poem for discussion in a poetry class, and a news crew may videotape a small portion of a song at a concert to include in a news report of that concert. Copyrights apply to both published and unpublished works and remain in effect until 70 years after the creator's death. Copyrights for works registered by an organization or as anonymous works last 95 years from the date of publication or 120 years from the date of creation, whichever is shorter.

It is important to realize that purchasing a copyrighted item (such as a book, painting, or movie) does not change the copyright protection afforded to the creator of that item. Although you have purchased the right to use the item, you cannot legally duplicate it or portray it as your own creation. Some of the most widely publicized copyright-infringement issues today center around individuals illegally distributing copyright-protected music and movies via the Internet, as discussed later in this chapter.

To protect their rights, some creators of digital content (such as art, music, photographs, and movies) use **digital watermarks**—a subtle alteration of digital content that is not noticeable when the work is viewed or played but that identifies the copyright holder. For instance, the digital watermark for an image might consist of slight changes to the brightness of a specific pattern of pixels that are imperceptible to people but are easily read by software. Digital watermarks can also be made visible, if desired, such as to add the name of a company or Web site URL to a photo being posted online, or to inform individuals that the photo is copyrighted and should not be used elsewhere.

Digital watermarks can be added to images, music, video, TV shows, and other digital content found online or distributed in digital form to identify their copyright

---

>**Copyright.** The legal right to sell, publish, or distribute an original artistic or literary work; it is held by the creator of a work as soon as it exists in physical form. >**Digital watermark.** A subtle alteration of digital content that is not noticeable when the work is viewed or played, but that identifies the copyright holder.

holders, their authorized distributors, and other important information. They are typically added with software, though digital cameras may soon be available that can add a digital watermark to each photo as it is created. As shown in Figure 6-2, digital watermarks added to photos are invisible until they are read with appropriate software. The purpose of digital watermarking is to give digital content a unique identity that remains intact even if the work is copied, edited, compressed, or otherwise manipulated. For instance, movies sent to movie theaters typically include a digital watermark that can be used to trace a pirated movie back to the theater where the pirated movie was created in order to help authorities locate and prosecute the criminal. Primarily because of the vast amount of copyrighted content distributed via the Internet today, the market for digital watermarking technology is growing rapidly and it is expected to reach nearly $600 million by 2012, according to one study.

Another rights-protection tool used with digital content is **digital rights management (DRM) software**. DRM software is used to control the use of a work. For instance, DRM used in conjunction with business documents (called *enterprise rights management*) can protect a sensitive business document by controlling usage of that document, such as by limiting who can view, print, or copy it. DRM used with digital content (such as movies and music) downloaded via the Internet can control whether or not the downloaded file can be copied to another device, as well as make a video-on-demand movie unviewable after the rental period expires. For a look at a tool used to verify authentic physical intellectual property and prevent counterfeiting of these products, see the Trend box.

The watermark embedded into this image is not visible.   The information contained in the watermark can be viewed using an image editing program.

FIGURE 6-2
Digital watermarks.

Trademarks

A **trademark** is a word, phrase, symbol, or design (or a combination of words, phrases, symbols, or designs) that identifies and distinguishes one product or service from another. A trademark used to identify a service is also called a *service mark*. Trademarks that are claimed but not registered with the *U. S. Patent and Trademark Office* (*USPTO*) can use the mark ™; nonregistered service marks can use the symbol ℠. The symbol ® is reserved for registered trademarks and service marks. Trademarks for products usually appear on the product packaging with the appropriate trademark symbol; service marks are typically used in the advertising of a service, since there is no product on which the mark can be printed. Trademarked words and phrases—such as iPod®, Chicken McNuggets®, Windows Vista™, and FedEx 3Day℠ Freight—are widely used today. Trademarked logos (see Figure 6-3) are also common. Trademarks last 10 years, but they can be renewed as many times as desired, as long as they are being used in commerce.

In addition to protecting the actual trademarked words, phrases, or logos, trademark law also protects domain names that match a company's trademark, such as Amazon.com and Lego.com. There have been a number of claims of online trademark infringement in recent years, particularly those involving domain names that contain, or are similar to, a trademark. For instance, several

FIGURE 6-3
Examples of
trademarked logos.

TREND

High-Tech Anticounterfeiting Systems

With counterfeiters increasingly trying to pass off copies of intellectual property as authentic (the International Anticounterfeiting Coalition estimates that counterfeits now make up 7% of the world's goods), many companies are turning to technology to help fight the fakes. One recent anticounterfeiting system developed by Kodak, called *TRACELESS*, is a new option for goods that are made of paper (like collectible trading cards) or that contain paper labels or product packaging (such as wine, prescription drugs, consumer electronics, apparel, and more). The TRACELESS system uses invisible chemical markers embedded in the product or packaging. The markers can be mixed with various inks, toners, varnishes, and other materials for printing, or they can be mixed into paper pulp, plastics, textiles, and other materials used to create a product or product packaging. The markers can only be detected using secure, handheld TRACELESS readers like the one shown in the accompanying photograph. Being able to determine easily and unequivocally if products are authentic can help retailers ensure they are selling legitimate products; it can also help law enforcement agencies identify counterfeit goods and prosecute counterfeiters. While

high-tech systems such as TRACELESS can help protect consumers and businesses from financial loss, they can also help save lives by preventing patients from ending up with fake prescription drugs masquerading as real drugs.

Invisible markers are embedded into this wine label.

The markers can be detected by this reader.

celebrities—such as Madonna and Jim Carrey—have fought to be given the exclusive right to use what they consider their rightful domain names (Madonna.com and JimCarrey.com, in these examples). Other examples include Microsoft's complaint against another organization using the domain name *microsof.com* and RadioShack's objection to a private individual using *shack.com* for the Web site of his design business.

While businesses and individuals can file lawsuits to recover a disputed domain name, a faster and less expensive option is to file a complaint with a dispute resolution provider, such as the *World Intellectual Property Organization* (*WIPO*). WIPO is a specialized agency of the United Nations and attempts to resolve international commercial disputes about intellectual property between private parties. This includes domain name disputes; in fact, WIPO has resolved more than 16,000 domain name dispute cases since it was formed 10 years ago. During the resolution process, WIPO has the power to award the disputed domain name to the most appropriate party. If the domain name was acquired with the intent to profit from the goodwill of a trademark belonging to someone else (such as by generating revenue from Web site visitors intending to go to the trademark holder's Web site or by trying to sell the domain name to the trademark holder at an inflated price) or to otherwise abuse a trademark, the act of acquiring that domain name is deemed to be **cybersquatting** and the trademark holder generally prevails. If the current domain name holder has a legitimate reason for using that name and does not appear to be a cybersquatter,

>**Cybersquatting.** The act of registering a domain name with the intent to profit from the goodwill of a trademark belonging to someone else.

however, WIPO may allow the holder to continue to use that domain name. For instance, WIPO ruled that microsof.com was confusingly similar to the trademark already owned by Microsoft and that its owner had no legitimate interest in that domain name, so WIPO transferred the disputed domain name to Microsoft Corporation. However, the owner of the design business (whose last name is Shackleton and whose nickname is "Shack") was allowed to keep the shack.com domain name because it was ruled that he had a legitimate interest in that name. The *Anticybersquatting Consumer Protection Act*, which was signed into law in 1999, makes cybersquatting illegal and it allows for penalties up to $100,000 for each willful registration of a domain name that infringes on a trademark.

Many recent cybersquatting cases deal with *typosquatting*—registering a domain name that is similar to a trademark or domain name but that is slightly misspelled in hopes that individuals will accidentally arrive at the site when trying to type the URL of the legitimate site. These sites often contain pay-per-click advertising used to generate revenue for the typosquatter; they can also be phishing sites that use spoofed Web pages to try to obtain sensitive information from visitors, or they can redirect visitors to sites for competing products or services. To prevent typosquatting and to protect their brands and other trademarks, many companies register variations of their domain names proactively. For instance, Verizon has registered more than 10,000 domain names related to its three most visible brands (Verizon, VZ, and FiOS). If a cybersquatter is causing enough damage to warrant it, companies can file a lawsuit against the cybersquatter. For instance, Verizon recently sued a company for unlawfully registering 663 domain names that were either identical or confusingly similar to Verizon trademarks. In late 2008, Verizon was awarded more than $33 million in that case—the largest cybersquatting judgment to date. Another form of cybersquatting involves individuals not affiliated with a company opening social media accounts using the company's brand names or variations of its brand names—typically either to use the account to sell pirated goods posing as the legitimate company, or in hopes the company will pay them to relinquish control of the accounts.

FIGURE 6-4
Patents. The patent shown here is for a new mobile phone.

Patents

Unlike copyrights (which protect artistic and literary works) and trademarks (which protect a company's logo and brand names), a **patent** protects inventions by granting exclusive rights of an invention to its inventor for a period of 20 years. A patented invention is typically a unique product, but it can also be a process or procedure that provides a new way of doing something or that offers a new technical solution to a problem. Like trademarks, U.S. patents are issued by the U.S. Patent and Trademark Office (USPTO). A recent patent issued for a new Nokia mobile phone design is shown in Figure 6-4.

The number of patent applications, particularly those related to computer and Internet products, has skyrocketed in recent years. In the U.S., patents have also been granted for Internet business methods and models, such as Priceline.com's name-your-own-price business model and Amazon.com's one-click purchase procedure. When a product or business model is patented, no other organization can duplicate it without paying a royalty to the patent holder or risking prolonged patent litigation. There have been many

> **Patent.** A form of protection for an invention that can be granted by the government; gives exclusive rights of an invention to its inventor for 20 years.

objections to some of the Internet business model patents that have been granted and some of these patents, including Amazon's one-click patent, have been challenged. Although several of Amazon's claims to its patent were initially rejected in late 2007 by the USPTO, the final outcome of this patent dispute had not been determined at the time of this writing, and the U.S. Supreme Court agreed in mid-2009 to consider the issue of the use of patents with business methods. There has also been a great deal of patent litigation recently surrounding computer technology. For instance, Apple has been sued in several patent infringement lawsuits related to its iPhone, and Microsoft has claimed that Linux infringed on many of its patents and is, therefore, attempting to collect royalties from vendors that use Linux in commercial products, such as computers and networking hardware.

Patents can be difficult, expensive, and time-consuming to obtain. However, patents can also be very lucrative. For instance, IBM, which has been the top patenting company for close to two decades, was issued over 4,100 patents in 2008 and earns an estimated $2 billion per year from its patents.

ETHICS

The term **ethics** refers to standards of moral conduct. For example, telling the truth is a matter of ethics. An unethical act is not always illegal, although it might be, but an illegal act is usually viewed as unethical by most people. For example, purposely lying to a friend is unethical but usually not illegal, while perjuring oneself in a courtroom as a witness is both illegal and unethical. Whether or not criminal behavior is involved, ethics guide our behavior and play an integral role in our lives.

Much more ambiguous than the law, ethical beliefs can vary widely from one individual to another. Ethical beliefs may also vary based on one's religion, country, race, or culture. In addition, different ethical standards can apply to different areas of one's life. For example, *personal ethics* guide an individual's personal behavior and *business ethics* guide an individual's workplace behavior. Ethics with respect to the use of computers are referred to as **computer ethics**. Computer ethics have taken on more significance in recent years because the proliferation of computers in the home and the workplace provides more opportunities for unethical acts than in the past. The Internet also makes it easy to distribute information that many individuals would view as unethical (such as computer viruses, spam, and spyware), as well as to distribute copies of software, movies, music, and other digital content in an illegal and, therefore, unethical manner.

ASK THE EXPERT

CEI **Dr. Ramon C. Barquin,** President, Computer Ethics Institute

If a person finds a lost device (such as a USB flash drive), is it ethical to look at the contents in order to try to determine its owner?

The answer is yes, you do have an ethical obligation to return something of value that you find to its rightful owner. If you find a wallet, it certainly is appropriate to look for a document that identifies its owner. But, with a USB drive, there has to be an element of proportionality. The comparison here is more along the lines of finding a briefcase full of documents. You can and should try to find the person who lost it, but it is more likely that you could do this by looking at the names and addresses on the envelopes than by reading every single letter. The key is to remember that your objective in browsing through content is to facilitate its return to the person who lost the briefcase (or USB drive) and not to satisfy your personal curiosity about that person's private affairs.

> **Ethics.** Overall standards of moral conduct. > **Computer ethics.** Standards of moral conduct as they relate to computer use.

TECHNOLOGY AND YOU

Virtual Gold and Income Taxes

While Second Life, World of Warcraft, and other virtual worlds only exist in cyberspace, there is nothing virtual about the money being made via virtual worlds and online multiplayer video games. For instance, in 2006, Ailin Graef (creator of Second Life resident and avatar Anshe Chung) became the first virtual world millionaire. In Second Life, Anshe buys and develops virtual real estate, owns virtual shopping malls, and performs other financial transactions for Graef. Graef announced in late 2006 that her Second Life assets topped $1 million in U.S. dollars (virtual money in Second Life is measured in Linden dollars and has an official market-driven exchange rate, approximately 260 Linden dollars per $1 U.S. at the time of this writing).

While a basic account with Second Life is free, buying land, building homes, and properly outfitting your avatar (see the accompanying illustration) is anything but free. For instance, a pair of new sneakers costs around $0.70 U.S., a plasma TV and leather couch for your avatar's condo costs about $2.15 U.S., a furnished split level retreat costs about $225 U.S., and a private island costs about $1,000 U.S., plus another $295 U.S. per month in maintenance use fees. The amount of real money exchanged in virtual worlds and online multiplayer games like World of Warcraft is staggering—one estimate is more than $1 billion U.S. per year. In addition to buying and selling goods and services within Second Life, World of Warcraft, and other virtual entities, individuals can also buy and sell virtual assets (such as Linden dollars, Second Life islands, World of Warcraft gold, and so on) on eBay and other online marketplaces.

As a result of the amount of money being exchanged within virtual communities, the issue of taxing that money has arisen in the U.S. and other countries. When virtual goods are cashed out for actual cash, it's clear that the profits should be reported as taxable income. But what about taxing virtual profits that never leave the virtual world? This issue is complicated by the fact that goods or services obtained through barter or as prizes are taxable in the U.S. under current law, and the fact that virtual transactions have real-world value. While the IRS has not yet specifically addressed the issue of whether or not virtual income is taxable in the U.S. before it is exchanged for real-life money and/or for goods or services, the issue is being looked into. Some countries have already made that decision, such as Australia, which implemented taxes on virtual income in late 2006, and South Korea, which has a value-added tax on individuals with virtual income over a certain amount. Whether the U.S. and other countries will follow suit remains to be seen.

The vitual money spent for goods and services in Second Life translates into real-world revenue for the sellers when exchanged for U.S. dollars.

Whether at home, at work, or at school, individuals encounter ethical issues every day. For example, you may need to make ethical decisions such as whether or not to accept a relative's offer of a free copy of a downloaded song or movie, whether or not to have a friend help you take an online exam, whether or not to upload a photo of your friend to Facebook without asking permission, whether or not to post a rumor on a campus gossip site, or whether or not to report as taxable income the virtual money you made in Second Life or another virtual world, as discussed in the Technology and You box.

As an employee, you may need to decide whether or not to print your child's birthday party invitations on the office color printer, whether or not to correct your boss if he or she gives you credit for another employee's idea, or whether or not to sneak a look at information that technically you have access to but have no legitimate reason to view. IT employees, in particular, often face this latter ethical dilemma since they typically have both access and the technical ability to retrieve a wide variety of personal and professional information about other employees, such as their salary information, Web surfing history, and personal e-mail.

ONLINE VIDEO

Go to the Chapter 6 page at **www.cengage.com/ computerconcepts/np/uccs4** to watch the "The Google Interview Process" video clip.

Businesses also deal with a variety of ethical issues in the course of normal business activities—from determining how many computers on which a particular software program should be installed, to identifying how customer and employee information should be used, to deciding business practices. **Business ethics** are the standards of conduct that guide a business's policies, decisions, and actions.

Ethical Use of Copyrighted Material

Both businesses and individuals should be very careful when copying, sharing, or otherwise using copyrighted material to ensure that the material is used in both a legal and an ethical manner. Common types of copyrighted material encountered on a regular basis include software, books, Web-based articles, music, and movies. Software ownership rights were discussed in Chapter 2; the rest of these topics are covered next.

Books and Web-Based Articles

Copyright law protects print-based books, newspaper articles, e-books, Web-based articles, and all other types of literary material. Consequently, these materials cannot be reproduced, presented as one's own original material, or otherwise used in an unauthorized manner. Students, researchers, authors, and other writers need to be especially careful when using literary material as a resource for papers, articles, books, and so forth, to ensure the material is used appropriately and is properly credited to the original author. To present someone else's work as your own is **plagiarism**, which is both a violation of copyright law and an unethical act. It can also get you fired, as some reporters have found out the hard way after faking quotes or plagiarizing content from other newspapers. Some examples of acts that would normally be considered or not considered plagiaristic are shown in Figure 6-5.

With the widespread availability of online articles and fee-based online term paper services, some students might be tempted to create their papers by copying and pasting excerpts of online content into their documents to pass off as their original work. But these students should realize that this is plagiarism, and instructors can usually tell when a paper is created in this manner. There are also online sources instructors can use to test the originality of student papers; the results of one such test are shown in Figure 6-6. Most colleges and universities have strict consequences for plagiarism, such as automatically failing the assignment or course, or being expelled from the institution. As Internet-based plagiarism continues to expand to younger and younger students, many middle schools and high schools are developing strict plagiarism policies as well.

TIP

For a review of how to cite online material properly, refer to Figure 3-16 in Chapter 3.

FIGURE 6-5

Examples of what is and what is not normally considered plagiarism.

PLAGIARISM	NOT PLAGIARISM
A student including a few sentences or a few paragraphs written by another author in his term paper without crediting the original author.	A student including a few sentences or a few paragraphs written by another author in his term paper, either indenting the quotation or placing it inside quotation marks, and crediting the original author with a citation in the text or with a footnote or endnote.
A newspaper reporter changing a few words in a sentence or paragraph written by another author and including the revised text in an article without crediting the original author.	A newspaper reporter paraphrasing a few sentences or paragraphs written by another author without changing the meaning of the text, including the revised text in an article, and crediting the original author with a proper citation.
A student copying and pasting information from various online documents to create her research paper without crediting the original authors.	A student copying and pasting information from various online documents and using those quotes in her research paper either indented or enclosed in quotation marks with the proper citations for each author.
A teacher sharing a poem with a class, leading the class to believe the poem was his original work.	A teacher sharing a poem with a class, clearly identifying the poet.

>**Business ethics.** Standards of moral conduct that guide a business's policies, decisions, and actions. >**Plagiarism.** Presenting someone else's work as your own.

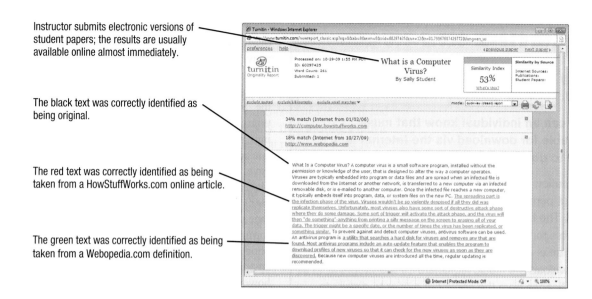

Instructor submits electronic versions of student papers; the results are usually available online almost immediately.

The black text was correctly identified as being original.

The red text was correctly identified as being taken from a HowStuffWorks.com online article.

The green text was correctly identified as being taken from a Webopedia.com definition.

support rec
individuals.
the Internet
a Web site f
legally at ri
delete it—ai
then share it
rented from
the *place sh*
recorded co
show obtain
rebroadcasti
another indi

While t
ing bootleg
many local,
focused on
music, and
the FBI intro
designed to
and other ir
this seal is c
additional p

The MI
movie pirate
gal DVDs, t
is also occu
MPAA uses
ies and then
being used
such as Bay
resources ii
graphics, m
cally use au
the firm is o
illegally, the
firm also ty
holder) deci

To pre
video-on-de
loaded mov
the movie f
only for a sp
starts to play
lar to the ob
as TiVo) hav
devices (suc
For a look a
you on your

Ethical U

A variety o
and types o
unethical m

Music

There have been many issues regarding the legal and ethical use of music over the past few years. The controversy started with the emergence and widespread use of *Napster* (the first P2P music sharing site that facilitated the exchange of music files from one Napster user's computer to another). Many exchanges via the original Napster service violated copyright law and a flood of lawsuits from the music industry eventually shut down Napster and other P2P sites that were being used to exchange copyright-protected content illegally. Additional issues arose with the introduction of recordable and rewritable CD and DVD drives, portable digital media players, and other technology that can be used to duplicate digital music. Some issues regarding the legal and ethical use of digital music have been resolved. For instance, downloading a music file from a P2P site without compensating the artist and record label is a violation of copyright law and an unethical act; so is transferring legally obtained songs to a storage medium to sell or give to others. To give individuals a legal alternative for obtaining digital music quickly and easily, music can be purchased and downloaded via a number of online music stores and services today. However, illegal music exchanges are still taking place and law enforcement agencies, as well as the Recording Industry Association of America (RIAA), are pursuing individuals who violate music copyrights. For instance, the RIAA won its first lawsuit against an individual in late 2007 when a young woman was found guilty of sharing music online and was ordered to pay a total of $222,000 to record companies. At a new trial in 2009, the verdict was the same but the award was increased to $1.92 million—$80,000 per downloaded song.

Once an MP3 file or audio CD has been obtained legally, however, most experts agree that it falls within the fair use concept for an individual to transfer those songs to a CD, computer, or portable digital media player, as long as it is for personal, noncommercial use and does not violate a user agreement. In the past, songs downloaded from some online music stores included DRM controls, which prevented the songs from being copied to other devices. While this helped prevent the illegal copying of downloaded songs from one user to another, it also prevented users from transferring legally downloaded music from one of their devices to another. In response to user protests, most music stores today (such as the one shown in Figure 6-7) offer their songs in the universal (and DRM-free) MP3 format, so they can be played on a wide range of devices.

FIGURE 6-6
Results of an online originality test on an essay that contained plagiarized content.

VIDEO PODCAST

Go to the Chapter 6 page at **www.cengage.com/ computerconcepts/np/uccs4** to download or listen to the "How To: Restore Your Computer's Music Library from Your iPod" video podcast.

FIGURE 6-7
Many music stores today offer DRM-free song downloads.

this temptation and have sold their customer lists, others believe that any short-term gains achieved through ethically questionable acts will adversely affect customer loyalty and will ultimately hurt the business in the long run.

To prepare future employees for these types of decisions, most business schools incorporate business ethics into their curriculum. However, there is the ongoing question of how effective the training is. In fact, AACSB International (an accrediting agency for business schools in the United States) recently reported that business schools have not done enough to raise the ethical awareness of MBA students. Ethics training is also becoming mandatory at some businesses. This may be even more important given the recent economic uncertainty because the Ethics Resource Center reports that workplace misconduct tends to increase by at least 11% during times of turmoil, such as layoffs and budget cuts. In addition, a recent survey of executives found that nearly one-half expected fraud levels within their companies to increase in the coming year.

Cheating and Falsifying Information

Just as computers and the Internet make it easier for individuals to plagiarize documents, computers and the Internet also make it easier for individuals to cheat on assignments or online exams, or to perform other similar unethical acts.

Unfortunately, cheating by students at both the high school level and the college level is rampant today. Cheating today is often performed via the Internet and mobile phones, such as creating a paper from material plagiarized from Web sites, storing notes on a mobile phone to view during a test, texting answers to another student during a test, or taking photos of an exam to pass on to a student taking the test later in the day. While technology does make it easier to cheat, it also may make it feel less like cheating. During one recent study of middle and high school students, for instance, about 25% of the students didn't think storing notes on a mobile phone or texting during an exam constituted cheating.

Traditionally, it was typically weaker students who cheated to prevent failing a course or an exam. Today, however, studies have shown that honor students and others with higher GPAs are more likely to cheat. For college students, MBA students tend to cheat more often than other graduate students—according to Donald McCabe of Rutgers University, this might be because the students are emulating behaviors they believe are necessary to succeed in the corporate world. But whether they realize it or not, students who choose to cheat are cheating themselves of an education. They are also being unfair to honest students by possibly altering the grading curve. Widespread cheating can also have a negative impact on society, such as if underprepared employees enter the workforce.

FIGURE 6-10

Academic honor codes. The honor code at the University of Denver is signed by virtually all incoming students.

To explain to students what behavior is expected of them, many schools are developing *academic honor codes*. These codes are usually published in the student handbook and on the school Web site; they may also be included in course syllabi. Research has shown that having an academic honor code effectively reduces cheating. For example, one McCabe study found that cheating on tests on campuses with honor codes is typically one-third to one-half less than on campuses that do not have honor codes, and the level of cheating on written assignments is one-quarter to one-third lower. To bring attention to their honor codes, some schools encourage incoming students to sign their honor codes upon admission. For instance, all incoming University of Denver students are asked to sign the school's honor code publicly (see Figure 6-10). Regardless of whether or not students choose to sign the honor code, they are required to abide by it.

Like academic cheating, lying on a job application or résumé is more common than most of us may think it is. The practice of providing false information in an attempt to look more qualified for a job, sometimes referred to as *résumé padding*, is both dishonest and unethical. It is also widespread. Recent research conducted by the *New York Times* found that almost half of hiring managers and 84% of job seekers believe that résumé padding is done by a significant number of candidates. In addition to being unethical, providing false information to a potential employer can have grave consequences. The majority of the companies surveyed in the *New York Times* study have a policy that lists termination as the appropriate action for employees who were hired based on falsified résumés or applications. Being blacklisted from an industry or being sued for breach of contract are also possibilities. Résumé writers should remember that background checks are easily available on the Web, which means credentials are easy to check and verify. Even if individuals believe they will not be caught, applicants should not embellish their résumés or job applications to any extent because it is an unethical thing to do. Another recent ethical issue surrounding IT employees is cheating on IT certification exams. Copies of certification questions and entire certification exams are available for purchase online, and some Web sites offer the services of "gunmen" (usually located in Asia) who take certification tests for individuals at a cost of up to several thousand dollars each. In response, companies that offer IT certifications are looking at the security of their testing processes to try to put a stop to this new type of cheating.

There are also situations in personal life that tempt some individuals to provide inaccurate personal information, such as when writing personal advertisements, when participating in chat rooms, and when individuals may otherwise wish to appear to be someone different from the person they really are. There are differing opinions about how ethical these actions are—some individuals believe that it is a person's right to portray himself or herself in any way desired; others feel that any type of dishonesty is unethical.

Computer Hoaxes and Digital Manipulation

Most people realize that information in print media can, at times, be misleading and that photos can be manipulated. Information found on the Internet may also be inaccurate, misleading, or biased. Some of this type of information is published on Web pages; other information is passed on via e-mail. Two types of computer-oriented misinformation include computer hoaxes and digital manipulation.

Computer Hoaxes

A **computer hoax** is an inaccurate statement or story—such as the "fact" that flesh-eating bacteria have been found in banana shipments or that Applebee's will send you a gift certificate for forwarding on an e-mail—spread through the use of computers. These hoaxes are sometimes published on Web pages, but they are more commonly spread via e-mail. Common computer hoax subjects include nonexistent computer viruses, serious health risks, impending terrorist attacks, chain letters, and free prizes or giveaways. Inaccurate information posted on a Web site or wiki just to be misleading can also be considered a computer hoax. E-mail hoaxes are written with the purpose of being circulated to as many people as possible. Some are started as experiments to see how fast and how far information can travel via the Internet; others originate from a joke or the desire to frighten people. Similar to spam, e-mail hoaxes can be annoying, waste people's time, bog down e-mail systems, and clog users' Inboxes. Because computer hoaxes are so common, it is a good idea to double-check any warning you receive by e-mail or read on a Web site before passing that warning on to another person, regardless of how realistic or frightening the information appears to be (sites like the one shown in Figure 6-11 can help you research potential hoaxes).

FIGURE 6-11

Hoax-Slayer. This is one site that can be used to research possible computer hoaxes.

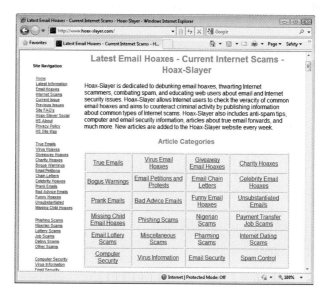

> **Computer hoax.** An inaccurate statement or story spread through the use of computers.

Digital Manipulation

Computers make it very easy to copy or modify text, images, photographs, music, and other digital content. In addition to being a copyright concern, **digital manipulation** (digitally altering digital content) can be used to misquote individuals, repeat comments out of context, retouch photographs—even create false or misleading photographs—and so is an ethical concern, as well. While there are some beneficial, ethical, noncontroversial applications of digital manipulation (such as aging photos of missing children to show what they may look like at the present time, or altering photos of wanted criminals or suspects to show possible alternate appearances for law enforcement purposes), the matter of altering photos for publication purposes is the subject of debate. Some publications and photographers see no harm in altering photographs to remove an offending item (such as a telephone pole behind someone's head), to make someone look a little more attractive, to illustrate a point, or to increase circulation; others view any change in content as unethical and a great disservice to both the public and our history. For example, fifty years from now, will anyone know that a staged or altered photograph of a historical event was not an actual depiction of the event?

Although manipulation of photographs has occurred for quite some time in tabloids and other publications not known as being reputable news sources, there have been several incidents of more reputable news publications using digitally altered photographs in recent years. Many of these became known because the unaltered photograph was used in another publication at about the same time. One of the most widely publicized cases occurred in 1994, just following the arrest of O. J. Simpson. While *Newsweek* ran Simpson's mug shot unaltered, *TIME* magazine darkened the photograph, creating a more sinister look and making Simpson's skin color appear darker than it actually is. This photo drew harsh criticism from Simpson supporters who felt the photograph made him appear guilty, the African-American community who viewed the alteration as an act of racial insensitivity, and news photographers who felt that the action damaged the credibility not only of that particular magazine, but also of all journalists.

A more recent example is the case of a one-time Pulitzer Prize finalist who resigned from a Toledo, Ohio, newspaper after it was discovered that he had submitted for publication nearly 80 doctored photos in just the 14 weeks prior to his resignation, including one sports photo of a basketball game with a digitally-added basketball placed in midair. Other recent instances of digitally manipulated images being printed in news media include a photo released by the U.S. Army of a U.S. soldier killed in action, whose picture was later discovered to be a composite of the soldier's head on another soldier's body; a photo printed in an Israeli newspaper of the Prime Minister, President, and members of the Cabinet of that country that the newspaper edited to replace the two female Cabinet members with male members; and a photo of an Iranian missile test that appeared in many newspapers but that contained a digitally added missile to replace one that did not fire during the test (see Figure 6-12).

Perhaps the most disturbing thing about known alterations such as these is that some may never have been noticed, and may consequently have been accepted as true representations. Adding to the problem of unethical digital manipulation is the use of digital cameras today, which eliminate the photo negatives that could be used with film cameras to show what photographs actually looked like at the time they were taken. Although some publications allow the use of "photo illustrations,"

FIGURE 6-12

Digital manipulation. The digitally manipulated photo (left) added an additional missile launching to the real photo (right) and appeared on the front page of many major newspapers.

DIGITALLY ALTERED PHOTO   **ORIGINAL PHOTO**

> **Digital manipulation.** The alteration of digital content, usually text or photographs.

INSIDE THE INDUSTRY

Click Fraud

Click fraud occurs when sponsored links (see the accompanying image)–such as on a search site results page–are clicked when there is no interest in the product or service associated with the sponsored link. The links can be clicked by a person or by an automated clicking program (sometimes referred to as a *clickbot* and often performed by botnets). The motive for click fraud is usually financial. For instance, although viewed as unethical in the business world, a company might click on a competitor's sponsored links in order to deplete that company's advertising budget. In addition, some companies or individuals create Web pages consisting primarily of sponsored links (usually sponsored links from Google, Yahoo!, or other search sites that are placed on other sites via ad networks) for the purpose of click fraud. Web sites hosting a sponsored link get a fee each time the link on that page is clicked, so these companies or individuals manually or automatically (via software or botnets) click the ads on their sites to fraudulently generate revenue. In fact, the independent click fraud monitoring and reporting service Click Forensics estimates that more than 60% of all ad traffic coming from these types of sites is fraudulent.

Click fraud is growing (Click Forensics estimates that approximately 13% of all online ad clicks are attributed to click fraud), and so it is the subject of some controversy and increasing litigation. For instance, Google recently agreed to pay $90 million to settle a class action lawsuit alleging the search site was charging companies for clicks not generated by legitimate users. To try to prevent overcharging companies due to click fraud, both Google and Yahoo! try to identify clicks associated with click fraud and credit the advertiser's account accordingly; however, many advertisers feel that the search sites could do a better job combating click fraud. The problem is compounded by the fact that, as search sites improve their ability to detect click fraud, the fraudsters continue to develop ways to disguise click fraud. Pay-per-click advertising is currently one of the fastest-growing types of advertising, but some fear that click fraud may inhibit further growth of Web-based advertising unless a solution is reached.

Sponsored Links

Nintendo Wii
Save on **Nintendo Wii** & Other Video Games at MSN Shopping - Shop Now!
Shopping.MSN.com

others have strict rules about digital manipulation—especially for news photojournalists. For instance, the *LA Times* fired a staff photographer covering the war in Iraq when he combined two of his photographs into one to convey a point better.

Ethical Business Practices and Decision Making

Most businesses must make a variety of ethics-related business decisions, such as whether or not to sell a product or service that some may find offensive or objectionable, whether or not to install video cameras in the workplace for monitoring purposes, whether or not to release potentially misleading information, or whether or not to perform controversial research. In addition, corporate integrity, as it relates to accounting practices and proper disclosure, is a business ethics topic that has come to the forefront because of the many recent incidents involving corporate scandals and bankruptcies. For a look at one new controversial topic related to *sponsored listings* on search sites—*click fraud*—see the Inside the Industry box.

Fraudulent Reporting and Other Scandalous Activities

Following the large number of corporate scandals occurring since 2002, business ethics have moved into the public eye. The scandals, such as the ones surrounding executives at Enron, Tyco International, and WorldCom, involved lies, fraud, deception, and other illegal and unethical behavior. This behavior forced both Enron and WorldCom into bankruptcy proceedings. When asked to comment on the scandals, 3Com Chief Executive Officer Bruce Claflin said on CNBC, "I would argue we do not have an accounting problem—we have an ethics problem."

In reaction to the scandals, Congress passed the *Sarbanes-Oxley Act of 2002*. This law includes provisions to improve the quality of financial reporting, independent audits, and accounting services for public companies; to increase penalties for corporate wrongdoing;

REVIEW ACTIVITIES

KEY TERM MATCHING

a. business ethics

b. computer ethics

c. computer hoax

d. copyright

e. digital manipulation

f. digital watermark

g. intellectual property rights

h. patent

i. plagiarism

j. trademark

Instructions: Match each key term on the left with the definition on the right that best describes it.

1. _____ A form of protection for an invention that can be granted by the government; gives exclusive rights of an invention to its inventor for 20 years.

2. _____ An inaccurate statement or story spread through the use of computers.

3. _____ A subtle alteration of digital content that is not noticeable when the work is viewed or played, but that identifies the copyright holder.

4. _____ A word, phrase, symbol, or design that identifies goods or services.

5. _____ Presenting someone else's work as your own.

6. _____ Standards of moral conduct as they relate to computer use.

7. _____ Standards of moral conduct that guide a business's policies, decisions, and actions.

8. _____ The alteration of digital content, usually text or photographs.

9. _____ The legal right to sell, publish, or distribute an original artistic or literary work; it is held by the creator of a work as soon as it exists in physical form.

10. _____ The rights to which creators of original creative works (such as artistic or literary works, inventions, corporate logos, and more) are entitled.

SELF-QUIZ

Instructions: Circle **T** if the statement is true, **F** if the statement is false, or write the best answer in the space provided. **Answers for the self-quiz are located in the References and Resources Guide at the end of the book.**

1. **T F** All unethical acts are illegal.

2. **T F** Changing the background behind a television newscaster to make it appear that he or she is reporting on location instead of from inside the television studio would be an example of digital manipulation.

3. **T F** Patents are used to protect artistic works, such as music or books.

4. **T F** Copying a song from a CD you own to your computer to create a custom music CD for personal use is normally considered fair use.

5. **T F** Résumé padding or lying on a job application would be viewed as unethical by most employers.

6. A software program would be protected by _____ law, while a corporate logo would be protected by _____ law.

7. Turning in a copy of a poem you found on a Web site as your original composition for a poetry class assignment is an example of _____.

8. _____ software is used to protect and manage the rights of creators of digital content, such as by allowing a digital music file to be copied a limited number of times.

9. The overturning by the U.S. Supreme Court of the _____ Act, which made it illegal to distribute patently indecent or offensive material online, is considered a landmark decision for free speech advocates.

10. Match each term to its description or example, and write the corresponding number in the blank to the left of each description or example.

   a. _____ What the symbol © stands for.

   b. _____ Can vary from another's depending on his or her values, culture, and so forth.

   c. _____ A warning about a nonexistent virus spread via e-mail.

   d. _____ A subtle alteration of digital content that identifies the copyright holder.

   1. Computer hoax
   2. Copyright
   3. Digital watermark
   4. Ethics

---

1. For each of the following situations, write the appropriate letter—E (ethical) or U (unethical)—in the blank to the right of the situation to indicate how most individuals would view the act.

   Situation

   Type of Situation

   a. A teenager rips a new CD she just bought and e-mails the MP3 files to all her friends.

   _____

   b. A photographer combines two of his photographs to create a new composite artistic piece.

   _____

   c. A physician incorporates another doctor's research into her journal article submission, including the researcher's name and article in her submission.

   _____

2. Match each term with its related example, and write the corresponding number in the blank to the left of each example.

   a. _____ Copying and pasting Web page text without recognizing the source.

   b. _____ Online age verification systems.

   c. _____ Service marks.

   1. Plagiarism
   2. Intellectual property rights
   3. Business ethics

3. Assume that you have created a Web site to display your favorite original photographs. Is the site and/or your photographs protected by copyright law? Why or why not?

4. Explain the difference between a copyright and a trademark.

5. Under what circumstances might a business need to consider cultural differences when creating a Web site? List at least two examples.

---

1. There are research services available online that can be used by students preparing term papers. Is the use of these services ethical? Is the use of programs to detect plagiarism by instructors ethical? How can the problem of plagiarism and other forms of cheating at schools today be resolved? Whose responsibility is it to ensure students do not cheat themselves out of a proper education?

2. While the Web contains a vast amount of extremely useful information, some content can be harmful. Think about suicide Web sites that explain in detail how to kill oneself, Web sites that broadcast the beheadings by terrorists, and Web sites that explain how to build bombs. If a Web site instructs visitors how to perform an illegal act, should the site's creators be criminally liable if a visitor carries out those instructions? Who, if anyone, is responsible for preventing potentially harmful information from being shared via the Web? Is there any Internet content that you believe a government has the right or obligation to censor? If so, what? Where should the line between freedom of speech and national or personal safety be drawn?

TECHNOLOGY AND YOU

Mobile Coupons

For years we have had coupons in the Sunday newspaper, and then digital coupons became available via the Internet. The newest trend in digital coupons is delivery to your mobile phone.

Although common in Asia and Europe for several years, digital coupons delivered to mobile phones is relatively new to the United States. But with businesses and consumers alike now viewing the mobile phone as an essential productivity and communications tool, mobile phone coupon use is growing rapidly. Digital coupons typically are delivered to mobile phones via e-mail or text message, and they can be redeemed by showing the coupon code or having the coupon's barcode scanned at the store or restaurant issuing the coupon, similar to using a paper coupon (and like other mobile phone applications, standard text messaging or data charges apply). To increase effectiveness and prevent unwanted intrusions—particularly because of the potential fees involved with receiving text messages—many mobile coupon companies require consumers to sign up or *opt-in* to coupon delivery. Some include software that can be downloaded to the phone to locate coupons for desired products and services in the user's geographical area, as well as to organize stored coupons and automatically delete expired coupons. Redemption rates for mobile coupons are much higher than for paper coupons—in part, because the coupons aren't forgotten at home.

What is the next step for electronic coupons expected to be? One likely possibility is sending electronic coupons to a mobile phone based on an individual's current geographical location (determined via the GPS capabilities built into most mobile phones today). For instance, an individual who walks by a Starbucks might get an electronic coupon via his or her mobile phone for 50 cents off a mocha Frappuccino. Now that's effective impulse marketing!

When you begin to notice the symptoms of burnout, experts recommend reevaluating your schedule, priorities, and lifestyle. Sometimes, just admitting that you are feeling overwhelmed is a good start to solving the problem. Taking a break or getting away for a day can help put the situation in perspective. Saying no to additional commitments and making sure that you eat properly, exercise regularly, and otherwise take good care of yourself are also important strategies for coping with and alleviating both stress and burnout.

Internet and Technology Addiction

When an individual overuses, or is unable to stop using, the Internet, it becomes a problem and is referred to as **Internet addiction** (also called *Internet addiction disorder* (*IAD*), *cyberaddiction, computer addiction disorder* (*CAD*), and *technology addiction*, depending on the technology being used). According to Dr. Kimberly Young, an expert on Internet addiction and the director of the Center for Internet Addiction Recovery in Pennsylvania, Internet addiction is an established psychological condition. And it is growing; in fact,

>**Internet addiction.** The problem of overusing, or being unable to stop using, the Internet.

researchers at Stanford University Medical School estimate that 1 in 8 Americans suffer from at least one sign of problematic Internet use. Internet addiction is considered a serious disorder and is being considered for inclusion as a new diagnosis in the upcoming revision of the *Diagnostic and Statistical Manual of Mental Disorders (DSM-V)*.

Originally, Internet addiction sufferers were stereotyped as younger, introverted, socially awkward, computer-oriented males. However, with the increased access to computers and the Internet today, this stereotype is no longer accurate. Internet addiction can affect anyone of any age, race, or social class and can take a variety of forms. Some individuals become addicted to e-mailing or text messaging. Others become compulsive online shoppers or online gamblers,

> Do you feel preoccupied with the Internet (think about previous online activity or anticipate next online session)?
>
> Do you feel the need to use the Internet with increasing amounts of time in order to achieve satisfaction?
>
> Have you repeatedly made unsuccessful efforts to control, cut back, or stop Internet use?
>
> Do you feel restless, moody, depressed, or irritable when attempting to cut down or stop Internet use?
>
> Do you stay online longer than originally intended?
>
> Have you jeopardized or risked the loss of a significant relationship, job, educational, or career opportunity because of the Internet?
>
> Have you lied to family members, a therapist, or others to conceal the extent of involvement with the Internet?
>
> Do you use the Internet as a way of escaping from problems or of relieving a dysphoric mood (e.g., feelings of helplessness, guilt, anxiety, depression)?

FIGURE 7-10
Signs of Internet addiction. You may be addicted to the Internet if you answer "yes" to at least five of these questions.

or become addicted to social networking activities. Still others are addicted to cyber-sex, cyberporn, or online gaming, or struggle with real-world relationships because of virtual relationships. Currently, the most common forms of addictive behaviors include multi-user online role-playing games, instant messaging, online chatting, online pornography, and social networking. See Figure 7-10 for Dr. Young's list of Internet addiction symptoms.

Like other addictions, addiction to using a computer, the Internet, or other technology may have significant consequences, such as relationship problems, job loss, academic failure, health problems, financial consequences, loss of custody of children, and even suicide. There is also growing concern about the impact of constant use of technology among teenagers. In addition to texting via mobile phones and posting to Facebook via portable computers during the day, many teens are taking these devices to bed with them, raising concerns about sleep deprivation and its consequences, such as concentration problems, anxiety and depression, and unsafe driving. In fact, one recent Belgian study found that late-night texting is affecting the sleep cycles of 44% of that country's 16-year-olds, with 12% of the youths studied waking up every night or every other night to text. Internet addiction is also increasingly being tied to crime and even death in countries (such as China and South Korea) that have high levels of broadband Internet access. For instance, Internet addiction is blamed for much of the juvenile crime in China, a number of suicides, and several deaths from exhaustion by players unable to tear themselves' away from marathon gaming sessions.

Internet addiction is viewed as a growing problem worldwide. Both China and South Korea have implemented military-style boot camps to treat young people identified as having Internet addiction, and the growing number of Internet-addicted youth prompted the Chinese government to ban minors from Internet cafés. In the U.S., there are a number of inpatient treatment centers that treat Internet addiction, such as the Illinois Institute for Addiction Recovery and the reSTART program in Washington, which recently opened as the first intensive 45-day residential program specially designed to treat Internet addiction.

Many experts believe that while Internet addiction is a growing problem, it can be treated, similar to other addictions, with therapy, support groups, and medication. Research to investigate its impact, risk factors, and treatment possibilities, as well as investigate treatment differences among the various types of technology abuse, is ongoing. New studies are also looking at the overall impact of technology and how its overuse or abuse may also impact people's lives, in order to identify other potential problems and possible solutions.

ACCESS TO TECHNOLOGY

For many, a major concern about the increased integration of computers and technology into our society is whether or not technology is accessible to all individuals. Some believe there is a distinct line dividing those who have access and those who do not. Factors such as age, gender, race, income, education, and physical abilities can all impact one's access to technology and how one uses it.

The Digital Divide

The term **digital divide** refers to the gap between those who have access to information and communications technology and those who do not—often referred to as the "haves" and "have nots." Typically, the digital divide is thought to be based on physical access to computers, the Internet, and related technology. Some individuals, however, believe that the definition of the digital divide goes deeper than just access. For example, they classify those individuals who have physical access to technology but who do not understand how to use it or are discouraged from using it in the "have not" category. Groups and individuals trying to eliminate the digital divide are working toward providing real access to technology (including access to up-to-date hardware, software, Internet, and training) so that it can be used to improve people's lives. In addition to access to computers and the Internet, digital divides related to other technologies may exist as well. For instance, one recent study revealed a digital divide in electronic health records (EHRs) at hospitals in the United States. The study found that hospitals that primarily serve low-income patients are less likely to have adopted EHRs and other safety-related technologies (such as clinical decision supports, electronic medication lists, and computerized discharge summaries) than hospitals with more affluent patients.

The digital divide can refer to the differences between individuals within a particular country, as well as to the differences between countries. Within a country, use of computers and related technology can vary based on such factors as age, race, education, and income.

The U.S. Digital Divide

Although there is disagreement among experts about the current status of the digital divide within the United States, there is an indication that it is continuing to shrink. While the digital divide involves more than just Internet use—it involves the use of any type of technology necessary to succeed in our society—the growing amount of Internet use is an encouraging sign. As discussed in Chapter 3, nearly 75% of the United States population are Internet users, using the Internet at work, home, school, or another location. Free Internet access at libraries, school, and other public locations, as well as the availability of low-cost computers and low-cost or free Internet access in many areas today, has helped Internet use begin to approach the popularity and widespread use of telephones and TVs, and has helped it become more feasible for low-income families today than in the past. In general, however, according to recent reports by the Pew Internet & American Life Project, individuals with a higher level of income or a higher level of education are more likely to go online, and younger individuals are more likely to be online than older Americans. Some overall demographic data about Internet use in the United States is shown in Figure 7-11.

Because the United States is such a technologically advanced society, reducing—and trying to eliminate—the digital divide is extremely important to ensure that all citizens have an equal chance to be successful in this country. Although there has been lots of

> **Digital divide.** The gap between those who have access to technology and those who do not.

progress in that direction, more work still remains. For instance, the Navajo Nation (a sovereign tribal nation with more than 250,000 citizens living across 27,000 square miles in New Mexico, Arizona, and Utah) has lagged significantly behind the rest of the U.S. in terms of technology. Many schools lack computers and Internet access, many residents (63%, according to the 2000 Census) have no telephone, and even some government entities within the Navajo Nation have dial-up or no Internet access. However, this is slowly changing as a result of the *Internet to the Hogan* project—a project to build an integrated wired and wireless network infrastructure to enable communications for government entities, as well as for individuals (via connections at community-based chapter houses) within the Navajo Nation. Once the basic infrastructure is in place, the goal is to expand to schools, medical clinics, hospitals, firehouses, and homes within a 15 to 30 mile radius of each chapter house, in order to provide additional services (such as telemedicine and distance learning) and to open up new job opportunities (such as personal Web-based businesses or telecommuting) that are not possible without high-speed Internet connectivity.

Many individuals view computers and the Internet as essential for all Americans today. For instance, students need access to technology and Internet resources to stay informed and be prepared for further education and careers. As already discussed, most jobs in the U.S. require some sort of computer or Internet use. And the Internet is becoming an increasingly important resource for older Americans, particularly for forming decisions about health and healthcare options. However, it is important to realize that not all individuals want to use computers or go online. Just as some people choose not to have televisions, mobile phones, or other technologies, some people—rich or poor—choose not to have a computer or go online. Sometimes this is a religious decision; at other times, it is simply a lifestyle choice.

The Global Digital Divide

While the digital divide within a country is about some individuals within that country having access to technology and others not having the same access, the global digital divide is about some countries having access to technology and others not having the same level of access. It is becoming increasingly important for all countries to have access to information and communications technology in order to be able to compete successfully in our global economy. The global digital divide is perhaps more dramatic than the U.S. digital divide. According to InternetWorldStats.com, about 1.6 billion people globally are online—only about 24% of the world's population. With nearly 74% of its population online, North America is the

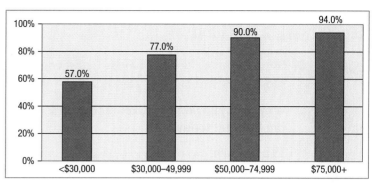

INCOME

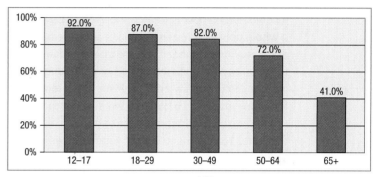

AGE

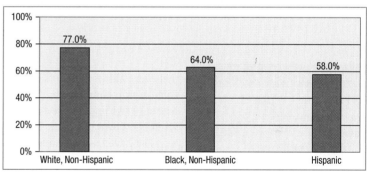

RACE

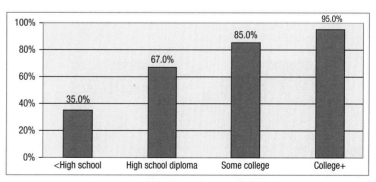

HIGHEST LEVEL OF EDUCATION OBTAINED

FIGURE 7-11
Key U.S. Internet use statistics. Shows the percent of individuals in each category who use the Internet.

ONLINE VIDEO

Go to the Chapter 7 page at **www.cengage.com/ computerconcepts/np/uccs4** to watch the "Intel World Ahead Program" video clip.

FIGURE 7-12
The OLPC XO laptop.

leading world region in Internet users; with less than 7% of its population online, Africa has one of the lowest percentages of Internet users.

For some, it is difficult to imagine how computers and the Internet would benefit the world's hungry or all of the billion people in the world without access to reliable electricity. Others view technology as a means to bridge the global digital divide. For instance, mobile phones and computers with solar-rechargeable batteries can be used in developing countries for education and telemedicine. New wireless Internet projects, such as the *Wildnet* technology that is being used to extend Wi-Fi in remote areas in order to connect areas up to 60 miles apart, are also helping to bridge the gap. Currently deployed in several countries, Wildnets are already being used to provide Internet access to rural schools in Ghana and the Philippines, and to connect doctors in a main hospital in India with technicians in remote eye-care clinics in remote villages.

For personal computer use, new products are emerging that could help lessen the global digital divide. Perhaps the most widely known project in this area is the *One Laptop Per Child (OLPC)* project. The goal of OLPC is to ensure that every child in the world between the ages of 6 and 12 has immediate access to a personal laptop computer by 2015, in order to provide them with access to new channels of learning, sharing, and self-expression. The current model of the *XO laptop* developed by OLPC is shown in Figure 7-12.

The XO laptop is made of thick plastic for durability with a display that can be viewed in direct sunlight. The rubber keyboard is sealed to keep out dirt and water, and the XO is very energy-efficient, consuming just a fraction of the energy required for a standard notebook computer. It can be charged via an electrical outlet, as well as from a car battery, foot pedal, or pull string. The XO is relatively small and light, has a 7.5-inch display, and is designed to be power efficient. It is Linux-based; contains a variety of communications and connectivity capabilities, including a Wi-Fi adapter, USB ports, a flash memory slot, and a built-in video camera and microphone; and uses 1 GB of flash memory for storage. The XO is currently being sold to governments of developing countries to be distributed to school-aged children—more than 1.5 million units have been deployed across the world in countries such as Peru, Uruguay, Rwanda, Ethiopia, Iran, Mongolia, and Afghanistan. The cost is currently $188 per computer, but the goal is to decrease the cost to $75 per computer eventually. According to OLPC, making it possible for students in developing countries to have a laptop will greatly impact their education, as well as society as a whole. They believe that by empowering children to educate themselves, a new generation will ultimately be better prepared to tackle the other serious problems (poverty, malnutrition, disease) facing their societies.

Assistive Technology

Research has found that people with disabilities tend to use computers and the Internet at rates below the average for a given population. Part of the reason may be that some physical conditions—such as visual impairment or limited dexterity—make it difficult to use a conventional computer system. That is where **assistive technology**—hardware and software specially designed for use by individuals with physical disabilities—fits in. While assistive technology is not currently available to help with all types of computer content (primarily streaming video and other multimedia content increasingly found on Web pages), there has been much improvement in assistive technology in recent years. In addition, researchers are continuing to develop additional types of assistive technology, such as *multimedia accessibility tools* to help individuals with visual impairments better control and experience Web-based multimedia. This growth in assistive technology is due in part to demands by disabled individuals and disability organizations for equal access to computers and Web content, as well as *Section 508* of the *Rehabilitation Act* (which requires federal agencies to make their electronic and information technology accessible to people with disabilities) and the *Americans with Disabilities Act* (*ADA*), which requires companies with 15 or more employees to make reasonable accommodations for known physical or mental limitations of otherwise qualified individuals. In order to be accessible to users of assistive technology, Web pages need to use features like *alternative text descriptions* (text-based descriptions sometimes called *alt tags* that are assigned to Web page images) and meaningful text-based hyperlinks—such as *How to Contact Us* instead of *Click Here*. Some states have additional accessibility laws and there has been an increase in accessibility lawsuits recently. For instance, blind visitors to the Target Web site sued Target for its lack of accessibility. Target recently settled the suit for $6 million to be distributed to the plaintiffs and agreed to make the Target.com site fully accessible to blind visitors.

To help provide individuals with physical disabilities equal access to technology, assistive input and output devices—such as *Braille keyboards*, specialized pointing devices, large monitors, and *screen readers*—are available for personal computers, as well as some mobile phones and mobile devices.

Assistive Input Systems

Assistive input devices allow for input in a nontraditional manner (see Figure 7-13). For example, *Braille keyboards*, large-key keyboards, or conventional keyboards with Braille or large-print key overlays are available for visually impaired computer users. *Keyguards*—metal or

ONLINE VIDEO

Go to the Chapter 7 page at **www.cengage.com/computerconcepts/np/uccs4** to watch the "The Importance of Alt Tags" video clip.

FIGURE 7-13
Assistive input devices.

BRAILLE KEYBOARDS
The keys on this keyboard contain Braille overlays.

ONE-HANDED KEYBOARDS
Each key on this half keyboard contains two letters (one for the right half and one for the left) so all keys can be reached with one hand.

EYE TRACKING SYSTEMS
Cameras track the user's eye movements, which are used to select icons and other objects on the screen.

>**Assistive technology.** Hardware and software specifically designed for use by individuals with physical disabilities.

HOW IT WORKS

Mobile Voice Search

You know you can do many things with your mobile phone—including accessing and searching the Web on most of today's phones. Web searching has traditionally been text based, but *mobile voice search* is now available. Mobile voice search allows you to speak, rather than type, search terms into your mobile phone, and then see the results of that search. The newest systems—such as Yahoo!'s *oneSearch* service shown in the accompanying illustration—allow the user to just press a button on the phone and speak the search terms into the phone, and then the search results are immediately displayed, just as with a text-based Web page search. Commonly requested information includes movie show times, information about and directions to local businesses, stock quotes, sports scores, weather information, airline flight updates, and more. In addition to providing the requested information, Yahoo! oneSearch also supplies other relevant information (such as displaying weather information for the departure and arrival cities when flight information is requested), as shown in the accompanying illustration. Usually, search results are filtered by proximity to the user's geographical area (which is determined by the GPS information or nearby cell tower locations relayed by the mobile phone being used)—a feature called *geobrowsing*. Geobrowsing (discussed in more detail in the Chapter 3 Trend box) is based on the assumption that mobile users are likely searching for something nearby. When used in conjunction with geobrowsing, mobile voice search essentially turns your mobile phone into your personal concierge.

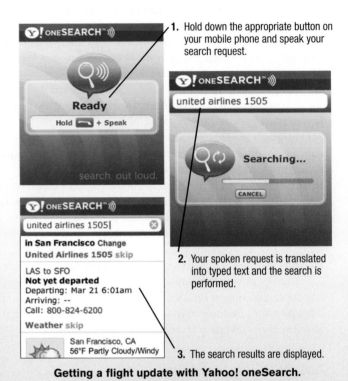

1. Hold down the appropriate button on your mobile phone and speak your search request.

2. Your spoken request is translated into typed text and the search is performed.

3. The search results are displayed.

Getting a flight update with Yahoo! oneSearch.

plastic plates that fit over conventional keyboards—enable users with limited hand mobility to press the keys on a keyboard (using his or her fingers or a special device) without accidentally pressing other keys. *One-handed keyboards* are available for users who have the use of only one hand, and speech recognition systems can be used to input data and commands to the computer hands-free, as discussed in Chapter 2. *Switches*—hardware devices that can be activated with hand, foot, finger, or face movement, or with sips and puffs of air—can be used to input data and commands into a computer. Some conventional input devices can also be used for assistive purposes, such as scanners, which—if they have optical character recognition (OCR) capabilities—can input printed documents as editable text.

For mouse alternatives, there are assistive pointing devices that can be used—sometimes in conjunction with a switch—to move and select items with an on-screen pointer; they can also be used to enter text-based data when used in conjunction with an on-screen keyboard. For example, *foot-controlled mice* are controlled by the feet, *head pointing systems* control the on-screen pointer using head movement, and *eye tracking systems* allow users to select items on-screen using only their gaze.

In addition to its use by disabled computer users, assistive hardware can also be used by the general population. For example, one-handed keyboards are sometimes used by people who wish to keep one hand on the mouse and one hand on the keyboard at all times; voice input systems are used by individuals who would prefer to speak input instead of type it; and head pointing systems are available for gaming and virtual reality (VR) applications. For a look at a new mobile voice input application—*mobile voice search*—see the How It Works box.

SCREEN READER SOFTWARE   **BRAILLE DISPLAYS**   **BRAILLE PRINTERS**

FIGURE 7-14
Assistive output devices.

Assistive Output Systems

Once data has been input into the computer, a variety of *assistive output devices* can be used. For instance, some examples of assistive output devices that can be used by blind and other visually impaired individuals are shown in Figure 7-14. A *screen reader* is a software program that reads aloud all text information available via the computer screen, such as instructions, menu options, documents, and Web pages. *Braille displays* are devices that can be attached to conventional computers (or built into portable computers and mobile devices designed for visually impaired individuals) and that continuously convert screen output into Braille form. *Braille printers* print embossed output in Braille format on paper instead of, or in addition to, conventional ink output.

Some operating systems also include accessibility features. For instance, recent versions of Windows and Mac OS include a screen reader, on-screen keyboard, speech recognition capabilities, and settings that can be used to magnify the screen, change text size and color, convert audio cues into written text, and otherwise make the computer more accessible.

FIGURE 7-15
Eco-labels.

ENVIRONMENTAL CONCERNS

The increasing use of computers in our society has created a variety of environmental concerns. The amount of energy used to power personal computers, servers, and computer components, as well as the heat generated by computing equipment, is one concern. Another is our extensive use of paper, CDs, and other disposables, and how much of it ends up as trash in landfills. The hazardous materials contained in computer equipment or generated by the production of computers and related technology, as well as the disposal of used computing products, are additional concerns.

Green Computing

The term **green computing** refers to the use of computers in an environmentally friendly manner. Minimizing the use of natural resources, such as energy and paper, is one aspect of green computing. To encourage the development of energy-saving devices, the U.S. Department of Energy and the Environmental Protection Agency (EPA) developed the **ENERGY STAR** program. Hardware that is ENERGY STAR compliant exceeds the minimum federal standards for reduced energy consumption and can display the ENERGY STAR label shown in Figure 7-15. The most recent ENERGY

UNITED STATES

EUROPEAN UNION

KOREA

BRAZIL

GERMANY

> **Green computing.** The use of computers in an environmentally friendly manner. > **ENERGY STAR.** A program developed by the U.S. Department of Energy and the Environmental Protection Agency to encourage the development of energy-saving devices.

STAR requirements for computers (version 5.0) focus on efficiency while the devices are being used, as well as power management features that can put the devices into sleep or hibernation mode after a designated period of inactivity. **Eco-labels**—environmental performance certifications—are also used in other countries; Figure 7-15 show some examples.

Energy Consumption and Conservation

With the high cost of electricity today and the recent increase in data center energy usage, power consumption and heat generation by computers are key concerns for businesses today. Today's faster and more powerful computers tend to use more energy and run hotter than computers from just a few years ago, which leads to greater cooling costs. Servers, in particular, are power-hungry, so consolidating servers (such as by the use of virtualization) is a common energy saving tactic used by businesses today. But energy use is still growing. In fact, a recent Environmental Protection Agency (EPA) study showed that servers and data centers use more than 1.5% of all electricity generated in the U.S. and that number is expected to double in the next five years. To help IT managers compare energy consumption in their facilities with other data centers, in order to help them improve data center efficiency, the EPA is in the process of developing an energy performance rating system for data centers. The EPA estimates that even a 10% reduction in energy consumption by U.S. data centers would save enough energy to power up to 1 million homes per year and save U.S. businesses $740 million annually.

In response to the growing emphasis on green computing today, hardware manufacturers are working to develop more energy efficient personal computers, servers, microprocessors, storage systems, and other computer components. Some energy-saving features found on computer hardware today include devices (such as computers and printers) that can go into very low-power sleep mode when not in use, low-power-consumptive chips and boards, high-efficiency power supplies, energy-efficient flat-panel displays, liquid cooling systems, and CPUs that power up and down on demand. The energy savings by using more energy-efficient hardware can be significant. For instance, moving to an LED flat-panel display instead of a conventional LCD display saves around 12% in energy consumption.

While ENERGY STAR 5.0-compliant computers are more efficient in standby and sleep mode than in the past, computers can still draw quite a bit of power when they are in these modes—particularly with a screen saver enabled. Because of this, businesses and schools are also increasingly using software to shut down computers automatically when they are not in use to save power. Mobile phone manufacturers are also working to reduce the environmental impact of their products, such as displaying reminders on mobile phones to unplug them from their chargers when they are fully charged because chargers can draw up to five watts per hour even if nothing is plugged into them. Other devices that draw power when they are turned off (sometimes called *energy vampires*) include computers, home electronics, and home appliances. In fact, it is estimated that the average U.S. household spends $100 per year powering devices that are turned off or in stand-by mode. To determine how much power a device is using, you can use a special device like the *Kill a Watt EZ* shown in Figure 7-16. This device displays the amount of power (in kilowatts or dollar value) any device plugged into it is currently using. To save on vampire power costs, unplug your devices when you are not using them (you can connect your electronic devices to a power strip and just switch off the power at the power strip to make this process easier). However, don't cut the power to any device (such as a wireless router, DVR, or cable box) that will need to be active to perform a needed function. A *smart power strip* that turn off outlets on the strip when it senses those devices aren't being used, is another alternative.

ONLINE VIDEO

Go to the Chapter 7 page at **www.cengage.com/ computerconcepts/np/uccs4** to watch the "Climate Savers Computing Initiative" video clip.

FIGURE 7-16

Energy usage monitors. This monitor displays in real time the amount of electricity (in kilowatt-hours or approximate cost) a connected device is using.

> **Eco-label.** A certification, usually by a government agency, that identifies a device as meeting minimal environmental performance specifications.

Alternate Power

In addition to more energy-efficient hardware, other possibilities for greener computing are being developed, such as alternate power sources for computers and mobile devices. For instance, *solar power* is a growing alternative for powering electronic devices, including mobile phones and portable computers. With solar power, *solar panels* convert sunlight into direct current (DC) electricity, which is then stored in a battery.

Although it has been expensive to implement in the past, improvements in solar technology are making its use more feasible for a greater number of individuals. Solar technology is now considered to be in its third generation, with *thin-film solar panels* being created by printing nanoparticles onto rolls of thin, flexible panels to create the panels at a fraction of the cost of earlier generations. As a result, solar panels are becoming available for an increasing number of applications. For instance, solar panels to be built into the covers of notebook computers are being designed and both solar-powered and hand-powered chargers (see Figure 7-17) are available for use with portable computers, mobile phones, and other small portable devices. These devices can be used wherever dependable electricity is not available, such as in developing countries and while outdoors. In addition, there are solar panels that are designed to be placed on the roof of the Toyota Prius, in order to add an additional 2 miles to the gallon, and the U.S. Army is testing prototypes of emergency tents with built-in solar panels to power radios, heaters, and other critical devices. The messenger bag shown in Figure 7-17 includes enough solar panels to fully charge a typical notebook computer, and, as an added environmental plus, the bag uses fabrics made from recycled plastics like soda bottles. For a look at another emerging option for powering your devices—*portable fuel cell chargers*—see the Trend box.

Solar power can be also used to power more permanent computer setups, as well. For instance, some Web hosting companies in the U.S. (including Solar Energy Host and AISO.Net) are now 100% solar powered and the solar panels that cover most of the rooftops at Google's Mountain View, California, headquarters power 30% of the energy needs for that complex. Solar power plants are also being developed, and some experts predict that many buildings in the future will be *solar buildings* with solar cells integrated into the rooftop, walls, and windows of the building to generate electricity.

Green Components

In addition to being more energy-efficient, computers today are being built to run quieter and cooler, and they are using more recyclable hardware and packaging. Many computer manufacturers are also reducing the amount of toxic chemicals being used in personal computers. For instance, Dell bans the use of some hazardous chemicals, such as cadmium and mercury; has reduced the amount of lead used in several desktop computers; and meets the European Union requirement of being completely lead-free for all electronics shipped to the EU. Some mobile phones are also going green, being made out of recycled plastics, including solar panels to charge the phone's battery, and including a pedometer and other applications to calculate the volume of CO_2 emissions you have avoided by not driving.

Recycling and Disposal of Computing Equipment

Another environmental concern is the amount of trash—and sometimes toxic trash—generated by computer use. One concern is paper waste. It now appears that the so-called *paperless office* that many visionaries predicted would arrive is largely a myth. Instead, research indicates that global paper use has grown more than six-fold since 1950, and one-fifth of all wood harvested in the world today ends up as paper. The estimated number of pages generated by computer printers worldwide is almost one-half billion a year—an

Solar panels are built into the bag.

SOLAR COMPUTER BAGS

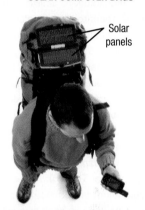

Solar panels

SOLAR-POWERED CHARGERS

HAND-POWERED CHARGERS

FIGURE 7-17

Alternate power.

Solar and hand power can be used to power mobile phones, portable digital media players, GPS devices, portable computers, and other devices.

TREND

Portable Fuel Cell Chargers

Tired of your mobile phone or laptop battery running out of power at inopportune times? Well, *portable fuel cells* just might be the solution. Unlike conventional batteries, which need to be recharged with electricity when they run out of electrons, fuel cells produce electricity using a chemical reaction between a fuel (originally hydrogen, but also sometimes methanol or butane today) and air. When more electricity is needed, more fuel is added to the fuel cell device.

While fuel cells may eventually be economical enough to power computers directly, the initial application today is powering mobile phones and other mobile devices on the go. One of the first consumer products on the market, released in Japan in late 2009, is *Dynario*, a methanol-based fuel cell charger developed by Toshiba. This palm-sized product (see the accompanying illustration) is connected to a mobile device via a USB cable to provide nearly instant power to the mobile device (the charger is refilled using dedicated methanol solution cartridges; one refill can charge a typical mobile phone two times).

In addition to their consumer applications, fuel cells are viewed as a possible option for powering devices used by U.S. soldiers on missions in order to reduce the number of batteries they have to carry. Currently, soldiers may carry up to 35 pounds of batteries with them for a 72-hour mission—the military would like to reduce that to 12 pounds. The goal is to develop efficient power sources that are lighter than current batteries, but are safe to carry and use in the field. Fuel cells, possibly in conjunction with other technologies like solar power, might help obtain this goal.

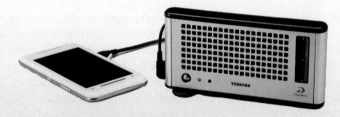

The Dynario portable fuel cell charger powers mobile devices with methanol.

amount that would stack more than 25,000 miles high. One possible solution for the future (electronic paper) is discussed in the Inside the Industry box. There are also utilities, such as the free *GreenPrint World* and *PrintWhatYouLike.com* services, designed to reduce paper consumption. These utilities eliminate images, blank pages, and other non-critical content located on documents and/or Web pages, in order to print just the necessary content on the least number of pages possible.

In addition to paper-based trash, computing refuse includes used toner cartridges, obsolete or broken hardware, and discarded CDs, DVDs, and other storage media. Mobile phones that are discarded when individuals switch providers—as well as new disposable consumer products, such as disposable digital cameras—also add to the amount of **e-trash** (also called *electronic trash* and *e-waste*) generated today. A surge in discarded televisions is also expected as prices of plasma TVs continue to decrease and many consumers replace their older TVs with flat-screen displays and TVs that support digital TV.

Compounding the problem of the amount of e-trash generated today is the fact that computers, mobile phones, and related hardware contain a variety of toxic and hazardous materials. For instance, the average CRT monitor alone contains about eight pounds of lead, and a single desktop computer may contain up to 700 different chemical elements and compounds, many of which (such as arsenic, lead, mercury, and cadmium) are hazardous and expensive to dispose of properly.

A global concern regarding e-trash is where it all eventually ends up. The majority of all discarded computer equipment (at least 70%, according to most estimates) ends up in

FURTHER EXPLORATION

Go to the Chapter 7 page at
**www.cengage.com/
computerconcepts/np/uccs4**
for links to further information
about green computing.

>**E-trash.** Electronic trash or waste, such as discarded computer components.

INSIDE THE INDUSTRY

E-Paper

Electronic paper (*e-paper*) is a type of flat panel display device that attempts to mimic the look of ordinary printed paper. The purpose of an *Electronic Paper Display* (*EPD*) is to give users the experience of reading from paper, while providing them with the ability to update the information shown on the device electronically. EPDs display content in high-contrast, so they can be viewed in direct sunlight. They also require much less electricity than other types of displays, since they don't require a backlight and they don't require power to maintain the content shown on the display—they only require power to change the content. Because the content stored in an EPD can be erased when it is no longer needed and then replaced with new content, EPDs are more environmentally friendly than conventional paper documents. An additional benefit is portability; an *e-book reader* (such as the *Amazon Kindle* and the *Sony Reader* shown in the accompanying photograph), for instance, can hold over a thousand books stored in electronic format in a device about the size of a paperback novel. In fact, with an e-book reader, you could carry a small library in your backpack.

E-paper is also widely used for *e-signs*, which look like ordinary paper signs, but their text can be changed wirelessly. Their low power consumption means that e-signs can run off battery power for an extended period of time, even with moving data. Some e-signs don't even require a battery; instead, the wireless signal used to transmit data to the display is strong enough to update the sign content by itself. Other retail applications currently on the market include e-paper shelf price tags that can communicate electronically with the store's database so the current price is always displayed, e-paper displays on wristwatches and USB flash drives, destination displays on trains, and e-paper newspapers that can be updated periodically during the day to reflect the latest news. For instance, in late 2007, the French newspaper *Les Echos* announced an electronic paper edition. This e-newspaper is delivered automatically to subscribers via a Wi-Fi connection and it is updated every hour during the day on weekdays. The Amazon Kindle e-book reader can also receive newspaper content (in addition to e-book content)—and thanks to its proprietary high-speed wireless connection, it can download 1,000 pages in less than one minute. E-paper technology used with fabric, plastic, metal, and other materials is in development and is expected to be used to enable keyboards to be printed onto military uniform sleeves, light switches to be printed onto wallpaper, and radio

circuitry and controls to be printed onto clothing and other everyday objects. It may also allow e-paper to be used on billboards, T-shirts, and even paint for easy redecorating, as well as regular-sized e-paper that can be inserted into a special computer printer to be printed electronically and then reused over and over. One improvement that has already occurred is the incorporation of touch and pen input with e-paper displays. For instance, both touch and pen input can be used in conjunction with the Sony e-book reader shown in the accompany photograph to flip the "pages" of the book and otherwise control the device.

So how does e-paper work? It is based on a display technology called *electrophoretic*, which was invented and is now manufactured and marketed by E Ink® Corporation. An electrophoretic display contains *electronic ink*—essentially charged ink that consists of millions of tiny beads or *microcapsules* about half the diameter of a human hair. These beads contain positively charged white particles and negatively charged black particles suspended in a clear fluid. When voltage is applied to the beads (through the circuitry contained within the display), either the white or the black particles rise to the top and the opposite colored particles are pulled to the bottom of the bead, depending on the polarity of the charge applied. Consequently, the beads in each pixel appears to be either white or black (see the accompanying illustration) and remain in that state until another transmission changes the pattern.

The white particles are at the top, so this pixel appears white.

AN E-BOOK   **AN E-INK MICROCAPSULE**

FIGURE 7-18

E-trash. The vast majority of the 40 million or so computers that become obsolete each year end up as e-trash in landfills.

landfills and in countries, such as China, India, and Nigeria, with lower recycling costs, cheaper labor, and more lax environmental standards than found in the United States. Much of the e-trash exported to these countries is simply dumped into fields and other informal dumping areas. Unaware of the potential danger of these components, rural villagers often sort through and dismantle discarded electronics parts looking for precious metals and other sources of revenue (see Figure 7-18)—potentially endangering their health as well as polluting nearby rivers, ponds, and other water sources. Compounding the problem, the remaining waste is often burned, generating huge clouds of potentially toxic smoke. Activists believe unchecked dumping by the United States and other countries— such as England, Japan, Australia, and Singapore—has been going on for at least 10 years. The primary reason for exporting e-trash is expense—proper disposal of a computer in the United States normally costs between $5 and $10, compared to $1 or less in third-world countries. Another reason is that some states in the United States are beginning to ban the most dangerous computing equipment— such as CRT monitors—from landfills.

While it is difficult—or, perhaps, impossible—to correct the damage that has already occurred from e-trash, many organizations are working to develop ways to protect people and the environment from future contamination. For instance, the *Climate Savers Computing Initiative* is an industry group started by Google and Intel in 2007 that is dedicated to reducing greenhouse-gas emissions, and the *Green Grid Alliance* is a global consortium dedicated to advancing energy efficiency in data centers and business computing. There are also some environmental regulations (such as California's *Electronic Waste Recycling Act* and Europe's *Restrictions on Hazardous Substances Directive*) that prohibit throwing away some types of computer components. For instance, California does not allow computer monitors to be thrown out as trash and has implemented mandatory fees of $8 to $25 on all TV and computer monitor purchases; these fees are used to fund the collection, recycling, and proper disposal of discarded electronic components. In the United States, computer manufacturers are beginning to produce more environmentally friendly components, such as system units made from recyclable plastic, nontoxic flame-retardant coatings, and lead-free solder on the motherboard.

Even though recycling computer equipment is difficult because of the materials currently being used, proper disposal is essential to avoid pollution and health hazards. Some recycling centers will accept computer equipment, but many charge a fee for this service. Many computer manufacturers have recycling programs that will accept obsolete or broken computer equipment from consumers, typically for a fee of about $15 to $30 per unit. Expired toner cartridges and ink cartridges can sometimes be returned to the manufacturer (using the supplied shipping label included with some cartridges) or exchanged when ordering new cartridges; the cartridges are then *recharged* (refilled) and resold. Cartridges that cannot be refilled can be sent to a recycling facility. In addition to helping to reduce e-trash in landfills, using recharged printer cartridges saves the consumer money since they are less expensive than new cartridges. Other computer components—such as CDs, DVDs, USB flash drives, and hard drives—can also be recycled through some organizations, such as *GreenDisk*. GreenDisk accepts shipments of all types of storage media (plus printer cartridges, mobile phones, mobile devices, notebook computers, power cords, and more) for a modest charge (such as $6.95 for 20 pounds of items if you ship them yourself); it reuses salvageable items and recycles the rest. There are also a number of recycling programs specifically designed for discarded mobile phones. These programs typically refurbish and sell the phones; many organizations donate a portion of the proceeds to nonprofit organizations.

In lieu of recycling, older equipment that is still functioning can be used for alternate purposes (such as for a child's computer, a personal Web server, or a DVR), or it can be donated to schools and nonprofit groups. Some organizations accept and repair donated equipment and then distribute it to disadvantaged groups or other individuals in need of the hardware. In the United States, for instance, Operation Homelink refurbishes donated computers and sends them free of charge to families of U.S. military personnel deployed overseas, who then use the computers to communicate with the soldiers via e-mail and videoconferences (see Figure 7-19).

For security and privacy purposes, data stored on all computing equipment should be completely removed before disposing of that equipment so that someone else cannot recover the data stored on that device. As discussed in Chapter 5, hard drives should be wiped clean (not just erased) using special software that overwrites the data on the drive several times to ensure it is completely destroyed; storage media that cannot be wiped (such as rewritable DVDs) or that contain very sensitive data (such as business hard drives being discarded) should be shredded. The shredded media is then typically recycled.

Consumers and companies alike are recognizing the need for green computing. A growing number of computing equipment manufacturers are announcing that they are committed to environmental responsibility. Support for a nationwide recycling program is growing, and new classifications from the EPA are expected to encourage recycling of an even greater number of computer components. So, even though computer manufacturing and recycling have a long way to go before computing equipment stops being an environmental and health hazard, it is encouraging that the trend is moving toward creating a safer and less wasteful environment.

FIGURE 7-19
Operation Homelink.
Computers donated to this organization are used to help soldiers (such as this soldier in Iraq) communicate with their loved ones.

RELATED LEGISLATION

There has been some legislation related to health, access, and the environment in the past few years. For instance, many states make it illegal to use a mobile phone without a hands-free system while driving, in an attempt to cut down on the number of accidents due to distracted drivers. The most significant recent legislation regarding accessibility has been the 1998 amendment to *Section 508* of the *Rehabilitation Act* requiring federal agencies to make their electronic and information technology accessible to people with disabilities. This act applies to all federal Web sites, as well, creating a trend of Web sites that are Section 508 compliant. While there are currently no federal computer recycling laws in the U.S., federal agencies are required to purchase energy-efficient electronic products. In addition, some federal laws (such as the Sarbanes-Oxley Act and HIPAA) have established privacy and data protection standards for companies disposing of computer hardware that contained specific types of data and some states have implemented laws related to electronic waste.

ASK THE EXPERT

Lauren Ornelas, Campaign Director, Silicon Valley Toxics Coalition

What impact does U.S. e-waste have on other countries?

According to the California Department of Toxic Substances Control report that was released in 2007, roughly 20 million pounds of e-waste were shipped out of California alone in 2006 to places such as Brazil, China, India, South Korea, Malaysia, Mexico, and Vietnam. For some countries, we have some idea of the impact. When we visited India, for instance, we saw workers (including children) dismantling electronics without adequate protection for themselves or the environment. Consequently, the workers and those around them are exposed to lead and other hazardous substances. These toxic substances also get into the soil, water, and air. In some areas, the water is so polluted that they can no longer drink from local water sources and water has to be shipped in from other towns. Nigeria has become a place where our e-waste is essentially just dumped with the pretense of it being recycled. While many electronic products are shipped to Nigeria under the guise of reuse, up to 75% of what is being shipped cannot be repaired or recycled.

SUMMARY

COMPUTERS AND HEALTH

Chapter Objective 1:
Understand the potential risks to physical health resulting from the use of computers.

Since the entry of computers into the workplace and their increased use in our society, they have been blamed for a variety of physical ailments. **Carpal tunnel syndrome (CTS)**, **DeQuervain's tendonitis**, and other types of **repetitive stress injuries (RSIs)** are common physical ailments related to computer use; *computer vision syndrome (CVS)*, eyestrain, fatigue, backaches, and headaches are additional possible physical risks.

Ergonomics is the science of how to make a computer workspace, hardware, and environment fit the individual using it. Using an ergonomically correct workspace and **ergonomic hardware** (such as *ergonomic keyboards, ergonomic mice, document holders, antiglare screens, keyboard drawers, wrist supports,* and *computer gloves*) can help avoid or lessen the pain associated with some RSIs. In addition, all users should use good posture, take rest breaks, alternate tasks, and take other common-sense precautions. For portable computers, **docking stations** can be used to allow easy connections to more ergonomically correct hardware, and **notebook stands** can be used to elevate a notebook computer so its display screen can be set at an ergonomically correct height, in order to create more ergonomically correct workspaces.

Chapter Objective 2:
Describe some possible emotional health risks associated with the use of computers.

In addition to physical health issues, the extensive use of computers and related technology in the home and office has raised concerns about emotional side effects of computer use. The *stress* of keeping up with ever-changing technology, layoffs, always being in touch, fear of being out of touch, information overload, and **burnout** are all possible emotional problems related to computer use. Taking a break, reevaluating your schedule, and taking good care of yourself can help you avoid or reduce the stress that these problems may cause. To manage all the digital information you encounter, good search techniques, *RSS feeds*, and e-mail filters can be used.

Internet addiction (also referred to as *Internet addiction disorder (IAD), cyberaddiction, computer addiction disorder (CAD)*, and *technology addiction*) refers to not being able to stop using computers, the Internet, or other technology. Many experts believe it is a growing problem and is most prominent in countries with high levels of broadband Internet access. It can affect users of any age and is treated similarly to other addictions.

ACCESS TO TECHNOLOGY

Chapter Objective 3:
Explain what is meant by the term "digital divide."

The **digital divide** refers to the gap between those who have access to computers and communications technology and those who do not. Although the term "digital divide" normally refers to physical access to technology, its "have not" category is sometimes thought to include not only those who do not have access to technology, but also those who have physical access to technology but who do not understand it or are discouraged from using it. There can be a digital divide within a country or between countries. Globally, the digital divide separates countries with access to technology from those without access to technology.

Chapter Objective 4:
Discuss the impact that factors such as nationality, income, race, education, and physical disabilities may have on computer access and use.

In the United States, studies show that the digital divide may be lessening, as people of every income, education, race, ethnicity, and gender continue to go online at increased rates. However, individuals living in low-income households or having little education still trail the national average for computer use. While the United States has a high number of Internet users, continuing to reduce the digital divide is important to ensure all citizens have an equal chance of being successful.

There are several programs designed to bring computers, Internet access, and technology to developing countries, such as the *One Laptop Per Child (OLPC) project*. Research suggests that people with disabilities tend to use computers and the Internet at rates lower than the average population. Part of the reason may be because some types of conventional hardware—such as keyboards and monitors—are difficult to use with some types of physical conditions. **Assistive technology** includes hardware and software that makes conventional computer systems easier for users with disabilities to use.

Examples of assistive input devices include Braille keyboards, keyguards, voice input systems, switches, foot-controlled mice, and head pointing systems. Assistive output devices include screen readers, Braille displays, and Braille printers. In order to be compatible with screen readers and other assistive devices, Web pages need to use features, such as alternative text descriptions for Web page images and descriptive text-based hyperlinks.

Chapter Objective 5:
List some types of assistive hardware that can be used by individuals with physical disabilities.

ENVIRONMENTAL CONCERNS

Many people worry about the environmental issues related to computer use, such as high energy use and the massive amount of paper computer users consume. **Green computing** refers to using computers in an environmentally friendly manner. It can include using environmentally friendly hardware (such as devices approved by an **eco-label** system like the **ENERGY STAR** certification used in the United States), as well as using procedures (such as consolidating servers and using power management features to place devices into standby or sleep mode when not in use) to reduce energy consumption. Environmentally friendly computers are just starting to come on the market, and alternate-powered hardware is beginning to become available.

Chapter Objective 6:
Suggest some ways computer users can practice "green computing" and properly dispose of obsolete computer equipment.

In addition to practicing green computing when buying and using computer equipment, discarded equipment should be reused whenever possible. Computer equipment that is still functioning may be able to be donated and refurbished for additional use, and toner and ink cartridges can often be refilled and reused. Hardware that cannot be reused should be recycled if possible, or properly disposed of if not recyclable so that it does not end up as hazardous **e-trash** in landfills. Recycling programs and initiatives may help obsolete products be disposed of in a more environmentally friendly manner.

For security and privacy purposes, storage media containing personal or sensitive data should be disposed of properly, such as wiped or shredded before being reused or recycled.

RELATED LEGISLATION

There are some laws in place to help protect our health, access to technology, and the environment. The most significant legislation regarding accessibility is the 1998 amendment to the *Rehabilitation Act* requiring federal agencies to make their electronic and information technology accessible to people with disabilities. In the U.S., some federal regulations and state laws impact the disposal of computer hardware.

Chapter Objective 7:
Discuss the current status of legislation related to health, access, and the environment in relation to computers.

REVIEW ACTIVITIES

KEY TERM MATCHING

a. assistive technology

b. carpal tunnel syndrome (CTS)

c. DeQuervain's tendonitis

d. digital divide

e. docking station

f. eco-label

g. ergonomic hardware

h. green computing

i. Internet addiction

j. notebook stand

Instructions: Match each key term on the left with the definition on the right that best describes it.

1. _____ A certification, usually by a government agency, that identifies a device as meeting minimal environmental performance specifications.

2. _____ A condition in which the tendons on the thumb side of the wrist are swollen and irritated.

3. _____ A device designed to easily connect a portable computer to conventional hardware, such as a keyboard, mouse, monitor, and printer.

4. _____ A device that elevates the display of a notebook or tablet computer to a better viewing height; can contain USB ports to connect additional hardware.

5. _____ A painful and crippling condition affecting the hands and wrist that can be caused by computer use.

6. _____ Hardware and software specifically designed for use by individuals with physical disabilities.

7. _____ Hardware, typically an input or output device, that is designed to be more ergonomically correct than its nonergonomic counterpart.

8. _____ The gap between those who have access to technology and those who do not.

9. _____ The use of computers in an environmentally friendly manner.

10. _____ The problem of overusing, or being unable to stop using, the Internet.

SELF-QUIZ

Instructions: Circle **T** if the statement is true, **F** if the statement is false, or write the best answer in the space provided. **Answers for the self-quiz are located in the References and Resources Guide at the end of the book.**

1. T F A repetitive stress injury is related to the emotional health issue of stress.

2. T F The ENERGY STAR program is an energy conservation program developed by the United States government.

3. T F Carpal tunnel syndrome can be caused by using a computer keyboard.

4. T F As computer use has become more common, the potential for stress related to computer use has decreased.

5. T F Assistive technology is hardware and software designed to help all beginning computer users learn how to use a computer.

6. The science of fitting a work environment to the people who work there is called _____ .

7. A state of fatigue or frustration usually brought on by overwork is referred to as _____.

8. The _____ can be used to describe discrepancies in access to technology by individuals within a country, as well as to compare access from country to country.

9. Craving more and more time at the computer can be an indicator of _____.

10. _____ power refers to electricity generated by the sun.

1. For each of the following situations, write the appropriate letter—Y (yes) or N (no)—in the blank to the right of the situation to indicate if the act is an example of green computing.

Situation

a. You adjust the power settings on your computer to never go into sleep mode.

b. Your boss requires you to print all of his e-mail messages so he can read them on paper.

c. You drop your old mobile phone off in a recycling box instead of throwing it in the trash.

2. Match each term with its related example, and write the corresponding number in the blank to the left of each example.

a. _____ Assistive hardware.

b. _____ Server consolidation.

c. _____ Docking stations.

d. _____ E-mail filters and flags.

3. List at least two assistive input or output devices designed for individuals with a visual impairment and explain the function of each.

4. List three possible negative physical effects that can result from computer use and describe one way to lessen each effect.

5. List three possible negative effects on the environment that can result from computer use and describe one way to lessen each effect.

EXERCISES

Green Computing?

_____

_____

_____

1. Green computing
2. Ergonomics
3. Digital divide
4. Information overload

DISCUSSION QUESTIONS

1. It is becoming increasingly common for biometric devices to be used to grant or deny access to facilities, as well as to identify consumers for financial transactions. In order to facilitate this, some data about each participant's biometric features must be stored in a database. How do you feel about your biometric characteristics being stored in a database? Does it depend on whether the system belongs to your bank, employer, school, or the government? Since biometric features cannot be reset, are you at risk using a biometric ID system? Can the use of biometric systems and other systems that require less actual use of the computer by individuals help the issue of accessibility and lessen the digital divide? If, for instance, the norm for controlling a computer was the voice, would that level the technological playing field for all individuals? Why or why not?

2. While gaming and texting are both popular pastimes, it is possible to become injured by performing these activities. For instance, some Wii users have developed tennis elbow and other ailments from some Wii Sports games and heavy texters have developed problems with their thumbs. Think of the devices you use regularly. Have you ever become sore or injured from their use? If so, was it the design of the input device being used, overuse, or both? What responsibilities do hardware manufacturers have in respect to creating safe input devices? If a user becomes injured due to overuse of a device, whose fault it is? Should input devices come with warning labels?

PROJECTS

1. **E-Paper** The chapter Inside the Industry box discusses e-paper—an erasable, reusable alternative to traditional paper and ink. While e-paper has many societal benefits (such as reducing the use of traditional paper and ink, as well as the resources needed to create and dispose of them), it has been slow to catch on.

   For this project, research the current state of e-paper. What products are available now and what products are due out soon? When a new technology, such as e-paper, that has obvious benefits to society is developed, who (if anyone) should be responsible for making sure it gets implemented in a timely fashion? Do you think businesses or individuals will choose to use e-paper products if the only incentive is a cleaner environment? Or will there need to be economic incentives, such as savings on paper and ink surpassing the cost of e-paper? Would you be willing to switch to a new technology (such as e-paper) that is beneficial to society if it costs more than the existing technology? Is it ethical for an industry or the government to mandate the use of new technologies if they create an additional cost or inconvenience to individuals? At the conclusion of your research, prepare a one-page summary of your findings and opinions and submit it to your instructor.

2. **Section 508** Section 508 is a section of the Rehabilitation Act that refers to requirements for making electronic and information technology accessible to people with disabilities.

   For this project, research Section 508 and the Rehabilitation Act in general to see how the law applies to Web site design and to whom the law applies. If you were to set up a personal or small business Web site, would you be legally obligated to conform to Section 508 regulations? What types of features or modifications does a Web site need to include to be Section 508 compliant? How would one go about testing to see if a Web site is Section 508 compliant? Prepare a one-page summary of your findings and submit it to your instructor.

3. **Ergonomic Workspaces** Some aspects of an ergonomic workspace, such as a comfortable chair and nonglaring light, may feel good right from the beginning. Others, such as using an ergonomic keyboard or wrist rest, may take a little getting used to.

   For this project, find at least one local store that has some type of ergonomic equipment—such as adjustable office chairs, desks with keyboard drawers, ergonomic keyboards, or notebook stands—on display that you can try out. Test each piece, adjusting it as needed, and evaluate how comfortable it seems. Next, evaluate your usual computer workspace. Are there any adjustments you should make or any new equipment you would need to acquire to make your workspace setup more comfortable? Make a note of any changes you could make for free, as well as a list of items you would need to purchase and the estimated cost. Prepare a short summary of your findings to submit to your instructor. If you made any adjustments to your regular workspace during this project, be sure to include a comment regarding whether or not you think it increased your comfort.

4. **Toxic PCs** As discussed in the chapter, computer hardware can contain a variety of toxic and hazardous materials. Is it ethical for computer manufacturers to continue to use hazardous materials in their products? What if a restriction on these compounds severely limited the types of computer equipment that could be manufactured or significantly increased the price? Is it ethical for consumers to buy products that are made of hazardous materials or are not recyclable? What efforts should be made to recycle e-trash in the U.S. and who is ethically responsible for the cost—the manufacturers, the consumers, or the government? Should the government require the recycling of e-trash? Should it ban the exportation of e-trash?

   For this project, form an opinion about the ethical ramifications of toxic PCs and e-trash and be prepared to discuss your position (in class, via an online class discussion group, in a class chat room, or via a class blog, depending on your instructor's directions). You may also be asked to write a short paper expressing your opinion.

5. **Internet Access: Luxury or Necessity?** A luxury can be defined as something that is an indulgence, rather than a necessity. Most people in the world would view items such as food, shelter, and water as necessities. In the United States, many would likely add electricity and indoor plumbing to that list. Today, many individuals are beginning to view Internet access as a necessity. But, while most people would agree that the Internet offers many conveniences, the question remains: Is it a necessity—that is, is it essential for existence? For instance, are there activities that must be performed online? If so, what about the people that do not have Internet access or chose not to use it? How does this lack of Internet access affect them? Do you view computers and/or Internet access as necessities? Can Internet access be viewed as a necessity even if there are alternative methods for accomplishing the same tasks you might accomplish using the Internet? Why or why not? Are there any products or services you view as a luxury today that might be viewed as a necessity in five years?

   For this project, consider whether Internet access in the United States should be viewed as a luxury or a necessity, and form an opinion on this issue. Be prepared to discuss both sides of this issue and your opinion (in class, via an online class discussion group, in a class chat room, or via a class blog). You may also be asked to write a short paper or prepare a short presentation expressing your opinion, depending on your instructor's directions.

Instructions: Go to the Chapter 7 page at **www.cengage.com/computerconcepts/np/uccs4** to work the following Web Activities.

6. **Interactive Activities** Work the interactive **Crossword Puzzle**, watch the **Video Podcasts** and **Online Videos**, and explore the **Further Exploration** links associated with this chapter.

   If you have a SAM user profile, you may have access to hands-on instruction, practice, and assessment of the skills covered in this chapter. Check with your instructor for instructions and the correct URL/Web site to access those assignments.

7. **Student Edition Labs** Work the following interactive **Student Edition Labs**.
   ➤ **Web Design Principles**   ➤ **Creating Web Pages**

8. **Test Yourself** Review the **Online Study Guide** for this chapter, then test your knowledge of the terms and concepts covered in this chapter by completing the **Key Term Matching** exercise, the **Self-Quiz**, the **Exercises**, and the **Practice Test**.

SAM

Student Edition Labs

expert insight on...
Computers and Society

DELL

Frank Molsberry is a Technologist in Dell's Office of the CTO. Prior to his current position, he helped found Dell's Workstation Architecture and Development team and, more recently, the Enterprise Architecture and Technology Group. In all, he has over 25 years of management and engineering experience in advanced system software development and PC system architectures. Frank has a Bachelor's degree in Computer Science and has several patents in the area of computer security. He does regular customer briefings on security and emerging technology trends.

A conversation with **FRANK MOLSBERRY**

Technologist for Dell Inc.

" Security is a mindset. In the same way you look at the features, usability, and performance of a solution, you need to specifically look at the security characteristics, as well. "

My Background . . .

I've been in the field of computer software and hardware development for over 25 years. I joined Dell in 1998 after working at IBM for 15 years. I am currently a Technologist in the Office of the CTO. My focus area is on Security Architecture and Technology. In that role, I support the current engineering efforts for incorporating security hardware and software into Dell products, work with the various security technology companies to evaluate and influence current and planned offerings, and participate with standards organizations, such as the Trusted Computing Group (TCG), in the definition of future security standards.

In many cases the subjects we focus on now (such as security) are not about stand-alone systems anymore, but instead involve an entire ecosystem of hardware devices, software applications, and the infrastructure connecting them. Because this can entail a great deal of breadth and depth of knowledge, I've found that it is important to have a "big-picture" vision and the ability to rapidly drill into the details as needed, but only to the level needed to answer the questions in front of you.

It's Important to Know . . .

The recommendations presented in these chapters are not one time things. Managing your security and privacy needs to be a regular routine—like brushing your teeth.

Technology is a double–edged sword and can always have a dark side. As you develop new and innovative hardware or software applications, you must always look at the threats that can be brought against it and, more importantly, how the technology could be misused beyond its intended purpose. By stepping back and identifying these issues up front, the developers and users of the technology can be better prepared to combat it. Security is a mindset. In the same way you look at the features, usability, and performance of a solution, you need to specifically look at the security characteristics, as well.

We now have a global economy. The products and services you provide must consider a global culture and have the flexibility to satisfy the varying customs, rules, and requirements of a global economy.

How I Use this Technology . . .

I use all the standard precautions on my personal computer—such as antivirus software, antispyware software, and backing up my data—to avoid data loss. I keep my systems on a UPS/surge protector and use power management features to save electricity. When traveling, I use a privacy screen to prevent others from viewing my work and I use encryption software to protect the data on my computer and portable media, such as USB flash drives.

What the Future Holds . . .

The next big thing is not usually a revolution as much as it is a continued progression that, when looked at over a long window of a time, shows up as a major change in technology or use model. So the trends of faster, smaller, cheaper will continue for the next decade.

The impact of security and privacy technology on society is huge. One of the biggest issues is identity theft and the tremendous effort it takes to recover from it. Tasks like shredding papers and monitoring your credit report activity can help prevent identity theft or alert you to suspicious activity. Social media and cloud-based services are seeing explosive growth, but little consideration is given to the use, security, and privacy of the personal information stored via these services, or to what happens when one of these entities is purchased or goes out of business. One must ask, "Can the collection of information I provide about myself online be used to compromise my identity?"

Methods to protect the environment from the impact of technology on the environment will continue to expand. Major manufacturers like Dell have implemented initiatives to reduce or eliminate hazardous materials like lead from their systems, and there are major programs for computer recycling and for returning consumables, such as printer cartridges. A possible development for the future is using more modular architectures, allowing the average user to easily change or upgrade the capabilities of a computer, TV, or printer without having to purchase an entirely new system.

It's important to realize that the digital divide is not new. It occurs when each new method of information communication is developed, such as with the introduction of radio and television. The continued decreases in the cost of computing, new categories of devices like netbooks, and improvements in wireless connectivity will help to close the current divide, but there may be new digital divides in the future. However, we must not lose sight of where information and communications fit in the hierarchy of needs. For those populations where the basic needs of food, clothing, and shelter are not being met, solutions to those problems may need to be reached before focusing on access to computing resources. Another key is connectivity—it does little good to have a computer today without Internet access. Advancements in 4G wireless communications like WiMAX and LTE are crucial.

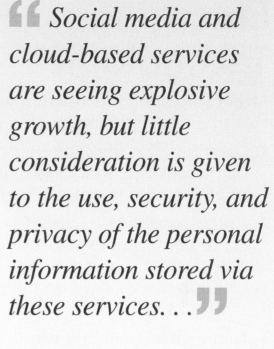

"Social media and cloud-based services are seeing explosive growth, but little consideration is given to the use, security, and privacy of the personal information stored via these services. . ."

My Advice to Students . . .

Computers and the ever changing technology they are based on are just tools. It is important not to just focus on the "coolness" of something new, but the problem it is trying to solve, the user experience, and the barriers to adoption.

Discussion Question

Frank Molsberry believes that developers must look at how new products could be misused. Think about a few recent new technologies or products. Have they been used in an illegal or unethical manner? What responsibility, if any, does a developer have if its product is used inappropriately? Be prepared to discuss your position (in class, via an online class discussion group, in a class chat room, or via a class blog, depending on your instructor's directions). You may also be asked to write a short paper expressing your opinion.

> For more information on Dell, visit www.dell.com and www.dell.com/innovation. For security information, visit www.trustedcomputinggroup.org and searchsecurity.techtarget.com. For a summary of many online tech news sites, visit www.dailyrotation.com.

chapter 8

Emerging Technologies

After completing this chapter, you will be able to do the following:

1. Describe what the computer of the future might look like, including some examples of emerging types of hardware.

2. Understand the effect that emerging computer technologies, such as nanotechnology, quantum computers, and optical computers, may have on the computer of the future.

3. Name some emerging wired and wireless networking technologies.

4. Explain what is meant by the term "artificial intelligence" (AI) and list some AI applications.

5. List some new and upcoming technological advances in medicine.

6. Name some new and upcoming technological advances in the military.

7. Discuss potential societal implications of emerging technologies.

outline

Overview

The Computer of the Future
Emerging Hardware
The Impact of Nanotechnology
Quantum and Optical Computers

Emerging Networking Technologies
Wired Networking Improvements
Wireless Networking Improvements

Artificial Intelligence (AI)
What Is Artificial Intelligence (AI)?
AI Applications

Technological Advances in Medicine
Electronic Monitoring and Electronic Implants
Telemedicine and Telesurgery

Technological Advances in the Military
Battlefield Robots
Exoskeleton Systems

Societal Implications of Emerging Technology

OVERVIEW

No study of computers would be complete without a look to the future. The rapid technological advancements that we've seen in the last few decades have been extraordinary, but some believe the best is yet to come. New advances are being made all the time in areas such as computer hardware, and Internet and networking technologies. In general, technology is continuing to become more user-friendly and more integrated into our daily lives, and that trend is expected to continue. For instance, imagine the following scenario: You walk up to your locked front door and gain access simply by touching the doorknob or speaking your name. When you enter a room, the lights, stereo system, and digital artwork on the walls change automatically to reflect your preferences. Your refrigerator and pantry keep up-to-the-moment inventories of their contents, and your closet automatically selects outfits for you based on the weather and your schedule for the day. Sounds like something out of a science fiction movie, doesn't it? Yet, all the technologies just mentioned are either available or in development.

Many of us are excited to see what new applications and technological improvements the future will bring, as well as how computers, the Internet, and other technologies will evolve. However, our enthusiasm for this progress should be balanced with the understanding that some future applications may not turn out the way we expect or may actually have a negative impact on society. One of the biggest challenges in an era of rapidly changing technologies is evaluating the potential impact of new technology and trying to ensure that new products and services do not adversely affect our security, privacy, and safety.

This chapter focuses on some of the emerging technologies that are already beginning to impact our lives. Topics include the computer of the future, emerging networking technologies, artificial intelligence (AI), and technological advances in medicine and in the military. The chapter closes with a discussion of the societal implications of emerging technologies. ■

THE COMPUTER OF THE FUTURE

While the exact makeup of future personal computers is anyone's guess, it is expected that they will keep getting smaller, faster, more powerful, and more user-friendly, and that they will eventually use alternative input methods more than keyboards. Portable computers will continue to grow closer in capabilities to conventional desktop computers and to be used for a wide variety of everyday activities while on the go. Tomorrow's home and business computers will likely not even look like today's computers—instead they may be built into walls, desks, appliances, and perhaps even jewelry and clothing. In addition to their changing appearance, computers are expected to keep converging with other devices and continue to take on multiple roles to serve our personal needs, as well as to control our household or office environment. Computers in the future may also be able to offer multisensory output—enabling users to see, hear, feel, taste, and smell output—and they will likely become even more environmentally friendly.

Some examples of emerging new hardware are discussed next, followed by a discussion of some technologies that may change the overall makeup of computers in the future—namely, nanotechnology, quantum computers, and optical computers.

VIDEO PODCAST

Go to the Chapter 8 page at **www.cengage.com/ computerconcepts/np/uccs4** to download or listen to the "How To: Navigate the Firefox Browser Using Mouse Gestures" video podcast.

Emerging Hardware

The overall size and appearance of computers seem to change on a continual basis. We now have fully functioning personal computers that are small enough to fit in a pocket or be worn on the body. Technologies are continuing to be developed to make computers and computer components smaller, faster, and more capable. Some of the exciting emerging input, processing, output, and storage hardware and technologies are discussed next.

Emerging Input Devices

Voice input and speech recognition capabilities are increasingly being incorporated into computers, mobile phones, GPS systems, and other devices to enable hands-free input. They are also commonly built into cars to enable hands-free control of navigation systems and sound systems, as well as to allow hands-free mobile phone calls to take place via the car's voice interface. Specialty speech recognition systems are frequently used to control machines, robots, and other electronic equipment, such as by surgeons during surgical procedures. While voice input is expected to be even more prominent in the future, using touch, pen, and *gestures* for input is also growing rapidly and expected to be the norm in the future. The use of *gesture input* started with motion sensitive gaming controllers, such as the *Wii Remote* used with the Nintendo Wii gaming system. However, used in conjunction with digital cameras to detect the gestures, gesture input may soon be incorporated into the computer of the future. For a closer look at gesture input, see the Trend box.

One new trend in the area of touch input is *surface computing*—using a combination of multi-touch input from multiple users and object recognition to interact with computers that are typically built into tabletops and other surfaces. One example is *Microsoft Surface*. This product (shown in Figure 8-1) uses touch and gestures performed via the screen, as well as objects placed on the screen, as input. It can recognize input from multiple users and multiple objects placed on the table simultaneously. According to Panos Panay, the general manager of Microsoft Surface, Microsoft Surface breaks down the barriers between people and technology—moving beyond the traditional mouse and keyboard experience to blend the physical and virtual worlds—and allows for effortless interaction with digital information in a simple, intuitive way.

FIGURE 8-1

Examples of emerging input devices.

SURFACE COMPUTING DEVICES   **2D BARCODES**   **NFC MOBILE PAYMENTS**

TREND

Gesture Input

We already have some devices that support gestures—such as the Nintendo Wii and the Apple iPhone—but some view gesture input as the next step toward making computer input easier and more natural to use. While devices like the Wii and iPhone use special hardware (such as an *accelerometer*) to detect gestures, gesture-based input systems used with computers typically use cameras to detect input based solely on a user's movements. For instance, hand gestures can be used to select and manipulate objects on the screen, similar to the system used by Tom Cruise's character in the movie *Minority Report* to change the images on his display by gesturing with his hands. Gesture input is noncontact, which avoids the fingerprint and germ issues related to public keyboard and touch screen use; it also enables input to be performed from a slight distance (such as through a glass storefront window). In addition, gesture input allows for full body input and, because cameras are used, it can enable the user's image to be imported into the application, such as to have the user's image displayed in a game or virtual world, showing his or her current movements in real time.

Currently, gesture input devices are being used primarily with consumer gaming applications and large screen interactive displays used for advertising purposes (see the accompanying

photo) or to convey information in public locations. However, they are also beginning to be used with mobile phones and personal computers and, according to the president and co-founder of Gesturetek (one of the leading companies in gesture input), 3D gesture input is expected to make its way to televisions in 2010.

Gesture input enables the user to control a computer with noncontact hand movements.

The digital camera capabilities built into most mobile phones today allow for several types of emerging input applications. As discussed in the Trend box, they allow for gesture input; in addition, they can be used with *two-dimensional (2D) barcodes* and *augmented reality applications* to retrieve and display useful information. **Two-dimensional (2D) barcodes**—such as the *QR (Quick Response) code* that represents data with a matrix of small bars—store information both horizontally and vertically and so can hold significantly more data than conventional one-dimensional barcodes. Today, 2D barcodes are just emerging, but they are expected to soon be used by consumers for activities such as viewing a video clip or photo (stored either in the code or online) or downloading a coupon or ticket when the barcode (such as one displayed on a sign, included in a magazine ad, or some other physical form) is captured with the phone's camera (refer again to Figure 8-1). In Japan, 2D barcodes are even beginning to appear on tombstones to enable graveside visitors to access information about the deceased via their mobile phones. **Augmented reality** is another emerging mobile phone application. With augmented reality, computer generated images are overlaid on top of real-time images. Mobile augmented reality applications typically use GPS information, the video feed from the mobile phone's camera, a digital compass, and other data obtained from the phone, and overlay appropriate data (based on the data

> **Two-dimensional (2D) barcode.** A barcode that represents data with a matrix of small bars and stores information both horizontally and vertically so it can hold significantly more data than a conventional one-dimensional barcode. > **Augmented reality.** When computer generated images are overlaid on top of real-time images, such as to overlay information over the photo or video displayed on a mobile phone.

applications include "instant-on" computers and mobile devices that can be turned on and off like an electric light, without any loss of data. It is possible that a form of nonvolatile RAM (such as one of the types discussed in this section or flash memory) will eventually replace *SDRAM* as the main memory for a computer.

Emerging Output Devices

Some of the most recent improvements in display technology center on more versatile output devices and new flat-screen technologies. For instance, recent improvements in flat-panel display technology and graphics processing have led to several emerging *three-dimensional (3D) output devices*, including *3D display screens* for computers. While traditional 3D displays require special 3D glasses, the newest 3D products use filters, prisms, multiple lenses, and other technologies built into the display screen to create the 3D effect and, as a result, do not require 3D glasses. Some 3D displays resemble conventional monitors; others are shaped differently, such as the dome-shaped *Perspecta* 3D display. Perspecta is used primarily for medical imaging; scientists, architects, and other professionals who routinely view detailed graphics or diagrams in the course of their work also frequently use 3D displays. Other 3D displays are designed to be wearable. A *3D wearable display* (such as the eyeglasses-based display shown in Figure 8-4) projects the image from a mobile device (usually a mobile phone or portable digital media player today) to a display screen built into the glasses. Typically, the technology allows the user to see the image as if it is on a distant large screen display. Many 3D wearable displays overlay the projected image on top of what the user is seeing in real time in order to provide situational awareness while the display is being used. While 3D wearable displays have entertainment applications, there are also wearable 3D displays designed for soldiers and other mobile workers.

3D projectors, such as those used to display *holograms* (three-dimensional projected images), are also in the works. For instance, holograms of individuals and objects can be projected onto a stage for a presentation, and hologram display devices can be used in retail stores, exhibitions, and other locations to showcase products or other items in 3D. Another emerging projector application is the *integrated projector*—tiny projectors that are beginning to be built into phones, portable computers, portable digital media players, and other portable devices to enable the device to project an image (such as a document, presentation, or movie) onto a wall or other flat surface from up to 12 feet away (refer again to Figure 8-4). These integrated projectors typically create a display up to 10 feet wide in order to easily share information on the device with others on the go without having to crowd around a tiny screen. This same technology is also being incorporated into very small stand-alone *portable projectors* that can be used for making presentations while on the go.

For display screens used with computers, mobile devices, and other electronic devices, there are a number of technologies under development designed to create displays that are

FIGURE 8-4
Examples of emerging output devices.

3D WEARABLE DISPLAYS
Images from the mobile device connected to the eyeglasses are displayed on top of the user's normal vision.

HOLOGRAPHIC PROJECTORS
Project 3D images of objects or individuals.

INTEGRATED PROJECTORS
Images displayed on the device (such as the mobile phone shown here) are projected onto any surface.

more visible, while at the same time using less energy. Some of these technologies are based on *organic light emitting diode (OLED)* technology. **Organic light emitting diode (OLED) displays** use layers of organic material, which emit a visible light when electric current is applied. While conventional flat panel displays based on *LCD (liquid crystal display)* technology do not produce light and so require *backlighting*), OLEDs emit a visible light and, therefore, do not use backlighting. This characteristic makes OLEDs more energy efficient and lengthens the battery life of portable devices using OLED displays. Other advantages of OLEDs include that OLEDs are thinner than LCDs, that they have a wider viewing angle than LCDs and so displayed content is visible from virtually all directions, and that their images are brighter and sharper than LCDs. Today, OLED displays are incorporated into many digital cameras, mobile phones, portable digital media players, and other consumer devices. They are also beginning to appear in television and computer displays and are expected to be more prominent in the near future.

In addition to the overall advantages of using OLED technology, some special types of OLEDs support applications not possible with CRT or LCD technology. For instance, *flexible OLED (FOLED)* displays—a technology developed by Universal Display Corporation—are OLED displays built on flexible surfaces, such as plastic or metallic foil. Flexible displays using FOLED technology, such as displays that can roll up when not in use (see Figure 8-5), are being developed by several companies. Other possible uses for flexible screens include making lighter desktop and portable computer monitors, integrating displays on military uniform sleeves, and allowing retractable wall-mounted big screen televisions and monitors. The flexibility of FOLED displays also adds to their durability, and their thinness makes FOLED technology extremely suitable for mobile devices. Another form of OLED developed by Universal Display Corporation is *transparent OLED (TOLED)*. TOLED displays are transparent and can emit light toward the top and bottom of the display surface. The portion of the display that does not currently have an image displayed (and the entire display device when it is off) is nearly as transparent as glass, so the user can see through the screen. TOLEDs open up the possibility of displays on home windows, car windshields, helmet face shields, and other transparent items.

 FIGURE 8-5
Examples of emerging display and printer technologies.

FOLEDS
Used to create flexible displays on plastic or another type of flexible material.

IMODS
Display is bright and readable, even in direct sunlight.

INTEGRATED PRINTERS
This printer uses no ink and is integrated into the digital camera to print digital photographs.

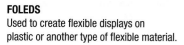

>**Organic light emitting diode (OLED) display.** A type of flat-panel display that uses emissive organic material to display brighter and sharper images.

Another emerging flat-panel display technology is *interferometric modulator* (*IMOD*) *displays*. Designed initially for mobile phones and other portable devices, an IMOD display is essentially a complex mirror that uses external light, such as from the sun or artificial light inside a building, to display images. Because IMOD displays are utilizing light instead of fighting it the way LCD displays do, images are bright and clear even in direct sunlight (see Figure 8-5). And, because backlighting isn't used, power consumption is much less than what is needed for LCD displays. In fact, similar to the e-paper discussed in the Chapter 7 Inside the Industry box, devices using IMOD displays use no power unless the image changes, which means they can remain on at all times without draining the device battery. Beginning to be used initially with mobile devices, IMODs could eventually be used for outdoor television screens, large digital signs, and other outdoor display devices that normally consume a great deal of power.

Some emerging printing applications involve the use of ink-jet technology in conjunction with applications other than printing documents. For instance, ink-jet technology may eventually be used for dispensing liquid metals, aromas, computer chips and other circuitry, and even "printing" human tissue and other organic materials for medical purposes. A recent advancement in printers that we will likely see more of in the near future is the integration of printers into other devices. For instance, the digital camera shown in Figure 8-5 contains an *integrated printer* that is based on a new technology developed by *ZINK* (for "zero ink") *Imaging*. This printer uses no ink; instead, it uses special paper that is coated with special color dye crystals. Before printing, the embedded dye crystals are clear, so ZINK Paper looks like regular white photo paper. The ZINK printer uses heat to activate and colorize these dye crystal when a photo is printed, creating a full color image. In addition to being integrated into a variety of consumer electronics devices, including digital cameras and digital picture frames, stand-alone *ZINK printers* are also available.

Emerging Storage Devices

Improvements in magnetic disk technology are continuing to increase the data than can be stored on hard drives. Traditionally, the magnetic particles on a hard disk have been aligned horizontally, parallel to the hard disk's surface (referred to as *longitudinal magnetic recording*). To increase capacity and reliability, most new hard drives today use *perpendicular magnetic recording* (*PMR*), in which the bits are placed upright to allow them to be closer together than is possible with a horizontal layout. For instance, PMR currently allows a recording density up to 400 *gigabits per square inch* (*Gb/inch²*), which results in internal hard drives with capacities up to 2 TB. Researchers believe that the theoretical limit for recording density with today's hard drive technology will be 1 *terabit per square inch* (*Tb/inch²*), which translates into about 4 TB of storage for a 3.5-inch hard drive, 1 TB for a 2.5-inch hard drive, and 100 GB for a 1-inch hard drive. To allow for higher capacities in the future, new hard drive technologies are under development. For instance, *Heat-Assisted Magnetic Recording* (*HAMR*), which uses lasers to temporarily heat the surface of the hard disks when storing data in order to pack more data onto the surface than is normally possible, may eventually boost the storage capacity of a hard drive to 50 Tb/inch². Another emerging possibility for high-capacity storage—*holographic storage*—is discussed shortly.

ASK THE EXPERT

 Josh Tinker, Market Development Manager, Seagate Technology

What do you expect will be the capacity of a typical internal desktop hard drive in five years?

The top capacity of an internal desktop hard drive today is 2 TB, but by 2015 we expect the top capacity of internal desktop hard drives to exceed 10 TB and possibly approach 15 TB. Today, a common consumer internal desktop hard drive capacity is 500 GB. By 2015, the hard drive industry could provide a similarly priced internal hard drive that holds 2 TB or even 3 TB.

Many emerging storage devices today are focused on creating even more convenient portable personal storage or packing an increasing amount of data on an optical disc or similar storage medium. For portable personal storage, USB flash drives are continuing to be built into a variety of everyday formats, such as watches, sunglasses, Swiss Army knives, wristbands, and wallet cards for easy portability (see Figure 8-6). USB flash drives and flash memory cards are also beginning to be used for media delivery—particularly for mobile phones, portable digital media players, and other mobile devices that typically contain a flash memory slot. For instance, a new option for portable music is *slotMusic*—music albums that come stored on microSD cards. These cards can be used with any phone or portable digital media player that has a microSD slot and they typically contain extra storage space to add additional files as desired. Movies are also beginning to be delivered via flash memory media. Panasonic and Disney have announced plans to begin releasing movies on microSD cards in 2010 and Sonic Solutions has announced movies stored on USB flash drives should begin to become available at about the same time. These new options for portable multimedia are geared toward individuals who would like access to this content via a mobile phone, car navigation system, netbook, or other device often used while on the go that has a flash memory card slot or a USB port.

Another storage possibility that, after many years of research and development, is finally a reality is **holographic storage**. *Holographic drives* record data onto *holographic discs* or *holographic cartridges*. To record data, the holographic drive splits the light from a blue laser beam into two beams (a *reference beam* whose angle determines the address used to store data at that particular location on the storage medium and a *signal beam* that contains the data). The signal beam passes through a device called a *spatial light modulator (SLM)*, which translates the data's 0s and 1s into a *hologram*—a three-dimensional representation of data in the form of a checkerboard pattern of light and dark pixels. The two beams intersect within the recording medium to store the hologram at that location (see Figure 8-7) by changing the optical density of the medium. Over one million bits of data can be stored at one time in a single flash of light, so holographic storage systems are very fast. And, because the hologram goes through the entire thickness of the medium, much more data can be stored on a holographic disc or cartridge than on a CD, DVD, or BD of the same physical size. In fact, hundreds of holograms can be stored in an overlapping manner in the same area of the medium—a different reference beam angle or position is used for each hologram so it can be uniquely stored and retrieved when needed. To read data, the reference beam projects the hologram containing the requested data onto a *detector* that reads the entire data page at one time. Today's holographic storage systems typically use removable recordable holographic cartridges that hold 300 GB per cartridge; 1.6 TB cartridges are expected by 2011. Holographic data storage systems are particularly suited to applications in which large amounts of data need to be stored or retrieved quickly, but rarely changed, such as for business data archiving, high-speed digital video delivery, and image processing for medical, video, and military purposes. Rewritable holographic drives and media are currently in the development stage and are expected to be available in 2010.

USB FLASH DRIVE WRISTBANDS

USB FLASH DRIVE WALLET CARDS

FIGURE 8-6
USB flash drives are becoming available in a wide range of convenient formats.

ONLINE VIDEO ▷

Go to the Chapter 8 page at **www.cengage.com/ computerconcepts/np/uccs4** to watch the "Holographic Storage: Data at the Speed of Light" video clip.

> **Holographic storage.** An emerging type of storage technology that uses multiple blue laser beams to store data in three dimensions.

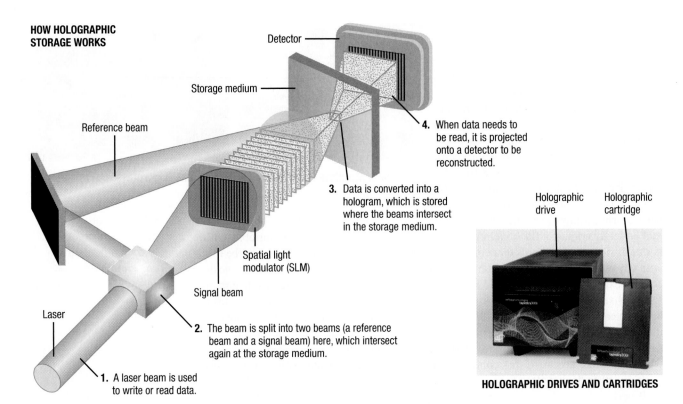

HOW HOLOGRAPHIC STORAGE WORKS

Detector

Storage medium

Reference beam

4. When data needs to be read, it is projected onto a detector to be reconstructed.

3. Data is converted into a hologram, which is stored where the beams intersect in the storage medium.

Holographic drive

Holographic cartridge

Spatial light modulator (SLM)

Signal beam

Laser

2. The beam is split into two beams (a reference beam and a signal beam) here, which intersect again at the storage medium.

1. A laser beam is used to write or read data.

HOLOGRAPHIC DRIVES AND CARTRIDGES

FIGURE 8-7

Holographic storage. Holographic drives store up to one million bits of data in a single flash of light.

The Impact of Nanotechnology

Although there are varying definitions, most agree that **nanotechnology** involves creating computer components, machines, and other structures that are less than 100 nanometers in size. Consequently, today's CPUs contain components that fit the definition of nanotechnology. However, some experts believe that, eventually, current technology will reach its limits. At that point, transistors and other computer components may need to be built at the atomic and molecular level—starting with single atoms or molecules to construct the components. Prototypes of computer products built in this fashion include a single switch that can be turned on and off like a transistor but is made from a single organic molecule, as well as tiny nickel-based *nanodots* that would, theoretically, allow about 5 TB of data to be stored on a hard drive roughly the size of a postage stamp. In other nanotechnology developments, researchers at the University of Arizona recently discovered how to turn single molecules into working transistors and they created transistors as small as a single nanometer. In addition, prototypes of tiny *nanogenerators* have been developed that may someday power mobile devices with low-frequency vibrations, such as a heartbeat or simple body movements like walking. For a look at a concept mobile device that nanotechnology may make possible in the future, see the Technology and You box.

One nanotechnology development that is already being used in a variety of products available today is **carbon nanotubes**—tiny, hollow tubes made up of carbon atoms. The wall of a single-walled carbon nanotube is only one carbon atom thick and the tube diameter is approximately 10,000 times smaller than a human hair. Carbon nanotubes have great potential for future computing products since they conduct electricity better than copper, are stronger than steel, conduct heat better than diamonds, and transmit electronic

> **Nanotechnology.** The science of creating tiny computers and components by working at the individual atomic and molecular levels. > **Carbon nanotubes.** Tiny, hollow tubes made of carbon atoms.

TECHNOLOGY AND YOU

The "Morph" Concept

While still a concept device, the *Morph* concept (developed by researchers at Nokia and the University of Cambridge Nanoscience Centre) demonstrates how nanotechnology may allow future mobile devices to be stretchable and flexible, allowing users to transform their mobile devices into radically different shapes. For instance, the Morph concept can be worn on the wrist, folded into a phone, or opened into a larger handheld device that features a touch pad or keyboard (see the accompanying illustration). Nanotechnology enables the material to repel water, dirt, and fingerprints and to be self-cleaning. Integrated sensors can monitor pollution and chemicals and notify the user as needed of any possible risks. The device is solar-powered via a covering of *Nanograss* that harvests solar power. According to Dr. Bob Iannucci, Chief Technology Officer, Nokia, "Nokia Research Center is looking at ways to reinvent the form and function of mobile devices; the Morph concept shows what might be possible."

Possible configurations for the Morph concept device.

impulses faster than silicon. Lithium ion batteries that use nanotubes are currently on the market and several nanotube-based computing products—like nanotube-based display screens and memory—are currently under development. Since carbon nanotubes can transmit electricity and are transparent, they are also being used for product development in the areas of TVs, solar cells, light bulbs, and other similar noncomputing applications. In addition, because of their strength and lightness for their size, carbon nanotubes are being integrated into products that benefit from those characteristics, such as automobile panels, airplanes, tennis rackets, and racing bikes. In fact, the frame of the bike model that several professional cyclists ride are built with carbon nanotubes (see Figure 8-8)—the entire bike frame weighs less than one kilogram (2.2 pounds). Carbon nanotubes are also beginning to be combined with other materials, such as plastic, to increase the durability of materials used to produce other consumer items, such as surfboards.

Two recent developments are *nanoparticles* that can remove contaminants from water sources and *nanosensors* that can detect small amounts of cancer-causing toxins or cancer drugs inside single living cells. Possible future applications of nanotechnology include disposing of e-trash by rearranging dangerous components at the atomic level into inert substances, microscopic devices that can enter the bloodstream and perform tests or irradiate cancerous tumors, improved military uniforms that protect against bullets and germ warfare, and computers and sensors that are small enough to be woven into the fibers of clothing or embedded into paint and other materials. Some of the devices generated by nanotechnology research may contain or be constructed out of organic material. Complete *organic computers* are a long way off, but researchers have already created biological computing devices—such as the *MAYA-II* computer that uses strands of DNA to perform computations. Although very slow and only programmed to play tic-tac-toe, the computer has never lost at that game.

ONLINE VIDEO

Go to the Chapter 8 page at **www.cengage.com/computerconcepts/np/uccs4** to watch the "Introducing the Morph Concept" video clip.

FIGURE 8-8
Carbon nanotubes make this bike frame very strong, but light.

Quantum and Optical Computers

Computers a few decades from now will likely use technology that is very different from the silicon chips and electronic bits and bytes we are accustomed to today. In addition to being miniature—based on nanotechnology—and likely incorporated into a variety of everyday devices, computers in the future may be *quantum* or *optical computers*.

Quantum Computing

The idea of **quantum computing** emerged in the 1970s, and it has received renewed interest lately. Quantum computing applies the principles of quantum physics and quantum mechanics to computers, going beyond traditional physics to work at the subatomic level. Quantum computers differ from conventional computers in that they utilize atoms or nuclei working together as *quantum bits* or *qubits*. Qubits function simultaneously as both the computer's processor and memory, and each qubit can represent more than just the two states (one and zero) available to today's electronic bits; a qubit can even represent many states at one time. Quantum computers can perform computations on many numbers at one time, making them, theoretically, exponentially faster than conventional computers. Physically, quantum computers in the future might consist of a thimbleful of liquid whose atoms are used to perform calculations as instructed by an external device.

Even though quantum computers are still in the pioneering stage, working quantum computers do exist. For instance, in 2001 the researchers at IBM's Almaden Research Center created a 7-qubit quantum computer (see Figure 8-9) composed of the nuclei of seven atoms that can interact with each other and be programmed by radio frequency pulses. This quantum computer successfully factored the number 15—not a complicated computation for a conventional computer, but the fact that a quantum computer was able to understand the problem and compute the correct answer is viewed as a highly significant event in the area of quantum computer research. More recently, Canadian scientists developed a 16-qubit quantum computer that can solve Sudoku puzzles, and Yale University researchers developed the first rudimentary electronic quantum processor (based on a 2-qubit chip) that can successfully perform a few simple tasks. In addition, Hewlett-Packard scientists have developed a *crossbar latch*—a switch just a single molecule thick that can store binary data and might one day function as a transistor in a quantum computer. One of the obstacles to creating a fully functional quantum computer has been the inability of researchers to control the actions of a single qubit inside a matrix of other qubits. In 2009, researchers successfully accomplished this in an experiment; this breakthrough is viewed as a significant step toward the ability to create more sophisticated working quantum computers in the future.

Quantum computing is not well suited for general computing tasks but it is ideal for, and expected to be widely used in, the areas of encryption and code breaking.

Optical Computing

Optical chips, which use light waves to transmit data, are also currently in development. A possibility for the future is the **optical computer**—a computer that uses light, such as from laser beams or infrared beams—to perform digital computations. Because light beams do not interfere with each other, optical computers can be much smaller and faster than electronic computers. For instance, according to one NASA senior research scientist, an optical computer could solve a problem in one hour that would take an electronic

FIGURE 8-9

Quantum computers.
The vial of liquid shown here contains the 7-qubit computer used by IBM researchers in 2001 to perform the most complicated computation by a quantum computer to date—factoring the number 15.

computer 11 years to solve. While some researchers are working on developing an all-optical computer, others believe that a mix of optical and electronic components—or an *opto-electronic computer*—may be the best bet for the future. Opto-electronic technology is already being used to improve long-distance fiber-optic communications. Initial opto-electronic computer applications are expected to be applied to the area of speeding up communications between computers and other devices, as well as between computer components. In fact, prototypes of chips that have both optical and electrical functions combined on a single silicon chip—a feat that was thought to be impossible until recently—already exist. One recent breakthrough in optical computing is the development by researchers of ways to make lasers smaller than was originally thought possible. These *nanolasers* could conceivably be incorporated into small electronic components in order to speed up communications inside a computer, such as within a CPU or between a CPU and other computer components.

EMERGING NETWORKING TECHNOLOGIES

Improvements are being made on a continual basis to both wired and wireless networking technologies to increase speed and connectivity options for both *local area networks* (*LANs*) and Internet connections, as well as to support the continued growth in Internet-based multimedia and communications applications used by computers and mobile devices that require fast, dependable connections, such as Voice over IP (VoIP), video-on-demand (VOD), mobile TV, and teleconferencing. For instance, one new improvement to videoconferencing technology to make it more closely mimic a real-time meeting environment is referred to as *telepresence videoconferencing*. With telepresence videoconferencing, participants see high-quality, life-sized video images of each other in real time (see Figure 8-10); the corresponding audio even appears to be coming from the appropriate individuals. Although telepresence videoconferencing setups are expensive, with travel becoming increasingly more expensive and time-consuming, many businesses view videoconferencing as a viable replacement for face-to-face meetings involving individuals in different locations.

Other emerging networking applications involve location information, such as the *geobrowsing applications* discussed in the Chapter 3 Trend box and monitoring systems that utilize GPS. For instance, *vehicle monitoring systems* are becoming available that can be installed in cars by parents and employers to monitor the use of the vehicles (by children or employees, respectively) using networking technology. These monitoring systems typically record factors such as where the vehicle is driven and how fast it was driven; some also allow the location of a vehicle to be tracked in real time via a Web site (see Figure 8-11). Some vehicle monitoring systems can even

◭ FIGURE 8-10
Telepresence videoconferencing.

◮ FIGURE 8-11
GPS-based vehicle monitoring systems. Allow parents or employers to track a vehicle in real time.

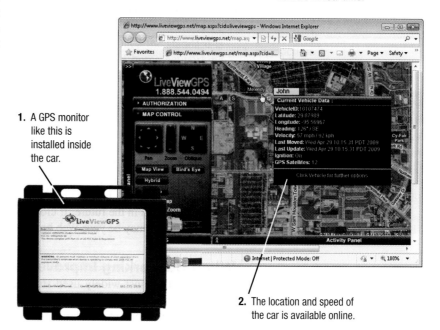

1. A GPS monitor like this is installed inside the car.

2. The location and speed of the car is available online.

Wireless Networking Improvements

Developed in the late 1990s, **Wi-Fi** (for *wireless fidelity*) is a family of wireless networking standards that use the IEEE standard **802.11**. Wi-Fi is the current standard for wireless networks in the home or office, as well as for public Wi-Fi hotspots. Wi-Fi capabilities are built into virtually all portable computers sold today; they are becoming increasingly integrated into everyday products, such as printers, digital cameras, portable digital media players, handheld gaming devices, gaming consoles—even SD cards—to allow those devices to wirelessly network with other devices or to access the Internet. Like Ethernet, the Wi-Fi standard is continually evolving to support increased speed and other capabilities. The speed of a Wi-Fi network and the area it can cover depend on a variety of factors, including the *Wi-Fi standard* and hardware being used, the number of solid objects (such as walls, trees, or buildings) between the access point and the computer or other device being used, and the amount of interference from cordless phones, baby monitors, microwave ovens, and other devices that also operate on the same radio frequency as Wi-Fi (usually 2.4 GHz). In general, Wi-Fi is designed for medium-range data transfers—typically between 100 and 300 feet indoors and 300 to 900 feet outdoors. There are a number of different versions of the 802.11 standard; the *802.11g* and *802.11n* standards are the most widely used today. Emerging 802.11 standards under development are expected to offer increased speed, security, and other factors in the future.

While Wi-Fi is very widely used today, it does have some limitations—particularly its relatively limited range. For instance, an individual using a Wi-Fi hotspot inside a Starbucks coffeehouse will lose that Internet connection when he or she moves out of range of that network and will need to locate another hotspot at his or her next location. In addition, other wireless technologies are in development for specific purposes, such as *multimedia networking*. These emerging wireless technologies are discussed next. For a look an emerging wireless technology—powering your hardware devices via *wireless power*—see the Inside the Industry box.

FURTHER EXPLORATION

Go to the Chapter 8 page at **www.cengage.com/ computerconcepts/np/uccs4** for links to information about wireless networking standards.

ONLINE VIDEO

Go to the Chapter 8 page at **www.cengage.com/ computerconcepts/np/uccs4** to watch the "WiMAX vs. Wi-Fi" video clip.

FIGURE 8-13

WiMAX vs. Wi-Fi. WiMAX hotzones can provide service to anyone in the hotzone, including mobile users, while the range of Wi-Fi hotspots is fairly limited.

WiMAX and Mobile WiMAX

An emerging standard designed for longer range wireless networking connections is **WiMAX** (*Worldwide Interoperability for Microwave Access*). Similar to Wi-Fi, WiMAX (also known as *802.16a*) is designed to provide Internet access to fixed locations (sometimes called *hotzones*), but the coverage area is significantly larger (a typical hotzone radius is close to 2 miles, though WiMAX can transmit data as far as 6 miles or so without line of sight). With WiMAX, it is feasible to provide coverage to an entire city or other geographical area by using multiple WiMAX towers (see Figure 8-13).

Mobile WiMAX (*802.16e*) is the mobile version of the WiMAX wireless networking standard. It is designed to deliver fast wireless networking to mobile users via a mobile phone, portable computer, or other WiMAX-enabled device. WiMAX capabilities are beginning to be built into portable

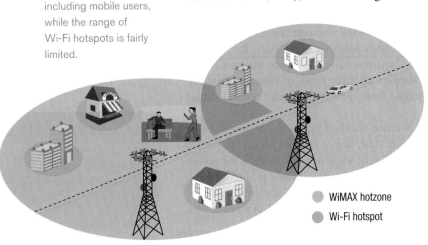

WiMAX hotzone
Wi-Fi hotspot

>**Wi-Fi (802.11).** A widely used networking standard for medium-range wireless networks. >**WiMAX.** An emerging wireless networking standard that is faster and has a larger range than Wi-Fi. >**Mobile WiMAX.** A version of WiMAX designed to be used with mobile phones.

INSIDE THE INDUSTRY

Wireless Power

Imagine recharging your notebook computer or mobile phone automatically, without plugging it into an electrical outlet. That scenario may soon be possible with *wireless power*. Researchers have been working on the concept of wireless power transmission for decades, but recent developments indicate that the concept may be feasible in the relatively near future. For instance, researchers recently demonstrated making a 60-watt light bulb glow with 75% efficiency from an energy source 3 feet away—an important development because one of the biggest challenges in transmitting power wirelessly is preventing too much power from escaping during transit. Other challenges are ensuring that wireless power is safe for humans and other living things in the areas where power will be broadcast, as well as creating a standard for wireless power so that multiple devices from different manufacturers can be charged at the same time using the same technology.

One company working toward this standard is Fulton Innovation. This company, along with other members of the *Wireless Power Consortium* (such as Olympus, Philips, and Texas Instruments), supports wireless power technology that uses *magnetic induction* to transfer power wirelessly from a charging power supply device to a target device containing the appropriate receiving technology. Ideally, wireless power systems will power devices without any direct physical contact, will automatically adjust the power transmitted to each device being charged to meet the needs of that device, and will deactivate the charging process when the device is fully charged.

Initial consumer applications for wireless power will likely be wireless charging bases that recharge devices (such as mobile phones, digital media players, remote controls, notebook computers, and small kitchen appliances) located on or near them—called *near-field wireless power transfer*. These charging bases could be stand-alone devices or they could be built into car consoles (see the accompanying illustration), desks, kitchen countertops, and other objects. As the technology matures and if the safety issues can be resolved, future wireless power applications could even include charging transmitters built into walls and furniture to power all of the devices located in the home on a continual basis.

computers and other devices, and WiMAX is currently being used to provide Internet access to selected geographical areas by a number of companies in over 135 countries. In the U.S., for instance, Sprint Nextel's WiMAX division and WiMAX leader Clearwire have merged and are in the process of building a new WiMAX-based nationwide high-speed network designed to deliver both fixed and mobile WiMAX-based Internet service to businesses and individuals. This new network is expected to be able to provide service to at least 140 million users by the end of 2010.

3G/4G Cellular Standards

Cellular standards have also evolved over the years to better fulfill the demand for mobile Internet, mobile multimedia delivery, and other relatively recent mobile trends. The current standard for cellular networks today in the U.S. and many other countries is *3G* (*third generation*). *3G cellular standards* are designed to support both data and voice. Users of 3G mobile phones and other 3G mobile devices can access broadband Internet content (such as online maps, music, games, TV, videos, and more) at relatively fast speeds—up to about 1.7 Mbps at the present time, with speeds expected to reach 3 Mbps in the near future. These speeds are equivalent to the speeds many home broadband

ONLINE VIDEO

Go to the Chapter 8 page at **www.cengage.com/ computerconcepts/np/uccs4** to watch the "Wireless Power: eCoupled Overview" video clip.

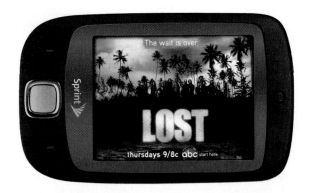

Internet users experience; consequently, Internet access via a 3G network is often referred to as *mobile broadband* (see Figure 8-14). In addition to mobile phones, computers can access the Internet via a 3G network with appropriate hardware. The next generation for mobile networks—*4G* (*fourth generation*)—is under development and two standards have emerged at the present time: the mobile WiMAX standard already discussed and *Long Term Evolution* (*LTE*). LTE (supported by AT&T Wireless, Verizon Wireless, and T-Mobile) is a cellular standard and is based on 3G *UMTS* (*Universal Mobile Telecommunications System*) standard. LTE networks are expected to arrive in the U.S. by 2011.

FIGURE 8-14

Mobile broadband.

3G networks provide mobile phone users with broadband access to multimedia content.

Short-Range Wireless Standards

Bluetooth is the original wireless standard designed for very short-range (10 meters, approximately 33 feet, or less) connections. It is designed to replace cables between devices, such as to connect a wireless keyboard or mouse to a desktop computer, to send print jobs wirelessly from a portable computer to a printer, or to connect a mobile phone to a wireless headset. The Bluetooth standard is continually evolving to be faster and support new applications. For instance, Bluetooth now includes support for Near Field Communications (NFC) and is fast enough to support multimedia applications, such as transferring music, photos, and videos between computers, mobile phones, and other devices. One interesting emerging Bluetooth application that is intended to protect teenagers from texting or talking on their mobile phones while driving is a special Bluetooth-enabled car key, which prevents the driver's mobile phone from being used while the car is on.

A new standard that is designed to connect peripheral devices, similar to Bluetooth, but that transfers data more quickly is **wireless USB**. The speed of wireless USB depends on the distance between the devices being used, but it is approximately 100 Mbps at 10 meters (about 33 feet) or 480 Mbps at 2 meters (about 6.5 feet). While Bluetooth and wireless USB can be used for similar applications, it is possible they might coexist. For example, wireless USB might be used to connect computer hardware in more permanent setups, while Bluetooth might be used in short-range mobile situations with portable computers and mobile devices. One of the first wireless USB devices to come on the market is the *wireless USB hub*. As shown in Figure 8-15, USB peripheral devices are plugged into the wireless USB hub and the hub is connected to the computer via a wireless connection and a *wireless USB adapter* plugged into a USB port on the computer.

FIGURE 8-15

Wireless USB.

Plug this adapter into the computer's USB port to connect the wireless USB hub to the computer.

Plug up to four USB devices to this hub to connect them wirelessly to the computer.

For transferring multimedia content quickly between nearby devices, a number of different standards are emerging. For instance, *Ultra Wideband* (*UWB*) is designed for applications that require high-speed transfers over short distances, such as wirelessly delivering multimedia content—such as video, music, and photos—between computers, TVs, digital cameras, DVD players, and more. A similar, but faster, standard is *wirelessHD* (*WiHD*). WiHD is backed by seven major electronics companies and is designed to transfer full-quality uncompressed high-definition audio, video, and data within a single room at speeds up to 25 Gbps, though those speeds have not been obtained yet. A new wireless standard designed

> **Wireless USB.** A wireless version of USB designed to connect peripheral devices.

for very fast transfers between devices that are extremely close together (essentially touching each other) is *TransferJet*. Developed by Sony, TransferJet is designed to transfer large files (such as digital photos, music, and video) quickly between devices as soon as they come in contact with each other, such as to transfer data between mobile phones or between digital cameras, to download music or video from a consumer kiosk or digital signage system to a mobile phone or other mobile device, or to transfer images or video from a digital camera to a TV set or printer. TransferJet-compatible devices are expected to be available in 2010.

ARTIFICIAL INTELLIGENCE (AI)

Although they cannot yet think completely on their own, computers and software programs have become more sophisticated, and computers are being programmed to act in an increasingly intelligent manner.

What Is Artificial Intelligence (AI)?

According to John McCarthy, who coined the term **artificial intelligence (AI)** in 1956 and is considered by many to be one of its fathers, AI is "the science and engineering of making intelligent machines." In other words, AI researchers are working to create intelligent devices controlled by intelligent software programs; in essence, machines that think and act like people and that perform in ways that would be considered intelligent if observed in humans. In 1950, Alan Turing—one of the first AI researchers—argued that if a machine could successfully appear to be human to a knowledgeable observer, then it should be considered intelligent. To illustrate this idea, Turing developed a test—later called the *Turing Test*—in which one observer interacts electronically with both a computer and a person. During the test, the observer submits written questions electronically to both the computer and the person, evaluates the typed responses, and tries to identify which answers came from the computer and which came from the person. Turing argued that if the computer could repeatedly fool the observer into thinking it was human, then it should be viewed as intelligent.

Many Turing Test contests have been held over the years, and in 1990, Dr. Hugh Loebner initiated the Loebner Prize, pledging a grand prize of $100,000 and a solid gold medal (see Figure 8-16) for the developer of the first computer whose responses to a Turing Test were indistinguishable from that of a human's responses. A contest is held every year, awarding a prize of $2,000 and a bronze medal to the developer of the most human computer but, so far, the gold medal has not been awarded. Although the

FIGURE 8-16
The Loebner Prize gold medal has yet to be awarded.

>**Artificial intelligence (AI).** When a computer performs actions that are characteristic of human intelligence.

to the data stored in the knowledge base in order to reach decisions). For instance, as shown in Figure 8-19, an expert system used to authorize credit for credit card customers would have a knowledge base with facts about customers and rules about credit authorization, such as "Do not automatically authorize purchase if the customer has exceeded his or her credit limit."

Expert systems are widely used for tasks such as diagnosing illnesses, making financial forecasts, scheduling routes for delivery vehicles, diagnosing mechanical problems, and performing credit authorizations. Some expert systems are designed to take the place of human experts, while others are designed to assist them. For instance, medical expert systems are often used to assist physicians with patient diagnoses, suggesting possible diagnoses based on the patient's symptoms and other data supplied to the expert system. Because it has access to an extensive knowledge base, the expert system may provide more possible diagnoses to the attending physician than he or she may have thought of otherwise.

When using an expert system, it is important to realize that its conclusions are based on the data and rules stored in its knowledge base, as well as the information provided by the users. If the expert knowledge is correct, the inference engine program is written correctly, and the user supplies accurate information in response to the questions posed by the expert system, the system will draw correct conclusions; if the knowledge base is wrong, the inference engine is faulty, or the user provides inaccurate input, the system will not work correctly.

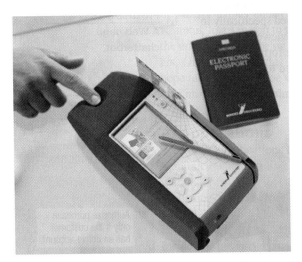

Neural Networks

Artificial intelligence systems that attempt to imitate the way a human brain works are called **neural networks**. Neural networks (also called *neural nets*) are networks of processors that are connected together in a manner similar to the way the neurons in a human brain are connected. They are designed to emulate the brain's pattern-recognition process in order to recognize patterns in data and make more progressive leaps in associations and predictions than conventional computer systems. Neural networks are used in areas such as handwriting, speech, and image recognition; medical imaging; crime analysis; biometric identification (see Figure 8-20); and *vision systems* that use cameras to inspect objects and make determinations—for example, the systems that check products for defects at manufacturing plants or that recognize stamps during postal processing.

FIGURE 8-20

Neural network systems. Often used in biometric identification systems, such as to analyze fingerprints.

Robotics

Robotics is the field devoted to the study of **robots**—devices, controlled by a person or a computer, that can move and react to sensory input. Robots are widely used by the military and businesses to perform high-precision but monotonous jobs, as well as to perform tasks that are dangerous or impossible for people to perform. There are also robots designed to perform personal tasks for individuals. The appearance of robots varies depending on their purpose, such as robot arms permanently connected to an assembly line, robots built on sturdy mobile platforms designed to travel over rough terrain, robots with fins for water tasks, robots shaped like animals (such as snakes or spiders) for special climbing abilities, and robots that resemble pets or humans for consumer applications. Robots used for medical and military applications are discussed shortly; robots used for business and consumer applications are discussed next.

> **Neural network.** An expert system in which the human brain's pattern-recognition process is emulated by the computer system.
> **Robotics.** The study of robot technology. > **Robot.** A device, controlled by a human operator or a computer, that can move and react to sensory input.

Robots are used in business for a variety of purposes, such as for looking for intruders, gas leaks, and other hazards, working on factory assembly lines, and other monotonous tasks (see Figure 8-21). Robots are also used for mining coal, repairing oil rigs, locating survivors in collapsed mines and buildings, and other dangerous tasks. They can also be used to facilitate videoconferencing by sitting in for a remote participant and relaying video and audio images to and from that participant. For instance, the videoconferencing robot shown in Figure 8-21 can be controlled by a remote participant to enable him or her to "move" around a factory, hospital, or other facility and view it remotely. In addition, robots are used in search and rescue missions, firefighting, and other service tasks.

There are also a number of *personal robots* available or in development to assist with personal tasks. Some are primarily entertainment robots. They typically use sensors, cameras, microphones, and other technologies to input data about their current surroundings, and then interact with people (such as by reciting phrases, delivering messages, taking photos or video, or singing and dancing). Others, such as the toy robot shown in Figure 8-21, are designed to be toys or companions for children. Still other personal robots are designed for household tasks, such as to mow the lawn, clean the pool, or clean the floor (refer again to Figure 8-21).

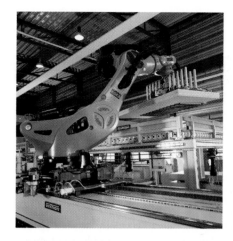

ASSEMBLY LINE ROBOTS

VIDEOCONFERENCING ROBOTS

TOY ROBOTS

HOUSEHOLD ROBOTS

 FIGURE 8-21
Business and personal robots.

FURTHER EXPLORATION (Go)

Go to the Chapter 8 page at **www.cengage.com/ computerconcepts/np/uccs4** for links to information about robots.

Household robots that can assist individuals with more complex tasks, such as putting away the dishes or picking up toys before vacuuming the living room, are a little further in the future, when robot technology improves to allow for better navigation and improved physical manipulation and as prices come down. Expected to have a more *humanoid* form than the household robots currently on the market, these future robots could be used to assist the elderly and wheelchair bound individuals, in addition to helping with household tasks. In fact, it has been reported that the South Korean government expects to have at least one robot in every South Korean household by 2020.

Many would agree that the use of robots has numerous benefits to society—such as adding convenience to our lives, replacing humans for dangerous tasks, and, potentially, monitoring and assisting the disabled and the elderly. But some individuals are concerned that, as true artificial intelligence becomes closer to reality, a class of robots with the potential for great harm could be created. In response, several organizations—including the South Korean government and the European Robotics Research Network—are in the process of developing standards for robots, users, and manufacturers concerning the appropriate use and development of robots. The U.S. military is also studying ways to ensure robotic soldiers can be programmed to recognize and obey international laws of war and the U.S. military's rules of engagement, in order to prevent them from performing acts such as firing on a hospital or crowd of civilians, even if enemy forces are nearby. Regardless of the progress in the area of implementing controls on robots, the issue of the role robots should take in our society is likely to continue to be debated for quite some time.

> **CAUTION CAUTION CAUTION CAUTION CAUTION CAUTION CAUT**
>
> While some robots are designed to be durable and used in adverse conditions, remember that robotic devices are electronic. To avoid the risk of electric shock and damage to robotic devices, do not use them in the water or in other adverse conditions unless the instructions specifically state that the action is safe.

TECHNOLOGICAL ADVANCES IN MEDICINE

Technological advances in the area of medicine in the past several years include computers that can analyze test results to identify precancerous cells too small for a person to see, implanted devices that enhance the functions of a current organ (such as cochlear implants that can restore hearing), electronic monitors that detect potentially dangerous medical conditions, and digital cameras the size of a pill that are swallowed to photograph the patient's digestive tract. Other topics in the forefront of medical technology research include *electronic monitoring* and *electronic implants*, as well as *telemedicine* and *telesurgery*.

Ⓐ **FIGURE 8-22**
Home medical monitoring systems.

ONLINE VIDEO

▷ Go to the Chapter 8 page at
**www.cengage.com/
computerconcepts/np/uccs4**
to watch the "Digital Hospitals:
A Look at Germany's Jena
University Hospital" video clip.

Electronic Monitoring and Electronic Implants

There are a number of *electronic monitoring systems* used for medical purposes today. Some use RFID technology to monitor the status of the objects; others use GPS technology to monitor the locations of objects. Electronic monitoring systems are increasingly being used in hospitals for patient identification, medical equipment asset tracking, and prescription drug identification. They are also frequently used in home healthcare. With the U.S. population aging, a variety of home medical monitoring systems are available to monitor elderly or infirm individuals and notify someone if a possible problem is detected. For instance, *electronic medical monitors* (see Figure 8-22) take the vital signs of an individual (such as weight, blood-sugar readings, or blood pressure) or prompt an individual to answer questions (such as if he or she ate yet that day, took prescribed medication, or feels well). These monitors then transfer readings or the individual's responses to a healthcare provider via the Internet or a telephone network for evaluation and feedback and to detect potential problems as early as possible.

While many electronic medical monitoring devices are external, some are implanted inside the individual. One example is an implanted cardiac device that continually monitors heart rhythms and records the rhythms for a set period of time in order to replay that information to the attending physician if the patient faints or otherwise does not feel well. Another example is the **VeriChip**—a tiny RFID chip about the size of a grain of rice (see Figure 8-23) that is implanted under a person's skin (usually on the hand or arm) and is used for identification purposes. Like the chips used to identify pets and to track the migration habits of animals, each VeriChip contains a unique verification number that can be read when a proprietary scanner is passed over the implanted chip. Although the VeriChip itself does not contain any personal data, it is designed to be used in conjunction with a database to access personal data, as needed, such as to provide hospital emergency room personnel with the medical health records of an unconscious patient. A version of the VeriChip under

> **VeriChip.** A tiny RFID chip about the size of a grain of rice that is implanted under a person's skin for identification purposes.

development will be able to continuously monitor the glucose levels of a diabetic without a blood sample; another is being designed to detect the H1N1 virus. The VeriChip also has nonmedical applications, such as access control to government installations, nuclear power plants, and other highly secure facilities; identity verification for airport security purposes and financial transactions; and emergency record retrieval and access control for personal computers, cars, homes, and other personal security applications. Versions of the VeriChip with GPS capabilities could also be used to find missing individuals, such as kidnap victims and lost Alzheimer's patients, like the clip-on and wristwatch monitoring systems available today that allow location information to be broadcast continuously to a proprietary receiver. Although privacy-rights advocates worry that a chip like the VeriChip could someday be used by the government to track citizens, others view it as no different from a medical ID bracelet and are not concerned because it is available on a purely voluntary basis.

An emerging possibility is *brain-to-computer interfacing (BCI)*—the process of connecting the brain with a computer, such as implanting electrodes directly into the brain to restore lost functionality to or facilitate the communications of severely disabled individuals. For instance, a severely paralyzed individual implanted with such a device can, after training, move a mouse, click it to type text, and perform other computer-related tasks using only his or her thoughts. In BCI experiments conducted with monkeys, the monkeys were able to control both a cursor and a robotic arm with their thoughts—raising the possibility that paralyzed individuals will someday be able to control robot assistants with their thoughts. Despite the potential benefits of brain implants, there is the concern that this technology could be misused. Medical ethicists are currently working on setting up standards and criteria to ensure that brain implant devices allow, according to medical ethicist Joseph Fins of Cornell University, ". . . patients to have control, not be under control." Currently the focus of brain implants and thought-controlled computers is bringing communications capabilities to the severely disabled. Some researchers, however, foresee the technology someday becoming mainstream—viewing brainwave input as the next step in the evolution of the human-computer input interface. Expanding on BCI research, one experiment in late 2009 focused on using BCI technology in conjunction with the Internet to communicate directly between the brains of two individuals—called *brain-to-brain communication*—and designed to help disabled individuals communicate directly with others, without requiring the use of a computer as an intermediary.

Telemedicine and Telesurgery

Telemedicine is the use of networking technology to provide medical information and services and is most often used to provide care to individuals who may not otherwise have access to that care, such as allowing individuals living in remote areas to consult with a specialist. For instance, physicians can use videoconferencing to communicate remotely with other physicians or with hospitalized patients (see Figure 8-24). Physicians can also use telemedicine to perform remote diagnosis of patients (for example, healthcare workers at rural locations, childcare facilities, and other locations can use video cameras, electronic stethoscopes, and other devices to send images and vital statistics of a patient to a physician located at a medical facility).

Another example of telemedicine is **telesurgery**—a form of *robot-assisted surgery* (where a robot controlled by a physician operates on the patient) in which at least one of the surgeons performs the operation by controlling the robot remotely over the Internet or another network (refer again to Figure 8-24). Robot-assisted surgery systems typically use cameras to give the human surgeon an extremely close view of the surgical area. As a result, robot-assisted surgery is typically more precise and results in smaller incisions than those made by a human surgeon,

>**Telemedicine.** The use of networking technology to provide medical information and services. >**Telesurgery.** A form of robot-assisted surgery in which the doctor's physical location is different from the patient's physical location and the doctor controls the robot remotely over the Internet or another network.

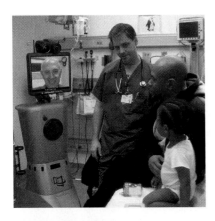

REMOTE CONSULTATIONS
Using remote-controlled teleconferencing robots, physicians can "virtually" consult with patients or other physicians in a different physical location (left); the robot transmits video images and audio to and from the doctor (via his or her computer) in real time (right).

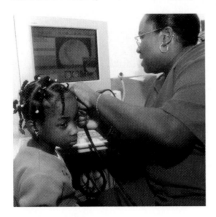

REMOTE DIAGNOSIS
At remote locations, such as the New York childcare center shown here, trained employees provide physicians with the real-time data (sent via the Internet) they need to make a diagnosis.

TELESURGERY
Using voice or computer commands, surgeons can now perform operations via the Internet; a robotic system uses the surgeon's commands to operate on the patient.

FIGURE 8-24
Examples of telemedicine applications.

allowing for less invasive surgery (for example, not having to crack through the rib cage to access the heart) and resulting in less pain for the patient, a faster recovery time, and fewer potential complications.

Telemedicine has enormous potential for providing quality medical care to individuals who live in rural or underdeveloped areas and who do not have access to sufficient medical care. Telemedicine will also be necessary for future long-term space explorations—such as a trip to Mars and back that may take three years or more—since astronauts will undoubtedly need medical care while on the journey. In fact, NASA astronauts and physicians recently performed telesurgery experiments in the Aquarius Undersea Laboratory 50 feet below the ocean surface to help in the development of a robotic unit that will eventually allow physicians to perform surgery remotely on patients who are in outer space. Some individuals envision the eventual use of portable robot-assisted telesurgery units in space, war zones, and other environments where access to surgeons is extremely limited.

TECHNOLOGICAL ADVANCES IN THE MILITARY

The U.S. military works on a continual basis with technological and research organizations to improve military equipment, such as weapons, protective gear for soldiers, and surveillance tools. The military is also involved in researching many of the other emerging technologies already discussed, such as nanotechnology and artificial intelligence. Two specific areas of research related to the military—*battlefield robots* and *exoskeleton systems*—are discussed next.

Battlefield Robots
Robots are used extensively by the U.S. military. For instance, **battlefield robots** are used in areas of conflict to investigate caves, buildings, trails, and other locations before soldiers enter them to make sure the locations are safe (see Figure 8-25), and to help soldiers locate and dispose of bombs, landmines, and other explosive devices. In addition to land-based robots, there are also military robots designed for underwater use, such as to detect mines or perform underwater surveillance and reconnaissance. Currently, military robots

>**Battlefield robot.** A robot used by the military to ensure that locations are safe prior to sending in soldiers.

are controlled remotely by soldiers, though researchers are working on more *autonomous robots* that can navigate on their own, perceiving obstacles and determining their course without continuous directions from a human operator, to accompany soldiers into combat. According to national security expert John Pike, autonomous armed robotic soldiers may become a reality as soon as 2020.

BATTLEFIELD ROBOTS
Designed to investigate hostile and inaccessible areas prior to human entry.

EXOSKELETON SYSTEMS
Designed to give soldiers enhanced mobility and endurance while carrying heavy loads.

FIGURE 8-25
Military robotic applications.

ONLINE VIDEO

Go to the Chapter 8 page at **www.cengage.com/ computerconcepts/np/uccs4** to watch the "A Look at the HULC Exoskeleton" video clip.

Exoskeleton Systems

An emerging military robotic application is the **exoskeleton suit**, whose name refers to a hard protective or supportive outer structure. Currently being researched and developed by several organizations under grants from the Defense Advanced Research Projects Agency (DARPA), exoskeleton suits are wearable robotic systems designed to give an individual additional physical capabilities and protection. For instance, an exoskeleton suit can give a soldier the ability to run faster and carry heavier items than he or she could without the suit—up to 200 pounds at a top speed of 10 mph for the *Human Universal Load Carrier* (*HULC*) exoskeleton suit shown in Figure 8-25. While lower-body exoskeleton suits like the HULC are in development and are expected to be field tested by soldiers in 2010, full exoskeleton suits are expected to be available in the future and may include additional capabilities, such as being made of bulletproof material that is able to solidify on demand to form a shield or turn into a medical cast if a soldier is injured. Other possible features include changing its color automatically for camouflage purposes; relaying information via sensors about a soldier's health, injuries, and location to field headquarters; and administering painkillers or applying pressure to a wound when directed by a physician. DARPA is also involved with the development of robotic prosthetic arms that feel, look, and perform like natural arms— these robotic arms will be used by military personnel who are injured in the line of duty.

SOCIETAL IMPLICATIONS OF EMERGING TECHNOLOGY

A new computing technology usually provides many benefits, since it normally would not become widely available for consumers if it was not designed to solve a problem or add convenience to our lives. However, not all advances are embraced by all individuals. For instance, security and privacy issues are areas of continual concern with emerging technologies. Potential dangers include trusting "intelligent" computers and robots so much that they become a personal safety hazard, allowing medical technology to enable people to be controlled by others, and spending resources on some areas of research and development that might be better spent elsewhere. Some people also worry that technology is advancing at such a rapid pace that we cannot possibly envision all the potential repercussions until it is too late. It is important to evaluate new and emerging technologies in terms of the entire picture—their benefits, as well as their possible risks and societal implications.

> **Exoskeleton suit.** A wearable robotic system designed to give an individual additional physical capabilities and protection.

SUMMARY

THE COMPUTER OF THE FUTURE

Chapter Objective 1:
Describe what the computer of the future might look like, including some examples of emerging types of hardware.

While the exact makeup of future computers is not certain, they will likely continue to get smaller, smarter, and more user-friendly. Portable computers will continue to grow more powerful and useful and home; business computers may be built into furniture, walls, desks, and other objects. Emerging input devices include gesture-based devices; input for consumer applications that may soon become the norm include **two-dimensional (2D) barcodes**, **augmented reality**, and a variety of RFID payment systems. CPU technology is continuing to evolve and it is possible that a form of **nonvolatile RAM (NVRAM)** may eventually replace the RAM we know today. Emerging output devices include *3D display screens*, *3D projectors*, *wearable personal displays*, and displays based on variations of **organic light emitting diode (OLED) display** technology. For storage, new formats of USB flash memory drives and flash memory cards are emerging and **holographic storage** has finally arrived.

Chapter Objective 2:
Understand the effect that emerging computer technologies, such as nanotechnology, quantum computers, and optical computers, may have on the computer of the future.

Future computers will likely be influenced by **nanotechnology** research, which focuses on building computer components at the individual atomic and molecular levels. Both computing and noncomputing products that use **carbon nanotubes** are being developed. **Quantum computing** (which use atoms or nuclei working together as quantum bits or *qubits*) and **optical computers** (which perform operations using light instead of electrical current) are in the early stages of development.

EMERGING NETWORKING TECHNOLOGIES

Chapter Objective 3:
Name some emerging wired and wireless networking technologies.

Improvements are being made on a continual basis to wired and wireless networking to increase speed and connectivity options, and to support an ever-growing number of new applications. Faster versions of the *Ethernet* standard are under development, and **Power over Ethernet (PoE)**—which sends both electrical power and data over Ethernet cables—is a new option for business networks. For easy home networks, the *Phoneline* or *Powerline* standards can be used; an emerging standard for delivering Internet over existing power lines *is broadband over power lines (BPL)*.

New versions of the **Wi-Fi (802.11)** standard for wireless networks (such as for improved speed and security) are being developed on a regular basis. **WiMAX** is an emerging wireless standard with a greater range than Wi-Fi; **mobile WiMAX** is a version of WiMAX designed for use with mobile phones and other mobile devices. The **wireless USB** standard is a new option for connecting peripheral devices to a computer, and several new wireless standards—such as *Ultra Wideband (UWB)* and *wirelessHD (WiHD)* are designed for wirelessly delivering multimedia content between computers, TVs, digital cameras, DVD players, and other consumer devices.

ARTIFICIAL INTELLIGENCE (AI)

Chapter Objective 4:
Explain what is meant by the term "artificial intelligence" (AI) and list some AI applications.

When a computer performs in ways that would be considered intelligent if observed in people, this is referred to as **artificial intelligence (AI)**. Some of the earliest advances in AI were in the area of chess; the most common test for AI is the *Turning Test*. One AI application is the **intelligent agent**. Examples include *application assistants*, *search agents*, *shopping bots*, *entertainment bots*, and *chatterbots*. Intelligent agents typically act as *virtual assistants* and modify their behavior based on the user's actions. They are frequently built into application programs and operating systems and are beginning to be used on Web pages. Some—like many chatterbots—use a *natural language interface*.

Expert systems perform tasks that would otherwise be performed by a human expert, such as diagnosing medical conditions, making financial forecasts, and performing credit authorizations. Expert systems use a *knowledge base* (a database containing specific facts and rules about the expert area) and an *inference engine* (a software program used to apply rules to the data stored in the knowledge base to reach decisions).

Neural networks and *robotics* are two other areas of artificial intelligence. A neural network is an AI system that tries to imitate the way the human brain works and is typically used for pattern recognition, such as speech analysis, crime analysis, and biometric identification. **Robotics** is the study of **robots**—devices, controlled by a person or a computer, that can move and react to sensory input. Robots are commonly used for repetitive and dangerous tasks; they are also being used for household tasks, for entertainment purposes, and to assist with business and personal tasks.

TECHNOLOGICAL ADVANCES IN MEDICINE

Technological advances in recent years include computers that analyze test results, implanted devices that assist an organ's functioning, and digital cameras that can be ingested to record images of a person's digestive tract. *Electronic monitoring* can take the form of internal or external monitors. Certain electronic implant applications—such as the **VeriChip** used for identification purposes and electrodes implanted in the brain—are embraced by some, but are not without controversy.

Telemedicine is the use of communications technology to provide medical information and services and can take a variety of forms. One application is **telesurgery**—a form of *robot-assisted surgery* where a robot (controlled by a physician) operates on a patient. With telesurgery, the robot is controlled remotely, such as over the Internet. Robots can use smaller incisions in some types of surgeries, which results in less pain for the patient and a faster recovery period. Other forms of telemedicine include remote professional consultations and diagnosis, such as via a videoconferencing system.

Chapter Objective 5:
List some new and upcoming technological advances in medicine.

TECHNOLOGICAL ADVANCES IN THE MILITARY

Recent and expected future technological advances in the military include newly designed weapons, protective gear, and surveillance tools. Surveillance tools in the future may include an increased use of **battlefield robots** and the use of *autonomous robots* that can navigate on their own. The uniform of the future may include an **exoskeleton suit**—a wearable robotic system that not only protects the user, but gives him or her additional physical capabilities.

Chapter Objective 6:
Name some new and upcoming technological advances in the military.

SOCIETAL IMPLICATIONS OF EMERGING TECHNOLOGY

There are many potential societal implications associated with emerging technologies, such as unexpected results, trusting "intelligent" computers and robots so much that they become a personal safety hazard, and allowing medical technology to enable people to be controlled by others. Since virtually any new technology could be used for both good and evil, we need to weigh the societal risks and benefits of emerging technologies in order to make educated and informed decisions about what we would like our lives and society to be like.

Chapter Objective 7:
Discuss potential societal implications of emerging technologies.

REVIEW ACTIVITIES

KEY TERM MATCHING

a. artificial intelligence (AI)

b. augmented reality

c. exoskeleton suit

d. expert system

e. nanotechnology

f. neural network

g. optical computer

h. robot

i. telemedicine

j. WiMAX

Instructions: Match each key term on the left with the definition on the right that best describes it.

1. _____ A computer system that provides the type of advice that would be expected from a human expert.

2. _____ A computer that uses light, such as from laser beams or infrared beams, to perform digital computations.

3. _____ A device, controlled by a human operator or a computer, that can move and react to sensory input.

4. _____ An emerging wireless networking standard that is faster and has a greater range than Wi-Fi.

5. _____ An expert system in which the human brain's pattern-recognition process is emulated by the computer system.

6. _____ A wearable robotic system designed to give an individual additional physical capabilities and protection.

7. _____ The science of creating tiny computers and components by working at the individual atomic and molecular levels.

8. _____ The use of networking technology to provide medical information and services.

9. _____ When a computer performs actions that are characteristic of human intelligence.

10. _____ When computer generated images are overlayed on top of real-time images, such as to overlay information over the photo or video displayed on a mobile phone.

SELF-QUIZ

Instructions: Circle **T** if the statement is true, **F** if the statement is false, or write the best answer in the space provided. **Answers for the self-quiz are located in the References and Resources Guide at the end of the book.**

1. **T** **F** Two-dimensional (2D) barcodes can store more data than conventional one-dimensional barcodes.

2. **T** **F** Nonvolatile RAM (NVRAM) chips do not lose their contents when the power to the computer is turned off.

3. **T** **F** Computers that process data with light are referred to as quantum computers.

4. **T** **F** Diagnosing a patient from a distance is referred to as telesurgery.

5. **T** **F** One advantage of robot-assisted surgery is faster recovery time.

6. In quantum computing, _____ (which can represent more than two possible states) are used instead of electronic bits.

7. _____ is an emerging wireless networking standard that is designed to provide access to larger geographical areas than Wi-Fi.

8. The _____ is an RFID chip approved to be implanted under a person's skin for identification purposes.

9. A _____ robot is used by the military in combat, such as to ensure locations are safe prior to sending in soldiers.

10. Many products today use carbon _____, which are a byproduct of nanotechnology research.

1. For the following list of emerging devices or technologies, write the appropriate letter (I, P, O, S, or C) in the space provided to indicate whether each device or technology is used for input (I), processing (P), output (O), storage (S), or communications (C).

   a. _____ WiHD   c. _____ 2D barcode   e. _____ NVRAM

   b. _____ OLED   d. _____ holographic cartridge   f. _____ IMOD

2. Supply the missing words to complete the following statements.

   a. _____ storage systems use multiple blue laser beams to store data in three dimensions.

   b. _____ is a form of robot-assisted surgery in which the doctor's physical location is different from the patient's physical location and the doctor controls the robot remotely over the Internet or another communications medium.

3. Write the number of the networking standard that best matches each of the following descriptions in the blank to the left of each description.

   a. _____ Used to create a wired home or business network.

   b. _____ Used to create a home network via existing telephone jacks.

   c. _____ Used to send power along with data over networking cables.

   d. _____ Used to connect a building to the Internet over existing power lines.

   1. PoE
   2. BPL
   3. Ethernet
   4. Phoneline

4. Would an OLED display or an LCD display use more battery power? Explain why.

5. Would Wi-Fi or WirelessHD be better for wirelessly networking two computers within a home? Explain.

1. More and more everyday devices—including cars and other vehicles—are being controlled by computers. There are advantages, such as avoiding possible driver errors and the ability to change the speed of or reroute trains automatically to avoid collisions. But are there potential risks, as well? For example, Thailand's Finance Minister once had to be rescued from inside his limousine after the onboard computer malfunctioned, leaving the vehicle immobilized and the door locks, power windows, and air conditioning not functioning. Do you think the benefits of increased automation of devices that could put us in danger if they malfunction outweigh the risks? What types of safeguards should be incorporated into computer-controlled cars, subway trains, and other automated vehicles? What about medication dispensers and other automated medical devices?

2. Interference with wireless devices is happening much more often than in the past. For instance, unlicensed walkie-talkies used on TV sets have interfered with police radios, and British air traffic control transmissions have been interrupted by transmissions from nearby baby monitors. If devices that use unlicensed radio frequencies interfere with each other, whose fault is it? The individual for buying multiple products that use the same radio frequency? The manufacturers for not ensuring their products can switch channels as needed to use a free channel? The government for allowing unregulated airwaves? Is there a solution to this problem? Who, if anyone, should be responsible for fixing this problem?

PROJECTS

HOT TOPICS

1. **WiMAX vs. Wi-Fi** As discussed in the chapter, WiMAX and Wi-Fi are both wireless networking standards.

   For this project, research WiMAX and Wi-Fi to determine their current status and the differences between the two standards. Are they designed for the same or different purposes? Explain. How are they being used today? Do you think the standards will coexist in the future, or will one eventually replace the other? At the conclusion of your research, prepare a one-page summary of your findings and opinions and submit it to your instructor.

**SHORT ANSWER/
RESEARCH**

2. **Today's Robots** As discussed in the chapter, robots can be used today for a variety of activities in businesses and the military, as well as in the home.

   For this project, select one type of robotic device on the market today—for instance, a robotic toy, vacuum cleaner, or lawn mower; a security or manufacturing robot; a robot used by the military or NASA; or a robotic personal assistant—and research it. Find out what the product does, what it costs, how it is powered and controlled, and if it can be reprogrammed. What are the advantages of the robotics part of the product? Do you think this is a worthwhile or beneficial product? At the conclusion of your research, prepare a one- to two-page summary of your findings and opinions and submit it to your instructor.

HANDS ON

3. **Online/Cloud Storage** There are a number of online or cloud storage services (such as ADrive, SkyDrive, and Box.net) designed to allow individuals to back up files online and share specific files with others; specialty online storage services designed for digital photo sharing include Flickr, Photobucket, and SnapFish.

   For this project, visit at least one online/cloud storage site designed for backup and file exchange, and at least one site designed for digital photo sharing. You can try the sites listed above or use a search site to find alternative sites. Tour your selected sites to determine the features each service offers, the cost, the amount of storage space available, and the options for sending uploaded files to others. Do the sites password protect your files, or are they available for anyone with an Internet connection to see? What are the benefits for using these types of storage services? Can you think of any drawbacks? Would you want to use any of the storage sites you visited? Why or why not? At the conclusion of this task, prepare a short summary of your findings and submit it to your instructor.

4. **Emotion Recognition Software** An emerging application is *emotion recognition software*, which uses camera input to try to read people's current emotion. The first expected application of such a system is for ATM machines, since they already have cameras installed. Possibilities include changing the advertising display based on the customer's emotional response to displayed advertising, and enlarging the screen text if the customer appears to be squinting. Is it ethical for businesses using emotion recognition software to read the emotions of citizens without their consent? Proponents of the technology argue that it is no different than when human tellers or store clerks interpret customers' emotions and modify their treatment of the customer accordingly. Do you agree? Why or why not? Is this a worthy new technology or just a potential invasion of privacy? Would you object to using an ATM machine with emotion-recognition capabilities? Why or why not?

For this project, form an opinion about the ethical ramifications of emotion recognition systems and be prepared to discuss your position (in class, via an online class discussion group, in a class chat room, or via a class blog, depending on your instructor's directions). You may also be asked to write a short paper expressing your opinion.

ETHICS IN ACTION

5. **Ubiquitous Computing vs. Big Brother** Ubiquitous computing—also known as pervasive computing—suggests a future in which few aspects of daily life will remain untouched by computers and computer technology. Computers and related technology will become embedded into more and more devices, and people will depend on computing technology for an ever-increasing number of everyday activities. But, if all the electronic devices in our lives can communicate with one another automatically, how can we control what they say and whom they say it to? Will these devices be used to track our movements so that the government will always know where we are? Will there really be a "Big Brother" computer that knows everything about everybody? What about personal privacy? How will it be protected? Does the idea of ubiquitous computing concern you or interest you? Is it something that you would like to see become a reality in the near future? Why or why not?

For this project, consider the potential impact of ubiquitous computing on our lives and our privacy and form an opinion about this issue. Be prepared to discuss both sides of this issue and your opinion (in class, via an online class discussion group, in a class chat room, or via a class blog). You may also be asked to write a short paper or prepare a short presentation expressing your opinion, depending on your instructor's directions.

BALANCING ACT

Instructions: Go to the Chapter 8 page at **www.cengage.com/computerconcepts/np/uccs4** to work the following Web Activities.

WEB ACTIVITIES

6. **Interactive Activities** Work the interactive **Crossword Puzzle**, watch the **Video Podcasts** and **Online Videos**, and explore the **Further Exploration** links associated with this chapter.

   If you have a SAM user profile, you may have access to hands-on instruction, practice, and assessment of the skills covered in this chapter. Check with your instructor for instructions and the correct URL/Web site to access those assignments.

7. **Student Edition Labs** Work the following interactive **Student Edition Labs**.
   - **Project Management**
   - **Visual Programming**
   - **Advanced Spreadsheets**

8. **Test Yourself** Review the **Online Study Guide** for this chapter, then test your knowledge of the terms and concepts covered in this chapter by completing the **Key Term Matching** exercise, the **Self-Quiz**, the **Exercises**, and the **Practice Test**.

Student Edition Labs

REFERENCES AND RESOURCES
GUIDE

INTRODUCTION

When working on a computer or taking a computer course, you often need to look up information related to computers. For instance, you may need to find out when the IBM PC was first invented, you may want tips about what to consider when buying a computer, or you may want to find out more about how numbering systems work. To help you with the tasks just mentioned and more, this References and Resources Guide brings together in one convenient location a collection of computer-related references and resources. These resources plus additional resources (such as a variety of interactive activities and study tools) are located on this textbook's Web site, at www.cengage.com/computerconcepts/np/uccs4.

OUTLINE

Computer History Timeline R-2

Guide to Buying a PC R-8

A Look at Numbering Systems R-11

Coding Charts R-15

Answers to Self-Quiz R-17

COMPUTER HISTORY TIMELINE

The earliest recorded calculating device, the abacus, is believed to have been invented by the Babylonians sometime between 500 B.C. and 100 B.C. It and similar types of counting boards were used solely for counting.

500 B.C.

Blaise Pascal invented the first mechanical calculator, called the Pascaline Arithmetic Machine. It had the capacity for eight digits and could add and subtract.

1642

Dr. John V. Atanasoff and Clifford Berry designed and built ABC (for Atanasoff-Berry Computer), the world's first electronic computer.

1937

Precomputers and Early Computers

1621

The slide rule, a precursor to the electronic calculator, was invented. Used primarily to perform multiplication, division, square roots, and the calculation of logarithms, its wide-spread use continued until the 1970s.

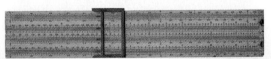

1804

French silk weaver Joseph-Marie Jacquard built a loom that read holes punched on a series of small sheets of hardwood to control the weave of the pattern. This automated machine introduced the use of punch cards and showed that they could be used to convey a series of instructions.

1944

The Mark I, considered to be the first digital computer, was introduced by IBM. It was developed in cooperation with Harvard University, was more than 50 feet long, weighed almost five tons, and used electromechanical relays to solve addition problems in less than a second; multiplication and division took about 6 and 12 seconds, respectively.

Precomputers and Early Computers (before approximately 1945)

Most precomputers and early computers were mechanical machines that worked with gears and levers. Electromechanical devices (using both electricity and gears and levers) were developed toward the end of this era.

First Generation (approximately 1946–1957)

Powered by vacuum tubes, these computers were faster than electromechanical machines, but they were large and bulky, generated excessive heat, and had to be physically wired and reset to run programs. Input was primarily on punch cards; output was on punch cards or paper. Machine and assembly languages were used to program these computers.

The UNIVAC 1, the first computer to be mass produced for general use, was introduced by Remington Rand. In 1952, it was used to analyze votes in the U.S. presidential election and correctly predicted that Dwight D. Eisenhower would be the victor only 45 minutes after the polls closed, though the results were not aired immediately because they weren't trusted.

The COBOL programming language was developed by a committee headed by Dr. Grace Hopper.

The first floppy disk (8 inches in diameter) was introduced.

UNIX was developed at AT&T's Bell Laboratories; Advanced Micro Devices (AMD) was formed; and ARPANET (the predecessor of today's Internet) was established.

IBM unbundled some of its hardware and software and began selling them separately, allowing other software companies to emerge.

1951   1960   1967   1969

| First Generation | Second Generation | Third Generation |

1947   1957   1964   1968

The FORTRAN programming language was introduced.

Robert Noyce and Gordon Moore founded the Intel Corporation.

John Bardeen, Walter Brattain, and William Shockley invented the transistor, which had the same capabilities as a vacuum tube but was faster, broke less often, used less power, and created less heat. They won a Nobel Prize for their invention in 1956 and computers began to be built with transistors shortly afterwards.

The first mouse was invented by Doug Engelbart.

The IBM System/360 computer was introduced. Unlike previous computers, System/360 contained a full line of compatible computers, making upgrading easier.

Second Generation (approximately 1958–1963)

Second-generation computers used transistors instead of vacuum tubes. They allowed the computer to be physically smaller, more powerful, more reliable, and faster than before. Input was primarily on punch cards and magnetic tape; output was on punch cards and paper; and magnetic tape and disks were used for storage. High-level programming languages were used with these computers.

Third Generation (approximately 1964–1970)

The third generation of computers evolved when integrated circuits (IC)—computer chips—began being used instead of conventional transistors. Computers became even smaller and more reliable. Keyboards and monitors were introduced for input and output; magnetic disks were used for storage. The emergence of the operating system meant that operators no longer had to manually reset relays and wiring.

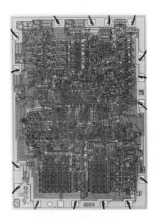

The first microprocessor, the Intel 4004, was designed by Ted Hoff. The single processor contained 2,250 transistors and could execute 60,000 operations per second.

Bill Gates and Paul Allen wrote a version of BASIC for the Altair, the first computer programming language designed for a personal computer. Bill Gates dropped out of Harvard to form Microsoft with Paul Allen.

Software Arts Inc's Visi-Calc, the first electronic spreadsheet and business program for personal computers, was released. This program is seen as one of the reasons personal computers first became widely accepted in the business world.

IBM introduced the IBM PC. This DOS-based PC used a 4.77 MHz 8088 CPU with 64 KB of RAM and quickly became the standard for business personal computers.

1971   1975   1979   1981

Fourth Generation

1972   1976   1980

The C programming language was developed by Dennis Ritchie at Bell Labs.

Seymour Cray, called the "father of supercomputing," founded Cray Research, which would go on to build some of the fastest computers in the world.

Steve Wozniak and Steve Jobs' founded Apple computer and released the Apple I (a single-board computer), followed by the Apple II (a complete personal computer that became an instant success in 1977). They originally ran the company out of Jobs' garage.

Sony Electronics introduced the 3.5-inch floppy disk and drive.

Seagate Technology announced the first Winchester 5.25-inch hard disk drive, revolutionizing computer storage.

IBM chose Microsoft to develop the operating system for its upcoming personal computer. That operating system was PC-DOS.

Fourth Generation (approximately 1971–present)

The fourth generation of computers began with large-scale integration (LSI), which resulted in chips that could contain thousands of transistors. Very large-scale integration (VLSI) resulted in the microprocessor and the resulting microcomputers. The keyboard and mouse are predominant input devices, though many other types of input devices are now available; monitors and printers provide output; storage is obtained with magnetic disks, optical discs, and memory chips.

The first general-interest CD-ROM product (*Grolier's Electronic Encyclopedia*) was released, and computer and electronics companies worked together to develop a universal CD-ROM standard.

Intel introduced the Intel386 CPU.

Compaq Corporation released the first IBM-compatible personal computer that ran the same software as the IBM PC, marking the beginning of the huge PC-compatible industry.

The first version of Microsoft Windows, a graphical environment, was released.

Tim Berners-Lee of CERN invented the World Wide Web.

Linus Torvalds created Linux, which launched the open source revolution. The penguin logo/mascot soon followed.

Intel introduced the Intel486 chip, the world's first million transistor CPU.

1983

1985

1989

1994

1982

1984

1986

1993

Intel introduced the 80286 CPU.

The Apple Macintosh debuted. It featured a simple, graphical user interface, used an 8 MHz, 32-bit Motorola 68000 CPU, and had a built-in 9-inch black and white screen.

Intel introduced the Pentium CPU.

NCSA released the Mosaic Web browser, developed by students at the University of Illinois. Mosaic was one of the first browsers to support graphics, and it was the first to support both Windows and Macintosh computers. Three million people were connected to the Internet.

Apple's Steve Jobs founded Pixar.

TIME magazine named the computer its "Machine of the Year" for 1982, emphasizing the importance the computer had already reached in our society at that time.

Microsoft was listed on the New York Stock Exchange and began to sell shares to the public; Bill Gates became one of the world's youngest billionaires.

The first DVD players used for playing movies stored on DVD discs were sold.

After winning 2 of 6 games in their first contest in 1996, the IBM computer Deep Blue beat chess master Garry Kasparov in a chess match.

The number of Internet users worldwide surpassed 100 million.

Shawn Fanning, 19, wrote the software to drive his Napster P2P service and began the debate about P2P filesharing and online music.

Palm released the Palm VII, its first handheld computer with wireless Internet access.

The Intel Pentium III CPU was introduced.

Apple introduced the iPod personal music player.

Intel's first 64-bit CPU, the Itanium, was introduced.

Microsoft released its XP line of products, including Windows XP and Office XP.

1997

1999

2001

1995

1998

2000

2003

Windows 95 was released and sold more than 1 million copies in 4 days.

Microsoft shipped Windows 98.

Both eBay and Amazon.com were founded.

The first USB flash drives were released.

Apple released the iMac, a modernized version of the Macintosh computer. Its futuristic design helped to make this computer immensely popular.

AMD released the 64-bit Opteron server CPU and the Athlon 64, the first 64-bit CPU designed for desktop computer use.

Microsoft shipped the Office 2003 editions of its Microsoft Office System.

Digital camera sales in the United States exceeded 14 million, surpassing film camera sales for the first time.

Sun Microsystems released Java, which is still one of the most popular Web programming languages.

Intel introduced its Pentium 4 CPU chip. A popular advertising campaign, launched in 2001, featured the Blue Man Group.

The Internet and wireless networks enabled people to work and communicate with others while on the go.

Spyware became a major problem; some studies indicated that over 80% of computers had spyware installed.

2004

New Internet-enabled gaming consoles, like the Wii shown here, were released.

Broadband Internet access approached the norm and improvements to wireless networking (such as WiMAX) continued to be developed.

Delivery of TV shows and other media to mobile phones became more common.

Blu-ray Disc and HD-DVD movies, discs, and players became available in the U.S.

Use of the Internet for online shopping, as well as downloads of music, movies, games, and television shows, continued to grow.

2006

Netbooks were introduced.

Google introduced the Chrome operating system.

facebook

Use of social networking sites exploded; Facebook announced it had more than 100 million users.

The HD-DVD format was discontinued, leaving Blu-ray Disc the HD format winner.

2008

2005

Phishing and identity theft became household words as an increasing number of individuals fell victim to these Internet scams.

The capabilities of mobile devices continued to grow; Palm's LifeDrive came with a 4 GB hard drive and built-in Wi-Fi and Bluetooth support.

Portable media players, such as the iPod, were common; digital music capabilities were built into a growing number of objects and devices.

Intel and AMD their first dual-core CPUs both released

2007

The Twitter microblogging service was launched.

Apple released the revolutionary iPhone.

Microsoft released Windows Vista and Office 2007.

Windows Vista

Quad-core CPUs were released by both Intel and AMD.

2009

Geobrowsing applications became more prominent; 4G phones became available.

Cloud computing entered the main-stream for both individuals and businesses.

Microsoft released Windows 7.

Windows 7

GUIDE TO BUYING A PC

Before buying a new computer, it is important to give some thought to what your needs are, including what software programs you wish to run, any other computers with which you need to be compatible, how you might want to connect to the Internet, and how much portability is needed. This section of the References and Resources Guide explores topics related to buying a new personal computer. ∎

Analyzing Needs

When referring to a computer system, a need refers to a functional requirement that the computer system must be able to meet. For example, at a video rental store, a computer system must be able to enter barcodes automatically from videos or DVDs being checked in and out, identify customers with overdue movies, manage movie inventories, and do routine accounting operations. Portability is another example of a possible need. For example, if you need to take your computer with you as you travel or work out of the office, you will need a portable computer instead of a desktop computer.

Selecting a computer for home or business use must begin with the all-important question "What do I want the system to do?" Once you have determined what tasks the system will be used for and the amount of portability that is needed, you can choose among the software and hardware alternatives available. Making a list of your needs in the areas discussed in the next few sections can help you get a picture of what type of system you are shopping for. If you are not really sure what you want a system to do, you should think twice about buying one yet—you can easily make expensive mistakes if you are uncertain about what you want a system to do. Some common decision categories are discussed next; Figure R-1 provides a list of questions that can help you define the type of computer that will meet your needs.

FIGURE R-1

Questions to consider when getting ready to buy a personal computer.

POSSIBLE QUESTIONS

What tasks will I be using the computer for (writing papers, accessing the Internet, watching TV, making telephone calls, composing music, playing games, etc.)?

Do I prefer a Mac or a PC-compatible? Are there any other computers I need my documents and storage media to be compatible with?

How fast do I need the system to be?

Do I need portability? If so, do I need a powerful desktop replacement or will a netbook or UMPC suffice?

What size screen do I need? Do I need two monitors?

What removable storage media will I need to use (such as DVDs, flash memory cards, or USB flash drives)?

What types of Internet access will I be using (such as conventional dial-up, DSL, cable, satellite, or mobile wireless)?

Do I need to be able to connect the computer to a network? If so, is it a wired or wireless network and what type of network adapter is needed to connect to that network?

What additional hardware do I need (scanner, printer, TV tuner/antenna, wireless router, or digital camera, for example)?

What brand(s) do I prefer? When do I need the computer?

Do I want to pay extra for a better warranty (such as a longer time period, more comprehensive coverage, or on-site service)?

Application Software Decisions

Determining what functions you want the system to perform will also help you decide which application software is needed. Most users start with an application suite containing a word processor, spreadsheet, and other programs. In addition, specialty programs, such as tax preparation, drawing, home publishing, reference software, games, and more, may be needed or desired.

Not all software is available for all operating systems. Consequently, if a specific piece of software is needed, that choice may determine which operating system you need to use. In addition, your operating system and application software decisions may already be made for you if your documents need to be compatible with those of another computer (such as other office computers or between a home and an office computer).

Platforms and Configuration Options

If your operating system has already been determined, that is a good start in deciding the overall platform you will be looking for—most users will choose between the PC-compatible and Apple Macintosh platform. PC-compatible computers usually run either Windows or Linux; Apple computers almost always use Mac OS.

Configuration decisions initially involve determining the size of the machine desired (see Figure R-2). For nonportable systems, you have the choice between tower, desktop, or all-in-one configurations; in addition, the monitor size needs to be determined. Fully functioning personal computers can be notebook or tablet computers. For tablet computers, you need to decide if you will require keyboard use on a regular basis; if so, a convertible tablet computer would be the best choice. If a powerful fully functioning computer is not required, you may decide to go with a more portable option, such as a netbook or UMPC.

You should also consider any other specifications that are important to you, such as the size of the hard drive, types of other storage devices needed, amount of memory required, and so forth. As discussed in the next section, these decisions often require reconciling the features you want with the amount of money you are willing to spend.

Power vs. Budget Requirements

As part of the needs analysis, you should look closely at your need for a powerful system versus your budgetary constraints. Most users do not need a state-of-the-art system. Those who do should expect to pay more than the average user. A computer that was top of the line six months or a year ago is usually reasonably priced and more than adequate for most users' needs. Individuals who want a computer only for basic tasks, such as using the Internet and word processing, can likely get by with an inexpensive computer designed for home use.

When determining your requirements, be sure to identify the features and functions that are absolutely essential for your primary computing tasks (such as a large hard drive and lots of memory for multimedia applications, a fast video card for gaming, a fast Internet connection, a TV tuner card for individuals who wish to use the computer as a TV set, and so forth). After you have the minimum configuration determined, you can add optional or desirable components, as your budget allows.

Listing Alternatives

After you consider your needs and the questions mentioned in Figure R-1, you should have a pretty good idea of the hardware and software you will need. You will also know what purchasing options are available to you, depending on your time frame (while some retail stores have systems that can be purchased and brought home the same day, special orders or some systems purchased online will take longer). The next step is to get enough information from possible vendors to compare and contrast a few alternative systems that satisfy your stated needs. Most often, these vendors are local stores (such as computer stores, warehouse clubs, and electronic stores) and/or online stores (such as manufacturer Web sites and *e-tailers*—online retailers). To compare prices and specifications for possible computer systems, find at least three systems that meet or exceed your needs by looking through newspaper advertisements, configuring systems online via manufacturer and e-tailer Web sites, or calling or visiting local stores. A comparison sheet listing your criteria and the systems you are considering, such as the one in Figure R-3, can help you summarize your options. Although it is sometimes very difficult to compare the prices of systems since they typically have somewhat different configurations and some components (such as CPUs) are difficult to compare, you can assign an approximate dollar value to each extra feature a system has (such as $50 for an included printer or a larger hard drive). Be sure to also include any sales tax and shipping charges when you compare the prices of each total system.

If your budget is limited, you will have to balance the system you need with extra features you may want. But do not skimp on memory or hard drive space because sufficient memory can help your programs to run faster and with fewer problems and hard

DESKTOPS

NOTEBOOKS

NETBOOKS

ULTRA-MOBILE PCS (UMPCs)

FIGURE R-2

Types of personal computers.

COMPONENT	EXAMPLE OF DESIRED SPECIFICATIONS	SYSTEM #1 VENDOR:	SYSTEM #2 VENDOR:	SYSTEM #3 VENDOR:
Operating system	Windows 7 Home Premium			
Manufacturer	HP or Dell			
Style	Notebook			
CPU	Intel dual core			
RAM	2 GB or higher			
Hard drive	500 GB or higher			
Removable storage	8-in-1 and flash memory card reader			
Optical drive	DVD-RW			
Monitor	Widescreen 15.4" minimum			
Video card and video RAM	Prefer dedicated video RAM			
Keyboard/mouse	Portable USB mouse with scroll wheel			
Sound card/speakers	No preference			
Modem	None			
Network card	Wi-Fi (802.11n)			
Printer	Ink-jet if get deal on price with complete system			
Included software	Microsoft Office			
Warranty	3 years min. (1 year onsite if not a local store)			
Other features	3 USB ports minimum, TV tuner, ExpressCard module			
Price				
Tax				
Shipping				
TOTAL COST				

FIGURE R-3

Comparing computer alternatives. A checklist such as this one can help to organize your desired criteria and evaluate possible systems.

drive space is consumed quickly. Often for just a few extra dollars, you can get additional memory, a faster CPU, or a larger hard drive—significantly cheaper than trying to upgrade any of those features later. A good rule of thumb is to try to buy a little more computer than you think you need. On the other hand, do not buy a top-of-the-line system unless you fall into the power user category and really need it. Generally, the second or third system down from the top of the line is a very good system for a much more reasonable price. Some guidelines for minimum requirements for most home users are as follows:

> A relatively fast multi-core CPU (generally, any multi-core CPU currently being sold today is fast enough for most users).

> 3 GB of RAM for desktop and notebook users.

> 320 GB or more hard drive space.

> Recordable or rewritable DVD drive.

> Network adapter or modem for the desired type(s) of Internet access.

> Sound card and speakers.

> At least 3 USB ports.

> A built-in flash memory media reader.

A LOOK AT NUMBERING SYSTEMS

As discussed in Chapter 2 of this text, a numbering system is a way of representing numbers. People generally use the *decimal numbering system* explained in Chapter 2 and reviewed next; computers process data using the *binary numbering system*. Another numbering system related to computer use is the *hexadecimal numbering system*, which can be used to represent long strings of binary numbers in a manner more understandable to people than the binary numbering system. Following a discussion of these three numbering systems, we take a look at conversions between numbering systems and principles of computer arithmetic, and then close with a look at how to perform conversions using a scientific calculator. ■

The Decimal and Binary Numbering System

The *decimal (base 10)* numbering system uses 10 symbols—the digits 0, 1, 2, 3, 4, 5, 6, 7, 8, and 9—to represent all possible numbers and is the numbering system people use most often. The *binary (base 2)* numbering system is used extensively by computers to represent numbers and other characters. This system uses only two digits—0 and 1. As mentioned in Chapter 2, the place values (columns) in the binary numbering system are different from those used in the decimal system.

The Hexadecimal Numbering System

Computers often output diagnostic and memory-management messages and identify network adapters and other hardware in *hexadecimal (hex)* notation. Hexadecimal notation is a shorthand method for representing the binary digits stored in a computer. Because large binary numbers—for example, 1010100010011101—can easily be misread by people, hexadecimal notation groups binary digits into units of four, which, in turn, are represented by other symbols.

The hexadecimal numbering system is also called the *base 16 numbering system* because it uses 16 different symbols. Since there are only 10 possible numeric digits, hexadecimal uses letters instead of numbers for the additional 6 symbols. The 16 hexadecimal symbols and their decimal and binary counterparts are shown in Figure R-4.

The hexadecimal numbering system has a special relationship to the 8-bit bytes of ASCII and EBCDIC that makes it ideal for displaying addresses and other data quickly. As you can see in Figure R-4, each hex character has a 4-bit binary counterpart, so any combination of 8 bits can be represented by exactly two hexadecimal characters. For example, the letter N (represented in ASCII by 01001110) has a hex representation of *4E* (see the Binary Equivalent columns for the hexadecimal characters *4* and *E* in Figure R-4).

FIGURE R-4

Hexadecimal characters and their decimal and binary equivalents.

HEXADECIMAL CHARACTER	DECIMAL EQUIVALENT	BINARY EQUIVALENT
0	0	0000
1	1	0001
2	2	0010
3	3	0011
4	4	0100
5	5	0101
6	6	0110
7	7	0111
8	8	1000
9	9	1001
A	10	1010
B	11	1011
C	12	1100
D	13	1101
E	14	1110
F	15	1111

Converting Between Numbering Systems

The concept of interpreting binary numbers was discussed in Chapter 2. Specifically, to convert from binary to decimal, you need to multiply each digit of the binary number by the appropriate power of 2 for that place value, such as by 2^0 or 1 for the right-most digit, 2^1 or 2 for the next digit, and so forth, and then add those products together. Three other types of conversions are discussed next.

Hexadecimal to Decimal

As shown in Figure R-5, the process for converting a hexadecimal number to its decimal equivalent is similar to converting a binary number to its decimal equivalent, except the base number is 16 instead of 2. To determine the decimal equivalent of a hexadecimal number (such as 4F6A, as shown in Figure R-5), multiply the decimal equivalent of each individual hex character (determined by using the table in Figure R-4) by the appropriate power of 16 and then add the results to obtain the decimal equivalent of that hex number.

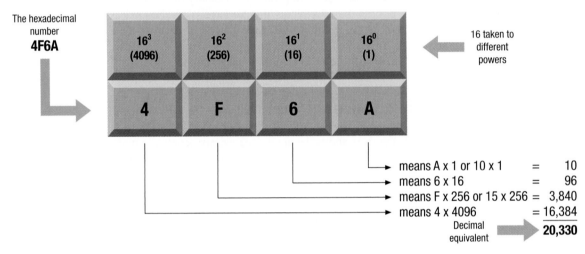

FIGURE R-5
The hexadecimal (base 16) numbering system. Each digit in a hexadecimal number represents 16 taken to a different power.

Hexadecimal to Binary and Binary to Hexadecimal

To convert from hexadecimal to binary, we convert each hexadecimal digit separately to 4 binary digits (using the table in Figure R-4). For example, to convert F6A9 to binary, we get

F	6	A	9
1111	0110	1010	1001

or 1111011010101001 in binary representation. To convert from binary to hexadecimal, we go through the reverse process. If the number of digits in the binary number is not divisible by 4, we add leading zeros to the binary number to force an even division. For example, to convert the binary number 1101101010011 to hexadecimal, we get

0001	1011	0101	0011
1	B	5	3

or 1B53 in hexadecimal representation. Note that three leading zeros were added to change the initial 1 to 0001 before making the conversion.

Decimal to Binary and Decimal to Hexadecimal

To convert from decimal to either binary or hexadecimal, we can use the *remainder method*. To use the remainder method, the decimal number is divided by 2 (to convert to a binary number) or 16 (to convert to a hexadecimal number). The *remainder* of the division operation is recorded and the division process is repeated using the *quotient* as the next dividend, until the quotient becomes 0. At that point, the collective remainders (written backwards) represent the equivalent binary or hexadecimal number (see Figure R-6).

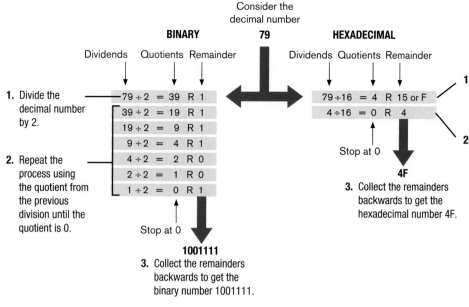

Consider the decimal number **79**

BINARY

Dividends Quotients Remainder

1. Divide the decimal number by 2.

79 ÷ 2	=	39	R	1
39 ÷ 2	=	19	R	1
19 ÷ 2	=	9	R	1
9 ÷ 2	=	4	R	1
4 ÷ 2	=	2	R	0
2 ÷ 2	=	1	R	0
1 ÷ 2	=	0	R	1

2. Repeat the process using the quotient from the previous division until the quotient is 0.

Stop at 0

1001111

3. Collect the remainders backwards to get the binary number 1001111.

HEXADECIMAL

Dividends Quotients Remainder

| 79 ÷ 16 | = | 4 | R | 15 or F |
| 4 ÷ 16 | = | 0 | R | 4 |

Stop at 0

4F

3. Collect the remainders backwards to get the hexadecimal number 4F.

1. Divide the decimal number by 16.

2. Repeat the process using the quotient from the previous division until the quotient is 0.

FIGURE R-6
The remainder method. The remainder method can be used to convert decimal numbers to binary or hex format.

A table summarizing all the numbering system conversion procedures covered in this text is provided in Figure R-7.

FIGURE R-7
Summary of conversions.

FROM BASE	TO BASE		
	2	10	16
2		Starting at the right-most digit, multiply binary digits by 2^0, 2^1, 2^2, etc., respectively, and then add products.	Starting at the right-most digit, convert each group of four binary digits to a hex digit.
10	Divide repeatedly by 2 using each quotient as the next dividend until the quotient becomes 0, and then collect the remainders in reverse order.		Divide repeatedly by 16 using each quotient as the next dividend until the quotient becomes 0, and then collect the remainders in reverse order.
16	Convert each hex digit to four binary digits.	Starting at the right-most digit, multiply hex digits by 16^0, 16^1, 16^2, etc., respectively, and then add products.	

Computer Arithmetic

To most people, decimal arithmetic is second nature. Addition and subtraction of binary and hexadecimal numbers is not much different than the process used with decimal numbers—just the number of symbols used in each system varies. For instance, the digits in each column are added or subtracted and you carry to and borrow from the column to the left as needed as you move from right to left. Instead of carrying or borrowing 10, however—as you would in the decimal system—you carry or borrow 2 (binary) or 16 (hexadecimal).

Figure R-8 provides an example of addition and subtraction with decimal, binary, and hexadecimal numbers.

FIGURE R-8
Adding and subtracting with the decimal, binary, and hexadecimal numbering systems.

	DECIMAL	BINARY	HEXADECIMAL
Addition	1 144 + 27 171	111 100101 + 10011 111000	1 8E + 2F BD
Subtraction	3 1̸4̸4 - 27 117	0 0 1̸0̸0101 - 10011 10010	7 8̸E - 2F 5F

Using a Scientific Calculator

A scientific calculator can be used to convert numbers between numbering systems, or to check conversions performed by hand. Many conventional calculators have different numbering system options; scientific calculator programs can be used for this purpose, as well. For example, Figure R-9 shows how to use the Windows Calculator program to double-check the hand calculations performed in Figure R-6 (the Scientific option must be selected using the View menu to display the options shown in the figure). Arithmetic can also be performed in any numbering system on a calculator, once that numbering system is selected on the calculator. Notice that, depending on which numbering system is currently selected, not all numbers on the calculator are available—only the possible numbers are displayed, such as only 0 and 1 when the binary numbering system is selected, as in the bottom screen in the figure.

FIGURE R-9

Using a scientific calculator. A physical calculator or calculator program can be used to convert between numbering systems, as well as to perform arithmetic in different numbering systems.

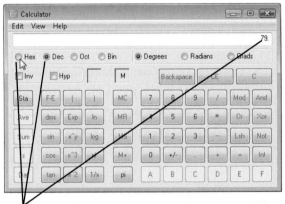

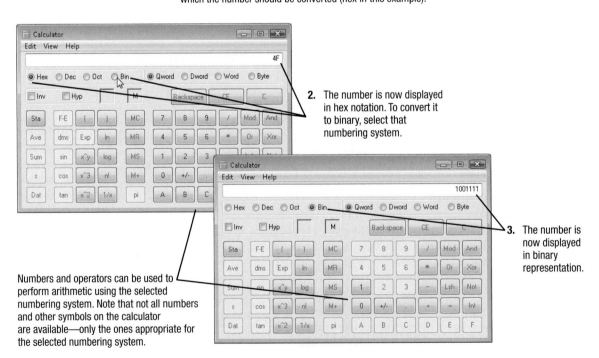

WINDOWS CALCULATOR
The Calculator program is typically located under Accessories on the Windows Start menu; select the *Scientific* option using the Calculator's View menu.

1. After entering a number (such as the decimal number 79 with the decimal numbering system selected shown here), select the numbering system to which the number should be converted (hex in this example).

2. The number is now displayed in hex notation. To convert it to binary, select that numbering system.

3. The number is now displayed in binary representation.

Numbers and operators can be used to perform arithmetic using the selected numbering system. Note that not all numbers and other symbols on the calculator are available—only the ones appropriate for the selected numbering system.

CODING CHARTS

As discussed in Chapter 2 of this text, coding systems for text-based data include ASCII and Unicode; *EBCDIC* is another coding system for text-based data that was developed primarily for use with mainframes. ∎

⊽ **FIGURE R-10**
ASCII and EBCDIC binary codes for typical keyboard symbols.

ASCII and EBCDIC

Figure R-10 provides a chart listing the 8-digit ASCII and EBCDIC representations (in binary) for most of the symbols found on a typical keyboard.

SYMBOL	ASCII	EBCDIC	SYMBOL	ASCII	EBCDIC	SYMBOL	ASCII	EBCDIC
A	0100 0001	1100 0001	e	0110 0101	1000 0101	8	0011 1000	1111 1000
B	0100 0010	1100 0010	f	0110 0110	1000 0110	9	0011 1001	1111 1001
C	0100 0011	1100 0011	g	0110 0111	1000 0111	(	0010 1000	0100 1101
D	0100 0100	1100 0100	h	0110 1000	1000 1000	)	0010 1001	0101 1101
E	0100 0101	1100 0101	i	0110 1001	1000 1001	/	0010 1111	0110 0001
F	0100 0110	1100 0110	j	0110 1010	1001 0001	-	0010 1101	0110 0000
G	0100 0111	1100 0111	k	0110 1011	1001 0010	*	0010 1010	0101 1100
H	0100 1000	1100 1000	l	0110 1100	1001 0011	+	0010 1011	0100 1110
I	0100 1001	1100 1001	m	0110 1101	1001 0100	,	0010 1100	0110 1011
J	0100 1010	1101 0001	n	0110 1110	1001 0101	.	0010 1110	0100 1011
K	0100 1011	1101 0010	o	0110 1111	1001 0110	:	0011 1010	0111 1010
L	0100 1100	1101 0011	p	0111 0000	1001 0111	;	0011 1011	0101 1110
M	0100 1101	1101 0100	q	0111 0001	1001 1000	&	0010 0110	0101 0000
N	0100 1110	1101 0101	r	0111 0010	1001 1001	\	0101 1100	1110 0000
O	0100 1111	1101 0110	s	0111 0011	1010 0010	$	0010 0100	0101 1011
P	0101 0000	1101 0111	t	0111 0100	1010 0011	%	0010 0101	0110 1100
Q	0101 0001	1101 1000	u	0111 0101	1010 0100	=	0011 1101	0111 1110
R	0101 0010	1101 1001	v	0111 0110	1010 0101	>	0011 1110	0110 1110
S	0101 0011	1110 0010	w	0111 0111	1010 0110	<	0011 1100	0100 1100
T	0101 0100	1110 0011	x	0111 1000	1010 0111	!	0010 0001	0101 1010
U	0101 0101	1110 0100	y	0111 1001	1010 1000			0111 1100	0110 1010
V	0101 0110	1110 0101	z	0111 1010	1010 1001	?	0011 1111	0110 1111
W	0101 0111	1110 0110	0	0011 0000	1111 0000	@	0100 0000	0111 1100
X	0101 1000	1110 0111	1	0011 0001	1111 0001	_	0101 1111	0110 1101
Y	0101 1001	1110 1000	2	0011 0010	1111 0010	'	0110 0000	1011 1001
Z	0101 1010	1110 1001	3	0011 0011	1111 0011	{	0111 1011	1100 0000
a	0110 0001	1000 0001	4	0011 0100	1111 0100	}	0111 1101	1101 0000
b	0110 0010	1000 0010	5	0011 0101	1111 0101	~	0111 1110	1010 0001
c	0110 0011	1000 0011	6	0011 0110	1111 0110	[	0101 1011	0100 1010
d	0110 0100	1000 0100	7	0011 0111	1111 0111	]	0101 1101	0101 1010

A 0041	N 004E	a 0061	n 006E	o 0030	{ 007B	* 002A	■ 25A0	ও 0985
B 0042	O 004F	b 0062	o 006F	1 0031	| 007C	+ 002B	□ 25A1	র 0997
C 0043	P 0050	c 0063	p 0070	2 0032	} 007D	, 002C	▲ 25B2	ে 09C7
D 0044	Q 0051	d 0064	q 0071	3 0033	~ 007E	- 002D	% 2105	৶ 09F6
E 0045	R 0052	e 0065	r 0072	4 0034	! 0021	. 002E	℞ 211E	č 0685
F 0046	S 0053	f 0066	s 0073	5 0035	" 0022	/ 002F	⅓ 2153	﮴ 06B4
G 0047	T 0054	g 0067	t 0074	6 0036	# 0023	£ 20A4	⅔ 2154	ﮪ 06AA
H 0048	U 0055	h 0068	u 0075	7 0037	$ 0024	Σ 2211	♕ 2655	α 03B1
I 0049	V 0056	i 0069	v 0076	8 0038	% 0025	∅ 2205	☂ 2602	β 03B2
J 004A	W 0057	j 006A	w 0077	9 0039	& 0026	√ 221A	❐ 2750	Δ 0394
K 004B	X 0058	k 006B	x 0078	[005B	' 0027	∞ 221E	☀ 2742	φ 03A6
L 004C	Y 0059	l 006C	y 0079	\ 005C	(0028	≤ 2264	● 27B2	Ω 03A9
M 004D	Z 005A	m 006D	z 007A	] 005D	) 0029	≥ 2265	♥ 2665	Ÿ 03AB

Ⓐ **FIGURE R-11**
Selected Unicode codes.

Ⓥ **FIGURE R-12**
Using Unicode.

Unicode

Since consistent worldwide representation of symbols is increasingly needed today, use of Unicode is growing rapidly. Unicode can be used to represent every written language, as well as a variety of other symbols. Unicode codes are typically listed in hexadecimal notation—a sampling of Unicode is shown in Figure R-11.

The capability to display characters and other symbols using Unicode coding is incorporated into many programs. For instance, when the Symbol dialog box is opened using the Insert menu in Microsoft Office Word, the Unicode representation (as well as the corresponding ASCII code in either decimal or hexadecimal representation) can be viewed (see Figure R-12). Some programs allow you to enter a Unicode symbol using its Unicode hexadecimal value. For instance, in Microsoft Office programs you can use the Alt+X command when the insertion point is just to the right of a Unicode hex value to convert that hex value into the corresponding symbol. For example, the keystrokes

2264Alt+X

result in the symbol corresponding to the Unicode code 2264 (the less than or equal sign ≤) being inserted into the document; entering 03A3 and then pressing Alt+X inserts the symbol shown in the Word screen in Figure R-12.

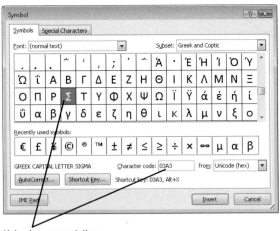

Unicode representation for Greek capital letter sigma Σ symbol.

UNICODE REPRESENTATION
The Symbol dialog box shown here lists the Unicode representation of each symbol as it is selected. If preferred, the ASCII representation can be displayed.

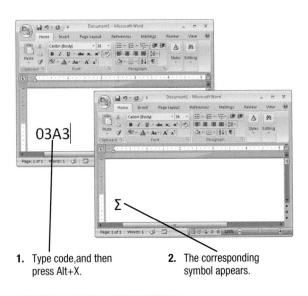

1. Type code, and then press Alt+X.

2. The corresponding symbol appears.

INSERTING SYMBOLS USING UNICODE
In Microsoft Office programs, typing the hexadecimal Unicode code for a symbol and then pressing Alt+X displays the corresponding symbol.

ANSWERS TO SELF-QUIZ

Chapter 1
1. T 2. F 3. F 4. F 5. T 6. Input 7. tablet 8. Virtualization 9. electronic mail or e-mail 10. a. 4 b. 2 c. 1 d. 3

Chapter 2
1. T 2. T 3. F 4. F 5. T 6. scanner, optical scanner, flatbed scanner, or portable scanner 7. quad-core 8. flash memory 9. folders 10. a. 2 b. 5 c. 1 d. 4 e. 3

Chapter 3
1. F 2. F 3. T 4. T 5. F 6. Digital Subscriber Line or DSL 7. keyword; directory 8. social networking site 9. online auction 10. a. 2 b. 4 c. 1 d. 3

Chapter 4
1. F 2. T 3. F 4. T 5. F 6. war driving 7. Biometric 8. virtual private network or VPN 9. digital signature 10. a. 3 b. 4 c. 1 d. 2

Chapter 5
1. F 2. T 3. T 4. F 5. F 6. disaster recovery 7. digital counterfeiting 8. filter 9. opt out; opt in 10. a. 3 b. 4 c. 1 d. 2

Chapter 6
1. F 2. T 3. F 4. T 5. T 6. copyright; trademark 7. plagiarism 8. Digital rights management (DRM) 9. Communications Decency 10. a. 2 b. 4 c. 1 d. 3

Chapter 7
1. F 2. T 3. T 4. F 5. F 6. ergonomics 7. burnout 8. digital divide 9. Internet addiction 10. Solar

Chapter 8
1. T 2. T 3. F 4. F 5. T 6. qubits 7. WiMAX 8. VeriChip 9. battlefield 10. nanotubes

CREDITS

Throughout the chapters: Screen shots of Microsoft Access®, Excel®, Paint®, PowerPoint®, Word®, and Windows® reprinted with permission from Microsoft Corporation. Copyright © Microsoft Explorer® reprinted with permission from Microsoft Corporation.

Chapter 1

Figure 1-1a, Photo courtesy of Nokia; **Figure 1-1b**, Courtesy Microsoft Corporation; **Figure 1-2a**, Courtesy Dell Inc.; **Figure 1-2b**, Courtesy Epson America; **Figure 1-2c**, Courtesy of Nintendo; **Figure 1-3a**, Courtesy Intel Corporation; **Figure 1-3b**, Courtesy General Dynamics Itronix; **Figure 1-3c**, Courtesy U.S. Army; **Figure 1-4a**, Courtesy of iStockphoto © Steve Cole; **Figure 1-4b**, Courtesy General Dynamics Itronix; **Figure 1-4c**, BlackBerry®, RIM®, Research In Motion®, SureType®, SurePress™ and related trademarks, names and logos are the property of Research In Motion Limited and are registered and/or used in the U.S. and countries around the world.; **Figure 1-4d**, Courtesy Ingersoll Rand Security Technologies; **You box,** Courtesy Abilene Christian University; **Figure 1-5a**, Courtesy Bluetooth SIG; **Figure 1-5b**, Courtesy 3M Touch Systems; **Figure 1-5c**, Courtesy MasterCard Worldwide; **Figure 1-5d**, Courtesy Ingersoll Rand Security Technologies; **Figure 1-7acde**, Courtesy IBM Corporate Archives; **Figure 1-7b**, Courtesy U.S. Army; **Figure 1-9a**, Courtesy of Gateway, Inc.; **Figure 1-9b**, Courtesy, Hewlett-Packard Company; **Figure 1-9c**, ©2009 Logitech. All rights reserved. Images/materials on page 13 used with permission from Logitech.; **Figure 1-9d**, Courtesy D-Link Systems, Inc.; **Figure 1-9e**, Courtesy Kingston Technology Company, Inc.; **Figure 1-11c**, Courtesy RedLobster.com; **Trend box a,** Courtesy of HTC; **Trend box b,** Courtesy Acer America Corporation; **Trend box c,** Courtesy Microsoft Corporation; **Trend box d,** Courtesy Dell Inc.; **Figure 1-12**, Courtesy Volvo Cars of North America; **Figure 1-13**, Courtesy of HTC; **Figure 1-14a**, Courtesy, Hewlett-Packard Company; **Figure 1-14b**, Courtesy Dell Inc.; **Inside box,** Courtesy of iStockphoto © Carsten Madsen; **Figure 1-15a**, Courtesy Belkin International, Inc.; **Figure 1-15b**, Courtesy Fujitsu America; **Figure 1-15c**, Courtesy MSI Computer Corporation; **Figure 1-15d**, Courtesy General Dynamics Itronix; **Figure 1-16a**, Photo by Dom Miguel Photography for Seaport; **Figure 1-16b**, Courtesy Chumby Industries. Chumby and the Chumby Logo are the registered trademarks of Chumby Industries, Inc.; **Figure 1-16c**, Courtesy of Nintendo; **Figure 1-17a**, Courtesy Ergotron Inc.; **Figure 1-17b**, Courtesy Dell Inc.; **Figure 1-18**, Courtesy of IBM; **Figure 1-19**, Courtesy of IBM; **Figure 1-20acd**, Courtesy of Gateway, Inc.; **Figure 1-20b**, Courtesy Dell Inc.; **Figure 1-20e**, Courtesy, Hewlett-Packard Company; **Figure 1-21a**, Image ©2009 by Kelty; **Figure 1-21b**, Google screenshot © Google Inc. and used with permission.; **Figure 1-21c**, Used by Permission of Clear Channel Radio.; **Figure 1-21e**, Courtesy Classmates.com; **Figure 1-21f,** Courtesy CastTV; **Figure 1-23a,** Courtesy of Gateway, Inc.; **How box**, Courtesy e2Campus by Omnilert, LLC; **Figure 1-25**, Courtesy of Stanford University; **Figure 1-26**, Google Chrome screenshot © Google Inc. and used with permission.; **Figure 1-27ac**, Courtesy of Gateway, Inc.; **Figure 1-27b**, Courtesy Dell Inc.; **Figure 1-28**, The Survivor: Tocantins Logo is a registered trademark of Survivor Productions, LLC. CSB.com website contents © CBS Broadcasting Inc. Used by permission. CBS and the CBS Eye are registered trademarks of CBS Broadcasting Inc.; **Figure 1-29**, Courtesy of Symantec Corp; **Figure 1-31**, Courtesy www.snopes.com; **Ask the Expert 2**, Courtesy Jack in the Box Inc.; **Ask the Expert 3**, Courtesy TabletKiosk; **Expert Insight**, Courtesy D-Link Systems, Inc.

Chapter 2

Figure 2-4, Courtesy HTC; **Figure 2-5**, ©2009 Logitech. All rights reserved. Images/materials on page 50 used with permission from Logitech; **Figure 2-6b**, Courtesy Kensington; **Figure 2-7a**, Courtesy Intermec Technologies; **Figure 2-7b**, Courtesy Motion Computing; **Figure 2-7c**, Courtesy Wacom Technology Corp.; **Figure 2-7d**, Courtesy of NCR Corporation; **Figure 2-8a**, Courtesy of Sony Electronics Inc.; **Figure 2-8b**, Courtesy Dell Inc; **Figure 2-8c**, SanDisk is a trademark of SanDisk Corporation, registered in the United States and other countries. Other brand names mentioned herein are for identification purposes only and may be the trademarks of their respective holder(s).; **Figure 2-8d**, ©Fujitsu Siemens Computers; **Figure 2-9a**, Courtesy, Hewlett-Packard Company; **Figure 2-9b**, Courtesy of Motorola; **Figure 2-9c**, Courtesy Intermec Technologies; **Figure 2-9d**, Courtesy of UPEK, Inc.; **Figure 2-10a**, Courtesy Canon USA; **Figure 2-10b**, Courtesy of Sony Electronics Inc.; **You box**, Courtesy of Mitek Systems; **Figure 2-12**, Courtesy Dell Inc.; **Inside box**, Courtesy of IBM; **Figure 2-13**, Courtesy of Intel Corporation; **Figure 2-14**, Courtesy Kingston Technology Company, Inc.; **Figure 2-15**, Photo courtesy of Nokia; **Figure 2-16a**, Courtesy Acer America Corporation; **Figure 2-18b**, Courtesy, Hewlett-Packard Company; **Figure 2-19**, Courtesy of Gateway, Inc.; **Figure 2-20a**, Courtesy of Hitachi Global Storage Technologies; **Figure 2-20b**, Courtesy Western Digital; **Figure 2-21**, SanDisk is a trademark of SanDisk Corporation, registered in the United States and other countries. Other brand names mentioned herein are for identification purposes only and may be the trademarks of their respective holder(s).; **Figure 2-22a**, Copyright © Iomega Corporation. All Rights Reserved. Iomega, the stylized "i" logo and all product images are property of Iomega Corporation in the United States and/or other countries.; **Figure 2-22b**, Courtesy Transcend Information USA; **Figure 2-24ab**, Courtesy Verbatim America LLC; **Figure 2-24c**, Courtesy CD Digital Card www.cddigitalcard.com; **Figure 2-25**, Copyright © Iomega Corporation. All Rights Reserved. Iomega, the stylized "i" logo and all product images are property of Iomega Corporation in the United States and/or other countries.; **Figure 2-26adfg**, SanDisk, the SanDisk logo, SanDisk Extreme and ImageMate are trademarks of SanDisk Corporation, registered in the United States and other countries. SD and SDHC are trademarks. SanDisk is an authorized licensee of the xD trademark. Other brand names mentioned herein are for identification purposes only and may be the trademarks of their respective holder(s).; **Figure 2-26b**, Courtesy Kingston Technology Company, Inc.; **Figure 2-26c**, Courtesy of Sony Electronics Inc.; **Figure 2-26e**, © 2009 Micron Technology, Inc. All Rights Reserved. Used with permission.; **Figure 2-27a**, © 2009 Micron Technology, Inc. All Rights Reserved. Used with permission.; **How box a**, Courtesy Kingston Technology Company, Inc.; **How box b**, Courtesy PortableApps.com; **Figure 2-29**, Photo by HID Global Corporation; **Figure 2-30aef**, Courtesy D-Link Systems, Inc.; **Figure 2-30bc**, Courtesy Belkin International, Inc.; **Figure 2-30d**, Courtesy Cricket Wireless; **Figure 2-31**, Courtesy of Symantec Corp.; **Trend box**, Courtesy Microsoft Corporation; **Ask the Expert 1**, Courtesy Kingston Technology Company, Inc.; **Ask the Expert 2**, Courtesy McDonald's Corporation; **Ask the Expert 3**, Courtesy of Tucows; **Expert Insight**, Courtesy Acer America Corporation.

Chapter 3

Figure 3-1a, Courtesy of Gateway, Inc.; **Figure 3-1b**, The Survivor: Tocantins Logo is a registered trademark of Survivor Productions, LLC. CSB.com website contents © CBS Broadcasting Inc. Used by permission. CBS and the CBS Eye are registered trademarks of CBS Broadcasting Inc.; **Figure 3-2a**, Use of the AT&T logo is granted under permission by AT&T Intellectual Property.; **Figure 3-2b**, Courtesy of Verizon Communications; **Figure 3-2c**, Courtesy Comcast; **Figure 3-2d**, Photo(s) courtesy of Hughes Network Systems, LLC; **Figure 3-2e**, Courtesy EarthLink, Inc.; **Figure 3-2f**, Courtesy Clearwire; **Figure 3-4**, Courtesy CinemaNow; **Inside box,** Courtesy U.S. Air Force; **Figure 3-5a**, Courtesy of Gateway, Inc.; **Figure 3-5b**, Courtesy of HTC; **Figure 3-5c**, Courtesy of Yahoo!; **Figure 3-8**, Courtesy Tranzeo Wireless USA; **Figure 3-9a**, Courtesy of iStockphoto © Sean Locke; **Figure 3-9b**, Courtesy Fujitsu America; **Figure 3-9c**, Courtesy Abilene Christian University; **Figure 3-11ab**, Google screenshot (c) Google Inc. and used with permission.; **Figure 3-13b**, Google screenshot (c) Google Inc. and used with permission.; **Figure 3-17**, Courtesy Microsoft Corporation; **Trend box,** Courtesy of Helio By Virgin Mobile USA; **Figure 3-18a**, Courtesy of Yahoo!; **Figure 3-18b**, Courtesy Microsoft Corporation; **Figure 3-19b**, Courtesy Vonage; **Figure 3-19c**, Courtesy D-Link Systems, Inc.; **Figure 3-20**, Courtesy of Intel Corporation; **Figure 3-21a**, Courtesy Facebook, Inc.; **Figure 3-21b**, Courtesy LinkedIn; **You box,** Courtesy Yoono; **Figure 3-24a**, Courtesy MobiTV; **Figure 3-24b**, Courtesy CastTV; **Figure 3-24c**, Courtesy Roku, Inc.; **Figure 3-25b**, MapQuest and the MapQuest logo are registered trademarks of MapQuest, Inc. Map content (c) 2009 by MapQuest, Inc. and its respective copyright holders. Used with permission.; **Figure 3-26**, iGoogle screenshot (c) Google Inc. and used with permission.; **How box a,** "Audacity" is a trademark of Dominic Mazzoni; **Figure 3-27**, Courtesy FactCheck.org; **Figure 3-29**, Courtesy Software Secure, Inc.; **Figure 3-30**, Courtesy of Zach Sunderland www.zacsunderland.com; **Ask the Expert 1**, Courtesy McDonald's Corporation; **Ask the Expert 2**, Courtesy Throw the Fight www.myspace.com/throwthefight, www.throwthefight.com.; **Ask the Expert 3**, Courtesy of IDPI. **Expert Insight**, Courtesy Microsoft, Inc.

Chapter 4

Figure 4-2, Courtesy JiWire, Inc.; **Figure 4-6a**, Courtesy ActivIdentity; **Figure 4-6b**, Joseph Mehling, Dartmouth College; **Figure 4-7a**, Courtesy Fujitsu America; **Figure 4-7b**, Courtesy Ingersoll Rand Security Technologies; **Figure 4-7c**, Courtesy L-1 Identity Solutions; **Figure 4-7d**, DoD photo by Staff Sgt. Jonathan C. Knauth, U.S. Marine Corps.; **How box**, Courtesy D-Link Systems, Inc.; **Figure 4-10**, Courtesy of Symantec; **Trend box**, Courtesy WiTopia and Viscosity; **Figure 4-13**, Courtesy Centennial Software Limited; **Figure 4-14ad**, Courtesy of Gateway, Inc.; **Figure 4-14bcf**, Courtesy Acer America Corporation; **Figure 4-14e**, Courtesy Kingston Technology Company, Inc.; **Figure 4-15**, Courtesy BleepingComputer.com; **Figure 4-16ac**, Courtesy, Hewlett-Packard Company; **Figure 4-16b**, Courtesy Dell Inc.; **Figure 4-17a,** Courtesy of Symantec; **Figure 4-17b**, Courtesy Lavasoft AB; **Inside box,** Google screenshot (c) Google Inc. and used with permission.; **You box,** Courtesy Mint.com; **Ask the Expert 1**, Courtesy ACM; **Ask the Expert 2**, Courtesy of Symantec; **Ask the Expert 3**, Courtesy of Symantec; **Expert Insight**, Courtesy of Symantec.

Chapter 5

Figure 5-1, Courtesy of Verizon Communications; **Figure 5-2**, Courtesy Kensington; **Trend box**, Courtesy TraceSecurity; **Figure 5-3**, Courtesy Kanguru Solutions; **How box**, Courtesy Absolute Software Corporation; **Figure 5-5a**, Courtesy of OtterBox; **Figure 5-5b**, Courtesy Targus, Inc.; **Figure 5-6a**, Courtesy General Dynamics Itronix; **Figure 5-6b**, Courtesy Trimble; **Figure 5-6c**, Courtesy of Motorola; **Figure 5-7ab**, Courtesy Kensington; **Figure 5-7cd**, Courtesy of APC by Schneider Electric; **Figure 5-8**, Courtesy General Dynamics Itronix; **Figure 5-10**, Photo courtesy of United States Secret Service; **Figure 5-11**, Courtesy Vi Labs; **Figure 5-12**, Photo courtesy of United States Secret Service; **Figure 5-13c**, © 2009 Idearc Media Corp. All Rights Reserved.; **Figure 5-16d**, Courtesy Chris Conrad; **Figure 5-17**, Gmail screenshot © Google Inc. and used with permission.; **Figure 5-18**, Courtesy Anonymizer, Inc.; **Figure 5-19b**, Google Chrome screenshot © Google Inc. and used with permission.; **Figure 5-21**, Courtesy Fellowes, Inc.; **Inside box**, Courtesy Turtle Wings, Inc. 301-583-8399; **Figure 5-22**, Courtesy SpectorSoft; **Figure 5-23a**, Courtesy of EPIC; **Figure 5-24**, Photo courtesy of Nokia; **Figure 5-25**, Photo by HID Global Corporation; **Figure 5-26**, Courtesy Agito Networks; **Figure 5-27**, Courtesy Omniquad Ltd. **Ask the Expert 1**, Courtesy Jack in the Box Inc.; **Ask the Expert 2**, Courtesy of DriveSavers, Inc. www.drivesavers.com; **Ask the Expert 3**, Courtesy of EPIC; **Expert Insight**, Courtesy eBay. The eBay logo is a trademark of eBay Inc.

Chapter 6

Figure 6-1b, Courtesy RedLobster.com; **Figure 6-2**, Courtesy of Digimarc; **Figure 6-3a**, Courtesy McDonald's Corporation; **Figure 6-3b**, Copyright © 1995-2009 RealNetworks, Inc. All rights reserved. RealNetworks, Real.com, RealAudio, RealVideo, RealSystem, RealPlayer, RealJukebox and RealMedia are trademarks or registered trademarks of RealNetworks, Inc.; **Figure 6-3c**, The eBay logo is a trademark of eBay Inc.; **Figure 6-3d**, Courtesy Eye-Fi; **Trend box,** Courtesy Eastman Kodak Company; **Figure 6-4**, Courtesy of United States Patent and Trademark Office; **You box**, Second Life is a trademark of Linden Research, Inc.; **Figure 6-6**, Courtesy of iParadigms, developers of Turnitin; **Figure 6-7**, eMusic and the eMusic logo are either registered trademarks or trademarks of eMusic.com Inc. in the USA or other countries. All rights reserved. (C) eMusic.com Inc.; **How box b,** Courtesy Belkin International, Inc.; **Figure 6-10**, Courtesy of University of Denver; **Figure 6-11**, Courtesy Hoax-Slayer; **Figure 6-12**, AP Images/Sepahnews.com; **Figure 6-14**, Imageinechina via AP Images; **Ask the Expert 1**, Courtesy Computer Ethics Institute; **Ask the Expert 2**, © 1995-2009 RealNetworks, Inc. All rights reserved. RealNetworks, Real.com, RealAudio, RealVideo, RealSystem, RealPlayer, RealJukebox and RealMedia are trademarks or registered trademarks of RealNetworks, Inc.; **Ask the Expert 3**, Courtesy WGBH Interactive; **Expert Insight a**, Courtesy ACM; **Expert Insight b**, image © Google Inc. and used with permission.

Chapter 7

Figure 7-1, Courtesy Aegis Mobility, Inc.; **Figure 7-3a**, Courtesy Kensington; **Figure 7-3b**, Courtesy of LapWorks Inc., the market leader in ergonomic and heat reducing laptop desks, stands, and accessories.; **Figure 7-5a**, Courtesy Kinesis Corporation; **Figure 7-5bcde**, Courtesy Kensington; **Figure 7-5fg**, Courtesy IMAK Products Corporation; **Figure 7-7a**, Courtesy of Motorola; **Figure 7-7b**, Courtesy General Dynamics Itronix; **Figure 7-7c**, Courtesy Intermec Technologies; **Figure 7-7d**, Courtesy of IBM; **Figure 7-8**, BlackBerry®, RIM®, Research In Motion®, SureType®, SurePress™ and related trademarks, names and logos are the property of Research In Motion Limited and are registered and/or used in the U.S. and countries around the world.; **You box**, Courtesy Cellfire; **Figure 7-10**, Courtesy of Dr. Kimberly Young, Director of the Center for Internet Addiction Recovery; **Figure 7-12**, Courtesy One Laptop per Child; **Figure 7-13a**, Courtesy Hooleon Corporation; **Figure 7-13b**, Courtesy Matias Corporation; **Figure 7-13c**, Courtesy of Prentke Romich; **How box**, Courtesy Yahoo! Inc.; **Figure 7-14ab**, Courtesy of Freedom Scientific, Inc.; **Figure 7-14c**, Courtesy Enabling Technologies; **Figure 7-14d**, Courtesy of NanoPac, Inc. www.nanopac.com; **Figure 7-15a**, Courtesy of U.S. Environmental Protection Agency; **Figure 7-15b**, Courtesy of European Commission, Environment Directorate-General; **Figure 7-15c**, Directorate-General Courtesy of Korea Environmental Labeling Association (KELA); **Figure 7-15d**, Courtesy of ABNT - ASSOCIAÇÃO BRASILEIRA DE NORMAS TÉCNICAS; **Figure 7-15e**, The Blue Angel is the Environmental Label for Germany; **Figure 7-16**, Courtesy P3 International; **Figure 7-17a**, Courtesy Voltaic Systems Inc.; **Figure 7-17b**, Courtesy ICP Solar Technologies Inc.; **Figure 7-17c**, Courtesy IST Designs, Inc.; **Trend box**, Courtesy Toshiba Corporation; **Inside box a**, Courtesy of Sony Electronics Inc.; **Inside box b**, Courtesy E Ink Corporation; **Figure 7-18**, © Basel Action Network 2006; **Figure 7-19**, Courtesy U.S. Marines; **Ask the Expert 1**, Courtesy AdMob; **Ask the Expert 3**, Courtesy SVTC; **Expert Insight**, Courtesy of Dell Inc.; the Dell logo is a trademark of Dell Inc.

Chapter 8

Figure 8-1a, Courtesy Microsoft Corporation; **Figure 8-1b**, Photo courtesy of Nokia; **Figure 8-1c**, Courtesy MasterCard Worldwide; **Trend box**, Courtesy GestureTek; **Figure 8-2**, Copyright IMEC; **Figure 8-3a**, Courtesy of IBM; **Figure 8-3b**, Courtesy of ABS Computer Technologies Inc. All rights reserved; **Figure 8-4a**, Courtesy Lumus Ltd.; **Figure 8-4b**, Courtesy Laser Magic Productions, Inc.; **Figure 8-4c**, Courtesy Microvision, Inc.; **Figure 8-5a**, Courtesy of Universal Display Corporation; **Figure 8-5b**, Courtesy of QUALCOMM MEMS Technologies, Inc.; **Figure 8-5c**, Courtesy ZINK Imaging; **Figure 8-6**, Courtesy CustomUSB.com; **Figure 8-7**, Courtesy InPhase Technologies; **You box**, Photo courtesy of Nokia; **Figure 8-8**, Courtesy BMC Cycling; **Figure 8-9**, Image reproduced by permission of IBM Research, Almaden Research Center. Unauthorized use not permitted.; **Figure 8-10**, Courtesy Cisco Systems, Inc.; **Figure 8-11**, Courtesy LiveViewGPS Inc. www.liveviewgps.com; **How box**, Google Docs screenshot (c) Google Inc. and used with permission.; **Figure 8-12**, Courtesy D-Link Systems, Inc.; **Inside box**, © 2009 Fulton Innovation LLC. All Rights Reserved. Used with Permission.; **Figure 8-14**, Courtesy Sprint Nextel; **Figure 8-15**, Courtesy D-Link Systems, Inc.; **Figure 8-16**, Courtesy of Dr. Hugh Loebner; **Figure 8-17**, Courtesy ChessBase.com; **Figure 8-18**, Courtesy Agentland.com; **Figure 8-19b**, © Fujitsu Siemens Computers; **Figure 8-20**, Courtesy Bundesdruckerei GmbH; **Figure 8-21a**, Photo courtesy of KUKA Robotics Corporation; **Figure 8-21b**, Courtesy InTouch Health, Inc.; **Figure 8-21c**, Courtesy Wowwee Robotics™ RS Media™; **Figure 8-21d**, Courtesy of iRobot; **Figure 8-22**, Courtesy Intel Corporation; **Figure 8-23**, Courtesy PositiveID Corporation; **Figure 8-24ab**, Courtesy InTouch Health, Inc.; **Figure 8-24c**, Courtesy, University of Rochester; **Figure 8-24d**, Photo made available by St. Joseph's Healthcare Hamilton; **Figure 8-25a**, Courtesy of iRobot; **Figure 8-25b**, Courtesy of Lockheed Martin; **Ask the Expert 1**, Photo courtesy of TabletKiosk; **Ask the Expert 2**, Courtesy of Seagate Technology LLC; **Ask the Expert 3**, Courtesy of Google Inc.

References and Resources Guide

Computer History Timeline: 1, 2, 5, 6, 9, 11, 15, Courtesy of IBM Archives; **3,** Courtesy Iowa State University; **4,** Courtesy Jim Bready; **7,** Courtesy Unisys Corporation; **8,** Courtesy U.S. Navy; **10,** Courtesy of Bootstrap Institute/Alliance; **12, 21, 25, 31,** Courtesy of Intel Corporation; **13, 35,** Courtesy Microsoft Corporation; **14,** Courtesy of Dan Bricklin. (c) www.jimraycroft.com 1982; **16,** Courtesy Cray Inc.; **18, 34,** Courtesy, Hewlett-Packard Company; **19,** Fabian Bachrach, courtesy W3C; **20,** Courtesy Larry Ewing lewing@isc.tamu.edu and The GIMP; **22,** Courtesy NCSA/University of Illinois; **23,** Courtesy of Panasonic; **24,** Image courtesy of Palm, Inc. Palm, Treo, Zire, Tungsten, logos, stylizations, and design marks associated with all the preceding, and trade dress associated with Palm, Inc.'s products, are among the trademarks or registered trademarks owned by or licensed to Palm. Inc.; **26, 32, 42, 45,** Microsoft, Windows and the Windows logo are either registered trademarks or trademarks of Microsoft Corporation in the United States and/or other countries.; **27,** Courtesy Microsoft Museum; **28,** The eBay logo is a trademark of eBay Inc.; **29,** Java and the Java Coffee Cup logo are trademarks or registered trademarks of Sun Microsystems, Inc.; **30,** Courtesy Kingston Technology Company Inc.; **33,** (C) 2003, 2005, 2006 2007 Advanced Micro Devices, Inc., Reprinted with permission. AMD, the AMD Arrow logo, AMD Opteron, AMD Turion and combinations thereof as well as certain other marks listed at http://www.amd.com/legal/trademarks.html are trademarks of Advanced Micro Devices, Inc.; **36,** Photo courtesy of Nokia. Copyright © 2007 Nokia. All rights reserved. Nokia and Nokia Connecting People are registered trademarks of Nokia Corporation. **37,** Courtesy Nintendo; **38,** Courtesy Dell Inc.; **39,** Courtesy Facebook, Inc.; **40, 43.** Google image (c) Google Inc. and used with permission.; **41,** Courtesy Belkin International, Inc.; **44,** Courtesy T-Mobile USA; **R-1a,** Courtesy Dell Inc.; **R-1b,** Courtesy Belkin International, Inc.; **R-1c,** Courtesy MSI Computer Corporation; **R-1d,** Courtesy General Dynamics Itronix.

@ (at sign), 29, 30
/ (forward slash)), 30
$ (dollar sign), 48
. (period), 30, 48
802.11. *See* Wi-Fi (802.11)

A

abacus, 10, R-2
access control systems, 147–149
    biometric, 150–151
    possessed knowledge, 148–149
    possessed object, 149–150
Acer Pan America, 90–91
acronyms, use of, 36
ACU (Abilene Christian University), 7
AdMob, 268
adware, 132–133
Agnihotry, Sumit, 90–91
AI. *See* artificial intelligence (AI)
all-in-one cases, 19
Amazon
    EC2 (Elastic Compute Cloud), 17
    intellectual property rights and, 238
    Kindle, 283
American Standard Code for Information
    Interchange. *See* ASCII (American
    Standard Code for Information
    Interchange)
anonymity, 37
antiglare screens, 268
antiphishing tools, 174–175
antispyware software, 221
antitheft tools, 193–195
antivirus software Software used to
    detect and eliminate computer
    viruses and other types of malware.
    See also viruses
    described, **165**
    overview, 35, 165–166
Apple Macintosh, 12
application service provider (ASP)
    A company that manages and
    distributes software-based services
    over the Internet. **97**
application software Programs that
    enable users to perform specific
    tasks on a computer, such as writing

letters or playing games. **15**, 16. *See
    also* specific *application software*
ARPANET The predecessor of the
    Internet, named after the Advanced
    Research Projects Agency (ARPA),
    which sponsored its development.
    93, **94**
artificial intelligence (AI) When a
    computer performs actions that are
    characteristic of human intelligence.
    12, **313**. 314–318
**ASCII (American Standard Code
    for Information Interchange)** A
    fixed-length, binary coding system
    used to represent text-based data
    for computer processing on many
    types of computers. **48**, 49, R-11,
    R-15–R-16
ASP. *See* application service provider
    (ASP)
assistive technology Hardware and
    software specifically designed for
    use by individuals with physical
    disabilities. **277**, 278–279
at sign (@), 29, 30
AT&T (American Telephone &
    Telegraph), 98, 104
ATMs (automatic teller machines). *See*
    automatic teller machines (ATMs)
Audacity, 124
augmented reality When computer
    generated images are overlayed on
    top of real-time images, such as to
    overlay information over the photo
    or video displayed on a mobile
    phone. 297
authentication, 6, 8
    cognitive, 148–149
    e-mail and, 166
automatic teller machines (ATMs), 7,
    148, 150

B

backups, 199–200
Baker, Paul, 10
bandwidth limits, 100, 101
banking, 56, 169–171

barcode A machine-readable code that
    represents data as a set of bars. **54**
barcode printers, 64
barcode reader An input device that
    reads barcodes. 9, 53, **54**
Barquin, Ramon C., 238
battlefield robot A robot used by the
    military to ensure that locations are
    safe prior to sending in soldiers.
    320, 321
Baustert, Ryan, 115
BD. *See* Blu-ray Disc (BD)
BD-R disc, 71
BD-RE disc, 72
BD-ROM disc, 71
Bell Labs, R-4
Berners-Lee, Tim, 94, R-5
binary numbering system The
    numbering system that represents all
    numbers using just two symbols
    (0 and 1). **48**, R-11, R–12-R–13
biometric access system An access
    control system that uses one
    unique physical characteristic of an
    individual (such as a fingerprint,
    face, or voice) to authenticate that
    individual. 74, **150**, 151
biometric reader A device used to
    input biometric data, such as an
    individual's fingerprint or voice. 53,
    55, 149
BIOS (basic input/output system), 61
bit The smallest unit of data a digital
    computer can recognize; represented
    by a 0 or a 1.
    described, **48**
    overview, 47–48
Blackberry, 20
Blackboard, 126
blade servers, 23
blade workstations, 23
blades, 23
blog A Web page that contains short,
    frequently updated entries in
    chronological order, typically by just
    one individual.
    described, **127**
    overview, 127–128

Blu-ray Disc (BD) A high-capacity (typically 25 MB or 50 MB) that is often used to deliver high-definition movies, as well as to store user data. **70**, 244

Bluetooth, 163, 312

BoF. *See* broadband over fiber (BoF) Internet access

bookmarks, 32

Boolean operators, 109

boot To start up a computer. **14**

bot A computer that is controlled by a hacker or other computer criminal. **160**

botnet A group of bots that are controlled by one individual. **160**

Braille display, 279

Braille keyboard, 277

Braille printer, 279

broadband connections, 78, 101. *See also* broadband over fiber (BoF) Internet access; broadband-enabled TVs

broadband over fiber (BoF) Very fast, direct Internet access via fiber-optic networks; also referred to as fiber-to-the-premises (FTTP) Internet access. 102, **104**

broadband-enabled TVs, 101, 121

Brown, Michelle, 169

browser. *See* Web browser

burnout A state of fatigue or frustration usually brought on by overwork. **271**, 272

business ethics Standards of moral conduct that guide a business's policies, decisions, and actions.

business partners, 238, **240**, 246, 249

business practices, 249–252

byte A group of 8 bits. **48**

C

cable Internet access Fast, direct Internet access via cable TV lines. 102, **103**

cable locks, 191

cache memory, 60, 61

campus emergency notification systems, 30

carbon nanotubes Tiny, hollow tubes made of carbon atoms. **304**, 305

carpal tunnel syndrome (CTS) A painful and crippling condition affecting the hands and wrist that can be caused by computer use. **264**, 268

CAs (Certificate Authorities). *See* Certificate Authorities

CD disc A low capacity (typically 650 MB) optical disc that is often used to deliver music and software, as well as to store user data. **70**, 71

CD-R disc, 71

CD-ROM disc, 71

CD-RW disc, 72

censorship, 128–130

central processing unit (CPU) The chip located on the motherboard of a computer that performs the processing for a computer. Also called the processor.

described, **58**

emerging technologies for, 298–300

location of, inside the system unit, 57

memory and, 60–61

overview, 12–13, 58–60

speed of, R-1–10

supercomputing clusters and, 25

Certificate Authorities, 155, 175

cheating, 246–247

chief privacy officer (CPO), 213–214

children, safety tips for, 178–179

Christopher, John, 199

Chrome (Google), 31–32, 106, 132, 308. *See also* Web browser

Chumby device, 22–23

circuit board, 57

citations, 111

C-level attacks, 190

click fraud, 249

clock speed, 59–60

cloud operating system, 308

cloud storage. *See* online storage

code of conduct A policy, often for a school or business, that specifies allowable use of resources, such as computers and other equipment. **245**

code of ethics A policy, often for an organization or industry, that specifies overall moral guidelines adopted by that organization or industry. **245**

coding systems, overview of, 48–49

.com filename extension, 35

communications The transmission of data from one device to another. *See also* communications device

described, **9**

interception of, 147

online, differences in, 36–37

port addresses, 153–154

communications device A piece of hardware that allows one device to communicate with other devices via a network or the Internet.

described, 77

overview, 14, 78

computer A programmable, electronic device that accepts data input, performs processing operations on that data, and outputs and stores the results.

arithmetic, R-13

described, **8**

disposal of, 281–285

future of, 295–307

generations of, 10–12, R-2–R-4

guide to buying, R-8

history of, 4, 10–12, R-2–R-7

in the home, 5

overview, 8–17

professionals, 16

reasons to learn about, 3–4

tracking software, 193–195

computer chips, 12. *See also* central processing unit (CPU)

computer crime Any illegal act involving a computer. **143**

computer ethics Standards of moral conduct as they relate to computer use. **238**, 239–253

computer hoax An inaccurate statement or story spread through the use of computers. **247**

computer literacy The knowledge and understanding of basic computer fundamentals. **4**

computer monitoring software Software that can be used to record an individual's computer usage, such as capturing images of the screen, recording the actual keystrokes used, or creating a summary of Web sites and programs accessed. 214, **215**, 216–217

computer network A collection of computers and other hardware devices that are connected together to share hardware, software, and data, as well as to communicate electronically with one another. *See also* Internet; wireless networks; World Wide Web

accessing, 27

components of, 26

described, **25**

emerging technologies for, 307–313

legislation, 179

overview, 25–32

security overview for, 148–187

computer sabotage An act of malicious destruction to a computer or computer resource.

described, **160**
overview, 160–166
protecting against, 165–166
computer tracking software, 193–195
computer virus A software program
installed without the user's knowledge
and designed to alter the way a
computer operates or to cause harm to
the computer system. 142, 160
definitions for, 165
described, **161**
overview, 35
computer vision syndrome, 264, 269
computer worm A malicious program
designed to spread rapidly to a large
number of computers by sending
copies of itself to other computers. **162**
computing generation, 5
Coney, Lillie, 204
Constitution (United States), 129
consumer kiosks, 7–8
continuous data protection (CDP), 199
conventional dial-up Internet access
Dial-up Internet access via standard
telephone lines. 78, 102, **103**
convergence, 4, 5
cookie A small file stored on a user's hard
drive by a Web server; commonly
used to identify personal preferences
and settings for that user. 204, **131**,
132, 213
copyright The legal right to sell, publish,
or distribute an original artistic
or literary work; it is held by the
creator of a work as soon as it exists
in physical form. 233, 252. *See also*
intellectual property rights
described, **234**
ethical use of material covered by,
240–247
CPU. *See* central processing unit (CPU)
CRT monitor, 62
CTS. *See* carpal tunnel syndrome (CTS)
cultural considerations, 251
cyberbullying Children or teenagers
bullying other children or teenagers
via the Internet. **177**, 178–179
cybersquatting The act of registering
a domain name with the intent
to profit from the goodwill of a
trademark belonging to someone
else. **236–237**
cyberstalking Repeated threats or
harassing behavior between adults
carried out via e-mail or another
Internet communications method.
177, 178
cyberterrorism, 145. *See also* terrorism

D

data Raw, unorganized facts.
alteration, 164
centers, 24
described, **9**
destruction, 214, 215
information versus, 9–10
-leakage prevention, 159
projectors, 62
representation, 47–49
theft, 167–168, 173
databases, 205–208
Davis, Collin, 186–187
Dead on Demand technology, 194
decimal numbering system The
numbering system that represents
all numbers using 10 symbols. 48,
R-11, R–12–R–13
decision making, 249–252
Dell Computer, 292–293
denial of service (DoS) attack An act
of sabotage that attempts to flood a
network server or a Web server with
so much activity that it is unable to
function. **163**, 164, 166
DeQuervain's tendonitis A condition in
which the tendons on the thumb
side of the wrist are swollen and
irritated. **264**
desktop computer A personal computer
designed to fit on or next to a desk.
See also computer
cable locks for, 191
described, **19**
overview, 17, 19–20
dial-up connection A type of Internet
connection in which the computer
or other device must dial up and
connect to a service provider's
computer via telephone lines before
being connected to the Internet. 101,
102, 103
dialog boxes
opening, 82
overview, 15
digital camera An input device that takes
pictures and records them as digital
images.
described, **55**
overview, 55–56
digital cash, 76
digital certificate A group of electronic
data that can be used to verify the
identity of a person or organization;
includes a key pair that can be used
for encryption and digital signatures.
175, 176

digital counterfeiting The use of
computers or other types of digital
equipment to make illegal copies of
currency, checks, collectibles, and
other items. 200, **201**, 202–203
digital divide The gap between those who
have access to technology and those
who do not. **274**, 275–276
digital forms, 52
digital manipulation The alteration
of digital content, usually text or
photographs. **248**, 249
digital photos, 5, 62, 248, 249
**digital rights management (DRM)
software** Software used to protect
and manage the rights of creators of
digital content, such as art, music,
photographs, and movies. **235**, 241,
243. *See also* intellectual property
rights
digital signage systems, 62
digital signature A unique digital code
that can be attached to a file or an
e-mail message to verify the identity
of the sender and guarantee the file
or message has not been changed
since it was signed. 175, **176**
Digital Subscriber Line. *See* DSL (Digital
Subscriber Line) Internet access
digital video recorders (DVRs), 5, 55–56,
242–243
digital watermark A subtle alteration
of digital content that is not
noticeable when the work is
viewed or played, but that
identifies the copyright holder. 203,
234, 235
direct connection A type of Internet
connection in which the computer
or other device is connected to the
Internet continually. 27, 101, **102**
directory search A type of Internet
search in which categories are
selected to locate information on the
Internet. **107**, 108
disabled individuals. *See* assistive
technology
disaster recovery plan A written plan
that describes the steps a company
will take following the occurrence of
a disaster. **199–200**
display device An output device that
contains a viewing screen.
described, **62**
overview, 62–63
display screen A display device built
into a notebook computer, netbook,
UMPC, or other device. **62**

distance learning A learning environment in which the student is physically located away from the instructor and other students; commonly, instruction and communications take place via the Web. 5–6, **126**

D-Link, 44–45

docking station A device designed to easily connect a portable computer to conventional hardware, such as a keyboard, mouse, monitor, and printer. 22, **266**, 267

document(s)
  editing, **82**
  formatting, **83**
  holders, 267, 268

dollar sign ($), 48

domain name A text-based Internet address used to uniquely identify a computer on the Internet.
  described, **28**
  top-level (TLDs), 28

domain name system (DNS) servers, 28

door locks, 191

DoS. *See* denial of service (DoS) attack

dot con A fraud or scam carried out through the Internet.
  described, **166–167**
  protecting against, 173–177

dots per inch (dpi), 54, 63

drive-by pharming, 171

DriveSavers, 199

DRM. *See* digital rights management (DRM) software

DSL (Digital Subscriber Line) Internet access Fast, direct Internet access via standard telephone lines. **103**

dual-core CPU A CPU that contains two separate processing cores. **59**

dual-mode mobile phones, 5

dumb terminals, 22

DVD disc A medium capacity (typically 4.7 MB or 8.5 MB) optical disc that is often used to deliver software and movies, as well as to store user data. 242–244
  described, **70**
  types of, 71

DVD-R discs, 71

DVD+R discs, 71

DVD-ROM discs, 71

DVD-RW discs, 72

DVD+RW discs, 72

E

e2Campus, 30

earbuds, 65

earphones, 65

eBay, 230–231. *See also* online auction

EBCDIC, 49, R-15–R-16

e-book readers, 62, 283

eco-label A certification, usually by a government agency, that identifies a device as meeting minimal environmental performance specifications. **280**

e-commerce
  overview, 118–119
  self-checkout systems, 8
  shopping carts, 118

editing Changing the content of a document, such as inserting or deleting words. **82**

E Ink Corporation, 283

elections, 11, 125

electronic circuits, 11

electronic mail (e-mail) Electronic messages sent from one user to another over the Internet or other network. *See also* e-mail address; e-mail filter
  described, **32**
  disaster recovery plans and, 200
  offline, 33
  overview, 32–33
  privacy, 133
  security and, 155–156, 166, 169–177, 209–210
  software, 15–16, 33

Electronic Privacy Information Center (EPIC), 204, 217

electronic profiling Using electronic means to collect a variety of in-depth information about an individual, such as name, address, income, and buying habits. 205, **207**, 208

electronic surveillance, 214–222

e-mail. *See* electronic mail (e-mail); e-mail address; e-mail filter

e-mail address An Internet address consisting of a username and computer domain name that uniquely identifies a person on the Internet.
  described, **29**
  throw-away, **209**, 210

e-mail filter A tool that automatically sorts your incoming e-mail messages based on specific criteria. **211**, 212

embedded computer A tiny computer embedded in a product and designed to perform specific tasks or functions for that product. 17, **18**

emoticons, 36

emotional health, 269. *See also* health

employee monitoring Observing or reviewing employees' actions while they are on the job. **219**, 220, 251

employee policy, 222

encryption A method of scrambling the contents of an e-mail message or a file to make it unreadable if an unauthorized user intercepts it.
  described, **154**
  e-mail and, 133
  hard drives and, 67, 192–193
  overview, 152, 154–156
  wireless networks and, 151–152

end user(s)
  cloud computing and, 17
  overview, 16

end-user license agreement (EULA), 201

energy consumption, 279, 280–281, 285

ENERGY STAR A program developed by the U.S. Department of Energy and the Environmental Protection Agency to encourage the development of energy-saving devices. **279**, 280

ENIAC, 11

enterprise rights-management software, 159

environmental concerns, 279–285

e-paper, 283

e-portfolio A collection of an individual's work accessible via the Web. 119, **128**

equipment locks, 191

ergonomic hardware Hardware, typically an input or output device, that is designed to be more ergonomically correct than its non-ergonomic counterpart. **267**, 268–270

ergonomics The science of fitting a work environment to the people who work there. 22, **265**, 266–267

escrow services, 177

Ethernet, 78, 308–309

ethics Overall standards of moral conduct.
  business practices and, 249–252
  copyrights and, 240–247
  cultural considerations and, 251–252
  described, **238**
  information use and, 243–244
  legislation, 253
  overview, 232
  questionable products/services and, 250–251
  using resources and, 243–245

e-trash Electronic trash or waste, such as discarded computer components. **282**, 284

evil twin, 158
.exe filename extension, 35
exoskeleton suit A wearable robotic system designed to give an individual additional physical capabilities and protection. **321**
expert system A computer system that provides the type of advice that would be expected from a human expert. **315**, 316
Explorer (Windows), 83
ExpressCard hard drives, 69
ExpressCard modules, 58

F

Facebook, 8, 32, 36, 116–117. *See also* social networking site
  online storage and, 75
  privacy issues and, 205
  security and, 177
FactCheck.org, 125
Favorites feature, 31, 32
FDE. *See* full disk encryption (FDE)
Feldman, Stuart, 260–261
fiber-to-the-premises (FTTP) Internet access. *See* broadband over fiber (BoF) Internet access
file Something stored on a storage medium, such as a program, a document, or an image.
  described, **83**
  management, 83
  working with, 83
filename A name given to a file by the user; it is used to retrieve the file at a later time.
  described, **83**
  extensions, 35
fingerprint recognition, 67, 150, 151
Firefox (Mozilla), 31–32. *See also* Web browser
firewall A collection of hardware and/or software intended to protect a computer or computer network from unauthorized access. 103, **152**, 153–154
Fitzgerald, Cantor, 200
fixed wireless Internet access Fast, direct Internet access available in some areas via the airwaves. 102, **103–104**
flash memory. Nonvolatile memory chips that can be used for storage by the computer or user; can be built into a computer or a storage medium. 61, 66. *See also* flash memory card

described, **72**
development of, 12
overview, 72–74
flash memory card A small, rectangular flash memory medium, such as a CompactFlash (CF) or Secure Digital (SD) card; often used with digital cameras and other portable devices. *See also* flash memory
described, **72**
overview, 13, 72–74
flat-panel display. *See also* monitor
  overview, 62
  technologies, 301–302
Flickr, 75, 117
floppy drives, 66
folder A named place on a storage medium into which files can be stored to keep the files stored on that medium organized.
  described, **83**
  working with, 83
fonts, 83
foreign languages, 49, 313
formatting Changing the appearance of a document, such as changing the margins or font size. **83**
forward slash (/), 30
fraudulent reporting, 249–250
FTP (File Transfer Protocol), 29
FTTP. *See* broadband over fiber (BoF) Internet access
full disk encryption (FDE) A technology that encrypts everything stored on a storage medium automatically, without any user interaction. **193**

G

gadgets, 121
gaming devices, 5, 19, 22–23
  display devices and, 62
  input devices for, 52
  Internet access via, 101
GB. *See* gigabyte (GB)
geobrowsing, 113
Germany, Julie Barko, 125
gesture input, 296, 297
gigabyte (GB) Approximately 1 billion bytes. **48**
global positioning system (GPS), 8, 52, 113, 163, 221, 297, 307, 308
Gmail (Google), 33, 209
Google, 32–33, 260–261
  Docs, 75
  Gmail, 33, 209
  Maps, 20, 203
  security and, 167, 205–206

Site Search, 107
translation features, 313
government database A collection of data about people that is collected and maintained by the government. 205, **206**
Graef, Ailin, 239
graphics tablet, 52
green computing The use of computers in an environmentally friendly manner. **279**, 280–281
grid computing, 17
Griffith, Jim, 230–231
GUI (graphical user interface), 95

H

hacking Using a computer to break into another computer system. 16, 144–145, 164
  described, **144**
  keystroke logging and, 216
handheld computer. *See* ultra-mobile PC (UMPC)
handwriting recognition, 52
hard drive The primary storage system for most computers; used to store most programs and data used with a computer.
  described, **66**
  development of, 11
  emerging technologies for, 302
  external, 66–67, 69
  internal, 66–67, 69
  overview, 66–67
  self-encrypting, 192, **193**
hardware The physical parts of a computer system, such as the keyboard, monitor, printer, and so forth. *See also* hardware theft; *specific devices*
  damage, 189–200
  described, **12**
  disposal, 214, 281–285
  emerging, 296–304
  input, 49–56
  loss, 189–200, 238
  output, 62–65
  overview, 12–14, 57–61
  processing, 57–61
  proper care of, 195–198
  storage, 65–77
hardware theft The theft of computer hardware. **190**
headphones, 65, 264
headsets, 56, 65
health. *See also* ergonomics
  emotional, 269

issues overview, 263–273
legislation, 285
technological advances and, 318–320
hexadecimal numbering system, R–11, R–12-R–13
History list, 32
Hollerith, Herman, 10, 11
holographic projectors, 300
holographic storage An emerging type of storage technology that uses multiple blue laser beams to store data in three dimensions. **303**, 304
home pages, 30, 31
hotspot. *See* Wi-Fi hotspot
.htm filename extension, 29
HTML (HyperText Markup Language), 15
HTTP (HyperText Transfer Protocol), 29
hybrid hard drive A hard drive that contains both a large amount of flash memory and magnetic hard disks. **68**
hyperlinks, using, 31–32

I

IBM (International Business Machines), 59, 306, 314
history of, 10, 12, 19–20, R-2, R-3, R-4
mainframes, 11, 24
malware and, 163
servers, 24
supercomputers, 25
Watson system, 59
icons, overview of, 14–15
identity theft Using someone else's identity to purchase goods or services, obtain new credit cards or bank loans, or otherwise illegally masquerade as that individual. 35, 158, 167
described, **168**
protecting against, 173–174
IM. *See* instant messaging (IM)
income taxes, 239
information Data that has been processed into a meaningful form.
data versus, 9–10
described, **9**
ethical use of, 243–247
falsifying, 246–247
integrity, 37
overload, 270–271
personal, protecting, 209–215
processing cycle, 9
theft, 167–168, 173
information privacy The rights of individuals and companies to control how information about them is

collected and used. **204**. *See also* privacy
infrastructure companies, 97
ink-jet printer An output device that sprays droplets of ink to produce images on paper. **64**
input The process of entering data into a computer; can also refer to the data itself. *See also* input hardware
described, **8**
hardware, 49–56
overview, 8–9
input device A piece of hardware that supplies input to a computer. *See also* input
described, **49**
emerging, 296–208
overview, 12–13
installed software Software that must be installed on a computer in order to be used. **80**
instant messaging (IM) A way of exchanging real-time typed messages with other individuals.
described, **112**
netiquette and, 36
security and, 170
spam and, 208
Institute for Politics, Democracy, & the Internet, 125
integrated circuits (ICs), 11
integrated projectors, 300
intellectual property rights The legal rights to which creators of original creative works (such as artistic or literary works, inventions, corporate logos, and more) are entitled. *See also* copyrights; digital rights management (DRM) software; patents; trademarks
described, **233**
legislation, 253
overview, 232–238
intelligent agent A program that performs specific tasks to help make a user's work environment more efficient or entertaining and that typically modifies its behavior based on the user's actions. 314, 315
internet, use of the term, 94
Internet The largest and most well-known computer network, linking millions of computers all over the world.
accessing, 27, 98–99
backbone, 95
citing resources from, 111
community today, 96
connection types, 101–102

control of, 99
described, **25**
evolution of, 93–99
getting set up to use, 99–106
legislation, 179
myths about, 98–99
overview, 25–27, 92–141
searching, 106–111
security overview for, 148–187
World Wide Web and, distinction between, 99
Internet addiction The problem of overusing, or being unable to stop using, the Internet. 121, **272**, 273
Internet address An address that identifies a computer, person, or Web page on the Internet, such as an IP address, domain name, or e-mail address. **30**, 31
pronouncing, 30–31
Internet appliance A specialized network computer designed primarily for Internet access and/or e-mail exchange. **22**
Internet content provider A person or an organization that provides Internet content. **96**
Internet Explorer browser (Microsoft). *See also* Web browser
cookies and, 131–132
Internet searches with, 106
RSS and, 123
using, 31–32
Internet filtering Using a software program or browser option to block access to particular Web pages or types of Web pages. **129**, 130
Internet service provider (ISP) A business or other organization that provides Internet access to others, typically for a fee.
bandwidth limits and, 100, 101
connection types and, 102
described, **25**
ethics and, 245
fees, 99
home pages, 31
mail servers, 33
overview, 96
privacy and, 133
security and, 147, 166, 209
selecting, 105–106
VoIP and, 114
Internet2, 95–96
IP address A numeric Internet address used to uniquely identify a computer on the Internet.
described, **28**

ethics and, 245
security and, 171, 203, 217, 194
iPhone (Apple), 7, 244
iPod (Apple), 7, 19, 163, 244
ISP. *See* Internet service provider (ISP)

J

Java applets, 119
Jensen, Debra, 20
Jeopardy! television show, 58, 59

K

Kaspersky Lab, 167
KB. *See* kilobyte (KB)
keyboard An input device containing
numerous keys that can be used to
input letters, numbers, and other
symbols.
assistive technology systems, 277–279
described, **49**
ergonomics and, 266–268
introduction of, 11
shortcuts, 81–82
keyword A word typed in a search box
on a search site or other Web page
to locate information related to that
keyword.
described, **107**
Internet filtering and, 129
using appropriate, 109–110
keyword search A type of Internet search
in which keywords are typed in a
search box to locate information on
the Internet. 32, **107**, 109–110
kilobyte (KB) Approximately 1 thousand
bytes (1,024 bytes to be precise). **48**
Kingston Technology, 61
Kodak, 236

L

laptop computer. *See* notebook computer
laser printer An output device that uses
toner powder and technology similar
to that of a photocopier to produce
images on paper. **63**, 64
Lawrence Livermore National Laboratory,
25
learning management systems, 126
LinkedIn, 116
Linux, 14
locks
door, 191
equipment, 191–192
Loebner, Hugh, 313
Los Alamos National Lab, 25

M

Macintosh (Apple)
operating system, 14, 20
overview, 19–20
magnetic hard drive A hard drive
consisting of one or more metal
magnetic disks permanently sealed,
with an access mechanism and
read/write heads, inside its drive.
67, 68
magnetic tape, 11
mail servers, 29, 33
mainframe computer A computer
used in large organizations (such
as hospitals, large businesses, and
colleges) that need to manage large
amounts of centralized data and run
multiple programs simultaneously.
described, **24**
IBM, 11, 24
overview, 18
virtualization and, 23
malware Any type of malicious software.
See also computer virus
described, **160**
mobile devices and, 163
new tools to fight, 167
overview, 35, 160–163
marketing database A collection of data
about people that is stored in a large
database and used for marketing
purposes. **205**, 206–208
markup languages, 15
MB. *See* megabyte (MB)
McAfee, 167
McDonald's Corporation, 77, 95
mechanical calculator, 10
medicine. *See* health
megabyte (MB) Approximately 1 million
bytes. **48**
Melfi, Joe, 44–45
memory. *See also* random access memory
(RAM)
adding more, 61
cache, 60, 61
described, **60**
modules, 57, 60
overview, 60–61
read-only (ROM), 60, 61
menu(s)
bar, 15, 81–82
overview, 81–82
Merritt, Marian, 160, 169
message board A Web page that enables
individuals to post messages on
a particular topic for others to
read and respond to; also called a
discussion group or online forum.
37, **114**

microcomputer. *See also* personal
computer (PC)
described, **19**
history of, 4
microphones, 56
microprocessor A central processing unit
(CPU) for a personal computer. 12,
58. *See also* central processing unit
(CPU)
Microsoft Corporation, 140–141
Microsoft Internet Explorer browser. *See
also* Web browser
cookies and, 131–132
Internet searches with, 106
RSS and, 123
using, 31–32
Microsoft Office, 19, 80
anti-piracy tools and, 202
common commands, 81–83
online testing and, 127
Picture Manager, 54
security and, 155
version 2010, 81
Microsoft Outlook, 33, 198, 213, 271
Microsoft SkyDrive, 75, 76, 81
Microsoft Windows. *See also* Windows
desktop
memory and, 61
overview, 14
midrange server A medium-sized
computer used to host programs and
data for a small network. 18, **23**, 24
military research, 11, 17, 317, 320–321
Mint.com, 175
Mitek Systems, 56
m-learning (mobile learning), 7
mobile coupons, 272
mobile device A very small
communications device that has
built-in computing or Internet
capability. *See also* mobile phones
assistive technology systems, 278
cases for, 195–196
described, **18**
overview, 18–19
security and, 163, 194–195
mobile phones. *See also* mobile device
banking and, 56
hands-free devices for, 264–265
health risks related to, 264–265
Internet access via, 100–101
security and, 163
use of, on the job, 20
mobile WiMAX A version of WiMAX
designed to be used with mobile
phones. **310**
mobile wireless Internet access Internet
access via a mobile phone network.
102, **104**

modem A device that enables a computer to communicate over telephone lines.
cable, 103
conventional, 103
described, **78**
DSL, 103
overview, 14
satellite, 103
Molsberry, Frank, 292–293
monitor A display device for a desktop computer.
described, **62**
flat-panel, 62
introduction of, 11
Morph concept, 305
Mosaic browser, 95. *See also* Web browser
motherboard The main circuit board of a computer, located inside the system unit, to which all computer system components connect. **57**, 58
mouse A common pointing device that the user slides along a flat surface to move a pointer around the screen and clicks its buttons to make selections.
common operations with, 51
described, **50**
movies. *See* online movies
MP3 files, 241–242. *See also* music
multi-core CPU A CPU that contains the processing components or core of more than one processor in a single CPU. **59**, 60
music, 234–235, 241–242
MySpace, 115, 116, 117, 170, 177. *See also* social networking site

N
nanotechnology The science of creating tiny computers and components by working at the individual atomic and molecular levels. 12, **304**, 305
Near Field Communications (NFC), 298
netbook A very small notebook computer. **21**
netiquette, 36
network. *See* computer network
network adapter A network interface, such as an expansion card or external network adapter.
described, **78**
overview, 14
network servers, 22, 25
networked economy, 34–35

neural network An expert system in which the human brain's pattern-recognition process is emulated by the computer system. described, **316**, 317–318
news sites, 122
Nigerian letter fraud scam, 172
nonvolatile RAM (NVRAM) Memory chips that do not lose their contents when the power to the computer is turned off. 60, **299**, 300
notebook computer A fully functioning portable computer that opens to reveal a screen and keyboard; also called a laptop computer. *See also* portable computer
bags/cases, 8, 195–196
cable locks for, 191
described, **21**
digital divide and, 276
m-learning and, 7
notebook stand A device that elevates the display of a notebook or tablet computer to a better viewing height; can contain USB ports to connect additional hardware. 197, 264, 266, **267**
numbering systems, 48–49, R-11–R-16
NVRAM. *See* nonvolatile RAM (NVRAM)

O
Obama, Barack, 20
Office (Microsoft), 19, 80
antipiracy tools and, 202
common commands, 81–83
online testing and, 127
Picture Manager, 54
security and, 155
version 2010, 81
offline e-mail, 33
OLED. *See* organic light emitting diode (OLED) display
Omnilert, 30
One Laptop Per Child (OLPC) project, 276
online auction An online activity for which bids are placed for items, and the highest bidder purchases the item. **118**, 119
online auction fraud When an item purchased through an online auction is never delivered after payment, or the item is not as specified by the seller. **171**, 172, 176–177
online banking Performing banking activities via the Web. **119**

online brokers, 119
online education, 125–126
online financial alerts, 175
online fraud, 166–172. *See also* online auction fraud
online gaming Playing games via the Web. **121**
online investing Buying and selling stocks or other types of investments via the Web. **119**
online movies Feature films available via the Web. **120**, 121, 242–244
online music Music played or obtained via the Web. **119**, 120
online news, 122
online pornography, 178
online shopping Buying products or services over the Internet. **118**, 119
online storage Remote storage devices accessed via the Internet; also called cloud storage. **75**, 76
online testing, 126–127
online theft, 166–177
online TV Live or recorded TV shows available via the Web. **120**, 121
online video Video watched or downloaded via the Web. **120**, 121
operating system The main component of system software that enables the computer to manage its activities and the resources under its control, run application programs, and interface with the user.
browsers as, 308
described, **14**
updates, 198
opt in To request that you be included in marketing activities or that your information be shared with other companies. **213**, 272
opt out To request that you be removed from marketing activities or that your information not be shared with other companies. 211, **212–213**
optical character recognition (OCR), 53, 55
optical computer A computer that uses light, such as from laser beams or infrared beams, to perform digital computations. 12, **306**, 307
optical disc A type of storage medium read from and written to using a laser beam.
described, **69**
overview, 69–72
recordable, 71
rewritable, 72

organic light emitting diode (OLED) display A type of flat-panel display that uses emissive organic material to display brighter and sharper images. **301**

Ornelas, Lauren, 285

outbound-content monitoring systems, 159

Outlook (Microsoft), 33, 198, 213, 271

output The process of presenting the results of processing; can also refer to the results themselves. *See also* output device

described, **9**

hardware, 62–65

overview, 8–9

output device A piece of hardware that presents the results of processing in a form the user can understand. *See also* output

emerging, 300–302

overview, 13

outsourcing companies, 159

P

P2P file sharing, 159, 161, 241

packet sniffing, 147

password A secret combination of characters used to gain access to a computer, computer network, or other resource.

described, **148**

encryption and, 155

hardware loss and, 190

one-time (OTP), 149, 150

possessed knowledge access systems and, 148–149

strong, 148

patent A form of protection for an invention that can be granted by the government; gives exclusive rights of an invention to its inventor for 20 years. 233, **237**, 238

PB. *See* petabyte (PB)

PC. *See* personal computer (PC)

PDAs (personal digital assistants), 19

pens, 51–52

people-drive security, 166, 167

period (.), 30, 48

peripheral devices, 57. *See also specific devices*

personal computer (PC) A type of computer based on a microprocessor and designed to be used by one person at a time; also called a microcomputer. *See also* computer; desktop computer; notebook computer

described, **19**

guide to buying, R-8–R–10

history of, 4

Internet access via, 100, 101

overview, 17, 19–20

protecting your, 198

personal safety issues, 177–179

petabyte (PB) Approximately 1,000 terabytes. **48**

pharming The use of spoofed domain names to obtain personal information to be used in fraudulent activities. **171**, 173–174

phishing The use of spoofed e-mail messages to gain credit card numbers and other personal data to be used for fraudulent purposes. 35, **169**, 170–171, 173–174

phrase searching, 108–109

PINs (personal identification numbers), 148

pixel The smallest colorable area in an electronic image, such as a scanned image, a digital photograph, or an image displayed on a display screen. **62**

plagiarism Presenting someone else's work as your own. **240**

podcast A recorded audio or video file that can be played or downloaded via the Web. **123**, 124

PoE. *See* Power over Ethernet (PoE)

point-of-sale (POS) systems, 7–8, 52, 54

pointing device An input device that moves an on-screen pointer, such as an arrow, to allow the user to select objects on the screen.

described, **49**

overview, 49–52

portable computer A small personal computer, such as a notebook, tablet, netbook, or ultra-mobile PC (UMPC), designed to be carried around easily. *See also* notebook computer

described, **21**

overview, 17, 21–22

portable fuel cell charters, 281, 282

portable hard drives, 69

portal Web page A Web page designed to be designated as a browser home page; typically can be customized to display personalized content. **123**

ports, 58

possessed knowledge access system An access control system that uses information only the individual should know to identify that individual. **148**, 149

possessed object access system An access control system that uses a physical object an individual has in his or her possession to identify that individual. **149**, 150

Power over Ethernet (PoE) A wired networking standard that allows electrical power to be sent along with data over standard Ethernet cables. **309**

power supplies, 196, **197**, 281, 309

presence technology Technology that enables one computing device (such as a computer or mobile smart phone) to locate and identify the current status of another device on the same network. **220**, 221

printer An output device that produces output on paper.

overview, 63–64

special-purpose, 64–65

privacy The state of being concealed or free from unauthorized intrusion. *See also* privacy policy

browsers and, 130–133

described, **204**

e-mail, 133

legislation, 222–223

overview, 35–36, 128–133

protecting, 209–215, 221–222

software, 210

privacy policy A policy, commonly posted on a company's Web site, that explains how personal information provided to that company will be used. **36**, 207, 210. *See also* privacy

private key encryption A type of encryption that uses a single key to encrypt and decrypt the file or message. **155**

processing Performing operations on data that has been input into a computer to convert that input to output. **8**, 9

processor, **58**. *See also* central processing unit (CPU)

product(s)

ethically questionable, 250–251

information sites, 125

program(s)

alteration, security issues related to, 164

overview, 8

programmers, 16
programming languages
history of, 11
overview, 15
public key encryption A type of
encryption that uses key pairs to
encrypt and decrypt the file or
message. **155**
punch cards, 10, 11, R-2

Q

quad-core CPU A CPU that contains four
separate processing cores. **59**
quantum computing A technology that
applies the principles of quantum
physics and quantum mechanics
to computers to direct atoms or
nuclei to work together as quantum
bits (qubits), which function
simultaneously as the computer's
processor and memory. **306**

R

Radicati Group, 33
RAM. *See* random access memory
(RAM)
random access memory (RAM) Chips
connected to the motherboard that
provide a temporary location for the
computer to hold data and program
instructions while they are needed.
60, 61
read-only memory (ROM), 60, 61
RSS (Really Simple Syndication) A tool
used to deliver selected Web content
to subscribers as the content is
published to a Web site. **123**, 124
recycling equipment, 281–285
reference sites, 32, 122
registers, 60, 61
remote storage A storage device that
is not directly connected to the
computer being used, such as one
accessed through a local network or
the Internet. **75**, 76
repetitive stress injury (RSI) A type
of injury, such as carpal tunnel
syndrome, that is caused by
performing the same physical
movements over and over again.
263, 264–265, 268
RFID reader A device used to read RFID
tags. 53, **54**
RFID tag A device containing a tiny chip
and a radio antenna that is attached
to an object so it can be identified
using RFID technology. **54**

RFID technology, 221, 298. *See also*
RFID reader; RFID tag
employee monitoring and, 219, 220
health care and, 318
overview, 54–55
security and, 149
Ribbon A feature found in recent versions
of Microsoft Office that uses
tabs to organize groups of related
commands. 15, 81, **82**
Roadrunner supercomputer, 25
robot A device, controlled by a human
operator or a computer, that can
move and react to sensory input.
316, 317–318, 319
robotics The study of robot technology.
316, 317–318
Rouch, Sonny, 276
routers, 153
RSI (repetitive stress injury). *See*
repetitive stress injury (RSI)
ruggedized device A device (such as
a portable computer or mobile
phone) that is designed to withstand
much more physical abuse than a
conventional device. **196**

S

Safari browser, 132. *See also* Web
browser
salami shaving, 167
satellite Internet access Fast, direct
Internet access via the airwaves and
a satellite dish. 102, **103**
scalability, 17
scandals, 249–250
scanner An input device that reads
printed text and graphics and
transfers them to a computer in
digital form. **53**, 54–55
scientific calculators, R-14
Scott, Kevin, 268
scripting languages, 15
Seagate Technology, 302
search engine A software program used
by a search site to retrieve matching
Web pages from a search database.
106, 107. *See also* search site
search site A Web site designed to help
users search for Web pages that
match specified keywords or selected
categories. *See also* search engine
described, **106–107**
evaluating results from, 110–111
search strategies and, 108–109
tools, 108
using multiple, 109
Second Life, 239

secure Web page A Web page that uses
encryption to protect information
transmitted via that Web page. **154**
security. *See also* computer virus;
encryption; passwords
authentication, 6, 8, 148–149, 166
databases and, 205–208
e-mail and, 155–156, 166, 169–177,
209–210
firewalls, **152**, 153–154
importance of, 189–200
IP addresses and, 171, 203, 217, 194
ISPs and, 147, 166, 209
legislation, 179, 222–223
mobile devices and, 163, 194–195
network, 148–186
overview, 35, 183–231
people-driven, 166, 167
servers and, 171, 213–214
social networking and, 177, 210
software, 35
specialists, 16
threads, 203
security software Software, typically a
suite of programs, used to protect
your computer against a variety of
threats. 35, 198
described, **165**
overview, 165–166
self-checkout systems, 8
self-destructing devices, 194
self-encrypting hard drive. A hard drive
that uses full disk encryption (FDE).
192, **193**
semiconductors, 11
servers. *See also* Web server
domain name system (DNS), 28
mail, 29, 33
midrange, 18, **23**, 24
network, 22, 25
security and, 171, 213–214
virtualization and, 23–24
services, ethically questionable, 250–251
Sheth, Rajen, 313
shopping carts, 118
Short Message Service (SMS), 33, 112
Shribman, Bill, 250
signature capture devices, 52
Silicon Valley Toxics Coalition, 285
sizing buttons, 15
SkyDrive (Microsoft), 75, 76, 81
slide rule, 10
smart card A credit card-sized piece of
plastic containing a chip and other
circuitry that can store data.
described, **76**
readers, 76, 149, 150
smart appliances, 5
smart homes, 5

smartphone A mobile device based on a mobile phone. **18**

Smekal, Martin, 22, 296

Snopes Web site, 37

social engineering tests, 191, 192

social networking site A site that enables a community of individuals to communicate and share information. 8, 26–27

described, **115**

ethics and, 250

management tools, 117

netiquette and, 36

overview, 115–118

security and, 177, 210

spam and, 208, 209

software The instructions, also called computer programs, that are used to tell a computer what it should do.

common commands, 81–83

companies, 97–98

described, **14**

desktop versus mobile, 80–81

guide to buying, R-8

overview, 12, 14–15, 78–83

ownership rights, 79

Software as a Service (SaaS), 80, 97

software license An agreement, either included in a software package or displayed on the screen during installation, that specifies the conditions under which a buyer of the program can use it. **79**

software piracy The unauthorized copying of a computer program. **200**, 201–203

solar power, 281

solid-state drive (SSD) A hard drive that uses flash memory media instead of metal magnetic hard disks. **68**

Sonny's Redwoods Web site, 276

spam Unsolicited, bulk e-mail sent over the Internet. *See also* spam filter

described, **208–209**

proliferation of, 34–35, 36

spam filter An e-mail filter used to redirect spam from a user's Inbox. **211**, 212

speakers Output devices that provide audio output. **65**

spear phishing A personalized phishing scheme targeted at an individual. 169, **170**, 171

spyware A software program that is installed without the user's permission and that secretly gathers information to be sent to others. **132**, 133

SSD. *See* solid-state drive (SSD)

Stanford University, 29

Start button, 15

status bar, 31

status updates, 113

stealthware, 133

storage The operation of saving data, programs, or output for future use. *See also* storage device

alternatives, evaluating, 76–77

described, **9**

hardware, 65–77

system characteristics, 65

storage device A piece of hardware, such as a DVD drive, into which a storage medium is inserted to be read from or written to. *See also* storage

described, **65**

emerging, 302–304

overview, 13, 65–66

storage medium The part of a storage system where data is stored, such as a DVD disc. **65**, 66

stress, effects of, 269–270

student response systems, 126

stylus An input device that is used to write electronically on the display screen. **51**, 52

supercomputer The fastest, most expensive, and most powerful type of computer.

described, **24**

overview, 18, 24–25

supercomputing cluster A supercomputer comprised of numerous smaller computers connected together to act as a single computer. **25**

surface computing, 296

surfing the Web, use of the term, 31

surge suppressor A device that protects a computer system from damage due to electrical fluctuations. **196**

Symantec, 160, 167, 169, 186–187, 198, 208

system analysts, 16

system failure The complete malfunction of a computer system. 189, **190**, 191

system tray, 15

system unit The main box of a computer that houses the CPU, motherboard, memory, and other devices. 12, **57**, 58–61

T

tabbed browsing, 31

tablet computer A portable computer about the size of a notebook that is designed to be used with an electronic pen.

described, **21**

m-learning and, 7

TabletKiosk, 22

taskbar

buttons, 15

overview, 15

toolbar, 15

TB. *See* terabyte (TB)

teenagers, safety tips for, 178–179

Tekunoff, Mark, 61

telemedicine The use of networking technology to provide medical information and services. 275, 276, 318, **319**, 320

telesurgery A form of robot-assisted surgery in which the doctor's physical location is different from the patient's physical location and the doctor controls the robot remotely over the Internet or another network. **319**, 320

television, broadband-enabled, 101, 121

terabyte (TB) Approximately 1 trillion bytes. **48**

terrorism, 145, 191, 200

text messaging A way of exchanging real-time typed messages with other individuals via a cellular network and, typically, cell phones.

described, **112**

spam and, 208

thin client A personal computer designed to access a network for processing and data storage, instead of performing those tasks locally; also called a network computer (NC). **22**

threads, 114

3D printers, 65

3D projectors, 300

3G networks, 104, 311–312

throw-away e-mail address An e-mail address used only for nonessential purposes and activities that may result in spam; the address can be disposed of and replaced if spam becomes a problem. **209**, 210

thumb drives, 73, 74. *See also* USB flash drives

Tinker, Josh, 302

toggle keys, 50

toolbars, 15, 31, 81–82

top-level domains (TLDs), 28

Torvalds, Linus, R-5

touch screen A display device that is touched with the finger to issue commands or otherwise provide input to the connected device. **52**

tower cases, 19

TRACELESS system, 236

TraceSecurity (company), 192
trackballs, 268
trademark A word, phrase, symbol, or design that identifies goods or services. 233, **235**, 236–237
transistors, 11
translation, 313
Trojan horse A malicious program that masquerades as something else. **62**, 163
Tucows, 79
Twitter, 29, 112–113, 115, 117, 164, 170
Twittering Sending short status updates about your current activities via the Twitter service. **112–113**
two-dimensional (2D) barcode A barcode that represents data with a matrix of small bars and stores information both horizontally and vertically so it can hold significantly more data than a conventional one-dimensional barcode. **297**
two-factor authentication Using two different methods to authenticate a user. **149**
typefaces, 83

U

ultra-mobile PC (UMPC) A portable personal computer that is small enough to fit in one hand; also called a handheld computer. 19, 80–81
described, **21**
display devices for, 62
input and, 49, 51
system unit and, 57
unauthorized access Gaining access to a computer, network, file, or other resource without permission. **144**, 145–159
unauthorized use Using a computer resource for unapproved activities. **144**, 145–159
Unicode An international coding system that can be used to represent text-based data in any written language. **49**, R-16
uniform resource locator (URL) An Internet address (usually beginning with http://) that uniquely identifies a Web page.
described, **28**
Favorites feature and, 31, 32
overview, 28–29
RSS and, 123
search engines and, 106
security and, 154, 167, 171, 174

using, 31–32
Web searches and, 32
uninterruptible power supply (UPS) A device containing a built-in battery that provides continuous power to a computer and other connected components when the electricity goes out. 196, **197**
UNIVAC, 11
UPS. *See* uninterruptible power supply (UPS)
URL. *See* uniform resource locator (URL)
USB 3.0, 298
USB flash drive A small storage device that plugs into a USB port and contains flash memory media. *See also* USB ports
described, **73**
overview, 73–74
security and, 149–150, 165, 194
USB ports, 57, 58, 77
username A name that uniquely identifies a user on a specific computer network. **29**

V

vaporware, 251
Vardi, Moshe, 145
.vbs filename extension, 35
VeriChip A tiny RFID chip about the size of a grain of rice that is implanted under a person's skin for identification purposes. **318**, 319
video surveillance The use of video cameras to monitor activities of individuals, such as employees or individuals in public locations, for work-related or crime-prevention purposes. **217**, 218–219
videoconferencing, 114–115
video-on-demand (VOD) The process of downloading movies and television shows, on demand, via the Web. 121
Virginia Tech, 30
virtual private network (VPN) A private, secure path over the Internet that provides authorized users a secure means of accessing a private network via the Internet.
described, **156**
evil twins and, 158
overview, 152–157
virtualization Creating virtual (rather than actual) versions of a computing resource, such as several separate environments that are located on a

single server but act like different servers. **23–24**
virus. *See* computer virus
VOD. *See* video-on-demand (VOD)
Voice over Internet Protocol (VoIP) The process of placing telephone calls via the Internet. 5, 307
described, **114**
phone adapters, 114
security and, 154
VoIP. *See* Voice over Internet Protocol (VoIP)
volatile A characteristic of memory or storage in which data is not retained when the power to the computer is turned off. **60**
VPN. *See* virtual private network (VPN)

W

W3C (World Wide Web Consortium), 98
Walt Disney Imagineering, 10
war driving Driving around an area with a Wi-Fi-enabled computer or mobile device to find a Wi-Fi network to access and use without authorization. **146**, 147
Watson, Graham, 140–141
WBT. *See* Web-based training (WBT)
Web browser A program used to view Web pages. 15–16, 106. *See also specific browsers*
described, **26**
Favorites feature, 31, 32
history of, 4, 94–95
as operating system, 308
overview, 31–32
privacy issues and, 130–133
security and, 210–211
tabbed browsing and, 31
updates, 198
using, 31–32
Web conference A face-to-face meeting taking place via the Web; typically uses video cameras and microphones to enable participants to see and hear each other. 114, **115**
Web mail (Web-based e-mail), 33
Web page A document, typically containing hyperlinks to other documents, located on a Web server and available through the World Wide Web.
described, **26**
home pages, 30, 31
Web server A computer that is continually connected to the Internet and hosts Web pages that are

accessible through the Internet. **26**. *See also* servers

Web service A self-contained business application that operates over the Internet. **97**

Web site A collection of related Web pages usually belonging to an organization or individual.
 alteration, security issues related to, 164
 described, **26**
 spoofing, 169

Web Slices, 31–32

Web-based articles, 240

Web-based software Software that is delivered on demand via the Web; also referred to as Software as a Service (SaaS) and cloudware. 80

Web-based training (WBT) Instruction delivered on an individual basis via the Web. **126**

Webinar A seminar presented via the Web. 114, **115**

Websense, 164

Weick, Dave, 77, 95

Weir, Greg, 79

WGBH Interactive, 250

wheels, 52

whitelisting, 166, 167

Wi-Fi (802.11) A widely used networking standard for medium-range wireless networks. 5, 78. *See also* Wi-Fi hotspot; wireless networks
 described, **310**

e-paper and, 283
global digital divide and, 276
security and, 145, 146–147, 151–152, 157

Wi-Fi hotspot A location that provides wireless Internet access to the public. 77, **104–105**, 146–147, 157–158

Wi-Fi piggybacking Accessing an unsecured Wi-Fi network from your current location without authorization. **146**, 147

widgets, 121

Wiki A collaborative Web page that is designed to be edited and republished by a variety of individuals. **128**

wildcard characters, 109–110

WiMAX An emerging wireless networking standard that is faster and has a larger range than Wi-Fi.
 described, **310**
 network adapters, 78
 overview, 310–311
 standards, 312

Windows (Microsoft). *See also* Windows desktop
 memory and, 61
 overview, 14

Windows Calculator, R-14

Windows desktop The background work area displayed on the screen in Microsoft Windows. **14**, 15

wireless networks. *See also* Wi-Fi (802.11)
 connection types, 102
 overview, 5
 security and, 146–147, 151–152, 157–158, 163–164
 standards, 311–313

wireless power, 311

wireless USB A wireless version of USB designed to connect peripheral devices. **312**

WISPs (wireless Internet Service Providers), 96

word processing programs, 15–16

workstations, 20, 23

World Trade Center attack, 191, 200. *See also* terrorism

World War II, 11

World Wide Web (WWW) The collection of Web pages available through the Internet. *See also* Web browser; Web page; Web site
 described, **26**
 Internet and, distinction between, 99
 overview, 25–27, 92–141
 searching, 32

WWW. *See* World Wide Web (WWW)

Y

Yahoo! Mail, 209

Young, Kimberly, 272

YouTube, 116, 177